Contents at a Glance

Table of Contents

About the Authors

Michael Lisin has been in the software industry for more than 17 years, with 10 of those years working with Microsoft. Most of his career, Michael has been consulting on SQL Server and business intelligence solutions for Microsoft's enterprise customers. He has worked with SQL Server Reporting Services since the product's first pre-beta version in 2002 and has taught Reporting Services classes and presented topics related to SQL Server at various events. Michael earned his MBA at Texas A&M University in 2006 and continues to be a dedicated scholar of Reporting Services. He is now working with business development for Microsoft.

Jim Joseph is an independent contractor with 10 years of experience developing custom software solutions in a variety of industries. He has worked with SQL Server Reporting Services since the first beta release in 2000. He earned his MBA from the University of St. Thomas in 2002. He has worked in a number of roles from developer to database administrator.

Amit Goyal is a senior lead manager for the SQL Server Reporting Services team at Microsoft. Before joining Microsoft, Amit was a director at Yahoo! and worked on development of the Panama search monetization platform. He has 14 years of industry experience at high-tech companies such as Microsoft, Yahoo!, Oracle, and Broadbase Software. He earned his bachelor of science degree from UIUC (University of Illinois at Urbana Champaign) and master's degree from Stanford University.

Dedications

Michael Lisin: *Dedicated to my family: my wife, Anna; my children (Helen, Noah, and Alexander); my mother; and the memory of my grandfather. Thank you all for always being extremely supportive in my life endeavors.*

Jim Joseph: *Dedicated to my wife, Deseere, and my son, Christopher. Thanks for having the patience to deal with an absent daddy.*

Amit Goyal: *Dedicated to my loving parents, Mr. Ram Charan and Mrs. Manju Goyal; my wife, Meenakshi Agarwal; my daughter, Aditi; and my sister, Rashmi.*

Acknowledgments

The authors would like to thank the publishing team for working with us on this book. Special thanks to Brook, Keith, Mark, Neil, J. Boyd, Seth, and others. Thank you for your valuable feedback, answers, and hard work on this book. Without you all, this book would not be possible.

Thank you to Matt Whitten and Stephen Rauch for getting Michael started with Reporting Services and to Dr. John Groth of Texas A&M for instilling creativity in your students. Thank you to Kevin Swailes for pointers about exception reports.

Amit Goyal would like to thank his colleagues on the SQL Server Reporting Services team for help with content from their areas of expertise, especially Prash Shirolkar, Lukasz Pawlowski, Neeraja Divakaruni, Robert Bruckner, Nico Cristache, and Sean Boon.

We Want to Hear from You!

As the reader of this book, *you* are our most important critic and commentator. We value your opinion and want to know what we're doing right, what we could do better, what areas you'd like to see us publish in, and any other words of wisdom you're willing to pass our way.

You can email or write me directly to let me know what you did or didn't like about this book—as well as what we can do to make our books stronger.

Please note that I cannot help you with technical problems related to the topic of this book, and that due to the high volume of mail I receive, I might not be able to reply to every message.

When you write, please be sure to include this book's title and authors as well as your name and phone or email address. I will carefully review your comments and share them with the author and editors who worked on the book.

Email: feedback@samspublishing.com

Mail: Neil Rowe
Executive Editor
Sams Publishing
800 East 96th Street
Indianapolis, IN 46240 USA

Reader Services

Visit our website and register this book at www.informit.com/title/9780672330261 for convenient access to any updates, downloads, or errata that might be available for this book.

Introduction

SQL Server 2008 Reporting Services (SSRS) is a server-based, extensible, and scalable platform that delivers and presents information based on data that a business collects during its operation.

Information, in turn, helps business managers to evaluate the current state of the enterprise and make decisions on how to increase revenues, reduce costs, and increase customer and employee satisfaction.

The Reporting Services scope extends from traditional paper reports to interactive content and various forms of delivery: email, file shares, and so on. SSRS is capable of generating reports in various formats, such as Hypertext Markup Language (HTML), Extensible Markup Language (XML), and Excel formats, thus allowing users to manipulate their data in whatever format is required.

Before diving into this book, let's take a moment to understand the layout and some of the conventions used in the book. First, we cover how this book is organized and what you can expect in each section. Second, we cover the style and formatting conventions used in this book. It is particularly noteworthy to note the style changes in reference to code lines, including SQL Server and .NET code.

How This Book Is Organized

This book begins with an introductory overview of SSRS and covers a broad range of topics in the areas of report authoring, Reporting Services deployment and administration, and custom code development for Reporting Services.

The chapters in Part I, "Introduction to Reporting Services," provide a high-level overview of Reporting Services and highlight key features of the Reporting Services, deployment scenarios, typical users of Reporting Services, and Reporting Services architecture. This part allows for leisurely reading and does not require you to have access to a computer.

The chapters in Part II, "Report Authoring from Basic to Advanced," take you through report development tools and processes. This part describes report building blocks and walks through building a report from simple to complex.

The chapters in Part III, "Reporting Services Management," discuss advanced topics of Reporting Services administration, such as setting proper security, managing Reporting Services as individual servers and in a web farm, and gathering report-execution information.

The chapters in Part IV, "Reporting Services Customizations," are for those of you who might want to extend Reporting Services and incorporate reports into your applications. This part covers key programmable aspects of Reporting Services.

The chapters in Part V, "SharePoint Integration," provide detailed drill-down into running Reporting Services in SharePoint integrated mode. If you are interested in allowing your users to view and manage reports from their SharePoint sites, this section provides comprehensive information on architecture, installation, tools, and management.

Conventions Used in This Book

SQL Server 2008 Reporting Services is frequently abbreviated as SSRS, and where appropriate we may distinguish between versions of the product such as SSRS 2005 or SSRS 2008.

Business Intelligence Development Studio is frequently abbreviated as BIDS.

New features available in SQL Server 2008 Reporting Services as compared to SQL Server 2005 Reporting Services are labeled with "New in 2008."

Names of products, tools, individual windows (docking or not), titles, and abbreviations are capitalized: for example, SQL Server, SQL Server Reporting Services, Visual Studio, Report Designer, Report Builder, Report Manager, Windows, and so on.

`Monospace` is used to highlight the following:

- **Sections of code that are included in the flow of the text:** "Add a text box to a report and place the following code in the `Background Color` property: `=Code.Highlight(value)`."
- **Filenames:** "Visual Studio creates a project with a single class `Class1`. Let's rename file `Class1.cs` in Solution Explorer to `MainClass.cs`."
- **Pathnames:** Report Server (the default directory is `C:\Program Files\Microsoft SQL Server\MSRS10.MSSQLSERVER\Reporting Services\ReportServer\bin`).
- **Error numbers, codes, and messages:** "`[rsRuntimeErrorInExpression] The Value expression for the textrun 'Textbox1.Paragraphs[0].TextRuns[0]' contains an error: Request for the permission of type 'System.Security.Permissions.FileIOPermission, mscorlib, Version=2.0.0.0, Culture=neutral, PublicKeyToken=b77a5c561934e089' failed.`"
- **Names of permissions, constants, properties, collections, and variables:** `Execute`, `Fields`, `ReportParameter`, `Parent`.

To indicate adjustable information, we use the following:

- {}, mostly where the variable information can be confused with XML (for example, `<Value>{EXPRESSION}</Value>`). In this example, an `{EXPRESSION}` is any valid expression, such as `=Fields!ProductImage.Value`.
- <>, where the variable information cannot be confused with XML (for example, `=Fields!<Field Name>.Value`).

CHAPTER 1

Introduction to SQL Server Reporting Services (SSRS)

IN THIS CHAPTER

- What Is SSRS?
- SSRS for End Users
- Overview of Features
- SSRS in the Report Development Life Cycle
- Editions of Reporting Services
- How Is SSRS Licensed?

In today's ultracompetitive business environment, having good information is essential. Companies are awash in information, and with the advent of technologies such as radio frequency identification (RFID), more and more information is coming. Technology has made the job of gathering information trivial, but making sense of it all still remains elusive. This makes good reporting and business intelligence tools essential.

This first chapter is strictly nontechnical. This chapter focuses on the following:

- Capabilities of SSRS
- How it fits into the Microsoft Business Intelligence platform
- Report development life cycle as it relates to SSRS
- Editions of SSRS
- Licensing SSRS

NOTE

This book abbreviates SQL Server 2008 Reporting Services as SSRS and SQL Server 2005 Reporting Services as SSRS2K5.

New features available in SSRS and not in SSRS2K5 are labeled with "New in 2008."

What Is SSRS?

SSRS is Microsoft's answer to business reporting. It provides a unified, server-based, extensible, and scalable platform from which to deliver and present information. Its scope extends from traditional paper reports to web-based delivery and interactive content. SSRS can also be configured to deliver reports to people's inboxes, file shares, and so on. SSRS is capable of generating reports in various formats, such as the web-oriented Hypertext Markup Language (HTML) and desktop application (Microsoft Excel and CSV) formats, thus allowing users to manipulate their data in whatever format is required. In addition, SharePoint can be used as a front end for SSRS, allowing reports to be presented directly in corporate portals.

SSRS is just one of the components in the Microsoft Business Intelligence (BI) platform. Combined, those components provide an excellent platform for enterprise data analysis. The Microsoft BI platform includes the following:

- **SQL Server:** The traditional database engine, which also stores SSRS catalog data.
- **SQL Server Analysis Services (SSAS):** A component for online analytical processing (OLAP) and data mining. OLAP performs data aggregation and allows users to traverse from aggregations to details looking through the dimensions (such as geography or time) of data. Data mining helps users to discover patterns in data.
- **SQL Server Integration Services (SSIS):** A component for extracting, transforming, and loading (ETL) data.

SSRS for End Users

SSRS is unique in the Microsoft BI suite because it covers a variety of information users. Microsoft divides users into three groups: information consumers, information explorers, and analysts.

Table 1.1 briefly summarizes the percentages of users in each group, the level of technical experience, and the expectations from an enterprise reporting tool. All of these factors will vary from company to company, but generally the breakdown holds true.

TABLE 1.1 Breakdown of Information Workers

Type of User	Percentage	Technical Expertise	Expectation
Analysts	5%–10%	High	Analysts can develop reports, work with ad hoc reports, and perform sophisticated calculations (such as linear regressions and trend analysis). Analysts often publish reports to explorers and consumers.

TABLE 1.1 Continued

Type of User	Percentage	Technical Expertise	Expectation
Information explorers	15%–30%	Medium	Information explorers want to interact with reports to some degree, such as applying filters or performing drill down through.
Information consumers	55%–85%	Low	Information consumers use static, predefined, and preformatted reports.

To address the varying needs of these types of users, SSRS provides three main tools from the user perspective:

- **Report Viewer:** The primary mechanism for viewing reports over the Web. Report Manager is the name of the website that SSRS sets up. It provides a very clean and neatly organized user interface for end users. Developers can also embed a `ReportViewer` control into both ASP.NET and Windows Forms applications.
- **Report Builder:** The tool that provides users with a front end for ad hoc reporting against a SQL Server or Analysis Services database. Unlike most ad hoc reporting tools, users of Report Builder do not need to know Structured Query Language (SQL) or anything about joins or grouping to create reports.
- **Report Designer:** The tool that takes on the job of building advanced reports. Although Report Builder does a good job as an ad hoc reporting tool, Report Designer was made to tackle really advanced reports.

Figure 1.1 summarizes the types of reporting users, and mentions some of the tools SSRS provides for them.

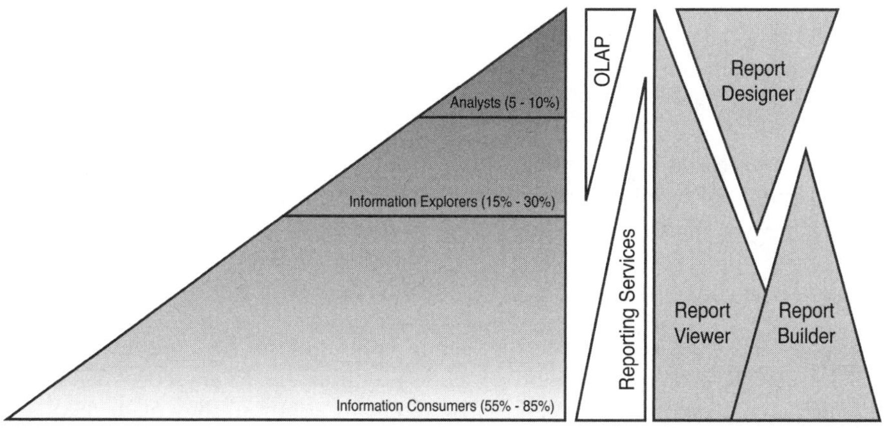

FIGURE 1.1 Reporting Services users and tools.

Overview of Features

SSRS has a number of features to address complex business reporting needs. Over the course of this book, these features are explored more closely. For now, here is a brief overview.

As far as creating reports, SSRS is a full-featured report engine. Reports can be created against any data source that has a managed code provider, OLE DB, or ODBC data source. This means you can easily retrieve data from SQL Server, Oracle, Analysis Services, Access, or Essbase, and many other databases. This data can be presented in a variety of ways. Microsoft took the feedback from SSRS2K5 and enhanced 2008 with new Chart and Gauge controls, and a new Tablix control, which is a mix of the Table and the Matrix controls from the earlier release. Combined, these new presentation formats give a whole new experience out of the box. Other enhancements include new output presentation formats, including Word and Excel, and direct integration with SharePoint.

Here is a concise list of SSRS features:

- Retrieve data from managed providers, OLE DB, and ODBC connections
- Display data in a variety of ways, including tabular, free form, and charts
- Export to many formats, including HTML, PDF, XML, CSV, TIFF, Word reports (New in 2008), and Excel
- Aggregate and summarize data
- Add in report navigation
- Create ad hoc reports and save them to the server
- Create custom controls using a report-processing extension
- Embed graphics and images and external content
- Integrate with SharePoint
- Provide a Simple Object Access Protocol (SOAP) application programming interface (API) and pluggable architecture
- Provide subscription-based reports and on-demand reports
- Allow users to store and manage their own custom reports built with SSRS's Report Builder 2.0 and manage subscriptions to the reports (New in 2008)
- URL-based report access
- Gauge and Chart controls to display KPI data (New in 2008)

As you can see, SSRS provides a comprehensive set of features out of the box. Another nice feature of SSRS is its extensibility. Because there is no way that the developers of SSRS could have anticipated every need of an enterprise reporting solution, they made SSRS extensible. This extensibility enables developers to use SSRS in any number of ways, from embedded reports to customized reporting solutions.

Enterprise Report Examples

Each user is likely to have favorite reports to make timely and effective business decisions, and although it is not possible to cover a whole gamut of reports in this book, some common ideas can help you think through practical applications of SSRS.

Scorecard reports are frequently used in today's businesses and provide information for each manager on how well his group is doing as compared to the goals set for the group. Usually, a scorecard implements a "traffic light" type of highlight or a "gauge" indicator. Values on the scorecard are highlighted in green when the group is meeting its goals, in yellow when the group is doing so-so, and in red when the group's performance requires immediate attention. Scorecard reports can take advantage of the key performance indicators (KPIs) features of Analysis Services 2008. Gauges and charts have been significantly enhanced in SQL Reporting Services 2008 by the acquisition of the Dundas Gauge and Chart controls by Microsoft.

When users are looking to combine a comprehensive set of business health and "speed" gauges (scorecard) and related information in a small space, a dashboard is used to accomplish this goal. A dashboard provides a short, typically one-page, summary view of a business (much like a car's dashboard summarizes a car's status) and allows drill down through the items on the top page to retrieve detailed information. SharePoint is an excellent platform to host dashboards and greatly simplifies arranging reports in a meaningful fashion on a page.

Today, when everybody is so short on time, it might be easy to miss an information point that could prove fatal for a business. Exception reporting is what comes to the rescue of a time-constrained user. Unlike regularly scheduled reports or summaries provided by scorecards, exception reports are created and delivered to a user when an unusual event occurs. An exception report removes the "noise" created in periodic reports, focusing instead on mission-critical anomalies. An example of such an anomaly could be a sudden drop in daily sales for a particular region.

Other typical reports include various views of sales (geographic, demographic, product, promotion breakdowns), inventory, customer satisfaction, production, services, and financial information.

SSRS in the Report Development Life Cycle

To understand all the ways SSRS can be used and deployed, you can simply walk through the report development life cycle and see what features are useful in each stage.

A typical reporting application goes through three stages (see Figure 1.2): authoring, managing, and delivery. SSRS provides all the necessary tools to work with a reporting application in all three stages.

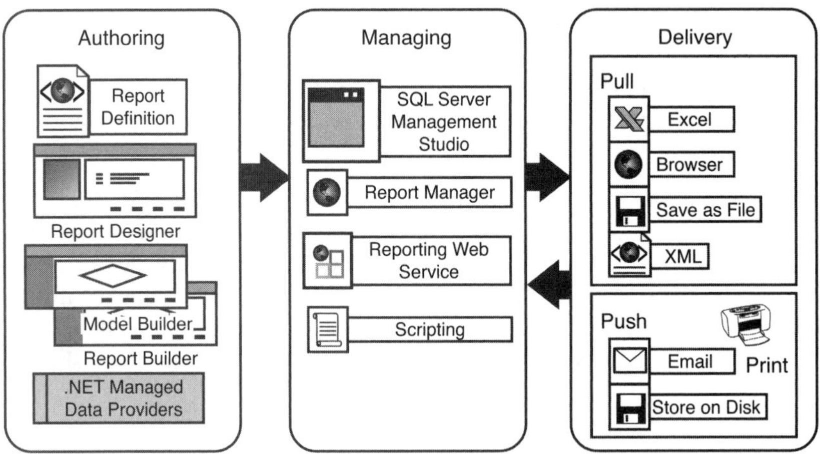

FIGURE 1.2 Reporting life cycle.

Authoring Stage

During this stage, the report author defines the report layout and sources of data. For authoring, SSRS maintains all the features of SSRS2K5 and adds some new features. SSRS still maintains Report Designer as its primary tool for developing reports in the 2008 release. Report Builder 1.0 is also available as a tool for developing reports against report models. Report models are metatdata models describing the physical structure and layout of the underlying SQL Server database. The biggest new enhancement for SSRS as far as tools for authoring go is the addition of Report Builder 2.0. Report Builder 2.0 fits nicely into the high-powered analyst space and gives them almost all the power of Business Intelligence Development Studio (BIDS), but with an Office 2007 look and feel.

NOTE

Report Builder 2.0 is not installed along with the SQL Server Reporting Services, but is available as a free download in the SQL Server 2008 feature pack.

Figure 1.3 shows the Report Designer interface.

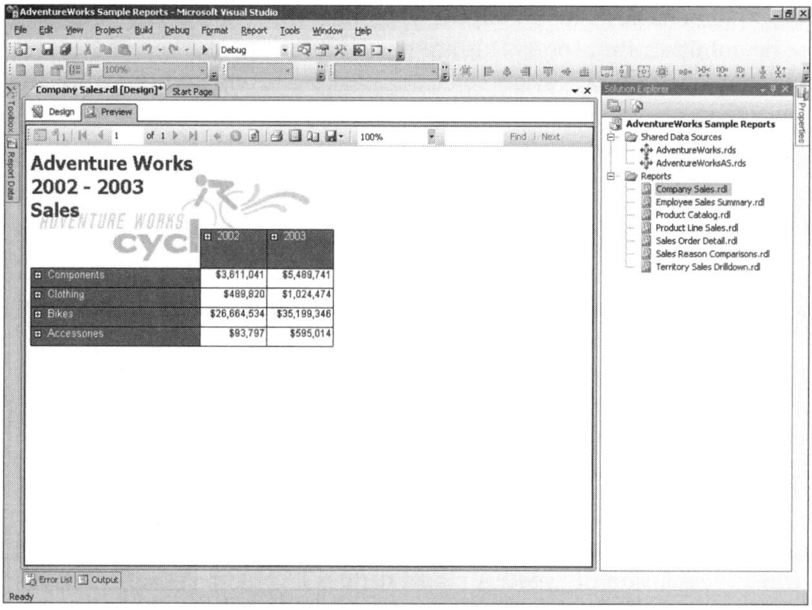

FIGURE 1.3 Report Designer.

Report Designer is a full-featured report-authoring tool that targets developers and provides extensive design capabilities and can handle a variety of data sources. Report Designer can work with all reports generated for SSRS, including reports generated by Report Builder. Report Designer incorporates the following productivity features:

- Import Access Reports, a feature that enables report designers to import Microsoft Access reports and create a report definition in turn. In complex cases, it might not be able to successfully or completely import an Access report. The general rule of thumb is that SSRS will be able to convert approximately 80% of the existing Access reports.
- IntelliSense for Expression Editing, which provides assistance with the syntax of a function used in expressions, names of class members, and indicates syntax errors in expressions by underlining them with squiggly red lines. You will see more details about this feature in Chapter 10, "Expressions."
- Multidimensional Expressions (MDX) and Data Mining Expressions (DMX) Query Designer, which provides a drag-and-drop interface for writing MDX and DMX queries. This feature is covered in more detail in Chapter 17, "Working with Multidimensional Data Sources."
- Relational Query Designer, which provides a drag-and-drop interface for writing SQL queries.
- Report Wizard, which provides step-by-step instructions to create a report.

- Preview mode, which enables a report author to preview the report design and layout before he publishes the report. This is a powerful feature of a Report Designer that does not require Reporting Services to be installed on a computer on which the preview is generated.
- Publishing and deployment functionality, which allows a report designer to publish a report to a target server. For example, the developer might choose to publish to a development or to a test reporting server.

SSRS also allows end users to design reports with SSIS. Three tools make this possible: Report Builder and Model Builder, and the new Report Builder 2.0. For those familiar with SSRS2K5, Report Builder and Model Builder are carryovers with little to no changes. Report Builder 2.0, however, is a brand new addition, which is a break from the previous edition. It is a smart client application that enables users to design reports with the full capability of SSRS. It also works directly against the client database.

With Report Builder 1.0, before an end user can develop a report, a developer must create a model, using the Model Builder tool. Figure 1.4 depicts the Model Builder's interface. A model is similar to a report, in that a model is a file written in Extensible Markup Language (XML) with an extension of `.smdl`. A model defines layout, data sources, data entities, and relationships in terms that are understood by end users and not in terms of SQL or MDX.

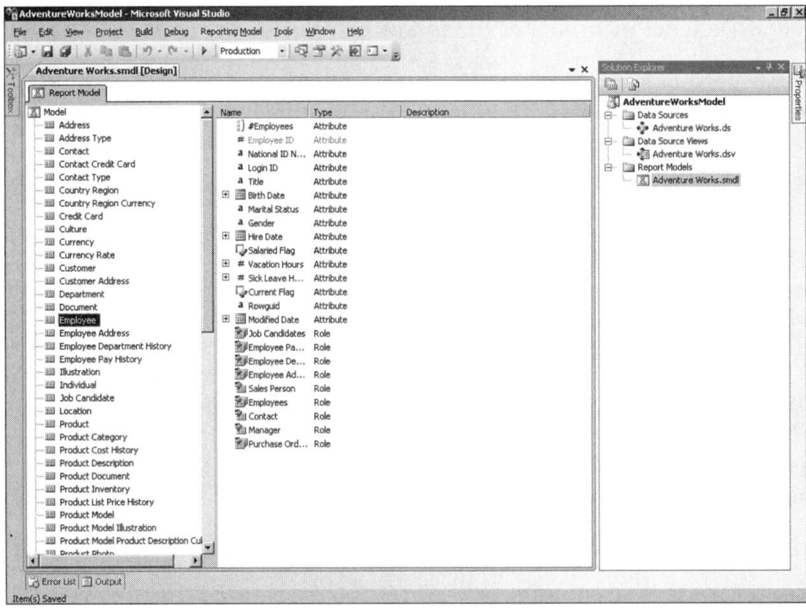

FIGURE 1.4 Model Builder 1.0.

When a model is published, an end user can choose a report's layout and drag and drop model items on a report. This is how an end user can create ad hoc reports, based on the published model. Figure 1.5 shows the Report Builder interface.

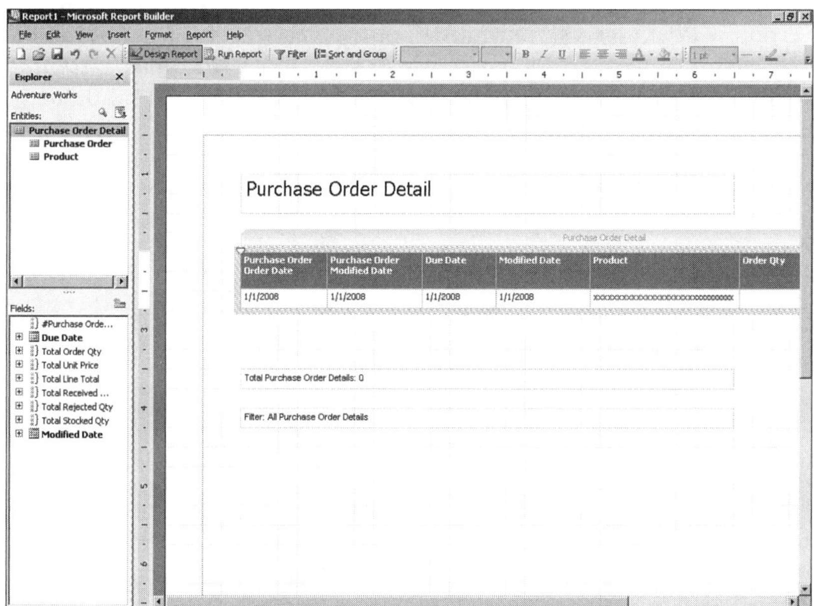

FIGURE 1.5 Report Builder 1.0.

Report Builder 1.0 targets end users and provides access to data sources predefined in a mode.

NOTE

Report Builder 1.0 cannot modify reports generated by Report Designer.

Report Builder 1.0 is a click-once .NET-smart client application that is launched from Report Manager's toolbar.

Report Designer and Report Builder (both versions) generate reports in Report Definition Language (RDL). RDL is an XML-based language, a code presentation of a report that defines data, presentation elements of a report, calls to the outside .NET assemblies, custom VB.NET functions, and expressions. RDL has powerful design elements (controls), such as the familiar Table, Chart, Subreport, and Matrix. SSRS has the capability to parameterize, sort, filter, drill down through, and aggregate data. RDL can be saved as a file on a file system or as data in the Reporting Services database. RDL is an open language that allows third-party vendors to develop custom authoring tools.

Report Builder 2.0 (New in 2008) represents a clean break with Report Builder 1.0. It is a full-featured smart client application that enables you to design and preview reports, then publish them either to the Report Server or to a SharePoint site. Report Builder 2.0 does not use metadata models; instead, it queries data directly from any .NET provider data source, including relational, multidimensional, XML, and ODBC data sources.

Report Builder 2.0 also breaks in terms of user interface (UI). It is not a click-once application like the 1.0 version. Rather, it is a separate install distributed with the SQL Server 2008 feature pack. It has an Office 2007 Ribbon look and feel. Unlike the earlier version, it is also a full-featured Report Designer fixing many limitations in Report Builder 1.0, from difficulty assigning print margins to using complicated expressions.

Figure 1.6 shows Report Builder 2.0.

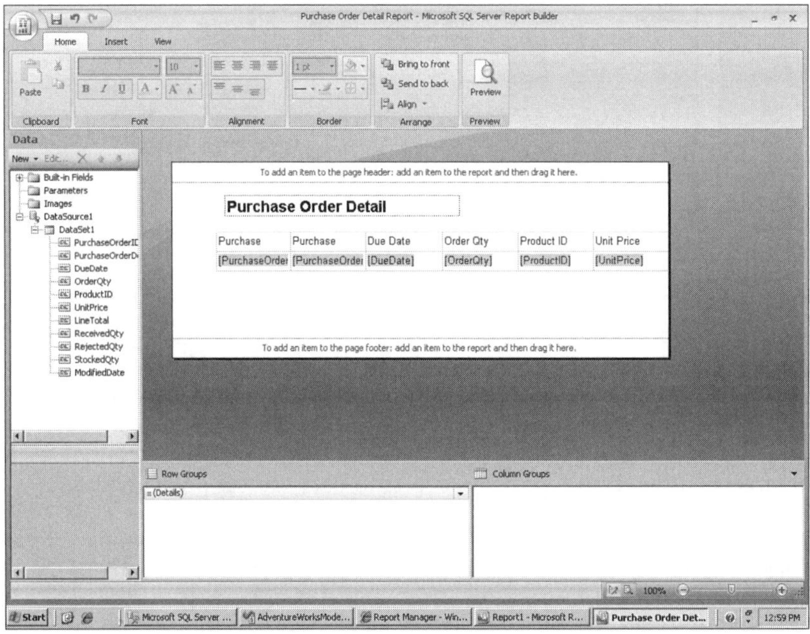

FIGURE 1.6 Report Builder 2.0

Managing Stage

During this stage, the report author publishes the report to a central location where it can be managed by a report administrator in terms of security and delivery. This central location is an SSRS database. After the report is published, the administrator can use Report Manager, SharePoint, custom written scripts, third-party tools, or SQL Server Management Studio to manage published reports. The report administrator can

- Assign the report's security or the right a user might have to a report.
- Establish execution control, such as selecting a time of an execution or caching options.
- Access and organize subscriptions from a single location.

- Control report-execution properties, which control how and when reports are processed. For example, the administrator can set processing options to prevent a large report from running on demand.
- Set timeout values to prevent a single report from overloading system resources.
- Automate report delivery through a standard subscription. Users can use subscriptions to set report presentation preferences. Users who prefer to view a report in Excel, for example, can specify that format in a subscription.
- Automate report distribution through data-driven subscriptions. A data-driven subscription generates a recipient list and delivery instructions at runtime from an external data source. A data-driven subscription uses a query and column-mapping information to customize report output for a large number of users.
- Set delivery methods for a report, such as file share, printer (this would require a custom extension in the current release, which is discussed in Chapter 29, "Extending Reporting Services"), or email.

Figure 1.7 shows the Report Manager's interface.

The default URL for Report Manager is http://<server>/reports (as shown in Figure 1.7). This is a default virtual directory in which Report Manager is installed. A report administrator can later change this URL by editing configuration files or using the Reporting Services Configuration Manager, as shown in Figure 1.8.

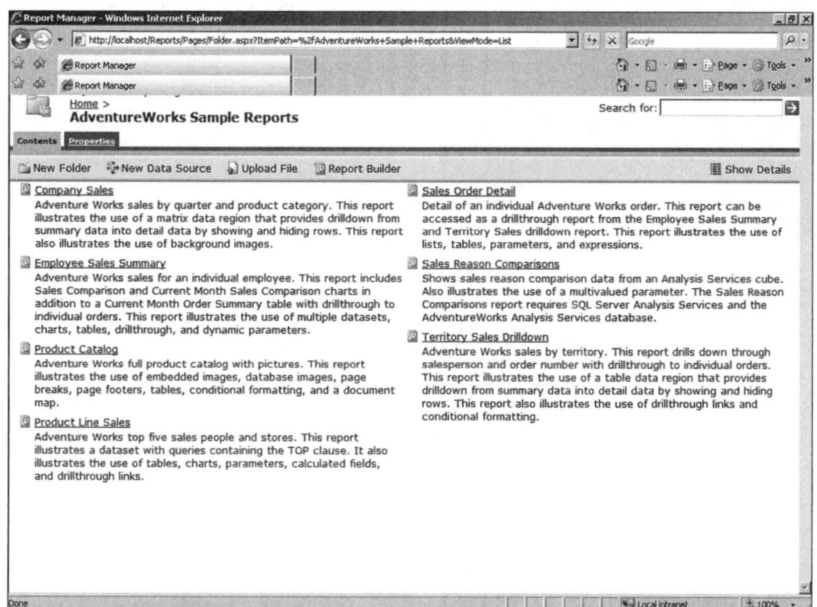

FIGURE 1.7 Report Manager.

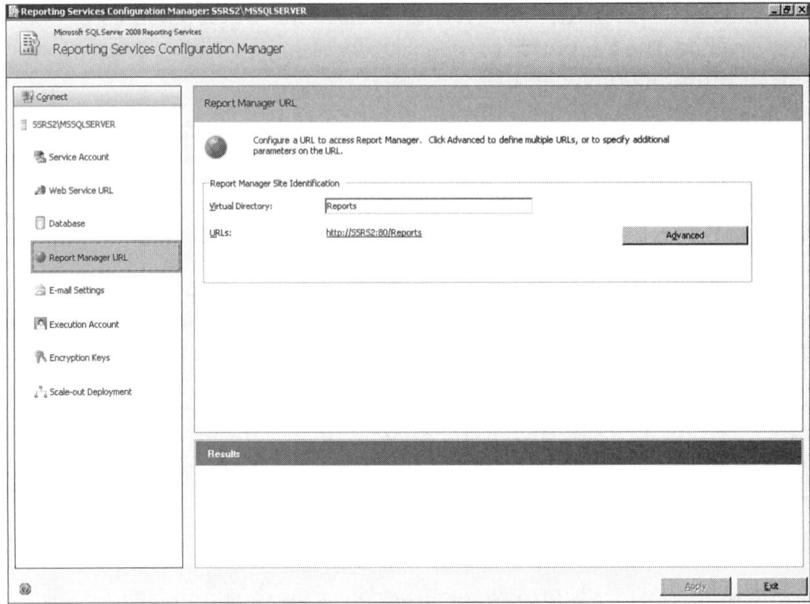

FIGURE 1.8 Reporting Services Configuration Manager.

Using SQL Server Management Studio, shown here in Figure 1.9, an administrator can perform most of the operations that she would otherwise perform through Report Manager. SQL Server Management Studio can access the SSRS catalog directly and does not require the SSRS Windows Service to be running to change the report's properties. However, an administrator will not be able to view the report if the SSRS Windows Service is not running.

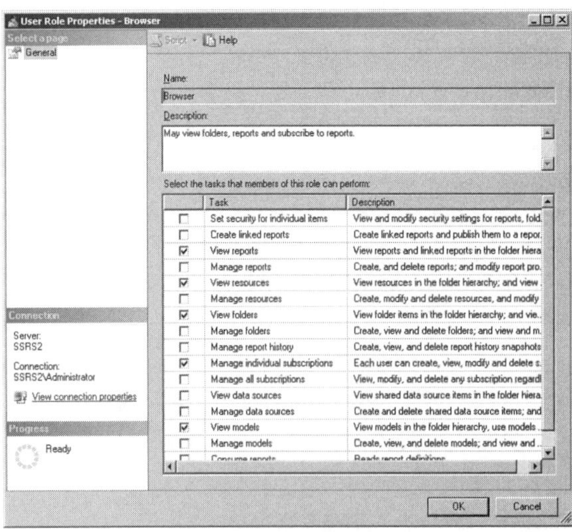

FIGURE 1.9 Managing within SQL Server Management Studio.

Table 1.2 presents a summary of the management features of SSRS.

TABLE 1.2 SSRS Management Features

Feature	Details
Browser-based management: Report Manager	Manages and maintains reports and the reporting environment.
Windows-based management: SQL Server Management Studio	Provides slightly better performance than the browser-based tool, in addition to the convenience of a single point of access (SQL Server Management Studio) for management of all SQL Server–related components.
Command-line utilities	Configure, activate, manage keys, and perform scripted operations.
Scripting support	Helps automate server administration tasks. For example, an administrator can script deployment and security settings for the group of reports, instead of doing the same one by one using Report Manager.
Folder hierarchy	Organizes reports by certain criteria, such as reports for specific groups of users (for example, a folder for the sales department).
Role-based security	Controls access to folders, reports, and resources. Security settings get inherited through the folder structure, similar to Windows folders security inheritance. Security can be inherited through the hierarchy or redefined at any level of hierarchy: folder or report. Role-based security works with Windows authentication. Security is installed during SSRS installation.
Job management	Monitors and cancels pending or in-process reports.
Shared data sources	Share data source connections between multiple reports, and are managed independently from any of the reports.
Shared schedules	Share schedules between multiple reports, and are managed independently from any of the reports.
History	Allows storing snapshots of a report at any particular moment of time. You can add report snapshots on an ad hoc basis or as a recurring scheduled operation. History can be used to view past versions of a report and see how information on a report has changed.
Linked reports	Create a link to an existing report that provides a different set of properties, parameter values, or security settings to the original report. To the user, each linked report appears to be a standalone report.
XML-based server configuration	Edits configuration files to customize email delivery, security configuration tracing, and more.

TABLE 1.2 Continued

Feature	Details
Database server and report logging capability	Contains information about the reports that execute on a server or on multiple servers in a single web farm. You can use the report execution log to find out how often a report is requested, what formats are used the most, and what percentage of processing time is spent on each processing phase.

The true test of an enterprise system is its ability to scale from a single user to up to thousands across an enterprise. The second test of an enterprise system is to maintain uptime and reliability. SSRS passes both tests.

SSRS manages these tasks by using underlying Windows technologies. The simplest deployment of SSRS just places all the components on a single machine. That single machine can then be updated with bigger and better hardware. The single machine deployment model provides a relatively cheap and cost-effective way to get up and running with SSRS.

SSRS can also be deployed across a network load-balanced (NLB) cluster, giving it scalability and availability. The database catalog that SSRS uses can also be deployed across a clustered database server apart from the web servers. This allows for nearly limitless growth in terms of number of users (scalability) and, at the same time, maximum availability.

Delivery Stage

During this stage, the report is distributed to the report's users and is available in multiple output formats. The SSRS retrieval mechanism enables users to quickly change an output format.

SSRS supports various delivery methods: email, interactively online (usually through a web browser, a portal such as SharePoint, or custom application), printer (requires custom extension), or file system. If the delivery method of interest is not available by default from SSRS, you can relatively easily develop custom delivery extensions. SSRS Books Online provides a complete set of samples for various custom delivery extensions. You can learn more about custom extensions in Chapter 29.

Reports are structured as items in a folder structure and allow for easy browsing and execution. You can see an example of viewing a report online in Figure 1.10. Note that the report is shown inside of Report Manager. Report Manager provides an additional functionality, such as assigning security or subscribing to a report. You can also view the report directly in the browser without Report Manager.

Alternatively, a user can subscribe to a report that subsequently will be delivered via email, as shown in Figure 1.11. Email delivery is a push model of report delivery. The push model is especially useful for the cases in which report generation takes a long time, the report needs to be delivered to an outside user, or there is an emergency situation that generates an exception report.

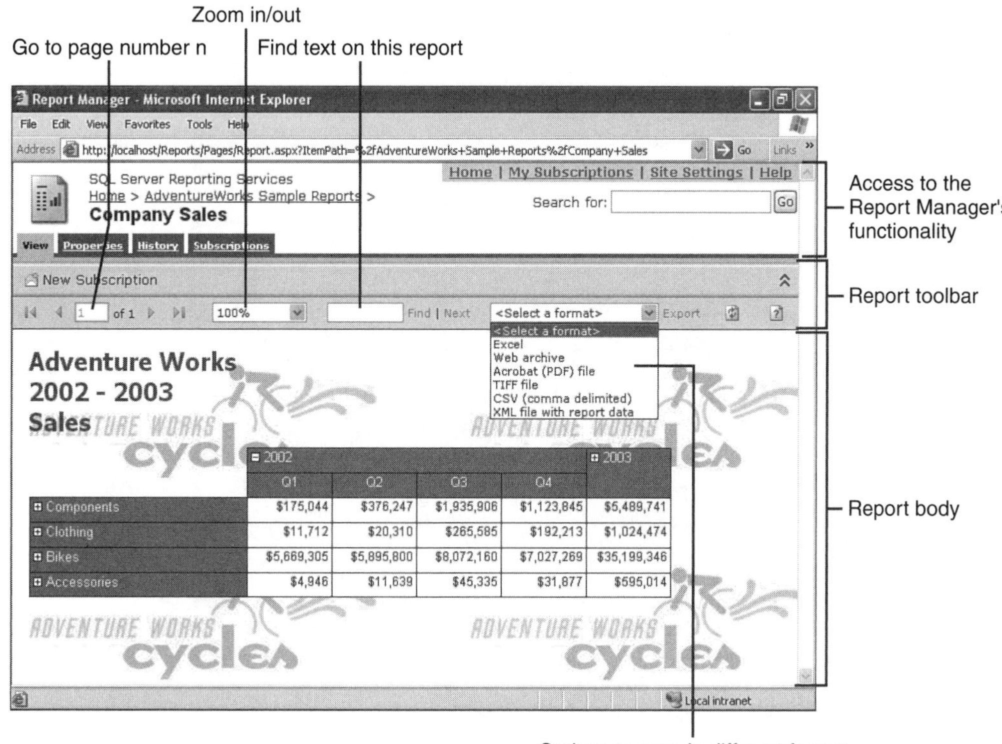

FIGURE 1.10 Online viewing.

Online and scheduled deliveries are great, but for a single solution to be truly ubiquitous, it has to offer more. SSRS does this, again, by making itself extensible rather than being all-encompassing.

A perfect example of this is via embedded reporting. With Visual Studio 2008, Microsoft has developed an integrated `ReportViewer` control. This control enables developers to embed SSRS reports into their Windows and web applications. Figure 1.12 shows the `ReportViewer` control.

If developers need to do more than just view reports, they can access the SSRS web services directly. This set of SOAP-based calls (SOAP API) provides access to just about every function on the Report Server. In fact, Report Manager does nothing more than make the same web service calls. For example, with the API, developers can modify permissions and create custom front ends.

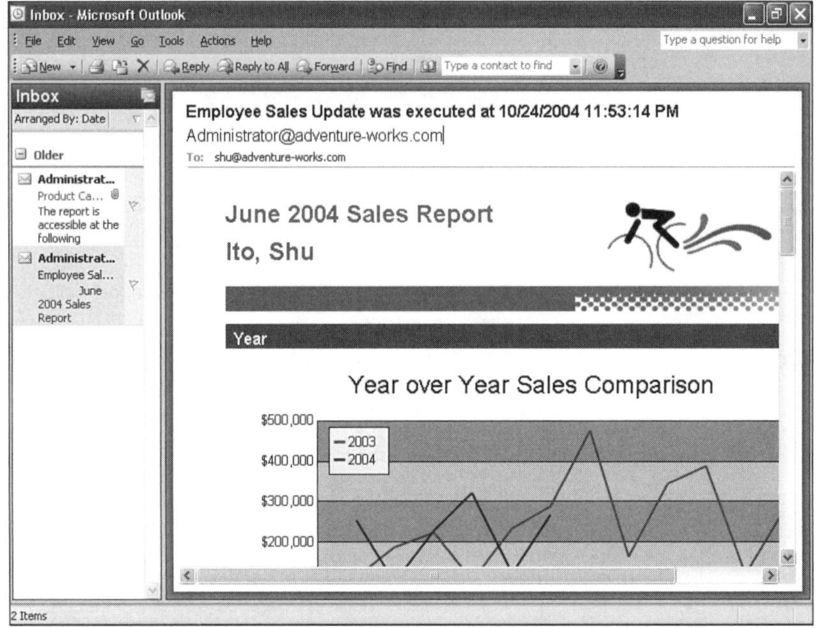

FIGURE 1.11 Email delivery.

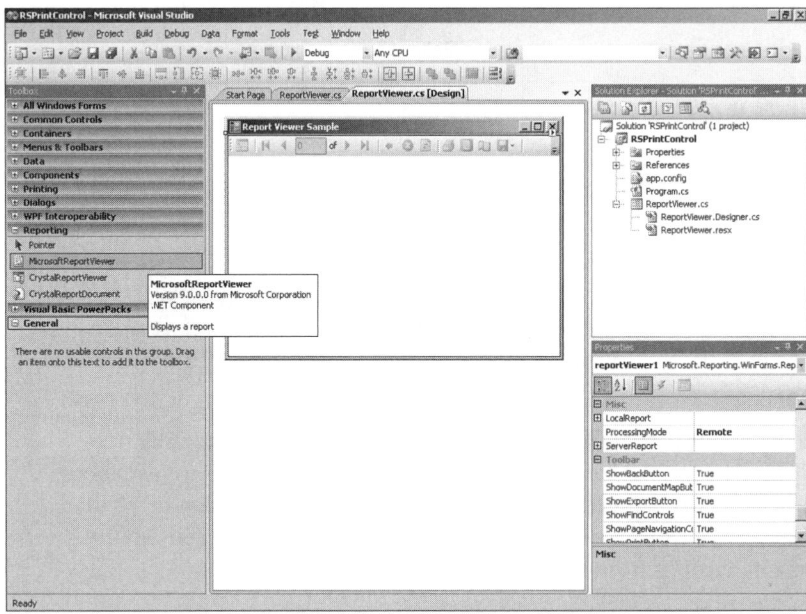

FIGURE 1.12 `ReportViewer` control.

Editions of Reporting Services

SSRS comes in four editions, which mirror the editions of SQL Server and Visual Studio. These editions range from free starter editions to full-scale Enterprise editions.

Chapter 5, "Reporting Services Deployment Scenarios," has more information about the different editions and supported features. Table 1.3 offers a high-level overview of the different editions of SSRS.

TABLE 1.3 Overview of SSRS Editions

Edition	Quick Overview
Express	Express Edition offers a lightweight edition of SSRS for developers who want to learn how to use SSRS.
Workgroup	Workgroup is for use in small departmental organizations or branch offices. Should the need arise, Workgroup Edition can be upgraded to Standard or Enterprise editions.
Standard	Standard Edition is for use in small- to medium-sized organizations or in a single-server environment. Standard Edition supports all the features of SSRS, except highly specialized data-driven subscriptions, and infinite drill down through Report Builder.
Enterprise	Enterprise Edition is for use in large organizations with complex database and reporting needs. Enterprise Edition is fully functional, and supports scale-out functionality across a web farm.
Developer	Developer Edition is essentially the same as Enterprise Edition, but has different licensing requirements to make it easy for people to develop enterprise applications. Developer Edition is licensed per developer in development (nonproduction) environments.

How Is SSRS Licensed?

The short answer is that every machine running SSRS has to be licensed as if it were running SQL Server. This means that any machine running SQL Server is automatically licensed for not just SQL Server, but for the entire Microsoft BI platform. This includes SSRS, SSAS, SSNS, and SSIS. This makes it really easy to get one's feet wet with SSRS. Just install SQL Server on one machine, and then install SSRS. On the flip side, if the choice is made to use the Enterprise Edition in a web farm scale-out scenario, every machine in the web farm must be licensed to run SQL Server.

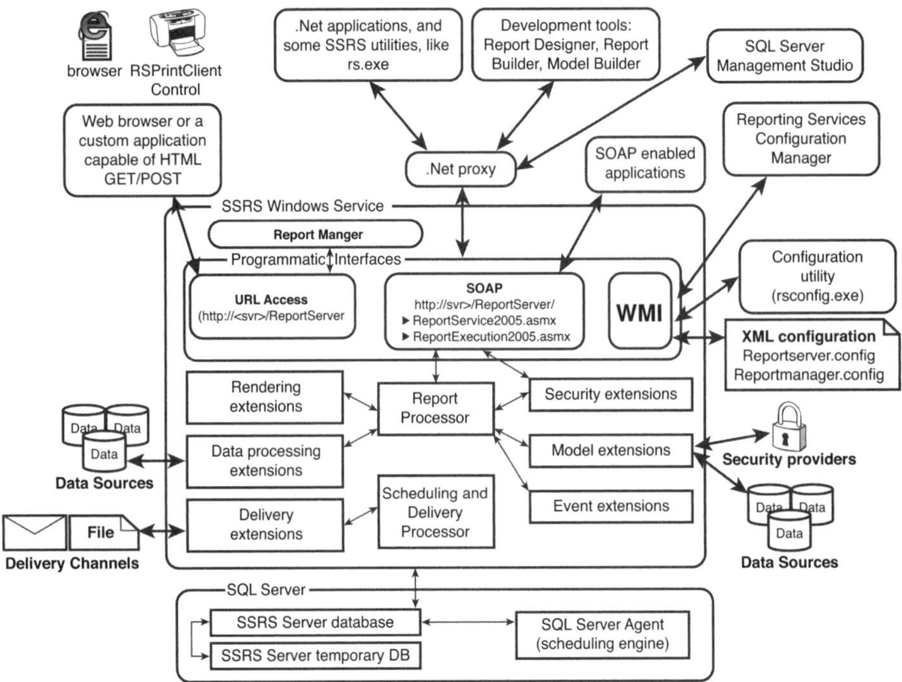

FIGURE 2.1 Reporting Services architecture.

Removal of IIS Dependency and Impact on SSRS

If you are coming from SQL Server 2005 Reporting Services (SSRS2K5), the first thing you will realize is that SSRS is no longer dependent on IIS. At first glance, this might seem like a shock, but IIS was a limiting factor for SSRS in a number of ways. Why remove IIS? The short answer is that IIS itself was having too big of an impact on SSRS and the ability to deploy it out in the field. Many IT departments refused to put IIS and SQL Server on the same machine. On top of that, things such as the `web.config` hierarchy could impact SSRS inadvertently. Web servers are often misconfigured. Most important, though, is that hosting the Report Server's delivery components inside IIS prohibited better resource governance. As you'll see, SSRS leverages the SQL operating system to better control resources.

In earlier releases, IIS used to function as the Hypertext Transfer Protocol (HTTP) server for Report Server. In SSRS, Report Server directly uses `HTTP.SYS` from the host operating system to handle HTTP and Secure Sockets Layer (SSL) requests. However, SSRS is not a general-purpose web server, and you should continue using IIS for web-based applications other than SSRS.

Because IIS is no longer present, Report Server handles registration and management of URLs for Report Manager and Report Server Simple Object Access Protocol (SOAP) endpoints by making URL reservations with `HTTP.SYS`. The Reporting Services Configuration tool supports setting up these URLs with information such as protocol, path, port, and virtual directory. This information is stored in the `rsreportserver.config` file under `<URLReservations>`.

The most common IIS settings that were used in SSRS2K5 continue to be supported by Report Server in SSRS. This includes IP address, host headers, multiple ports, SSL certificates, and IIS security modes such as NTLM, Kerberos, Negotiate, Basic, and Custom. Some IIS authentication functionality is not supported, such as anonymous, digest, and passport authentication or client certificates.

The biggest loss in removing dependency on IIS may be the use of Internet Server Application Programming Interface (ISAPI) filters. If you were using ISAPI filters (for instance, to integrate with single sign-on solutions), an Industry Security and Acceleration (ISA) server is the recommended alternative. Some other uses of ISAPI may be mimicked or replaced by using custom ASP.NET HTTP modules.

NOTE

Even though SSRS doesn't need IIS any longer, it can coexist with IIS on the same box. Both IIS and Report Server use `HTTP.SYS` and can share a single port. The way this works is that `HTTP.SYS` figures out whether to send the request to Report Server or IIS. If both Report Server and IIS map the same virtual directory, Report Server will get the request first. If you are using Windows XP 32-bit machines, be aware that different ports need to be used for SSRS and IIS.

SSRS maintains a similar monitoring experience as IIS. It has a W3C-compliant HTTP request log and preserves a subset of IIS/ASP.NET performance counters.

SSRS Windows Service

As you can probably tell from Figure 2.1, SSRS consolidated all of its services into a single Windows service. The service actually consists of several different subsets that can be turned on or off based on the configuration file settings. These subsets include the following:

- Report Manager
- Report Server web service
- Scheduling service
- Notification service
- Event service

Because all the services are consolidated, they all run under a single process (default: `ReportingServicesService.exe`). The process, however, hosts multiple application domains. Report Manager, Report Services web services, and all background processing tasks (Scheduling service, Notification service, and Event service) all use separate application domains.

Each of the subsets can be turned on or off individually. However, there are certain interdependencies.

Report Manager provides the main UI for SSRS. Because SSRS no longer requires IIS, URL reservations are made directly with HTTP.SYS. Report Manager can be effectively rendered useless just by removing the URL reservation for it. However, that does not turn it off. Report Manager is not available in SharePoint integrated mode, even if it is configured.

The Report Server web service processes all on-demand requests, and serves as the primary integration point for most third-party or external components. For example, the Report Manager uses the Report Server web service.

The background processing application domain includes the Scheduling, Notification, and Event services, and some database maintenance. It handles tasks that are initiated by the Report Server. Scheduling- and subscription-based processing tasks can be turned off. Scheduled tasks and subscriptions have to be defined through the UI either through Report Manager or SharePoint.

Memory Management

In spite of using separate application domains, memory management is shared between each service. SSRS uses components from the SQL operating system to manage memory consumption. Therefore, unlike earlier releases in which memory usage could not be configured and which were often limited to constraints within IIS, SSRS can use all the memory on a machine. Like SQL Server (the database engine), Reporting Services can set upper and lower limits on memory consumption per instance. SSRS also defines thresholds for memory consumption. When one of the thresholds is reached, the behavior of Reporting Services changes to stay available and responsive to the end user.

Each application domain hosted by Reporting Services is subject to the memory manager. Just like in SQL Server, when application domains start, they each request a minimum amount of memory to speedily respond to requests. Afterward, they start reporting their memory usage and listening for notifications that come from the memory manager as to how much memory they should use and free, and respond accordingly.

When a request comes to shrink the amount of RAM used for each of the consumers, the server calculates the minimum amount of memory to free and receives from the application domains information about how much memory can be freed and how easy it would be to do so. It then starts to free memory based on the lowest cost and largest memory consumption. As memory is released, that forces the Report Server to serialize some state information to disk. Because the algorithm is a weighted cost algorithm, the desired effect is to pause some of the very large reports while saving state information, and keep the small reports going.

That being said, there are three states for memory pressure in SSRS: high, medium, low.

Table 2.1 explains the three states.

TABLE 2.1 Memory Pressure

Memory Pressure	Server Response
Low	All requests get processed with new requests being accepted. Requests that require background processing tasks continue with a lower priority.
Medium	Requests that are currently executing continue to process while new requests are accepted on a case-by-case basis. Memory allocations to all the application domains start to be reduced with larger reductions to the background-processing application domain. Requests to web services and URL access are given a higher priority.
High	No longer accepts new requests, and requests for memory start getting denied. The server starts the process of swapping state information to disk, and current requests slow down.

When no memory is available, the Report Server responds with a `HTTP 503` error. In extreme cases, the Report Server might have to recycle the application domain.

Four new memory configuration options are available in SSRS (`rsreportserver.config`), as listed in Table 2.2.

TABLE 2.2 Memory Configuration Options

Configuration Option	Usage
`WorkingSetMinimum`	Defines the minimum amount of memory the Reporting Server Service can use
`WorkingSetMaximum`	Defines the maximum amount of memory the Reporting Server Service can use
`MemorySafetyMargin`	Defines the upper limit of the low-memory section
`MemoryThreshhold`	Defines the upper limit of the medium-memory pressure section

The report processor performs the following operations:

- **Execution:** Retrieves a report definition and combines it with data retrieved by the data-processing extension. This operation generates an intermediate format.
- **Rendering:** Renders the intermediate format to a requested output format using rendering extensions.
- **Processing of models:** This is similar to the execution operation for reports that are generated by Report Builder and that contain a semantic model (or simply a model, which serves as a data source for a report) and a semantic query. Semantic query refers to a query performed against a model that, in turn, just like a SQL query, generates a report's data set.

This is how the report processor responds to user requests:

- **New interactive report request:** An intermediate format is generated and passed to the rendering extension; the user receives the rendered report.
- **Request to generate cache or snapshot:** An intermediate format is generated and stored in the database.
- **Request for cached report or snapshot:** An intermediate format is retrieved from cache (or snapshot) and passed to the rendering extension; the user receives the rendered report.

Command-Line Utilities

Three administration assistance utilities are installed automatically during the Reporting Services install:

- **`rs.exe`**: Host scripting operations. Developers can, for example, create a VB.NET script to deploy a set of reports. You can find more details about this utility in Chapter 24 "RS Utility."
- **`rsconfig.exe`**: Use to modify encrypted connection information to the Report Server database.
- **`rskeymgmt.exe`**: Back up/restore symmetric keys for encrypted data used by a Report Server or delete encrypted data if the key is lost. For more information, see Chapter 23, "SSRS Administration."

NOTE

The `rsactivate.exe` utility, which was used in the earlier release to activate new SSRS instances in a web farm, is no longer included. Activation is performed using the Reporting Services Configuration tool.

Reporting Services Extensions

An extension is a .NET assembly that is invoked by the report processor to perform certain processing functions. There are several types of extensions: data processing, delivery, rendering, security (authentication and authorization), semantic query, model generation, and event processing.

For an extension to be used by a Report Server, it has to be installed (assuming default SSRS configuration) to the `C:\Program Files\Microsoft SQL Server\MSRS10.MSSQLSERVER\Reporting Services\ReportServer\bin` directory and configured in `C:\Program Files\Microsoft SQL Server\MSRS10.MSSQLSERVER\Reporting Services\ReportServer\ReportingServicesService.exe.config`.

The last part of an extension filename usually implies the extension's functionality. For example, the HTML rendering extension's filename is `Microsoft.ReportingServices.HtmlRendering.dll`.

Custom extensions enable developers to add complementing functionality that is not available in SSRS "out of the box." For example, a company can implement an extension that delivers reports to a phone or a fax. You can learn more about extensions in Chapter 29, "Extending Reporting Services."

NOTE

This release of SSRS does not allow custom semantic query, model-generation, or event-processing extensions.

Data-Processing Extensions

Data-processing extensions retrieve data from the report data source. Some of the tasks performed by data-processing extensions include open connections to data sources, analyze queries and return field names, pass parameters, and retrieve and iterate data sets. Table 2.3 outlines some of the more popular data-processing extensions included and configured with SSRS.

TABLE 2.3 Data-Processing Extensions Configured with SSRS

Extension	Description/Notes
SQL Server	Connects to and retrieves data from the SQL Server database engine versions 7.0 through 2008.
OLE DB	Connects to and retrieves data from OLE DB-compliant data sources.
SQL Server Analysis Services	Connects to and retrieves data from the SQL Server Analysis Server Services 2000 and 2005. For Analysis Services 2005, this extension supports both Multidimensional Expressions (MDX) and Data Mining Expressions (DMX).

TABLE 2.3 Continued

Extension	Description/Notes
Oracle	Connects to and retrieves data from an Oracle database; requires Oracle client 8i Release 3 (8.1.7) to be installed on a computer on which Reporting Server is installed.
ODBC	Connects to and retrieves data from ODBC-compliant data sources.
XML	Retrieves XML data from any XML web source (such as a web server) that can be accessed through a URL.

All data-processing extensions that are installed with SSRS (except XML), leverage corresponding .NET data providers. The `Microsoft.ReportingServices.DataExtensions` library provides wrapper classes that supply SSRS data-processing extension interfaces to .NET data providers.

Developers can create additional custom data-processing extensions.

Delivery Extensions

Delivery extensions deliver reports to specific devices or formats. Extensions included with SSRS include email and file share delivery. The delivery method and, therefore, corresponding extension are selected when a user (or an administrator) creates a subscription.

A sample of printer delivery extension is included with SQL Server samples and discussed in Chapter 26, "Creating and Calling a Custom Assembly from a Report." Table 2.4 outlines the delivery extensions included and configured with SSRS.

TABLE 2.4 Delivery Extensions Included with SSRS

Extension	Purpose
Email delivery	Delivers a rendered report to an email inbox. Allows setting delivery options that control an output format and whether the report is delivered as a link or as an attachment.
File share delivery	Delivers a rendered report to a shared folder. Allows setting delivery options that control a destination folder path, an output format, and whether the report overrides an older version or is added as a new version.

Developers can create additional custom delivery extensions.

Rendering Extensions

Report Server rendering extensions transform a report's layout and data into a device-specific format. Extensions included with SSRS include HTML (3.2 and 4.0), Microsoft Excel, Microsoft Word, Text/CSV, XML, image (BMP, EMF, GIF, JPEG, PNG, TIFF, WMF), and PDF rendering.

NOTE

With SSRS, Microsoft added the ability to export to Microsoft Word as a new rendering extension.

Because the final rendering phase is only loosely coupled with data processing, users can choose different rendering options for the same report without the need to re-query data sources.

Developers can create additional custom rendering extensions.

Security Extensions

This book frequently uses the term *security extension* as if it refers to a single unit. In actuality, there are two interrelated extensions:

- Authentication extension, which handles a process that establishes user identity
- Authorization extension, which handles a process that checks whether an identity has access to a particular SSRS resource

SSRS includes a security extension based on Windows authentication. After a user's identity is established, an authorization process determines whether a Windows user (or a Windows group that contains a user) is configured to access a particular resource on a reporting server.

Developers can create additional custom security extensions. An instance of SSRS can use only one security extension. In other words, either the Windows or a custom extension can be used, but not both at the same time.

NOTE

SSRS by default attempts to use Kerberos for authentication as opposed to NTLM, which was the default for SSRS2K5. You can reconfigure this in the `ReportingServicesService.exe.config` file.

Report Server Databases

The SSRS catalog encompasses two databases: the Report Server database (the default name is ReportServer) and Report Server temporary database (the default name is ReportServerTempDB). The Report Server database is a SQL Server database that stores parts of the SSRS configuration, report definitions, report metadata, report history, cache policies, snapshots, resources, security settings, encrypted data, scheduling and delivery data, and extension information.

NOTE

Although users can certainly directly access databases in the SSRS catalog and directly modify objects that SSRS uses, this is not a recommended (or supported) practice. Underlying data and structures within the SSRS catalog are not guaranteed to be compatible between different releases of SSRS, service packs, or patches.

Treat the Report Server database as a production database. A loss of snapshot data can negatively impact a business. For example, users might make some business decisions using a snapshot's capabilities to report "frozen-in-time" data.

Another database that SSRS uses is the Report Server temporary database. This database is responsible for storing intermediate processing products, such as cached reports, and session and execution data.

NOTE

To store temporary snapshots in the file system, rather than in the database, administrators should complete the following steps:

1. Modify `RSReportServer.config` and set `WebServiceUseFileShareStorage` and `WindowsServiceUseFileShareStorage` to `True`.
2. Set `FileShareStorageLocation` to a fully qualified path. The default path is `C:\Program Files\Microsoft SQL Server\MSRS10.MSSQLSERVER\Reporting Services\RSTempFiles`.

Unlike SQL Server's tempdb, data in ReportServerTempDB survives SQL Server and Report Server restarts. Report Server periodically cleans expired and orphan data in ReportServerTempDB.

All data in ReportServerTempDB can be deleted at any time with minimal or no impact. The minimal impact that a user might experience is, for example, a temporary performance reduction due to lost cache data and a loss of an execution state. The execution state is stored in the table SessionData. Loss of the execution state results in an error: `Execution 'j4j3vfblcanzv3qzcqhvml55' cannot be found (rsExecutionNotFound)`. To resolve the loss of the execution state, a user would need to reopen a report.

TIP

SSRS does not recover deleted ReportServerTempDB or tables within this database. To quickly recover from erroneous deletions of objects in this database, keep a script or a backup of an empty ReportServerTempDB handy.

In a scale-out deployment, the SSRS catalog is shared across all the Report Servers in the deployment.

Scheduling and Delivery Processor

The scheduling and delivery processor is hosted in SSRS Windows service and monitors for events. When the scheduling and delivery processor receives an event, the scheduling and delivery processor collaborates with the report processor to render a report. After a report is rendered, the scheduling and delivery processor uses delivery extensions to deliver a report.

The scheduling and delivery processor leverages the SQL Server Agent as a scheduling engine. The schedule is based on the local time of the Report Server that owns the schedule. When an administrator creates a new schedule, the SSRS creates a SQL Server Agent job to run on the requested schedule. Then SSRS adds a row in the Schedule table of the Report Server database. The row's ScheduleId field is the job's identifier. Administrators can schedule subscriptions, report history, and snapshot execution.

When the scheduled time comes, the SQL Server Agent generates an event by executing the scheduled job. The job inserts a row in the Event table of the Report Server database. This row serves as an event for the scheduling and delivery processor.

The scheduling and delivery processor checks the Event table and initiates appropriate actions as a response to an event.

NOTE

The polling interval is specified in the `rsreportserver.config` configuration file, and is set to 10 seconds by default.

The scheduling and delivery process "breaks" when either (or both) the SSRS Windows service is not running (the scheduling and delivery processor is not processing events) or the SQL Server Agent is not running (the agent is not generating events).

NOTE

When the SSRS Windows service is not running and the SQL Server Agent is running, the job history for SQL Server Agent will indicate that the scheduled request ("insert event") ran successfully. The job will be successful despite the fact that the scheduled operation cannot complete because the scheduling and delivery processor is not running to process the event.

Report Builder 1.0

One of the most popular features in the first version of SSRS was the ability to develop end-user reports. Microsoft delivered this functionality in SSRS2K5 with Report Builder 1.0. In SSRS, Report Builder 1.0 remains unchanged, and Report Builder 2.0 is offered alongside as an alternate Report Designer.

Report Builder 1.0 is a click-once, ad hoc, end-user report-authoring and -publishing tool that provides drag-and-drop, easy-to-use report design functionality.

NOTE

You can find more information about click-once applications by searching www.microsoft.com and reading http://msdn.microsoft.com/msdnmag/issues/04/05/clickonce/default.aspx.

As a typical click-once application, Report Builder 1.0 is deployed from a browser and executes on a client's computer. Report Builder does not require administrative permissions during installation and runs in a secure sandbox provided by .NET code access security.

To deploy Report Builder, click the Report Builder button on the Report Manager's toolbar. Alternatively, you can use http://<server>/ReportServer/ReportBuilder/ReportBuilder.application to launch Report Builder. Report Builder is deployed to `C:\Documents and Settings\<Username>\Local Settings\Apps\2.0\<obfuscated directory>` (Windows 2003) or `C:\Users\<Username>\AppDation\Local\Apps\2.0\<obfuscated directory>` (Windows 2008).

Before you can use Report Builder

- You must have appropriate permissions, and be a member of the Report Consumer role or a custom role that includes the Consume Reports task.
- At least one report model has to be published.
- An Internet browser must allow you to download files.

Report Model Designer

The Report Model Designer creates report models for use by Report Builder. A model abstracts complexities of underlying data. For example, a model allows mapping names of tables and columns to business terms that an end user can easily understand.

The Report Model Designer is hosted in Business Intelligence Development Studio (BIDS) or Visual Studio and is intended for use by developers. Actually, BIDS is a Visual Studio shell with only BI projects and no language projects. One of the BI projects is the Report Model Project, which launches the Report Model Designer and allows developers to create models.

Report models and, therefore, ad hoc reports can work only with SQL Server data sources: SQL Server database engine and SQL Server Analysis Services. However, developers can work around this limitation and access other data sources by using link servers or Analysis Services Unified Data Model. Both provide a thin layer of abstraction and allow access to any OLE DB- or ODBC-compliant data source, including Oracle.

Report Builder 2.0

Report Builder 2.0 is very different from Report Builder 1.0. Report Builder 1.0 works entirely on metadata models generated by Report Model Designer or through Report Manager. Report Builder 2.0 works directly against defined data sources or shared data sources. In short, Report Builder 2.0 is a full-featured Report Designer in its own right.

Report Builder 2.0 is installed via the feature pack and is meant to be an end-user tool. It displays an Office 2007 Ribbon-like UI. It can also publish report and data sources directly to the Report Server or a SharePoint site when the Report Server is running in SharePoint integrated mode.

As mentioned earlier, Report Builder 2.0 uses a report's services native data sources directly. Therefore, it can use the full range of data sources available for SSRS, including SQL Server, Oracle, SQL Server Analysis Services (multidimensional), and any OLE DB or ODBC data source. It can also use custom data extensions that have been developed for SSRS.

Because it is a full-featured Report Designer, it can produce standard tabular, matrix, chart, and free-form reports. It is can also use the new gauges within SSRS. Reports published with Report Designer can be opened, viewed, and edited with Report Builder 2.0, which is a big advantage. Report Builder 1.0 could not open reports developed with Report Designer. Likewise, Report Builder 2.0 supports all the standard presentation formats supported by SSRS, including HTML, MHTML, PDF, TIFF, Excel, and Word. It includes support for aggregations, drill through, and other navigation tools such as bookmarks and document maps.

Report Designer

Report Designer is a developer-oriented comprehensive report-authoring, -previewing, and -publishing tool hosted in BIDS or Visual Studio.

To organize the report development process, Report Designer provides three views of a report: Report Data, Design, and Preview.

The Report Data window helps developers to define data sources and design data set queries. Report Designer provides three drag-and-drop graphical query designers to assist with SQL queries, Analysis Services MDX (introduced as a new feature in SSRS2K5), and Analysis Services DMX (another feature introduced in SSRS2K5).

The Design tab allows developers to design graphical presentations of a report and associate that graphical presentation with data. Report Designer provides a drag-and-drop Layout Designer and Toolbox with reporting controls. Layout design is similar to a UI design that Visual Studio provides for Windows and web applications: You can drag and drop reporting controls to a report, arrange them as needed, set properties, and establish associations with data sets that were designed through the Data tab.

The Preview tab provides a preview for a report so that developers can test and adjust the report as needed.

Report Designer provides the Report Wizard that takes developers through the guided steps to create a report. The wizard provides a limited number of layouts to choose from, but a report developer can modify the layout as needed by using the Layout tab after completing the wizard's steps.

Finally, Report Designer enables developers to build and deploy reports to SSRS.

NOTE

Reports developed by Report Designer cannot be interpreted or edited by Report Builder 1.0.

Report Manager

Report Manager is a web-based report access and management tool providing access to a single instance of a Report Server. Among other things, via Report Manager users can view, search, and subscribe to reports; manage security (report access and roles); create folders and move reports around folders; manage data sources; and set report parameters. Security permissions determine the actions a user can perform using Report Manager. The default URL that invokes Report Manager is http://<server>/reports. The default directory that contains the Report Manager's binaries, pages, and so on is `C:\Program Files\Microsoft SQL Server\MSRS10.MSSQLSERVER\Reporting Services\ReportManager`.

Although Report Manager provides for limited customization, it is not designed to support customization. This leaves companies with a few customization options, but these can be combined:

- Accept limited customization capabilities of Report Manager, such as modification of style sheets it uses (by default located at `C:\Program Files\Microsoft SQL Server\MSRS10.MSSQLSERVER\Reporting Services\ReportManager\Styles`), and adjust the name the Report Manager displays through the site settings (http://<server>/Reports/Pages/Settings.aspx).
- Understand how Report Manager functions internally through the use of classes in the `ReportingServicesWebUserInterface` assembly and leverage its undocumented functionality.
- Write custom management pages to replace one or more management pages in Report Manager (by default located at `C:\Program Files\Microsoft SQL Server\MSRS10.MSSQLSERVER\Reporting Services\ReportManager\Pages`).
- Write a custom façade that displays a company's information and eventually takes a user to the Report Manager pages.
- Write a custom report management application to replace Report Manager.

SQL Server Management Studio

SQL Server Management Studio provides a Windows Forms-based integrated environment that can manage various SQL Server components. From the SSRS perspective, the Management Studio has similar functionality to Report Manager when used to manage a single instance of SSRS.

The advantages of using the SQL Server Management Studio include a consolidated content view for SSRS web farm (scale-out) deployment, slightly better performance, an ability to script and replay administrative tasks, and a finer granularity for role-based security settings.

TIP

Use SQL Server Management Studio for a consolidated view of an SSRS web farm.

Reporting Services Configuration Tool

The Reporting Services Configuration tool is a Windows Forms application that can be used to start and stop the Report Server Windows service and reconfigure Report Servers. For example, administrators can change the Report Server's database and SQL Server names, change the SSRS Windows service identity, and change the virtual directories used to access the Report Server and Report Manager. Administrators can start the Reporting Services Configuration tool from SQL Server 2005 by selecting Configuration Tools, Reporting Services Configuration, or from the SQL Server Configuration Manager by clicking the Configure button in the SQL Server Reporting Services Properties dialog box.

`RSPrintClient` Control

The `RSPrintClient` ActiveX control provides client-side printing for reports viewed in Report Manager. The control presents the Print dialog box for a user to initiate a print job, preview a report, specify pages to print, and change the margins. Developers can access this control programmatically in the code to enable report-printing functionality in their applications.

WMI Provider

SSRS includes a Windows Management Instrumentation (WMI) provider that maps SSRS XML configuration files to a set of classes to simplify configuration management of the Report Server and Report Manager, and to minimize configuration errors. The WMI provider also supplies a class that provides basic properties and status information for an SSRS instance, and thus assists with discovery of SSRS instances on a network.

Both the Reporting Services Configuration tool and the `rsconfig.exe` utility use the SSRS WMI provider.

Performance Monitoring Objects

SSRS Windows service and web service include performance objects that supply performance counters that provide information about report processing and resource consumption. The objects are called the RS Windows service and RS web service, respectively.

To have a more complete picture and to gather more information, an administrator can also monitor SQL Server, ASP.NET, processor, memory, and physical or logical disk counters.

Summary

This chapter discussed the SSRS architecture. Table 2.5 provides an SSRS components summary.

TABLE 2.5 Reporting Services Components Summary

Component	Brief Description
Programmatic interfaces	Provides access to SSRS functionality through SOAP and HTTP requests.
Report processor	Facilitates a set of report-generation operations from data retrieval to rendering. The report processor invokes other components, such as data extensions, to assist with report generation.
Command-line utilities	Three utilities, designed to assist with scripting of administrative tasks, installed automatically during the Reporting Services install.
Data-processing extensions	Retrieve report data from a data source. Developers can develop additional custom data-processing extensions.
Rendering extensions	Transform the report's intermediate format (a combination of the report's layout and data) into a device-specific format, such as HTML. Developers can create new rendering extensions.
Delivery extensions	Deliver reports to specific devices, such as email or a file system. Developers can create new delivery extensions.
Security extensions	Enable authentication and authorization of users and groups. Developers can (excluding SQL Server Express Edition) create new security extensions.
Report Server database	Stores report definitions, report metadata, report history, cached reports, snapshots, resources, security settings, encrypted data, scheduling and delivery data, and more.
Scheduling and delivery processor	Monitors for events (such as timed subscription) and collaborates with report processor (to render a report) and delivery extensions (to deliver scheduled reports to a location specified in the subscription).
Report Manager	Provides web-based report access and management capabilities. The default URL that invokes Report Manager is http://<server>/reports.

TABLE 2.5 Continued

Component	Brief Description
Report Builder 1.0	Provides drag-and-drop, easy-to-use report design functionality. Report Builder is an ad hoc end-user report-authoring and -publishing tool executed on a client computer.
Report Model Designer	Generates report models for use in Report Builder 1.0.
Report Designer	Enables developers to develop complex reports. Report Designer is a comprehensive report-authoring and -publishing tool hosted in BIDS or Visual Studio.
SQL Server Management Studio	Provides administrators with a Windows Forms-based integrated environment to manage SQL Server components, including SSRS. From the report management perspective, Management Studio has similar functionality to Report Manager, but provides additional capabilities, such as consolidated web farm management.
Reporting Services Configuration tool	Provide administrators with functionality to start and stop the Report Server Windows service and reconfigure report servers. This is a Windows Forms application.
WMI provider	Provides a set of WMI interfaces to manage settings of a Report Server and assists with SSRS instance discovery on a network.
Performance monitoring objects	Provide a view of SSRS Windows service and web service performance.

The next chapter covers various SSRS deployment scenarios and features of SSRS editions.

CHAPTER 3

Getting Started with Reporting Services Tools

IN THIS CHAPTER

- Report Manager
- Business Intelligence Development Studio
- Report Designer
- Report Builder 1.0
- Report Builder 2.0
- Reporting Services Configuration Manager
- SQL Server Management Studio

SSRS uses a number of tools to develop and deploy reports, and to configure the Report Server. These tools include Report Designer, Business Intelligence Development Studio (BIDS), and Report Builder 1.0 and 2.0 for report development. On the configuration front, you can use the Reporting Services Configuration tool to configure most settings on the Report Server. Security, schedules, and jobs can be managed with SQL Server Management Studio. Reports, data sources, and permissions can be viewed and managed with Report Manager. This chapter introduces you to these tools.

Report Manager

Report Manager is the primary UI for SSRS. It is accessible with a simple web browser and requires no tools be installed on the client. The primary purpose of Report Manager is to navigate and view the Report Server's content. It can also be used to upload new reports, create new folders in the report hierarchy, and manage data sources.

Report Manager can also be used to subscribe to reports, manage security, set properties, manager report history and parameters, and serve as the launch point for Report Builder.

There are a couple of caveats about Report Manager. First, it is recommended to use Report Manager with only Internet Explorer 6 and later. Other browsers are not supported. Second, if a Report Server is in SharePoint integrated mode, Report Manager is not available.

Like most web applications, Report Manager enables you to perform actions based on the user's security rights. A user with full access will see screens similar to Figure 3.1. Users with less access will see different results depending on their level of access.

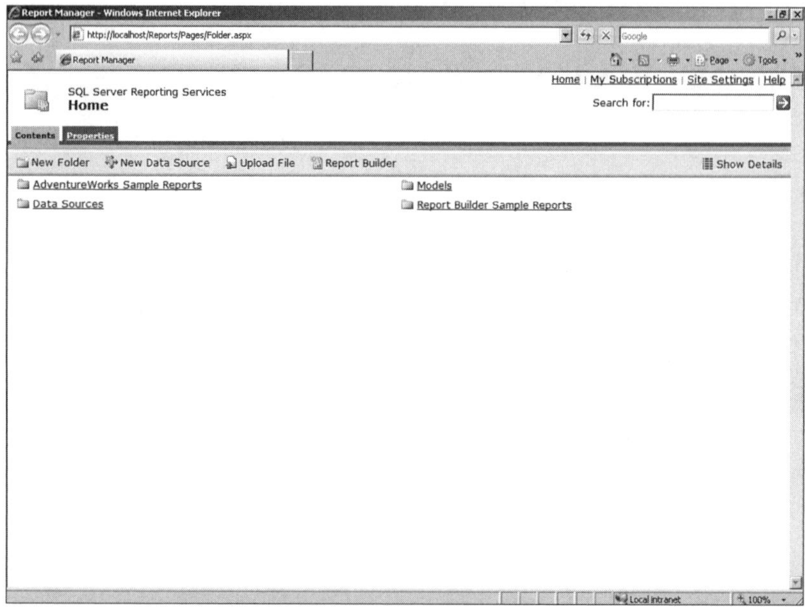

FIGURE 3.1 Report Manager.

In case you are thinking about customizing Report Manager, realize that you have limited customization options. For example, you can modify the application title from within the Site Settings menu. You can also modify the style sheet to give it a customized look and feel. Remember to fully test any modification you make as changes may not be covered by Microsoft support.

Business Intelligence Development Studio

Business Intelligence Development Studio (BIDS) is the Visual Studio 2008 shell with specific project types related to business intelligence. These project types include Reporting Services, Analysis Services, and Integration Services.

Reporting Services has two different project types. The first is the Report Server project, which initiates the Report Designer interface so that we can create reports in BIDS. The second project type is the Report Model project, which enables us to create semantic models for use in Report Builder 1.0.

Once a project is open inside of BIDS, four panes are available:

- Solution Explorer

- Properties
- Design
- Toolbox

Solution Explorer, the Properties window, and the Toolbox can be moved around and docked into different locations depending on user preferences. Figure 3.2 shows them in their default locations.

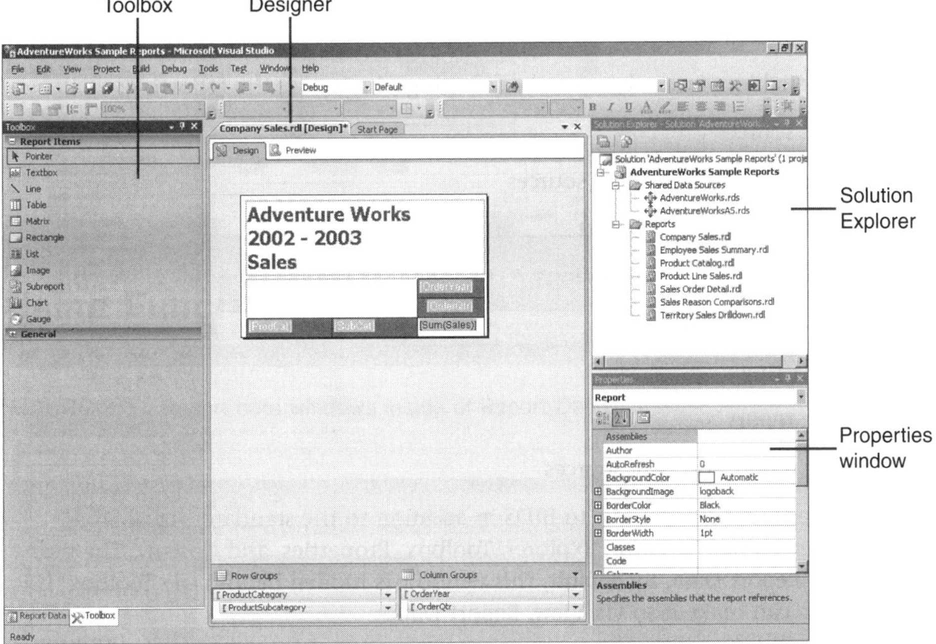

FIGURE 3.2 BIDS open with a report project.

First is the Solution Explorer. Visual Studio, and hence BIDS, organizes groups of projects into a "solution." This way, if you have reports that are related to an application, you can view the reports and the application's code at the same time (as long as the application is a .NET application). If for some reason the Solution Explorer is not visible, you can open it via View, Solution Explorer.

The second of these is the Properties window. A Properties window enables you to view and change properties on the items you select (such as project properties, report items, and the report itself). Different items have different kinds of controls displayed when you select them. These could be simple text boxes or complex custom dialogs that display when you click an ellipsis (...). The Properties window can also be shown by clicking the View menu.

The Toolbox is another popular pane. This contains items that you can drag onto the Design window to create a report. Depending on the project type, items may be grouped into different tabs. The default tab is the General tab.

ests them. One key difference between Report Builder 1.0 and any other report-authoring tools included in SSRS is that Report Builder 1.0 can use only report models as data sources. Report Builder 1.0 cannot edit or preview reports from other report-authoring tools.

Report Builder 1.0 can build tabular, matrix, and chart reports. The Gauge data region and the ability to combine data regions are not available in Report Builder 1.0. Report Builder 1.0 can also publish reports to the Report Server.

Report Builder 1.0 uses the Office 2003 look and feel. It does not include a Ribbon like its successor Report Builder 2.0.

NOTE

Report Builder 1.0 is considered deprecated in SSRS 2008. It is included to ease migrations to Report Builder 2.0, which is also included in the SQL Server feature pack.

Report Builder 2.0

Report Builder 2.0 is a new addition in SSRS 2008. Unlike its predecessor, it is a full-featured Report Designer that does not depend on difficult-to-manage report models. It is also a full-featured report-authoring tool, and unlike Report Builder 1.0 reports developed in Report Builder 2.0 can be edited in Report Designer and reopened again in Report Builder 2.0. Therefore, reports can originate with end users and can be upgraded by software developers.

Report Builder 2.0 features a Ribbon, similar to the ones found in Office 2007. This creates a look similar to some other popular tools used by high-power analysts such as Excel.

Report Builder 2.0 can create tabular, matrix, chart, and even gauge reports and free-form reports (via the List control). All these report items are available through the Ribbon interface. You can also edit report properties such as the page layout and size. You can also include subreports and add page headers and footers.

The UI of Report Builder 2.0 is similar to 1.0 in other ways, too. It includes a Data pane in which you can add and configure report parameters, embedded images, and the data set included in the report. There is also a grouping pane, which enables you to easily manage the grouping in the report. It also includes a Properties window, which enables you to edit properties of the selected item.

Unlike Report Builder 1.0, in which you could only publish a report to the server that hosted the model, Report Builder 2.0 enables you to publish reports to a Report Server of your choosing. This is another side effect of reports using "standard" Reporting Services data sources. Figure 3.5 shows Report Builder 2.0 with all windows displayed.

With all the similarities to Report Designer, there still remains a key difference. Report Builder 2.0 looks at the RDL file primarily as a document. Report Designer/BIDS includes multiple RDL files within projects and projects within solutions. This is in keeping with

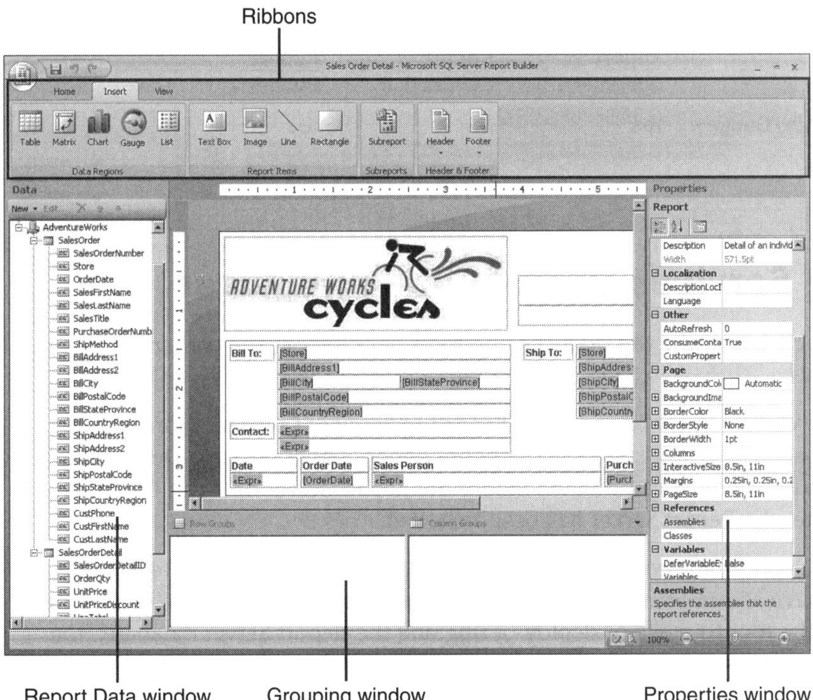

FIGURE 3.5 Report Builder 2.0.

the intended audiences. Report Designer/BIDS was written primarily with software developers in mind. Report Builder 2.0's intended market is the advanced data analyst.

Table 3.1 compares the report-authoring tools delivered with SSRS.

TABLE 3.1 SSRS Report-Authoring Tools

	Report Designer	**Report Builder 1.0**	**Report Builder 2.0**
Full-featured report-authoring tool	Yes	No	Yes
Data sources	All supported SSRS data sources	Metadata models	All supported SSRS data sources
Access method	BIDS	Click-once application	SQL Server feature pack
Project/solution support	Yes	No	No

SQL Server Management Studio's primary responsibility is for the management of SQL Server instances. Two windows are unique to SQL Server Management Studio:

- Registered Servers
- Object Explorer

The Register Servers window enables you to keep a list of different SQL Server instances that you would normally connect to and manage. The window then groups them by type: SQL Server, Analysis Services, Reporting Services, and SQL Server Compact Edition. Each different type is accessible via icons at the top of the window. Inside each group, the end user can group them again into server groups based on preference.

By double-clicking an instance in the Register Servers windows, you can then connect to the instance. The instance will show up in the Object Explorer window. As far as SQL Server Reporting Services is concerned, this is where the meat of the action is.

SQL Server Management Studio can be used to do the following with SQL Server Reporting Services:

- Enable/disable features
- Set server properties
- Set server defaults
- Manage schedules
- Manage running jobs
- Manage server security roles

All of these tasks can be done whether the Report Server is in native mode or in SharePoint integrated mode.

NOTE

In SSRS2K5, SQL Server Management Studio could be used to manage content, too. This functionality has been removed for SSRS 2008 and consolidated into either Report Manager or SharePoint.

You can set most of the properties on a SSRS instance by right-clicking the Report Server in Object Explorer and selecting Properties. Figure 3.7 shows the Properties dialog box. As you can see from the image, you can select pages on the left side and edit the values on the right side.

Jobs, shared schedules, and security can be managed by right-clicking the items in the Object Explorer and selecting the appropriate context menus. Actions that can be performed via context menus include canceling jobs and creating/editing/deleting security roles on the Report Server.

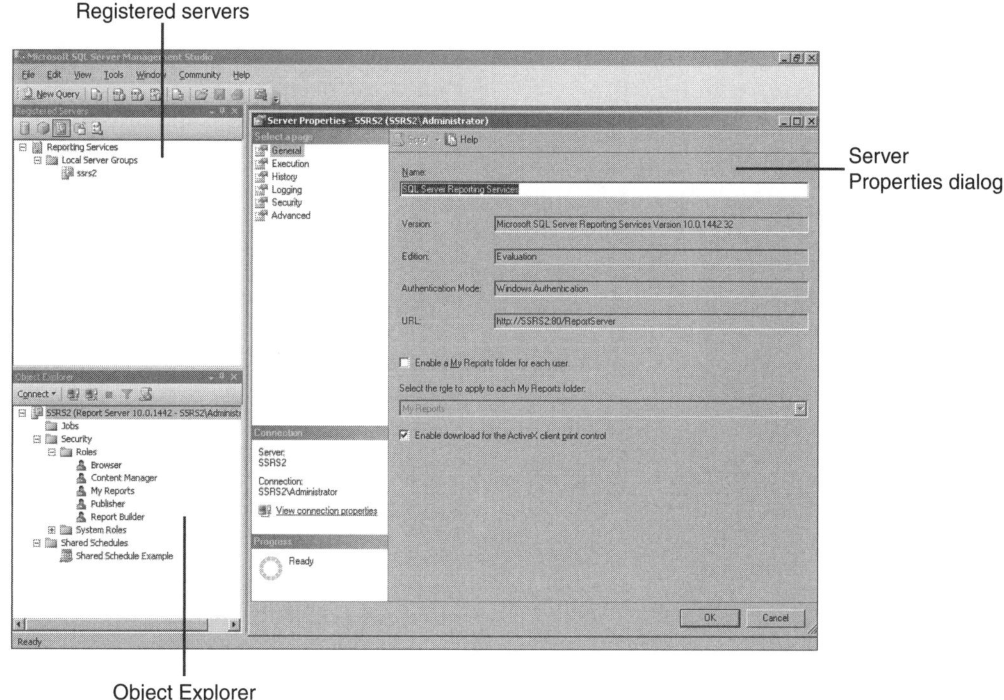

FIGURE 3.7 SQL Server Management Studio Properties dialog box.

Summary

SSRS provides a number of tools for authoring reports and managing Report Servers. The most useful of these tools are BIDS and Report Builder 2.0 for report authoring and Reporting Services Configuration Manager and SQL Server Management Studio for configuring and managing the server.

This chapter introduced these tools and the key menu items they each contain. Later chapters build on this material and provide more detail about what you can do with these tools.

CHAPTER 4

What's New in SQL Server Reporting Services 2008

IN THIS CHAPTER

- Report Server Architecture Changes
- Reporting Services Configuration Manager
- SQL Server Management Studio Updates for Administrators
- Report Manager Update
- Report Engine Architecture Changes
- Report-Processing Scalability Enhancements
- Report-Rendering Enhancements
- `ReportViewer` Control Enhancements
- Report Designer Enhancements
- Report Builder 2.0
- Tablix
- Data-Visualization Controls
- Rich-Text Support
- RDL Enhancements
- Teradata as a Data Source
- SharePoint Integration Enhancements
- Programming and API Changes
- Upgrading from Earlier Versions

SQL Server Reporting Services 2008 introduces an updated architecture and new reporting features on top of SSRS2K5. The result is a better experience for report designers and end users of reports. It is also easier for IT staff to manage the SSRS deployment. This chapter covers the new features and architecture changes.

When it comes to performance and scalability, here are some benefits worth noting:

- SSRS 2008 can handle up to three to four times the number of concurrent users on the same hardware as SSRS2K5.
- SSRS 2008 throughput is significantly better than SSRS2K5 at any level of load.
- In a scale-up environment with higher memory and parallelization, SSRS2K5 used to start failing with errors at very high level of parallel threads. SSRS 2008 continues to work with higher throughput than 2005.

Report design enhancements in SSRS 2008 include an advanced report layout structure called Tablix, data-visualization controls for charts and gauges, and a better report-authoring design experience in the Business Intelligence Development Studio (BIDS). In addition, a new Report Builder 2.0 tool is available as a web download for end users to create reports against SSRS 2008.

SSRS 2008 has added support for exporting reports in Microsoft Office Word format and has enhanced rendering to Excel and CSV. There is better consistency of report layout and pagination between different report-rendering formats in SSRS 2008 over SSRS2K5.

SSRS 2008 also extends support for SharePoint integration, which was first made available in the SSRS2K5 SP2 release. Features in Report Server native mode such as data-driven subscriptions and URL access are now supported in SharePoint mode, too.

Here is an overview of the key architecture changes in SSRS 2008:

- Report Server is no longer hosted in Internet Information Services (IIS) and can independently take care of its networking and memory management needs.
- Unlike SSRS2K5, reports are no longer bound to memory on the box because the report engine will page memory to disk as required. Therefore, large reports don't fail or starve smaller reports of memory. Memory limits can be set to better control how much memory is used by SSRS.
- The report-processing engine can now do on-demand processing. For example, in a 100-page report, each page layout is computed only when the user actually wants to view the page.
- A new report-rendering object model provides more consistency in layout and pagination between report-rendering formats.

One of the key design goals for Microsoft was to not break anything with SSRS 2008 architecture changes. Deployment topologies haven't changed, and SSRS 2008 continues to support single-instance and scale-out deployments. Upgrades from SSRS 2000 and SSRS2K5 to SSRS 2008 are supported.

Finally, configuration and management tools for SSRS have been updated in 2008 to support the new architecture.

The architecture changes, updates to SSRS tools, and new features are described in this chapter.

Report Server Architecture Changes

Take a look at Figures 4.1 and 4.2 to compare the architectures of SSRS2K5 to SSRS 2008.

Here are the key changes to Report Server:

- SSRS server applications and services have been combined into a single Windows service. This makes SSRS easier to deploy, configure, and manage.
- Report Server is no longer dependent on IIS. It now includes components and tools to manage any relevant IIS capabilities.
- Report Server uses shared components from SQL Server, such as SQL CLR for ASP.NET management, network interfaces, and memory management capabilities. This implies that any advances in administration and logging in SQL Server can be leveraged in SSRS in future releases.

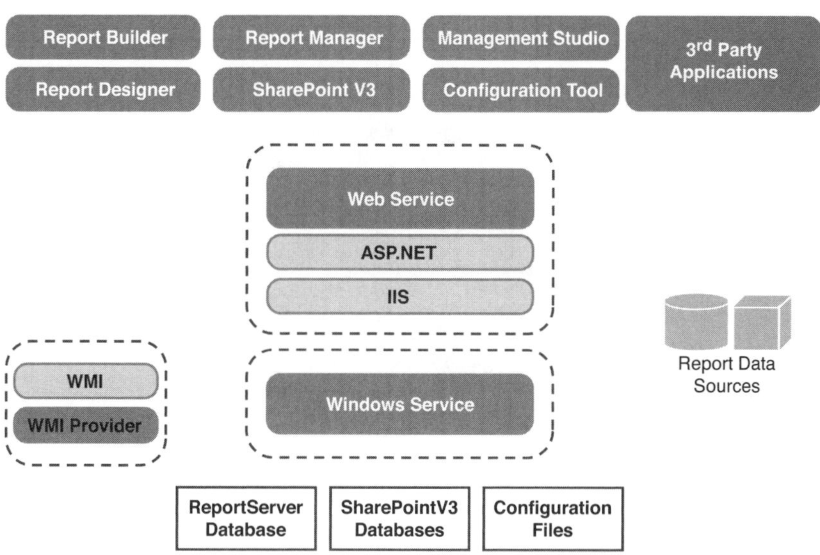

FIGURE 4.1 Reporting Services 2005 architecture.

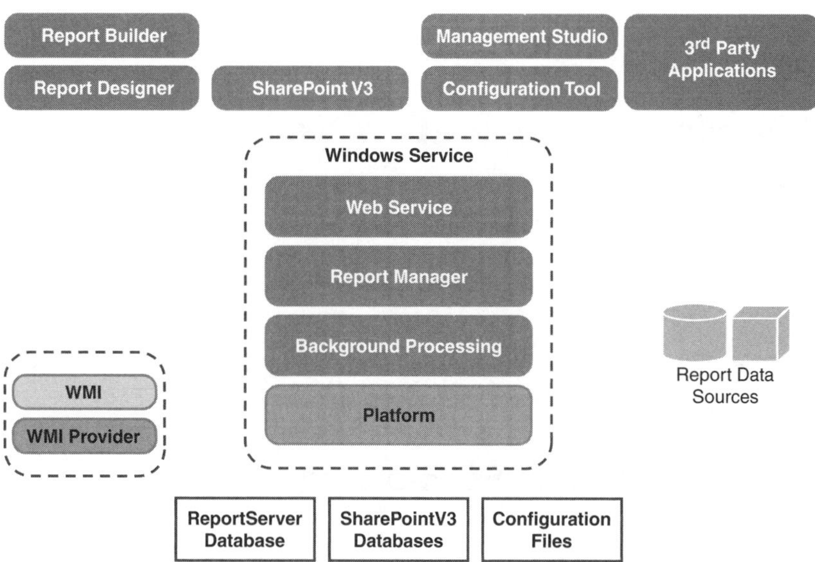

FIGURE 4.2 Reporting Services 2008 architecture.

Compared to the SSRS2K5 architecture in Figure 4.1, the Report Manager application and the Report Server web service have been combined into a single Windows service in Figure 4.2. The box called Platform represents the core capabilities that IIS used to handle for SSRS2K5 but are now managed natively by Report Server. Figure 4.3 shows a summary of these capabilities.

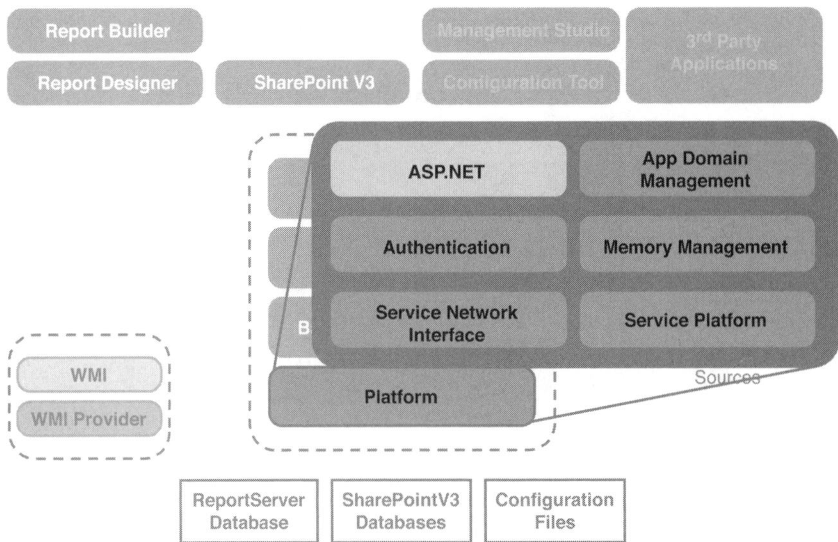

FIGURE 4.3 Report Server native platform capabilities.

The impact of removing the SSRS dependency on IIS is described in Chapter 2, "Reporting Services 2008 Architecture."

Reporting Services Configuration Manager

The Reporting Services Configuration Manager enables you to configure Report Server settings. In SSRS 2008, it has usability enhancements such as wizards to configure the Report Server database and credentials. Figure 4.4 shows the Report Server database summary page.

Because IIS is no longer needed with SSRS 2008 and Report Server handles Hypertext Transfer Protocol (HTTP) communication, the Configuration Manager enables administrators to configure the Report Server and Report Manager URL (see Figure 4.5).

SQL Server Management Studio Updates for Administrators

SQL Server Management Studio (SSMS) is the primary tool for SSRS administrators to manage one or more Report Server instances. Administration covers enabling server features, setting server properties and defaults, defining roles, creating schedules, and job management.

Here are the key changes in SSMS 2008 compared to SSMS 2005:

- Administrators can connect to any Report Server, whether it is configured in native mode or SharePoint mode. In 2005 SP2, it was not possible to connect to a Report

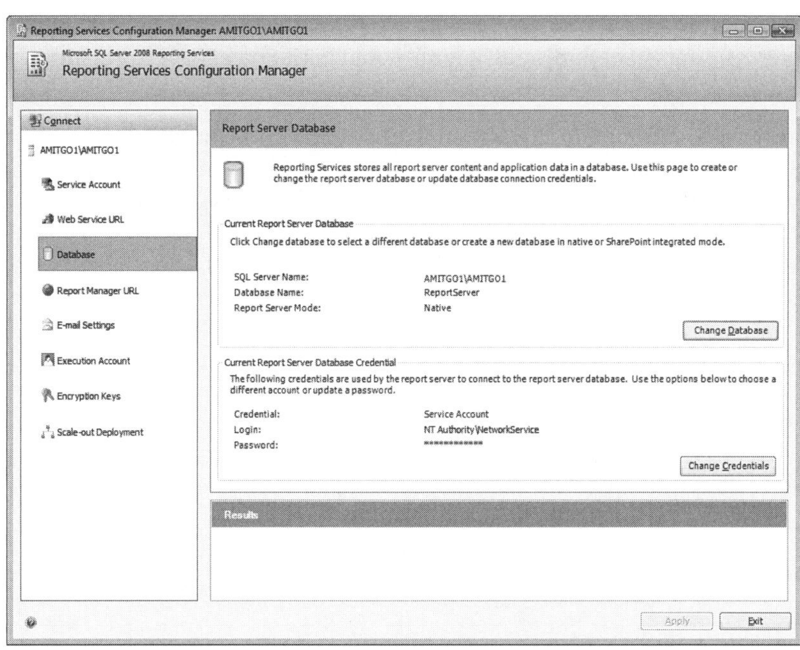

FIGURE 4.4 Reporting Services Configuration Manager: Report Server DB.

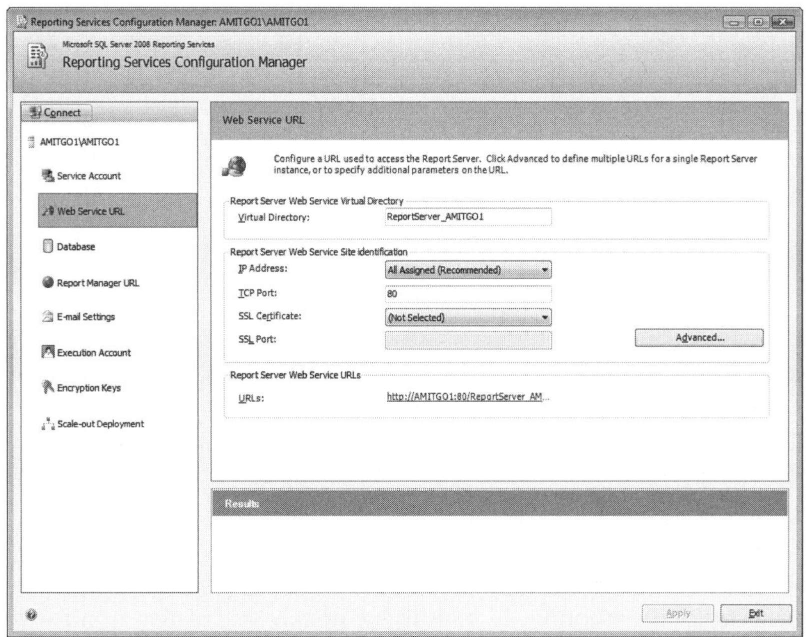

FIGURE 4.5 Reporting Services Configuration Manager: URL reservation.

Server in SharePoint mode. If you are going to use SSRS in SharePoint integrated mode, Chapter 34, "Tools Support for SSRS Integrated with SharePoint," provides more information about tools that support SharePoint integrated mode.

- A Report Server system Properties dialog box has been added. Right-click the connected Report Server name and choose Properties to launch the dialog box. It has pages to view and set properties for execution, history, logging, and security. A General page shows the SSRS version, edition, authentication, and Report Server URL (see Figure 4.6). An Advanced page shows all the properties, and it is the fastest place to view or edit them in one place (see Figure 4.7).

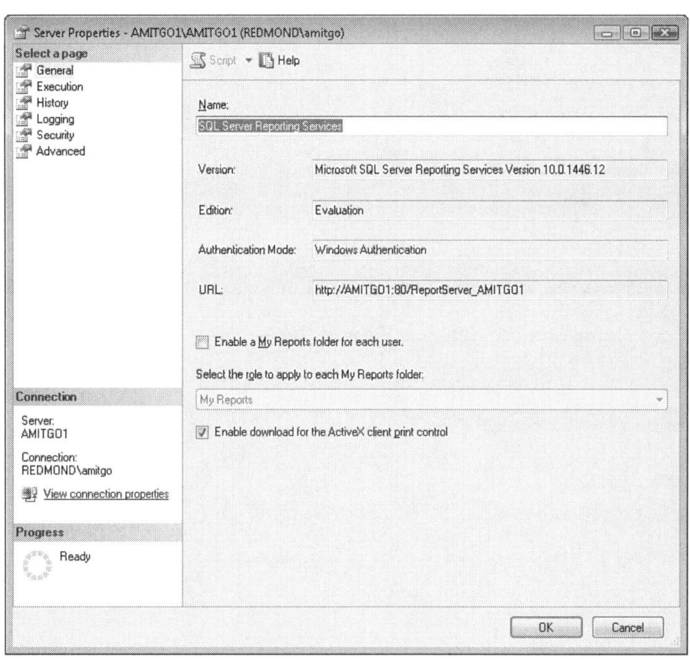

FIGURE 4.6 SSMS 2008: Report Server System Properties General page.

- A dialog box to enable or disable Report Server features has been added. Right-click the connected Report Server name and choose Facets to launch the dialog box. It has a page to allow the administrator to enable or disable Report Manager, SSRS web services, and report scheduling and delivery (see Figure 4.8).

- Report content management has been removed from SSMS in 2008 (see Figure 4.9; the Home node from SSRS2K5 is no longer there). Therefore, SSMS cannot be used to assign permissions or to manage reports, models, data sources, or subscriptions. These management features continue to be available from Report Manager (in native mode) and the SharePoint user interface (in SharePoint mode). The purpose behind this change was to avoid duplication of features in the Report Management tools and the Report Server Administration tool.

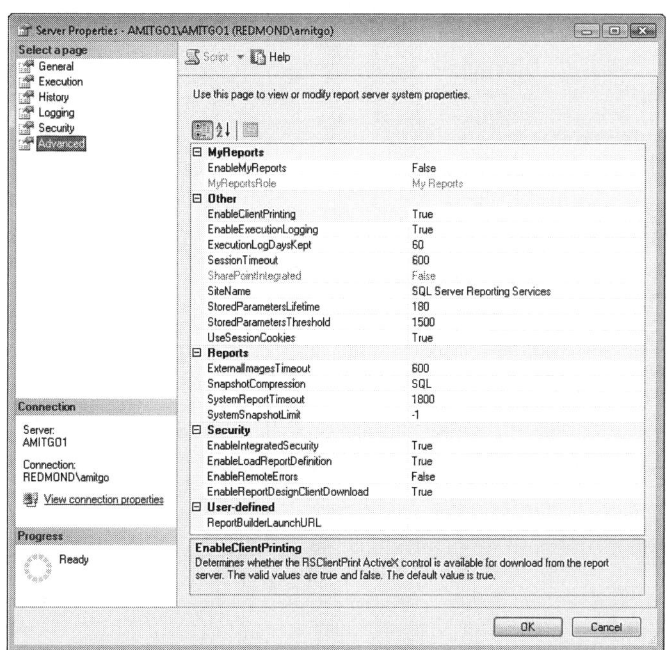

FIGURE 4.7 SSMS 2008: Report Server System Properties Advanced page.

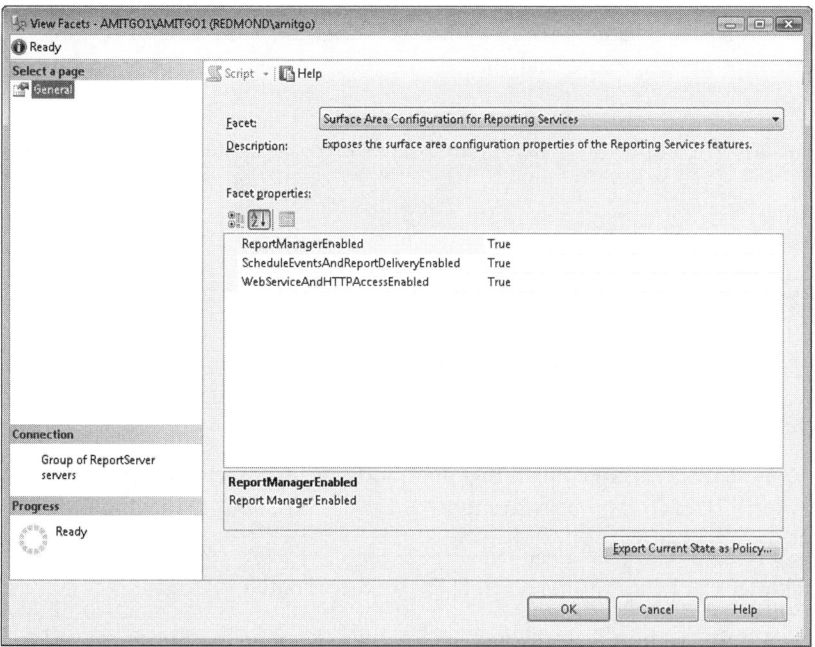

FIGURE 4.8 SSMS 2008: Report Server Facets page to enable or disable features.

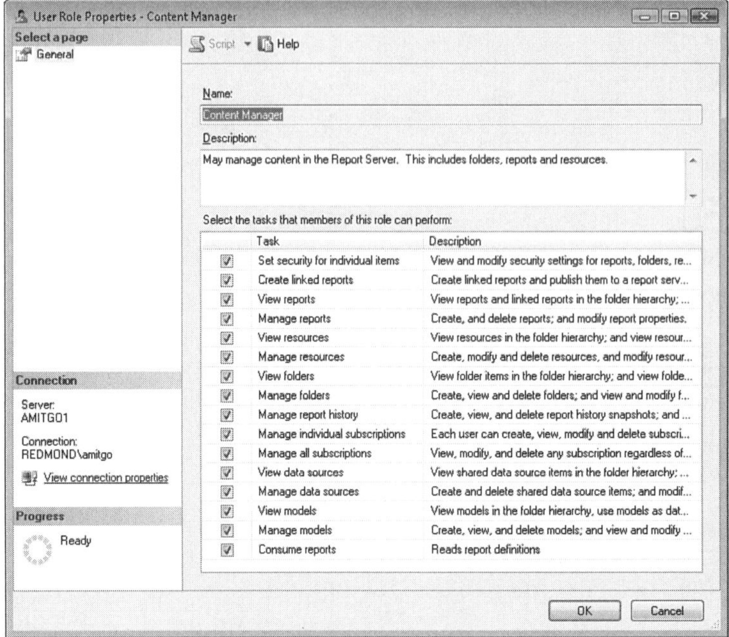

FIGURE 4.9 Report Server tree view in SSMS 2008.

- Job management has been added so that administrators can view scheduled jobs and cancel them if needed. Note that there is a Cancel All Jobs menu option on the Jobs folder.

Roles management and the ability to create shared schedules continue to be supported in SSRS 2008.

Report Manager Update

Report Manager remains the default tool for end users to view and manage report content for Report Server in native mode. It is now the only tool available to manage reports, models, data sources, subscriptions, and permissions.

If you are going to use SSRS in SharePoint integrated mode, see Chapter 36, "Managing Reports in SharePoint." That chapter provides more information about managing reports via the SharePoint user interface.

Here are the key changes in Report Manager in SSRS 2008 compared to 2005:

- Report Server administration features such as job management have been moved to SSMS, whereas report content management features have been removed from SSMS. This avoids duplication of features between the two tools.

- Model management, model clickthrough, and model item security have been added in Report Manager. Users can set model item security (see Figure 4.10) and associate clickthrough reports to entities in a model (see Figure 4.11).

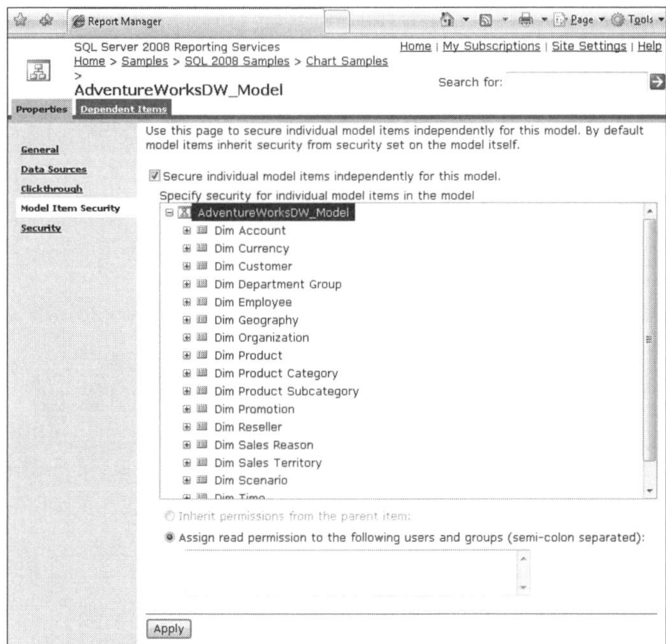

FIGURE 4.10 Report Manager: model item security.

On the Data Source page, a Generate Model button is available. This button brings up a page that enables you to specify the name, description, and location of the model. After a model has been created, it can be managed in Report Manager. Figure 4.12 shows a general view of a model. Note the Edit and Update links. Edit allows saving the model `.smdl` file so that it can be edited. Update allows uploading the latest `.smdl` file to replace the existing one in Report Manager.

Report Engine Architecture Changes

The report engine is responsible for processing and rendering reports. A primary goal behind architecture changes in SSRS 2008 was to make the report engine capable of scalable enterprise reporting.

SSRS2K5 suffered from a few limitations with regard to scalability and rendering consistency:

- Reports were bound by memory. This meant that large data sets and pages in reports could cause out-of-memory exceptions. A single large report could block or fail many small reports.

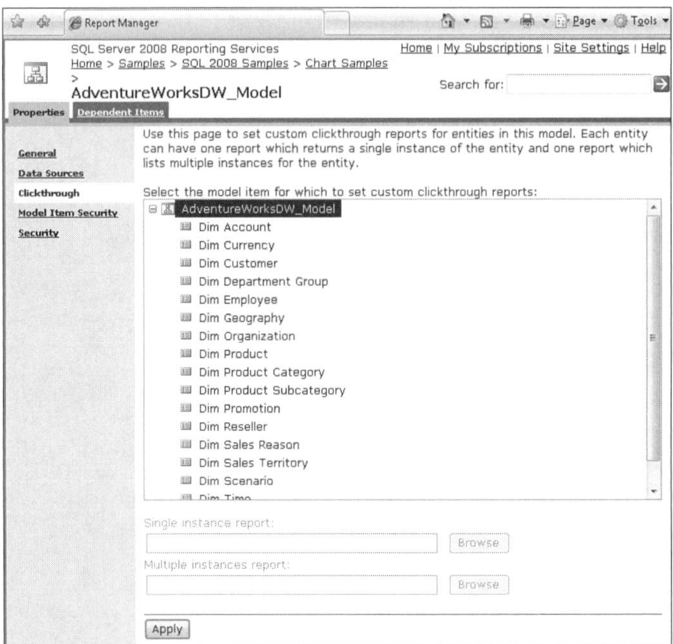

FIGURE 4.11 Report Manager: associate clickthrough reports.

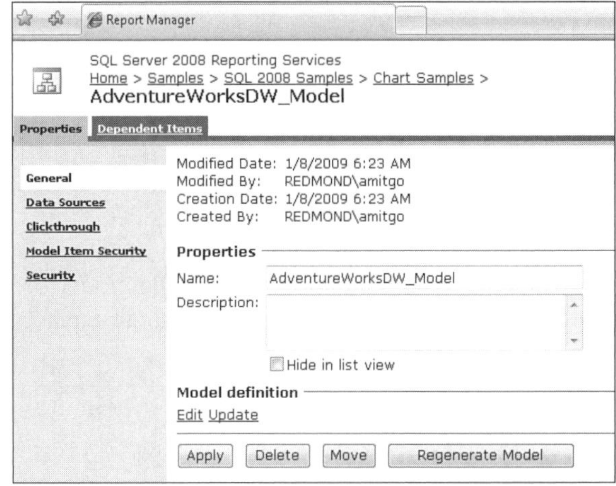

FIGURE 4.12 Report Manager: model management.

- End users had to wait for a long time if a report had hundreds of pages, even though they wanted to see only the first few pages.
- Report-rendering layout and page breaks were inconsistent across various report export formats (Excel, PDF, CSV, and so on).

Here are the key changes that were made in the report engine in SSRS 2008 to address these problems:

- The processing engine takes advantage of new memory management capabilities in SSRS 2008 to swap memory to disk for large reports and to balance memory usage between large and small reports.
- Processing has been changed to follow an on-demand processing model, where each page of the report is processed and rendered only when the user wants to view it. This avoids handling of large amounts of report data at runtime.
- There is a new report-rendering object model in SSRS 2008 that supports on-demand report processing and consistent layout and pagination between different report-rendering formats.

Report-Processing Scalability Enhancements

SSRS 2008 enables administrators to specify minimum and maximum memory settings, and SSRS tries to keep within that bound by swapping memory to the file system when under memory pressure. For more information, see the "Memory Management" section in Chapter 2. Figure 4.13 shows the difference in behavior between memory usage in SSRS2K5 and 2008. In 2005, memory pressure could cause SSRS to fall over and recycle the application domain, which essentially kills all reporting requests. In 2008, memory pressure causes the report engine to swap memory to a file system cache and reduce the memory usage to remain below the maximum memory allocated to SSRS. This allows SSRS to scale to meet the needs of executing large reports and a large number of report-execution requests.

The primary enhancement in the processing engine in SSRS 2008 is on-demand processing, which allows processing each page of a report when the user actually wants to view it. This avoids the burden on the report processor to handle large amounts of data processing up front for all runtime requests.

Figure 4.14 and Figure 4.15 show how the SSRS report-processing engine behaves in 2005 and 2008, respectively.

In 2005, report processing and rendering follows this workflow:

1. Execute queries and retrieve data sets.
2. Perform grouping, sorting, and filtering, and calculate aggregates as defined in the report definition.
3. Report items such as images and text boxes are evaluated and stored in an intermediate format (snapshot).
4. The entire intermediate format is exposed through the Rendering Object Model (ROM), and the report gets rendered.

In 2008, the renderers are invoked right after the data-fetch stage. Subsequent processing is triggered by each page-rendering request. Computations such as grouping, sorting, and

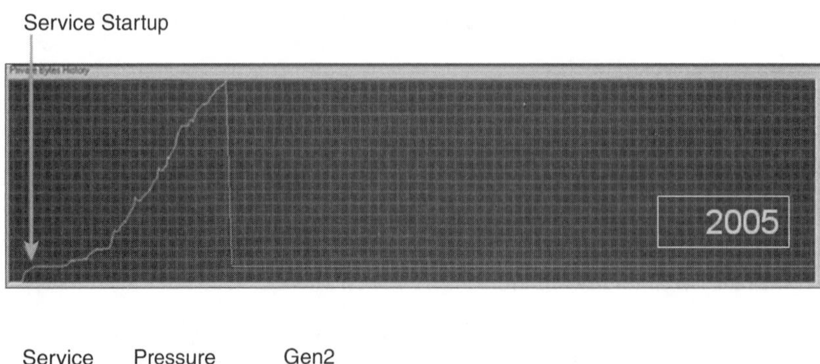

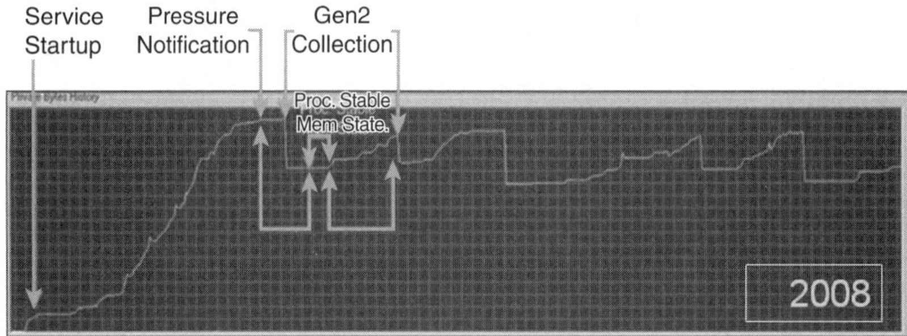

FIGURE 4.13 SSRS2K5 versus 2008 memory usage.

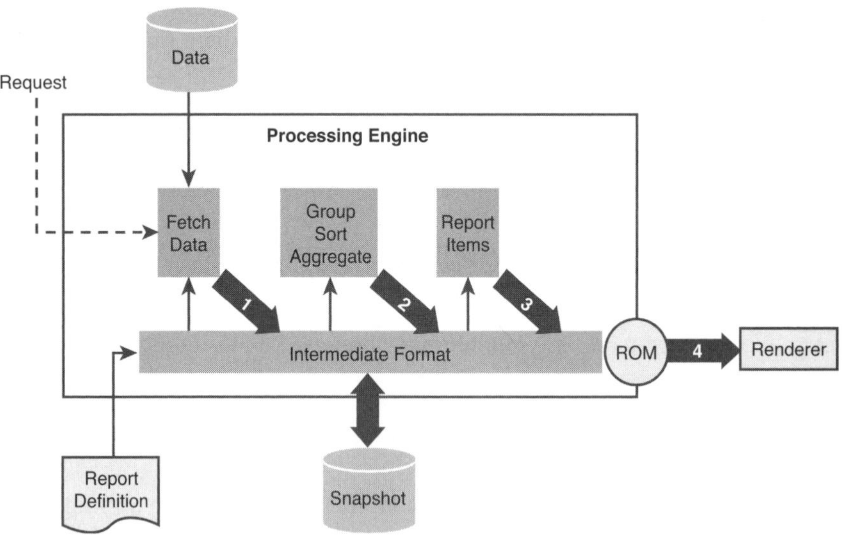

FIGURE 4.14 SSRS2K5 report-processing flow.

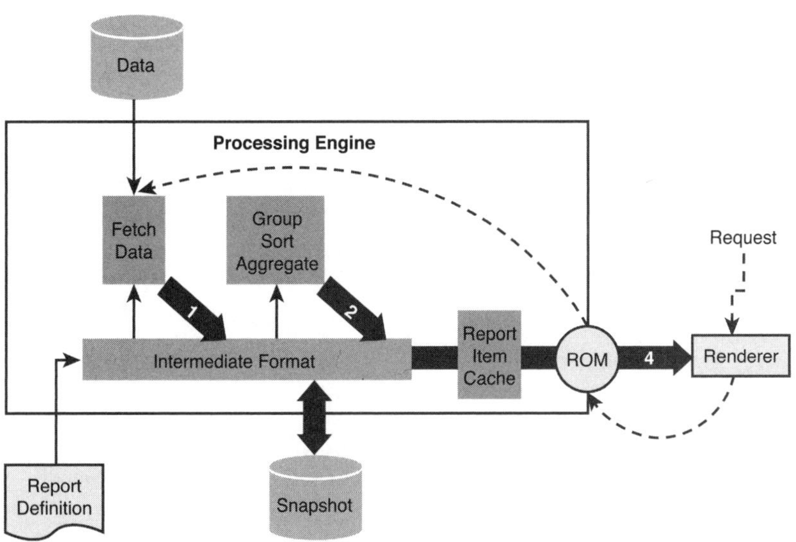

FIGURE 4.15 SSRS 2008 report-processing flow.

aggregation are done the first time a data region is accessed through the ROM. Report items such as text box values and style expressions are evaluated only when the relevant page is rendered. A report item cache is used to help optimize performance.

As a result of the on-demand processing enhancements in SSRS 2008, there is a reduced and predictable data-processing and computation cost for each page-rendering request. Figure 4.16 shows a comparison of page response time when running reports with the SSRS2K5 report-processing engine versus the page response time with the SSRS 2008 report-processing engine. Notice that the response time for rendering any arbitrary page number with SSRS 2008 is lower and predictable.

Report-Rendering Enhancements

The new Rendering Object Model (ROM) in SSRS 2008 provides more consistent rendering layout between different renderers. When you set a page break in your report, 2008 pagination provides more consistent paging behavior when you are viewing or exporting a report.

Here are some key new report-rendering changes in SSRS 2008:

- Word rendering is now supported. Reports can be exported as a Microsoft Word document that is compatible with Microsoft Office Word 2000 or later.
- An Excel rendering extension can now be used to export reports with subreports and nested data regions to Microsoft Office Excel.

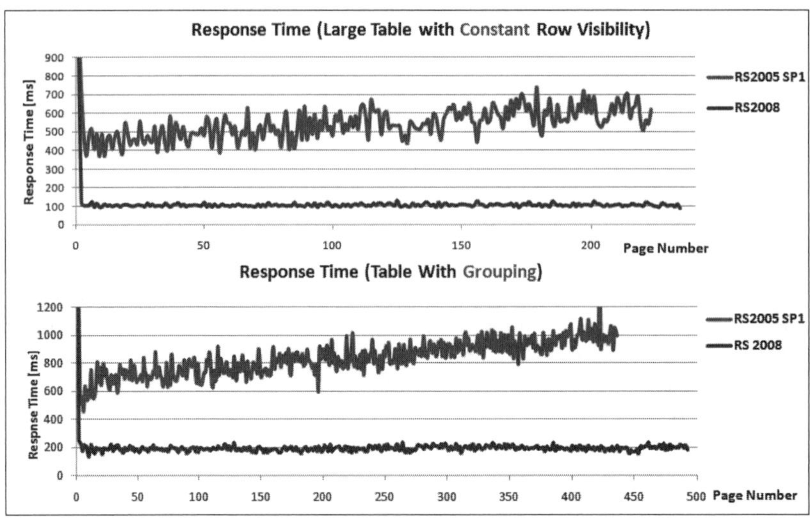

FIGURE 4.16 Report page response-time comparison.

- The CSV rendering extension has been changed to produce data-only content, as opposed to a combination of data and layout in 2005. Data-only output files can be consumed more readily by other applications.

Figure 4.17 shows the report-rendering architecture in SSRS 2008. Renderers are grouped as soft page-break renderers (such as HTML, MHTML, Word, and Excel), hard page-break renderers (such as PDF and Image), or data-only renderers (such as CSV and XML).

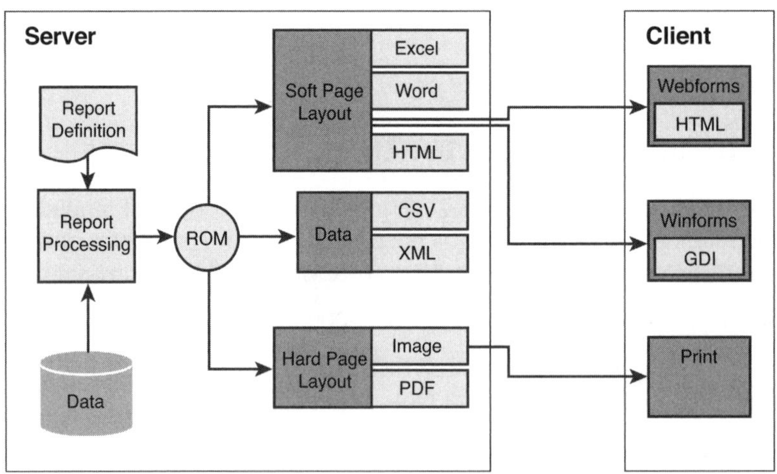

FIGURE 4.17 SSRS 2008 report-rendering architecture.

ReportViewer Control Enhancements

The ReportViewer control was updated in SSRS 2008 to work against the new ROM and the RPL (Report Page Layout) format that is generated by renderers. Some of the rendering load is handled by the client-side controls, which helps with performance and scalability. The WebForms/WinForms controls request output from the RPL renderers and then generate HTML/drawing to the screen based on the RPL.

To increase performance, there is a new setting for PageCountMode, which can be Actual or Estimated. If it is set to Estimated, the total page count is not calculated upon rendering the first page. The ReportViewer control shows a question mark (?) in place of the total page count and changes it to the actual page count when the last page is displayed.

Report Designer Enhancements

Report Designer is the primary report development tool available from the SQL Server Business Intelligence Development Studio (BIDS). The design surface now supports a richer designer experience with rulers and snap lines. The Data tab in Report Designer has been replaced with a Report Data pane that organizes all report data into one place, and it is always visible as you create the report layout. It shows data sources, data sets, parameters, images, and built-in fields. Other changes include a new grouping pane that provides a convenient way to create groups for a Tablix data region and new property dialog boxes to set report item properties.

Report Builder 2.0

Report Builder 2.0 (RB 2.0) is the new end-user report-authoring tool for SSRS 2008, but you must install it via either the SSRS 2008 feature pack or by installing the SQL Server Service Pack 1. Go to www.microsoft.com/downloads and search for "Report Builder 2.0."

RB 2.0 is a full-fledged Report Designer that lives outside the Visual Studio environment, and unlike RB 1.0 this version doesn't have a requirement for metadata models to act as data sources. The definitive feature for RB 2.0 is an Office 2007 Ribbon-like user interface. End users can use this tool to publish report and data sources directly to the Report Server or a SharePoint site when the Report Server is running in SharePoint integrated mode.

NOTE

Report Builder 2.0 can be used to edit and save all reports regardless of whether they were designed in the BIDS Visual Studio–oriented Report Designer or via Report Builder 1.0.

RB 2.0 supports all the new design, visualization, and rendering features of SSRS 2008. End users can create reports with multiple data regions and pull data from multiple data sources. Figure 4.18 shows a sample report in RB 2.0 with its Office Ribbon-style authoring environment.

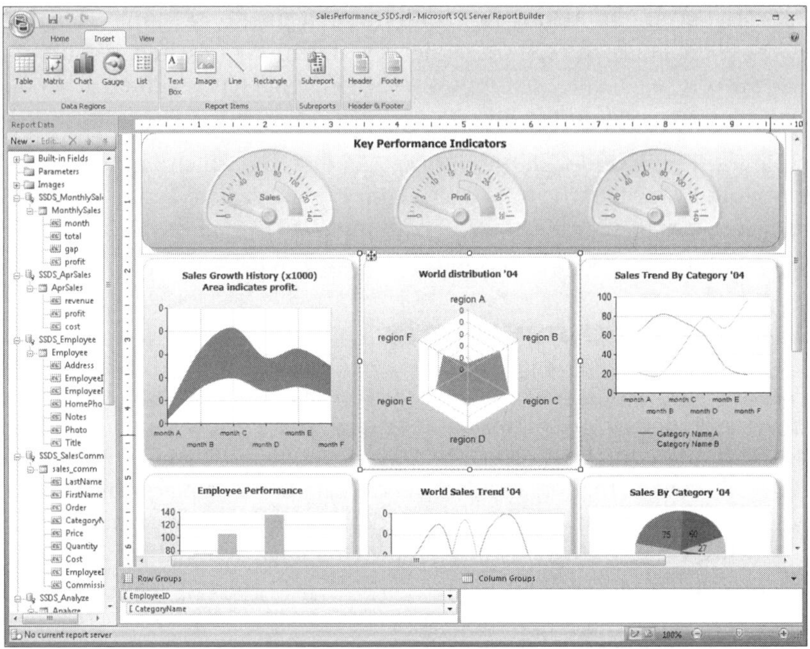

FIGURE 4.18 Report Builder 2.0 Office Ribbon-style UI.

RB 2.0 is intended to eventually replace Report Builder 1.0 in later releases.

Tablix

Tablix is a new data region item that has been added in SSRS 2008 to provide a flexible grid layout and to combine the best of `Table` and `Matrix` controls. Figures 4.19, 4.20, and 4.21 show examples of how report layouts from SSRS2K5 can be combined into a more powerful Tablix layout in SSRS 2008.

Tablix improves report layout flexibility and provides a more consistent rendering behavior. It can support multiple row groups and column groups. Groups can be nested, adjacent, or recursive. The Tablix data region automatically adjusts to include rows and columns for displaying group and summary data.

One way to think about it is that SSRS 2008 Tablix = SSRS2K5 Table, Matrix, and List controls with added features. Report Designer provides templates for Table, Matrix, and List that can be dragged from the toolbox, and under the covers all these actually generate a Tablix data region in the RDL. You can extend a simple table with matrix-like features or extend a simple matrix with table-like features.

To learn more about Tablix, see Chapter 13, "Working with Report Items."

			2005	2006
West	Total		140	180
	Washington	Total	80	100
		Seattle	50	60
		Spokane	30	40
	Oregon	Total	60	80
		Portland	40	50
		Eugene	20	30
East	Total		200	220

	2005	2006
West	140	180
Washington	80	100
Seattle	50	60
Spokane	30	40
Oregon	60	80
Portland	40	50
Eugene	20	30
East	200	220

FIGURE 4.19 Tablix example: hierarchical rows with dynamic headers.

		2005	2006
WA	Seattle	50	60
	Spokane	30	40
OR	Portland	40	50
	Eugene	20	30

State	City	Pop	Area
WA	Seattle	20	30
WA	Spokane	10	20
OR	Portland	10	10
OR	Eugene	25	5

State	City	2005	2006	Pop	Area
WA	Seattle	50	60	20	30
	Spokane	30	40	10	20
OR	Portland	40	50	10	10
	Eugene	20	30	25	5

FIGURE 4.20 Tablix example: mixed dynamic and static columns.

Data-Visualization Controls

SSRS 2008 includes a redesigned `Chart` control that allows many new chart types, such as histograms, pareto, pyramid, funnel, bar/column cylinder, polar, radar, stock, candlestick, range column/bar, smooth area/line, stepped line, and box plot. Figure 4.22 shows a few examples of charts.

NOTE

Dundas Software is a company that specializes in data-visualization software for Microsoft technologies. Dundas controls have been popular with SSRS2K5 customers. Microsoft bought the code base for Dundas data-visualization controls such as Chart, Gauge, Calendar, Map, and Barcode. Chart and Gauge controls have been integrated into SSRS 2008 and are available at no extra cost. Other controls, such as Map, will be added to SSRS in later releases.

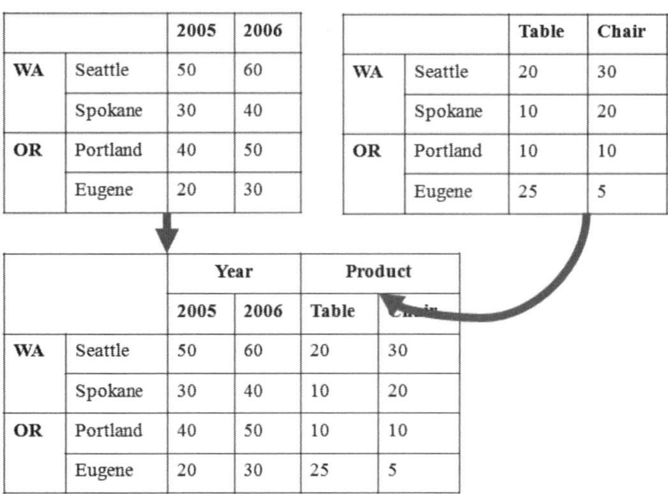

		2005	2006
WA	Seattle	50	60
	Spokane	30	40
OR	Portland	40	50
	Eugene	20	30

		Table	Chair
WA	Seattle	20	30
	Spokane	10	20
OR	Portland	10	10
	Eugene	25	5

		Year		Product	
		2005	2006	Table	Chair
WA	Seattle	50	60	20	30
	Spokane	30	40	10	20
OR	Portland	40	50	10	10
	Eugene	20	30	25	5

FIGURE 4.21 Tablix example: parallel dynamic groups.

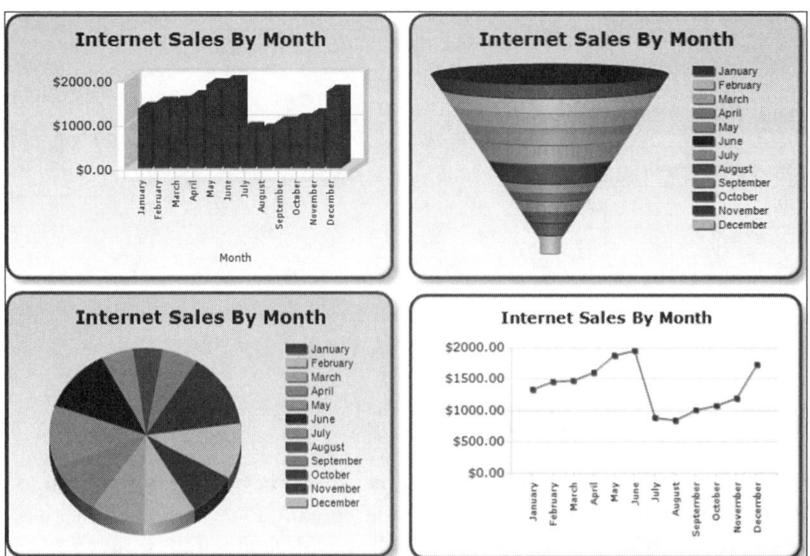

FIGURE 4.22 Chart examples.

Charts have a much improved user interface with enhanced series, secondary axes, automatic interval labeling, tooltips, drawing effects, and many other features that have been popular with Dundas `Chart` controls.

A new data-visualization control is available from SSRS 2008 for gauges to provide a highly visual way to emphasize key performance indicators. A gauge uses a pointer to show a single value and can have different visual representations such as a linear or radial gauge or even a thermometer gauge for indicating temperature. A range can be added to highlight a subset of values on the scale, and multiple gauges can be added in a single gauge data region. Figure 4.23 shows examples of gauges.

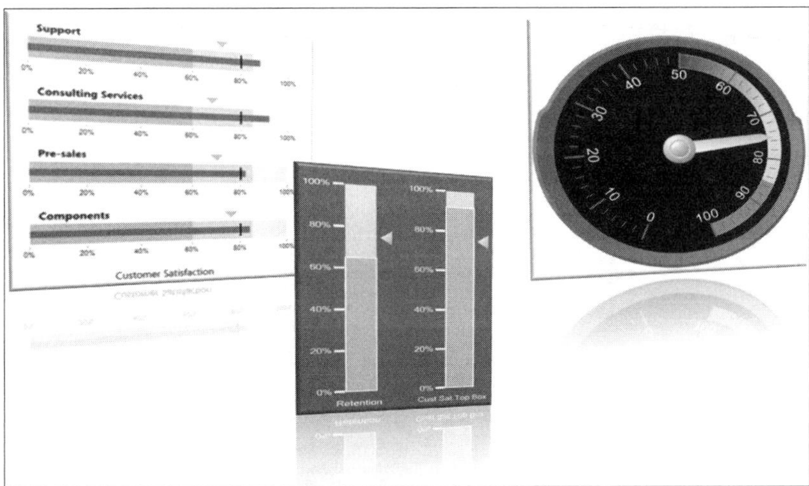

FIGURE 4.23 Gauge examples.

To learn more about charts and gauges in SSRS 2008, see Chapter 13.

Rich-Text Support

The Textbox report item has been enhanced to support rich text with a mix of fonts, colors, text formatting, styles, paragraphs, hyperlinks, and international complex scripts. You can import basic HTML from a field in your database for render within the report.

Support for rich text opens up opportunities, such as creating template reports that mix data from a database, expressions, and text on the design surface. This might take the form of form letters, notices, invoices, or receipts. Figure 4.24 shows a simple example.

To learn more about the Textbox report item, see Chapter 13.

RDL Enhancements

Report Definition Language (RDL) has changed in SSRS 2008 to reflect new processing and rendering features such as Tablix, chart, gauge, and the report engine architecture changes.

SSRS 2008 RDL has redesigned page elements to provide more control over page beaks when the report is exported to different renderers.

New RDL elements include `PageSections`, `PageSection`, and `PageBreak`. Page headers and footers, page margins, columns, column spacing, the `InteractiveHeight`, and `InteractiveWidth` elements have moved from the `Report` parent element to the `Page`

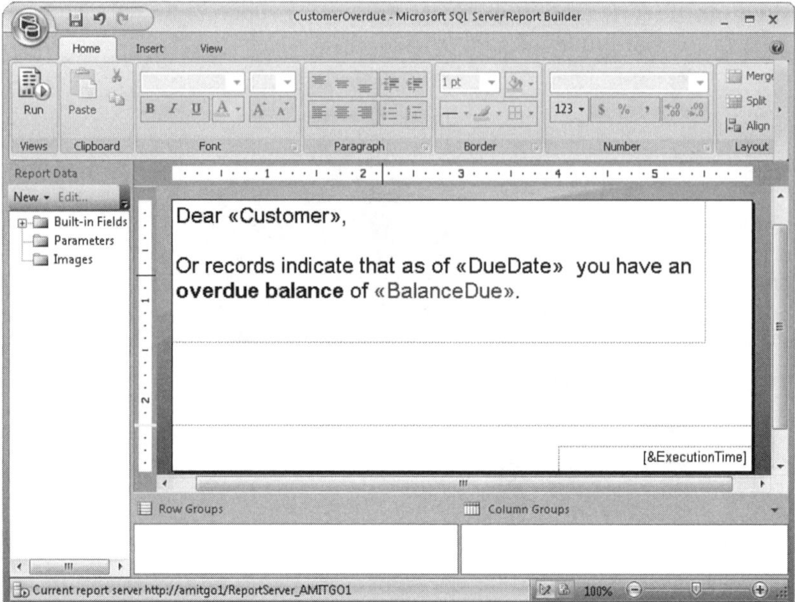

FIGURE 4.24 Example of rich text in text box.

parent element. New support for `KeepTogether` and `KeepWithGroup` has been added to support better control over pagination.

In SSRS 2008, processing-time variables can be declared that are global throughout the report or local to particular group scopes. The `DeferVariableEvaluation` element controls whether a variable is evaluated during on-demand processing of the report.

There is a new attribute `xsi:nil="true"` to distinguish between an element that is explicitly null from one that is not specified. Constants now have data types via the `DataType` attribute on the `Value` element. The default is `String`, but it can be set to other data types as needed.

Teradata as a Data Source

A Teradata data-processing extension was added to SSRS 2008 to enable querying Teradata as a data source for reports and report models.

SharePoint Integration Enhancements

Starting with SSRS2K5 SP2, the core architecture and features for SharePoint integration have been available.

The key enhancements added in SSRS 2008 are support for data-driven subscriptions (DDS), URL access parameters, and for the ability to manage a Report Server in SharePoint mode via SSMS.

Starting with the SQL 2008 release, SSMS supports management of Report Server in SharePoint integrated mode. You can connect to a Report Server in SharePoint mode by entering the URL to the SharePoint site in the Connect to Server dialog box (example syntax, `http://<server>/<site>`) and entering the appropriate credentials. For more information about Report Server management features via SSMS, see Chapter 34.

DDS are now supported in SharePoint integrated mode (just as they have already been available in native mode). DDS provide a way to dynamically filter results, decide on an output format, and generate a list of subscribers at runtime. Figure 36.17 through Figure 36.20 in Chapter 36 show the new SharePoint UI for setting up a DDS.

URL access to the Report Server is available as a way to access individual reports in a customized fashion. This is useful for integrating report viewing and navigation in custom web applications. URL requests contain parameters that are processed by the Report Server and impact how the URL request will be handled. These parameters were not supported in SharePoint integrated mode in SSRS2K5 SP2, but are newly supported in SSRS 2008. See Chapter 35, "Viewing Reports in SharePoint," for more information about using URL access in SharePoint mode.

Programming and API Changes

SOAP endpoint namespaces for SSRS2K5 have not changed for SSRS 2008. Therefore, SSRS2K5 clients or custom applications will continue to work against the SOAP application programming interfaces (APIs). The approach taken for SSRS 2008 by Microsoft was to add new methods to the existing SOAP endpoints like `ReportService2005.asmx` and `ReportExecution2005.asmx`. `ReportService2006.asmx` was added for SharePoint integrated mode in SSRS2K5 SP2, and new methods have been added to it in SSRS 2008 for managing DDS and to list/cancel jobs.

NOTE

The Simple Object Access Protocol (SOAP) namespace is the same for SSRS2K5 and SSRS 2008, and new methods were added for SSRS 2008. If you need to write a 2008-compatible custom client, we recommend checking whether a method exists before calling it. This way, you can catch failures if the client is run against SSRS2K5.

The SSRS 2000 SOAP endpoint (`ReportService.asmx`) has been removed from SSRS 2008. It had already been deprecated. URL access continues to work, but if a custom application was built using RS 2000 SOAP APIs, it will need to be ported to use the newer SOAP endpoints.

SSRS 2008 has a new Windows Management Instrumentation (WMI) namespace. The 2005 WMI namespace is not supported in SSRS 2008. The old namespace was `\root\Microsoft\SqlServer\ReportServer\v9`. The new namespace is `\root\Microsoft\SqlServer\ReportServer\RS_<InstanceName>\v10`.

SSRS 2008 has introduced a new ROM to support the on-demand report-processing changes. It is not backward compatible with the SSRS2K5 ROM. Therefore, if you have written custom rendering extensions with SSRS2K5, you will have to port them over to work with the SSRS 2008 ROM.

Custom report items (CRIs) for 2008 have changed from 2005 to sync with the new ROM. There is a new interface for 2008 CRIs, but the 2005 CRI interface remains supported.

In the area of server extensibility, a new extension was added called Report Definition Customization Extension (RDCE). It allows customization of RDL at runtime. You can find more information about RDCE in Chapter 29, "Extending Reporting Services."

Upgrading from Earlier Versions

You can upgrade from earlier versions of SSRS to SSRS 2008. An upgrade to SSRS 2008 moves settings out of IIS and into the Report Server.

The Report Server database will be auto-upgraded by the Reporting Services Service (RS service). When an older version of the database is detected, you are prompted to upgrade it. If you proceed, the schema is updated to the new format, and you cannot then roll it back to a previous format.

The auto-upgrade feature means customers no longer have to create a database-upgrade script (and there's no longer a manual upgrade option in the Reporting Services Configuration tool). Those features from SSRS2K5 have been removed from the Reporting Services Configuration tool in SSRS 2008.

NOTE

SSRS 2008 has a new Rendering Object Model (ROM). Therefore, custom rendering extensions from SSRS2K5 will not work with SSRS 2008 and have to be rewritten using the SSRS 2008 ROM.

Custom security and rendering extensions block upgrade because there is no way for the installer to determine all the files needed for such extensions. The way to deal with this is to un-configure the custom extensions from SSRS2K5, upgrade to SSRS 2008, and then reconfigure the custom extensions.

RS 2000 or RS 2005 RDL can be published to the 2008 Report Server and will continue to work. Older RDL files are upgraded to new RDL when loaded with the 2008 Report Designer. Table 4.1 lists the various report-authoring usage scenarios and the corresponding SSRS 2008 support.

TABLE 4.1 Report-Authoring Support Table

Usage Scenario	Support
RS 2005 RDL, RS 2000 RDL	Can publish directly to 2008 Server using Report Manager or the SOAP API. 2005 RDL will be preserved (not upgraded).
Report Designer 2000	Not supported; cannot deploy reports to a 2008 server.
Report Designer 2005	Authors 2005 RDLs. Can deploy reports to 2008 Server.
Report Designer 2008	Will upgrade 2000 and 2005 RDLs to 2008. Authors 2008 RDLs. Deploy to 2008 server only.
Visual Studio 2005 Viewer and Visual Studio 2008 Viewer	Can view 2008 Server report. 2008 RDLs are not supported in Local mode.
Visual Studio 2005 and Visual Studio 2008 RDLC Designer	Authors SQL 2005 RDLs. Does not support 2008 RDLs.
RS 2005 RDL, RS 2000 RDL	Can publish directly to 2008 Server using Report Manager or the SOAP API. 2005 RDL will be preserved (not upgraded).

4

Summary

SSRS 2008 has introduced a new Report Server architecture that includes native support for functionality previously provided by IIS. SSRS 2008 has more control over memory management and can page memory to the file system to keep within specified limits. The report-processing engine architecture has changed to improve performance and scalability for large reports and many concurrent users. An on-demand processing architecture and new report ROM provides higher throughput and faster performance for rendering report pages. Even the `ReportViewer` control enhances performance/scalability by doing some of the work on the client side.

A key design goal for the architecture changes in SSRS 2008 was to not break anything. Upgrades from SSRS2K5 are supported smoothly; IIS settings are migrated, and an auto-upgrade is performed on the Report Server catalog.

SSRS management tools such as the Configuration tool, SSMS, and Report Manager have been updated in SSRS 2008 to reflect the architecture changes. Report Server SharePoint integrated mode continues to be strengthened via more feature parity with native mode (for example, DDS support).

Report authoring has been enhanced via Report Designer and Report Builder 2.0 tools. SSRS 2008 provides new features such as Tablix, Chart, and Gauge data-visualization controls, support for rich text in text boxes, and Teradata data source integration. There is a new renderer for Microsoft Word and enhancements for the Excel and CSV renderers.

CHAPTER 5

Reporting Services Deployment Scenarios

IN THIS CHAPTER

This chapter provides an overview of Reporting Services deployment scenarios (including Internet deployment), including SSRS hardware and software requirements, licensing, and security. More technical information about security is covered in Chapter 20, "Securing Report Server Items."

NOTE

Although the test (staging) environment might not be as "powerful" as production, it is best to have a total match for the most effective and realistic scalability testing.

In a SQL Server Reporting Services enterprise production environment, support for web farms and scale-up capabilities of Enterprise Edition come in handy for high-volume reporting. Web farm deployment is flexible and enables administrators to add capacity to a Report Server web farm as demand grows. In addition, if one of the servers in the web farm fails, the remaining servers pick up the load. Thus, a web farm provides high availability for a report-processing layer, but not the SSRS catalog (database).

To achieve complete high availability for a reporting solution, a company can install a Reporting Services catalog on a SQL Server 2008 cluster.

For an environment that does not have high-performance or -availability requirements, you can simplify deployment and use a single Report Server instance with a catalog placed in a nonclustered instance of SQL Server 2008.

You can further simplify deployment in a development environment, install all the Reporting Services components on a single server, and install development tools on a set of workstations.

If a developer or a user needs to be completely mobile, that user can install all the necessary components and a subset of data sources on a laptop, as depicted in the Single Server Deployment in Figure 5.1.

NOTE

There is no separate Books Online for SSRS. Books Online covers all the SQL Server 2008 components: Reporting Services, SQL Server engine, T-SQL, and so on.

SSRS is a fairly memory- and CPU-intensive application. It is hard to be precise with the exact hardware configuration that an administrator might need for installation. Table 5.1 presents approximate CPU needs that depend on the number of concurrent users.

TABLE 5.1 Estimates of Reporting Server CPUs Needs

Concurrent Users	Approximate Number of CPUs
< 150	1
< 700	2
700 > < 2,000	4–8
2,000 > < 4,000	8–16
4,000 >	16+

Table 5.1 provides estimates for a 3GHz 32-bit Intel Xeon CPU server and is based on SSRS performance for rendering a report of an average layout complexity, which retrieves approximately 5,000 rows of data from a data source and provides users with HTML output and reasonable completion times of no more than 25 to 30 seconds. The data source used in this analysis is well tuned and available without significant latency.

Keep in mind that your results will likely differ from the result in the table. A test is the best way to determine precise configuration needs best suited for your deployment scenario.

Configuration tips that you might want to consider when deploying SSRS (or specifically a Report Server) include the following:

- A 32-bit instance of a Report Server can use memory up to 3GB (requires the /3GB switch in `boot.ini`). Because of this, efficient hardware use would be at 4GB per instance (3GB for a Report Server and 1GB for the OS). To effectively use servers with larger amounts of memory, consider installing multiple instances of SSRS per server.
- For performance, start with scaling up (fastest CPU available, 4GB of RAM, and capable I/O subsystem), then move to scale out, and add capacity as necessary (add

Report Servers to a web farm). Host the Report Server catalog in a SQL Server instance on a separate box from your data sources (transactional, data warehouse, or line-of-business database) or at least make sure that a SQL Server instance can handle additional workload.

- For scale-up scenarios, SSRS 2008 supports a 64-bit platform for both x64 (Opteron, Athlon64, and Xeon EMT64T CPUs) and IA64 (Itanium CPU). A 64-bit platform overcomes the 4GB memory limitation of the 32-bit platform and should be considered for reporting applications with high memory demand. A reporting application that renders a fair amount of or large Microsoft Excel or PDF reports is an example of a high-memory-demand application.
- For reliability, use redundant components: at least two SSRS web servers and a database cluster for the Reporting Services catalog database, redundant disk arrays, and network pathways. Although high availability requires at least two servers, three is better. With three servers, you can do maintenance on one of the servers and still have a high-availability configuration running in your environment.
- For cost evaluation when deciding whether to buy more servers with a smaller number of CPUs versus fewer servers with a larger number of CPUs in each, consider the price of the hardware, the additional costs associated with extra servers, and the cost of a reporting-solution failure. As the number of servers grows, so do the server management overhead and other costs, such as the cost of additional space, cooling, and energy.

High-Availability Deployment Considerations

To create a highly available Reporting Services installation, an administrator can deploy Reporting Services on a web farm and use clustering for the Reporting Services catalog database. Enterprise Edition of Reporting Services is the only edition that supports web farm deployment in the production environment. Developer Edition and Evaluation Edition can be deployed on a web farm, but only in a testing environment. No other editions support the web farm feature.

Although the Enterprise Edition of SSRS supports a web farm, it does not include a functionality to create and manage a web farm. This is why a company would have to use separate software (or hardware) to create and manage a web farm. An example of web farm management software is the Network Load Balancing (NLB) feature of Windows Server. The steps to install Reporting Services on a web farm (scale-out configuration) are covered in Chapter 6, "Installing Reporting Services."

To protect the catalog database, companies can deploy a SQL Server 2008 cluster. If Windows authentication is being used between the Report Server and the SQL Server 2008, both Report Server and the SQL Server 2008 cluster have to be in either the same or in the trusted domains. Both nodes of the SQL Server 2008 cluster must have an exact match and all hardware and software installed on a cluster must be supported.

Alternative high-availability options can be used to protect from a database server failure: hardware-based data replication or peer-to-peer replication in SQL Server 2008.

NOTE

The database mirroring functionality of SQL Server 2008 is another high-availability option.

Overview of Deployment Scenarios

SSRS has two main deployment scenarios. The first is possibly the simplest: the single-server deployment. In this scenario, a single machine is responsible for hosting both major components of SSRS: the database and the Report Server.

The second major scenario is the scale-out deployment, in which the database is on one machine, possibly a clustered virtual machine, and the Report Server is on another machine or on a web farm.

Figure 5.1 shows a sample SSRS deployment. When administrators install SSRS, they have a choice to install one or more client- and server-side components, as outlined in Table 5.2.

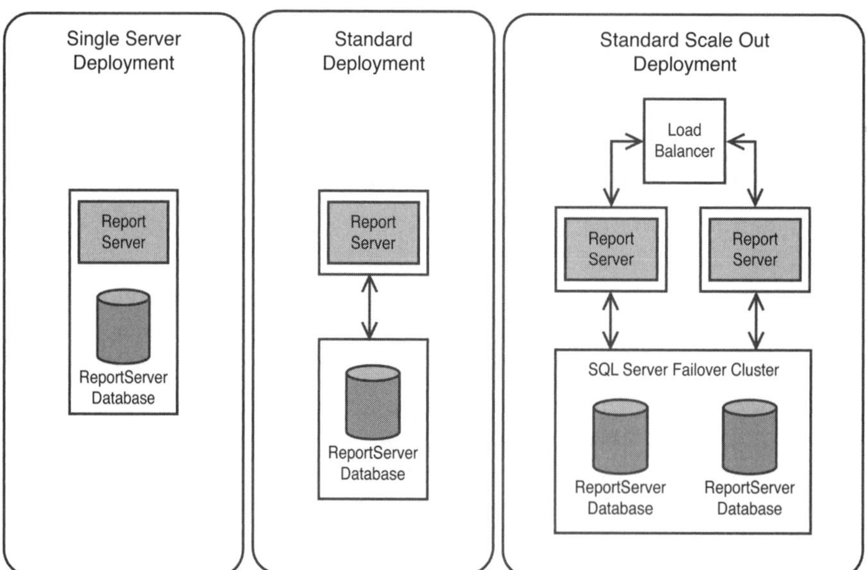

FIGURE 5.1 Deployment scenarios.

TABLE 5.2 Reporting Services Deployable Elements

Component	Approximate Size	Typical Install Location
Reporting Services	230MB	Deployed on the server

TABLE 5.2 Continued

Component	Approximate Size	Typical Install Location
Books Online	160MB	Developer's or administrator's workstation
Basic management tools - command-line tools	880MB	Developer's or administrator's workstation
SQL Server Management Studio (includes basic management tools)	900MB	Developer's or administrator's workstation, .NET Framework
Business Intelligence Development Studio	1GB	Developer's workstation

SSRS 2008 added the ability to separate out servers to do simply scheduled batch or subscription processing. Figure 5.2 shows an advanced scale-out scenario where servers are isolated for doing simply on-demand or batch processing.

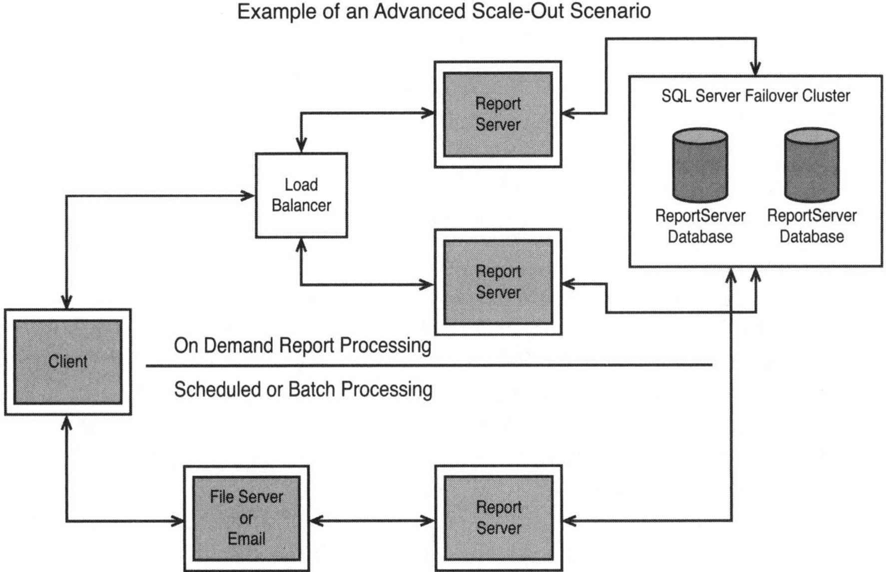

FIGURE 5.2 Advanced deployment scenario.

Advantages/Disadvantages of the Standard Model

The standard model, or single-server deployment model, might sound simple and easy to do at first, and it is certainly the way to do it for a development workstation, or a simple trial or proof of concept. However, you should consider a couple of things when debating whether to use this model in a production environment.

Performance Impact of the Standard Model

The primary consideration for most administrators after cost is performance. Having both the database and the Report Server on the same machine might sound tempting on the financial front because SSRS is included with the SQL Server relational engine. However, both the relational engine and Report Server love RAM and CPU cycles. Although SSRS 2008 has made huge strides in rendering efficiency, SSRS is still going to use all the RAM it can get or whatever it needs (the lower of the two numbers) to render a report. Rendering reports, and especially rendering large reports, also chews up lots of CPU cycles. Adding this overhead to an older machine that is already struggling with the database server is not advisable.

Disk Space Requirements for SSRS

Anyone who has known a DBA, or who has been one, knows there is one thing all DBAs love: storage. They just can't seem to get enough of it. Even in today's environments with large storage area networks (SANs) and hundreds of spindles, the DBA always wants more. This is for good reason.

SSRS, like most databases, installs with a very small footprint. It's almost, and possibly is, negligible. However, depending on how SSRS is used, the disk space requirements can grow pretty large. To understand how space is used inside the SSRS database, an overview of the different types of objects and how they are stored is required.

By now, it should be understood that the SSRS database holds the Report Definition Language (RDL) files, data sources, models, and all metadata, such as folders and access control lists (ACLs). This might seem like a lot to store, but in reality this is rather small, and only in the most extreme cases should this cause issues. Session state information for SSRS is stored in the Report Server temporary database. Because only one row is generated per user session, this should not get very large, and grows at a predictable rate.

Other things stored in the database can, however, grow to be very large. Resources for reports are stored in the catalog as a binary large object (BLOB). It's a sure bet that your friendly neighborhood DBA hates BLOBs. When a BLOB is stored initially with the report RDL, it might not be such a big deal. However, if a resource is stored as part of a report in an archive solution, this can get very large very quickly. Cached reports or temporary snapshots are stored in the Report Server temporary database as a BLOB in intermediate format. Because cached reports include raw query results, the BLOB can get pretty large. Another disk space consideration when using cached reports with parameterized reports is that a separate copy of the cached report is generated for each combination of report parameters. The bottom line is that if you are using temporary snapshots, prepare to use disk space. In addition, you must consider report history snapshots, too. The only difference between them and temporary snapshots is that the report history is saved inside the Report Server database and not inside the Report Server temporary database.

Availability Impact of Standalone Deployment

If the performance impact of the single-server deployment can be shrugged off, the availability impact of it can't be. Having one machine be the central data store and Report Server creates a single point of failure in an enterprise environment. This makes having a backup essential to save the system from some unforeseen calamity. Not much more can be said about it. It is up to the administrator to decide how critical the functionality SSRS provides is. If it can be down for as much time as needed to restore from tape, or if SSRS is not yet important enough to be deployed in a redundant manner, a standalone deployment should suffice.

Advantages/Disadvantages of the Scale-Out Model

The scale-out model of deployment has two main advantages over the standalone model: performance and availability. However, it has one major downside: cost. Because in the scale-out model the database server is separate from the web server, the performance penalty of combining the database engine with the Report Server's rendering engine gets nullified. In addition, the database can be clustered in a virtual server to provide high availability.

With modern SAN technologies, the database can even be replicated to a remote site. The SSRS application server lives on a separate server. The server is simply the first node in what could become an NLB cluster. The cluster makes it possible to scale out for performance/availability or both. Scaling out also helps with dispersing the workload generated by scheduled subscriptions, because each machine on the cluster looks for events that trigger a subscription to process. The cluster also allows one node to be removed for upgrades/maintenance and then be placed back online when the maintenance is complete.

NOTE

NLB clusters are not a function of SSRS. Instead, they are a function of the OS or hardware. SSRS is just an application that can be placed on an existing NLB cluster.

All of this flexibility comes at a price (literally). The only editions to support a scale-out deployment are Developer and Enterprise. Microsoft does not offer support for the Developer Edition, and does not license it for use in a production environment. In addition, every machine in a scale-out deployment has to be licensed separately for Enterprise Edition. More than anything, the cost of a scale out is what keeps most shops from adopting it.

Requirements for a Standard Deployment

In a standard deployment, the web server/application server and the database server are installed on the same machine. For this reason, it is important that the minimum hardware requirements be met or exceeded. It is also helpful to have the NetBIOS name or IP address of the Simple Mail Transfer Protocol (SMTP) server handy and the service account used to execute the reports in unattended mode and the credentials with which to log in to the database.

After collecting all the necessary information, you just need to run setup and configure the Report Server. Sounds easy, doesn't it? While running, the installation program offers two main options. The first option is the default installation. This is the option used for running the standard deployment. This option sets up the database server and the Report

Server on the same machine. The second option is called the Files Only option. This option is used primarily in scale-out deployments. For the brave or simply curious, this option can be used to set up SSRS locally; however, the administrator must run the Report Services Configuration tool after the install completes and configure the options herself.

Requirements for a Scale-Out Deployment

As discussed earlier in this chapter, SSRS can be deployed in a scale out on a web farm. Each machine in the web farm runs SQL Server Reporting Services Windows service, which contains the Report Server web services, and the scheduling and delivery processor. As anyone who has managed a web farm knows, in theory any machine on the farm should be easily replaceable with another in the same configuration, and ideally state should not be stored on any box on the farm. SSRS accomplishes this task by using data source configuration information and reports inside the Report Server database. The application servers just need to register themselves with the database server. This might sound simple, but it is not trivial. SSRS 2008 has given administrators much better tools to aid in this configuration process.

Overview of Report Server Initialization

Because SSRS uses potentially sensitive information, it is important to secure it appropriately. In addition, in a scale-out situation, multiple Report Servers need to encrypt and decrypt the data stored in the database. To understand how SSRS accomplishes this, you need a bit of knowledge about encryption and decryption techniques.

In general, there are two kinds of encryption: symmetric and asymmetric. Symmetric is very fast because it uses only one possible key to encrypt and decrypt the data. However, this form of encryption has its drawbacks. How can you share information that has been encrypted with the symmetric key without compromising the key? The answer is to use asymmetric encryption. Asymmetric encryption uses a combination of keys, one public and one private. The public key can be shared with another host and can be used to decrypt messages encrypted with the private key. The same can be said for the private key. Asymmetric encryption is relatively slow, so it should not often be used to encrypt/decrypt.

SSRS uses both types of encryption in a simple, yet intelligent way. For every Report Server database, SSRS generates a unique symmetric key that can then be used to encrypt the data. At this point, every Report Server that needs access to the data must publish its public asymmetric key along with its unique installation ID and client ID to the Report Server database. The Report Server database then uses the public to encrypt the internal symmetric key and share it with the client. After being encrypted with the client's public asymmetric key, the symmetric key cannot be decrypted by anyone else without the private key. Administrators can actually watch this process unfold by watching the changes in the Keys table during the activation process. The process of exchanging public keys and symmetric keys is called activation.

Activation is a two-phase process. The first phase is the Announce Self phase, and the second phase is the Activated phase. The Announce Self phase covers the reading of the keys from the Keys tables and, if needed, the writing of the client's public key to the Keys table. The Activated phase is the time the Report Server gets the symmetric key in encrypted form.

NOTE

Because the private keys are stored under the user's profile in SSRS, changing the user the service runs under could force a reactivation.

The process of adding and removing machines in the scale-out deployment model is simply the process of running activation over again. The same is true for taking an SSRS installation and pointing it to a different database.

NOTE

To use ASP.NET with a web farm, the `validationKey` and `decryptionKey` should be the same on every machine in the web farm. You can find information about how to accomplish this in the Microsoft Knowledge Base article at http://support.microsoft.com/default.aspx?scid=kb;en-us;Q312906.

To remove a server, just uninitialize it by opening the Reporting Services Configuration tool from any node on the cluster, select the node to be removed, and click the Remove button. To move a node, remove the node from its existing setup and follow the steps to add it to the new cluster.

Internet Deployment Considerations

Reporting Services is not specifically designed for Internet-facing scenarios. This is, partially, because the default authentication mechanism of Reporting Services is Windows integrated security. For security reasons, SQL Server setup does not provide options to deploy SSRS with anonymous access to reports.

Several deployment options are available to an SSRS administrator to make reports accessible over the Internet:

- Keep only public data in the SSRS catalog and enable Report Server for anonymous access.
- Deploy SSRS with Windows authentication and leverage Kerberos delegation to authenticate users.
- Use programmatic options (such as custom security extensions) to authenticate and authorize users.

Internet Deployment Option 1: Enable Report Server for Anonymous Access

This scenario is designed to distribute public information. In this scenario, none of the reports are secured, and all the users would get the same information. When accessing Reporting Services deployed in this fashion, Internet users will not be prompted for login credentials. Best practice for this scenario is to place the SSRS catalog database on the same server with an instance of the Report Server. Because the Report Server has web components, this option means that the SQL Server 2008 instance that hosts catalog data will also be running on the web server and there are no queries that cross boundaries of the web server.

To reduce data exposure in this scenario, the catalog must contain only a limited subset of public data. To further reduce data exposure, reports can be configured to be rendered from an execution snapshot; in this latter case, the SSRS catalog would contain only the snapshot data.

NOTE

To configure a report's rendering from a report-execution snapshot, an administrator can use the Report Manager, navigate to a report that needs to be configured, then navigate to the Properties tab, Execution screen, and select the Render This Report from a Report Execution Snapshot option.

Because this scenario does not protect data from unauthorized access, it might only be used when a company intends to publish public data, such as a product catalog. Secure Sockets Layer (SSL) configuration is not required for this scenario.

To provide public data (or snapshots with public data) to the SSRS catalog in this configuration, an administrator can use replication or SQL Server Integration Services to "copy" public data (or snapshots) from an internal data source to the SSRS catalog placed on a web server.

Internet Deployment Option 2: Deploy Report Server with Windows Authentication

This scenario leverages a default authentication mechanism of SSRS and uses a corresponding security extension.

In this scenario

1. A company would have a domain associated with web-facing servers and use Kerberos delegation to validate a user by interacting with a corporate domain inside the firewall.
2. Customers can configure Reporting Services virtual directories with either Windows integrated or basic authentication.

3. When accessing Reporting Services deployed in this fashion, Internet users are prompted for credentials. After users are validated, they have the level of access to a report corresponding to their credentials.

If this option is chosen, an administrator must configure SSL for proper security, especially for basic authentication.

Internet Deployment Option 3: Use the Programmatic Approach

Situations in which a programmatic approach can be used include the following:

- Users do not have Windows accounts.
- User IDs and passwords are stored in a third-party security provider, which, in turn, is used for user authentication.
- Single sign-on technology (such as Microsoft Passport) is used in place of Windows authentication.

To programmatically handle security, a company can develop a custom security extension, handle security within a .NET application, or use the new `ReportViewer` control.

NOTE

Remember that security breaches can have far-reaching financial consequences for a business. Therefore, use custom security solutions with caution, especially when a reporting solution is exposed on the Internet.

This book discusses some aspects of security extensions in Chapter 29, "Extending Reporting Services." An example of a security extension is provided with SQL Server 2008.

On a high level, to handle security within an application, a developer could

- Authenticate a user in the code by either collaborating authentication processing with a third-party security provider or perhaps simply comparing the user's identifier and password to the values stored in a database.
- After the user has been successfully authenticated, the code would either query a third-party security provider or a database for the user's security access options.
- The code needs to control access to a report, based on the user's security access options.

You have several options to control a user's access to a report. Depending on the need of the reporting application, a code can impersonate a Windows user who mapped to the SSRS Content Manager role (an administrative access). In turn, the code itself would control which reports can be accessed by a user.

Alternatively, depending on the actions that the code must take, the code may impersonate different Windows users who have finer granularity of permissions. In this case, there could be a Windows user who has access to just a single report.

After a user is impersonated, the code can, for example, use the function `Render` to access the report's data stream or use the `ReportViewer` control.

The `ReportViewer` control can process remote server and local reports. When the `ReportViewer` control processes local reports, it does it internally and does not need access to a Report Server.

Most data sources (like SQL Server) that a `ReportViewer` control uses require user identification and a password to access data. In this case, an application can collect, for example, a user's SQL Server credentials and pass those credentials to a data source, thereby restricting the user's access to data.

Enabling a Report Manager for Internet Access

As previously stated, Report Manager was never specifically designed to be an Internet-facing application. But in case it is, a few tips can help make it more secure when exposed to the Internet. Figure 5.3 shows a possible Internet deployment scenario.

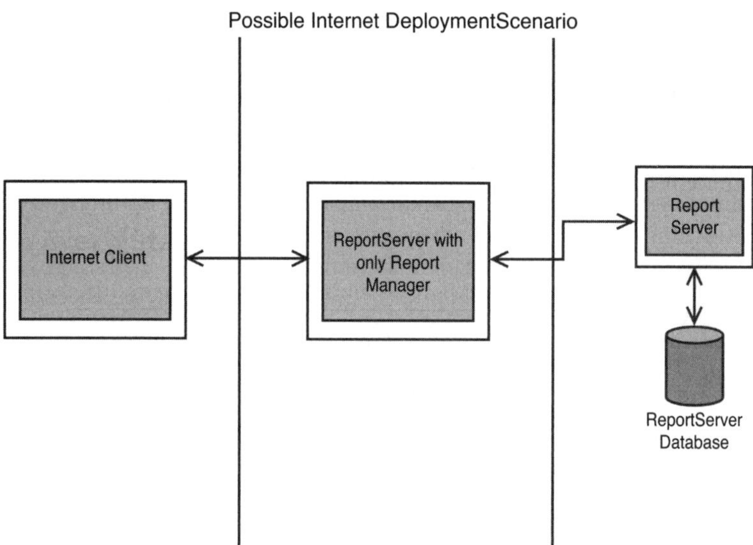

FIGURE 5.3 Internet deployment scenario.

The first of these is to see whether you can run Report Manager on its own server, separate from the Report Server web service, scheduling and delivery processor, and the database server. The key is to remember that SSRS 2008 consolidates all these services into a single Windows service. It is possible to turn off every feature of SSRS except for Report Manager and add the server to a scale-out deployment. This way, the server with Report Manager reaches out to another machine to render and process reports.

Another thing to consider is security. First, build a custom security extension that uses Forms authentication or another kind of technology. After authenticating your users, minimize their permissions on the Report Server. Two roles are required for viewing reports: Browser and System User.

In addition, minimize the footprint of the exposed server. Make sure Report Manager uses another Report Server to process reports by setting the `ReportServerURL` and `ReportServerVirtualDirectory` setting in the `RSReportServer.config` file. Also turn off any features you are not using. This may include My Reports, client-side printing, Report Builder, subscriptions, and so on.

If all of this fails, and you still end up running Report Manager on the same computer as the Report Server, go ahead and disable the `defaultProxy`. By default, this should be set to false, but go ahead and verify it. An example is shown here:

```
<configuration>
...
<system.net>
              <defaultProxy enabled="false" />
       </system.net>
...
</configuration>
```


Minimum Hardware Requirements

Table 5.3 outlines hardware requirements for SQL Server 2008 installations.

TABLE 5.3 Minimum Hardware Requirements

Hardware	Minimum Requirements 32-Bit	Minimum Requirements x64	Minimum Requirements IA64
CPU	Pentium III-compatible processor or faster. 1GHz minimum. Recommended 2GHz or faster.	Any Intel EMT64 or AMD x64 chip. Minimum 1.4GHz. Recommended 2GHz or faster.	Itanium processor. Recommended 1GHz or faster.
Memory (RAM)	512MB minimum, 2GB or more recommended. Report Server will use a maximum of 3GB (with /3GB switch in `boot.ini`).	512MB minimum, 2GB or more recommended. Maximum is the OS-specified maximum.	512MB minimum, 2GB or more recommended. Maximum is the OS-specified maximum.
Hard disk space	Total will vary depending on selected components. See Table 5.2.	Total will vary depending on selected components. See Table 5.2.	Total will vary depending on selected components. See Table 5.2.

TABLE 5.3 Continued

Hardware	Minimum Requirements 32-Bit	Minimum Requirements x64	Minimum Requirements IA64
Monitor	VGA or higher resolution. 1024x768 recommended for SQL Server graphical tools.	VGA or higher resolution. 1024x768 recommended for SQL Server graphical tools.	VGA or higher resolution. 1024x768 recommended for SQL Server graphical tools.
Pointing device	Microsoft mouse or compatible pointing device.	Microsoft mouse or compatible pointing device.	Microsoft mouse or compatible pointing device.
CD/DVD-ROM	CD or DVD drive as needed for given installation media.	CD or DVD drive as needed for given installation media.	CD or DVD Drive as needed for given installation media.

The following is the terminology used in relation to the 64-bit platform:

- IA64 refers to Itanium-compatible hardware architecture. This architecture can run IA64 software and 32-bit software using the Windows-On-Windows (WOW64) software emulator. The Itanium CPU cannot natively run 32-bit x86-compatible instructions and uses instruction emulation as a part of WOW64 processing.
- x64 refers to Extended Memory Technology support-compatible architecture and includes systems based on Opteron, Athlon 64, Intel Xeon EM64T, and Intel Pentium EM64T. x64 architecture can run classic 32-bit x86-compatible instructions natively on the CPU. One of the advantages of this architecture is an ability to support both 32- and 64-bit code. To ease an adoption of the 64-bit platform and optimize a hardware purchase, some companies might first deploy a 32-bit operating system and software on x64 hardware and then upgrade to 64-bit software on the same hardware requirements.

NOTE

System Configuration Check blocks setup from running if the CPU type (Pentium III or higher) requirement is not met. Setup issues a warning, but allows you to proceed, if the CPU speed or minimum memory requirement is not met.

Software Requirements

We recommend installing Reporting Services on Windows 2008. Although Windows 2003 SP2 is a fully supported platform, Windows 2008 reflects the latest technological advances, including enhanced coverage in the areas of security and high availability.

Windows Server 2008 also provides the Hyper-V virtualization systems. SQL Server 2008 and all of its components, including SSRS, are supported in virtual environments created using Hyper-V, provided of course sufficient CPU and RAM resources are allocated to the virtual machine and that the virtual machine runs an operating system supported by SSRS.

Tables 5.4, 5.5, and 5.6 list operating system requirements and additional software requirements for installation of Reporting Services on 32- and 64-bit platforms.

TABLE 5.4 Operating Systems That Can Run 32-Bit Versions of Report Server

	Enterprise Edition	**Enterprise Evaluation Edition**	**Developer Edition**	**Standard Edition**	**Workgroup Edition**
Windows XP Professional SP2	No	Yes	Yes	Yes	Yes
Windows XP SP2 Media Center Edition	No	Yes	Yes	Yes	Yes
Windows Vista Ultimate	No	Yes	Yes	Yes	Yes
Windows Vista Business	No	Yes	Yes	Yes	Yes
Windows Vista Enterprise	No	Yes	Yes	Yes	Yes
Windows Vista Home Premium	No	Yes	Yes	No	No
Windows 2003 SP2 Standard	Yes	Yes	Yes	Yes	Yes
Windows 2003 SP2 Enterprise	Yes	Yes	Yes	Yes	Yes
Windows 2003 SP2 Data Center	Yes	Yes	Yes	Yes	Yes
Windows 2008 Standard	Yes	Yes	Yes	Yes	Yes
Windows 2008 Enterprise	Yes	Yes	Yes	Yes	Yes
Windows 2008 Data Center	Yes	Yes	Yes	Yes	Yes

5

NOTE

Systems that are not explicitly listed in Table 5.4 are not supported by Reporting Services. For example, Reporting Services 32-bit is not supported on Windows 2003 64-bit Itanium.

For situations with heavy memory or I/O requirements, such as heavy graphics and PDF rendering, customers can benefit from deploying SSRS on a 64-bit platform. Table 5.5 outlines SSRS support on a 64-bit platform.

TABLE 5.5 Operating System Requirements, 64-Bit

	Enterprise x64	Standard x64	Workgroup x64	Web x64	Express x64
Windows XP Pro x64	No	Yes	Yes	Yes	No
Windows Server 2003 Standard x64	Yes	Yes	Yes	Yes	Yes
Windows Server 2003 Data Center x64	Yes	Yes	Yes	Yes	Yes
Windows Server 2003 Enterprise x64	Yes	Yes	Yes	Yes	Yes
Windows Vista x64 Ultimate	No	Yes	Yes	Yes	Yes
Windows Vista x64 Home Premium	No	No	Yes	No	Yes
Windows Vista x64 Home Basic	No	No	Yes	No	Yes
Windows Vista x64 Enterprise	No	Yes	Yes	Yes	Yes
Windows Vista x64 Business	No	Yes	Yes	Yes	Yes
Windows Server 2008 Standard x64	Yes	Yes	Yes	Yes	Yes
Windows Server 2008 Data Center x64	Yes	Yes	Yes	Yes	Yes
Windows Server 2008 Enterprise x64	Yes	Yes	Yes	Yes	Yes

The following operating systems are supported by SQL Server Enterprise/Developer Edition IA64:

- Windows Server 2008 64-bit Itanium
- Windows Server 2003 SP2 64-bit Itanium Data Center
- Windows Server 2003 SP2 64-bit Itanium Enterprise

Note that with any 64-bit operating system, management tools may be supported in WOW64. WOW64 allows native 32-bit code to execute natively on non-32-bit systems.

NOTE

Development tools such as Business Intelligence Development Studio (BIDS) are neither installed nor supported on the IA64 platform. For IA64 deployments, use development tools installed on a separate 32-bit or x64 workstation.

Table 5.6 outlines additional software requirements for both 32- and 64-bit platforms and optional software that can be installed to benefit Reporting Services.

5

TABLE 5.6 Additional Software Requirements, 32- and 64-Bit

Software	Requirement Notes
.NET Framework	Windows 2003 IA63 requires .NET Framework 2.0 SP1. Every other version of requires the .NET Framework 3.5.
Microsoft Data Access Components (MDAC)	All versions require MDAC 2.8 SP1 or higher.
Windows Installer	All versions require Windows Installer 4.5 or later.

Key Features of SSRS 2008 Editions

At least some components of SSRS are available in almost all editions of SQL Server 2008: Workgroup, Standard, Enterprise, Developer, and Evaluation.

Whether a customer is a large enterprise or a small company, the key features of Reporting Services that are always available include the following:

- **Manageability:** Reporting Services is easy to deploy and manage. In addition to having a convenient web-based management interface, both deployment and management of Reporting Services can be scripted.
- **Security:** Reporting Services keeps corporate data secure. Reports and information are not accessible, unless sufficient privilege is granted to a user.
- **Programmability:** Reporting Services allows developing of a custom functionality that can be embedded in a report, called from a report, or scripted.

- **Reporting controls and wizard:** Windows and web-based `ReportViewer` controls are supplied with Visual Studio 2008. Report controls simplify adding reporting functionality to Windows and web-based applications.

Additional features available in the Standard Edition of Reporting Services include the following:

- **Extensibility:** Reporting Services allows adding new server functionality. RDL is an XML-based language and is designed to be extensible. SSRS also allows for extending data-processing, data-rendering, and data-delivery extensions with your own custom implementations.

Additional features available in the Enterprise Edition of Reporting Services include the following:

- **Scalability:** Reporting Services Enterprise Edition supports large workloads and high-volume reporting. Support for web farms in Enterprise Edition allows easy scale out, providing an ability to add extra capacity as needed. In addition, Enterprise Edition scales up, supporting more than two CPUs.
- **Availability:** Web farm support of Reporting Services Enterprise Edition paired with the Reporting Services catalog installed on a SQL Server 2008 cluster enables high-availability reporting solutions.
- **Data-driven subscriptions:** Reporting Services Enterprise Edition allows customers to dynamically change the recipient list, report parameters, and processing options. In contrast, Standard Subscription, available in Standard Edition of Reporting Services, is for a single predefined user and single predefined parameter set.

To help determine the most appropriate version, refer to Table 5.7 to review key features of SSRS editions.

TABLE 5.7 Key Features by Reporting Services Editions

	Express	Workgroup	Standard	Enterprise
Data sources	Local SQL Server instance only	SQL Server and Analysis Services	Supports all data sources (relational and OLAP)	
Rendering formats	Excel, PDF, Image (RGDI, Print), HTML, Word	Excel, PDF, Image (RGDI, Print), HTML, Word	Supports all output formats	
Management	Report Manager	Supports SQL Server Management Studio and Report Manager		
Caching	No	No	Supported	
History	No	No	Supported	
Delivery	No	No	Supported	
Scheduling	No	No	Supported	

TABLE 5.7 Continued

	Express	Workgroup	Standard	Enterprise
Extensibility	No	No	Can add/remove data sources, renderers, and delivery	
Custom authentication	No	Supported		
Scale-out Report Servers	No	No	No	Supported
Subscriptions	No	No	Supported	
Data-driven subscriptions	No	No	No	Supported
Role-based security	Cannot modify roles	Cannot modify roles	Can add roles	
Report Builder	No	Supported		
Report models	No	Supported		
Model-level security	No	Supported		
Infinite clickthrough	No	No	No	Supported

NOTE

Developer and Evaluation editions have the same capabilities as the Enterprise Edition of SSRS. However, the Developer Edition is licensed and supported only in the development environment, and the Evaluation Edition expires after 180 days.

Licensing

In a "nutshell," a server license (for Workgroup, Standard, or Enterprise editions) is required for every operating system environment on which that edition of SQL Server software or any of its components (for example, Reporting Services) is running.

This means that a company does not have to buy a separate license if SSRS is installed with SQL Server 2005 together on a single computer. For scale-out (web farm) deployments, each web server that runs Report Server must have a SQL Server license.

Summary

In this chapter, you learned about various SSRS deployment choices. Deployment choices for SSRS components range from a developer's workstation, in which all SSRS components are installed on a single computer, to an enterprise high-availability and high-performance multiserver web-farm deployment.

This chapter also discussed SSRS deployment options for Internet access, and examined the hardware and software requirements, licensing, and key features of the various SSRS editions.

The next chapter delves into the SSRS installation process.

CHAPTER 6

Installing Reporting Services

IN THIS CHAPTER

- Installing Reporting Services
- Deployment Scenarios
- Feature Selection

By now, you should be able to approximate hardware requirements, have an idea about software prerequisites, and be ready to proceed with installation.

NOTE

Before running Setup, note the following:

1. You need access to an account with administrative privileges to run SQL Server 2008 Setup.
2. Set up several Windows accounts to run SQL Server services, such as Report Server and SQL Server.
3. Secure a computer on which you are planning to install SQL Server components; use a firewall, service accounts with least privileges, and so on.
4. Avoid hosting a Report Server on a computer that has an underscore in its name. Computers with underscores in the name break state management capabilities of the Report Server.

On computers on which autoplay functionality is enabled, SQL Server 2008 Setup starts automatically when the install disc is inserted into (depending on the install media) the CD or DVD drive.

If Setup does not start automatically, you can run `<setup directory>\servers\setup.exe`.

Splash.hta provides options to install additional components, such as SQL Server Upgrade Advisor and more. Because this book focuses on SSRS, it concentrates on the actions necessary to install SSRS.

To launch the SQL Server 2008 install, select Server Components, Tools, Books Online, and click the Samples link on the splash screen, or run <setup directory>\x86\setup10.exe directly. The directory name may vary depending on the platform required.

The following are the SSRS-related setup steps:

1. Select Installation from the leftmost menu of the SQL Server Installation Center (see Figure 6.1).

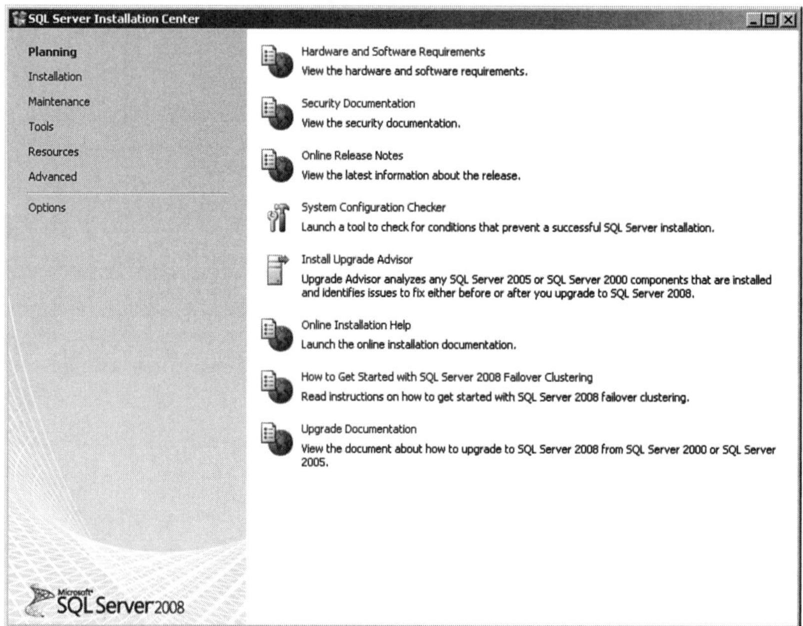

FIGURE 6.1 SQL Server Installation Center.

2. Click New SQL Server Stand-Alone Installation or Add Features to an Existing Installation as shown in Figure 6.2. Doing so launches the installation for SSRS. The other options are largely for the installation of SQL Server's relational engine or Analysis Services on a Microsoft Cluster Server (MCS) cluster.
3. The Setup Support Rules dialog box checks for minimum hardware requirements, whether Internet Information Services (IIS) is installed, and so on. The configuration check also reports whether any problems may require attention prior to installing SQL Server. Fix errors, if any, rerun Setup, and on the successful completion of this step click OK. Figure 6.3 shows the screen with the details list view.

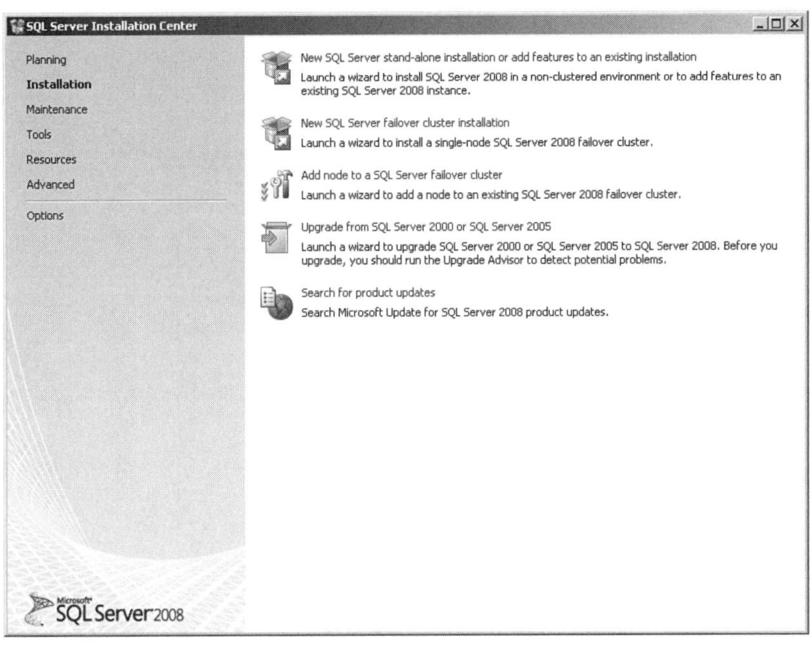

FIGURE 6.2 Installation menu of the SQL Server Installation Center.

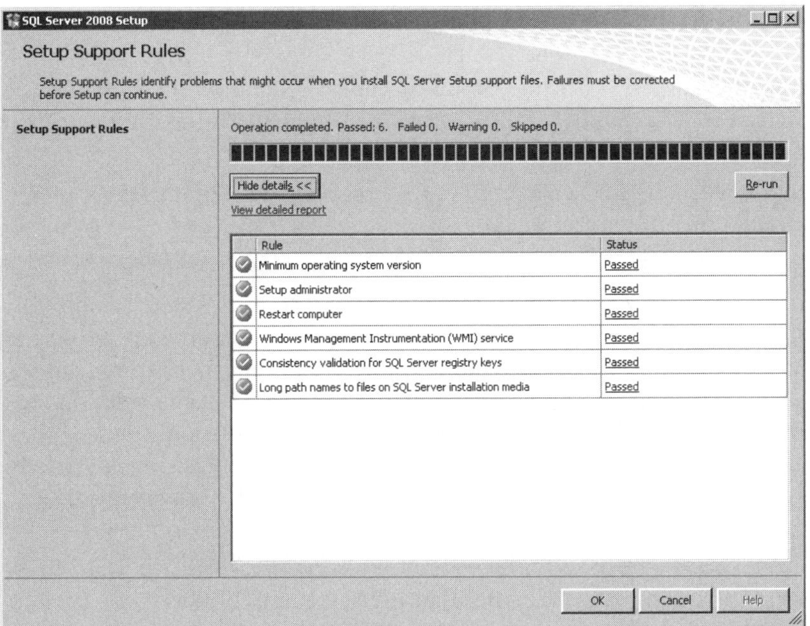

FIGURE 6.3 Setup Support Rules screen.

4. The next step is the installation of the SQL Server support files (the files needed by SQL Server Setup). They help SQL Server Setup install and update instances after the initial setup is complete. Click Install to start the process (see Figure 6.4).

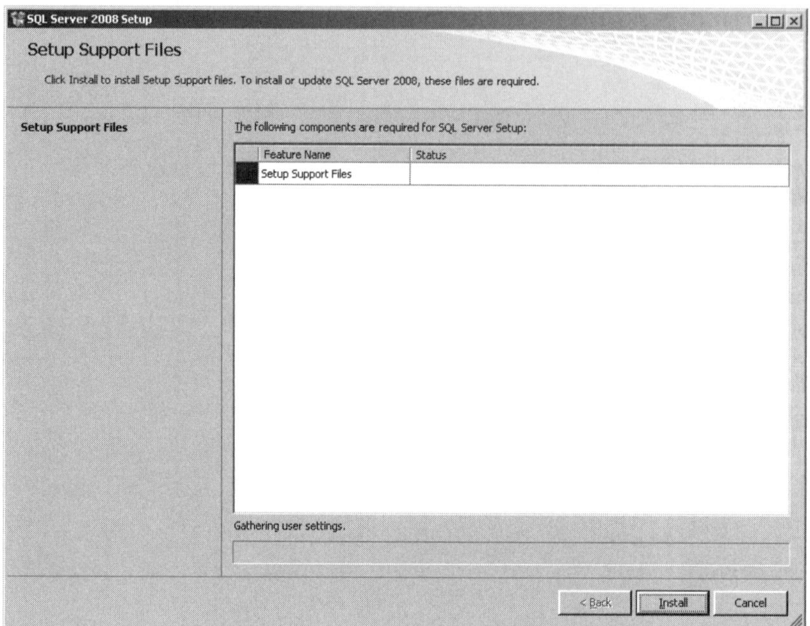

FIGURE 6.4 Setup support files.

5. After installing the setup support files, Setup executes a second round of checks. The title of the screen is Setup Support Rules. Before continuing with the installation, fix any issues the installer finds (see Figure 6.5).
6. Now you pick an edition of SQL Server or enter a product key. Enter a key or pick Enterprise Evaluation Edition (see Figure 6.6).
7. Click the check mark to accept the EULA, and then click Next (see Figure 6.7).
8. At this point, we are at the heart of the installation process. In this step, Setup enables you to select SQL Server–related services to install without the need to specify details. Basic setup options often suffice for a simple install. Advanced install options are also available. The Feature Select dialog box that selects SSRS server-side components is shown in Figure 6.8. For a server-side component installation, check Database Engine Services, Reporting Services. Database Engine Services is not required if you have another server that will serve as the database server. For a client-side component installation, check Management Tools – Basic and Management Tools - Complete, Business Intelligence Development Studio, Books Online.
9. Now you select the instance configuration setting. You can either select the default instance, if applicable, or a named instance (see Figure 6.9).
10. A disk summary displays. Click Next.

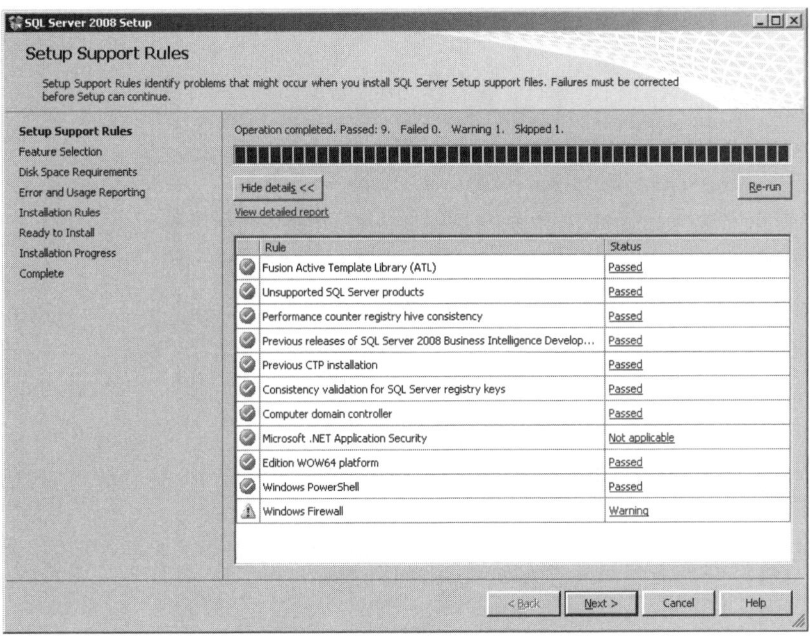

FIGURE 6.5 Setup support rules.

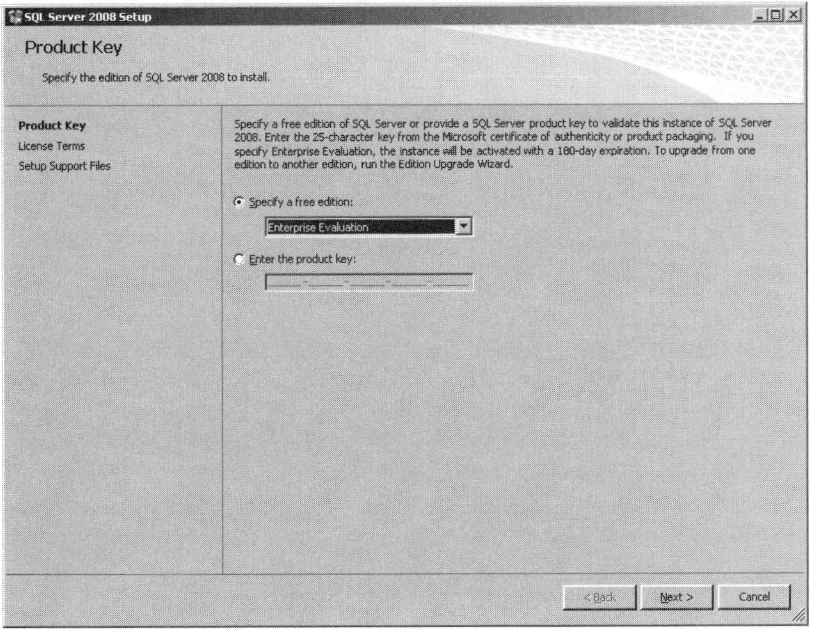

FIGURE 6.6 Enter a product key.

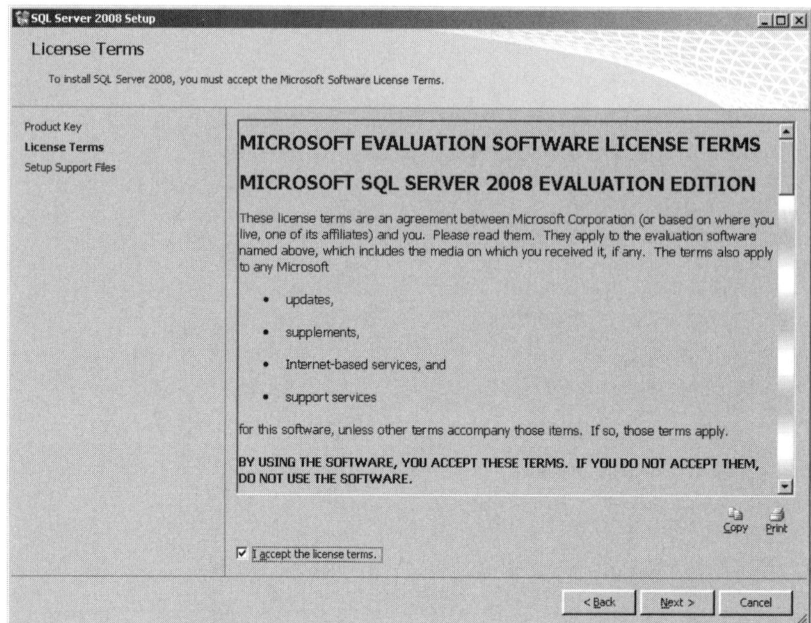

FIGURE 6.7 Accepting the EULA.

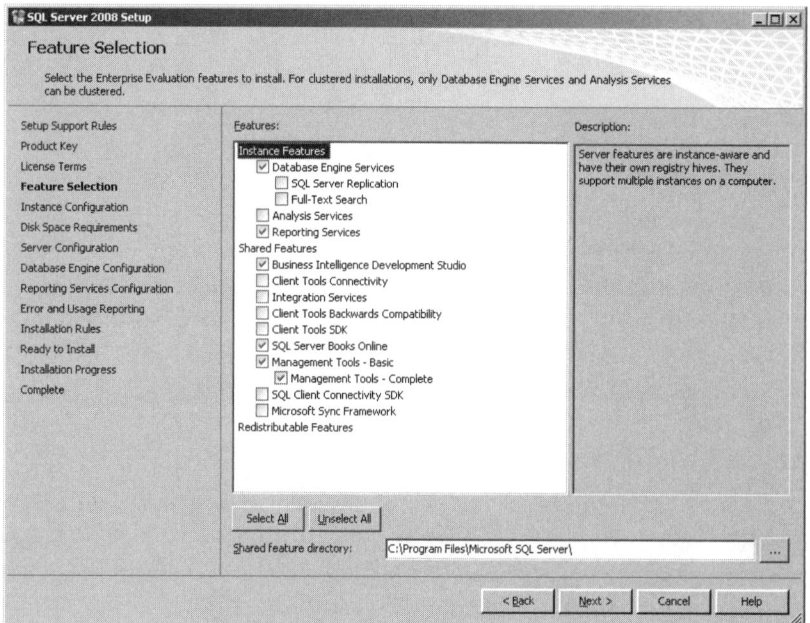

FIGURE 6.8 Feature selection process.

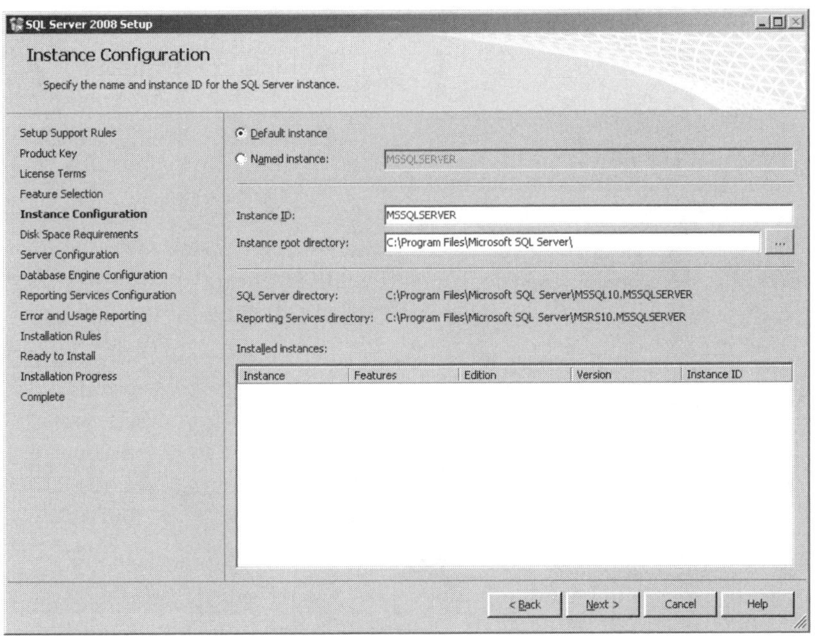

FIGURE 6.9 Instance configuration.

11. Now it is time to select service account information and enter their credentials. It is recommended to use a different service account for each service (see Figure 6.10).
12. At this stage we configure the relational engine. You may skip this step if you did not select Database Engine Services from the feature selection screen. Click the Add Current User button. This will add your user account as a SQL Server administrator for the database engine. If you want to change the default directories for data and log files or enable file stream access in the database engine, you can configure them using the other tabs. For our purposes, the default selection suffices (see Figure 6.11).
13. Depending on the features selected, you now choose the installation mode for SSRS: native mode, SharePoint integrated mode, or Files Only mode. Files Only mode allows you to lay down the Reporting Services files and leave the configuration and activation to later stages. Native mode default configuration will install and preconfigure SSRS with all the default options. Select Install the Native Mode Default Configuration (see Figure 6.12).
14. When the Error and Usage Reporting screen appears, check the check boxes if you want to send error information to Microsoft. Click Next when complete.
15. The next screen is Installation Rules. It runs some final checks before proceeding with the installation. Click Next to proceed with the installation, so long as there are no errors present (see Figure 6.13).

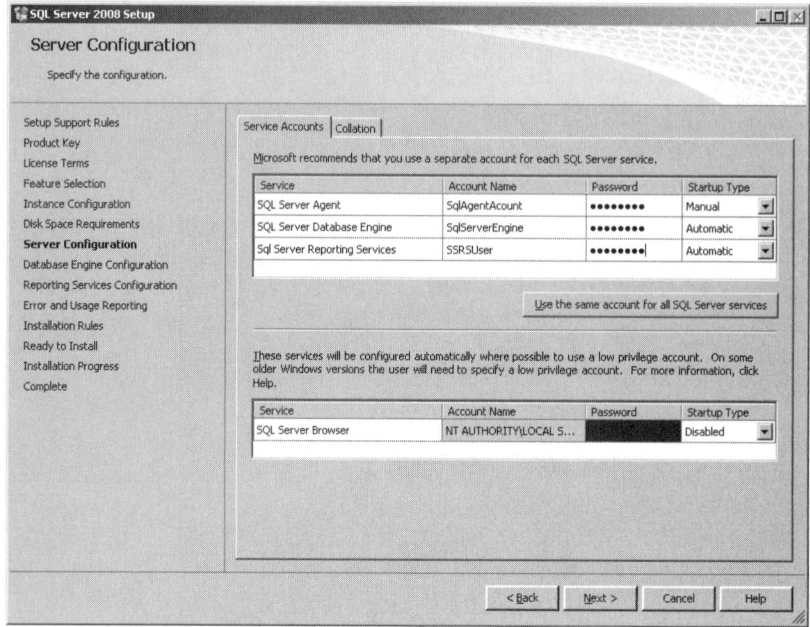

FIGURE 6.10 Service account configuration.

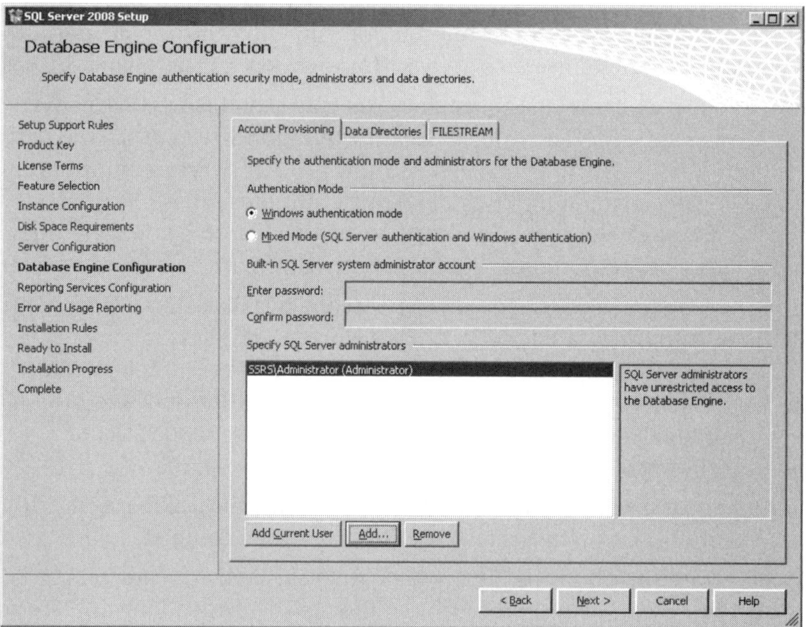

FIGURE 6.11 SQL Server configuration.

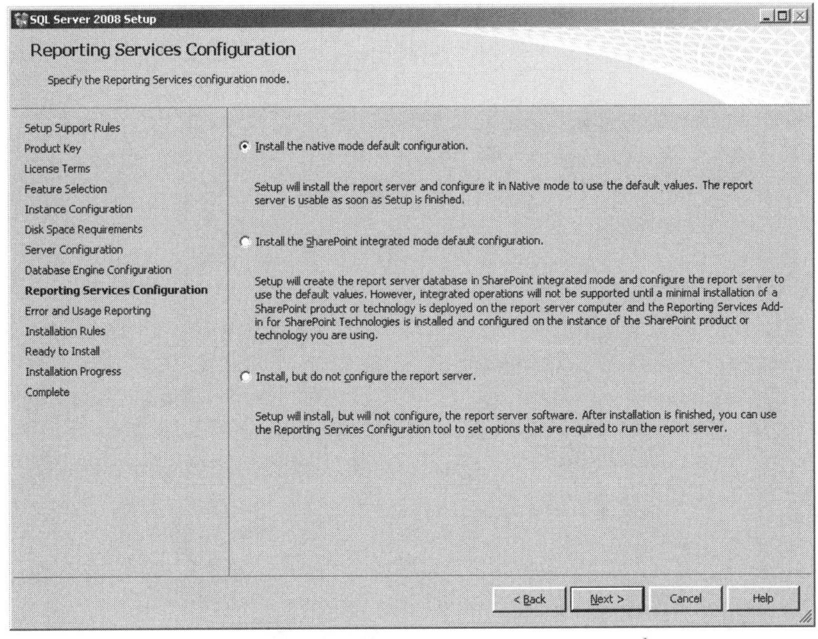

FIGURE 6.12 Reporting Services configuration.

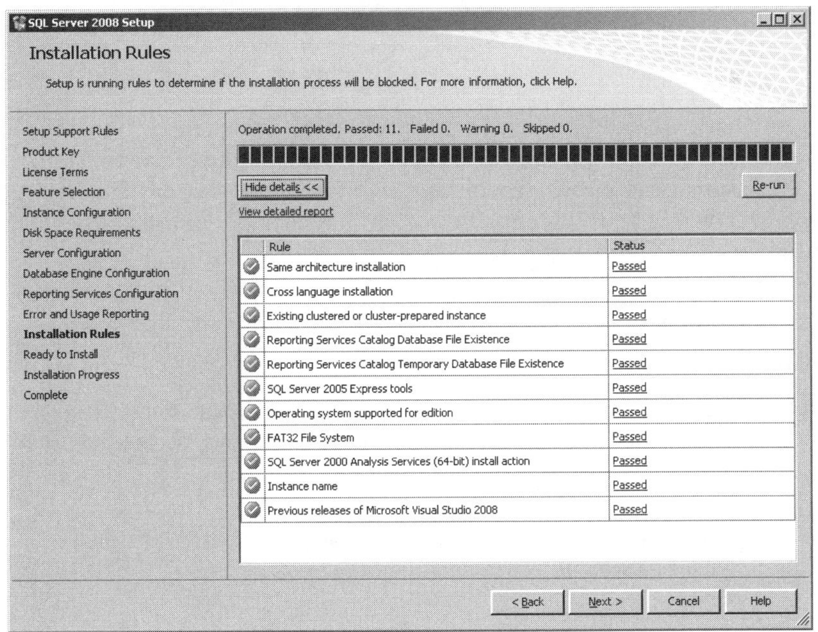

FIGURE 6.13 Last installation checks.

9

16. A summary screen displays that lists the actions that will be performed. Click Install to proceed with the installation (see Figure 6.14).

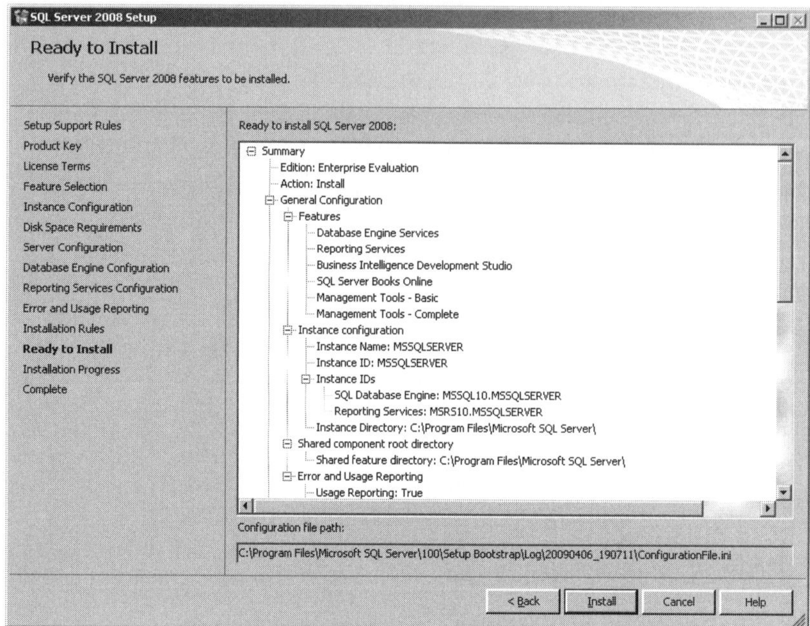

FIGURE 6.14 Installation summary.

At this point, the installation should proceed as planned. Unless some unexpected error happens, you should have a working instance of SSRS deployed on your machine, along with SQL Server. Everything is set up with the default settings. Therefore, you should be able to access Report Manager by just entering http://localhost/Reports in the address bar of you local web browser.

TABLE 6.1 SQL Server 2008 Installable Groups of Components

Component Group	Explanation
SQL Server Database Services	Core database services to store and manage data: database engine, replication, full text search, and shared tools, such as the BCP (Bulk Copy utility).
Analysis Services	Services that support online analytical processing (OLAP), data mining, and integration services (rewrite of DTS).
Reporting Services	Report-processing services: Report Servers, extensions, catalog database, Report Manager, and Report Builder.

TABLE 6.1 Continued

Component Group	Explanation
Integration Services	A set of tools and programmable objects for extracting, transforming, and loading data (ETL).
Shared Components	Includes SQL Server Management Studio, Configuration Manager, Profiler, Replication Monitor, and Books Online. Also includes libraries for OLE DB, Books Online, and ODBC communications. This option does not install samples.

NOTE

As you learned in Chapter 5, "Reporting Services Deployment Scenarios," System Configuration Check blocks Setup from running if the CPU type (Pentium III or later) requirement is not met. Setup issues a warning, but will allow you to proceed, if the CPU speed or minimum memory requirements are not met.

NOTE

Report Manager provides access to the Report Builder and, therefore, the Report Manager must be installed if end-user ad hoc report design functionality is desired.

If you have chosen a default configuration, Setup installs SSRS with defaults:

- Report Server and ReportServerTemDB databases on the instance of the SQL Server database services installed during the same setup as SSRS
- Report Server virtual directory: `http(s)://<server>/ReportServer`
- Report Manager virtual directory: `http(s)://<Server>/Reports`

You can view the defaults by clicking the Details button in the Report Server Installation Options dialog box.

Setup configures Secure Sockets Layer (SSL) if the certificate is installed before Reporting Services installation. Administrators can always install an SSL certificate post SSRS installation, but would consequently need to adjust SSRS configuration (specifically whether https:// is used in URLs).

After SSRS has been installed, we are ready to move on to more advanced topics.

Summary

This chapter discussed the SSRS installation steps. To install Reporting Services, run SQL Server 2008 Setup, check Reporting Services on the Components to Install dialog box for

When the wizard completes, attach databases using the SQL Server Management Studio user interface or by executing the following command. Use AdventureWorks and AdventureWorksDB as database names for OLTP and DW, respectively:

```
USE [master]
GO
CREATE DATABASE [AdventureWorks] ON
( FILENAME = N'C:\Program Files\Microsoft SQL Server\MSSQL.1\MSSQL\Data\Adventure
Works_Data.mdf' ),
( FILENAME = N'C:\Program Files\Microsoft SQL Server\MSSQL.1\MSSQL\Data\Adventure
Works_Log.LDF' )
 FOR ATTACH
GO
```

Using the Report Server Project Wizard to Create a Simple Report

1. Click the Windows Start button, point to All Programs, point to Microsoft SQL Server 2008, and then click SQL Server Business Intelligence Development Studio.

NOTE

If you do not see SQL Server Business Intelligence Development Studio as a selection, then, most likely, it was not installed. In this case, run the SQL Server setup again and select Shared Features, Business Intelligence Development Studio.

2. Click the File menu, and then click New, Project. The New Project dialog box opens. To develop advanced examples for this book, we will install Visual Studio 2008 Professional Edition. Both BIDS and Visual Studio use the same shell. The difference: BIDS is limited to business intelligence projects, whereas Visual Studio 2008 Professional Edition also includes programming language projects, such as Visual C# or Visual Basic.
3. In the Project Types section on the left, click Business Intelligence Projects.
4. In the Templates section on the right, click Report Server Project Wizard, as shown in Figure 7.1.

   The Templates section should contain a number of options. You might notice that the Name (project name) and the Solution Name keep changing with each option. (These fields are located at the bottom of the dialog box.) You should also make note of the Location, because this is the folder where the project and solution files are stored.
5. For now, just type **`MyFirstReportProject`** in the Name field. Your New Project dialog box should look similar to Figure 7.1. You can modify the location of the project if

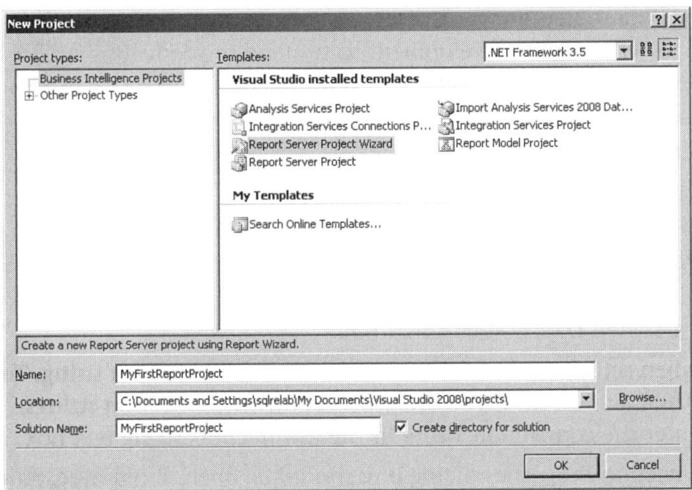

FIGURE 7.1 Creating a new Report Server project using the Report Server Project Wizard.

you choose. If you select Create Directory for Solution, the wizard will create a directory with the name specified in Solution Name field. By default, the solution name will be the same as the name.

6. Click OK and the Report Wizard starts.
7. Click Next on the Welcome to the Report Wizard screen. You may also want to enable the Do Not Show This Page Again check box.

Choosing quality data sources for the report is probably the most crucial step in the report development process, albeit one of the easiest. The difficulty involves judging the quality of the data presented to the analyst, as the saying goes "garbage in, garbage out."

Assuming that you have quality data it is a fairly straightforward task to connect Reporting Services to a data source. Using .NET technologies, you can connect to SQL Server, Oracle, and Analysis Services natively. Other possible data sources (installed with SSRS 2008) include Extensible Markup Language (XML; you can retrieve data either from a web service or a flat file), an ODBC- or an OLE DB-compliant data source, SQL Server Integration Services (SSIS) package (you must select Shared Features, Integration Services during the install to see this selection), SAP NetWeaver BI, Hyperion Essbase, and Teradata.

ODBC and OLE DB data sources open Reporting Services up to any number of third-party databases. As if this were not enough, you can also write your own data-processing extension using the interfaces provided by Microsoft. This way, report developers could report against any internal or proprietary data source.

Remember that a report data set can contain an embedded data source or it can be pointed to a shared data source. In most of the examples in this book, we leverage a shared data source. A shared data source allows you to change connection strings for all the reports by using a shared data source in a single change, instead of modifying

19. Click Next to continue to the next step: Select the Report Type. Leave Tabular (default) selected.

    Two key reporting structures enable you to present data: a table that expands vertically from top to bottom, and a matrix that expands both vertically and horizontally (from left to right). In SSRS 2008, Microsoft combines previously distinct report items in the report item called Tablix, which delivers the functionality of both a matrix and a table. This makes sense because a table, technically, has a subset of a matrix's capabilities. You will learn more about Tablix later in this book.

20. Click Next to continue to the next step: Design the Table. Select both Name and ListPrice from the Available Fields list, and then click the Details button. This indicates that you want to display all the available products in rows of a table. You should see a dialog box similar to that shown in the Figure 7.4.

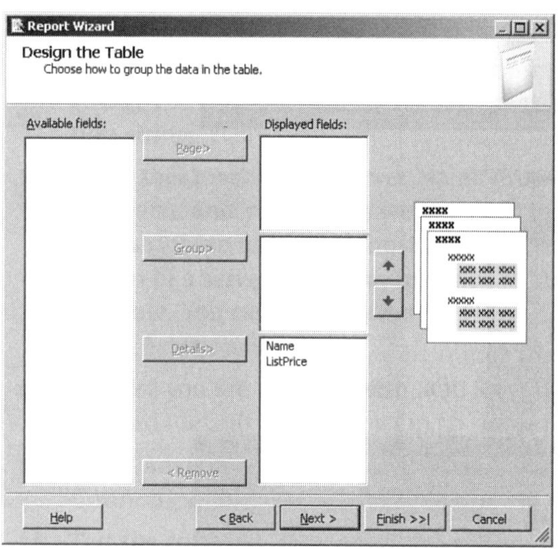

FIGURE 7.4 Design the Table dialog box.

21. Click Next to continue to the Choose the Table Style screen. Click through the style selection to see a preview on the right side of the Style Selection dialog box. Leave Slate (default) as the selection for the purpose of this exercise.

22. Click Next to continue to the Choose the Deployment Location screen. Enter the appropriate location of a Report Server. In our case, we have deployed it on a local machine `http://localhost/ReportServer` directory. Also enter the deployment folder information. By default, it will be the name of the project (for example, MyFirstReportProject). You should see a dialog box similar to the one shown in the Figure 7.5.

23. Click Next to give the report a name. Let's call it **`Product Price List`**.

24. Click Finish to complete the wizard. Your BIDS screen should look like the one shown in Figure 7.6.

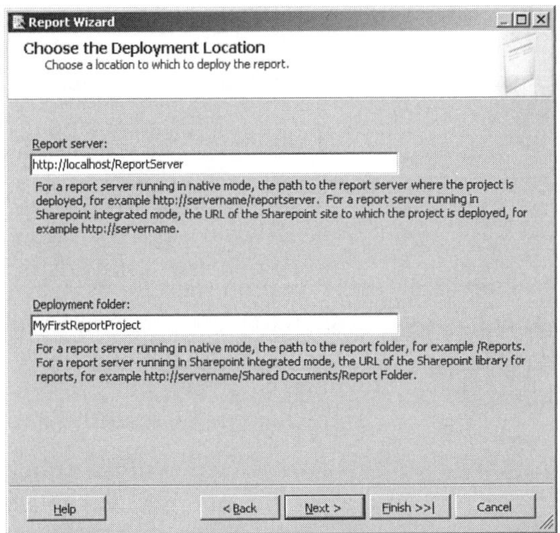

FIGURE 7.5 Choose the Deployment Location dialog box.

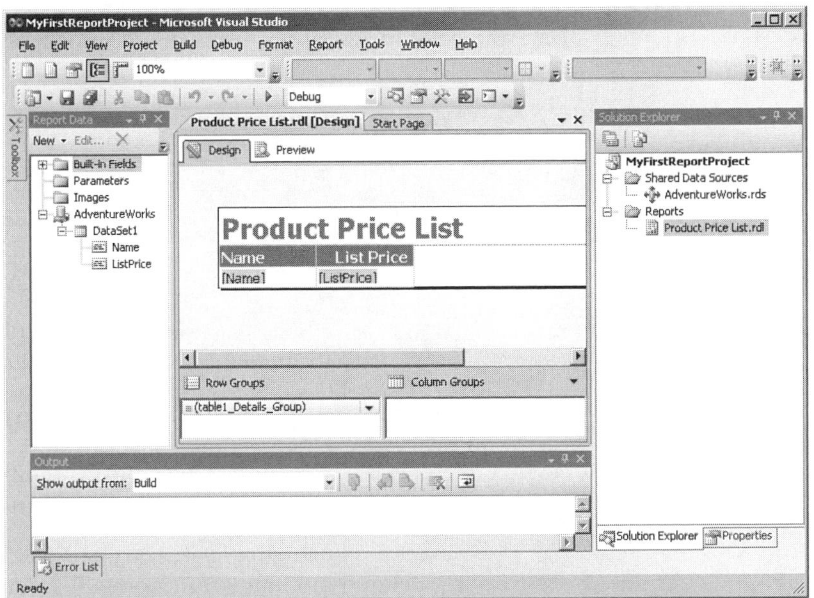

FIGURE 7.6 BIDS after completion of the Report Server Project Wizard.

Note the components of the project that the wizard created: the project itself, shared data source, a data set with two fields, and a report with a table. The table on the report contains product information in rows, and has column headings, based on the data set fields.

25. Display the Preview tab to see what the report will look like.

Try to experiment with the report that we just created. Although it looks great for the first report, there is obviously some work to do. You may have noticed that the column width is not sufficient to aesthetically accommodate most product names and that the price has four decimal digits (not quite a currency-style formatting).

Summary

The Report Server Project Wizard streamlines individual report-creation steps for us to a single workflow. In the next chapter, we further break down steps to create a report, learn basic formatting, and add parameters to a report.

CHAPTER 8

Report Designer(s)

IN THIS CHAPTER

- Three Main Report Designers from Microsoft
- Visual Studio Haves Versus Have Nots
- Solution, Project, File Hierarchy
- Generating Reports with Visual Studio

Report Designer is the main tool Microsoft provides for developers and tech-savvy information analysts to design and develop reports. For the end user, Microsoft provides two flavors of an ad hoc report design tool called Report Builder: a revamped Report Builder version 2.0 (New in 2008), which now has a Microsoft Office-like Ribbon interface and can support various data sources; and an SSRS2K5-style Report Builder version 1.0. In this chapter, we discuss both Report Designer and Report Builder and the relationship between Report Designer, Visual Studio, and SQL Server Business Development Studio. Then, you use Report Designer to author a report. For more information about client-side ad hoc reporting, see Chapter 18, "Ad Hoc Reporting."

Three Main Report Designers from Microsoft

Microsoft offers three main report designers. The first one is Microsoft SQL Server Report Designer, or simply Report Designer, integrated with Visual Studio. Starting from SQL Server 2005, if you do not have Visual Studio installed, SQL Server setup installs the Visual Studio shell and labels it SQL Server Business Intelligence Development Studio under the Microsoft SQL Server program group.

The other two report designers are standalone applications called Report Builder. SSRS 2008 ships with two versions of Report Builder: Report Builder 1.0, which is the same application used in SSRS2K5; and Report Builder 2.0, which is a new application for SSRS 2008. Report Builder 1.0 enables end users to create their own reports even if they know little to no SQL (because this product leverages entities defined in a model and builds queries internally). Report Builder 2.0, on the another hand, has pretty much the same capabilities as Report Designer, enabling users to develop and incorporate embedded code in a report and use various data sources, including a model.

The main difference between the Report Designer and the Report Builders is the target audience. Visual Studio/SQL Server Business Intelligence Development Studio (BIDS) and Report Designer target the developer community.

Whereas Report Builder 1.0 clearly targets an end user, Report Builder 2.0 blurs this differentiation and targets both an end user and a developer who focuses on reports only. In either version of Report Builder, users who do not know how to write queries can use a report model as a data source. A model will generate appropriate queries in turn. You can pick an appropriate Report Builder based on the following summaries.

Report Builder 1.0

- Is a part of the SSRS 2008 installation package.
- Launches within a browser window from the SSRS Report Manager application.
- Is a special type of Windows Forms application called "click-once." A click-once application installs and launches itself in a single click.
- Does not require a user to have administrative permissions to install. Unlike many Windows applications, click-once applications do not require a user to have administrative permissions to install. A click-once application installs in a user's local space.
- Does not have access to local storage resources.
- Can use only a report model as a data source.

NOTE

Keep in mind that although a user launches the Report Builder over the Web, it is still a Windows Forms application. Report Builder is a special type of application called click-once. A click-once application installs and launches itself in a single click.

At the time of this writing, Report Builder 2.0

- Is a part of the Microsoft SQL Server 2008 feature pack. You can download the feature pack from www.microsoft.com/download. Just search for "SQL Server 2008 Report Builder 2.0."
- Requires administrative permissions to install.
- Allows its users to save reports to a local storage.
- Allows creating reports even without access to a data source.
- Can leverage any data source, including a model.

NOTE

Unlike Report Builder 1.0, Report Builder 2.0 does provide access to a report model for you to build reports with. You can, however, create reports with Report Builder 2.0 without access to even a data source. For example, with Report Builder 2.0, you can create a report with a table where data is entered directly into the table's cells.

An SSRS administrator can configure SSRS to launch Report Builder 1.0, Report Builder 2.0, or even Custom Report Builder. (You can launch the latter from the SSRS Report Manager; just choose the Custom Report Builder Launch URL option. If this option is not specified, SSRS launches Report Builder 1.0 by default.)

Visual Studio Haves Versus Have Nots

At this point, you might be wondering what the difference is between Visual Studio and BIDS. Put simply, not much.

In the first version of SSRS, the only report development tool available was Visual Studio. Many report development shops wanted the ability to use SSRS without having to purchase Visual Studio. In response to this, Microsoft bundled BIDS with SSRS2K5 and subsequently with SSRS 2008. Effectively, BIDS is just a shell of Visual Studio with the capability to develop reports. In fact, when it relates to SQL Server, we use the terms *Visual Studio* and *Business Intelligence Development Studio (BIDS)* interchangeably.

During the installation, the setup program detects whether you have Visual Studio installed. If you do, the setup program simply installs the files needed to create reports. If you do not have Visual Studio, the setup program installs BIDS.

Solution, Project, File Hierarchy

As with anything else developed with Visual Studio, it helps to understand some basics about how Visual Studio handles files.

If you are developing reports, the developer's basic unit of work is the Report Definition Language (RDL) files and associated data sources. Developers can also include shared data sources, which have an `.rds` extension. Likewise, if you are working with report models, the default file extension is `.smdl`. (SMDL is short for Semantic Data Modeling Language).

Reporting-related files will be contained in a type of project called a Report Server project. If you are creating an SMDL file for use in the client-side Report Builder, the project type is called Report Model project. A Report Model project will likely also have Data Source View (DSV) and Data Source (DS) files. All SSRS-related files (RDL, SMDL, DSV, and DS) are plain-text Extensible Markup Language (XML) files. A project has folders to organize the different components.

A solution contains many projects. Combined, solutions and projects create a management hierarchy. A solution has one or more projects (the latter is more typical); a project

5. Click OK to close the Shared Data Source dialog box.

Now that you have the data source, you can create a report. To create an empty report, follow these steps:

1. In Solution Explorer, right-click Reports, hover over Add to expand the menu, and then click New Item (see Figure 8.3).

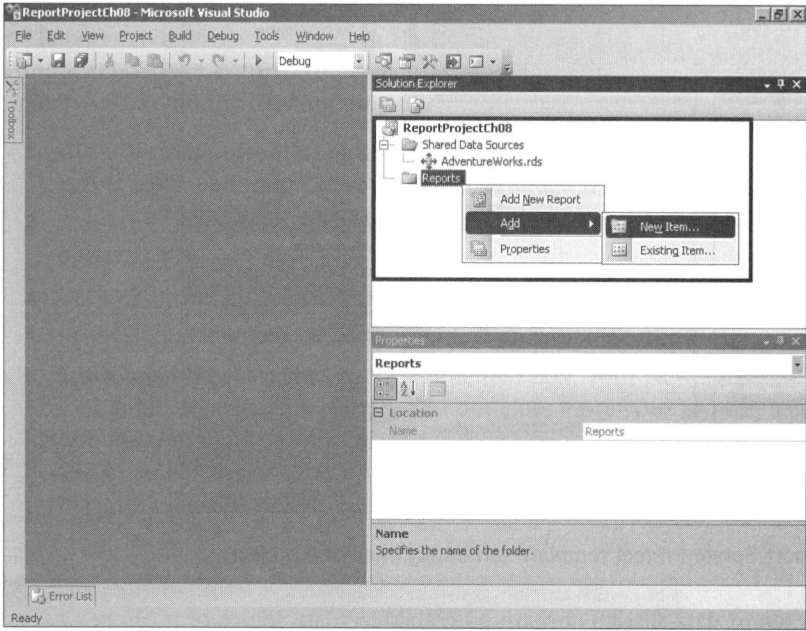

FIGURE 8.3 Adding a new item.

NOTE

If you selected Add New Report, the Report Wizard appears. Click Cancel to exit the wizard. Remember that our goal in this chapter is to follow report-creation steps more closely, instead of relying on wizards to develop our reports.

2. The Add New Item dialog box opens. From this dialog box, select Report from the Templates menu.
3. Enter the name of the report (`Sales by Territory by Salesperson.rdl`) in the Name text box. The screen should look similar to Figure 8.4. When you have finished, click Add.

At this point, you should have a new solution, project, and an empty report file. Figure 8.5 shows the empty report created inside the project. From here, we just need to collect

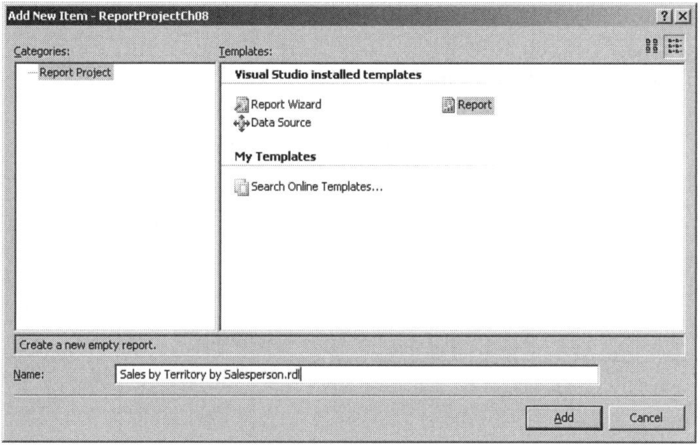

FIGURE 8.4 Add New Item dialog box.

data from the data source, choose a layout, and preview the report. Note that Report Designer conveniently lays out this process with a dockable Report Data window and two tabs across the top: Design and Preview.

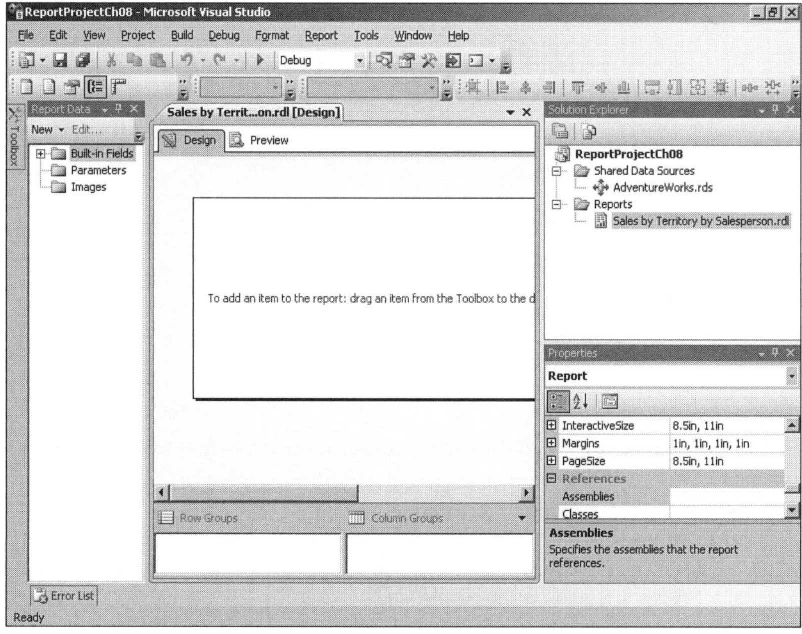

FIGURE 8.5 An empty report.

SSRS reports collect data into an object called a data set. The results of the query, the SQL statement used for the query, and a pointer to the data source are all stored in the data set. In fact, with a little work, you can make Reporting Services read from a `System.Data.DataSet` object over a web service. BIDS contains a Graphical Query Builder to help write queries. It also allows for free-form queries to be specified by the developer. As we continue, you will see both views.

To continue the life cycle of your report, let's continue by adding a data set to collect and store your data. The data set you create will use the shared data source to execute a SQL statement and return a resultset. To proceed, follow these steps:

1. From the Report Data window, select New, Data Source (see Figure 8.6). The Data Source Properties dialog box opens.

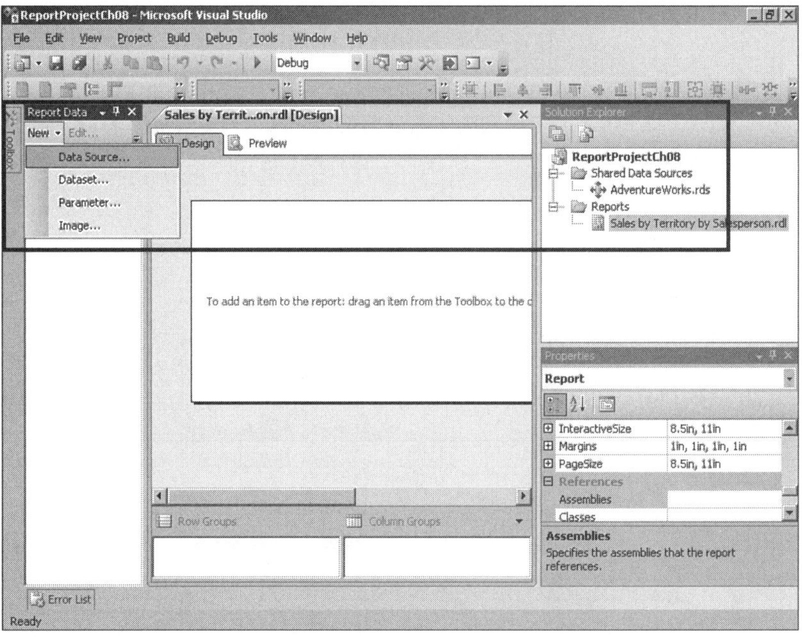

FIGURE 8.6 New Data Source option.

2. The first thing to do is to name the data source. Enter **`AdventureWorksDataSource`** in the Name text box. This uniquely identifies the data source throughout the course of a report. Select Use Shared Data Source Reference and pick AdventureWorks from a drop-down list. Note that all items on the Credentials tab are grayed out. The report will use credentials that we have defined for the shared data source. You should see a dialog box similar to that shown in Figure 8.7. Click OK to complete.

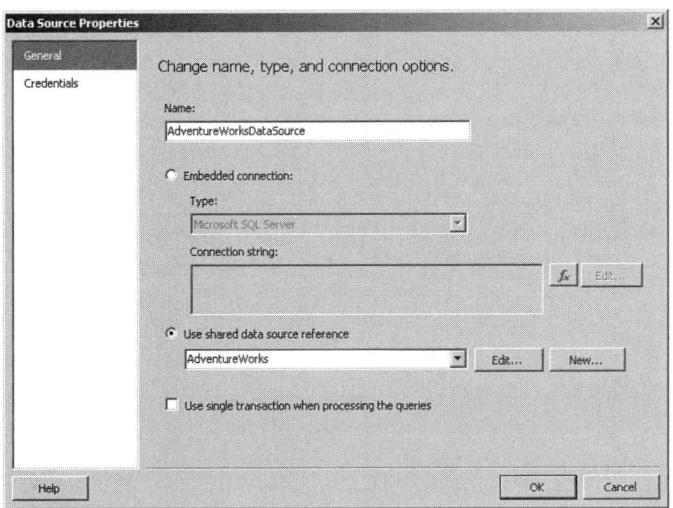

FIGURE 8.7 Data Source Properties dialog box.

3. From the Report Data window, select New, Dataset. The Dataset Properties dialog box opens. Enter **AdventureWorksDataset** in the Name text box. This uniquely identifies the data set throughout the course of a report. Select AdventureWorksDataSource from a drop-down list. At this point, there are also other text boxes, such as the Query Type, Query, and Time Out. The Query text box contains the text of the actual query. Query Type has the text, and Time Out specifies the command timeout value. A zero (0) value in the Timeout field lets the query run indefinitely. Other horizontal tabs of the Dataset Properties dialog box contain the more advanced options in the data set:

   - The Parameters tab contains a list of parameters to be passed on to the query. The most common use of the Parameters tab is to store stored procedure parameters.
   - The Fields tab contains the list of fields returned by the data set, and is the place where report developers can enter calculated fields.
   - The Options tab contains connection options (collation, case and accent sensitivity, and other) for the underlying database connection. It also enables you to select how you want SSRS to interpret subtotal rows for queries (such as MDX queries) that return subtotals. The default, Auto, indicates that you want to interpret subtotals as details if the report does not use the `Aggregate` function.
   - The Filters tab is used to filter the data from the resultset.

   The dialog box should now look similar to Figure 8.8.

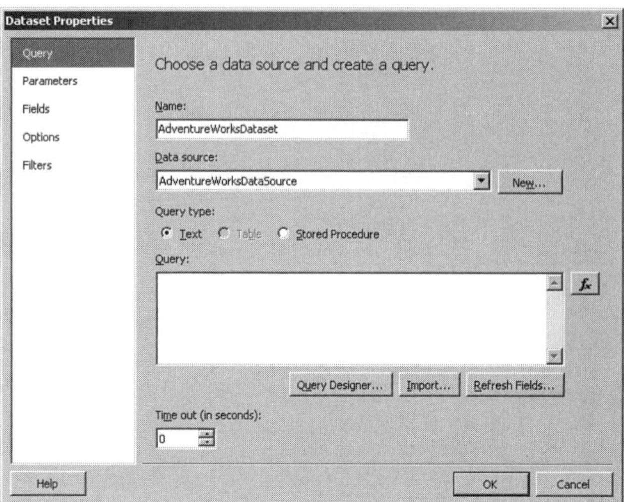

FIGURE 8.8 Dataset Properties dialog box.

Now you are ready to enter your query either directly in the Dataset Properties dialog box or by using one of the Query Designers. Two main views are available for creating queries. The first one is the Generic Query Designer. This provides a free text view for inputting the query. Basically, it assumes you know what you are doing as a developer or can simply copy a query from somewhere. Figure 8.9 shows the Generic Query Designer.

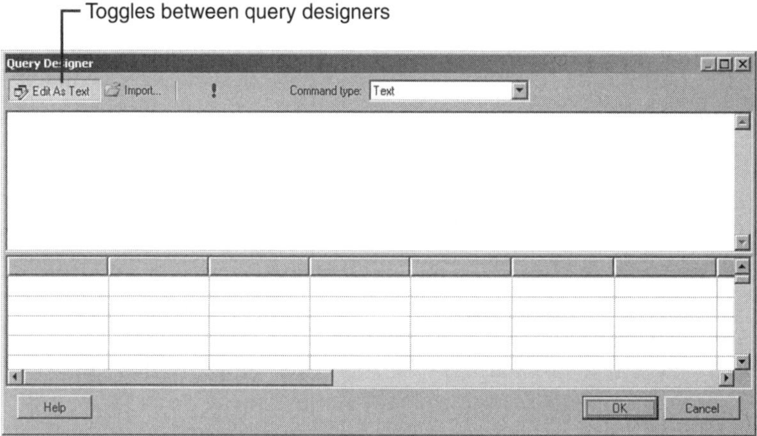

FIGURE 8.9 Generic Query Designer.

4. Click the Query Designer button to display the Generic Query Designer. If you are reading a printed copy of this book, you might find it a bit tedious to retype a query

that we propose for this exercise in the Dataset Properties dialog box or in the Generic Query Designer. So instead, let's leverage the Visual Query Designer to generate joins between tables and then pick fields. In the Generic Query Designer, click the Edit as Text button to display Visual Query Designer. Note that Edit as Text appears as depressed in the Generic Query Designer. Figure 8.10 shows the Generic Query Designer.

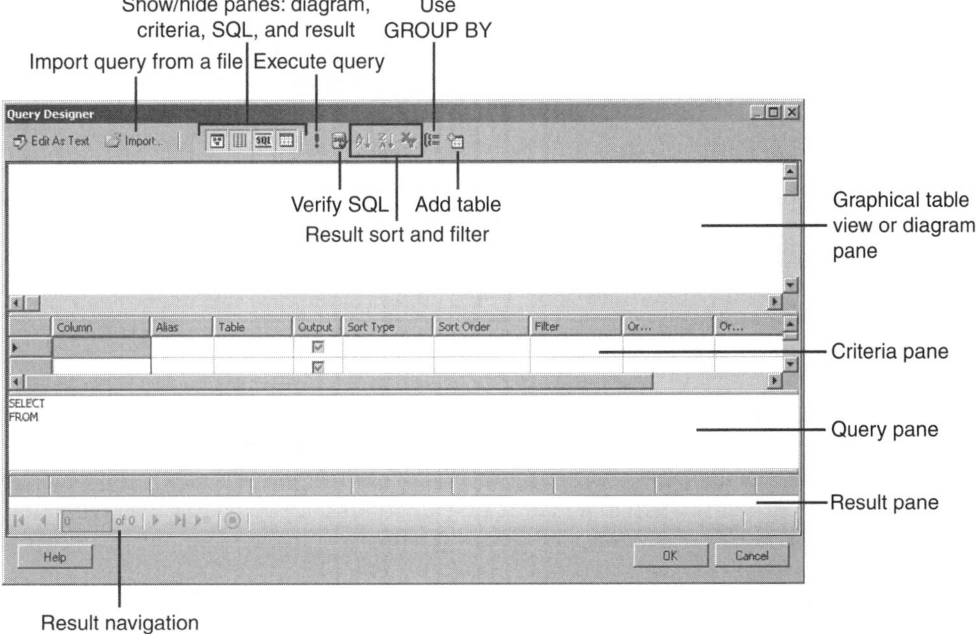

FIGURE 8.10 Visual Query Designer.

5. Right-click in the diagram pane of the Graphical Query Designer, select Add Table from the context menu, and while pressing and holding the Ctrl key select the following eight tables in the Add Table dialog: Address, Contact, CountryRegion, Employee, EmployeeAddress, SalesPerson, SalesTerritory, StateProvince. Note that in the Graphical Query Designer the table's schema is provided on the right side of the table name in parentheses.

NOTE

Samples in this book use the AdventureWorks *2005* sample database. If you intend to use AdventureWorks 2008 sample database, keep in mind that object names may differ. For example, in AdventureWorks 2005, we use `Person.Contact` table for the contact information, and in AdventureWorks 2008, we use `Person.Person` table for the same purpose.

6. Click the check box in front of a column name for each column that you want to have on the report. For the purpose of our example, let's use the following eight columns: Person.Contact.FirstName, Person.Contact.LastName, Person.CountryRegion.Name, Sales.SalesTerritory.Name, Sales.SalesPerson.SalesQuota, Sales.SalesPerson.SalesYTD, Sales.SalesPerson.SalesLastYear. Let's also add column aliases to clarify the meaning of the column or where we have duplication of column names. In our example, such duplication is CountryRegion.Name and SalesTerritory.Name.

   We came up with the following query in the Query pane of the Graphical Query Designer. If you are reading an electronic version of this book, you can just copy this query into either the Generic Query Designer or into the Query pane of the Graphical Query Designer:

```
SELECT
Person.Contact.FirstName, Person.Contact.LastName,
Person.CountryRegion.Name AS CountryRegionName,
Sales.SalesTerritory.Name AS TerritoryName,
Sales.SalesPerson.SalesQuota,
Sales.SalesPerson.SalesYTD,
Sales.SalesPerson.SalesLastYear
FROM
Sales.SalesPerson
INNER JOIN HumanResources.Employee ON HumanResources.Employee.EmployeeID =
Sales.SalesPerson.SalesPersonID
LEFT OUTER JOIN Sales.SalesTerritory ON Sales.SalesTerritory.TerritoryID =
Sales.SalesPerson.TerritoryID
INNER JOIN Person.Contact ON Person.Contact.ContactID =
HumanResources.Employee.ContactID
INNER JOIN HumanResources.EmployeeAddress ON HumanResources.Employee.
EmployeeID = HumanResources.EmployeeAddress.EmployeeID
INNER JOIN Person.Address ON HumanResources.EmployeeAddress.AddressID =
Person.Address.AddressID
INNER JOIN Person.StateProvince ON Person.StateProvince.StateProvinceID =
Person.Address.StateProvinceID
INNER JOIN Person.CountryRegion ON Person.CountryRegion.CountryRegionCode =
Person.StateProvince.CountryRegionCode
```

   As with any tool that purports to make life easier, you usually have to give up some control. Some queries are too complex to be displayed graphically. For example, derived tables did not display in the first release of SSRS. Starting from SSRS2K5, this capability is available, but you might run into other syntaxes that the designer does not know how to display graphically.

7. Run the query to preview the results by clicking the ! (Run) button on either designer's toolbar.
8. Click OK on a designer to confirm a query that you have just completed.
9. Click OK in the Dataset Properties dialog box to complete a data set.

Design Screen

After selecting your data, the next step is to design the presentation for the data. Layout assistance is provided by the Toolbox, Report Data, and Design dockable windows.

Design view is a default that BIDS displays after you add a report (see Figure 8.11).

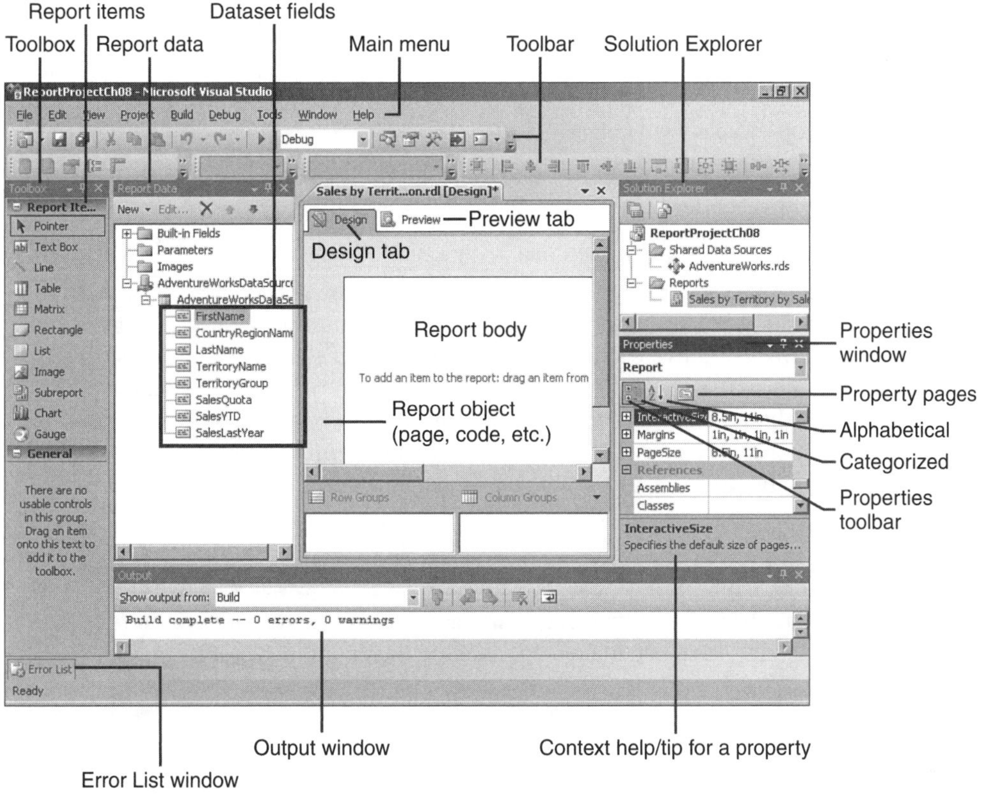

FIGURE 8.11 Report Design view.

The Toolbox (shown in Figure 8.11) is accessible by selecting Toolbox from the View menu. This has all the report item controls you might use while authoring reports. The simplest way to use them is to drag the control you want onto the body of a report.

Data can be inserted from the Report Data window. (Just choose Report Data from the View menu.) The Report Data window contains a tree list of available fields to use from the data sets. If you drag a field onto the report body, BIDS creates a text box to contain the field.

Any item on the report can be modified through the Properties window. The Properties window can be accessed by pressing F4 or by selecting Properties Window from the View menu. Figure 8.11 shows the Properties window for a report object.

At this point in the report development process, you need to take the results of your query and apply a layout and format to them. Let's make a simple tabular report and add a few bells and whistles. Complete the following steps using the Sales by Territory by Salesperson report:

1. Drag a text box from the Toolbox to the report body. In the Properties window (F4), select the text box. (Most likely, the text box you just added is already selected.) Enter **`Sales by Territory by Salesperson`** in the text box and change the following property values to those specified here:

   Name: ReportTitle

   Location: Top = 0, Left = 0

   Size: Height = .5in, Width = 4.5in

   Color: DarkBlue

   Font: FontFamily = Tahoma, FontSize = 18pt, FontWeight = Bold
2. Drag a table and place it on the report's body under the report title that you have just created. By default, the table comes with three columns, which are all 1-inch wide. Click the bar above each column; if selected successfully, the entire column should be selected. After a column is selected, you can use the Properties window and change the Width property to fit the information you are going to display. You can do this for each column individually or select columns you want to change to the same size by pressing and holding Ctrl key and selecting multiple columns.

NOTE

In SSRS 2008, the Table report item is actually represented by a new Tablix data region. Tablix represents both Table and Matrix report items. This is why some of the menu items and dialog boxes use Tablix even though we work with the Table report item.

3. From the Report Data window, drag the AdventureWorkDataset fields (CountryRegionName, TerritoryName, and FirstName) to the first three columns of the table. Note that when you drag a field over a column the entire column is selected. Report Designer will add a value of a field to a data row of the table and the name of a field to the header of the table. When adding a field name to table's header, the Report Designer will also insert spaces before each capital letter in the field's name.
4. To add more columns to the table, you can select the rightmost column of the table, right-click the column, and select Insert Column, Right (see Figure 8.12). Repeat three times. The table should now have six columns.
5. Alternatively you can continue dragging fields from the data set to the table, positioning your cursor where you want the column to be added, similar to Figure 8.13 where we add a column to the end of the table. Note how the cursor changes to indicate an addition to the table.

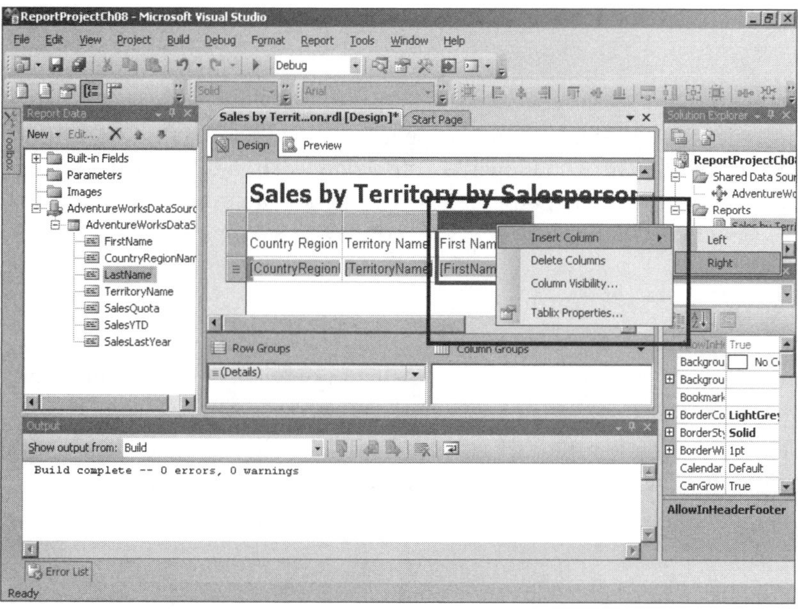

FIGURE 8.12 Adding columns to a table.

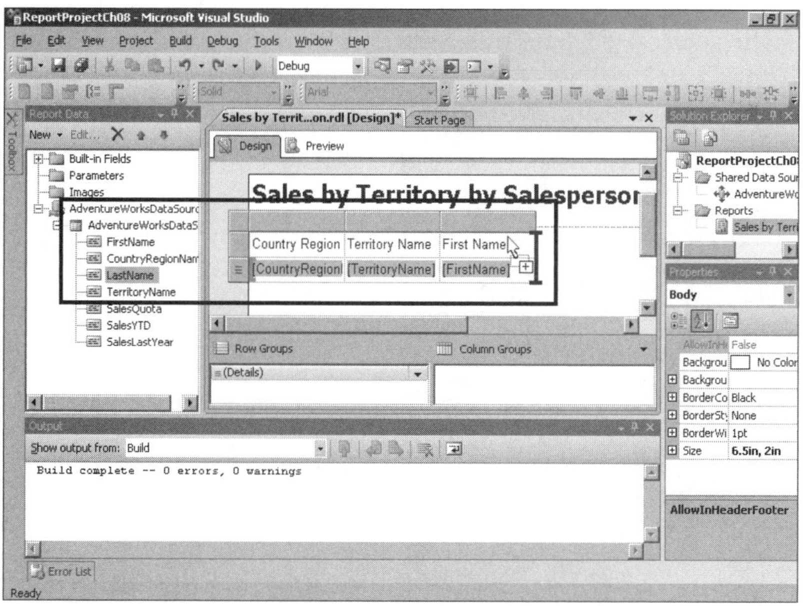

FIGURE 8.13 Adding columns to a table by dragging data fields.

6. Click the button next to the report header row. After the row is selected, use the Properties window to set the following properties:

BackgroundColor: #1c3a70

Color: White

Font: FontFamily = Tahoma, FontSize = 11pt, FontWeight = Bold

7. Click the button at the upper-left corner of the table. When you do this, the entire table should now be selected. The Properties window now should reflect the table's properties. You can modify table properties as you consider appropriate. For example, you can change table's `BorderStyle` property to `Solid` to display a border around the table.
8. Click the Preview tab to see what the report looks like.

   We should fix some formatting to make a report more visually appealing. You may have noticed that country and territory names are not ordered, and Sales columns are not formatted as currency.
9. Click the Design tab. Holding the Ctrl key, select cells that contain sales data. For the format, enter **`C`. (The single letter *C* is a formatting for currency.)**
10. Click anywhere on the table, and then right-click the button at the upper-left corner of the table.
11. Select Tablix Properties from the context menu.
12. Now display the Sorting tab.
13. Click the Add button three times to add three columns to sorting. Select the following columns for sorting: CountryRegionName, TerritoryName, and LastName. Leave the default sorting order A to Z (see Figure 8.14).

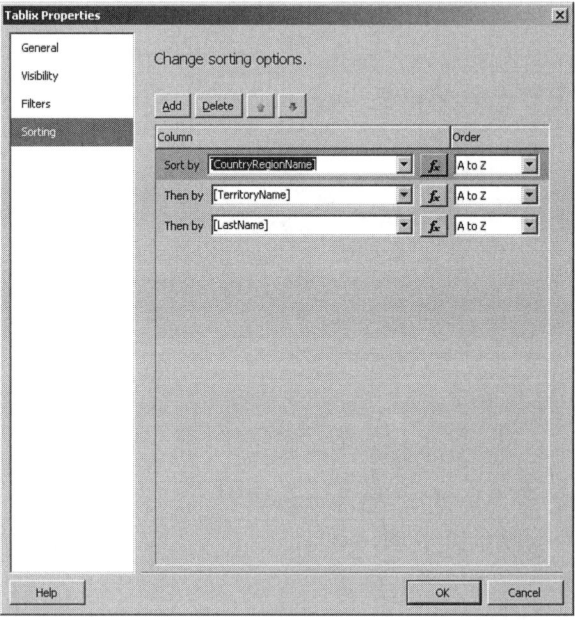

FIGURE 8.14 Adding columns for sorting.

14. Click OK to complete the sorting assignment, and display the Preview tab to see what the report looks like (see Figure 8.15).

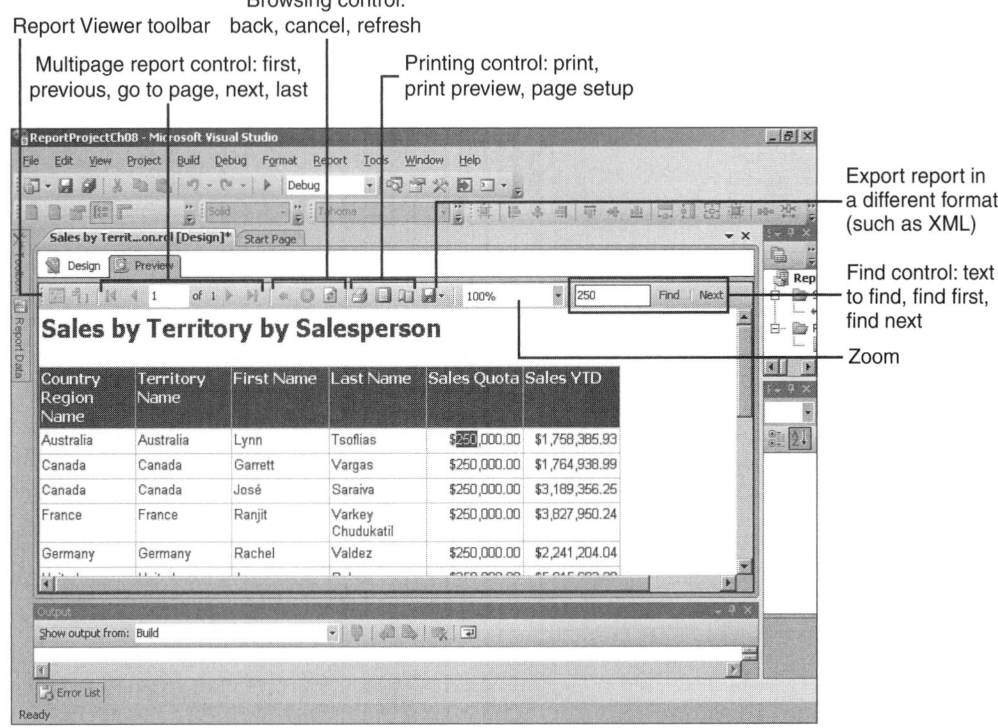

FIGURE 8.15 Completed report in Preview mode.

This concludes the starter report. Preview mode has full report-viewing capabilities and allows navigating multipage reports and exporting a report to a different format (such as XML, Word, and Excel). Preview mode also has print capabilities (such as print preview and page setup).

Summary

BIDS is nothing more than the shell of Visual Studio. Both products house the main report development tool from Microsoft: SQL Server Report Designer. Over the next several chapters, you will see how to use Report Designer to develop powerful and visually appealing reports for all kinds of end users. You'll learn more about client-side ad hoc reporting in Chapter 18.

CHAPTER 9

Report Definition Language

IN THIS CHAPTER

- Language: A Way to Communicate
- Use of XML
- Declarative Programming
- Report Elements

The preceding chapter introduced you to Report Designer and Report Builder. This chapter takes a look at the output from these tools.

SSRS is unique in that it uses Extensible Markup Language (XML) to generate reports. This chapter provides an insight into why Microsoft uses XML as their report-generation language, and then delves into the structure of the resulting document.

Language: A Way to Communicate

At first glance, the name Report Definition Language (RDL) might appear to be a misnomer. As you've already seen, it is nothing more than an XML document, just like any other XML document. Why would they call this a language? After all, there is no compiler necessary, and the syntax is nothing like C++, C#, or any other programming language. To answer this, you need to think of things at a bit higher level than most programming paradigms allow.

Remember, one of the goals of SSRS is to remain an open-ended environment.

Likewise, as you have already seen, SSRS is composed of many different components: There is the database server, the Windows Service, the Report Server Web Service, and so on.

Most important, at least from an end-user perspective, are the report designers and the rendering engine. As you have seen, Microsoft already offers three designers: Report Designer and Report Builder 1.0 and 2.0.

All designers use the same rendering engine, and even within this engine there are multiple formats. For all of this to work together seamlessly, all these components need to communicate with the same underlying principles. This is where the common language comes in to play; it is just a common way to communicate instructions between the various entities.

Use of XML

Most enterprise reporting solutions use proprietary binary formats. This locks developers into using that vendor's tools to generate and deploy reports. Obviously, this runs counter to the SSRS design goal of generating open standards. The other thing to note about SSRS is the idea to keep report designers and generators separate. This poses the fundamental challenge of what open format allows such disparate things to communicate. Thankfully, the answer already existed: XML.

XML is already in use throughout the Web and even in many non-Web systems as a communication mechanism. It easily allows anyone with a text editor to create an XML file. XML is similar to Hypertext Markup Language (HTML) in that it is a form of markup language. There are a few major differences.

With XML, a document has to be well formed, meaning every beginning markup tag (called a node) has to have a corresponding ending tag. Second, HTML only has a few keywords that can be used to mark up text. XML doesn't have any such limitation because the end user is the one responsible for the creation of tags. The tags are used to describe the data encompassed by them. This is in stark contrast to HTML, which describes how to handle presentation of data. This makes XML an ideal communication medium or language.

The one drawback about such a flexible medium is, ironically enough, its flexibility. Immediately, you might wonder the following: If any node can be in any place, and any node can have any attribute, how can this be effective? There have to be some rules. To solve this problem, you need to create an XML schema. An XML schema allows the creation of a contract to adhere to between different systems by defining when and where in the document a set of XML nodes should appear, and which nodes should have attributes describing them.

The RDL specification is the XML schema that describes the layout of the XML used to create reports. The XML itself basically becomes the programming language of the report.

Declarative Programming

Just as a programming language lets a programmer tell a computer how and what to produce to the end user, the RDL tells the Report Server what data to use and how to lay it out. Now, there is a little trick here: Most programming languages communicate a *what* and a *how* to do something. There is no way to tell ASP.NET to produce a web page just by giving it a template. However, that is what the RDL does. The RDL communicates what the output is to look like and where the source data is to come from. This leaves the application free to decide how to generate the defined look and feel, regardless of the programming language or underlying architecture. This model is called the declarative model.

A producer application is an application that is used to generate RDL files. Business Intelligence Development Studio (BIDS) and Report Builder fall into this category. For most users, it is helpful to have a graphical user interface (GUI), although you can develop a report purely in your favorite text editor.

A consumer application is simply one that takes the RDL from the producer and creates the desired output. In its simplest form, it queries for the data and displays the results in the specified format. This is where a lot of the custom elements come in. Using the custom elements, it is possible to send instructions for one output format, which could then be ignored by all others.

Report Elements

To create a report, you need to know a few things:

- Where and what is your source data?
- What is the report layout?
- Are there any other properties, such as external images or parameters?

To cover this much information, the RDL schema has many elements. The RDL specification (schema) itself is an open schema, and Microsoft fully expects third parties to add onto it to extend it. In the scope of this book, it would be time-consuming and arduous to cover every element, so this book covers just a few key elements. You can find more information about the RDL schema on the Microsoft website at http://schemas.microsoft.com/sqlserver/reporting/2008/01/reportdefinition/ReportDefinition.xsd.

If you'd prefer to see the RDL's elements in a graphical form, you can find it in the Books Online or in its web version at http://msdn.microsoft.com/en-us/library/ms153957.aspx or by simply searching for "Report Definition XML Diagrams" at http://www.microsoft.com.

You can also view the XML of any report by opening the report in BIDS and selecting the Code from the View menu while in Design view. Alternatively, you can view a report's XML by right-clicking the report in Solution Explorer and selecting View Code from a drop-down menu.

Let's examine several SSRS elements.

Report Element

The Report element is the highest-level element in the RDL's XML hierarchy. The Report element contains all the information needed to process the report. There can be only one Report element in every report. In fact, every other element is a child node of the Report element. Examples of these child elements include PageHeader, Body, PageFooter, DataSources, DataSets, and Parameters.

The following code listing shows an example of the Report element. The RDL is of an empty report with a Line report item:

```
<?xml version="1.0" encoding="utf-8"?>
<Report xmlns:rd="http://schemas.microsoft.com/SQLServer/reporting/reportdesigner"
xmlns="http://schemas.microsoft.com/sqlserver/reporting/2008/01/reportdefinition">
  <Body>
    <ReportItems>
      <Line Name="Line1">
        <Top>0.0175in</Top>
        <Height>0.25in</Height>
        <Width>1in</Width>
        <Style>
          <Border>
            <Style>Solid</Style>
          </Border>
        </Style>
      </Line>
    </ReportItems>
    <Height>2in</Height>
    <Style />
  </Body>
  <Width>6.5in</Width>
  <Page>
    <Style />
  </Page>
  <rd:ReportID>a045101c-aa05-4334-940f-b728efb81635</rd:ReportID>
  <rd:ReportUnitType>Inch</rd:ReportUnitType>
</Report>
```

ReportParameters Element

For the ReportParameters element, there are following entries in the RDL schema:

```
...
  <xsd:element name="Report">
    <xsd:complexType>
      <xsd:choice minOccurs="1" maxOccurs="unbounded">
```

```
...
        <xsd:element name="ReportParameters" type="ReportParametersType" minOc-
curs="0" />
...
  <xsd:complexType name="ReportParameterType">
    <xsd:choice minOccurs="1" maxOccurs="unbounded">
      <xsd:element name="DataType">
        <xsd:simpleType>
          <xsd:restriction base="xsd:string">
            <xsd:enumeration value="Boolean" />
            <xsd:enumeration value="DateTime" />
            <xsd:enumeration value="Integer" />
            <xsd:enumeration value="Float" />
            <xsd:enumeration value="String" />
          </xsd:restriction>
        </xsd:simpleType>
      </xsd:element>
      <xsd:element name="Nullable" type="xsd:boolean" minOccurs="0" />
      <xsd:element name="DefaultValue" type="DefaultValueType" minOccurs="0" />
      <xsd:element name="AllowBlank" type="xsd:boolean" minOccurs="0" />
      <xsd:element name="Prompt" type="StringLocIDType" minOccurs="0" />
      <xsd:element name="ValidValues" type="ValidValuesType" minOccurs="0" />
      <xsd:element name="Hidden" type="xsd:boolean" minOccurs="0" />
      <xsd:element name="MultiValue" type="xsd:boolean" minOccurs="0" />
      <xsd:element name="UsedInQuery" minOccurs="0">
        <xsd:simpleType>
          <xsd:restriction base="xsd:string">
            <xsd:enumeration value="False" />
            <xsd:enumeration value="True" />
            <xsd:enumeration value="Auto" />
          </xsd:restriction>
        </xsd:simpleType>
      </xsd:element>
      <xsd:any namespace="##other" processContents="skip" />
    </xsd:choice>
    <xsd:attribute name="Name" type="xsd:normalizedString" use="required" />
    <xsd:anyAttribute namespace="##other" processContents="skip" />
  </xsd:complexType>
```


You may notice that `ReportParameters` is a child of `Report` and is of a `ComplexType` called `ReportParametersType`. A complex element has child elements and, optionally, attributes, whereas a simple element does not have children or attributes. By this definition, the `Report` element itself is a complex type, and a `DataType` is a simple type that can be only one of the following values: `Boolean`, `DateTime`, `Integer`, `Float`, or `String`.

Graphical report designers, such as Report Designer in BIDS, map elements to some graphical presentation. Figure 9.1 presents the General tab of the Report Parameter Properties dialog box. Here you can clearly see a mapping between `ReportParametersType` and graphical elements: `Name`, `Prompt`, `Data Type`, and so on.

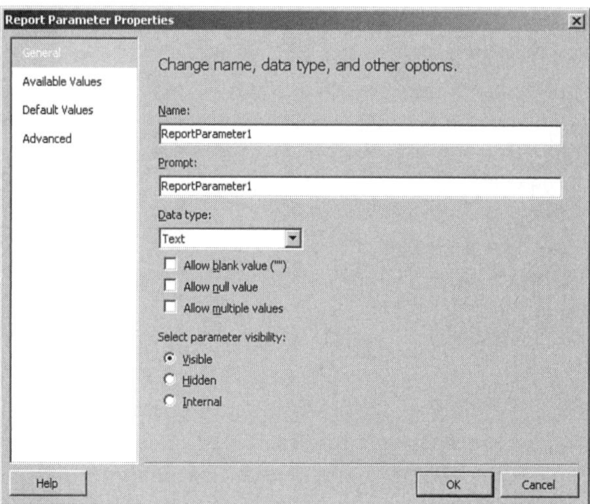

FIGURE 9.1 Report Parameter Properties dialog box.

Armed with an understanding of the RDL, you can write your own graphical report designers if you so choose. SQL Server Books Online have an example of such a generator under the title "Tutorial: Generating RDL Using the .NET Framework," which is also available online at http://msdn.microsoft.com/en-us/library/ms170667.aspx. The RDL generator in the example simply uses .NET's `System.Xml.XmlTextWriter` class to stream RDL elements to a file.

In limited scenarios, an understanding of the RDL would also help you edit RDL files manually. In general, we recommend minimizing manual RDL editing because text editors (such as Notepad) do not check the resulting changes against the RDL's schema, and if your changes are incorrect, the SSRS will return errors. However, in a few cases, you might be pressed to manually edit RDL. For example, you are troubleshooting a report that worked perfectly in a test environment and now fails in production. You have less than an hour to fix the report because it contains the company's quarterly financials and the submission deadline is coming up. You realize that the production database is case sensitive and that you can quickly solve the problem by manually editing a query in report's RDL using Notepad. In a perfect world, this would never happen; in reality, it might.

We present child elements of `ReportParametersType` and their description in the Table 9.1.

NOTE

Because all XML is character based, technically, any data type is a string. To be more specific about a range of possible string values, this book generally uses acceptable type names (Type column in the Table 9.1). For example, `Boolean` indicates that the string value could be `True` or `False`.

TABLE 9.1 Report Parameters

Element Name	Required or Optional	Type	Description
`Name`	Required	`String`	Unique name of the parameter. (The value of this element is used when other expressions need to refer back to this parameter.) Note: Parameter names must be unique within the `ReportParameters` parent element.
`DataType`	Required	`Enumeration`	Programmatic data type of the parameter. Because it is a required value, there is no default. `Boolean` | `DateTime` | `Integer` | `Float` | `String`.
`Nullable`	Optional	`Boolean`	Whether the value of the parameter can be null. Defaults to `False` if excluded.
`DefaultValue`	Optional	`Element`	Value used for the parameter when not supplied by the end user. If the `Prompt` element is omitted, the value is null. `DefaultValue` becomes required when there is no `Prompt` element and when either `Nullable` is `False` or a `ValidValues` element exists that does not contain `Null` (an omitted value).
`AllowBlank`	Optional	`Boolean`	Whether an empty string is an acceptable value for the parameter. The default value is `False`, and the element is ignored if the `DataType` is not `String`.
`Hidden`	Optional	`Boolean`	Determines whether a user should be prompted to enter a parameter. If this element is `False`, the user interface will prompt a user to enter the parameter.

9

TABLE 9.1 Continued

Element Name	Required or Optional	Type	Description
MultiValue	Optional	Boolean	Determines whether a parameter can have more than one value at runtime.
UsedInQuery	Optional	String enumeration = {True, False, Auto}	Default = Auto. If a ParameterA is included in an expression or a query for a ParameterB, this element determines how to handle a refresh of a default value for ParameterB when ParameterA changes. Auto relies on SSRS to determine whether a dependency exists.
ValidValues	Optional	String	Helps to improve security when you define a parameter of type String. If you do not use this option, your report may be vulnerable to a SQL injection attack.
Prompt	Optional	String	The Prompt element designates the text that the user interface should display when prompting the user for parameter values. If the element is omitted, the user will not be prompted for a parameter's value, and the parameter *cannot* be modified any other way. For example, it can't be modified through URL access. The Report Designer does not allow this element to be blank. If you edit RDL manually and set this element to blank (or remove this element), the effect is similar to setting the Hidden element to True.

DataSets Element

The DataSets element is a collection of individual DataSet elements (see Table 9.2). As a whole, the collection contains information about how to get the data used in the reports. Each individual DataSet element has to have a unique name element. The DataSet element itself contains elements for basic properties, such as AccentSensitivity, CaseSensitivity, Collation, and so on.

TABLE 9.2 DataSet Elements

Name	Required, Optional, or Multiple	Type	Description
Name	Required	String	Unique name given to the data set. This cannot be the same name given to any data region or grouping.
Fields	Optional	Element	List of fields that are included in the data set. They may map to columns in the data set.
Field	Multiple: 1-N	Element	The field name is the name of the field as it is referred to within the report.
Filters	Optional	Element, Filters-Type	List of filters. Each filter contains a Filter expression (such as =Fields!ProductID.Value), operator (such as Equal), and a value of one of a data types (such as Integer).
Interpret Subtotals AsDetails	Optional	String	Restricted to True, False, or Auto. Directs whether to interpret results of a query that returns subtotals as detail rows instead of aggregate rows. Subtotals are interpreted as detail rows when this element is set to True and the report does not use the Aggregate() function to access any fields in the data set.
Query	Required	Element	Information used to gather data from the data source. This parameter includes connection information, query text, query parameters, and so on required to get the data from the data source.

The actual database query is contained in the Query element. Each data set can have only one query. When using the Query element, you can see some of the influences of the .NET Framework, particularly ADO.NET. The child elements are CommandText, CommandType, DataSourceName, QueryParameters, and Timeout.

The Fields collection contains Field elements. In an online transaction processing (OLTP) system, the Fields collection usually maps to the columns returned by your database query. There is also the ability to add calculated fields. The field name is the name referenced in the layout sections of the report. The Field element must have either a DataField child element or a Value child element, but not both. As you might have guessed, the DataField simply maps to a query column. A Value element should contain an expression used to calculate a field. In the designer, this shows up as a calculated value. An example of the `Fields` collection follows:

```
<Fields>
  <Field Name="FirstName">
    <DataField>FirstName</DataField>
    <rd:TypeName>System.String</rd:TypeName>
  </Field>
  <Field Name="CountryRegionName">
    <DataField>CountryRegionName</DataField>
    <rd:TypeName>System.String</rd:TypeName>
  </Field>
</Fields>
```

In a lot of cases, a database query or stored procedure returns more information than most readers would like or need. In this case, you can apply a filter to the data set through the `Filters` collection. Each individual `Filter` element contains a collection of `FilterExpression`, `Operator`, and `FilterValues`. Basically, for every row in the data set, the report-processing engine is responsible for evaluating the expression against that row and using the operator to compare it to the list of values. So, keep in mind that depending on the expression, this can be time-consuming.

The following code listing displays an example of the `Query` and `Filter` elements:

```
<DataSets>
  <DataSet Name="AdventureWorks">
    <Fields>
      <Field Name="ProductID">
        <DataField>ProductID</DataField>
        <rd:TypeName>System.Int32</rd:TypeName>
      </Field>
      <Field Name="Name">
        <DataField>Name</DataField>
        <rd:TypeName>System.String</rd:TypeName>
      </Field>
    </Fields>
    <Query>
      <DataSourceName>DataSource1</DataSourceName>
      <CommandText>     SELECT ProductID, Name
           FROM Production.Product</CommandText>
      <rd:UseGenericDesigner>true</rd:UseGenericDesigner>
    </Query>
    <Filters>
      <Filter>
        <FilterExpression>=Fields!ProductID.Value</FilterExpression>
        <Operator>Equal</Operator>
        <FilterValues>
```

```
      <FilterValue DataType="Integer">866</FilterValue>
    </FilterValues>
  </Filter>
</Filters>
</DataSet>
</DataSets>
```

The schema definition element for a `DataSet` is in the following listing. To shorten the listing, we have skipped several child elements for a `DataSet` that determine how a Report Server sorts data: `AccentSensitivity` (when text is accent sensitive, the character `'a'` is not equal to the character `'ã'`), `WidthSensitivity` (determines whether single-byte and double-byte representation of the same character is identical), and `KanatypeSensitivity` (sensitivity to two types of Japanese characters).

```
...
        <xsd:element name="DataSets" type="DataSetsType" minOccurs="0" />
...
  <xsd:complexType name="DataSetsType">
    <xsd:sequence>
      <xsd:element name="DataSet" type="DataSetType" maxOccurs="unbounded" />
    </xsd:sequence>
    <xsd:anyAttribute namespace="##other" processContents="skip" />
  </xsd:complexType>
...
  <xsd:complexType name="DataSetType">
    <xsd:choice minOccurs="1" maxOccurs="unbounded">
      <xsd:element name="Fields" type="FieldsType" minOccurs="0" />
      <xsd:element name="Query" type="QueryType" />
      <xsd:element name="CaseSensitivity" minOccurs="0">
        <xsd:simpleType>
          <xsd:restriction base="xsd:string">
            <xsd:enumeration value="True" />
            <xsd:enumeration value="False" />
            <xsd:enumeration value="Auto" />
          </xsd:restriction>
        </xsd:simpleType>
      </xsd:element>
      <xsd:element name="Collation" type="xsd:string" minOccurs="0" />
...
      <xsd:element name="Filters" type="FiltersType" minOccurs="0" />
      <xsd:element name="InterpretSubtotalsAsDetails" minOccurs="0">
        <xsd:simpleType>
          <xsd:restriction base="xsd:string">
            <xsd:enumeration value="True" />
            <xsd:enumeration value="False" />
            <xsd:enumeration value="Auto" />
```

```
      </xsd:restriction>
    </xsd:simpleType>
  </xsd:element>
  <xsd:any namespace="##other" processContents="skip" />
</xsd:choice>
<xsd:attribute name="Name" type="xsd:normalizedString" use="required" />
```

ReportItems Element

ReportItems define the contents of the report. They are under the PageHeader, Body, and PageFooter elements. ReportItems contain user interface elements, such as Tablix, Image, Line, Subreport, and Rectangle. Because SSRS allows you to nest controls, you can also find report items within other report items. Each report item must contain at least one child element.

Because many elements inherit from a report item, it is advantageous to be familiar with the shared properties. These are mostly related to presentation. Height, Width, ZIndex, Top, and Left are all used to size and position an item. Each report item can have its own style section. The Action, Visibility, and DrillThrough elements all aid in reporting interactivity. Generic RDL of a report item that contains some common elements is shown in the following code listing. {REPORT ITEM} abbreviates any report item, such as Textbox, Tablix, and so on. Most common child elements of a report item are noted in the following listing:

```
<ReportItems>
       ...
        <{REPORT ITEM} Name="...">
              <Style>...</Style>
              <Top>...</Top>
              <Left>...</Left>
              <Height>...</Height>
              <Width>...</Width>
              <ZIndex>...</ZIndex>
              <Visibility>...</Visibility>
              <ToolTip>...</ToolTip>
              <Bookmark>...</Bookmark>
              <DocumentMapLabel>...</ DocumentMapLabel>
              <RepeatWith>...</RepeatWith>
              <CustomProperties>...</CustomProperties>
              <ActionInfo>...</ActionInfo>
              <ReportItems>...</ReportItems>
              <DataElementName>...</DataElementName>
              <PageBreakAtStart>...</PageBreakAtStart>
              <PageBreakAtEnd>...</PageBreakAtEnd>
        </{REPORT ITEM}>
       ...
</ReportItems>
```

Table 9.3 describes some common elements of a report item.

TABLE 9.3 Common `ReportItems` Elements

Name	Required or Optional	Type	Description
`Name`	Required	`String`	Unique name given to the report item.
`Style`	Optional	`Element`	The style information such as padding, color, font, and so on for the element.
`Action`	Optional	`Element`	An action such as a bookmark link or a drillthrough action that is associated with the report item. This aids in making reports interactive.
`Top`	Optional	`Size`	Distance between the top of the report item and the top of the containing object. If excluded, the value becomes 0 inches.
`Left`	Optional	`Size`	Distance between the left of the report item and the left of the containing object. If excluded, the value becomes 0 inches.
`Height`	Optional	`Size`	The vertical size of the item. If omitted, the value defaults to the height of the containing object minus the `Top` value.
`Width`	Optional	`Size`	The lateral size of the item. If omitted, the value defaults to the width of the containing object minus the `Left` value.
`PageBreakAtStart`	Optional	`Boolean`	Instructs the Report Server to put a page break before a report item.
`PageBreakAtEnd`	Optional	`Boolean`	Instructs the Report Server to put a page break after a report item.
`Visibility`	Optional	`Element`	Specifies the initial visibility of an item and a toggle trigger item for the visibility.

You can find additional information, including more discussion about RDL, in subsequent chapters.

Data Regions

Data regions are the primary mechanism used to display data and a base class of controls that generate repeating content based on data in a data set. Data regions include Tablix (implements a table, list, and a matrix), Chart, and Gauge. Each data region is unique in its own way and, therefore, has many of its own specialized elements and attributes. Because all the data regions display data, all have the `<DataSetName>` tag. We provide more information about the specifics of data regions later in this book.

Summary

This chapter covered why and how Microsoft chose to use XML in SSRS. This chapter also covered the programming model that arose as a result, and explained some of the key elements and their derivations.

The following chapters build on this information, some indirectly and some in a more direct way. Report Builder and Report Designer are nothing more than fancy RDL generators. Therefore, this chapter provided a cursory look at what they generate. The following chapters really do nothing more than show how to use them to build bigger and better reports by generating more advanced RDL. Later chapters of this book provide more information about RDL, specifically with regard to report items and data regions.

CHAPTER 10
Expressions

IN THIS CHAPTER

- What Is an Expression?
- Expression Syntax
- Adding Expressions
- Collections
- Using Functions
- Other Functions
- Expression and Built-In Function Security
- Using Expressions to Change Report Item Properties
- Emphasizing Certain Values

This might come as a bit of a shock, but much of the work you have done up to this point has been done using expressions. Expressions are central to SSRS. In fact, they are so central that just about everything depends on them. Every property on every report item is an expression. The designer just sets them to predefined values, instead of making them dynamic. This chapter covers making these properties dynamic, and how to use SSRS built-in tools to help you do so.

What Is an Expression?

Expressions are VB.NET statements that resolve to a single value of a .NET type, such as `Integer`, `String`, and so on. Much like VB.NET statements, expressions can be composed of constants, variables, functions, and operators. If you are wondering whether you can write C# expressions, the answer is no. All code embedded in a report, including expressions, has to follow VB.NET syntax. If you prefer to write C# code, see Chapter 26, "Creating and Calling a Custom Assembly from a Report." If writing C# is not a matter of principle (and for simplicity's sake), you can think about VB.NET expressions as C# expressions without semi-colons.

Most expressions are nothing more than simple strings or VBA constants. For example, the `FontWeight` property of a text box can be set to a number of values, including `Bold`, `Normal`, and `ExtraLight`. Other expressions are strings, such as the `Height` and `Width` properties.

Report Designer aids us by setting property values to predefined constants. They remain constant while the report is being rendered.

The real power of expressions comes when these formerly static values can be changed while the report is processing, which gives the report a level of dynamism that it otherwise would not have had.

Suppose, for example, that you are generating a report of products and their profit and loss. One of the requirements of the report is to show the products that are losing money in BIG, **bold**, red letters. We would not know the profitability information until a report pulls data from a data source. After data is retrieved, the report can use a simple expression logic `=IIf(Fields!ProductProfit.Value < 0, "Red", "Black")` in the `Color` property of a text box to highlight negative values in red.

Now let's look at the world of expressions.

Expression Syntax

Expressions are preceded by an equals (=) sign, which tells the report-processing engine that the statement following this sign has to be evaluated. It is certainly possible to turn even a constant to an expression. For example, the `VerticalAlign` property can have constant values: `Top`, `Middle`, and `Bottom`; alternatively, a developer can express those constants as expressions `="Top"`, `="Middle"`, or `="Bottom"`. (Note that we use a literal name of the constant in an expression.)

If you are more familiar with Microsoft Excel than VB.NET, expressions are similar to VBA expressions in Excel. Starting an expression with = only increases the resemblance.

Expressions can be used to achieve several goals: display the values on a report, and calculate values for style and formatting properties.

Style change can include variation of colors, highlights, and shapes of displayed data. To accomplish those goals, expressions are used in properties of reporting items. Most properties of the reporting items support expressions, but a few (such as `Name`) do not. Most of the expressions in properties are strings, but a few are VBA constants, such as `True` or `False`, and a few have numeric values.

Let's start our examination by taking a look at a simple yet common expression:

```
=Fields!FirstName.Value
```

This is a common expression for retrieving values from a data set. As expected, the expression starts with an equals sign. Next is the keyword `Fields`. This is in reference to the `Fields` collection of the parent data set. The next piece (`!FirstName.Value`) makes reference to the `FirstName` field in the `Fields` collections, and gets its value. It is also possible to use functions around fields to achieve a desired result. For example, you can retrieve a total sum of all `Price` fields using the following:

```
=Sum(Fields!Price.Value)
```

Expressions can contain one or more of the following:

- **Constants:** Constants can be static expressions (such as static text `="This is static text"` or numeric `=5`) or predefined (such as `Red` [for color], `Left` [for text alignment], and `Arial` [for font family]). Most of the properties accept predefined constants. For example, `TextAlign` can have one of the following values: `General`, `Left`, `Center`, or `Right`.
- **Collections:** Collections themselves and items of all collections are read-only. Therefore, you can neither add nor remove items from a collection, nor can you change an item in a collection. For example, you can't set `CommandText` for an item in the `DataSets` collection.

  The `Variables` collection is, in a way, an exception to the "read-only" rule. You still can't add items to a `Variables` collection programmatically, but you can set (or initialize) a `Variables` item once. Because you can initialize a variable with an expression, the item can contain variable values. See the "Variables Collection (New in 2008)" section later in this chapter for more information.

  A collection item can belong to one of the built-in collections outlined in Table 10.1. We discuss the `Parameters` collection in more detail in Chapter 12, "Report Parameters," and the rest of the collections further in this chapter.

TABLE 10.1 Collections

Collection	Brief Description
`DataSets` (New in 2008)	Contains the collection of data sets in a report Example: `DataSets("AdventureWorksDSet").CommandText`
`DataSources` (New in 2008)	Contains the collection of data sources in a report Example: `=DataSources("AdventureWorksDSrc").Type`
`Fields`	Contains collection of fields in a data set Example: `=Fields!Name.Value`
`Globals`	Contains global information for an entire report, such as the report name Example: `=Globals.ReportName`
`Parameters`	Contains report's single- and multiple-valued parameters Example: `=Parameters!Parameter1.Value`
`ReportItems`	Contains the report's text boxes, either standalone or text boxes that are part of other items, like `Tablix` Example: `=ReportItems("Textbox1").Value`
`User`	Contains data about the user running the report, such as user ID Example: `=User!UserID`

TABLE 10.1 Continued

Collection	Brief Description
Variables (New in 2008)	Contains variables and group variables that you define for a report Example: =Variables.Var1

- **Operators:** Operators include the programmatic symbols used for common mathematical operations, such as addition, subtraction, power, modulo, and so on, and operate on strings, such as string concatenation.
  - **Arithmetic** operators include ^, *, /, \, Mod, +, and -.
  - **Comparison** operators include <, >, <=, >=, =, <>, Like (compares two strings), and Is (compares two object reference variables).
  - **Concatenation** operators include & and +. Use the & operator for concatenation of two strings to avoid confusion with adding two numbers.
  - **Logical/bitwise** operators include And, Not, Or, Xor (logical exclusion operation), AndAlso (performs short-circuiting logical conjunction on two expressions), and OrElse (short-circuiting logical disjunction on two expressions).
  - **Bit shift** operators include << and >>.
- **Visual Basic runtime functions:** Keep in mind that the Expression Editor will provide only the most common functions from the VB runtime library, such as Right, Left, InStr, Format, and so on.
- **Custom functions:** See Chapter 25, "Implementing Custom Embedded Functions," for more information.

If you use an expression for the value of a property and you either receive an error or are not able to achieve the desired result (for example, text alignment does not work properly), you need to make sure that the type of the expression value is appropriate for the property. For example, if you use the =IIf(1=1,Top,Bottom) expression for the VerticalAlign property, SSRS returns a runtime error: The VerticalAlign expression for the text box '<textbox name>' contains an error: [BC30451] Name 'Top' is not declared.

The proper expression is =IIf(1=1,"Top","Bottom").

Alternatively, if you enter =IIf(1=1,10,0) in the BorderWidth property, there is no runtime error, and SSRS is not going to provide an expected width, because the property expects a string "10pt" as opposed to a numeric value of 10.

Adding Expressions

There are two ways to add an expression:

- Type an expression in a property value either in the Properties window (by default docked at the lower-right corner of the Report Designer interface) or in the Property Pages dialog box. You can open the Property Pages dialog box by right-clicking a control and selecting *Control Name* Properties from the shortcut menu, where *Control Name* is a name of a report item, such as Textbox.
- Compose an expression with the Expression Editor.

An Expression Editor provides a convenient way of entering expressions, including IntelliSense, a list of common VB and SSRS functions, operators, and collections that a developer can copy to an expression.

To start an Expression Editor, use one of the following methods shown in Figures 10.1, 10.2, and 10.3:

- Click the drop-down on the right of the property in the Properties window.
- Right-click the item and select *fx* Expression from the drop-down (only works for text box items).
- Click the *fx* button to the right of the expression box. This is available from the Properties dialog box only.

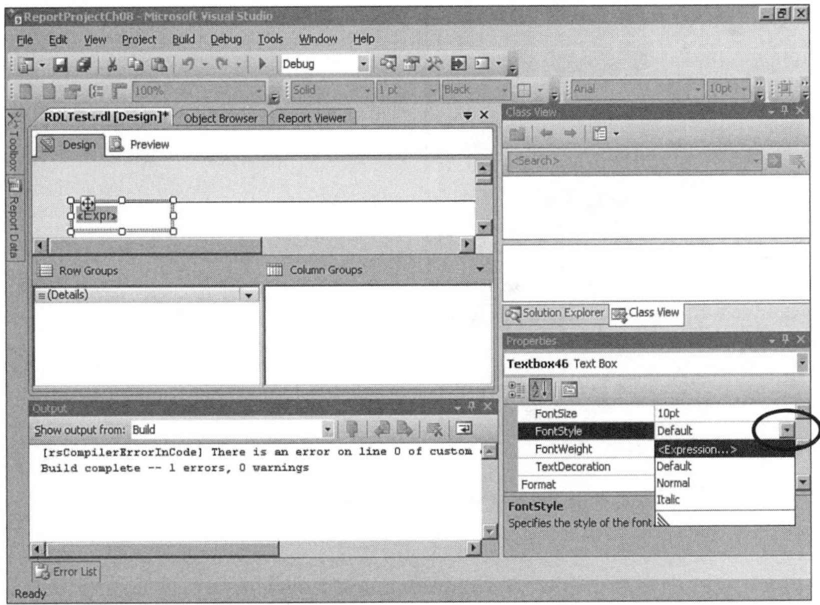

FIGURE 10.1 Click the drop-down on the right of the property.

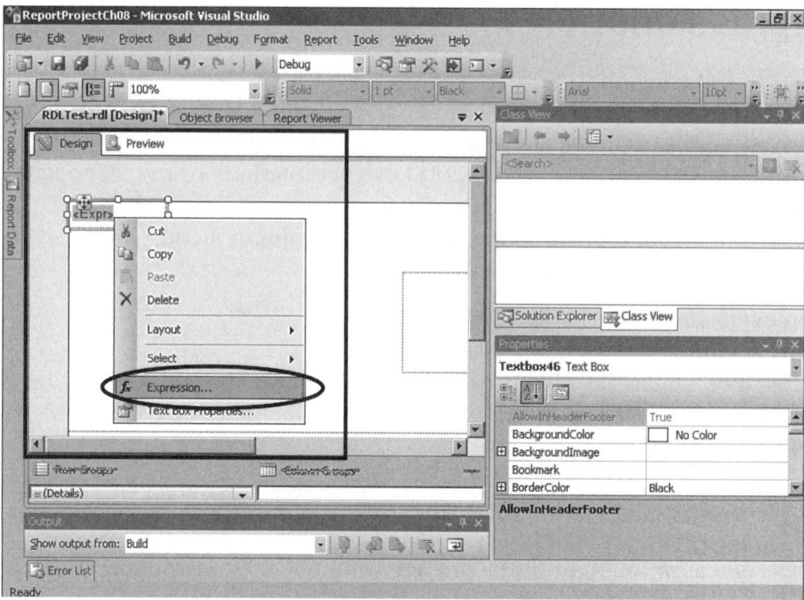

FIGURE 10.2 Right-click the item and select fx Expression from the drop-down.

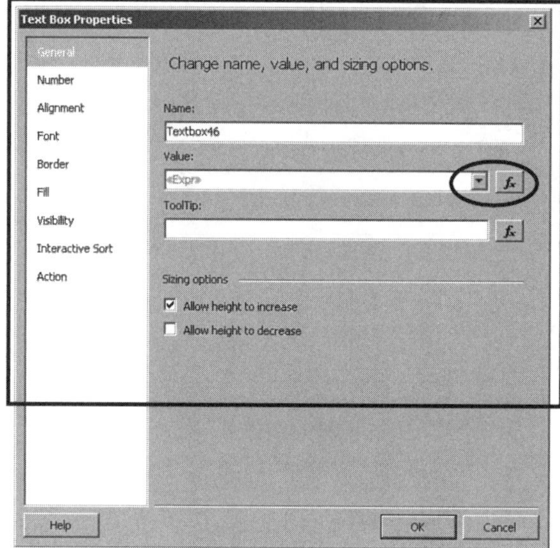

FIGURE 10.3 Click the fx button to the right of the expression box.

Any of the preceding methods will display the Expression Editor window, shown in Figure 10.4. The Expression Editor consists of an IntelliSense-enabled editing area, category browser, category member list, and multipurpose area.

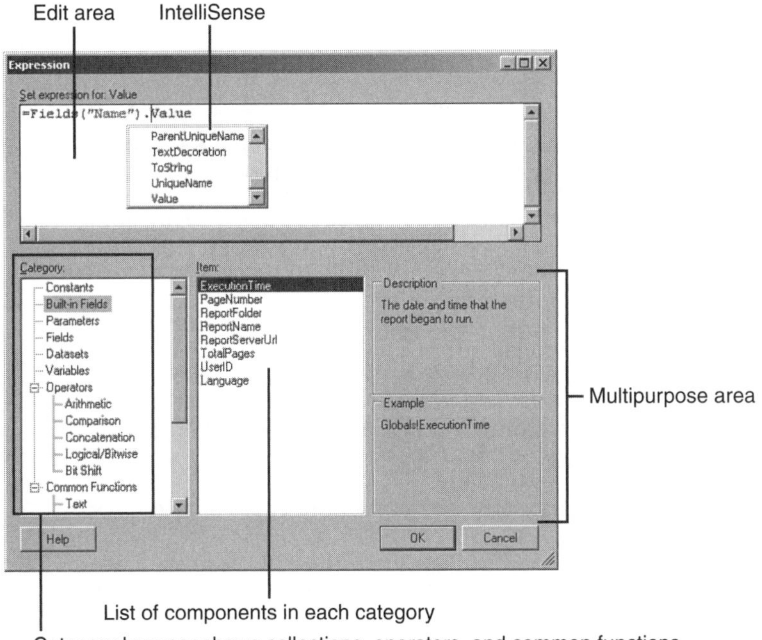

FIGURE 10.4 Expression window, also known as the Expression Editor.

The multipurpose area works in several capacities: When the category is a collection (such as `Parameters`), this area displays the collection member browser and an example for `Globals` and `User` collections. When the category is a constant, it displays a list of available constants.

The multipurpose area is pretty sophisticated when it comes to displaying constants. Depending on the property being edited, the Expression Editor displays constants available for this specific property only. The multipurpose area goes even further and, for example, for the `Color` property it will display a selectable color palette and for the `FontFamily` property it will display a sample of a font that you have selected.

When the category is operators and functions, the multipurpose area carries a description and an example.

NOTE

When you use an expression, you will see the value <<Expr>> on the design surface rather than an actual expression.

Collections

SSRS provides eight global collections to draw information from as it processes reports. There are several ways to access collection items (where `Collection` is a name of collection, `ObjectName` is a name of an object collection item, `Property` is a property of the accessed object, and `Member` is a collection member that has a simple data type, like `String`).

The following access methods demonstrate access to collections that contain simple data types, such as `String`:

```
=Collection!ObjectName.Property
=Collection("ObjectName").Property
=Collection.Item("ObjectName").Property
```

`=Fields("FirstName").Value` in the preceding is the same as `=Fields!FirstName.Value` and `=Fields.Item("FirstName").Value`.

The following access methods demonstrate access to collections that contain objects:

```
=Collection.Member
=Collection("Member")
=Collection.Item("Member")
```

NOTE

All objects in the SSRS object model are read-only. Therefore, for example, it is not possible to assign a value to a parameter during report processing. The `Variables` collection is, to a degree, an exception to the "read-only" rule. Although you still can't add items to a `Variables` collection programmatically, you can set (or initialize) a value of a `Variables` item once.

DataSets Collection (New in 2008)

The `DataSets` collection contains data sets referenced in a report. You may choose to include the query in the report in a text box so that a user interested in exactly which data is in the report can see the original command text. Table 10.2 shows member properties of `DataSets` collection items.

TABLE 10.2 `DataSets` Collection Item Properties

Property	Type	Description
`CommandText`	`String`	The original query of a data set. If a query contains a parameter, an original form of a query returned. For example, if you have a query `SELECT ProductID FROM Production.Product Where ProductId = @ProductId`, the `CommandText` will contain exactly the same query.

TABLE 10.2 Continued

Property	Type	Description
RewrittenCommand Text	String	Expanded original query (CommandText). When a provider supports the IDbCommandRewriter interface, the provider fills RewrittenCommandText with expanded CommandText converting parameters. At the time of this writing, very few providers support this interface. ReportModel is one of the providers that actually populate this member.

Books Online states that the DataSets collection is "not available in local preview." The actual behavior is rather different. For example, the DataSets.CommandText is Nothing (or Null) the first time you preview the report, but you should almost always be able to view the results if you click the Refresh button in Preview mode of the Report Designer.

Both members of a collection have relatively limited usability outside of report debugging. You can use the information contained in CommandText to display a query used to retrieve the data. You can do so by assigning a text box the following value: =DataSets("ProductsDataSet").CommandText. This proves helpful for debugging, especially if you are generating a SQL statement at the runtime (using dynamic SQL statements).

So that you do not distract users with the CommandText information, you can set a Color property of the text box where you are displaying CommandText to the same color as a background. This way the query is not visible on the screen, but you can still get it through View Source functionality of a browser. You can access this functionality in Internet Explorer by right-clicking a page and selecting View Source from a drop-down menu.

For security reasons, you might not want to keep this information in the final production reports, because even though invisible it is still available in a report's Hypertext Markup Language (HTML). Therefore, it might highlight a query's vulnerabilities, especially if the query contains parameters or dynamic SQL.

You can use RewrittenCommandText for a similar purpose, to view a query with its parameters expanded. However, because only a limited number of providers fill this member with data, the usability of this member is even further limited.

DataSources Collection (New in 2008)

Another collection that you might find useful for debugging is DataSources. Table 10.3 describes the members of this collection.

TABLE 10.3 DataSources Collection Items Properties

Property	Type	Description
DataSourceReference	String	The relative path of the data source Example: /DataSources/AdventureWorks
Type	String	The type of a data provider Example: SQL

Members of this collection are `Nothing` (or `Null`) if the data source is an embedded data source.

`Fields` Collection

The `Fields` collection contains references to fields within a data set. The most typical use of the `Fields` collection is to display data in text boxes. However, they can be used in calculating formulas for other properties and functions.

All fields have names. When a data set is created, Report Designer executes a query and retrieves column metadata, including names and a populated `Fields` collection for this data set with names retrieved. `Fields` can be either mapped to columns of a query or calculated by SSRS. Calculated fields are expressions (such as adding two database fields together) and are often used when they either add elegance to a report or the query language is not powerful enough to retrieve calculated fields (an infrequent occurrence with modern enterprise databases).

Report Designer enables you to add new fields or modify/delete existing fields. To add new fields, select Add from the shortcut menu. To modify or delete existing fields, right-click the field to modify and select Edit or Delete from the shortcut menu. The preceding steps assume that the Report Data window is visible; to open it from a main menu, navigate to View, Report Data.

Report Designer enables you to drag fields from the Report Data window to a report. If the report creator drops a field to a Tablix, a corresponding cell is filled with an expression, based on the field. If a field is dropped outside of the Tablix, a text box is created.

Recall that the Report Definition Language (RDL) schema allows each data set to have its own set of fields. The result of this is that while authoring reports, you will have multiple sets of `Fields` collections. The important thing to remember is that each data region can have a reference to only one data set, and, hence, one set of fields that belong to that data set. The data set name that the `Fields` collection refers to is actually a property of the data region, and not of the `Fields` collections.

SSRS must be able to match a field name to an appropriate data set or the scope has to be explicitly defined. For example, if a report has a single data set, using an expression like `=First(Fields!FirstName.Value)` is acceptable in an independent text box. However, if the report has multiple data sets, an expression `=First(Fields!FirstName.Value, "DataSet1")` is required. Because data regions have an associated data set, this association provides scope resolution for fields within a data region.

In SSRS 2008, Microsoft added extended (New in 2008) properties to the `Fields` collection. Table 10.4 shows a complete list of properties.

TABLE 10.4 `Fields` Collection Items Member Properties

Property	Type	Description
`Value`	`Object`	The value of the field from the data set.

TABLE 10.4 Continued

Property	Type	Description
IsMissing	Boolean	Tells you whether the field actually exists in the data set. Helpful if there is no way to be certain of the field's name. Also helps if you have misspelled a field's name.
UniqueName	String	The fully qualified name of a level in SSAS hierarchy. For example, the UniqueName value for a student might be School.&[123].
BackgroundColor	String	The background color.*
Color	String	The foreground color.*
FontFamily	String	The name of the font.*
FontSize	String	The font in points.*
FontWeight	String	The weight (Normal, Bold, and so on) of the font.*
FontStyle	String	The style (Normal, Italic) of the font.*
TextDecoration	String	Special text formatting.
FormattedValue	String	Contains a formatted value (for example, $3,000.00).
Key	Object	Contains the key of a level in the SSAS hierarchy.
LevelNumber	Integer	For parent-child hierarchies, contains the level or dimension number.
ParentUniqueName	String	For parent-child hierarchies, contains a fully qualified name of the parent level.

**In SSAS, this information can be specified as a property of an item and stored in a cube.*

The extended properties are properties other than `Value` and `IsMissing`. The extended properties have to be supported by a provider to contain values; otherwise, those properties are `Nothing` (or `Null`). An example of a provider that supports extended properties is the SQL Server Analysis Services (SSAS) data-processing extension. The thought behind extended properties is to have a consistent formatting of the data no matter what tool a user uses.

NOTE

The extended properties are properties other than `Value` and `IsMissing`. The extended properties have to be supported by a provider to contain values; otherwise, those properties are `Nothing` (or `Null`).

10

Globals Collection

The `Globals` collection is also fairly straightforward and has a predefined, fixed number of items. It is simply a list of global variables that are accessible while rendering the report.

Table 10.5 shows the properties available via the `Globals` collection.

TABLE 10.5 Globals Collection Item Properties

Property	Type	Description
ExecutionTime	DateTime	The date and time that the rendering engine began processing the report.
PageNumber	Integer	The page number of the current page. This parameter can be used only in headers and footers.
ReportFolder	String	The virtual path to the folder containing the report. This does not include the ReportServerName.
ReportName	String	The name of the report from the Report Server's catalog.
ReportServerUrl	String	The URL of the Report Server from which the report is being processed.
TotalPages	Integer	The value for the total number of pages in a report. This parameter can be used only in headers and footers.

One of the most frequent uses of the Globals collection is to display a page number in the report's footer, such as in the following expression, which can be placed in a text box in the report's footer:

```
=Globals.PageNumber & " of " & Globals.TotalPages.
```

Parameters Collection

The Parameters collection contains the list of parameters in the report. Table 10.6 shows the Parameters collection item properties.

TABLE 10.6 Parameters Collection Item Properties

Member	Type	Description
Count	Integer	The number of values: 1 for a single value parameter, 0 or more for a multivalue parameter
IsMultiValue	Boolean	True if the parameter is multivalue
Label	String	The friendly name of the parameter from the Prompt property of the parameter
Value	Object	The value of the parameter

The Parameters collection is similar to the Fields collection in that it can be used in any number of properties or functions. Unlike the Fields collection, the Parameters collection is global in scope and does not require scope resolution.

We work with this collection in Chapter 12.

ReportItems Collection

The ReportItems collection is simply a list of text boxes on the report. Only the Value property of a text box can be accessed. By accessing these values, developers can use them in calculating derived values.

> **NOTE**
>
> Keep in mind that text boxes can be hidden from the user. By using invisible text boxes, you can acquire data at runtime and use that data to process values for other visible items.

For example, the value of Textbox1 can be accessed with the following expression using the ReportItems collection:

```
=ReportIems!Textbox1.Value
```

The use of ReportItems enables developers to create page summaries. For example, the following expression creates a summary of values displayed in TextBox1:

```
=Sum(ReportItems!Textbox1.Value)
```

In addition, ReportItems can be used in complex expressions involving several items. ReportItems can also be passed to and used in a code, such as in the following example:

```
Function Incr(ReportItems As Object) '***This function increments passed parameter
    return ReportItems("Textbox1").Value+1
End Function
```

Although a ReportItems item can be used to access data from any text box in the report, to access the value of the current text box, use Me.Value or just Value.

The need to use Value might arise, for example, for conditional formatting. The following expression can be used in the property BackgroundColor:

```
=IIf(Value < 0, "Red", "White")
```

User Collection

The User collection is the simplest of collections. It contains just two properties related to the user running the report, and both properties are strings. The first item is UserID, and the second item is Language. The UserID is the user identity of the person running the report. By default, SSRS uses Windows authentication, which supplies the UserID in the form <DomainName>/<User Name>. The Language is the language identifier (used in localization) for the user. In the case of U.S. localization, this value is "en-US".

NOTE

When using Expression Editor, keep in mind that members of the `User` collection (`UserID` and `Language`) are both located under the `Globals` branch of the category member list.

Report designers can use the `User` collection to provide user-dependent formatting customization of a report. To do that, a report developer can create a parameter with the following properties:

```
Name: User
Internal: Checked (this eliminates prompt to a report user)
Available Values: Leave empty
Default Values: Non Queried with expression =User!UserID
```

Then, the report developer can use such parameters to conditionally format report items or to pass the parameter to a query. The benefit of using the parameter versus using `=User!UserID` directly (which is also an option) is an ability to modify the parameter's value. The parameter can be, for example, modified by a user, whereas `=User!UserID` is read-only.

Variables Collection (New in 2008)

IN SSRS 2008, you can define report and group variables. You can set (initialize) a variable only once. For an initialization, you can either set a value of a variable to a constant or an expression. In Figure 10.5, you might notice that `Var2` is set to a constant string expression `"This is a constant string"` and `Var1` is set to an expression. For example, you can use something like `=Code.GetInfo()` as an initialization expression for `Var2`, where `GetInfo()` is a function in a `Code` section of a report:

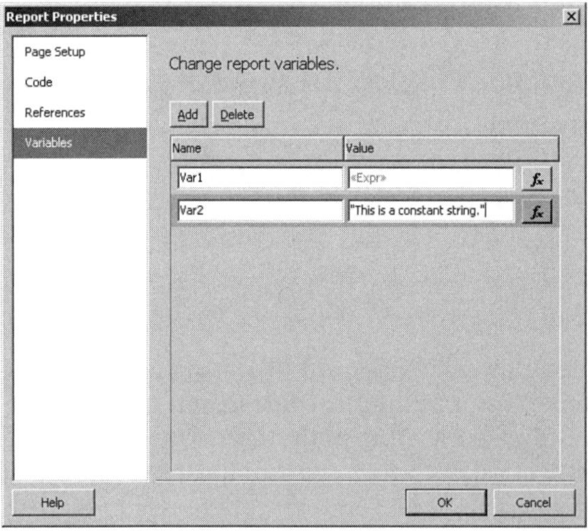

FIGURE 10.5 Initializing variables.

```
Public Function GetInfo() As String
     Dim data as String
     data = "Current date and time is:" & CStr(Now())
     return data
End Function
```

Each time you access `=Variables!Var1.Value` on your report, it will execute a function `GetInfo()` and return the current date and time. So in a sense, you have initialized the variable `Var1` with a function.

Similarly, you can define a variable `Var3`, initialize it with an expression `=Code.GetInfo()`, declare a public variable in the `Code` section of a report as `Public Info As String = "Hello"`, and then you can manipulate `Info` through the code and every time you access `=Variables!Var3.Value` you will get the latest value of the `Info`.

Similarly to the report variables, you define group variables through the Group Properties dialog box. A group variable is valid only in the scope of the group and its child groups. You can use group variables to calculate subtotals for a group.

Using Functions

Functions are really what make expressions so powerful and substantially simplify complex data manipulations for a report.

SSRS comes with two generic types of built-in functions: those used for aggregations of data, and those related to scope.

SSRS also allows you to reference any of the standard or custom assemblies that come with the Common Language Runtime. In fact, three of them are already referenced for you: `Microsoft.VisualBasic`, `System.Math`, and `System.Convert`.

In addition, SSRS enables you to write your own functions using custom code blocks (in VB.NET).

Visual Basic Runtime Functions

Runtime functions are provided through Microsoft .NET library's namespaces: `Microsoft.VisualBasic`, `System.Math`, and `System.Convert`.

Note that the Visual Basic namespace adds a couple of functions to `System.Math`; one of those functions is the random number generator, `Rnd`. The functions fall in the following categories:

- `Aggregate` (for example, `Avg`)
- `Conversion` (for example, `Str`)
- `Date & Time` (for example, `DateAdd`)
- `Financial` (for example, `NPV` [net present value calculation])
- `Inspection` (for example, `IsNull`),

TABLE 10.7 Continued

Action	Functions
Format a string	Format, FormatCurrency, FormatDateTime, FormatNumber, FormatPercent
Manipulate strings	InStr, Left, LTrim, Mid, Right, RTrim, Trim
Work with ASCII and ANSI values	Asc, AscW, Chr, ChrW
Replace a specified substring	Replace
Return a filter-based string array	Filter
String to ASCII value	Asc, AscW
ANSI value to string	Chr, ChrW
String to number	Val
Convert string to a date/time	DateValue, TimeValue
Splits/joins a string array on/from the specified number of substrings	Split, Join
Financial Functions	
Depreciation	DDB, SLN, SYD
Future value	FV
Interest rate	Rate
Internal rate of return	IRR, MIRR
Number of periods	NPer
Payments	IPmt, Pmt, PPmt
Present value	NPV, PV
Math Functions	
Random number generation	Randomize, Rnd
Absolute value and sign of a specified number	Abs, Sign

TABLE 10.7 Continued

Action	Functions
Reverse trigonometric functions (For example, Acos returns an angle for a specified Cos value.)	Acos, Asin, Atan, Atan2
Produce the full product of two 32-bit numbers; multiplies two big numbers	BigMul
Smallest/largest/nearest whole number greater/less than or equal to the specified number	Ceiling/Floor/ Round
Trigonometric functions	Cos, Cosh, Sin, Sinh, Tan, Tanh
Quotient (division result) of two numbers, also passing the remainder as an output parameter	DivRem
Result is the number e (its value approximately 2.72) raised to the specified (as parameter) power. The number e is frequently used in mathematical and statistical calculations.	Exp
Remainder resulting from the division of a specified number by another specified number	IEEERemainder
Logarithm and Base 10 Log of a specified number	Log, Log10
Larger and smallest of two specified numbers	Max, Min
Result of specified number raised to the specified power	Pow
Square root of a specified number	Sqrt
Information Functions	
Check whether the parameter of the specified type	IsNothing (or IS Nothing), IsDate, IsNumeric, IsError, IsArray, IsReference
Examine array bounds	LBound, UBound
Examine the type of the expression, return the string name of the type	TypeName

Function `IsNothing` can be used to check for the `Null` values. For example, an expression `=IsNothing(Fields!SalesPersonId.Value)` checks whether `SalesPersonId` is equal to `Null`. This expression is equivalent to `=Fields!SalesPersonId.Value IS Nothing` (that is, comparison to the keyword `Nothing`). Do not use `IsDBNull` in your expressions; this function does not have useful applications in SSRS expressions.

Table 10.8 lists the functions related to program flow. These functions help with programmatic decision making.

TABLE 10.8 Program Flow Functions

Function	Description	Example
`Choose`	Selects and returns a value from a list of arguments	`= CStr(Choose(Value, "Red", "Yellow", " Green "))` returns color depending on the value (1–3). This example can be used to control a "traffic light" highlight.
`IIf`	Selects and returns one of two objects, depending on the evaluation of an expression	`= IIf(TestMe < 0, "Red", "Green")` returns color, depending on the value. This example can be used to highlight negative values.
`Switch`	Evaluates a list of expressions and returns an `Object` value of an expression associated with the first expression in the list that is `True`	`=Switch(Fields!City.Value = "London", "English (United Kingdom)", Fields!City.Value = "Rome", "Italian (Italy)", Fields!City.Value = "Paris", "French (France)")` returns locale depending on the city. Can be used in the `Language` property to provide the appropriate format defaults.

Aggregate Functions

Aggregate functions are used to aggregate data over a certain scope. Two examples of these types of operations are `Sum` and `Average`.

Aggregate functions are simple to use. The big trick to them is scope. All aggregate functions contain `Scope` as a parameter. If `Scope` is not entered, it defaults based on a number of criteria. Because of this defaulting, you will usually see aggregates used without a reference to `Scope`. For example, with a sum in a table or a matrix, the scope is assumed to be the innermost grouping within the table or matrix.

Outside of a data region, the scope is just the name of the data set. For example, if you have a text box outside a table in which you intend to put a total sales value, you put the following expression inside the text box value property:

```
=Sum(Fields!Sales.Value,"SalesDataset")
```

If a report has only one data set, the `Scope` parameter does not need to be specified.

If you are in a data region, and you want to override the default group for an aggregate, just give the group name you want or `Nothing` to specify the outermost grouping available.

With that out of the way, Table 10.9 provides a list of available aggregate functions.

TABLE 10.9 Aggregate Functions

Function Signature	Expression Type	Return Type	Description
`Aggregate (Expression, [Scope])`			Returns a custom aggregate of the specified expression, as defined by the data provider
`Avg(Expression, [Scope, [Recursive]])`	`Float`	`Float`	Returns the average of all non-null values from the specified expression
`Count(Expression, [Scope, [Recursive]])`	`Object`	`Integer`	Returns a count of all non-null values of the specified expression
`CountDistinct(Expression, [Scope, [Recursive]])`	`Object`	`Integer`	Returns a count of all distinct values from the specified expression
`CountRows([Scope], [Recursive])`	`N/A`	`Integer`	Returns a count of rows within the specified scope
`First(Expression, [Scope])`	`Object`	Same as type of `Expression`	Returns the first value from the specified expression after all sorting has been applied to the data
`InScope (Scope)`	`String`	`Boolean`	Returns `True` if the current instance of an item is in the specified scope
`Last(Expression, [Scope])`	`Object`	Same as type of `Expression`	Returns the last value from the specified expression after all sorting has been applied to the data

10

TABLE 10.9 Continued

Function Signature	Expression Type	Return Type	Description
`Level([Scope])`	`String`	`Integer`	Returns the current level of depth in a recursive hierarchy; could be used to create level-based indentations
`Max(Expression, [Scope, [Recursive]])`	`Object`	Same as type of `Expression`	Returns the maximum value from all non-null values of the specified expression
`Min(Expression, [Scope, [Recursive]])`	`Object`	Same as type of `Expression`	Returns the minimum value from all non-null values of the specified expression
`StDev(Expression, [Scope, [Recursive]])`	`Integer or Float`	`Float`	Returns the standard deviation of all non-null values of the specified expression
`StDevP(Expression, [Scope, [Recursive]])`	`Integer` or `Float`	`Float`	Returns the population standard deviation of all non-null values of the specified expression
`Sum(Expression, [Scope, [Recursive]])`	`Integer` or `Float`	`Float`, `Decimal`, or `Double`*	Returns a sum of the values of the specified expression
`Var(Expression, [Scope, [Recursive]])`	`Integer` or `Float`	`Float`, `Decimal`, or `Double`*	Returns the variance of all non-null values of the specified expression

TABLE 10.9 Continued

Function Signature	Expression Type	Return Type	Description
`VarP(Expression, [Scope, [Recursive]])`	`Integer` or `Float`	`Float`, `Decimal`, or `Double`*	Returns the population variance of all non-null values of the specified expression

Depending on the type of expression

An aggregate function can be used in expressions for any report item. The call syntax for the majority of aggregate functions is as follows:

```
=Function(Expression,[Scope, [Recursive]])
```

This syntax indicates that both the `Scope` and `Recursive` parameters can be omitted. If `Recursive` is specified, however, scope also has to be present. Aggregate functions cannot call other aggregate functions.

- **`Expression`**: A valid SSRS expression on which to perform the aggregation. The expression cannot contain aggregate functions.
- **`Function`**: A name of an aggregate function.
- **`Recursive`**: A modifier directing aggregate function to include aggregations from lower levels plus aggregation of the current level.
- **`Scope`**: String, the name of a data set, grouping, or data region to which an aggregate function is applied.

Other Functions

Table 10.10 outlines additional scripting functions offered by SSRS. These functions don't directly aggregate or perform any other calculations on values.

TABLE 10.10 Additional Scripting Functions

Function Signature	Expression Type	Return Type	Description
`Previous(Expression, [Scope])`	`Object`	Same as type of `Expression`	Returns the previous instance (value) of the expression within the specified scope.

TABLE 10.10 Continued

Function Signature	Expression Type	Return Type	Description
`RowNumber(Scope)`	N/A	`Integer`	Returns a running count of all rows in the specified scope. `Scope` controls the reset of the running value, when `Scope` is equal to `Dataset`: Running value is not reset throughout the entire data set. `Group`: Running value is reset on group expression change. `Data region`: Running value is reset for each new instance of the data region.
`RunningValue(Expression, Function, [Scope])`	Determined by the `Function` parameter	Determined by the `Function` parameter	Uses a specified function to return a running aggregate of the specified expression. Same running value reset rules as for the `RowNumber()` function. The expression cannot contain aggregate functions.

The `RowNumber` function can be used to change the background color of a table row: `=IIf(RowNumber("DataSet1") Mod 2,"White","Gray")`.

Remember that in addition to built-in functions, developers can always write their own functions with custom code. If custom functions are used, the way to access the custom functions is by preceding the function name with `Code` (for example, `=Code.MyFunctionName()`).

Custom functions and assemblies are covered in Chapters 25, "Implementing Custom Embedded Functions," and 26, "How to Create and Call a Custom Assembly from a Report."

Expression and Built-In Function Security

The functions outlined in this chapter are those that SSRS allows to execute by default. By default, all reports run with `ExecuteOnly` permission. This means, for example, that functions such as `Dir` that access file system functionality will not execute by default. However, an administrator can give report processing additional permissions by editing the CAS policy file, but this would be applied to *all* reports on the server. In this case, the report-publishing right must be restricted to trusted personnel. This is because anybody who has the right to publish will be able to execute any method, which can in turn substantially compromise security.

To learn more about security, see the ".NET Security Primer for an SSRS Administrator" section of Chapter 26.

Using Expressions to Change Report Item Properties

Expressions are pretty basic in concept and exceptionally simple in implementation. They are the Swiss army knife in the report developer's toolbox. With the basics out of the way, it's time to create another report.

In this and the following section, we follow the steps that demonstrate how to leverage expressions to change a report item's appearance to highlight (or emphasize) certain values.

1. Open the solution that we developed in the Chapter 8, "Report Designer(s)." If you do not have it handy, create a new solution that contains a shared data source pointing to the AdventureWorks sample database.

> **NOTE**
>
> Keep in mind that we are using the AdventureWorks 2005 database for the examples in this book. For more information, see the section "Sample Database Setup" in Chapter 7, "Report Server Project Wizard."

2. Add a new report called **`Top Salespersons`**.
3. Using the shared data source, create a data set using the following query:

```
SELECT TOP 5
    C.LastName, C.FirstName, E.EmployeeID, SUM(SOH.SubTotal) AS SaleAmount
FROM
    Sales.SalesPerson SP
INNER JOIN HumanResources.Employee E ON SP.SalesPersonID = E.EmployeeID
INNER JOIN Person.Contact C ON E.ContactID = C.ContactID
INNER JOIN Sales.SalesOrderHeader SOH ON SP.SalesPersonID = SOH.SalesPersonID
INNER JOIN Sales.SalesOrderDetail SOD ON SOH.SalesOrderID = SOD.SalesOrderID
INNER JOIN Production.Product P ON SOD.ProductID = P.ProductID
INNER JOIN Production.ProductSubcategory PS ON P.ProductSubcategoryID =
➥PS.ProductSubcategoryID
INNER JOIN Production.ProductCategory PC ON PS.ProductCategoryID =
➥PC.ProductCategoryID
GROUP BY
     C.LastName, C.FirstName, E.EmployeeID
```

4. Name the data **`SalesDS`**.
5. In the Design window, add a table to the report and delete the last column. You should now have two columns in the table.
6. Drag the Last Name from the fields of SalesDS in the Report Data, and drag the SalesAmount field from the data set onto the second column. Format the SalesAmount text box with the format string `c0`.
7. Change the header `BackgroundColor` property to Blue and `Color` property to White. Make the font Bold.

8. Select the Table Details row. On the `BackgroundColor` property, enter the following expression:

```
=IIf(RowNumber("SalesDS") Mod 2,"Gray","White")
```

You should now be able to preview the alternating colors on each detail row.

Emphasizing Certain Values

Now suppose that you want to recognize salespeople who have more than $130,000,000 in sales. First, you might want to sort the data. Next, you would put an emphasis on the people by changing the font color for a row and possibly making the font size larger. The following steps enable you to do these things:

1. Select the table, right-click it, and select Tablix Properties from the context menu.
2. On the Sorting tab, click Add to add a sorting expression and select SaleAmount from the Sort By list box under the Column heading.
3. Select Z to A (meaning descending) as the order.
4. Click OK.
5. Select the detail row on the table.
6. On the `Color` properties of the selected table row, place the following expressions:

```
=IIf(Fields!SaleAmount.Value>=130000000,"Green","Black")
```

7. To increase the size of the font, enter the following in the `Font`, `Font Size` property:

```
=IIf(Fields!SaleAmount.Value>=130000000,"14pt", "10pt")
```

8. Preview the report. You should see something similar to what is shown in Figure 10.6.

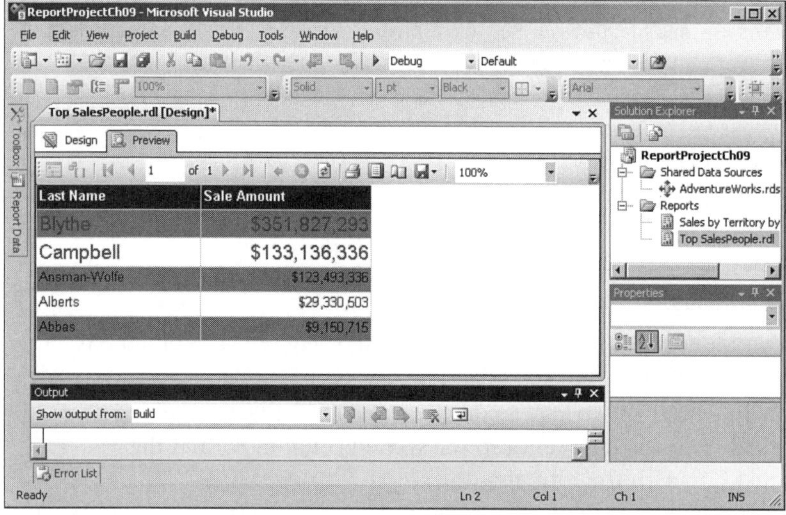

FIGURE 10.6 Alternating row colors and emphasizing values on a report.

Summary

Expressions are one of the major components that make SSRS flexible, yet powerful. Using them, you can make decisions at runtime and base decisions on the data being returned. Expressions are derivatives of VB.NET, or they can be constants.

Expressions contain constants, variables, operators, collection members, and functions.

There are eight major collections: `DataSets`, `DataSources`, `Globals`, `Fields`, `Parameters`, `ReportItems`, `User`, and `Variables`.

By combining these collections with either aggregate functions or any other kind of function, you can make powerful expressions that help to add a level of dynamism to reports.

CHAPTER 11
Accessing Data

IN THIS CHAPTER

- Data-Processing Extensions
- Types of Data Sources
- Connection Strings
- Querying Data
- Adding a Data Source

This chapter and the following chapter (Chapter 12, "Report Parameters") look more closely at data retrieval and parameters. The combination of these two items helps to add incredible flexibility to SSRS.

Parameters are values you can pass into the report to help make rendering decisions at runtime. Users can get prompted to input parameters at runtime. Leveraging data sets, you can draw a list of valid parameter values from your data sources. You can even make parameters dependent on each other in such a way that the lists of values for `ParameterB` are derived as a function of `ParameterA`.

As you have already seen, data sets retrieve the data that reports use, and they are critical to report processing. Data sets leverage data sources. A data source, in turn, points to a data store (most frequently a database) and consists of a name, type (such as Microsoft SQL Server), connection string, and credentials.

A data set consist of the following:

- A pointer to (or the name of) a data source.
- A query that the data set will process.
- Parameters for the query.
- Fields. When a query is a SQL statement, a list of fields will be generated by the Report Designer. When a query is a dynamic SQL statement or a stored procedure, you may need to add fields manually. You can also add your own calculated fields.
- Filters. A filter is similar to a `WHERE` clause.

- Options. Most of the options direct a data provider on how to process text data (for example, whether a data provider should be case sensitive with data [query results]).
- The result of the query processing (a single set of rows and columns).

Data-Processing Extensions

The first thing created during the report development process is, usually, a data source and then a data set. With that, a developer selects a source of data, creates a query, and can evaluate the quality of the data returned by the data set.

Data quality is something you, as the developer, must evaluate. However, the open-ended nature of SSRS helps tremendously by not putting any hard limits on the type of data you can use.

SSRS comes with the capability to connect to SQL Server, Analysis Services, Integration Services package (you must select Shared Features, Integration Services during the install to see this selection), Oracle, ODBC, OLE DB, Report Server Model, SAP NetWeaver BI, Hyperion Essbase, Teradata, and XML.

If these choices are not enough, it is possible to extend SSRS by writing a custom data-processing extension to be used within a data source. Extensions are covered in Chapter 29, "Extending Reporting Services."

NOTE

To connect to SQL Server 6.5, use OLE DB.

Types of Data Sources

There are three types of data sources. The first type of data source is the embedded data source. This type is kept within the report, and cannot be accessed by other reports. In the SSRS documentation, this is referred to as a report-specific data source.

The second type of data source is the shared data source. The largest difference between the two data sources is location. A shared data source lives on the Report Server as a separate entity from the reports, whereas the definition for a report-specific data source is that the source is stored within the report itself. This allows other reports to use them for their data sources.

The third type of data source is an expression that is used to dynamically choose the data source at runtime. This is called a data source expression. Remember that just about every property can be modified by an expression. Data sources are no different.

NOTE

Much like most other properties, a data source can be modified using an expression. This capability allows you to change connections during runtime.

Report-Specific Data Sources

The report-specific data source should be used only when the data needed to process a report should be restricted to that report. If multiple reports need to access the same data source with the same credentials, you should use a shared data source. This is because maintaining lots of embedded data sources can be cumbersome. After the report has been published to the Report Server, the embedded data source has to be maintained as part of that report. You can use the Report Manager web interface to change the reference from an embedded to a shared data source.

Shared Data Sources

A shared data source exists on the Report Server as a separate entity. Report developers can define a shared data source in Visual Studio, but it does not overwrite an existing data source by default in the same manner that it overwrites reports. To override a shared data source, you have to set `OverwriteDataSources` project property to `True` (see Figure 11.1).

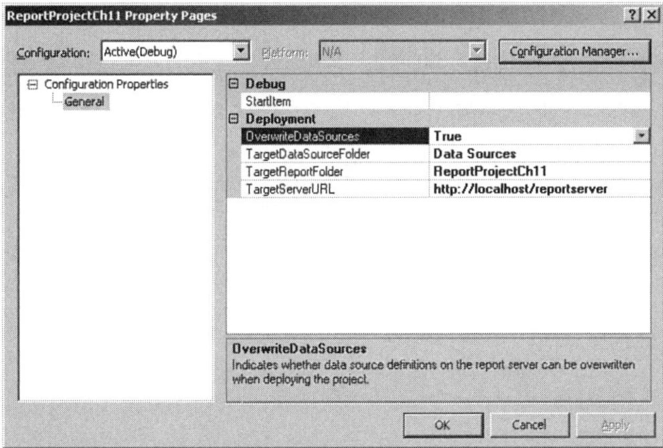

FIGURE 11.1 `OverwriteDataSources` project property.

A shared data source is useful when

- Many reports use data from the same location with the same credentials.
- An administrator needs to have an easy way to change the location of a data source for several reports. This is the case, for example, when moving reports from development to production.

Data Source Expressions

An expression can be used to define the connection at runtime. A classic case is the difference between an active online transaction processing (OLTP) database and historical data or a data warehouse. Many companies store historical data that is more than six months old in a data warehouse. You would have to determine an appropriate connection from some report-level parameter.

Like all expressions, a data source expression would have to be written in Visual Basic.NET and preceded by an equals (=) sign.

To define data source expressions, consider the following guidelines:

- Do not use a shared data source. You cannot use a data source expression in a shared data source. You must define a report-specific data source for the report instead.
- Design the reports using a static connection string.
- Do not include credentials in the connection string. When possible, Windows authentication is the best way to handle credentials. You can also hard code the credentials through the Data Source Properties dialog box (as discussed later in this chapter).
- Use a report parameter to specify the values to be passed to the expression. The parameter can pull from a list of valid values from a query using a separate data source. Later in this chapter, you will see how to set up parameter dependencies that enable you to do this.
- Make sure all the data sources implement the same schema.
- Before publishing the report, replace the static connection string with an expression.

The following is an example of an expression-based data source for SQL Server:

```
="Data Source=" &Parameters!DBServer.Value & ";Initial Catalog=NorthWind
```

The preceding example assumes that there is a parameter called `DBServer`.

Data Source Credentials

You have several options to supply credentials for a data source (see Figure 11.2):

- Windows authentication (integrated security). It is the easiest to use, and the credentials are handled separately from the data sources. Using this option, you are also leveraging time-tested Windows security. Because each Windows user has individual credentials, you can assign security restrictions down to a level of an individual user. You can also leverage Windows security groups to handle several users as a group with the same level of permissions. For example, you can set permissions in such a way that an employee's personal information is available only to the HR group and the employee herself.
- Hard-code the credentials. In this case, you just enter login credentials. Report Designer stores encrypted credentials separately from the data source, locally and in the file `ProjectName.rptproj.user` and then in the Reporting Services database, also in the encrypted form.
- Prompt a user for login credentials.

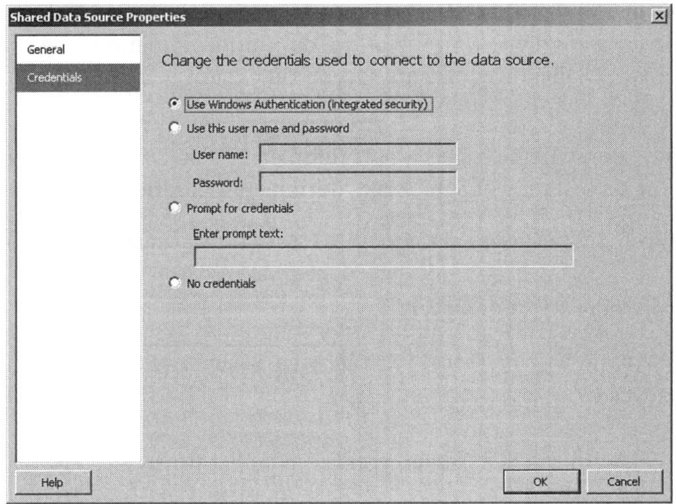

FIGURE 11.2 Shared Data Source Properties dialog box, Credentials tab.

- Use the No Credentials option. This is used for data sources that do not require credentials.
- Hard-code credentials in the connection string (*not recommended*). This approach is not recommended because of the security implications associated with this method. Because the credentials are not encrypted, this approach can easily lead to unauthorized information access.

Connection Strings

Connection strings vary widely by the type of processing extensions used in the data set. For example, if you use the OLE DB or ODBC process, you must specify the driver. For SQL Server, you should specify a database name, whereas for Oracle the database name is not required. For XML, just point it to the source by entering a URL in the connection string. In all cases, you should not specify the credentials used in accessing the data source inside the connection string. SSRS stores data source credentials separately.

The following are some common connection strings:

NOTE

We use `***Server` to denote a name or an IP address of a server that hosts a data source. For example, `SQLServer` is the name of a server that hosts a SQL Server database.

In addition to specifying a name or an IP address, you can use the following to point to a local server: `localhost`, `(local)`, and `.` (dot). All of those work for the .NET Framework data provider, but only `(local)` works for the SQL OLE DB provider.

- SQL Server RDBMS. You can connect the .NET Framework data provider, OLE DB data provider for SQL Server, and ODBC. In general, we do not recommend using ODBC because in many cases ODBC providers are several times slower than .NET or OLE DB providers.
  - SQL Server 2000 and later, where 1433 is a port number. The SQL Server administrator sets a port for an instance of SQL Server during configuration process:

    ```
    Data source=SQLServer\InstanceName,1433;Initial Catalog=DatabaseName
    ```

  - Microsoft OLE DB provider for SQL Server:

    ```
    Provider=SQLOLEDB.1;Data Source=(local);Integrated Security=SSPI;Initial
    Catalog=AdventureWorks
    ```

- Analysis Services. Much like with the SQL server, you can connect using several different providers:
  - The .NET Framework data provider for Analysis Services:

    ```
    data source= OLAPServer;initial catalog=AdventureWorksDW
    ```

    - The Microsoft OLE DB provider for OLAP 8.0. You can use it to connect to SQL Server 2000 and later:

      ```
      provider=MSOLAP.2;data source=OLAPServer;initial
      catalog=AdventureWorksDW
      ```

    - The Microsoft OLE DB provider for Analysis Services 10.0. You can use it to connect to SQL Server 2008:

      ```
      provider=MSOLAP.4;data source= OLAPServer;initial
      catalog=AdventureWorksDW
      ```

- Oracle. We recommend Oracle using network configuration tools and that you set an alias for an Oracle server. For example, where the actual server is at `OracleServerAddress:Port/Instance`, you can set an alias as `OracleServer`.
  - The .NET Framework data provider for Oracle. Oracle is running on Windows, and Windows authentication is set up:

    ```
    Data Source=OracleServer; Integrated Security=Yes;
    ```

- The OLE DB provider for Oracle:

```
Data Source=OracleServer;User ID=userId;
Password=userPassword;Provider=OraOLEDB.Oracle.1;Persist Security Info=True;
```

- XML via URL:

```
URL="http://MyWebServer.com/Queryresults.aspx"
```

- XML via web service:

```
URL=<url>;SOAPAction=<method-uri>[#¦/]<method-name>
URL=http://ReportServer/reportserver/reportservice.asmx;SOAPAction="http://sche
mas.microsoft.com/sqlserver/2004/05/reporting/reportservices/ListChildren"
```

NOTE

When specifying XML as a data source, the credentials should be set to Windows authentication or to No Credentials for anonymous access. Anything else generates an error during runtime.

- Report model data source for native mode SSRS:

```
Server=http://ReportServer/reportserver;
datasource=/models/AdventureWorks.smdl
```

- Report model data source for SSRS in SharePoint integrated mode:

```
Server=http://ReportServer;
datasource=http://ReportServer/SharePointSite/documents
/models/AdventureWorks.smdl
```

- SSIS package:

```
-f c:\packagename.dtsx
```

- SAP NetWeaver BI data source:

```
DataSource=http://SAPServer:8000/sap/bw/xml/soap/xmla
```

- Hyperion Essbase:

```
Data Source=http://HyperionServer:13080/aps/XMLA;Initial Catalog=SalesDB
```

- Teradata:

```
Data Source=TeradataServer;User ID=myUsername;Password=myPassword;
```

Microsoft supplies additional drivers that are not installed by default with SSRS. For example, the Microsoft SQL Server 2008 feature pack (www.microsoft.com/downloads/details.aspx?FamilyId=C6C3E9EF-BA29-4A43-8D69-A2BED18FE73C&displaylang=en) comes with an IBM DB2 OLE DB driver install. Once you install it, the report driver shows `Microsoft OLE DB Provider for DB2` in the OLE DB provider list.

Practically all the DBMS vendors supply .NET, OLE DB, or ODBC providers for their databases and supply setup and connection string information. In addition, Connectionstrings.com provides connection information for a variety of data sources.

Querying Data

After a connection is established, your next step is to query the data source. For most relational databases, this involves executing some type of SQL query against the catalog. In the case of Analysis Services, you use Multidimensional Expressions (MDX) queries, and for data mining, you use Data Mining Extensions (DMX) queries.

The Graphical Query Designer that comes with Report Designer aids developers in developing queries in any of the preceding languages. For more advanced queries or in cases when the data source is not relational database management system (RDBMS), you can use the Generic Query Designer.

Graphical Query Designer

The Graphical Query Designer is a tool to aid in the development of the query. Behind the scenes, it connects to the data store to pull tables and views. All you have to do is right-click the top pane to add the table you want and select the columns. If the database has referential integrity, the Graphical Query Designer picks that up, too, and makes the necessary joins automatically. You can also join database tables by dragging columns from one table to the other.

Table 11.1 outlines the four panes in the Graphical Query Designer.

TABLE 11.1 Panes of Graphical Query Designer

Pane	Function
Diagram	Displays graphic representations of the tables in the query. Use this pane to select fields and define relationships between tables.
Grid	Displays a list of fields returned by the query. Use this pane to define aliases, sorting, filtering, grouping, and parameters.

TABLE 11.1 Continued

Pane	Function
Query	Displays the Transact-SQL query represented by the Diagram and Grid panes. Use this pane to write or update a query using T-SQL query language.
Result	Displays the results of the query. To run the query, right-click in any pane, and then click Run.

Changing the diagram or grid affects the SQL and Result panes. For example, when you add a table to the diagram, it actually adds a database table to the SQL query as it is being generated. This is a good way for users to actually learn SQL. Figure 11.3 shows the Graphical Query Designer.

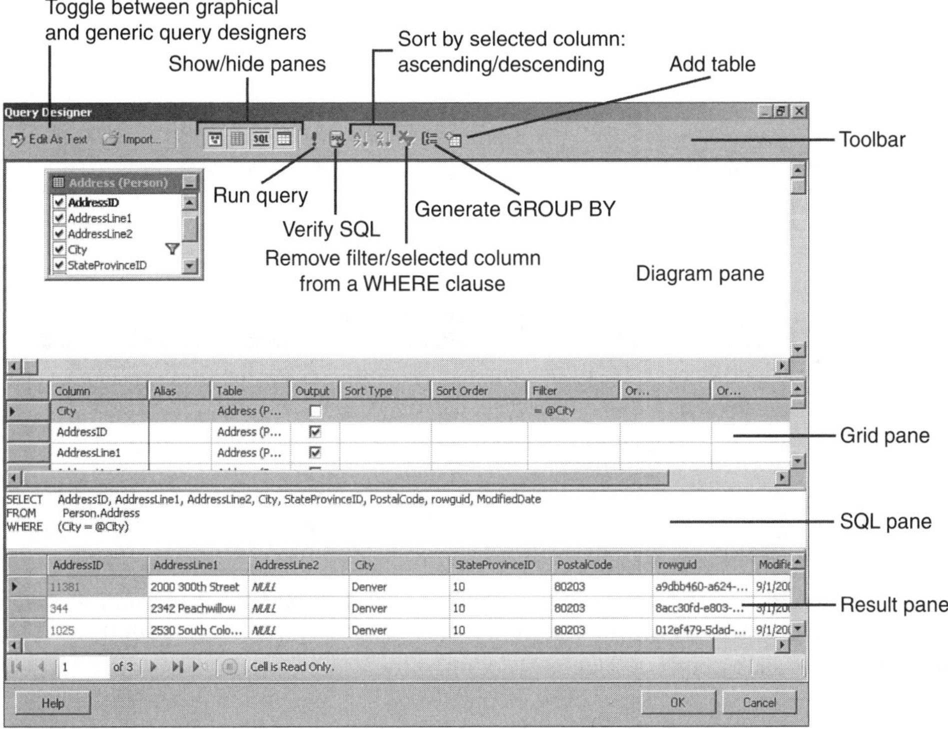

FIGURE 11.3 Graphical Query Designer.

Generic Query Designer

The Generic Query Designer is open ended. It is for times when you need more flexibility than the Graphical Query Designer allows. This flexibility is especially helpful for running multiple SQL statements to perform some preprocessing, or for writing dynamic statements based on parameters or custom code. Figure 11.4 shows the Generic Query Designer.

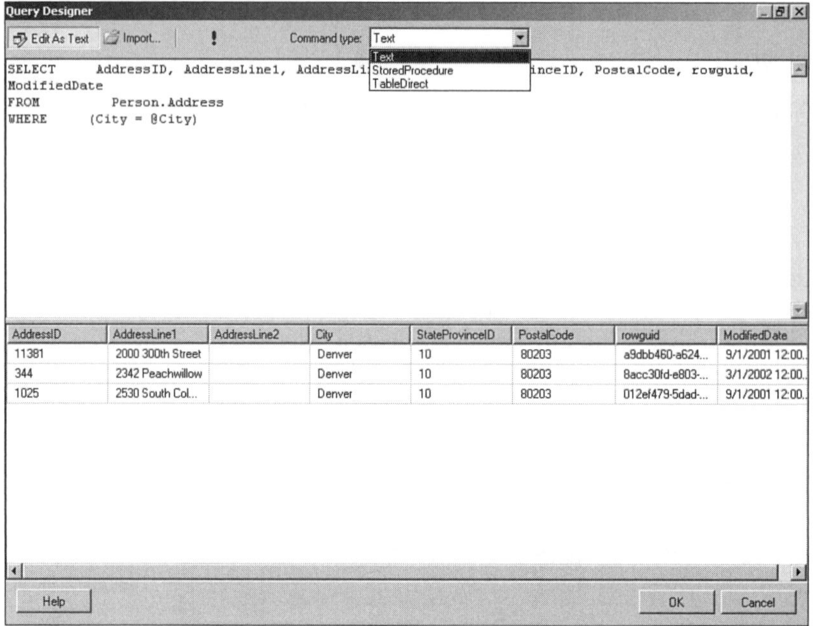

FIGURE 11.4 Generic Query Designer.

NOTE

For both Graphical and Generic Query Designers, make sure to click the OK button after you have completed query modifications. Just closing the Designer window will cancel changes, and you might lose a valuable work.

Data Set Properties

The data set contains a couple of properties of which developers should be mindful. Those properties are accessible through the Dataset Properties dialog box. To bring up the Dataset Properties dialog box (see Figure 11.5), open the Report Data dockable window (from the main BIDS screen, choose View, Report Data), right-click a data set, and select Dataset Properties from the drop-down menu.

The properties are as follows:

- The `Name` of the data set
- The `Data source` or a pointer to a shared data source
- The `Query type` or a type of query for a data set: `Text`, `Table`, or `Stored Procedure`
- The `Query`, which represents a query that retrieves data from the data source

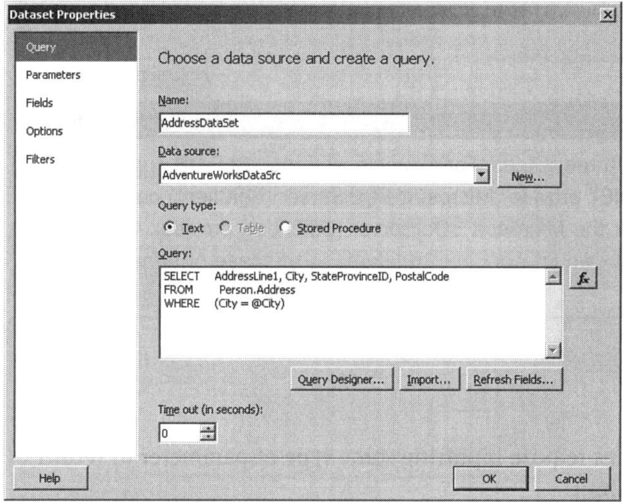

FIGURE 11.5 Dataset Properties dialog box.

- The `Fields` collections, which includes fields retrieved by the query and calculated fields
- The `Parameters` (a parameter in a query string, such as `SELECT * FROM Person.Address WHERE City = @City`) and `Dataset/Parameters`, which are used to limit selected data and must have matching parameters in each for proper report processing
- The `Filters` collection, which further filters result of the query inside of a Report Server after a data set returns data
- The `Options`, which provides instructions on how to execute a query (`Time out`) or how to sort (collation, sensitivity) and interpret the subtotals

`Query` is the only property available for access during runtime through the `CommandText` property of the `DataSets` collection. The rest of the properties are stored in Report Definition Language (RDL) and used by SSRS to process a data set.

Command Type

The command type is similar to the ADO.NET command type. It indicates the type of query that is contained in the query string and corresponding `CommandText` element of RDL. There are three values: `Table`, `Text`, and `Stored Procedure`. `Text` provides for execution of a free-form (but, of course, valid) query. `Stored Procedure` corresponds to a stored procedure call. Finally `Table` indicates for SSRS to use the `TableDirect` feature of SQL

from a query. However, the Report Designer will remove the association if the parameter is no longer present in the query.

Stored procedures can be executed by changing the command type to `Stored Procedure` and entering the SQL statement. There is no reason for the `EXEC` clause. If a stored procedure has default values, that value can be passed through to the procedure by passing the query parameter the keyword `DEFAULT`.

The `Timeout` property sets a limit as to the amount of time the query can run. If left empty or set to `0`, the query can run indefinitely.

Querying XML

The ability to directly query XML as a data source became available in SSRS2K5. Because querying XML is a little different from querying an RDBMS and fairly wide usage of XML, it is worth noting some special requirements unique to using XML as a data source. They are as follows:

- Set XML as the data source type.
- Use a connection string that points to either the URL of a web service, web-based application, or XML document. XML documents from inside SQL Server cannot be used. Instead, use `xquery` or `xpath` as a part of the query with SQL Server as the data source type.
- Use either Windows integrated security or no credentials. No other type of credentials is supported.
- The result of the query must be XML data.
- Define the XML query using either the element path, query element, or leave it empty.

The Generic Query Designer is the only way to create queries against XML. The Graphical Query Designer will not work. The good news is that developers can specify one of three types, as shown in Table 11.2.

TABLE 11.2 XML Query Types

XML Query Type	Description and Syntax

Element path	The element path specifies the path to the data to return without including namespaces.
	Syntax:
	`ElementPath = XMLElementName [/ElementPath]`
	`XMLElementName = [NamespacePrefix:]XMLLocalName`

Query element	The query element is similar to the element path, but it helps to define namespaces for the element path.
	Syntax:
	`<Query`
	`xmlns:es="http://schemas.microsoft.com/StandardSchemas/Extended`
	`Sales">`
	`<ElementPath>/Customers/Customer/Orders/Order/es:LineItems/es:Line`
	`Item</ElementPath>`
	`</Query>`

Empty	No query. It takes the first element path to a leaf node and applies it to the whole document.
	In the following document, an empty query will default to the following:
	`/Custs/Cust/Orders/Order:`
	`<Custs>`
	`<Cust ID=1>`
	`<Name>Bob</Name>`
	`<Orders>`
	`<Order ID=1 Qty=6>Chair</Order>`
	`<Order ID=2 Qty=1>Table</Order>`
	`</Orders>`
	`<Returns>`
	`<Return ID=1 Qty=2>Chair</Order>`
	`</Returns>`
	`</Cust>`
	`<Cust ID=2>`
	`Name>Aaron</Name>`
	`</Cust>`
	`</Custs>`

Fields

The result of processing the query is the `Fields` collection. When the Report Designer processes a query you have entered in the Dataset Properties dialog box, the Report Designer identifies fields returned by a query and populates the `Fields` collection. In the majority of the cases the Report Designer identifies fields returned by a query automatically as you either move to a different tab (like Fields) of the Dataset Properties dialog box or click OK to complete it. If this did not happen, you can click the Refresh Fields button to force the Report Designer to update the fields in the data set.

There are two types of fields. The first and most obvious is the database fields. Database fields are the direct result of running the query. As you might have noticed, the field name automatically gets set to the field name as expressed by the query.

The second type of field is a calculated field. This is the result of using expressions or custom code to derive a value. An expression value can, but does not have to, be based on one of the database fields. The value could just be a result of the function `Now()`.

Let's examine a calculated field. Suppose you want to determine the percent of a quota a salesperson has met.

You can add a calculated field to the data set and plug in this expression (see Figure 11.8):

```
=SalesYTD/SalesQuota * 100
```

Note that calculated expressions have `<<Expr>>` in the Field Source column and an *fx* button after it.

A word of caution on calculated fields: The calculation is performed for every row brought back from the data set. If it is a large data set, this can be rather time-consuming.

Fields and XML

In dealing with XML, every element along the element path and every attribute return as a field. All the fields are `String` data types. Some fields even include embedded XML.

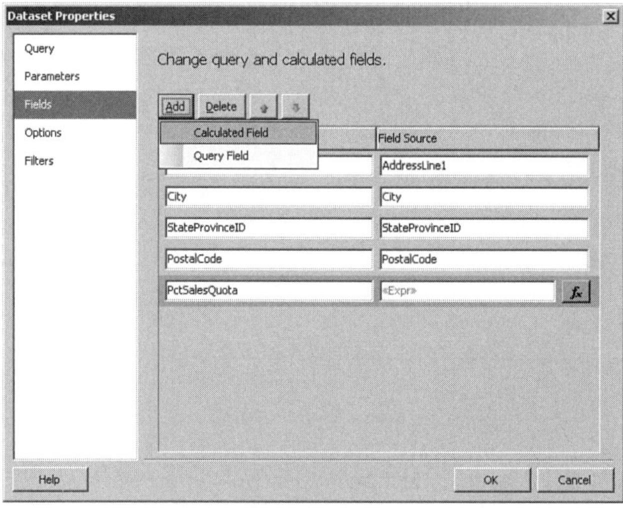

FIGURE 11.8 Adding a calculated field to a data set.

Filters

At first, it might seem strange that you would need a filter at the data set level. After all, why would you need them, if you can just modify the WHERE clause in the SQL? The dilemma comes when you need to run canned queries, such as stored procedures, or if you cannot pass in the appropriate value to filter inside the SQL.

A word of caution comes with this, too: It is much easier to filter at the database level than at the client level. Returning large data sets simply to filter it down to one or two rows on the Report Server is possible, but it might be an inefficient use of system resources.

Adding a Data Source

If you have closed the solution we have developed in the previous chapter, reopen it. To create a data source, complete the following steps:

1. From Solution Explorer, right-click the project name.
2. From the drop-down menu, select Add, New Item.
3. In the Project Items list box that appears, select Data Source.
4. For the name, enter **AdventureWorks**.
5. Select Microsoft SQL Server.
6. Enter the following connection string:

```
Data Source=(localhost);Initial Catalog=AdventureWorks
```

7. On the Credentials tab, select the Use This User Name and Password option and enter the username and password. This option allows the report to run unattended with the database credentials that you specified. The credentials will be encrypted and stored in the ReportServer database. If instead of database credentials you want to store Windows credentials, you can publish the data source, and edit it on the target server using Report Manager. Using Report Manager, specify the username and password in the format <domain>\<account>, and then select Use as Windows Credentials When Connecting to the Data Source.
8. Click OK (or click Apply if you used Report Manager to edit the data source).

Summary

Data sources provide the report with a connection to the data. Data sets use the data source along with a query of some kind to produce a resultset that the rendering engine takes and uses to process the report.

Data sources can be either specific to a report or shared among many reports. A number of data providers are installed with SQL Server and include SQL Server, SSAS, Oracle, XML, Teradata, SAP, and Essbase.

Many other data sources are supported through .NET, OLE DB, and ODBC. If a provider is not available, it can be custom developed. It is helpful from an administration point of view to use a shared data source whenever possible. An exception to this is when a data source needs specific credentials or elevated security.

Visual Studio offers two query designers: the Graphical Query Designer and the Generic Query Designer. SSRS leaves the processing of the query to the data source. After the data source is finished processing the data, it generates a data set, which is a collection of fields inside of rows.

Calculated fields can be added to the data set at design time to augment the returned results. Filters can also be applied to the resulting data sets. Both filters and fields are applied on a row-by-row basis and, if not used carefully, can lead to performance problems.

Parameters can either be static or bound to data sets. The value of certain parameters can also be passed in as input to a query. The output of that query can be used as the list of values for a parameter, in effect creating a dependency between parameters and data sets. This dependency can be used in many different ways to affect the data used in the final data set processed.

CHAPTER 12

Report Parameters

IN THIS CHAPTER

Report-level parameters can serve a number of functions, including the following:

- Manipulating report data
- Connecting related reports together
- Varying report layout and presentation

Parameters are used to pass information to a report to influence report processing. For example, a parameter can serve as a condition in a `WHERE` clause of a query that generates the report's data set. Parameters are relatively easy to set up and are very flexible.

Report parameters can be presented to the user in several ways, as shown in Table 12.1. Note that you as a report designer have control over the user's entry, but only if you specify available values for a parameter. If you specify both available values and default values, then

- When SSRS finds a match between available and default values, SSRS would present a parameter selection control (see Table 12.1) with default values preselected from a list of available values. For example, if you specify Value1 and Value2 as available and specify Value2 as default, SSRS would display Multiselect list as the parameter selection control and Value2 will be selected.
- Otherwise, default values are ignored.

When you specify the default values but not available values, SSRS would present a corresponding control with default values entered. The default values can be overridden. For example, if you specify Value2 as default and do not specify any available values, SSRS would display a Text box (or Multiline text box if it is a Multivalue parameter) with Value2 entered. You would be able to override Value2 with another value.

TABLE 12.1 Parameter Presentation Options

Control	Number of Values	Report Designer Has Control Over Entered Values	Presented When
Text box	1	No.	Single-value parameter, excluding `Boolean` and `DateTime` types.
Multiline text box	1-N	No.	Multivalue parameter with no available values specified. If a designer specifies default values, they will be presented, but can be overridden.
Text box with calendar control	1	No.	`DateTime` type single-value parameter.
Drop-down list	1	Yes.	Single-value parameter with multiple available values.
Multiselect list	1-N	Yes.	Multivalue parameter with multiple available values.
Check box titled NULL	1	N/A. Restricted to checked/unchecked state.	Presented when designer checks Allow Null Value option.
Toggle-able radio button	1	N/A. Restricted to `True` or `False` selections.	Single-value `Boolean` parameters only.

Parameters can also be hidden from the user. Although this might sound strange at first, hidden parameters can be used to alter report processing based on the input from other parameters, or based on the result from a data set.

Setting Up Parameters

You can set up parameters from the Report Designer through the following steps:

1. Select View, Report Data from the BIDS main menu. This will open Report Data dockable window.
2. In the Report Data dockable window, right-click the Parameters folder and select Add Parameter from the drop-down menu. The initial screen looks similar to Figure 12.1.

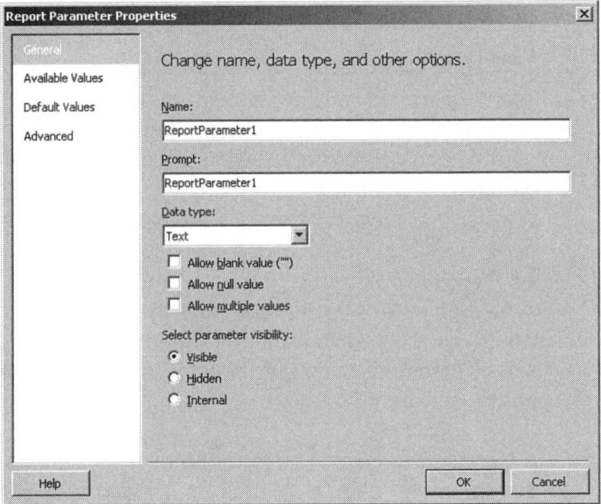

FIGURE 12.1 Report parameters.

Note the tabs General (shown on the figure), Available Values (allows you to enter a list of available values), Default Values (allows you to enter a list of default values), and Advanced. The Advanced tab controls how SSRS refreshes default values for dependent parameters:

- **Automatically Determine When to Refresh (default):** Asks SSRS to analyze dependencies and refresh when dependencies exist
- **Always Refresh:** Asks SSRS to always refresh, regardless of dependencies
- **Never Refresh:** Asks SSRS to never refresh

Parameter Properties

Table 12.2 outlines several properties of parameters.

TABLE 12.2 Parameter Properties

Property Name	Expected Value	Description
`Name`	`String`	The actual and unique name of the parameter within the scope of the report. This is what the parameter is referred to when referencing it in the `Globals` collection.

TABLE 12.2 Continued

Property Name	Expected Value	Description
`Data type`	`Enum:` `Text` (default), `Integer`, `Date/Time`, `Boolean`, `Float`	The data type in which to expect the parameter. It defaults to `String`, but you can choose a different data type from the drop-down list. If the report parameter values come from a query, the return type for the query must match the type specified here. Because .NET CLR is a strongly typed system, SSRS is too. It returns an error if a string is passed in for what is supposed to be a number value. For a `Boolean` value, the Report Server simply creates a radio button list with `true/false` as the only options.
`Prompt`	`String`	A friendly message to pass to the user who enters the parameter data. If it is left empty, and a default value is specified for the parameter, the user is not asked to input the value because the report will use the defaulted value. If the prompt is empty, and no default value is specified, the report will not run.
Allow blank value (empty string, "")	`Boolean`	An empty string is a valid value.
Allow null value	`Boolean`	A parameter that can have a null value. SSRS presents a check box with the title NULL. When checked, a data entry control for the parameter is grayed out.
Allow multiple values (`MultiValue`)	`Boolean`	Allows you to select multiple values by checking check boxes in a drop-down list, instead of displaying a single text box or drop-down list.
`Hidden`	`Boolean`	The value of this should not appear in the report, but it can still be set at runtime.
`Internal`	`Boolean`	A parameter that cannot be changed at runtime. A consumer of a published report will never see this as a parameter.

Later on in the chapter, you will walk through creating report parameters.

Data-Driven Parameters

Report parameter values can be driven from a list of valid values. This list can come from a data set. Under Available Values, just add a list of values for the values to remain hard-coded in the RDL. If you want to drive them from a data source, select Get Values from a

Query when you configure available values for a parameter. The screen should look similar to Figure 12.2.

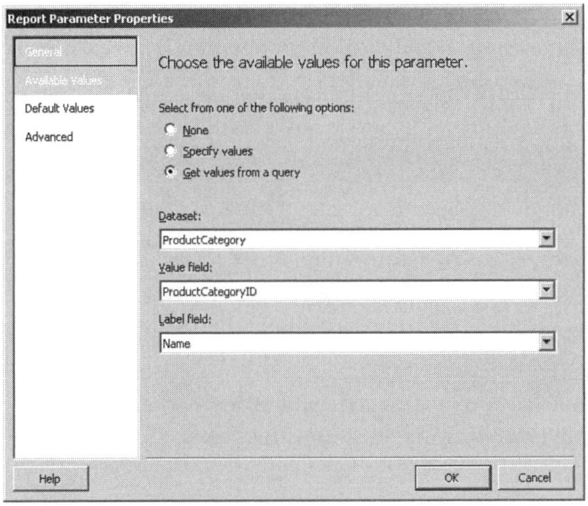

FIGURE 12.2 Query parameter values.

The same holds true for the default values. They can be either data driven through the same mechanism or hard-coded within the RDL.

The label is the value displayed to the user, whereas the value is the value passed back to the Report Server. For example, this is useful in a query parameter in which you want the user to select a familiar name from a drop-down list, yet the query expects the ID.

Expressions with Parameters

Up to this point, we have only talked about parameters within queries or queries being used as a source for data in parameters. Because the parameters are part of the `Parameters` collection, you can use a parameter in an expression.

For example, suppose you have a parameter called `Emphasis`. Its values come from a predefined list of controls within the report. The intention is to change the font style from normal to bold if the value of the parameter is set to the name of the control.

The following expression on the `bold` property of a fictitious `Location` control does exactly that:

```
=IIF(Parameters!Emphasis.Value="Location",True,False)
```

Taking this a step further, you can change the `visible` property or any of the other properties in any report item. This allows you to use parameters in all sorts of ways not necessarily related to the data retrieved for a report.

Dynamic SQL with Parameters

So far, you have seen how parameters can be passed on to query values, but can you rearrange the whole query with parameters? The answer is yes.

Believe it or not, the query is just an expression like any other expression. By default, it is evaluated as a constant string, but with the use of parameters and custom code blocks, you can make the query behind the report dynamic. There is a catch to all that flexibility: You must return the same number of columns with the same names no matter what the query.

A good example of this is in the `ORDER BY` or `GROUP BY` clause within a query. Although any of the controls can sort or group the results of a data set by any column, they are limited in speed and capacity of the Report Server. By contrast, most databases are built for exactly this sort of thing, and with the effective use of indexes, a lot of spare CPU cycles can be recovered.

To make a dynamic query, open the Generic Query Designer and type in an expression that evaluates to a query. The following is an example that uses the `Emphasis` parameter used previously:

```
="select * from test_tb order by " & Parameters!Emphasis.Value
```

You could also declare this in a custom code block:

```
Function fnGetSql(Byval parameter as String) as String
    Return "select * from test_tb order by " & Parameters!Emphasis.Value
End Function
```

And call it like this:

```
=Code.fnGetSql(Parameters!Emphasis.Value)
```

NOTE

To prevent a SQL injection attack, leverage available values for a parameter and restrict a user's permissions on a data source to read-only.

Parameter Dependencies

You can make parameter values dependent on other parameters. The trick to doing this is to derive the list of values from a data set. That data set must use the parent parameter to get its data.

For example, suppose you have two parameters: `ParameterA` and `ParameterB`. `ParameterB`'s values are queried from `DataSetB`. `DataSetB` needs a value from `ParameterA` to process.

From the user's perspective, the second parameter (ParameterB) does not display until a value is passed from ParameterA and DataSetB gets processed.

You will see parameter dependency in action from the example at the end of this chapter.

Using Multivalue Parameters

A multivalue Parameter1 stored as an array in the Parameters collection and the expression =IsArray(Parameters!ReportParameter1.Value) will return True. Thus we can access individual elements of an array using an element index. For example, to access the first (note that array's index starts with 0) value of the multivalue parameter, we will use the following expression:

```
=Parameters!ReportParameter1.Value(0)
```

And to access a label of the first element, we will use the following:

```
=Parameters!ReportParameter1.Label(0)
```

We can also get a count of values for Parameter1 using =Parameters!ReportParameter1.Count or issue an explicit check on whether the parameter is a multivalue parameter by using =Parameters!ReportParameter1.IsMultiValue.

To use a multivalue parameter in a query, you need an IN clause in your query, such as SELECT * FROM Person.Address WHERE City IN (@City). Then you associate a multivalue report parameter with a query parameter. In this case, SSRS substitutes a parameter with a list of its values separated by commas. When possible, this is a preferred method that requires less effort on your part.

For more advanced query expressions or when a data source does not support array parameters, you can use the Join function to generate a comma-separated list of values yourself:

```
=Join(Parameters!ReportParameter1.Value,",")
```

Example of Using Multivalue Dependent Parameters

Let's use a parameter to modify the Top Salespersons.rdl report to include product categories and subcategories. We have developed Top Salespersons.rdl in the Chapter 10, "Expressions."

First, let's open the project we have completed in the Chapter 10 and make a copy of Top Salespersons.rdl:

- In the Solution Explorer, right-click the **Top Salespersons.rdl** report and select Copy from the drop-down menu.

- Right-click the name of a project and select Paste from the drop-down menu. Note that the Paste option is available only when you right-click the project itself; it is not available if you right-click the folder Reports located under the project.

You will now see a new report called `Copy of Top Salespersons.rdl`. Let's rename it to **`Ch12.Top Salespersons by Category`**.

NOTE

Keep in mind that we are using AdventureWorks 2005 database for the examples in this book. For more information, see the "Sample Database Setup" section in Chapter 7, "Report Server Project Wizard."

In the following several steps, we modify the `SalesDS` data set and add the `ProductCategory` and `SubCategory` data sets using the `AdventureWorksDataSrc` data source:

1. Data set name: `SalesDS`. Query (added parts of the query are `WHERE` and `ORDER BY` clauses):

```
SELECT TOP 5
    C.LastName, C.FirstName, E.EmployeeID,
    SUM(SOH.SubTotal) AS SaleAmount
FROM        Sales.SalesPerson SP
    INNER JOIN HumanResources.Employee E ON SP.SalesPersonID = E.EmployeeID
    INNER JOIN Person.Contact C ON E.ContactID = C.ContactID
    INNER JOIN Sales.SalesOrderHeader SOH ON SP.SalesPersonID = SOH.
SalesPersonID
    INNER JOIN Sales.SalesOrderDetail SOD ON SOH.SalesOrderID = SOD.SalesOrderID
    INNER JOIN Production.Product P ON SOD.ProductID = P.ProductID
    INNER JOIN Production.ProductSubcategory PS ON P.ProductSubcategoryID =
PS.ProductSubcategoryID
    INNER JOIN Production.ProductCategory PC ON PS.ProductCategoryID =
PC.ProductCategoryID
WHERE
    PC.ProductCategoryID IN (@ProductCategory)
    ANDPS.ProductSubcategoryID IN (@ProductSubcategory)
GROUP BY
    C.LastName, C.FirstName, E.EmployeeID,
    PC.ProductCategoryID, PS.ProductSubcategoryID
ORDER BY SUM(SOH.SubTotal) DESC
```

2. Data set name: `ProductCategory`. Query:

```
SELECT DISTINCT ProductCategoryID, Name
FROM        Production.ProductCategory
ORDER BY    Name
```

3. Data set name: `SubCategory`. Query:

```
SELECT      ProductSubcategoryID, ProductCategoryID, Name
FROM        Production.ProductSubcategory
WHERE       ProductCategoryID in (@ProductCategory)
```

`SalesDS` and `SubCategory` data sets will not return any data until a user specifies values for the query parameters. This should not stop the field list from displaying the Report Data window.

We are now ready for a practical parameter implementation. In the following steps we will set up report parameters.

1. Switch to Design view. You should see a table with two columns: `Last Name` and `Sale Amount` from `SalesDS` data set.
2. Go to the Report Data window and expand the Parameters folder. There should be two parameters: `ProductCategory` and `ProductSubcategory`. Note that the Report Designer (BIDS) created parameters automatically based on the parameters of the query in `SalesDS` data set.
3. Right-click the `ProductCategory` parameter and select Parameters Properties.
4. Change the prompt on `ProductCategory` parameter to Category and change the data type to `Integer`. Check the Allow Multiple Values option. Note that the Report Designer inserted a space in the value of the prompt when it encountered the capital letter *C* in the second part of the parameter's name.
5. Under Available Values tab, select Get Values from a Query.
6. Select `ProductCategory` for the data set.
7. Change the Value field to **`ProductCategoryID`** and the Label field to **`Name`.**
8. Click OK to complete setting options for the `ProductCategory` parameter.
9. Right-click the `ProductSubcategory` parameter and select Parameters Properties.
10. Change the prompt to Subcategory; change the data type to `Integer`.
11. Under Available Values tab, select Get Values from a Query.
12. Select the `SubCategory` data set. Select ProductSubCategoryId for the Value field and Name for the Label field.
13. Click OK to complete the `ProductSubcategory` parameter configuration.
14. Preview the report by clicking the Preview tab of the Report Designer. Note that prompts for `ProductCategory` and `ProductSubcategory` parameters are Category and Subcategory. Also note that `ProductCategory` and `ProductSubcategory` are dependent parameters. Subcategory selection is grayed out until you make a category selection, and SSRS displays only appropriate subcategories for each category.
15. To run the report, select Category, Subcategory and click the View Report button. Note that some category and subcategory combinations do not have any data. Feel free to further experiment with the report.

Summary

Over the course of this chapter, you have learned what report parameters are and how they can be used. This includes their use in queries or in expressions that can be used throughout the report.

Parameters allow for dynamism by adding user input to the report-rendering process. A number of parameter options and a number of ways SSRS prompts the user are available by using familiar controls. Parameters can be data driven, or they can have a static list of valid values.

After being entered, a parameter can be used as a parameter for a data set's query or anywhere within the report as a part of an expression.

Multivalue parameters became available in SSRS2K5 and can be used in the `WHERE` clause of a data set query (`WHERE PC.ProductCategoryID in (@ProductCategory)`) or within an expression (`=Parameters!ProductCategory.Value(0)`).

CHAPTER 13

Working with Report Items

IN THIS CHAPTER

- ▶ Data Regions, Containers, and Independent Report Items
- ▶ Report Designer's Toolbox
- ▶ Line Report Item
- ▶ Rectangle Report Item
- ▶ Image Report Item
- ▶ Textbox Report Item (Improved in 2008)
- ▶ Tablix (New in 2008) = Table, Matrix, List
- ▶ Practical Application of Report Items
- ▶ Chart Report Item (Improved in 2008)
- ▶ Practical Application of a Chart
- ▶ Gauge Report Item
- ▶ Report Body Versus Page Header/Footer

Now that this book has covered what is necessary to retrieve data, let's move on to designing reports. This chapter goes into the Toolbox (literally and figuratively) and discusses the various controls used for building reports and the resulting Report Definition Language (RDL). Toward the end of the chapter, we generate a couple of reports.

Presentation elements in SSRS are called report items. The report items included in SSRS are: Tablix (New in 2008, Tablix handles List, Table, and Matrix), List, Chart, Textbox, Image, Line, Rectangle, Subreport, and Gauge (New in 2008).

Report items are similar to visual controls available in Visual Studio languages, such as Visual Basic or C#. We introduced you to report items earlier in this book, and you used report items to build samples. This chapter provides more information about each of these report items.

You might have noticed that on the surface the set of report items did not change much even since the original SSRS 2000 release. For instance, take a look at the list of report items in the Toolbox window of SQL Server Business Intelligence Development Studio (BIDS). The only new report item in the Toolbox window is Gauge. However, Microsoft has made substantial changes to the inner working of report items. For example, Microsoft has added the Tablix report item. Tablix, although not available for picking from the Toolbox, provides presentation functionality for List, Matrix, and Table report item.

In this book, we use Tablix to describe a related report item if we do not have to distinguish between List, Matrix, and Table.

Keep in mind that each RDL element is a property of a report item. You can set a property in the Report Designer through a Properties dialog box. (To open, right-click a report item and select *Item Name* Properties from the drop-down or through the Properties window.

Normally, the Properties window is located under the Solution Explorer window. If you do not see it, press F4 as a shortcut, or in BIDS choose Properties Window from the View menu.

Most of the properties can contain expressions, which allow a designer to change a visual appearance of an item during runtime. Some of the properties (such as a location or position of an item) are purely static and can be set only during design time.

Data Regions, Containers, and Independent Report Items

Report items (or presentation elements) in SSRS can be categorized as data regions (items that must be associated with data sets), containers (items that can contain other items), and independent report items. Some items can belong to more than one category.

Independent report items are items other than data regions. Textbox, Image, Line, Rectangle, and Subreport are independent report items. Independent report items do not have to be associated with any data sources.

Data regions function as a repetitive display of rows, groups of rows, or columns from a data source associated with a region. Tablix, Gauge, and Chart are data regions.

NOTE

A data region requires an associated data set to function. The `DataSetName` property of a data region contains a name of an associated data set. If a `DataSetName` property is not set, you will see errors during deployment and rendering of a report.

In addition, data regions support grouping and sorting of displayed information. For more information about grouping and sorting, see Chapter 14, "Grouping, Sorting, Aggregating Data, and Working with Scope." All the data regions except Chart are also containers.

Containers, as the name implies, can contain any reporting items, including containers and data regions. Tablix, Rectangle, Report Body, Page Header, and Page Footer are containers. Items placed in a container become the container's children, and the container becomes the parent. As a result, the `Parent` property of each child item is populated with the name of a container. All children move together with the container when the container is moved. When the container is deleted, all children are deleted. The container is fixed when the position of a report item within this container is fixed. For example, a `Table` is a fixed container because the position of each cell is fixed. Most, but not all, of the containers are also data regions. Therefore, data regions can be nested within other data regions.

TIP

If you delete a container by mistake, you can easily undo this action via Edit, Undo or by using the Ctrl-Z keyboard shortcut. For the shortcut to work properly, the focus of the action should be the `ReportName.rdl[Design]` (Design or Layout tabs) or `ReportName.rdl[XML]` window.

From the perspective of the RDL, the container has a `<ReportItems>` section, which is used to specify the beginning of a container for report items.

For example, Table 13.1 shows the RDL of a Rectangle that contains a single Line item.

TABLE 13.1 Rectangle's RDL Explained

RDL Fragment	Explanation
`<Rectangle Name="rectangle1">`	Opening RDL/XML tag indicating the beginning of the Rectangle item.

`<Left>0.375in</Left>`
`<Height>1in</Height>`
`<Top>0.25in</Top>`
`<Width>2in</Width>`
`<ZIndex>1</ZIndex>`
	`Left` and `Top`: Coordinates of the left top end of an item.
	`Width` and `Height`: Relative position of the right end of an item. `Height=0in` or not included indicates a horizontal line. `Width=0in` or not included indicates a vertical line.
	`ZIndex`: Drawing order. In case of overlapping items, an item with a higher number covers an item with a lower number.
	`ZIndex`, `Left`, `Top`, `Width`, and `Height` are abbreviated as `{LOCATION}` throughout the rest of this chapter.

`<ReportItems>`	Beginning of a container for report items. To simplify further discussion, one or many items in the `<ReportItems>` section are abbreviated as `{ITEMS}`.
`<Line Name="line1">`	Beginning of the line item.

`<Left>0.5in</Left>`
`<Top>0.25in</Top>`
`<Width>1in</Width><Height>0.5in</Height>`
`<ZIndex>1</ZIndex>`
	`{LOCATION}`: See earlier explanation.
	Note: `ZIndex` numbering starts anew within each container. The `ZIndex` tag is not shown in the subsequent RDL code examples unless attempting to pinpoint an explicit element of the style.

TABLE 13.1 Continued

RDL Fragment	Explanation

`<Style>`
`  <BorderColor>`
`   <Default>Blue</Default>`
`  </BorderColor>`
`  <BorderWidth>`
`   <Default>5pt</Default>`
`  </BorderWidth>`
`  <BorderStyle>`
`   <Default>Solid</Default>`
`  </BorderStyle>`
` </Style>`
	`Style`: Style of an item, such as color and width. You can find more information about style in Chapter 15, "Advanced Report Formatting." Report Designer inserts an empty tag, even if no style is specified.
	The `Style` tag is not shown in the subsequent RDL code examples unless attempting to pinpoint an explicit element of the style.

`</Line>`	Closing tag indicating the end of the `Line` item.
`</ReportItems>`	Closing tag indicating the end of the container.

`<Style>`
` <BorderStyle>`
`  <Default>Solid</Default>`
` </BorderStyle>`
`</Style>`
	Draw solid border around the rectangle.

`</Rectangle>`	Closing tag indicating the end of the `Rectangle` item.

Report Designer's Toolbox

The Toolbox window provides a convenient drag-and-drop interface for all report items. The Toolbox can be opened, closed, hidden, docked, or can float within Report Designer. If the Toolbox is closed, it can be opened via View, Toolbox or by pressing the Ctrl-Alt-X keyboard combination.

If the Toolbox is hidden, the designer can click the Toolbox tab on the left of the BIDS interface or mouse over the tab.

To add a report item to a report using the Report Designer, you can either drag and drop a report item from the Toolbox or copy a report item from the same or another report. Another method is to right-click any report item in the Toolbox and then click the report body on the Design tab and draw out an item. A less-common approach is to edit the RDL file by hand, but this is not recommended by Microsoft within the context of Report Designer.

Line Report Item

Line is, perhaps, the simplest report item and can be placed anywhere on a report. Line does not display any data values and serves as a decoration and navigation item. When used for navigation, a line can carry a bookmark or a label. Navigation is discussed in more detail in Chapter 16, "Report Navigation."

The RDL of the Line item is defined with the `<Line>` tag.

Rectangle Report Item

Rectangle is a graphical element that can provide three functions: decoration, container, and navigation. When used for navigation, a rectangle can carry a bookmark or a label.

Rectangle by itself is not able to display any data values and can be placed anywhere on a report. Because the rectangle is a container, it can contain other report items, including other containers and data regions. The RDL of the rectangle is defined with the `<Rectangle>` tag.

Image Report Item

An Image report item, as the name implies, is designed to display an image. SSRS supports BMP, JPG, JPE, GIF, and PNG image formats. If you come across a different format, you can use Microsoft Paint or your favorite editor to convert to formats accepted by SSRS.

An image can be embedded in a report, stored as a part of the project, stored in a database, or loaded from a URL.

You can add an image to a report in several ways. The most common is to drag an Image report item from the Toolbox and drop it onto a report (or generally on any container item). Report Designer displays the Image Properties dialog box with the window shown in Figure 13.1 at the drop completion.

Click Import and select the image you want to display. Report Designer assigns the name smiley2 to an image with the filename `smiley2.gif`.

You may have noticed the Select the Image Source option on the Image Properties dialog box. Understanding the underlying difference between embedded and project images will help you to understand differences in the handling of those images. An embedded image is actually a MIME-encoded image, stored as text in the RDL file.

An embedded image is stored in the RDL file and rendered during the render process.

When you add an embedded image, Report Designer does not compare it with other embedded images to determine whether there is duplication. Therefore, Report Designer adds more embedded images with the same content, automatically incrementing the name.

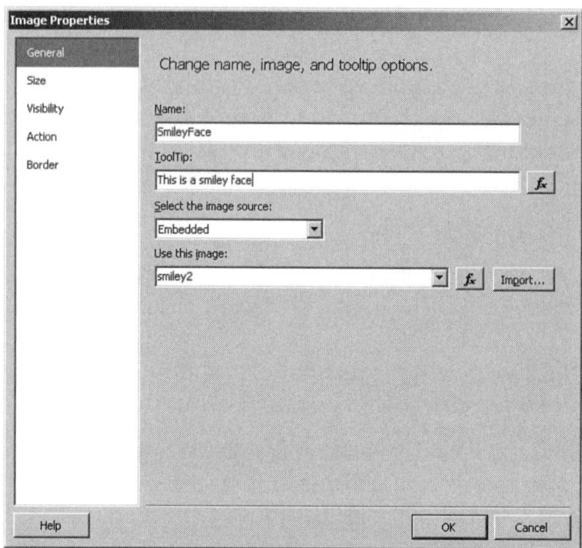

FIGURE 13.1 Image Properties window.

You can delete and add and rename embedded images through the Report Data window, Images folder.

Another common way to incorporate an image on a report is to add an image file to a project. We use a term *project image* to denote an image added to a project.

To add a project image, you either drag and drop an image onto a project in Solution Explorer or right-click the project's name, select Add, Existing Item from the drop-down menu, and then locate an image file to add. Report Designer will copy an image file to the project's directory from an original location and add it to Reports folder for the project. When you deploy your project, the project image will be deployed, too.

Because the project-level image is saved as a file, there can be only one file with the specific name. If you try to add a file with the same name, BIDS asks whether you want to override an existing file.

To add a project image to a report, you can either drag the image file from Solution Explorer to a report or add an Image report item. In either case, make sure to change Select the Image Source drop-down to External and pick one of the project images that BIDS prepopulated for you in the Use This Image list.

You can delete or rename project-level images through Solution Explorer.

Embedded images insert character-encoded information in the RDL file. `{MIME}` indicates the graphical format of the image (for example, `image/jpg`):

```
<EmbeddedImages>
    <EmbeddedImage Name="logo">
      <ImageData>{Character encoded binary Data}</ImageData>
```

```
        <MIMEType>{MIME}</MIMEType>
    </EmbeddedImage>
</EmbeddedImages>
```

The RDL for an image can be broken down into the sections shown in Table 13.2.

TABLE 13.2 Image's RDL Explained

Element	Explanation
`<Image Name="image1">` `{LOCATION}`	Open tag and image's position on a report.

`<Source>`
`{SOURCE}`
`</Source>`
	`{SOURCE}`: Location of the image. `{SOURCE}` can be `Embedded`, `Database`, or `External`. (This is for either project or web images.)

`<MIMEType>`
`{MIME}`
`</MIMEType>`
	`{MIME}` is a graphical format of the image, such as `image/gif`.

`<Sizing>`
`{SIZING}`
`</Sizing>`
	`{SIZING}`: Determines how to fit graphics within boundaries of an Image report item:
	▶ `AutoSize` or none: Keep an original image size.
	▶ `Clip`: Clip to fit inside of the item if the graphic is larger.
	▶ `Fit`: Fit graphics to the size of the item.
	▶ `FitProportional`: Same as `Fit`, plus keeps an original graphic's proportions. (This way, circles do not become ovals, for instance.)

`<Border>` `</Border >`	Specifies a border around the item.

`<Value>`
`{VALUE}`
`</Value>`
	`{ VALUE}` is an expression that evaluates to an image name or a constant. For example, a `{VALUE}` could be
	▶ `logo` for an embedded image.
	▶ `logo.gif` for a project-level image.
	▶ `http://sc.msn.com/global/c/lgpos/MSFT_pos.gif` for a web-based image.
	▶ `=Fields!ProductImage.Value` for a database image.

`</Image>`	Closing tag.

You may want to consider several factors to determine which type of image is preferable for your report. External or database images may be preferred in some cases because they

- Allow you to modify an image without redeploying a report. This is helpful when, for example, many reports share the same image, such as a logo. You have to keep track of all the reports that contain the image to make sure that there is no negative impact.

- Reduce storage requirements. For example, a relatively large image embedded in multiple reports increases the size of each report and, correspondingly, storage requirements for the SSRS database.

Textbox Report Item (Improved in 2008)

A Textbox report item is designed to display all sorts of text, including textual representation of numeric data on a report.

A standalone text box should always be used to display a single expression, such as the name of a report. The expression in this case is a constant string.

An individual text box can be placed anywhere on a report and can include almost any expression. If the data set associated with a report contains multiple rows and the following expression is used, only the last value is displayed. For example, the following expression will display the last product name in the data set:

```
=Fields!ProductName.Value
```

Aggregate functions, such as `First`, `Maximum`, `Minimum`, and `Average`, can be used to access other values. For more information about aggregate functions, see Chapter 14. In addition, conditional functions can be used to display a value matching a certain condition. Note that the default SSRS functionality does not allow you to access fields in a data set by index.

When displaying data, a text box does not distinguish between a null, an empty string, or a string of spaces (or blanks). You can use functions to ensure a predictable display of data on a report. To substitute a `Null` (or `Nothing`) value, you can use the following:

```
=IIF(Fields!FirstName.Value Is Nothing, "N/A", Fields!FirstName.Value)
```

Or

```
=IIF(IsNothing(Fields!FirstName.Value), "N/A", Fields!SaleAmount.Value)
```

NOTE

Although Textbox is one of the simpler report items, it is an important one to understand. Keep in mind that every text displaying cell in Tablix also uses a Textbox report item.

For SSRS 2008, Microsoft improved the Textbox item:

- You can mix various styles, fonts, and colors on a single text box. Any fragment of text on a text box can be formatted individually. This allows you, for example, to highlight portions of text in bold, increase the size of a font for headings, and more.
- Report Designer enables you to copy HTML from a web page to a Textbox item and maintain the formatting. In this particular scenario the Report Designer converts

HTML to RDL. Notice that although all the original links from a web page look like links (underscored blue text), the links are rendered as text and not as hyperlinks `<A HREF>`. As a result, copied links are not actionable if you click them.

- You can display simple HTML in a text box. HTML can come from a database, or can be entered directly in a text box as an expression. SSRS supports only simple HTML, replacing all the constructs it can't process with text. The following are supported HTML items:
  - Hyperlinks and fonts: <A HREF> and <FONT>
  - Header, style, and block elements: <H{n}>, <DIV>, <SPAN>, <P>, <DIV>, <LI>, <HN>
  - Text formatting: <B>, <I>, <U>, <S>
  - List processing: <OL>, <UL>, <LI>
- Textbox now provides full support for complex international writing, such as support of LTR (English) and RTL (Hebrew) languages in a single sentence, and languages that change the shape of characters depending on a position or surrounding characters (Arabic, Indic).

TABLE 13.3 Textbox's RDL Explained

Element	Explanation
<Textbox Name="Textbox1"> <CanGrow>true</CanGrow> <KeepTogether>true</KeepTogether>	Open tag.
<Paragraphs> <Paragraph> <TextRuns> <TextRun> <Value>="This is bold text."</Value> <Style> <FontWeight>Bold</FontWeight> </Style> </TextRun> </Paragraph>	Each new line in a text box is a paragraph. A text box can have multiple lines/paragraphs. TextRun is what makes different formatting possible. In this case, the TextRun specifies bold text. A text box can have multiple TextRuns. When the value is an expression, BIDS uses the term *placeholder* to refer to TextRun.

TABLE 13.3 Continued

Element	Explanation
<Paragraph> <TextRun> <Value ="<h1 id=Heading1>This is a Heading 1 </h1><P><B>This is a bold text</B><P id=Text2>This is a plain text<P><A HREF="" http://www.microsoft.com "">This is a link</A></P>" </Value> <MarkupType>HTML</MarkupType> <Style /> </TextRun> </TextRuns> <Style /> </Paragraph> </Paragraphs>	This is a paragraph that contains HTML. Note that the HTML is encoded; however, the value that a user enters as an expression is a bit easier: ="<h1 id=Heading1>This is a Heading 1 </h1><P><B>This is a bold text</B><P id=Text2>This is a plain text<P><A HREF=""http://www.microsoft.com"">This is a link</A></P>" Note that Markup Type determines whether SSRS should treat this text fragment as HTML.
<rd:DefaultName>Textbox1</rd:DefaulName> {LOCATION} <Style> <Border> <Style>None</Style> </Border> <PaddingLeft>2pt</PaddingLeft> <PaddingRight>2pt</PaddingRight> <PaddingTop>2pt</PaddingTop> <PaddingBottom>2pt</PaddingBottom> </Style> </Textbox>	Location, style (border, padding) and closing tag.

NOTE

To support the new functionality, the RDL in SSRS 2008 is more complex in comparison to the previous version. The increase in complexity is true for many report items, including Textbox, Tablix (provides functionality for List, Matrix, and Table), and Chart.

Where schema requires, a tag has to be present for a text box's RDL to be valid. For example, Textbox requires a <Value> tag, but it can be empty, such as <Value /> or <Value></Value>.

Reading through the RDL of a Textbox report item, you may have noticed that a text box uses `TextRun` to allow a mix of various text styles and HTML implementation. You may have also noticed that BIDS uses the term *placeholder* to refer to `TextRun`, which contains an expression. In other words, the following is a placeholder:

```
<Value>="This is bold text."</Value>
```

The following is not a placeholder:

```
<Value>This is bold text.</Value>
```


Let's see how the BIDS interface reflects this difference. To create a placeholder, follow these steps:

1. Click inside of a text box. Ensure that you have a vertical bar blinking cursor inside of the text box.
2. Right-click inside of the text box. You will see the context menu (see Figure 13.2).

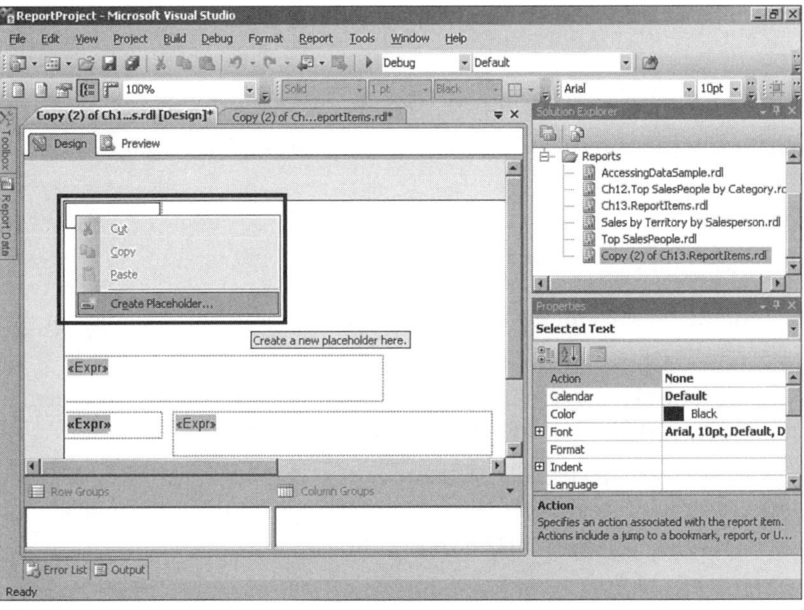

FIGURE 13.2 Adding a placeholder: context menu.

3. Select Create Placeholder from the menu.
4. BIDS displays the Placeholder Properties dialog box (see Figure 13.3).

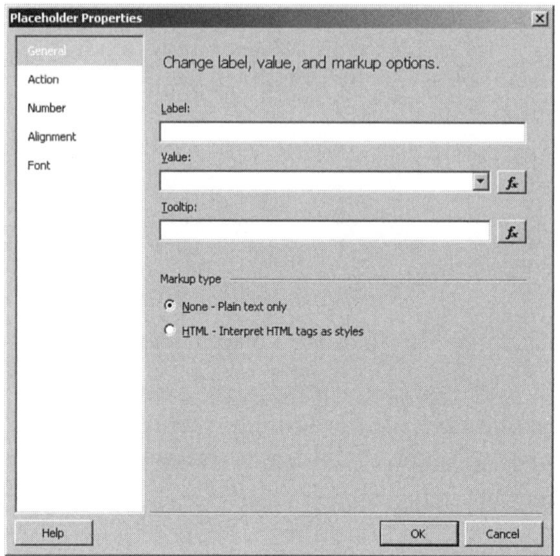

FIGURE 13.3 Adding a placeholder: Placeholder Properties dialog box.

5. At a minimum, complete the Value field. Make sure that you use an expression. (Remember that expressions have an equals sign before them.) Here is an example of a text expression: `="This is a text."`
6. Click OK to complete.
7. Note that the text box displays <<Expr>> for a placeholder.

If you add more placeholders, each will have <<Expr>> in place for it. For example, for two placeholders, you will see <<Expr>><<Expr>>.

To edit a placeholder, click inside of a text box where a placeholder is located, and then double-click <<Expr>> to display the Placeholder Properties dialog box.

A placeholder can contain HTML. By default, SSRS converts HTML to a plain text. To ensure that SSRS processes the context as HTML, set MarkupType on the Placeholder Properties dialog box to HTML - Interpret HTML Tags as Style.

You can also add HTML to a text box as follows:

1. Paste HTML into a text box.
2. Select the HTML that you have just added.
3. Right-click the selection and select Text Properties from the context menu.
4. In the Text Properties dialog box, select HTML - Interpret HTML Tags as Style.
5. Click OK to complete.
6. BIDS converts HTML into an expression (and therefore creates a placeholder).

Tablix (New in 2008) = Table, Matrix, List

Tablix is a data region that provides presentation for the Table, Matrix, and List. When you pick Table, Matrix, or List in the Toolbox window, you are picking a template for the Tablix. Tablix's templates allow a smoother transition to SSRS 2008 because by default each template provides behavior of earlier versions of SSRS:

- Table presents a grid layout with static columns and expands detail data row by row.
- Matrix presents group data in a grid layout that's capable of expanding both rows and columns.
- List presents data in a free-form fashion for complex repeating areas.

Much like Table or Matrix cells in earlier versions of SSRS, a cell in a Tablix can contain the following:

- A single report item, including a Textbox, an Image, or another data region, such as Tablix or Gauge. Note that the Textbox is a default for a Table and a Matrix.
- Multiple items if you first add a Rectangle item as a container. Rectangle is a default for a List template.

Tablix is designed to be flexible and allows a report designer to change between Table, Matrix, and List without losing all the work. Table 13.4 outlines actions to switch between Table and Matrix.

TABLE 13.4 Switching Between Table and Matrix

		To	
		Table	*Matrix*
From	*Table*		Add column groups. It is typical to remove the details row.
	Matrix	Remove column groups and add the details row.	

You can also transform a Table or a Matrix to a List and vice versa. However, because List contains a single cell, this type of change is less typical.

When you define a group for a Table, Matrix, or List, BIDS adds rows (when you add a row group) and columns (when you add a column group) to display grouped data.

NOTE

Remember that the name of a group implies expansion direction: A row group expands vertically down a page adding rows, and column groups expand horizontally adding columns.

13

Tablix's cells belong to one of the four Tablix's internal areas (see Figure 13.4). Only Body is a required area; the rest are optional:

- **Corner:** Report Designer automatically creates a corner when you have both row and column groups, whether added during a report design or coming from a Matrix template. You can merge corner cells, split previously merged cells, or add another report item.
- **Row Groups area:** BIDS automatically creates a row group area when you have row groups, whether added during a report design or coming from Table or Matrix templates. Cells in a row group area typically display row group headings. Any aggregations in this area have a scope of the entire Tablix.
- **Column Groups area:** Report Designer automatically creates a column group area when you have column groups, whether added during a report design or coming from a Matrix template. Cells in a row group area typically display column group headings. Any aggregations in this area have a scope of the entire Tablix.
- **Body:** Displays aggregate or detail data depending on the group a cell within the body belongs to. For example, a cell that belongs to the Details group will show details of the data from a data set.

Figure 13.4 shows each of theses four areas.

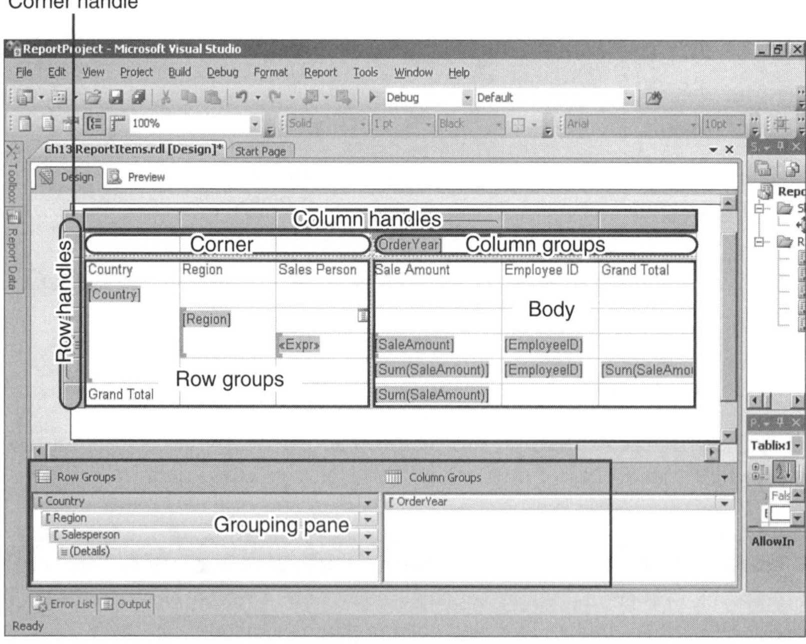

FIGURE 13.4 Tablix in Design view: Tablix areas.

NOTE

Keep in mind that the Body area is always present. If you do not see a second set of lines above the Body area, that column group area is not present. The lack of column groups is also reflected in the Column Groups pane of the Design window, and as a result you would not see any entries in that pane. You can apply the same logic to row groups.

In addition to four internal areas, a Tablix has three handle areas: corner handle, column handles, and row handles.

As mentioned earlier, BIDS provides visual clues for various elements of Tablix. Figure 13.5 provides a brief description of visual clues in Tablix.

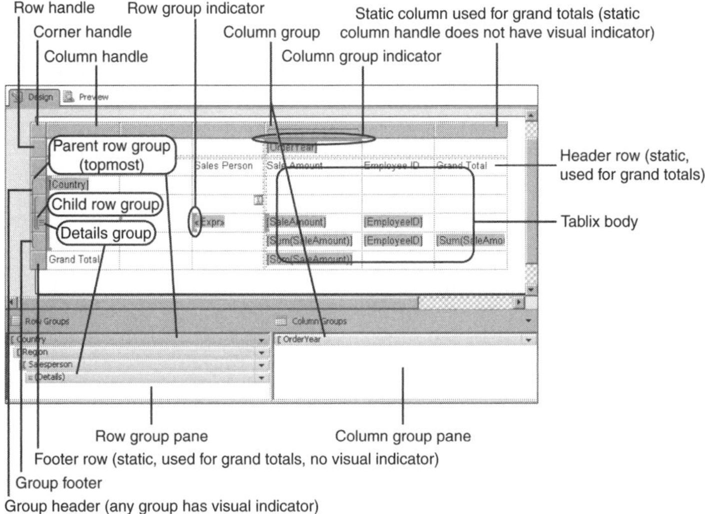

FIGURE 13.5 Tablix in Design view: visual indicators of grouping

Because the Report Designer (BIDS) does not have Tablix in its Toolbox, you start your design from either Table or Matrix. Both are templates of Tablix.

The flexibility of Tablix enables you to design beyond an original template and add or remove row and column groups as necessary in your design. For example, the initial report requirements may state that you need to break down sales by country, region, and salesperson. You may start your design with a table and then realize that the data really has one more dimension: time. The time would allow a report consumer to see the trend of sales over time and identify regions with declining sales for further evaluation. In earlier versions of SSRS, you had to replace a table with a matrix, which would, obviously, add time to your efforts. In SSRS 2008, you can simply add a column group, grouping data by a time period, such as year, quarter, or month. You can also use multiple periods (such as both month and year) to allow users of your reports to drill down and see a more detailed breakdown of data.

The interface to add a row and column groups is slightly inconsistent between Table and Matrix templates. Specifically, if a column is a part of a column group, you can right-click the column handler for such column and see a selection to add either a row or a column group. The same is not true for a row handler, however. Row handler allows you to see only a selection to add a row group.

NOTE

When you click a cell that belongs to a group, row/column group indicators turn from gray to orange.

If you want to follow the discussion and practice adding row and column groups, just complete these steps:

1. Create a copy of the Top Salespersons report. (We developed this report in Chapter 12, "Report Parameters.")
2. Rename the report. (We have used the name `Ch.13.ReportItems.rdl` as a new name for the copy of the Top Salespersons report.)
3. Delete the existing table from the body of the report.
4. Drag and drop Matrix from the Toolbox to the body of the report.
5. Set the `DataSetName` property of the Tablix to `SalesDS`.

Notice that the new Matrix has two groups: RowGroup and ColumnGroup.

You can use one of the following methods to add a row or a column group:

- Right-click any cell in the Body area, select Add Group from the drop-down menu, and select the type of group you want to add (see Figure 13.6). Note that the context menu provides you with two sections (Column Group and Row Group) and various types of groups (Parent, Child, or Adjacent).

- Right-click a group entry in either the Row Groups or Column Groups panes of the grouping window, select Add Group from the drop-down menu, and select the type of group (Parent, Child, or Adjacent) you want to add. This method enables you to add a row group from the Row Groups pane or a column group from the Column Groups pane. This also works if you click the drop-down indicator next to a group entry in either pane. If you do not see the grouping pane, click Report, Grouping to open it (see Figure 13.7).

- Right-click a cell that contains a group indicator, select Add Group from the drop-down menu, and select the type of group you want to add. This enables you to add a row group from a cell containing row group indicators or a column group from a cell containing a column group indicator.

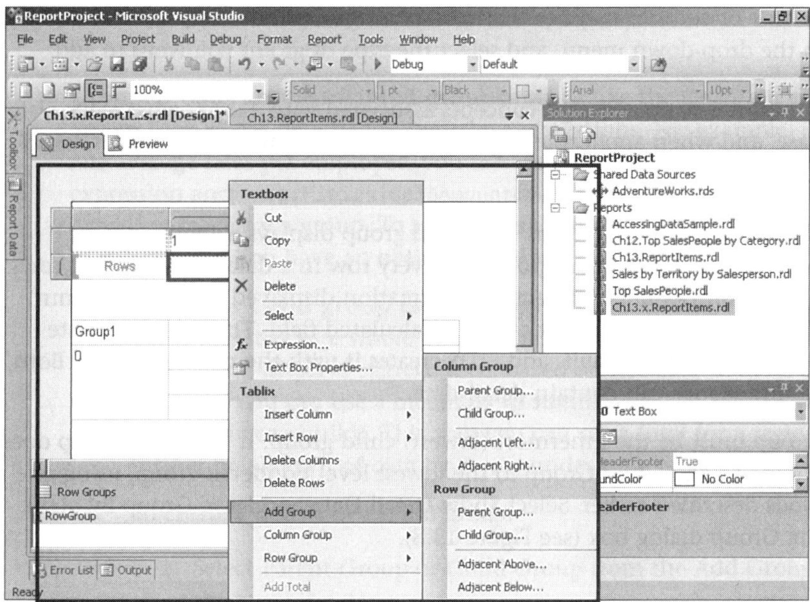

FIGURE 13.6 Add Group menu.

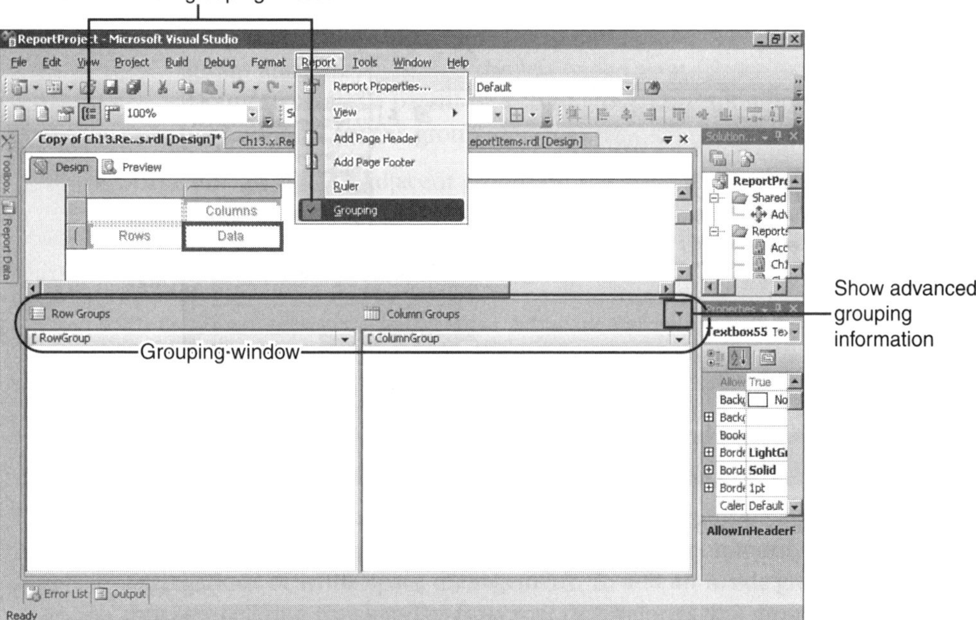

FIGURE 13.7 Grouping pane.

TABLE 13.5 Continued

Element	Explanation
<TablixBody> <TablixColumns> <TablixColumn> <Width>1in</Width> </TablixColumn> </TablixColumns> <TablixRows> <TablixRow> <Height>0.25in</Height> <TablixCells> <TablixCell> <CellContents> <Textbox Name="Textbox3"> </Textbox> </CellContents> </TablixCell> </TablixCells> </TablixRow> </TablixRows> </TablixBody>	RDL for the Tablix body. In this case, it contains one row, one column, and a single text box, `Textbox3`.
<TablixColumnHierarchy> <TablixMembers> <TablixMember> <Group Name="ColumnGroup"> <GroupExpressions> <GroupExpression /> </GroupExpressions> </Group> <TablixHeader> <Size>0.25in</Size> <CellContents> <Textbox Name="Textbox2"> </Textbox> </CellContents> </TablixHeader> </TablixMember> </TablixMembers> </TablixColumnHierarchy>	Single column with no group expression.

TABLE 13.5 Continued

Element	Explanation
<TablixRowHierarchy> <TablixMembers> <TablixMember> <Group Name="RowGroup"> <GroupExpressions> <GroupExpression> =First(Fields!Country.Value, "TopSalesPeople") </GroupExpression> </GroupExpressions> </Group> <TablixHeader> <Size>1in</Size> <CellContents> <Textbox Name="Textbox1"> </Textbox> </CellContents> </TablixHeader> <TablixMembers> <TablixMember> <Group Name="Details" /> </TablixMember> </TablixMembers> </TablixMember> </TablixMembers> </TablixRowHierarchy>	Row hierarchy contains a child group named `Details` and a parent group named `RowGroup`. The parent group uses a single group expression `=First(Fields!Country.Value, "TopSalesPeople")` with the scope of the entire data set `TopSalesPeople`.
<DataSetName> TopSalesPeople </DataSetName>	Explicit data set association. If the report contains a single data set, all data regions will be associated with such data set, and explicit association is not required. Otherwise, the `DataSetName` element has to be present.
<Height>0.5in</Height> <Width>2in</Width> <Style> <Border> <Style>None</Style> </Border> </Style> </Tablix>	The Tablix's overall size, style (including border), and closing tag.

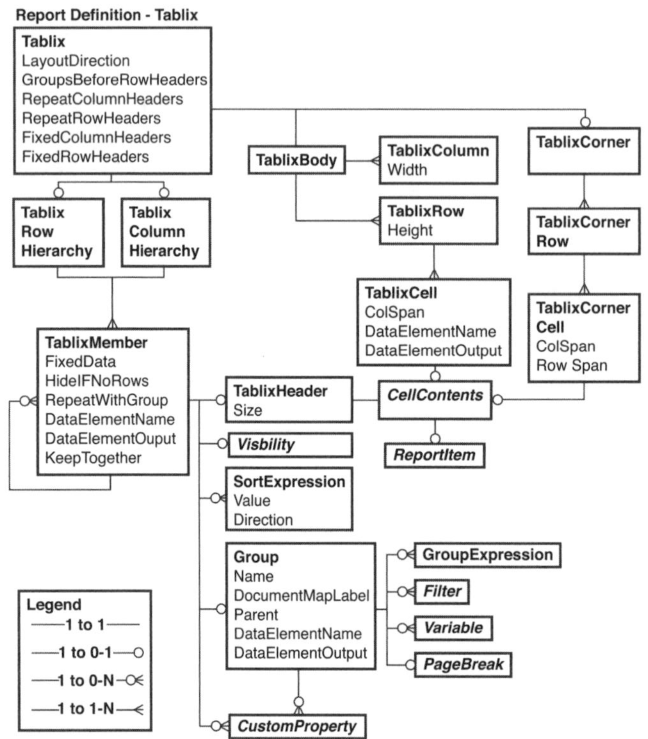

FIGURE 13.10 Tablix's XML structure diagram.

Formatting Tablix

You can merge multiple adjacent cells. Tablix's corner, row, and column group areas allow you to merge cells vertically across multiple rows and horizontally across multiple columns. If you need to merge a rectangular area of cells, you have to merge in one direction first. For example, if you need to merge 2×2 cells, you first merge two cells horizontally in both of two rows, and then you merge cells vertically. To split back a rectangular area, you perform actions in reverse, first splitting vertically, then horizontally. Keep in mind that BIDS may remove a column or a row entirely as a result of a merge. For example, if the 2×2 area that you are merging is all the Tablix has, merging it leaves you with a single cell and correspondingly a single column and a single row.

BIDS only allows horizontal merge on the Tablix's Body area.

When you merge cells, Report Designer preserves data from only the first cell; data in other merged cells is discarded. Report Designer enables you to split back to the original columns.

To merge or split cells, select the cells, right-click the selection, and then select Merge Cells or Split Cells, respectively, from the shortcut menu. Alternatively, Report Designer provides a toolbar button to perform this operation. Both menu and toolbar will reflect BIDS' ability to merge. For example, if you select vertical cells for a merge in the Tablix's Body area, BIDS grays out the toolbar button and hides the menu entry for merge/split.

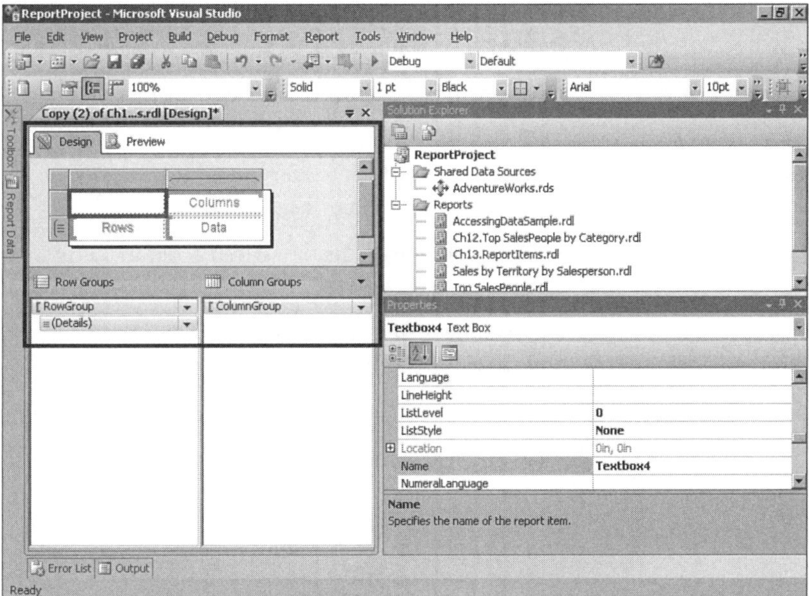

FIGURE 13.11 Simple Tablix design.

To properly color the entire row (or column), you can use the following expression in the `BackgroundColor` property of the innermost group, where `RowGroup1` is the name of the row group:

```
=IIF(Not InScope("RowGroup1"), "LightGrey", "White")
```

Because a cell in a Tablix contains one or more report items, you format the result by formatting those items. For example, a cell that presents textual information contains a Textbox report item. By setting properties and formatting text in a Textbox report item, you can manipulate the rendering outcome.

For example, you can conditionally hide row data by setting the `Hidden` property of each cell to `True`. Chapter 14 shows an example of this.

We frequently use several properties of a Tablix in our work. To set these properties, select the entire Tablix by either clicking the Tablix's corner handler or selecting the Tablix from the drop-down list on the Properties window. The frequently used properties are as follows:

- **`Filters`**: A set of filter expressions for a Tablix. Filters limit data displayed by a Tablix much like the `WHERE` clause limits results of a query. Whereas in most of the cases you want to actually leverage a `WHERE` clause to improve performance and reduce unnecessary network traffic, you still need to have a filter (for example, in situations when you can't change a data set).
- **`FixedColumnHeaders`** and **`FixedRowHeaders`**: When set to `True`, these keep column and row headers displayed when the user scrolls through Tablix.

13

- **GroupsBeforeRowHeader**: Skips the specified number of column groups before displaying row headers. Tablix will display columns of data and then row headers.
- **LayoutDirection**: A direction of column expansion. Left to right (`LTR`, default) or right to left (`RTL`).
- **NoRowsMessage**: When a data set returns no results, SSRS renders this message rather than an empty data region.
- **OmitBorderOnPageBreak**: Determines the border display when a report item spans multiple pages.
- **RepeatRowHeaders** and **RepeatColumnHeaders**: When `True`, SSRS will repeat column and row headers for a Tablix that spans multiple pages.
- **SortExpressions**: A set of sort expressions for a whole Tablix. You can also define sort expressions for a group.

Practical Application of Report Items

It is time to put your knowledge to practical use. By now, you have sufficient knowledge to put fairly complex reports together. Let's create a Sales Order summary report.

Adventure Works's management requested a report that displays selected properties of an order header (ship and bill to addresses, contact information, and billing summary) and selected properties of an order's line items (product name, unit price, order quantity, and line total). Adventure Works requires each report to have a company logo. To meet these requirements, let's complete the following steps:

1. Create a new report. For the purpose of this exercise, we will reuse the AdventureWorks shared data source that we created in earlier chapters. From the Report Data window, select New, Data Source. Name the data source **AdventureWorks**, select the Use Shared Data Source Reference option and choose AdventureWorks. (Yes, both data sources can have the same name.)
2. In the Report Data window, right-click the AdventureWorks data source and select Add Dataset. Name the data set **Order_Header**. `Order_Header` will contain data selected from a join between `SalesOrderHeader`, `Address`, and `StateProvince` tables.
3. To have a more complete picture of an order and include both shipping and billing addresses, you need to include `Address` and `StateProvince` tables twice in the `Order_Header` data set. Create aliases for the first set of `Address` and `StateProvince` tables as **BillToAddress** and **StateProvinceBill**, and use **ShipToAddress** and **StateProvinceShip** aliases for the second set of tables. To create an alias for a table, right-click a table in a Graphical Query Designer, select Properties from the shortcut menu, and fill the Alias field as needed. Alternatively, you can edit the query text directly.
4. Create an alias for each field you want to include on a report. You can prefix fields with `Ship` or `Bill` for tables related to shipping and billing addresses, respectively. For our sample, we have included the following fields from `SalesOrderHeader` table:

OrderDate, TaxAmt, SubTotal, Freight, TotalDue, Comment, ShipDate. We also included the following fields from Address (and StateProvince) tables: AddressLine1, City, PostalCode, and StateProvinceCode (this is from StateProvince table). Based on whether the address is shipping or billing, we have prefixed aliases for the fields with Ship or Bill, correspondingly.

5. Create an **Order_Detail** data set. This data set contains data selected from a join between SalesOrderHeader. (This table will provide a cross-reference between SalesOrderNumber and SalesId, SalesOrderDetail, and Product tables.) The fields that we have selected for our sample are SalesOrderDetail.OrderQty, SalesOrderDetail.UnitPrice, SalesOrderDetail.LineTotal, Product.Name.

6. To retrieve a specific order, let's use parameter @SalesOrderNumber in the WHERE clause of both data sets:

```
WHERE
SalesOrderHeader.SalesOrderNumber = @SalesOrderNumber).
```

The resulting queries are as follows:

```
Order_Header
```

```
SELECT Sales.SalesOrderHeader.OrderDate, Sales.SalesOrderHeader.TaxAmt,
    Sales.SalesOrderHeader.SubTotal, Sales.SalesOrderHeader.Freight,
    Sales.SalesOrderHeader.TotalDue, Sales.SalesOrderHeader.Comment,
    Sales.SalesOrderHeader.ShipDate, BillToAddress.AddressLine1 AS
BillAddressLine1,
    BillToAddress.City AS BillCity, BillToAddress.PostalCode AS BillPostalCode,
    StateProviceBill.StateProvinceCode AS BillStateProvinceCode,
    ShipToAddress.AddressLine1 AS ShipAddressLine1,
    ShipToAddress.City AS ShipCity, ShipToAddress.PostalCode AS ShipPostalCode,
    StateProviceShip.StateProvinceCode AS ShipStateProvinceCode
FROM
    Sales.SalesOrderHeader
    INNER JOIN Person.Address AS BillToAddress ON
    Sales.SalesOrderHeader.BillToAddressID =
    BillToAddress.AddressID AND
    Sales.SalesOrderHeader.ShipToAddressID = BillToAddress.AddressID AND
    Sales.SalesOrderHeader.BillToAddressID = BillToAddress.AddressID AND
    Sales.SalesOrderHeader.ShipToAddressID = BillToAddress.AddressID
    INNER JOIN Person.StateProvince AS StateProviceBill ON
    BillToAddress.StateProvinceID = StateProviceBill.StateProvinceID
    INNER JOIN Person.Address AS ShipToAddress ON
    Sales.SalesOrderHeader.BillToAddressID = ShipToAddress.AddressID AND
    Sales.SalesOrderHeader.ShipToAddressID = ShipToAddress.AddressID AND
    Sales.SalesOrderHeader.BillToAddressID = ShipToAddress.AddressID AND
    Sales.SalesOrderHeader.ShipToAddressID = ShipToAddress.AddressID AND
    Sales.SalesOrderHeader.BillToAddressID = ShipToAddress.AddressID AND
    Sales.SalesOrderHeader.ShipToAddressID = ShipToAddress.AddressID AND
```

```
    StateProviceBill.StateProvinceID = ShipToAddress.StateProvinceID
    INNER JOIN Person.StateProvince AS StateProviceShip ON
    BillToAddress.StateProvinceID = StateProviceShip.StateProvinceID AND
    ShipToAddress.StateProvinceID = StateProviceShip.StateProvinceID
WHERE
      Sales.SalesOrderHeader.SalesOrderNumber = @SalesOrderNumber
```

Order_Detail

```
SELECT Sales.SalesOrderDetail.OrderQty, Sales.SalesOrderDetail.UnitPrice,
    Sales.SalesOrderDetail.LineTotal, Production.Product.Name
FROM
    Sales.SalesOrderHeader
    INNER JOIN Sales.SalesOrderDetail  ON
    Sales.SalesOrderHeader.SalesOrderID = Sales.SalesOrderDetail.SalesOrderID
    INNER JOIN Production.Product  ON
    Sales.SalesOrderDetail.ProductID = Production.Product.ProductID
WHERE
      Sales.SalesOrderHeader.SalesOrderNumber = @SalesOrderNumber
```

7. Add the company logo image report item. From Windows File Explorer, drag the image item and drop it onto the report body. Change the name to **Logo**. (Refer back to Figure 13.1 to see the Image Properties dialog box.)
8. Add a list by dragging a List item from the Toolbox. As you remember, List is a template for Tablix. You can take advantage of the `Dataset` property of the List item to avoid typing scope resolution for each of the simple report items, such as Textboxes, included on the List report item.
9. As an experiment, drag and drop the `ShipCity` field of `Order_Header` outside of the List item. Note the value of the text box outside of the list is `=First(Fields!ShipCity.Value, "Order_Header")`. As a comparison, drag and drop the `ShipCity` field on the list. Note the value of the created text box is `=Fields!ShipCity.Value`. Also note that the `DataSetName` property of the list is now set to `Order_Header`, and it was blank originally. Be careful when dropping fields from other data sets to a list. If you do so, BIDS will update `DataSetName` to the data set associated with the last drop, potentially invalidating the scope resolution for other items.
10. Add a report heading. Drag and drop a text box from the Toolbox. Enter the following expression as a value: `="Sales Order Number" & " - " & First(Fields!SalesOrderNumber.Value, "Order_Header")`. This expression concatenates the constant `"Sales Order Number - SO#####"` and the value of the SalesOrderNumber field. To highlight the heading of the report, increase the font size and change the text box background.
11. Add and arrange data fields in the page header by dragging and dropping data set fields on the list: Street, City, State, and Zip from both billing and shipping addresses. Second, add billing summary fields. Add Textbox items to title values that

were added, such as a text box stating Ship To Address. Change the heading for information sections to bold font.

12. Add lines to help separate informational pieces as necessary. Note that not all the web browsers support overlapping controls, such as lines. If you need to cross lines, you might need to have several lines bordering each other.
13. Add a table to display details of an order. Drag and drop a Table item from the Toolbox. The default table has three rows and three columns. Drag and drop the `Order_Detail` fields to the Detail area of the table, and note how the heading is changed to the name of the field.
14. To summarize line-item charges, right-click the detail row and select Insert Row, Outside Group Below from the context menu. This row becomes a footer of the table.
15. In the rightmost cell of the row, enter the following summarization expression: **`=Sum(Fields!LineTotal.Value).`**

The resulting design-time view of the report should look similar to Figure 13.12.

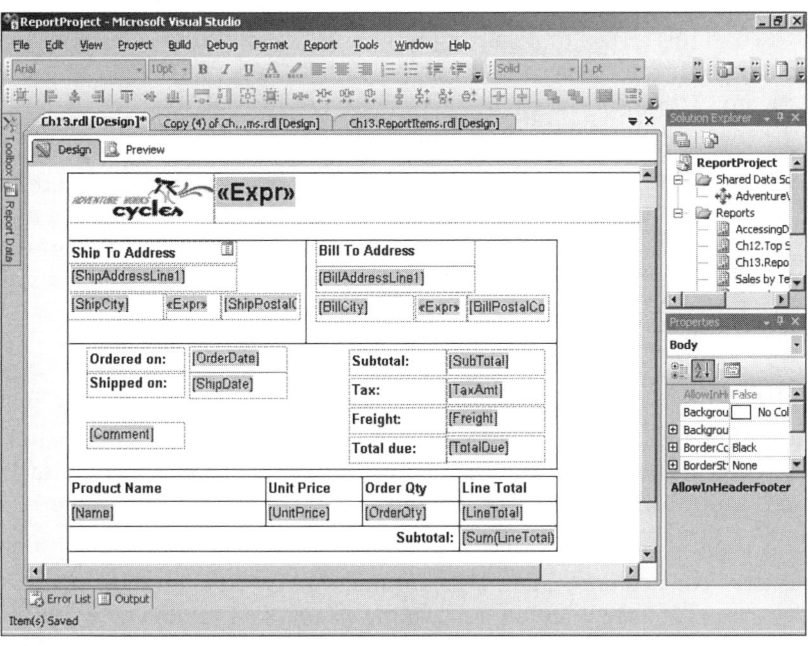

FIGURE 13.12 Design picture of the Sales Order Summary report.

Chart Report Item (Improved in 2008)

A Chart report delivers a graphic presentation of data from a single data set. Chart has comprehensive functionality and has similar capabilities to an Excel chart, including a variety of chart types, 3D effects, trend lines, and more.

Microsoft significantly overhauled chart capabilities in SSRS 2008 and added the following:

- New chart types, such as bar/column cylinder, pyramid, funnel, polar, radar, stock, candlestick, range column, range bar, smooth area, smooth line, stepped line, box plot, Pareto, and histogram.
- Secondary axes support.
- Calculated series functionality that allows you to select 15 commonly used calculations, including statistical analysis, moving averages, and financial indicators.
- More control over common chart elements like `Legends`, `Titles`, `Axes` (such as custom axis intervals, reverse direction, set alternating bands on a chart [interlaced lines]), and `Labels` (such as automatic label interval to avoid collisions, customizable rotation angles, font size, and text-wrap properties for axis label calculations).
- New interface and new, more appealing chart design.
- Support of multiple chart areas, multiple legends, and multiple titles on the same chart.

The Chart control used in this release of Reporting Services is licensed from Dundas Software (www.dundas.com). You can obtain an add-on pack for Reporting Services from Dundas Software. Figure 13.13 shows a design-time view of a chart after you click the design surface of the chart. Note the three drop areas: Series, Category and Data.

Unlike the previous version, the Chart Properties dialog box no longer provides comprehensive control over a chart's properties. A chart's context menu provides an interface to access properties for various chart components. To access this menu, right-click a chart to display a shortcut menu. This shortcut menu enables you to access various components of a chart (see Figure 13.14).

Chart Data (Value)

A chart requires at least one set of data values associated with it. You can simply drag and drop a field to the Design area (it has a Drop Data Fields Here note) of a chart. The data determines the y-axis value. For example, for a column chart, the data determines the height of a column.

Data is considered static. For a column chart, it means that a single data file added to a chart (and no series) results in a single column providing a sum of all values and a single legend. If you add one more data fields to a chart, SSRS shows a second column and adds a second legend.

In most charts, we group data by a series or a category. In this case, you must use an aggregate expression for a data value. This is similar to grouping in a Tablix where non-aggregate expressions are syntactically allowed. However, the result contains the last value of a field rather than a summary value for a group and, therefore, produces an unexpected result. Report Designer automatically adds an aggregate function, but changes are allowed. To verify or change the data value expression, you can right-click a field you added and select Series Properties from the context menu.

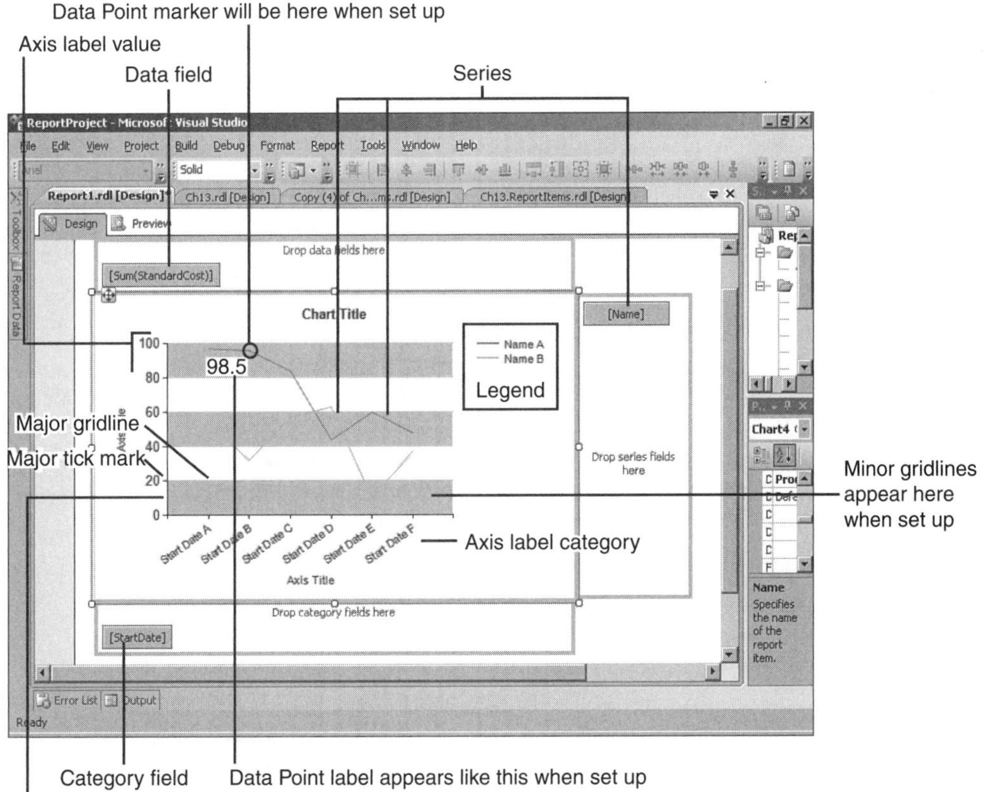

FIGURE 13.13 Design-time picture of a chart.

Chart can display only numeric data. You can convert formatted strings (such as `"123.123"`) to numbers either in a query or using SSRS expressions.

Different chart types handle `Null` (or empty) values from a data set differently: In an X-Y graphic chart, you will have gaps for empty values, for example, and a nonlinear chart (such as pie, doughnut, funnel, or pyramid) simply skips the display of `Null` values. You can eliminate `Null` values in a query or through expressions.

Alternatively, you can use the chart's empty-point-handling capability:

1. On the chart's design surface, click the series that contains `Null` values. BIDS displays properties for the series in the Properties pane.
2. Expand the EmptyPoint node and set the Color property.
3. In the EmptyPoint node, expand the Marker node.
4. Under the Marker node, set the MarkerType property.

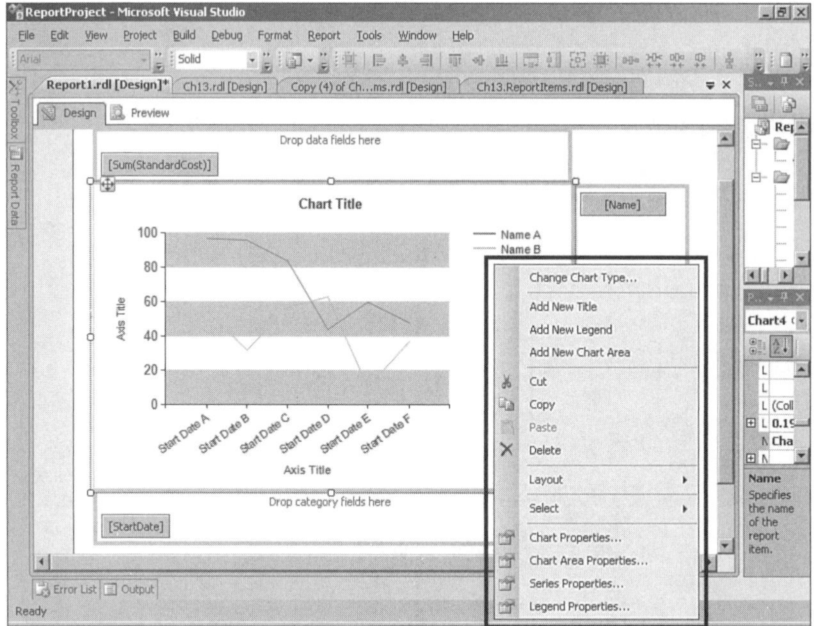

FIGURE 13.14 Chart context menu.

NOTE

Some chart types handle empty points automatically, by either connecting across a missing point or simply skipping a display of a missing value altogether.

Table 13.6 provides partial RDL of Chart Data. From this point forward in this book, the section surrounded by the `<ChartData>` tag is abbreviated as `{CHART DATA}`.

TABLE 13.6 Partial Set of Tags for Chart Data RDL

Element	Explanation
`<ChartData>`	Begin the Chart Data section.
`<ChartSeriesCollection>`	Collection of series. Each series in a collection has associated data points and describes how those points look on a chart.

`<ChartSeries Name="Standard-Cost">`
`<ChartDataPoints>`
`<ChartDataPoint>`
`<ChartDataPointValues>`
`<Y> =Sum(Fields!Standard-Cost.Value)`
	Names comes from a data field associated with a series, the value from the `StandardCost` field.

TABLE 13.6 Continued

Element	Explanation

`<ChartDataLabel>`
`<Label>`
 	
`=Sum(Fields!ProductID.Value, "ProductCostHistory")`
	Each point on chart can have a label. It is common to see an actual value next to a data point.

`<ChartMarker>`	Allows formatting a marker. A marker is a graphical highlight of a data point on a graph. On a line chart, a marker enables you to highlight the difference between a connector line and the actual data.
`<Type>Line</Type>`	Chart type. In this case, it is `Line`.
`<ChartEmptyPoints>`	Describes how to handle empty or null data in a series.
`<ValueAxisName>Primary` `<CategoryAxisName>Primary`	Axes and series association.

13

Chart Series

Data series are optional and when added create series labels that are placed in the legend of the chart. Series groups are dynamic. A chart that uses series groups displays a chart element for each series group for each category. For example, a column chart with sales data displays a column for each year returned by a series group expression.

Following is the RDL that describes series. From this point forward, the section surrounded by the `<ChartSeriesHierarchy>` tag is abbreviated as `{CHART SERIES}`:

```
<ChartSeriesHierarchy>
  <ChartMembers>
    <ChartMember>
      <Group Name="Chart4_SeriesGroup1">
        <GroupExpressions>
          <GroupExpression>=Fields!Name.Value</GroupExpression>
        </GroupExpressions>
      </Group>
      <Label>=Fields!Name.Value</Label>
    </ChartMember>
  </ChartMembers>
</ChartSeriesHierarchy>
```

Chart Category

Chart Category Groups is the optional mechanism of grouping data that provides the labels for chart elements.

For example, in a column chart, Country Name fields placed in the Category region generate country labels for x-axes (United States, Italy, and so forth).

You can nest categories. Multiple categories nest x-axes labels. For example, in a column chart with sales data, the first category group could be a county, and the second category group could be TerritoryId. The column chart would display groupings of products by TerritoryId on the x-axis.

Following is the RDL that describes a category grouping. From this point forward, the section surrounded by the `<ChartCategoryHierarchy>` tag is abbreviated as `{CHART CATEGORY}`:

```
<ChartCategoryHierarchy>
  <ChartMembers>
    <ChartMember>
      <Group Name="Chart4_CategoryGroup1">
        <GroupExpressions>
          <GroupExpression>=Fields!StartDate.Value</GroupExpression>
        </GroupExpressions>
      </Group>
      <Label>=Fields!StartDate.Value</Label>
    </ChartMember>
  </ChartMembers>
</ChartCategoryHierarchy>
```

Chart Areas

The Chart area contains the plotting area of a chart and axes related items such as axes labels and axes titles. A single chart may have multiple areas, but contains only one area by default. A data series could be connected to only one area through the `ChartArea, Name` property. When you add a new series, BIDS automatically assigns `ChartArea, Name = Default`. You will need to change `ChartArea, Name` property to associate series with a different Chart area.

While you can combine most of the charts types (like line and column) on a single Chart area, for some (such as bar, polar, and shape) you may need to add a new area to accommodate them. Table 13.7 provides a partial list of a chart area's RDL elements.

TABLE 13.7 Partial List of Elements for a Chart Area's RDL

Element	Explanation
<ChartAreas> <ChartArea Name="Default">	The Chart Area is a plotting area of a chart and axes-related items.
<ChartCategoryAxes> <ChartAxis Name="Primary">	Describes the x-axes of a chart (primary and secondary).
<ChartAxisTitle>	Title explains the meaning of the x-axes. For example, in the case of countries, it may simply state Countries.
<ChartMajorGridLines> <ChartMinorGridLines>	Properties of major and minor gridlines: style of gridline line, visibility.
<ChartMinorTickMarks> <ChartMajorTickMarks>	Properties of tick marks. A tick mark extends the gridlines through an axis. It is similar to marks on a ruler.
<Angle>-35</Angle> <LabelsAutoFitDisabled>true</ LabelsAutoFitDisabled>	Properties of labels for each axis. LabelsAutoFit ensures that labels do not overlap. When AutoFit is disabled, you can rotate a label yourself so that it does not overlap.
<ChartValueAxes> <ChartAxis Name="Primary">	Describes the y-axes of a chart (primary and secondary) .

Chart's RDL

A rudimentary chart is described by the following structure:

```
Chart Name="chart1">
       {CHART SERIES}
       {CHART CATEGORY}
       {CHART AREAS}
       {CHART LEGENDS}
       {CHART TITLES}
       {CHART DATA}
       {LOCATION}
       <DataSetName>DataSet1</DataSetName>
</Chart>
```

A real-life chart has additional elements in its RDL. These elements describe graphical presentation properties for a chart.

Reporting Services supports the following chart types: area, bar, column, line, polar, range, scatter, and shape. Table 13.8 provides a description of each type and each type's variants.

TABLE 13.8 Chart Types

Chart Type	Variants	Description
Area	Area, smooth area, stacked area, 100% stacked area, and 3D variations	Displays data as a set of points connected by a line, with a filled-in area below the line.
Bar	Bar, stacked bar, 100% stacked bar, and 3D variations	Displays data as sets of *horizontal* bars.
Column	Column, stacked column, 100% stacked column, and 3D variations	Displays data as sets of *vertical* columns. Includes information about hybrid column/line charts.
Line	Line, smooth line, stepped line, and line with markers	Displays data as a set of points connected by a line.
Polar	Polar, radar, and 3D radar	Displays a series as 360-degree points grouped by category. Values are displayed by the length (the farther, the greater value).
Range	Range, smooth range, range column, range bar, stock, candlestick, error bar, and boxplot.	Displays data as a set of lines with markers for high, low, close, and open values.
Scatter	XY	Displays data as a set of points in space.
	Bubble, 3D bubble	Displays data as a set of symbols whose position and size are based on the data in the chart.
Shape	Pie, exploded pie, doughnut, exploded doughnut, funnel, pyramid, and 3D variations.	Displays data as percentages of the whole.

Best Practices

Chart design best practices can be summed up as this: Make a picture that is worth a thousand words. With that in mind, a report designer wants to make sure that a chart is simple, meaningful, and efficient. A good chart:

- Includes relevant data (excludes irrelevant). For example, it does not make sense to chart daily values if your business client wants to see quarterly aggregations of data. Of course, as needed, you can allow your customer to drill through the data to determine whether a spike in the revenue is a result of the entire quarter or a single week when a company had a successful marketing campaign.

- Is clear to read and does not have overlaps. All labels, including axes and data point, are spaced appropriately and do not overlap. You either minimize the number of data points or format labels appropriately to avoid overlaps.
- Clearly marks empty values to avoid unclear gaps: Is this value zero or missing?
- Displays series of data and not a single value. A Gauge report provides better graphical representation of a single value.

Practical Application of a Chart

Let's apply the knowledge from this chapter to create a report.

To create a report that displays sales by country and by year, including graphical presentation of sales data, complete the following steps.

1. Similar to steps presented in the "Practical Application of Report Items" section of this chapter, add a new report with a data set based on the following query:

```
SELECT
  SUM(SOH.TotalDue) AS Sales,
  DATENAME(yyyy, SOH.OrderDate) AS Year,
  A.Name AS CountryName
FROM
  Sales.SalesOrderHeader AS SOH
  INNER JOIN   Sales.SalesTerritory AS ST ON SOH.TerritoryID = ST.TerritoryID
  INNER JOIN Person.CountryRegion AS A ON ST.CountryRegionCode =
  ➥A.CountryRegionCode
GROUP BY
  ST.Name, DATENAME(yyyy, SOH.OrderDate), A.Name
ORDER BY
     ST.Name, Year
```

2. Drag and drop a Chart item onto a report. Note the drop areas: Drop Data Fields Here, Drop Category Fields Here, and Drop Series Fields Here. Leave default chart selection (Column chart) and click OK to accept. Feel free to experiment with other chart types.
3. Drag and drop the Sales field onto the Data area, the CountryName field onto the Category area, and the Year field onto the Series area.
4. Set the chart's title to **`Sales By Country`**, the category (x) axes title to `Country`, and the value (y) axes to **`USD$`**.

   Click the y-axis label (you might need to click twice depending on the original state of a chart) to select it. Right-click the selection and choose Axis Properties from the context menu. Click the Number tab. This tab allows you to format axis labels. Choose appropriate formatting. We have chosen the options shown in Figure 13.15.

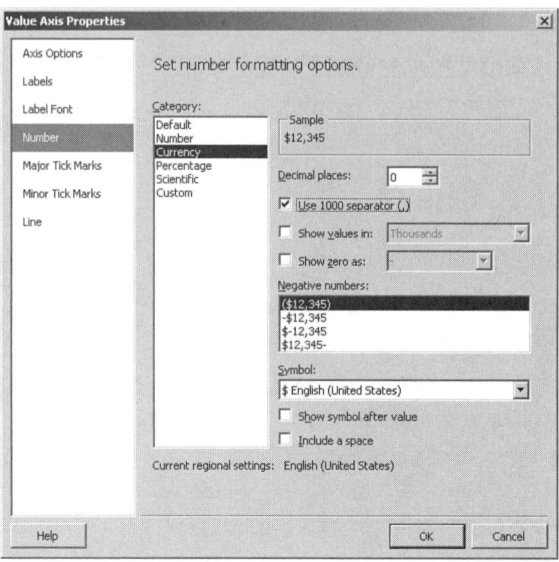

FIGURE 13.15 Number tab of the Axis Properties dialog box.

5. Click the x-axis label to select it. Right-click and select Axis Properties from the context menu. A Category Axis Properties dialog box will display. Click the Labels tab. Notice the Enable Auto-Fit selections (see Figure 13.16). You can experiment with options and disable Auto-Fit, choosing instead to rotate labels by a specified angle.
6. Preview the results. Suppose we manage U.S. sales and by looking at the chart we see that somehow 2004 was a bad year as compared to 2003. We also see that this was the case across all counties. Is this a global recession or another anomaly? Let's design a chart that shows us the monthly breakdown of the U.S. sales.
7. Drag and drop another Chart item onto a report. In this chart, we will present only U.S. sales aggregated on a monthly basis.
8. Add a new data set based on the following query. Note that the query is essentially the same as the earlier query, but with an added `Month` field and `HAVING` clause for the United States (changes in bold):

```
SELECT
  SUM(SOH.TotalDue) AS Sales,
  DATENAME(yyyy, SOH.OrderDate) As Year,
  MONTH(SOH.OrderDate) AS Month,
  A.Name AS CountryName
FROM
```

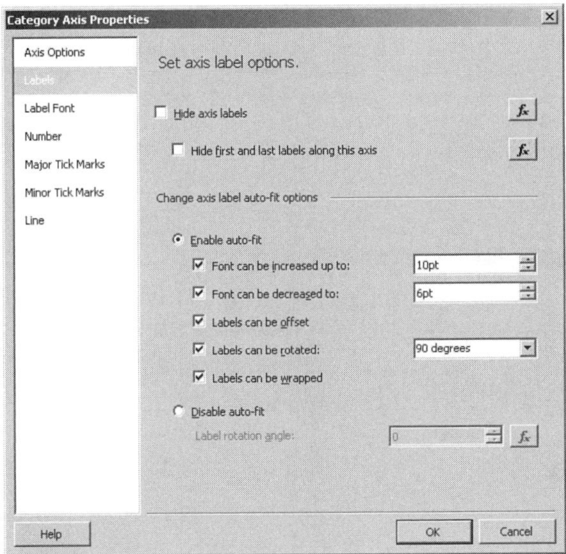

FIGURE 13.16 Labels tab of the Axis Properties dialog box.

```
    Sales.SalesOrderHeader AS SOH
    INNER JOIN   Sales.SalesTerritory AS ST ON SOH.TerritoryID = ST.TerritoryID
    INNER JOIN Person.CountryRegion AS A ON ST.CountryRegionCode =
    ➥A.CountryRegionCode
GROUP BY ST.Name, DATENAME(yyyy, SOH.OrderDate),
MONTH(SOH.OrderDate), A.Name
HAVING MAX(ST.CountryRegionCode) = 'US'
ORDER BY ST.Name, Year, Month
```

9. Drag and drop the Sales field onto the Data area, and both the Year and Month fields onto the Category area.
10. Format axis labels and change titles appropriately.
11. Preview the results. Now we can see that 2004 has only partial data available (six months specifically). It also looks like overall sales are increasing. Let's add a trend line to be sure.
12. In the Drop Data Fields Here area, right-click the Sales series and select Add Calculated Series from the context menu. BIDS then opens a Calculated Series Properties dialog box.

NOTE

If you happen to add fields to the Drop Series Fields Here area, BIDS will hide the Add Calculated Series option from the context menu.

13. Select Exponential Moving Average and use 12 periods to better see annual trends. Also check Start from First Point to see the trend line starting from the beginning of the graph and not 12 periods after.
14. Click the Border tab and set the line width to 3 points. This will make the trend line easier to view. Click OK to close and preview. You should see something similar to Figure 13.17.

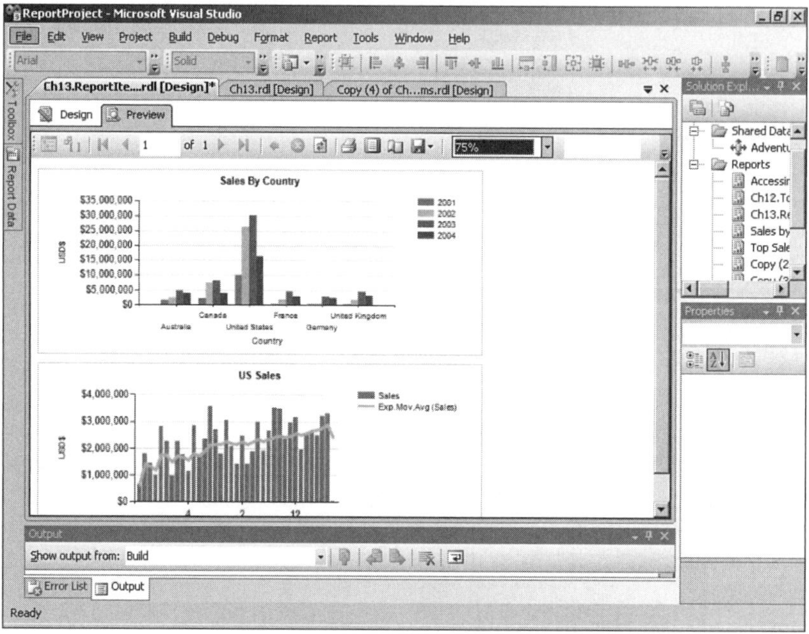

FIGURE 13.17 Chart at work.

Gauge Report Item

A Gauge report is a great tool to graphically display key performance indicators (KPIs). In the previous version of SSRS, you had to use a workaround and display various images, depending on the state of the KPI. (For example, for a thermometer, you had to display four images of a thermometer depending on what quartile the temperature value was in.)

You can still use the same technique in this version, especially if there is no gauge available to satisfy your needs. For example, because a smiley-face gauge is not available, you would instead display an *image* of a smiley face when the company is meeting its revenue targets and a sad face when it is not.

Figure 13.18 shows a design view of a gauge.

SSRS includes linear and radial charts. You select a gauge type when you add a Gauge item to your report. Because a gauge consists of multiple components, you cannot change the type of gauge after it has been added to a report. However, you can manipulate individual

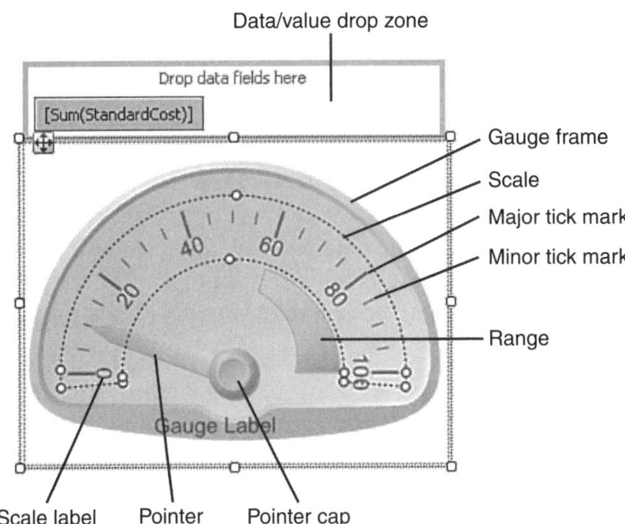

FIGURE 13.18 Design view of a gauge.

components of a gauge to "change" its type. For example, on a radial gauge, you can set `StartAngle=0` and `SweepAngle=360` to convert to a full circle scale.

By default, a gauge has one scale and one pointer. You can add scales and pointers and associate between scales and pointers. There are four types of pointers: marker, bar, thermometer, and needle. A needle pointer is available only for a radial chart.

To display values using a gauge, follow these steps:

1. Drag and drop a field onto the surface of a gauge.
2. Create a pointer and drag and drop a field to a pointer placeholder.

Upon drop completion, you might notice that a gauge uses `Sum()` aggregation for the numeric fields and `Count()` for non-numeric fields.

Table 13.9 lists some of the more commonly leveraged properties of a gauge.

TABLE 13.9 Gauge Properties

Property	Action
`MaximumValue` and `MinimumValue`	Ending and beginning value of the scale
`StartValue` and `EndValue`	Move, expand, and contract the gauge's range
`StartWidth`	Convert the beginning of the gauge range to a pointy or fat shape

You can add multiple gauges to a gauge panel. A panel is a container for gauges.

Chapter 17, "Working with Multidimensional Data Sources," includes an example of a gauge in use.

Report Body Versus Page Header/Footer

The report body can contain any SSRS items, including data regions. The page header and footer can only contain independent report items, such as Textbox, Line, and Rectangle. More complex page header and footer functionality can be implemented with Tablix and the `RepeatOnNewPage` property.

To add a page header or footer, right-click the Design area surrounding a report and select Add Page Header or Add Page Footer from the context menu. To remove, right-click the Design area surrounding a report and select Remove Page Header or Remove Page Footer from the context menu. Add and remove menu entries depending on whether a page header (or footer) is already visible. BIDS does not keep track of report items from a removed page header/footer. You effectively delete all the items from a removed page header/footer. You can, however, use an undo action (Edit, Undo) to restore a recently removed page's header/footer (together with original items).

Normally, you use page headers and footers to display page-related data, such as page number (`=Globals.PageNumber`). Other expressions that you may use in page header (or footer) include the following:

- Aggregation of data from a single page, `=Sum(ReportItems!TextboxSales.Value)`. This is possible because the `ReportItems` collection contains all the text boxes on a page.
- Aggregation of data from a data set, `=Sum(Fields!Sales.Value,"DataSet1")`.

Both page footer and page headers have `PrintOnFirstPage` and `PrintOnLastPage` properties, which are visible in the Properties window when you click the page header (or footer). Those properties control whether a header or footer is rendered on the first and last pages and are pretty much self-explanatory.

Summary

Report items are the presentation elements within SSRS.

Data regions function as a repetitive display of rows, groups of rows, or columns from a data set associated with a region. Data regions include Tablix (Table, Matrix, List), Chart, and Gauge. Data regions cannot be included in page headers or page footers.

Other report items are used for display purposes and are commonly called independent report items. These items include Line, Rectangle, Textbox, and Image.

Data regions and independent report items support navigation; see Chapter 16 for more information.

Containers can include other reporting items. Items placed in a container become the container's children, and the container becomes the parent. Tablix, Rectangle, Report Body, Page Header, and Page Footer are containers.

In the following chapter, you build on this knowledge by learning how to group, sort, and aggregate data within a given scope of a data region. By learning how to use report items and group data effectively, you will be able to create advanced reports in no time.

CHAPTER 14

Grouping, Sorting, Aggregating Data, and Working with Scope

IN THIS CHAPTER

- Grouping Data on a Report
- Sorting, Including Interactive Sorting and Data Source Sorting
- Scope Parameter of Aggregate Functions
- Level and InScope Functions

Grouping and sorting functionality provides some of the key motivators for purchasing reporting tools. Although every enterprise database management system (DBMS) can group and sort data, reports presented to business users usually have multiple levels of grouping inside of them, not to mention lots of pretty pictures, complex layouts, and graphs. A simple query tool is inadequate for this task. This chapter discusses grouping and sorting and when it is appropriate to do it in SSRS versus the DBMS. Note that in SSRS grouping and sorting functionality is available within data regions.

Grouping Data on a Report

Grouping enables you to aggregate items within a group and, in turn, to generate reports with complex formatting. Chapter 10, "Expressions," covered various aggregation functions. Aggregation functions help grouping scenarios by providing totals for groups and subtotals for subgroups. The relationship between an aggregation function and group is controlled by scope. This relationship becomes useful when, for example, a user needs to see what percentage of a total a particular line item represents.

In the examples in previous chapters, you have seen summarizations in data regions, such as the Tablix (Table, Matrix, List), Gauge, and Chart.

Most scenarios employ grouping in SSRS to aggregate data and generate summary information. Concepts applicable to aggregation in SSRS are similar to those applicable to the `GROUP BY` clause in a SQL query. However, unlike a query, which allows for very limited formatting, SSRS is practically unlimited in its formatting capabilities.

As in many cases in software development, choosing a particular approach (such as, query versus SSRS) is based on several key factors: performance, scalability, elegance, and development time. This is a "magic" formula. The complex part of this is to find the best balance between key factors that can solve this "magic." When time allows, the best solution is to experiment with various approaches and find the best for a particular application.

Through experiments you should see that in almost all cases, using SQL for grouping (`GROUP BY`) provides the best performance. However, a static SQL statement is not very flexible.

The SQL statement might be too complex, lose its elegance, and, especially, it may not provide the required formatting. In addition, complex SQL queries are hard to maintain and troubleshoot.

The following are some tips to help strike a balance between the grouping capabilities of SSRS and SQL:

- Ideally and where possible, use `GROUP BY` in a query.
- Make sure to use `WHERE` and `HAVING` clauses. Both clauses enable you to reduce the amount of data received by SSRS. This is especially important if you are not going to use the data in a report.
- Do not format or convert data in a query, unless needed for `GROUP BY`. A conversion function is called for each row of returned data, which adds an unnecessary burden to a database server. Because database servers are much harder to scale out using inexpensive commodity hardware than reporting servers, it makes sense to have conversion and formatting performed by SSRS.

For example, the following query retrieves a summary of all line items for every order. Displaying the resulting aggregated data in a Tablix would be much faster than using Tablix to aggregate the data:

```
SELECT
    Sales.SalesOrderHeader.SalesOrderNumber,
    SUM(Sales.SalesOrderDetail.LineTotal) AS SumOfDetails,
    SUM(Sales.SalesOrderHeader.SubTotal) AS OrderSubTotal
FROM
    Sales.SalesOrderDetail INNER JOIN
    Sales.SalesOrderHeader ON Sales.SalesOrderDetail.SalesOrderID =
    Sales.SalesOrderHeader.SalesOrderID
GROUP BY Sales.SalesOrderHeader.SalesOrderNumber
```

To add a new group, you can use one of the following methods:

- **Tablix row (column) group:** Refer to the Tablix report item discussion in Chapter 13, "Working with Report Items."
- **Gauge:** Right-click a Gauge panel (the space around a gauge), and select Add Data Group from the shortcut menu.

- **Chart:** Drag and drop a field from the Report Data window onto a chart. When you mouse over the chart, you should see category (Drop Category Fields Here) and series (Drop Series Fields Here) drop areas. When you drop a field, you create a category or a series group.

The Group Properties dialog box provides an interface to edit groups for Tablix, Gauge, and Chart. Although the interface has changed from the previous version of SSRS, many of the original concepts remain the same.

Figure 14.1 shows the Group Properties dialog box for a Tablix group. Note that Gauge and Chart will have three fewer tabs in comparison to Tablix. Gauge, and Chart do not have Page Breaks, Visibility, and Advanced on their Group Properties dialog box.

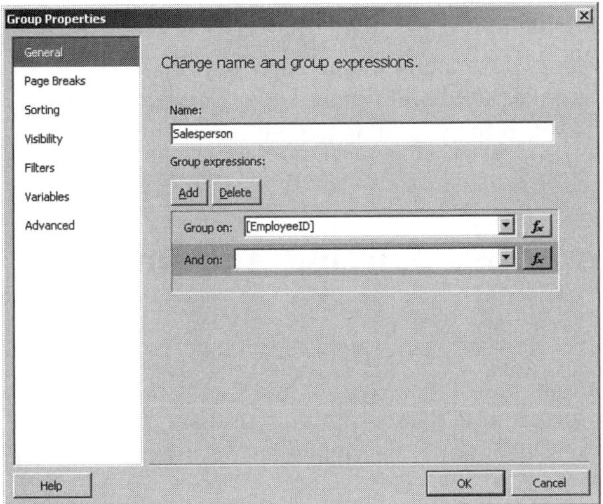

FIGURE 14.1 Group Properties dialog box.

The following are procedures to display the Group Properties dialog box:

- **Tablix row (column) group:** In the grouping pane (window), right-click a group (or click a down arrow at the right of a group) and select Group Properties from the shortcut menu.

  Or right-click in the cell with a group indictor and select Row Group (or Column Group), and then select Group Properties from the shortcut menu.

- **Gauge:** Right-click a Gauge pane (the space around a gauge), and then select Edit Data Group or Data Group Properties from the shortcut menu.

- **Chart:** Click a chart twice (do not double-click). You should see category (Drop Category Fields Here) and series (Drop Series Fields Here) drop areas. Each series group is represented by a button. Right-click the series that you want to edit and select Category Group Properties (or Series Group Properties).

You can also edit properties of a group from the Properties window (use the F4 shortcut to display). The Report Definition Language (RDL) that describes a group is as follows:

```
<Group Name="Group1">
  <GroupExpressions>
    <GroupExpression>=Fields!Country.Value</GroupExpression>
  </GroupExpressions>
</Group>
```

The Group Properties dialog box opens on the General tab, from where you can name a group and specify grouping expressions. The Page Breaks tab allows you to specify how a group affects the report's pagination. The Sorting tab specifies how the data within a group is sorted (similar to `ORDER BY` in Transact-SQL). The Visibility tab specifies the initial visibility of the group and an item that can interactively trigger visibility. If you need to exclude group items from a display on a report, you must use the Filters tab (this is similar to `WHERE` and `HAVING` clauses). The Variables tab enables you to specify group variables. A group variable is a new functionality of SSRS 2008. And finally, the Advanced tab enables you to specify a group's parent for recursive displays and document map items to allow quick navigation on a large report.

Sorting, Including Interactive Sorting and Data Source Sorting

You have three available options to sort results:

- Make the data source (database) sort data on data retrieval by using an `ORDER BY` clause. As SSRS processes a data set sequentially, it displays data in the order returned by a data set.
- Make SSRS sort data during report generation. SSRS sorts data regions and groups that have the `SortExpressions` property set. This option will re-sort data returned by a data set. This option is useful when you need to offload sort processing from a database server, when you need to leverage a single data set to display data in a specific order, or when you need to to fine-tune sorting within a group.
- Use interactive sort functionality (HTML-rendered reports only). This functionality makes SSRS regenerate a report with a new direction: ascending or descending. SSRS adds interactive sorting functionality to the items that have `UserSort` property set. This option proves useful when you need to enable a user to sort by various fields interactively.

Data Source Sorting

When a report developer uses the `ORDER BY` clause in a query, the database performs sorting. This provides the best performance, especially when you need to sort a large volume of data and have plenty of capacity on the database server. In many cases, it will not be an issue for a database server with sufficient capacity, but do consider performance implications for the database server. In addition, because the query approach has a scope of an entire data set, it might not provide needed fine-tuning for data sorting.

When necessary, a report developer can parameterize data source sorting by using the following expression used as the query in a data set:

```
="SELECT {fields} FROM {table} ORDER BY " & Parameters!MySort.Value
```

The `MySort` parameter should contain a valid list of database fields or numbers corresponding to the fields to use in `ORDER BY`.

For example, to retrieve a list of employees, use the following expression:

```
="SELECT FirstName, LastName, Title FROM Employee ORDER BY " & Parameters!MySort.
➥Value
```

In this example, `MySort` could be set to a nonqueried parameter with the values `FirstName` and `LastName` or values `1` and `2`. For more information about parameters, including information about how to pass a parameter value to a report, see Chapter 12, "Report Parameters."

For dynamic query expressions, report developers need to make sure that `Parameters!MySort.Value` properly corresponds to a database field or fields. In addition, a dynamic query expression has to return a valid query. Each properly placed space is crucial, such as the space between `ORDER BY` and a parameter.

Query design has to follow best practices to avoid SQL injection. You can find a good article about avoiding SQL injection attacks at http://msdn.microsoft.com/msdnmag/issues/04/09/SQLInjection/.

Data Region and Group Sorting

A report developer can implement sorting for a group or for a data region by providing one or many expressions for the `Sorting` property. A Sorting property tab of a data region (or a group) is shown in Figure 14.2.

Similar to data source sorting, an expression can, for example, sort by `FirstName` and `LastName`. Of course, fields used in expressions in this case will belong to the `Fields` collection. In other words, the sorting expressions will have the form of `=Fields!FirstName.Value` and `=Fields!LastName.Value`. `FirstName` and `LastName` by default have the same name as fields retrieved by the data source (or the same as database field names). Note that you can change default names.

Similar to data source sorting, sort expressions can take advantage of parameters. For more information about parameters, including information about how to pass a parameter value to a report, see Chapter 12. The expression that incorporates parameters has a form of `=Fields(Parameters!{ParameterName}.Value).Value`. For example, if the parameter `MySort` is used, the expression will be `=Fields(Parameters!MySort.Value).Value`.

In addition, expressions can include flow control functions, such as `IIf()`. Sorting is performed in the scope where the sort is specified. For example, if you have a table that

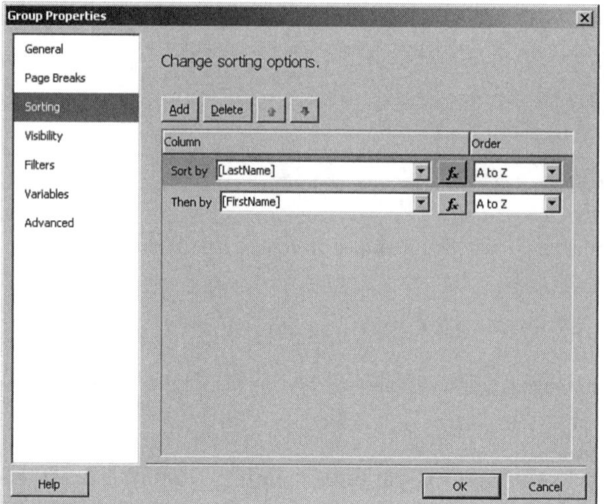

FIGURE 14.2 Sorting expressions.

contains a group, sorting expressions specified for a table will not affect the data sort in the group.

The RDL that describes sorting is as follows:

```
<SortExpressions>
  <SortExpression>
    <Value>=Fields!Country.Value</Value>
  </SortExpression>
</SortExpressions>
```

Interactive User Sorting

SSRS2K5 added an interactive sort action that enables users to sort an HTML-rendered report.

The RDL that describes interactive sorting is as follows:

```
<UserSort>
  <SortExpression>=Fields!Country.Value</SortExpression>
  <SortExpressionScope>Group1</SortExpressionScope>
</UserSort>
```

A report developer can set up this type of sorting through a text box's property `UserSort` or through the Interactive Sort tab of a text box's Properties dialog box (see Figure 14.3).

To determine the proper position of an interactive sorting control, visualize the output and decide what location makes sense for the interaction to occur. For example, to sort values within a group, a cell in a group header should contain an interactive sort control.

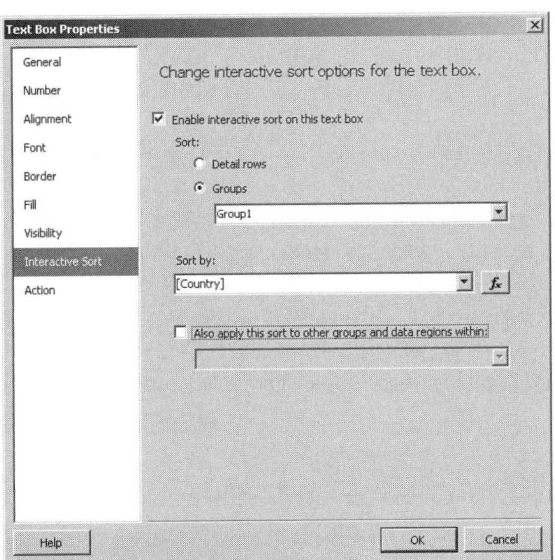

FIGURE 14.3 Interactive sorting.

Similarly, if you want to sort data in the entire Tablix, you pick a cell in the Tablix's row or column header.

The following are the components of an interactive sort:

- **Enable Interactive Sort on This Text Box:** When selected, this option enables interactive sorting functionality on the selected text box. It also enables all other entry fields.
- **Sort Detail Rows:** This option specifies to sort on the innermost (Detail) group.
- **Sort Groups:** This option specifies which group is sorted.
- **Sort By (required):** Normally, this option specifies a column expression for the column to be sorted. For example, if the designer needs to sort a column that contains the expression `=Fields!Country.Value`, the same expression is used for sorting. In a few cases, the designer might choose to use different expressions for sorting. For example, the designer might decide to use `=Fields!UserID.Value` if `UserID` is sequenced in the same sort order as `FirstName`. If you do not specify anything for Sort By, BIDS automatically disables sorting.
- **Also Apply This Sort to Other Groups and Data Regions check box:** This option specifies whether to apply the sort options to another group or a data region.
- **Apply This Sort to Other Groups and Data Regions list:** This option displays when the Also Apply This Sort to Other Groups and Data Regions check box is selected and specifies an additional data region or a group to apply sorting.

Behind the scenes, there is nothing magical about interactive sorting. If you look at the rendered report's source, you will notice that SSRS added the following fragments to the HTML to allow the data to be sorted:

```
<a tabindex="1" style="cursor:pointer;" onclick=
"ClientReport13a375a994924cd3901a2bc918df4104.ActionHandler
('Sort','10iT0_A');return false;" onkeypress="if(event.keyCode == 13 ||
➥event.which == 13){ClientReport13a375a994924cd3901a2bc918df4104.ActionHandler
('Sort','10iT0_A');}return false;">
<IMG SRC="/Reports/Reserved.ReportViewerWebControl.axd?ReportSession=
➥jvcab245onfgwp45bqgcub45&amp;ControlID=13a375a994924cd3901a2bc918df4104&amp;
➥Culture=1033&amp;UICulture=9&amp;ReportStack=1&amp;OpType=ReportImage&amp;
➥ResourceStreamID=unsorted.gif"/>
</a>
```

As you may notice from the HTML fragment, `ResourceStreamID` is initially `unsorted.gif` and changes to `sortAsc.gif` or `sortDesc.gif`, depending on the direction of the sort. This is internal functionality to SSRS, and you do not want to change it. However, it reveals that the "magic" is simply scripting. You can further explore this functionality by adding more interactive sort fields and observing changes in rendered HTML and the report's URL.

Keep in mind that it is also possible to make dynamic SQL and leverage the data source server for runtime sorting. In most cases, however, SSRS built-in interactive sorting will be more efficient overall, easier to develop and maintain, and thus more elegant.

Scope Parameter of Aggregate Functions

The `Scope` parameter of aggregate functions defines the scope in which the aggregate function is performed. A valid scope could be any of the following:

- A string name of an associated data set.
- A string name of a containing data region. Within the data region, `Scope` is optional for all aggregate functions except `RowNumber()`.
- A string name of a containing group.
- Omitted, when optional. In this case, the scope of the aggregate is the innermost data region or grouping to which the report item belongs. If the item is outside of a data region and there is a single data set, `Scope` refers to this single data set. If there are multiple data sets, `Scope` cannot be omitted. In the case of multiple data sets, SSRS provides an explicit reference if the designer drags and drops a field outside of the data region.

When you specify the `Scope` parameter, keep in mind that you can

- Specify only current or any containing scope. For example, for an aggregate function in a cell of a row group, you can specify a scope as a current row group, any parent group, the entire Tablix, or the name of a data set associated with Tablix.

- Specify only a single scope for a function. For example, you can't specify `Country` and `State` simultaneously as the scope for an aggregate function.
- Use either a column or row group in an expression, but not both.

A scope has an order of containment from the least to the most filtered set of data:

1. **Data set**: Contains results of a query after the data set filters are applied. It has the outermost scope.
2. **Data region**: Contains data set data after the data region's filters and sorts are applied.
3. **Group hierarchy**: Each group contains further filtered and sorted data, starting from data in the data region and moving through group hierarchy to the innermost child.
4. **Nested data regions**: A cell may contain a nested data region.
5. **Group hierarchy in a nested data region**: Same as a number 3 for a nested data region.

TIP

Scope is a case-sensitive string, and therefore `Dataset1` and `dataset1` are different `Scope` values.

If the containing group or data region is not used as scope, SSRS throws an error:

```
The Value expression for the <Item> '<Item Name>' has a scope parame-
ter that is not valid for an aggregate function. The scope parameter
must be set to a string constant that is equal to either the name of
a containing group, the name of a containing data region, or the name
of a dataset.
```

The `Scope` parameter cannot be used in page headers or footers.

For `RowNumber()` to generate expected results, the expression containing this function has to be in the "detail" row and not on the "summary" row like a group header or footer.

You can define multiple scopes for a Tablix. Depending on a Tablix's template and number of groups, the number of scopes will vary: The Table template can have multiple row scopes and the Matrix template can have multiple row and multiple column scopes.

For example, a Table with a single group (this is a default for a Table) has three scopes:

1. The data set scope, which allows you to apply aggregations to all the data in the data set. Note that the data set is associated with the table through the `DataSetName` property.
2. The entire Table scope, which allows you to apply aggregations to detail rows.
3. A group scope.

Similarly, a Matrix template (by default) has four scopes: the associated data set, whole Matrix (allows you to aggregate details), and one for each of the groups (a Matrix has at least one row and at least one column group).

`Level` and `InScope` Functions

`Level([Scope])` returns a zero-based (top level in a hierarchy is `0`) integer (the current level of depth in a recursive hierarchy).

To create a recursive hierarchy, you use the Group Properties dialog box (we talked about it in the "Grouping Data on a Report" section of this chapter); and on the General tab, set a group expression to the field that specifies child data (such as `EmployeeID`); and on Advanced tab, set the recursive parent to the field that specifies parent data (such as `ManagerID`). Both `EmployeeID` and `ManagerID` come from the Employee table of the Adventure Works database.

Note that when you specify a recursive parent for a group, such group can have one and only one group expression. Interestingly, you get the same message whether you specify more than one group expression or none at all:

```
[rsInvalidGroupingParent] A grouping in the tablix 'Table1' has Parent and more
than one group expressions. Parent is only allowed if the grouping has exactly one
group expression.
```

Also note the difference between the `Parent` property of a report item and the `Parent` property of a recursive group. The former is accessible from the Properties window when you click a control. The latter is accessible from the Properties window when you click a group in either Row Groups or Column Windows and is located under `Group` property, effectively making it `Group.Parent`.

`Level()` returns `0` when you use the `Scope` parameter and the `Scope` specifies one of the following: a nonrecursive grouping (or grouping with no `Parent` element), data set, or data region. If the `Scope` parameter is omitted, the function `Level()` returns the level of the current scope.

`Level` can be useful to provide indentation (for example, a hierarchy of employees in a sales department). To provide indentation, a report developer could do the following:

1. Add a blank report.
2. Create a data set that retrieves `EmployeeID` and `ManagerID` from a database using the following query:

```
SELECT
    Person.Contact.FirstName, Person.Contact.LastName,
    HumanResources.Employee.ManagerID, HumanResources.Employee.EmployeeID
FROM
    HumanResources.Employee INNER JOIN
    Person.Contact ON HumanResources.Employee.ContactID =
    Person.Contact.ContactID
```

3. Drag and drop a table on a report.
4. Drag and drop the `FirstName` field from the data set to the cell in the first column of the Data (or detail) row. Note that the Data row is the second row of the table. Open the expression for that cell and modify it to `=Fields!FirstName.Value & " " & Fields!LastName.Value`. In the cell above (first column of the Header row), enter **`Name`**. In the Properties window for this cell, set `Padding.Left = (2 + Level()*20) & "pt"`.
5. In the cell in the second column of the Data row, enter the following expression: **`=Level()`**. In the cell above (second column of the Header row), enter **`Level`**.
6. Open the Group Properties dialog box for the `(Details)` group and specify the hierarchy by opening the Advanced tab and setting the recursive parent to the `ManagerID`.
7. Preview the report and notice the indentation in the name hierarchy and level numbers.

14

The `InScope(Scope)` function returns `True` if the current instance of an item is within the specified scope. Practical usability of `InScope()` is mostly limited to data regions that have dynamic scoping, such as Tablix and Chart.

`InScope()` is often used to implement advanced formatting. For example, `InScope()` can be used to highlight rows with subtotals or to create a drill-through link with capabilities to access different reports, depending on the clicked cell.

For example, you have a Table with two row groups: `Order` (parent) and `OrderLineItem` (child). You want report users to navigate to an `OrderLineItemDetailReport` when a user clicks a cell in an `OrderLineItem` group. You can use the Go to Report action (see Chapter 16, "Report Navigation," for more information) and specify the following as the report expression:

```
=IIF(InScope("OrderLineItem"), "OrderLineItemDetailReport", "InvalidClickReport")
```

Similarly, we can format all the cells as clickable by setting `Color` and `TextDecoration` properties for the `OrderLineItem` group's cells:

```
Color =IIF(InScope("OrderLineItem"), "Blue", "Black")
TextDecoration =IIF(InScope("OrderLineItem"), "Underline", "None")
```

Summary

Grouping and sorting functionality allow SSRS to perform much more complex data manipulations than a query. When there is sufficient data source server capacity and for the best performance, use `GROUP BY` and `ORDER BY` in a query. Data regions provide additional options to sort and group data. In a way, grouping and sorting functionality is similar to `GROUP BY` and `ORDER BY` in a query, but with much more granularity and dynamic expression-driven control. SSRS also enables you to implement an interactive sort with little effort on your part.

CHAPTER 15

Advanced Report Formatting

IN THIS CHAPTER

- Formatting-Related Report Item Properties
- Formatting Numeric and Date/Time Values
- Creating Alternating Colors for the Lines on a Report
- Paging Report (Improved in 2008)

Thus far, this book has discussed some basic formatting, such as highlighting text in bold, changing background color, and adjusting report layout. This chapter provides a broader view on formatting.

Report Formatting, Report Border, and Layout toolbars (see Figure 15.1) are conveniently available to do some design-time formatting. The formatting toolbars are the same as in the last version of SSRS.

The Properties window and Properties (property pages) dialog box provide access to a full set of formatting properties. Both allow you to use expressions for most properties, which mean that you can dynamically modify formatting during runtime.

TIP

Try to preview a report (click the Preview tab of Report Designer) to verify whether the formatting is satisfactory.

Unlike the toolbar, property pages have been improved, mostly around number formatting (see Figure 15.2). The Number tab is new and helps you assign complex formatting to a number. For example, what you see on the figure translates to the `Format` property set to `'$'0.00;('$'0.00)`.

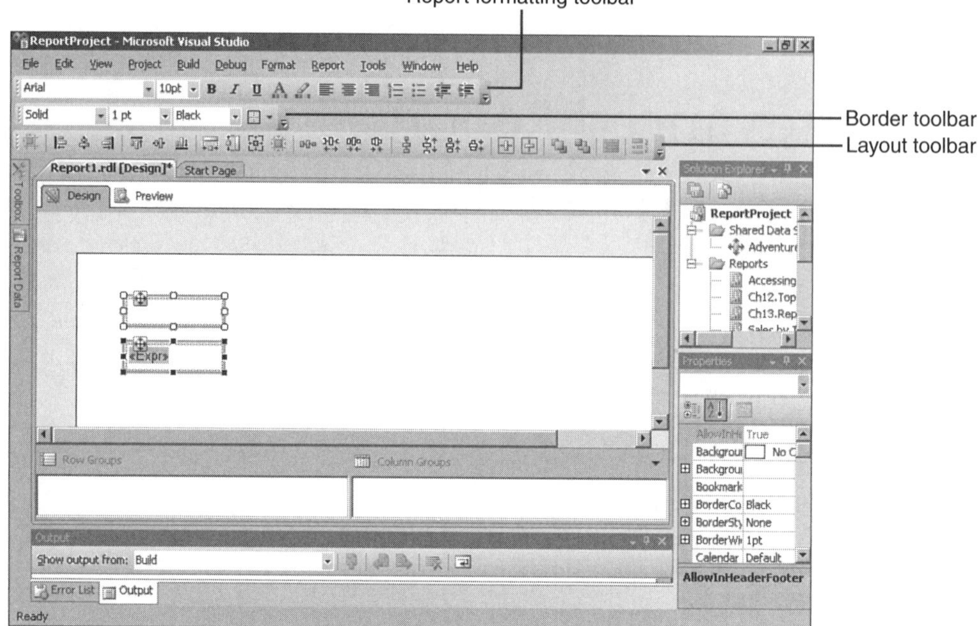

FIGURE 15.1 Report-formatting toolbars.

Formatting-Related Report Item Properties

Formatting properties can be divided into three categories:

- **Background control properties:** Designed to control background, such as background color, of data presented on a report. These properties are shown in Table 15.1.

TABLE 15.1 Background-Related Report Item Formatting Properties

Property	Description
`BackgroundColor`	The color of the background of the item. This property could be a name of the color, such as `Red`, or the HTML color string in the form `#RRGGBB`. Letters `R`, `G`, and `B` provide hexadecimal representation for red, green, and blue color intensity. For example `#FF0000` is red. If this property is omitted, the background becomes transparent. This property is not available for Line, Subreport, and Image report items.
`BackgroundGradientType`	The direction in which the background gradient is displayed: `None`, `LeftRight`, `TopBottom`, `Center`, `DiagonalLeft`, `DiagonalRight`, `HorizontalCenter`, `VerticalCenter` This property is available only for a chart's areas (plot, chart, and legend).

TABLE 15.1 Continued

Property	Description
BackgroundGradientEndColor	The end color of the background gradient. If omitted, the item has no background gradient. This property is available only for a chart's areas (plot, chart, and legend).
BackgroundImage	An image to display as the background of a report item. This property is available for Rectangle, Text Box, List, Matrix, Table, Body, Page Header and Footer, Subtotal, and a Chart's plot area (settable through the Properties window). The BackgroundImage property is not available for Line, Image, Subreport, Chart Legends, or Chart Areas.

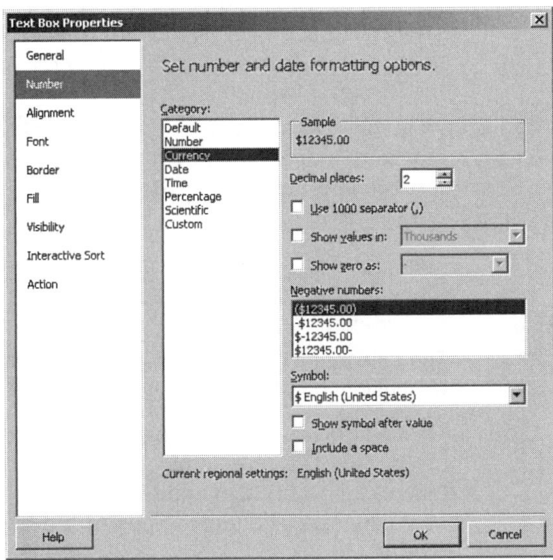

FIGURE 15.2 Item Properties window and Properties dialog box.

- **Output text control properties:** Designed to control textual (string, numeric, and date) output, such as color, font, currency, and date formatting. These properties are shown in Table 15.2.
- **Border appearance control properties:** Designed to control a border surrounding output. All report items, except Line, have a border. These properties are shown in Table 15.2.

Formatting properties accept expressions to provide dynamism of representation, based on, for example, the retrieved data or parameters. See Chapter 10, "Expressions," for more information about expressions.

NOTE

Note, for example, that a value `Red` is valid when used as a property value by itself, whereas an expression must evaluate to a string "`Red`".

Other formatting properties (See Table 15.2) control the appearance of text displayed in the item (font, color, international properties, alignment, and so on) and the appearance of the border (color, width).

TABLE 15.2 Other Formatting Properties

Property Type	Properties	Description

Border formatting	`BorderColor`
	`BorderStyle`
	`BorderWidth`
		The color of the border of the item: `Bottom`, `Default`, `Left`, `Right`, `Top`. The style of the border of the item: `Dotted`, `Dashed`, `Solid`, and so on. The width of the border of the item.
		All border-formatting properties have child elements to format the corresponding location of a border: `Bottom`, `Default`, `Left`, `Right`, `Top`.

General formatting	`Format` `Calendar`	The Microsoft .NET Framework formatting string to apply to the item. For example, `C` for currency. The calendar to use to format dates. Used in conjunction with the `Language` property.

Text formatting	`Color Direction`
	`FontFamily`
	`FontSize`
	`FontStyle`
	`FontWeight`
	`TextDecoration`
	`WritingMode`
	`Line Height`
		The color (`Red`), direction, font family name (such as `Arial`), size in points (`1pt`), style (such as `Italic`), weight (thickness, such as `Bold`), special effect to apply to the font for the text in the item (such as `Underline`), and the direction of the text.
		`Line Height` specifies the minimum height of a cell containing the text. If not specified, the height is based on the font size.

Locale control	`Language`
	`NumeralLanguage`
	`NumeralVariant`
		The primary language of the text. The digit format to use based on the `Language` property. Used for locale formatting. For example, `en-GB` changes formatting to Great Britain's locale. For example, currency formatting changes from `$` to `£` and the date changes from `mm/dd/yy` to `dd/mm/yy`. `NumeralLanguage` and `NumeralVariant` control numeric presentation of text.

TABLE 15.2 Continued

Property Type	Properties	Description
Padding	`Bottom/Left/Right/Top`	The amount of space to insert between the bottom/left/right/top edge of the item and the text or image in the item.
Text alignment	`TextAlign` `VerticalAlign`	The horizontal (left, right, or center) and vertical (top, middle, or bottom) alignment of the text in the item.

Formatting Numeric and Date/Time Values

Both numeric and date/time values allow for standard and custom formatting strings. A standard formatting string refers to a single character that specifies the desired output format for a value.

TIP

`Me.Value` or simply `Value` provides access to the `Value` property of an SSRS item and simplifies formatting expressions. Instead of using the same expression that was used to set the `Value` property, you can access the value of this expression through `Me.Value`. For example, to display negative values in red, the property `Color` can be set to the expression `=IIF(Fields!TotalDue.Value >= 0, "Black", "Red")`. Alternatively, you can use `=IIF(Value >= 0, "Black", "Red")` and achieve the same result.

Any numeric format string that does not fit the definition of a standard format string (either numeric or date/time) is interpreted as a custom format string. For example, format string `d!` is interpreted as a custom format string because it contains two alphabetic characters, even though the character `d` is a standard date/time format specifier. This is true even if the extra characters are white spaces. Similarly, character `h` is interpreted as a custom format because it does not match any standard format specifiers.

In addition, report developers can exercise greater control over how values are formatted by using custom format specifiers.

Resulting output strings are influenced by the settings in the Regional Options control panel and locale control properties: `Language`, `NumeralLanguage`, and `NumeralVariant`. Computers with different locale-specific settings generate different formatting for numbers and dates.

For example, `February 4, 2006` returns `2/4/2006` when run with the `United States English (en-US)` locale, but it returns `04.02.2006` when run with the `German (de-DE)` locale.

You can learn more about globalization and locale options at www.microsoft.com/globaldev/getWR/steps/WRG_lclmdl.mspx.

Standard Numeric Format Strings

Numeric format strings are used to format common numeric types. A standard format string takes the form Axx, where A is a single alphabetic character called the format specifier, and xx is an optional integer called the precision specifier. The format specifier must be one of the built-in format characters (see Table 15.3). The precision specifier ranges from 0 to 99 and controls the number of significant digits or zeros to the right of a decimal. The format string cannot contain white spaces.

TABLE 15.3 Standard Numeric Format Strings

Format Specifier	Name	Description[1]	Example[2]
C or c	Currency	The number is converted to a string that represents a currency amount. The conversion is controlled by the Language property. The precision specifier indicates the desired number of decimal places. If omitted, the default currency precision is controlled by the Language property.	Value=1234.567 Language=default Output=$1,234.57 Language=en-GB Output=[bp1,234.57
D or d	Decimal	This format is supported for integer types only. The number is converted to a string of decimal digits (0–9).	Value=1234 Output=1234
E or e	Scientific (exponential)	The number is converted to a string of the form d.ddd...E±ddd or d.ddd...e±ddd. One digit always precedes the decimal point, a minimum of three digits follow the ± sign, and the case determines the prefix of the exponent (E or an e). If the precision specifier is omitted, a default of E6 is used.	Value=1234.567 Output=1.234567+E0 03
F or f	Fixed-point	The number is converted to a string of the form ddd.ddd.... If the precision specifier is omitted, the default numeric precision given by the Language property is used.	Value=1234.567 Output=1234.57

TABLE 15.3 Continued

Format Specifier	Name	Description[1]	Example[2]
G or g	General	The number is converted to the most compact of either fixed-point or scientific notation, depending on the type of the number and whether a precision specifier is present. If the precision specifier is omitted or zero, the type of the number determines the default precision.	Value=1234.567 Output=1234.567
N or n	Number	The number is converted to a string of the form d,ddd,ddd.ddd.... Thousand separators are inserted between each group of three digits to the left of the decimal point. If the precision specifier is omitted, the precision is guided by the Language property.	Value=1234.567 Output=1,234.567
P or p	Percent	The number is converted to a string where the value is multiplied by 100 and presented with a percentage sign. If the precision specifier is omitted, the precision is guided by the Language property.	Value=123.4567 Output=12,345.67%
R or r	Round-trip	The round-trip specifier guarantees that a numeric value converted to a string will be parsed back into the same numeric value. SSRS examines data for the best output to accomplish this.	Value=1234.567 Output=1234.567
X or x	Hexadecimal	The number is converted to a string of hexadecimal digits. X produces uppercase (ABCDEF) for digits greater than 9; x produces lowercase (abcdef). Decimal number 123 is correspondingly converted to hexadecimal 7b. This format is supported for integer types only.	Value=1234 Output=4D2

[1]*The following abbreviations are used: Letter d indicates a digit (0–9), and letter E or e denotes an exponent.*

[2]*Uses uppercase, does not use a specifier, and uses default U.S. English* NumeralLanguage*. For example, format string* C *is used for currency.*

If the format string does not contain one of the standard format specifiers, the format string is ignored.

The following abbreviations are used: Letter d indicates a digit (0–9), letter E or e denotes an exponent, ± indicates that you can use either the plus or minus sign in the expression.

The exponent always consists of a plus or minus sign and a minimum of three digits. By default, SSRS prefixes negative numbers with a minus sign.

The precision specifier indicates the minimum number of digits desired. If required, the number is padded with zeros to produce the number of digits given by the precision specifier. The number is padded to its left for integer types formatted with decimal or hexadecimal specifiers and in digits after the decimal point for other specifiers. Padding is ignored for the R format specifier.

You can find additional information about standard numeric format strings in the .NET Framework Developer's Guide at http://msdn.microsoft.com/library/default.asp?url=/library/en-us/cpguide/html/cpconstandardnumericformatstrings.asp

Custom Numeric Format Strings

Table 15.4 shows custom numeric format strings, descriptions, and output examples. You can exercise greater control over how values are formatted by using custom format specifiers.

TABLE 15.4 Custom Numeric Format Strings

Format Specifier	Name	Description	Example
0	Zero placeholder	In the position where the 0 appears in the format string, copy the digit of the value to the result string. The number of 0s before and after the decimal point determines the exact number of digits. The number is rounded to the nearest decimal position.	Value=012.3 Format=000.00 Output=012.30 Format=000. Output=012
#	Digit placeholder	In the position where the # appears in the format string, copy the digit of the value to the result string. This specifier never displays 0 character if it is not a significant digit, even if 0 is the only digit in the string.	Value=012.30 Format=###.## Output=12.3 Format phone number Value=1234567890 Format=(###)###-#### Output=(123)456-7890

TABLE 15.4 Continued

Format Specifier	Name	Description	Example
.	Decimal point	The first period (.) character in the format string determines the location of the decimal separator in the formatted value; any additional period characters are ignored. The actual character used as the decimal separator is determined by the Language property. For example, the French decimal point is actually a comma (,).	Value=12.34 Format=###.## Language= "French" Output=12,3
,	Thousand separator and number scaling	The first occurrence of a comma (,) character when used in conjunction with 0 and # placeholders inserts thousand separators between each group of three digits to the left of the decimal separator. The actual character used as the decimal separator is determined by the Language property.	Value=10000000.5 Format=#,###,. Output=10,000
%	Percentage placeholder	Multiply Value by 100 and insert the % sign. The percent character used is dependent on the current Language.	Value=10.5 Format=###% Output=1050
E0 E±0 e0 e±0	Scientific notation	Format using scientific notation. The number of 0s determines the minimum number of digits to output for the exponent. The E+ and e+ formats indicate that a sign character (plus or minus) should always precede the exponent. The E, E-, e, or e- formats indicate that a sign character should only precede negative exponents.	Value=12000 Format=0.###E+000 Output=12E+004
'ABC' "ABC"	Literal string	Characters enclosed in single or double quotes are copied to the result string literally, and do not affect formatting.	Value=12 Format="AB"00.00 Output=AB12.00
;	Section separator	The semicolon (;) character is used to apply separate formatting for positive, negative, and 0 numbers in the format string. If there are two sections and the result is 0, it is formatted per the first section. If the second section is skipped, such as ##;;0, then 0 is formatted according to the third section.	Value=-123 Format=##;(##) Output=(123)

TABLE 15.4 Continued

Format Specifier	Name	Description	Example

`\c`	Escape character	Where c is any character, the escape character displays the next character as a literal. In this context, the escape character cannot be used to create an escape sequence (such as `\n` for newline).	`Value=-123`
			`Format= \z0000`
			`Output=-z0123`

`Other`	All other characters	All other characters are copied to the result string as literals in the position they appear.	

Numbers are rounded to as many decimal places as there are digit placeholders to the right of the decimal point. If the format string does not contain a decimal point, the number is rounded to the nearest integer. If the number has more digits than there are digit placeholders to the left of the decimal point, the extra digits are copied to the result string immediately before the first digit placeholder.

You can find additional information about custom numeric format strings in the .NET Framework Developer's Guide at http://msdn.microsoft.com/library/default.asp?url=/library/en-us/cpguide/html/cpconcustomnumericformatstrings.asp

Standard Date/Time Format Strings

A standard date/time format string consists of a single character format specifier character from Table 15.5.

TABLE 15.5 Standard Date/Time Format Strings

Format Specifier	Name/Note	Output of `Value= CDate("1/2/2003 23:59:11.15")`
`d`	Short date pattern.	`02/01/2003`
`D`	Long date pattern.	`02 January 2003`
`t`	Short time pattern.	`23:59`
`T`	Long time pattern.	`23:59:11`
`f`	Full date/time pattern (short time).	`02 January 2003 23:59`
`F`	Full date/time pattern (long time).	`02 January 2003 23:59:11`
`g`	General date/time pattern (short time).	`02/01/2003 23:59`
`G`	General date/time pattern (long time).	`02/01/2003 23:59:11`
`M` or `m`	Month day pattern.	`02 January`

TABLE 15.5 Continued

Format Specifier	Name/Note	Output of Value= CDate("1/2/2003 23:59:11.15")
R or r	The RFC 1123 pattern is the same as the custom pattern ddd, dd MMM yyyy HH:mm:ss G\MT.	Thu, 02 Jan 2003 23:59:11 GMT
s	Sortable date/time pattern; conforms to ISO 8601 and is the same as the custom pattern yyyy-MM-ddTHH:mm:ss.	2003-01-02T23:59:11
u	Universal storable date/time pattern; the same as the custom pattern yyyy-MM-dd HH:mm:ssZ. Does not do time zone conversion.	2003-01-02 23:59:11Z
U	Universal sortable date/time pattern; displays universal, rather than local time.	02 January 2003 05:59:11
Y or y	Year month pattern	January 2003
Any other single character	Unknown specifier. SSRS will use the default.	02/01/2003 23:59:11

You can find additional information about standard date/time format strings in the .NET Framework Developer's Guide at http://msdn.microsoft.com/library/default.asp?url=/library/en-us/cpguide/html/cpconstandarddatetimeformatstrings.asp.

Custom Date/Time Formatting

Table 15.6 describes the custom format specifiers and shows examples of output. Note how the percent sign (%) converts standard to custom specifiers. For example, d specifies short date pattern, but %d specifies day of the month. When % is used with a character not reserved for custom formatting, the character displayed is literal. For example, a format string %n results in the output n.

TABLE 15.6 Custom Date/Time Formatting

Format Specifier	Description	Output of Value= CDate("1/2/2003 23:59:11.15")
%d	Displays the current day of the month, measured as a number between 1 and 31, inclusive. Single digit only (1–9) is displayed as a single digit.	2

TABLE 15.6 Continued

Format Specifier	Description	Output of Value= CDate("1/2/2003 23:59:11.15")
dd	Displays the current day of the month, measured as a number between 1 and 31, inclusive. Single digit only (1–9) is prefixed with a preceding 0 (01–09).	02
ddd	Displays the abbreviated name of the day specified.	Thu
dddd (plus any number of additional d characters)	Displays the full name of the day specified.	Thursday
f to fffffff	Displays fractions of seconds represented in one to seven digits.	1 to 1500000
g or gg (or any number of additional g characters)	Displays the era (A.D., for example).	A.D.
%h	Displays the hour for the specified value in 12-hour format (undistinguished A.M./P.M., range 1–12). No rounding occurs; that is, a value of 4:45 returns 4.	11
hh (plus any number of additional h characters)	Same as above, but a single-digit hour (1–9) is preceded with 0 (01–09).	11
%H	Displays the hour for the specified value in 24-hour format (the range 0–23). The hour represents whole hours passed since midnight (displayed as 0). If the hour is a single digit (0–9), it is displayed as a single digit.	23
HH (plus any number of additional H characters)	Same as above, but a single-digit hour (1–9) is preceded with 0 (01–09).	23
%m	Displays the minute for the specified value in the range 0 to 59. The minute represents whole minutes passed since the last hour. If the minute is a single digit (0–9), it is displayed as a single digit.	59
mm (plus any number of additional m characters)	Same as above. A single-digit minute (0–9) is formatted with a preceding 0 (01–09).	59
%M	Displays the month, measured as a number between 1 and 12, inclusive. If the month is a single digit (1–9), it is displayed as a single digit.	1

TABLE 15.6 Continued

Format Specifier	Description	Output of Value= CDate("1/2/2003 23:59:11.15")
MM	Same as above. A single-digit month (1–9) is formatted with a preceding 0 (01–09).	01
MMM	Displays the abbreviated name of the month for the specified value.	Jan
MMMM	Displays the full name of the month for the specified value.	January
%s	Displays the seconds for the specified value in the range 0-59. The second represents whole seconds passed since the last minute. If the second is a single digit (0-9), it is displayed as a single digit only.	11
ss (plus any number of additional s characters)	Same as above. A single-digit second (0–9) is formatted with a preceding 0 (01–09).	11
%t	Displays the first character of the A.M./P.M. designator for the specified value.	P
tt (plus any number of additional t characters)	Displays the A.M./P.M. designator for the specified value.	PM
%y	Displays the year for the specified value as a maximum two-digit number. The first two digits of the year are omitted. If the year is a single digit (1–9), it is displayed as a single digit.	3
yy	Same as above. A single-digit year (1–9) is formatted with a preceding 0 (01–09).	03
yyyy	Displays the year for the specified value, including the century. If the year is represented with fewer than four digits, 0s are added to the left to display four digits.	2003
%z	Displays the time zone offset for the system's current time zone in whole hours only. The offset is always displayed with a leading sign, which indicates hours ahead of Greenwich mean time (+) or behind Greenwich mean time (-). The range of values is –12 to +13. Value is affected by daylight savings time.	-6 Note: -6 offset is for central standard time.
zz	Same as above. A single digit is formatted with a preceding 0 (00–09).	-06

15

TABLE 15.6 Continued

Format Specifier	Description	Output of Value= CDate("1/2/2003 23:59:11.15")
zzz (plus any number of additional z characters)	Same as above, but displays hours and minutes. The range of values is -12:00 to +13:00. Single-digit offset (0–9) is formatted with a preceding 0 (00–09).	-06:00
:	Displays the time separator.	
/	Displays the date separator.	
" " or ' '	Displays the literal value of a string enclosed.	
\	Displays the next character as a literal. Cannot be used to create an escape sequence.	

You can find additional information about custom date/time format strings in the .NET Framework Developer's Guide at http://msdn.microsoft.com/library/default.asp?url=/library/en-us/cpguide/html/cpconcustomdatetimeformatstrings.asp.

Creating Alternating Colors for the Lines on a Report

To alternate color of the lines in the table, you can use the function `RowNumber`.

To generate alternating colors for a table's Detail row, you can set the `BackgroundColor` property of all columns and the table's Detail row to the expression `=IIF((RowNumber("MyTable") Mod 2) = 0, "LightGrey", "White")`.

TABLE 15.7 Alternating Table Row Colors

Row Number ("MyTable")	Product Name
1	Adjustable Race
2	All-Purpose Bike Stand
3	AWC Logo Cap

What if alternating colors need to be set for the group header (or footer)? In this case, you can use the `RunningValue()` function to return a row number of a group's header.

If you have a table with a single group that uses `=Fields!ProductID.Value` as a group expression and you display only the group's header in the result, you can set the `BackgroundColor` property for all columns in the group's header equal to the expression

`=IIf(RunningValue(Fields!Name.Value, CountDistinct, Nothing) Mod 2=0,"Gainsboro", "White")` to generate alternating colors, similar to Table 15.8.

TABLE 15.8 Design of Alternating Colors for the Group Header

TH->[1]	Row Number (RunningValue)	Product Name	Items Sold
G1->[2]	=RunningValue(Fields!Name.Value, CountDistinct, Nothing)	=Fields!Name.Value	=RowNumber("G1")

[1]TH : *Table header row*

[2]G1: *Header of a single table group (named* G1*) with the group expression* =Fields!Name.Value

The resulting output is presented in Table 15.9. Note the number of items displayed in the Items Sold column. Although each group contains more than one hundred rows, each group's header is displayed only once, and thus Items Sold displays an aggregate number of rows in a group.

TABLE 15.9 Presentation of Alternating Colors for the Group Header/Footer

Row Number (RunningValue)	Product Name	Items Sold
1	Adjustable Race	1
2	All-Purpose Bike Stand	249
3	AWC Logo Cap	3,382

Similarly to a single group, to display alternating colors when there is more than one table group, you can use the `RunningValue()` function on the combination of all group expressions. For example if we also want to break down the number of items sold by product color, we can use an expression such as the following:

```
=IIf(RunningValue(CStr(Fields!ProductID.Value) & CStr(Fields!ColorID.Value),
CountDistinct, Nothing) Mod 2=0,"Gainsboro", "White")
```

The `RunningValue()` in this case will generate two distinct running values for `Adjustable Race Red` and `Adjustable Race Blue` combinations. You may have noticed we used product name concatenated with color in our explanation, but the actual formula above uses IDs. The benefit of using IDs is better performance, because a combination of IDs produces a shorter string, and therefore takes less time to process.

Paging Report (Improved in 2008)

Pagination support differs for each of the rendering extensions. As a result you would see a different visual pagination outcome, depending on the extension you use to render a report. For example, PDF and Image formats are page oriented and enable you to precisely set page properties. HTML, Word, and Microsoft Excel are not page oriented. CSV and XML do not support pagination at all and ignore pagination properties.

NOTE

If you see that a report does not render across pages as you intended, check page settings to ensure that everything can fit on a page, considering page size, margins, report body size, and the number of columns.

SSRS provides several properties to support pagination: `PageBreakAtEnd`, `PageBreakAtStart`, `PageHeight`, `PageWidth`, `InteractiveHeight`, `InteractiveWidth`, `KeepTogether` (New in 2008), `KeepWithGroup` (New in 2008), `PageBreak` (New in 2008), `PageSectionType` (New in 2008), and `HideIfNoRows` (New in 2008).

`PageSectionType` is a parent type of the `PageHeader` and `PageFooter` elements. `PageSectionType` is in the RDL's schema, but you will not find it in your report's RDL; instead, you would see `PageHeader` and `PageFooter` in the report's RDL.

PageHeight and PageWidth: Physical Page Sizing

These properties are used to control physical page (paper) sizing for PDF- and Image-rendering extensions. PDF- and Image-rendering extensions insert page breaks based on the value of those properties. These properties accept strings in the format `{FloatingNumber}.{unit designator}`, where a unit designator is a size measurement and could be `in`, `mm`, `cm`, `pt`, or `pc`.

A rendering extension will insert a hard page break based on the values specified by `PageHeight` and `PageWidth`. Keep in mind that rendering extensions do not automatically adjust paper size based on a size of a report's body when the report's body grows beyond page boundaries.

`PageHeight` and `PageWidth` do not allow expressions. In cases where you have to pass the size of a page to a rendering extension, you pass device information settings (or parameters to a rendering extension). For example, to pass a page size to Image-rendering extensions, you use the following URL command to change page size to 11x9 inches:

```
http://servername/reportserver?/SampleReports/MyReport&rs:Command=Render&
rs:Format=IMAGE&rc:OutputFormat=JPEG&rc:PageHeight=11in&rc:PageWidth=9in
```

When SSRS receives this URL command, it assembles the `DeviceInfo` XML element and passes it to the Image-rendering extension.

InteractiveHeight and InteractiveWidth

These properties dictate logical page sizing for the HTML-, Word-, and Excel-rendering extensions.

The HTML rendering extension accepts interactive page size, creates page breaks, and allows navigating through pages, using a toolbar.

Word- and Excel-rendering extensions insert "soft" page breaks into the resulting documents. When you render a spreadsheet and want to check the location of the page breaks, you can display page breaks in Excel by selecting View, Page Break Preview.

HTML, Word, and Excel pages are based on approximate page size and provide less-precise page breaks than page-oriented formats (IMAGE and PDF). `InteractiveHeight` and `InteractiveWidth` accept strings in the format `{FloatingNumber}.{unit designator}`, where a unit designator is a size measurement and could be `in`, `mm`, `cm`, `pt`, or `pc`.

You can disable soft page breaks by setting `InteractiveHeight` to `0`; however, if the report contains a large amount of data, this might negatively impact perceived performance. When `InteractiveHeight = 0`, the user can't see a report until all rendering completes. When `InteractiveHeight` is not zero, a user can access each page after the page's rendering completes.

PageBreak (New in 2008)

The `PageBreak` property replaces the `pageBreakAtEnd` and `PageBreakAtStart` properties from the previous version of SSRS. The `PageBreak` property is available for Rectangle, data regions (Tablix, Chart, Gauge), or a group within a data region. `PageBreak` can have the following values:

- **`Start`**: Insert a page break before.
- **`End`**: Insert a page break after.
- **`StartAndEnd`**: Insert a page break before and after.
- **`Between`**: Insert a page break between instances of a group. A group expression has the same value for all members of an instance.

All values, except `Between`, are allowed for Tablix, Gauge, Chart, and Rectangle. `Between` is allowed for a group only.

NOTE

SSRS ignores page breaks on column groups.

You can set page breaks using the `Group.PageBreak` property on the Properties window or using the Group Properties dialog.

To access the Group Properties dialog, right-click a group in the Row Groups pane and select Group Properties from the context menu. Use the Page Breaks tab to change pagination properties. You can set the `Between` value from this tab.

To use the Properties window, click a group in the Row Groups pane and find the `pageBreak` property under the parent property `Group`.

To dynamically adjust the number of rows on a page, a report developer can pass a report parameter and add the following group expression:

```
=System.Math.Floor(RowNumber(Nothing)/(Parameters!RowsPerPage.Value))
```

For physical page formatting, the `PageBreak` property adds page breaks in addition to breaks controlled by `PageHeight` and `PageWidth`. For example, when a report is rendered to Excel, `PageBreak` breaks down the report to individual sheets. If `PageBreak` is supplied for HTML rendering, `InteractiveHeight` and `InteractiveWeight` are ignored.

Different renderers include different amounts of data on a rendered report. For example, if a report developer used the toggle action on a report, then the PDF renderer does not include the collapsed section of the report.

Unlike PDF renderer, Excel renderer includes all sections (including collapsed ones) and provides an interface similar to the toggle action of an interactive report.

HTML pagination is based on visibility settings for items on a report. For example, if a part of a report is collapsed, it will be included on a single HTML page in a collapsed state, but only if it fits the page. This is true, even though expanding the collapsed section of a report will take the report's size outside of the intended page size.

Pagination might improve perceived performance of a report; the first page will be rendered and presented to a user while SSRS continues rendering the remaining pages.

To access a particular page of a report, you add the following to a URL command: `&rc:Section={PageNumber}`.

`Columns` Property: A Way to Multicolumn Reports

To add multiple columns to pages of your report, you leverage the `Columns` property of a report. When you add multiple columns to a report, SSRS fills all columns on a page before starting a new page.

This functionality is available only for page-oriented formats (PDF and Image). If you render a multicolumn report in HTML, you will see only a single column.

NOTE

If you see that a report does not render across columns as you intended, check page settings to ensure that everything can fit on a page, considering page size, margins, report body size, and the number of columns. If you do not have a proper fit, you may miss columns or you may have orphan columns.

To access the `Columns` property, either select Report in the Properties window (lower-right corner of BIDS) or click an area surrounding the report's body. Enter the number of columns that you want to have and spacing between. Figure 15.3 shows a multicolumn report design example.

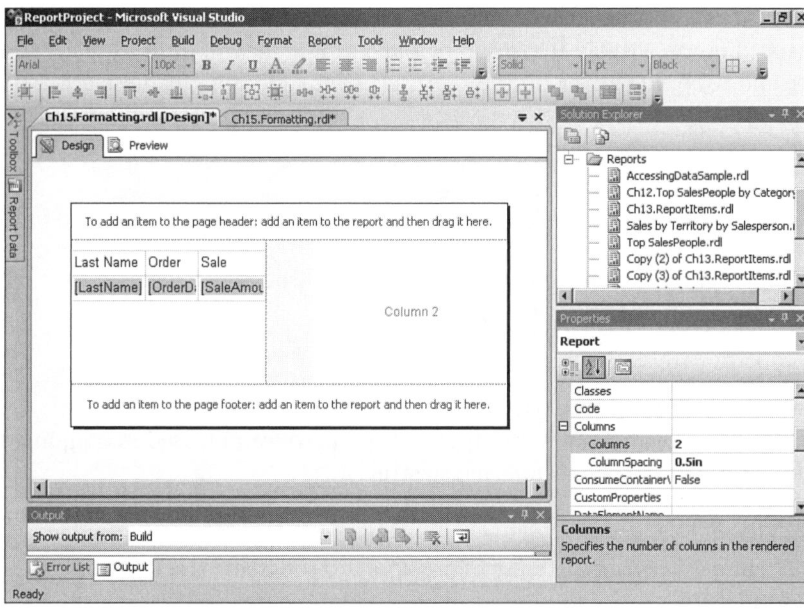

FIGURE 15.3 Multicolumn report design.

Advanced Group Properties: `RepeatOnNewPage`, `KeepTogether` (New in 2008), `KeepWithGroup` (New in 2008), and `HideIfNoRows` (New in 2008)

These properties are accessible in the Advanced mode of the grouping pane and enable you to do the following:

- **`RepeatOnNewPage`**: Repeat the group's row header on every page where the group has at least one row.
- **`KeepTogether`**: Force SSRS to attempt keeping the entire group together on a page, instead of inserting a page break between. Not supported for column groups.
- **`KeepWithGroup`**: Help to keep the group's header and footer together on the same page, instead of orphaning to another page. The property can have one of the following values:
    - **`Before`**: Keep this static member (mostly footer) with the previous group in a grouping pane. Note gray static members in the grouping pane.
    - **`After`**: Keep this static member (mostly header) with the previous group in a grouping pane.

- **None**: Let SSRS decide whether to use `Before` or `After`.
- **HideIfNoRows**: Hide a static element of a group when the group has no data. This property overrides other `Visibility` properties.

To access the Advanced mode, display the grouping pane (if not shown, in BIDS select Report, Grouping), and using the arrow on the right side of the grouping pane select Advanced Mode, and then select Tablix where you want to set those properties.

Summary

SSRS supports a comprehensive set of formatting capabilities through the report item's properties, which control output appearance.

Some of the key properties are as follows:

- **BackgroundColor**: Controls the background color of the item. When a report requires alternating colors for rows of output, this property can be used in conjunction with functions `RowNumber()` and `RunningValue`.
- **Color**: Controls the color of the text.
- **Format**: .NET Framework formatting string to apply to the item. The following are examples of format strings:
    - `###.##` formats a value of `012.30` to the output `12.3`.
    - `(###)###-####` formats a value of `1234567890` to the output `(123)456-7890`, which is typical presentation of a phone number.
    - `C` formats a value of `1234.56` to a typical presentation of currency `$1,234.56`.
    - `yyyy-MM-dd HH:mm` formats `11:59PM` on `1/2/2006` to `2003-01-02 23:59`.
- **Language**: Controls locale formatting. For example, when set to `English (United Kingdom)`, the currency sign in formatting changes from `$` to `£`.
- **PageBreak**, **KeepTogether**, and **KeepWithGroup**: Control pagination before and after an item.
- **PageHeight** and **PageWidth**: Control physical page sizing for PDF- and Image-rendering extensions.
- **RepeatOnNewPage** and **HideIfNoRows**: Control the behavior of a group's header (footer) and visibility of a group when it has no rows.
- **InteractiveHeight** and **InteractiveWidth**: Control logical page sizing by the HTML-, Word-, and Excel-rendering extensions.

The following chapter discusses functionality that SSRS provides to simplify navigation in large reports and within the hierarchy of reports.

CHAPTER 16

Report Navigation

IN THIS CHAPTER

- `Hyperlink` (Go to URL) Navigation
- `BookmarkLink` (Go to Bookmark) Navigation
- `Drillthrough` (Go to Report) Navigation
- Document Map
- Hide and Toggle Items
- Practical Application of Action Items

One of the main uses for navigation functionality is to simplify navigation of large reports and navigation of report hierarchies. To achieve this, report developers can add hyperlink actions (or simply actions) to a report. Reporting Services supports three types of actions:

- **`Drillthrough` (Go to Report):** Go to other reports. This action also provides an opportunity to provide parameters for the target report and the ability to jump to the same report with different parameters. This action is denoted with the `<Drillthrough>` element in a report's Report Definition Language (RDL).
- **`BookmarkLink` (Go to Bookmark):** Jump to other areas (bookmarked) within the report. This action is denoted with the `<BookmarkLink>` element in a report's RDL.
- **`Hyperlink` (Go to URL):** Jump to web pages and other `HREF` constructs, such as mail and news. This action is denoted with the `<Hyperlink>` element in a report's RDL.

Expressions can be used as a value for any action. Report developers can add an action from either the Item Properties (for example, Text Box Properties for a text box) dialog box or from the Properties window.

To open the Properties dialog, right-click a report item, select <Item Name> Properties from the shortcut menu, and then click the Action tab and select one of the actions: Go to Report, Go to Bookmark, or Go to URL.

Alternatively, you can modify the Action property from Properties window by just clicking the ellipsis to the right of the Action property (see Figure 16.1).

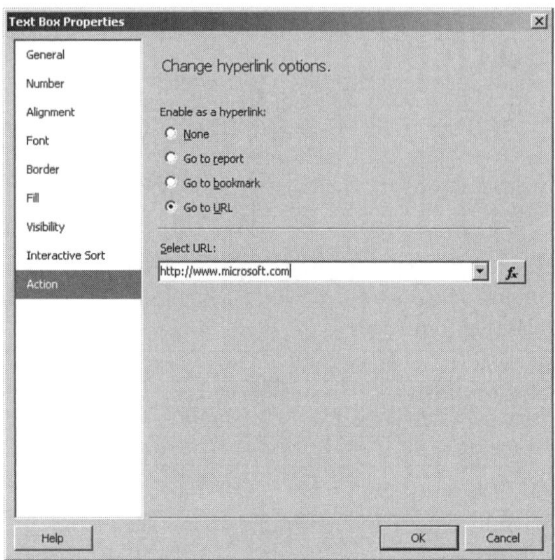

FIGURE 16.1 Action tab.

You can add actions to a Textbox, Image, Gauge, or Chart data series. Because a Tablix can contain a Textbox, Image, Gauge, or Chart, those, in turn, can provide actionable items within a Tablix.

Any Reporting Services item can have Bookmark and Document Map labels associated with it. Those labels assist in navigation by providing "landing marks" for navigation destinations. To illustrate this, imagine that you have a bookmark Bookmark10 located on page 10 of your report and a table of contents (TOC) on page one of your report. One of the TOC's lines contains the BookmarkLink action involving Bookmark10. If you click this action in the TOC, the focus of the view will switch to page 10. You can set Bookmark and Document Map via like-named properties in the Properties window.

TIP

Highlight an actionable item so that it is intuitive to a user that the item can be clicked. Blue in color, underlined text items usually provide good highlights.

Hyperlink (Go to URL) Navigation

When a report developer adds the Hyperlink action, SSRS generates HREF to create a navigable HTML link. For example, when you enter http://www.microsoft.com into a Go to URL text box and set the value of Textbox.Value equal to Visit Microsoft, the following is the link generated by SSRS when it renders the report to HTML format:

```
<a href="http://www.microsoft.com/" style="text-decoration:none;color:Black"
TARGET="_top">Visit Microsft</a>
```

Reporting Services allows navigation using other constructs valid for the `HREF` tag. For example, `javascript:history.back()` enables you to emulate a browser's Back button. This particular construct relies on Java support by the browser (Netscape 2 or later and Internet Explorer 3 or later) and enabled JavaScript. Other valid constructs are

- `mailto:support@adventureworks.com`, which allows creating a link that launches an email editor and places support@adventureworks.com on the To line
- `ftp://www.microsoft.com` to launch an FTP download
- `news:www.microsoft.com` to get to a newsreader

NOTE

Not all `HREF` constructs function in Preview mode. For example, `javascript:history.back()` will not deliver the action in Preview mode; also, this construct will function after the report is deployed to a Report Server.

To create a `Hyperlink` (Go to URL) action, enter a valid (such as http://www.microsoft.com or other described previously) `HREF` construct in the Go to URL action field. Figure 16.1 shows the Action property page that allows you to input the Go to URL action. `Action` has the following corresponding RDL:

```
<Action>
  <Hyperlink>http://www.microsoft.com</Hyperlink>
</Action>
```

Or

```
<Action>
  <Hyperlink>={Expression}</Hyperlink>
</Action>
```

In the preceding code fragment, an `{Expression}` is any expression that evaluates to a valid `HREF` construct as described previously, such as http://www.microsoft.com.

BookmarkLink (Go to Bookmark) Navigation

`BookmarkLink` (Go to Bookmark) simplifies navigation for large reports. This action allows navigation to a bookmarked line or page of the report. Keep in mind that you can associate multiple actions with a single bookmark link.

To create a `BookmarkLink` navigation, the first step is to set a bookmark. A bookmark can be set for any report item using the following:

- **Properties window:** The Properties window is normally docked in the lower-right corner of Report Designer. If you do not see this window, press F4 or choose Properties Window from the View menu.
- **Navigation tab of an item's Properties dialog box:** The Properties dialog box can be accessed by right-clicking a report item and selecting *Item* Properties from the shortcut menu, where *Item* is the name of an item, such as Text Box. The Action tab of an item's Properties dialog box is shown in Figure 16.1.

After `Bookmark` is set, Report Designer adds the following RDL:

```
<Bookmark>
  ={Expression}
</Bookmark>
```

The next step is to create a `BookmarkLink` action, which performs the navigation to the bookmark set in the previous step. The `BookmarkLink` action can be created for Textbox, Image, Gauge, and Chart data series. To create a `BookmarkLink` action, open the Action tab of an item's Properties dialog box, select **Go to Bookmark**, and enter a bookmark's expression.

After the `BookmarkLink` action is set, Report Designer adds the following RDL:

```
<Action>
  <BookmarkLink>
    ={Expression}
  </BookmarkLink>
</Action>
```

Drillthrough (Go to Report) Navigation

This type of action is commonly used when there is a need to have master (parent) and detail (child) reports. An action, which takes users to a detail report, is created on the master report.

To create a `Drillthrough` navigation (action), you need to set the Go to Report expression on the Action tab of the item's Properties dialog box. The Go to Report expression must evaluate to a name of a report.

You can also specify parameters to pass to a report by clicking the Add button under the Use This Parameters to Run the Report section (which becomes visible once you select Go to Report action on the Action tab). In the Parameters dialog box, you can enter a constant name of a parameter and an expression that will assign a value to the parameter.

The following is an example of the RDL for the `Drillthrough` action:

```
<Action>
  <Drillthrough>
    <ReportName>Product Detail</ReportName>
    <Parameters>
      <Parameter Name="ProductNumber">
        <Value>=Fields!Name.Value</Value>
      </Parameter>
    </Parameters>
  </Drillthrough>
</Action>
```

NOTE

The Back to Parent Report button on the Report Viewer's toolbar provides a convenient way to navigate back to a parent. This button is especially handy in Preview mode when a Back browser button is not available.

Document Map

Much like bookmarks, the document map is designed to simplify navigation for large reports. A document map is intended for interactive (HTML rendering) report viewing and is displayed as a side panel on a report.

PDF, Word, and Excel rendering extensions have a different way of articulating a document map. Excel rendering extension creates a separate worksheet with the name Document Map, which provides links to a worksheet with the report's data. PDF displays the document map in the Bookmarks navigation tab.

Document map labels are set similarly to bookmarks as they relate to report items. To create a document map for a report, you would fill the `DocumentMapLabel` property in the Properties window for each report item them that you would like to include on the map.

When a report has at least one document map label, Reporting Services automatically generates a document map and renders a treelike structure containing navigational items. SSRS builds a document map entry when it sees the following RDL:

```
<Label>={Expression}</Label>
```

Document map labels from report items are displayed on the same level (next after the root level) and ordered in the order of the report item's appearance on a report. The order is based first on the position of the top side (vertical ordering) of a report item and then on the position of the left side (horizontal ordering) of the report item.

The document map also supports a hierarchical display of labels. SSRS creates a hierarchical view on a document map when you set Document Map and Recursive Parent expressions using the Advanced tab of the Group Properties dialog box. PDF shows labels of a document map in the Bookmarks navigation panel. (In Adobe Reader 9.0, the panel is accessible from View, Navigation Panels, Bookmarks menu.) Note that early versions of the Adobe Reader did not support hierarchical bookmarks.

The document map has the same name as the name of the report. This name is used for the root node of a document map. There are no options that allow changing the name of a document map and only one document map is allowed per report.

Rendering of a document map by the Word rendering extension is a bit trickier and you have to perform a couple of additional steps. The steps are necessary because the Word rendering extension renders the document map as table entry fields. You can see table entry fields as `{TC "Text" [switches]}` if you show hidden fields (you can do this by using Ctrl-* shortcut) while viewing a Word document. To create a table of contents (TOC) from table entry fields, you would perform an "insert table of contents" action and set appropriate options. In Word 2007, you select the References tab on the Ribbon, click the Table of Contents button, and select Insert Table of Contents from the drop-down list. At this point, a Table of Contents dialog opens. Click the Options button, and in the Table of Contents Options dialog box unselect everything except the Table Entry Fields check box. Click OK until the TOC is inserted into the exported document.

Hide and Toggle Items

Hiding and toggling functionality supports interactive visibility for sections of a report and enables you to dynamically expand portions (of a report) that you want to see. This is yet another option to simplify navigation. Hide and toggle functionality can be used, for example, to implement master/detail functionality, category/subcategory functionality, or to simply shorten a large report.

To implement this functionality, you would leverage several properties:

- **`InitialToggleState`**: The `InitialToggleState` property indicates an image that is displayed for a toggle item: collapsed, expanded, or expression. Normally, the toggle control is a plus or minus symbol, which indicates an expanded or collapsed state, respectively. The `InitialToggleState` property only defines a picture of a state image, but does not change the visibility of an item. If not specified, the default toggle state is `False` (or collapsed). If a report developer clears the `InitialToggleState` property, the state reverts back to `False`.
- **`ToggleItem`**: A name of report item that will show or hide this report item.
- **`Hidden`**: Indicates an initial visibility of a report item.

NOTE

Note that the toggle state is not available for groups. It is available only for individual items.

BIDS adds the following RDL for the `InitialToggleState`:

```
<ToggleImage>
    <InitialState>true</InitialState>
</ToggleImage>
```

Reporting Services adds the following RDL for `ToggleItem` and `Hidden`. (When the item is visible, the `<Hidden>` tag is not included.)

```
<Visibility>
  <ToggleItem>{ToggleItem}</ToggleItem>
  <Hidden>={Expression}or {true}</Hidden>
</Visibility>
```

Practical Application of Action Items

For illustrative purposes, imagine that the Adventure Works Internet sales department wants to create an interactive product catalog. The initial screen of a report should not be larger than a single page. A report must provide effective navigation through the products (items in the catalog). A user of the catalog must be able to navigate through the product category and subcategory hierarchies.

Implementation

First, using any method described in earlier chapters, let's create a new report (Navigation) and a data set (you can name the data set **ProductCategories**) with the following query using the **AdventureWorks** data source:

```
SELECT Production.ProductCategory.Name  AS CategoryName,
       Production.ProductSubcategory.Name AS SubCategoryName,
       Production.Product.Name AS ProductName,
       Production.ProductPhoto.ThumbNailPhoto,
       Production.Product.ProductNumber
FROM
Production.ProductCategory
INNER JOIN
Production.ProductSubcategory ON Production.ProductCategory.ProductCategoryID =
Production.ProductSubcategory.ProductCategoryID
INNER JOIN Production.Product ON Production.ProductSubcategory.
ProductSubcategoryID = Production.Product.ProductSubcategoryID
INNER JOIN
Production.ProductProductPhoto ON Production.Product.ProductID =
Production.ProductProductPhoto.ProductID
INNER JOIN
Production.ProductPhoto ON Production.ProductProductPhoto.ProductPhotoID =
Production.ProductPhoto.ProductPhotoID
```

Create a report layout outline, as shown in Figure 16.2. This report uses Matrix (remember that Matrix is a template for Tablix) to provide category navigation.

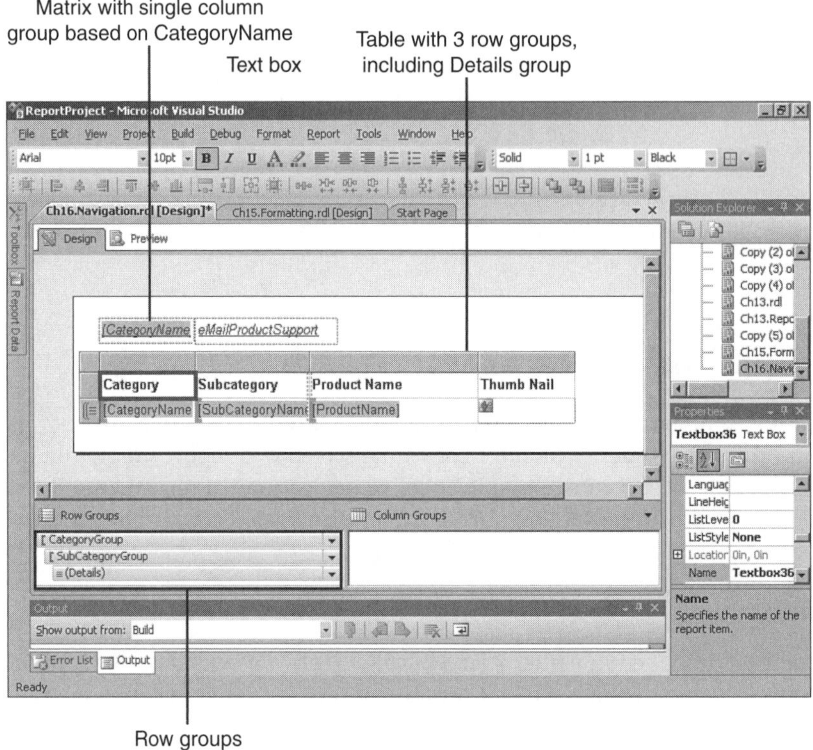

FIGURE 16.2 Navigation report Design view.

To show pictures from the database, add an Image report item from the toolbox to the last column of the Details row in the table.

To show pictures from a database, right-click the cell with an image in it and select Image Properties from the context menu. Set Select the Image Source to Database. Set Use This Field to [ThumbNailPhoto] and set Use This MIME Type to image/jpeg.

Right-click the Matrix's cell with `CategoryName` value in it and select Text Box Properties from the context menu. On the Action tab (see Figure 16.3), select Go to Bookmark and select [CategoryName] from the drop-down list. This adds the following expression to the Select Bookmark action:

```
=Fields!CategoryName.Value
```

This bookmark will allow users to access an appropriate category name on a report. Apply formatting so that a user can tell that this is a clickable item. For example, in the Text Box Properties dialog box (under the Font tab), select Italic, Blue, Underline font.

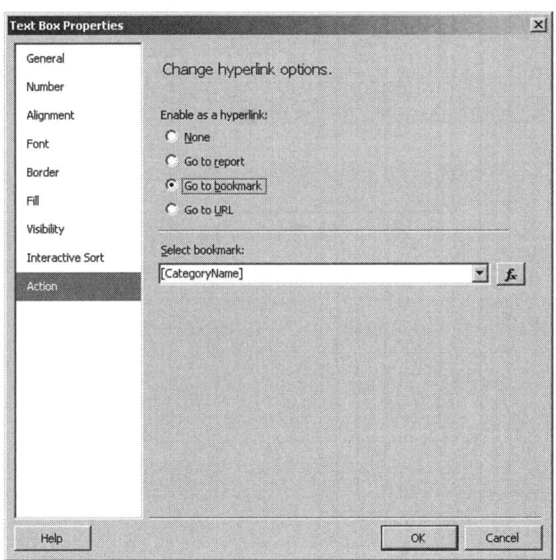

FIGURE 16.3 Go to Bookmark action.

Right-click the text box with eMail Product Support in it and view the Text Box Properties dialog box. On the Action tab, enter the following expression to the Go to URL action (see Figure 16.4):


```
mailto:support@adventureworks.com
```

This action starts the user's email application and places support@adventureworks.com in the To line.

Click the table and then right-click SubcategoryGroup (first parent of the Details group) in the grouping pane. Select Group Properties from the context menu and go to the Advanced tab.

Select [CategoryName] from the Recursive Parent drop-down list or enter the following expression as the recursive parent:

```
=Fields!CategoryName.Value
```

Select [SubCategoryName] from the Document Map drop-down list or enter the following expression in the document map:

```
=Fields!SubCategoryName.Value
```

Note that we use [CategoryName] as the grouping expression for CategoryGroup and also as a document map for the outer (parent) group (see Figure 16.5). Setting the recursive parent and document map as we have done creates a hierarchy in a document map.

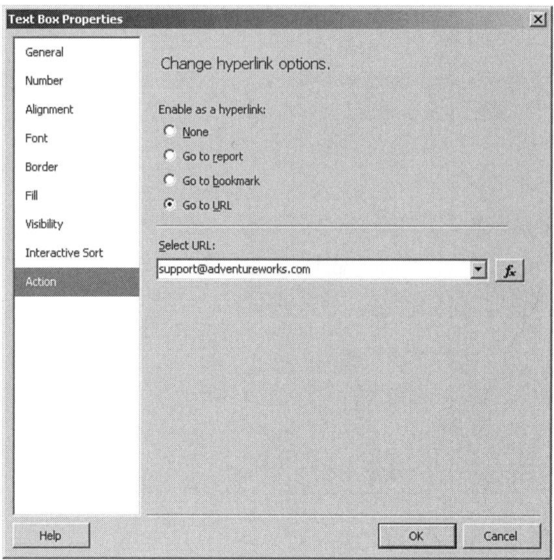

FIGURE 16.4 Go to URL action.

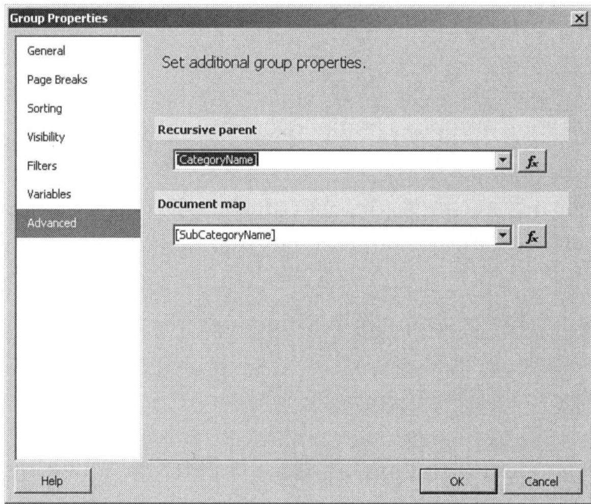

FIGURE 16.5 Document map and its hierarchy.

Click the text box that contains the [SubCategoryName] expression and a group indicator. Note that because it was a part of the first group that we created it has the name Group1. Let's set its name to **`SubCategoryGroupTxt`**.

Similarly, rename the text box with [CategoryName] to **`CategoryNameTxt`**.

In the grouping pane, right-click the Details group, select Group Properties from the context menu, and go to the Visibility tab. Set the When the Report Is Initially Run option (initial visibility) to Hide. Check the Display Can Be Toggled by This Report Item check box, and select SubCategoryGroupTxt from the drop-down list. Visibility information should look similar to Figure 16.6.

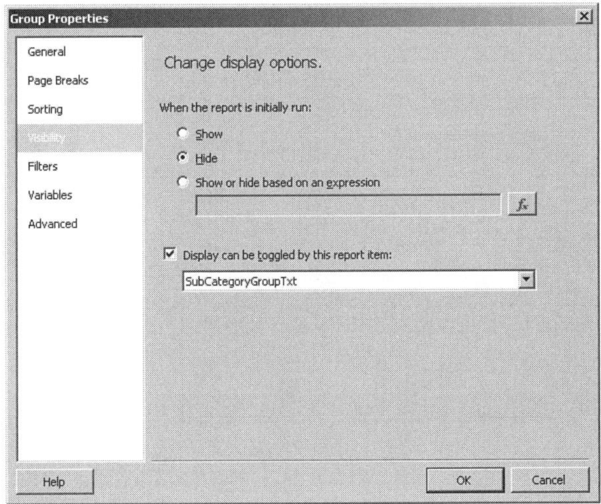

FIGURE 16.6 Setting item visibility.

For a clean display, set the `Hidden` property (from the Properties window) to `True` and set the `ToggleItem` property to `SubCategoryGroupTxt` for detail cells in the Product Name and Thumb Nail Photo columns.

Add formatting to make the display more visually appealing.

Figure 16.7 shows the final product.

NOTE

A report can use a hidden parameter to prevent a casual user from viewing some information, such as `HideCost` = `True`. However, when you create a `Drillthrough` action, you can set the `HideCost` parameter to `False` and thus reveal cost information.

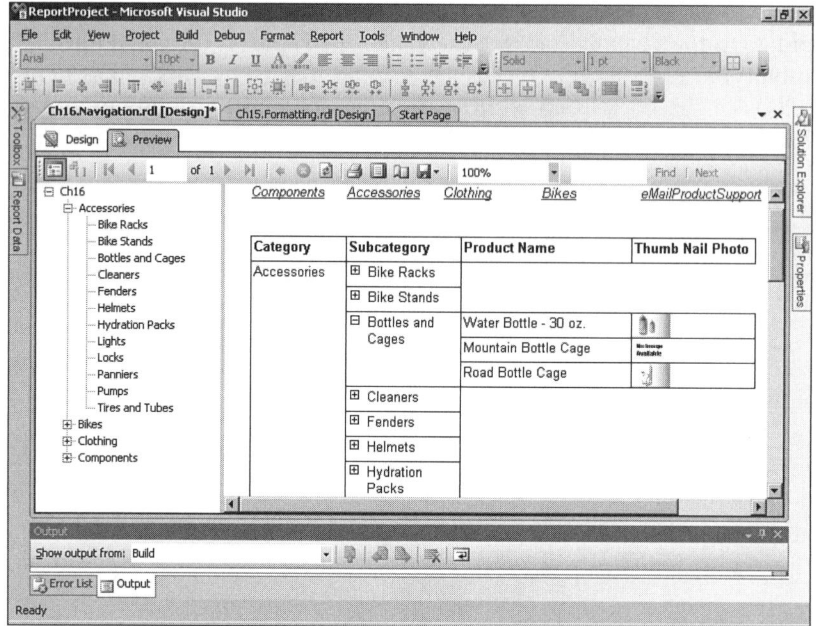

FIGURE 16.7 Sample report with navigation.

Summary

Actions, document maps, and bookmarks simplify navigation of complex reports, report hierarchies, and more. SSRS supports three types of actions: `Drillthrough` (or Go to Report), `BookmarkLink` (or Go to Bookmark), and `Hyperlink` (or Go to URL; general web navigation).

Actions can be added to a Textbox, Image, Gauge, or Chart data series. Because a Tablix can contain a Textbox, Image, Gauge, or Chart, those, in turn, can provide actionable items within Tablix.

Any Reporting Services item can have Bookmark and Document Map labels associated with it. Those labels assist in navigation by providing "landing marks" for navigation destinations.

After a report developer has defined `Document Map` labels, SSRS automatically renders a document map. Document maps are supported by HTML, Excel, Word, and PDF rendering extensions.

The next chapter explains how SSRS works with multidimensional data sources and how it integrates with Analysis Services and data-mining features of SQL Server 2008.

CHAPTER 17

Working with Multidimensional Data Sources

IN THIS CHAPTER

Analysis Services is a large subject and deserves an entire book by itself. Although the details of Analysis Services are beyond the scope of this book, a discussion of basic concepts will help you to get the most out of this chapter.

Analysis Services Concepts

It is no surprise that during the course of business every company accumulates data. It is common to divide databases into two categories: transaction processing and data warehouses.

Typical transaction-processing databases are used for current processing, such as online sales, customer management, employee management, production, and inventory management. Transaction-processing databases are small in size, usually less than 100GB, and tend to have only a small amount of historical data that is directly relevant to ongoing transaction processing. An online transaction processing (OLTP) database is tuned for fast processing of transactions, incurs many changes (volatile) throughout a day, and is normally not used for reporting. An OLTP database is typically normalized to optimize data storage and retrieval for transactions.

A data warehouse (DW) is a database that is used for reporting and data analysis. It is possible to use an OLTP database for reporting, but it often negatively impacts transactional performance and is certain to make online users unhappy. If an online purchasing transaction is slow, a user is likely going to another site that offers better performance.

A DW usually has the following attributes:

- It is large in size (it is not uncommon to have multiterabyte data warehouses) and might contain years of historical data. Part of the data might not be currently useful, but provides a view into the company's past and can be analyzed to determine why, for example, online sales were successful in a certain time frame, or how well a marketing campaign performed.
- It stores data in the matter understandable to business users as opposed to applications. In contrast, OLTP databases are designed to accommodate applications. A DW is designed to answer business questions, such as sales numbers for a particular region and time frame.
- It is updated on predetermined intervals (once daily, weekly, or monthly) from transactional databases and ideally does not change previously stored historical data.

A subset of a DW is called a data mart. A DW usually contains data from a variety of heterogeneous data sources. Data marts are designed to minimize the amount of data used in processing and can contain a subset of data, based on, for example, time or geography.

Unified Data Model (UDM) was a new feature that first appeared in SQL Server 2005. UDM greatly simplifies access to data and combines the best of relational and analytical models.

UDM allows Reporting Services to get data from Analysis Services in a similar fashion as from any relational data source. One way to think about UDM is as a view on data, which allows "combining" data from various data sources (SQL Server relational and OLAP databases, Oracle, Teradata, DB2, and so on), "defining" relationships between that data, "defining" calculated fields, and mapping between original column names and newly defined names that might be more understandable to users of UDM. Several words in the previous sentence are included in double quotes (`" "`). UDM does not really combine data, but rather creates a metadata (data describing) view. This does not affect the source data itself, but allows creating a metadata view that, for example, may have a "relationship" between SQL Server and an Oracle table. Then UDM can be queried, like a database, and UDM, in turn, will access original data sources to retrieve needed data. UDM blurs the usual differentiation between OLTP and DW data. In the past, a DW stored denormalized data for quick retrieval. This is standard in the industry, but with UDM, users no longer have to denormalize their DWs.

Analysis Services consists of two components: Online Analytical Processing (OLAP) and Data Mining (DM). OLAP is designed to summarize data, and DM is designed to look for patterns and trends in data.

Let's look at the example in which a manager wants to analyze sales by country. It is certainly possible to use aggregate functions such as `SUM()` in a query or in SSRS to calculate summaries by country, but for the large amounts of data, it is not very efficient. Depending on the amount of data, summarization could be slow, which would be unsatisfactory to online users.

Reporting Services provides caching mechanisms that enable you to prepare a summary report and then display it to a user in real time without waiting for data retrieval. However, OLAP provides a better choice when a user is looking for summarized (or aggregated) data. This is because OLAP is specially tuned to perform aggregations. One of the most useful OLAP modes is Multidimensional OLAP (MOLAP). MOLAP stores aggregated data in an Analysis Services multidimensional structure, called a cube, which is highly optimized to maximize query performance.

NOTE

This chapter discusses default OLAP aggregation mode: MOLAP. Analysis Services provides two modes in addition to MOLAP: Relational OLAP (ROLAP), which does not store summaries and queries relational data for each Multidimensional Expressions (MDX) query; and Hybrid OLAP (HOLAP, a combination of MOLAP and ROLAP). Details of various modes are beyond this book's scope.

A Transact-SQL (T-SQL) query against the AdventureWorks DW database to get a summary by country would look like the following:

```
SELECT DimSalesTerritory.SalesTerritoryCountry  AS [Country-Region],
     SUM(FactInternetSales.SalesAmount) AS [Internet Sales-Sales Amount]
FROM DimSalesTerritory INNER JOIN FactInternetSales  ON
     DimSalesTerritory.SalesTerritoryKey = FactInternetSales.SalesTerritoryKey
GROUP BY DimSalesTerritory.SalesTerritoryCountry
```

A comparative multidimensional (or MDX; you can find more about MDX later in this chapter) query to retrieve the same result would look like the following:

```
SELECT NON EMPTY
    { [Measures].[Internet Sales Amount]} ON COLUMNS,
       NON EMPTY { [Customer].[Customer Geography].[Country]}
DIMENSION PROPERTIES
    MEMBER_CAPTION,
    MEMBER_UNIQUE_NAME ON ROWS
FROM [Adventure Works]
```

As you can see, for a simple aggregation the complexity of either query is fairly comparable. The key difference is in the underlying structures that each query accesses.

At this point, you should not be concerned if you are not familiar with MDX. SQL Server 2008 has an extremely capable visual designer that makes creation of an MDX query a fairly easy endeavor.

The result of both queries is the same and is shown in Table 17.1 (OLAP).

TABLE 17.1 Query Results

Country-Region	Internet Sales-Sales Amount
Australia	9061000.5844
Canada	1977844.8621
France	2644017.7143
Germany	2894312.3382
United Kingdom	3391712.2109
United States	9389789.5108

The duration of either query is not significantly different if the amount of data is small. For large amounts of data, the MDX query is going to be significantly faster because a cube stores aggregate data. Aggregation of data can be done on multiple levels, such as country, state, and city, and can be subsequently stored in the cube. Thus, MOLAP does not have to query a large DW to generate needed summaries. All that needs to be queried is the cube. MOLAP summarizes and stores data when the cube is processed.

Data-Mining Concepts

Data mining is designed to analyze trends and patterns in the data. For example, a manager at Adventure Works wants to analyze purchasing patterns of Adventure Works customers and determine how to up-sell and cross-sell shoppers online and wants to determine how to best design a marketing (mailing) campaign. Multiple attributes of a customer can be analyzed (age, geographic location, number of cars, number of children, gender, and marital status). There are potential patterns of attributes that determine whether the customer is likely to purchase a certain product. Based on determined patterns, a manager can target likely shoppers with promotions. Data mining derives knowledge from data by examining it using mathematical models for predictions and statistical analysis.

Conversely to data mining, OLAP usability for trend analysis is limited. A user would have to come up with a hypothesis that he needs to verify by looking through the data and determining whether the hypothesis is true. If the number of attributes that needs to be taken into account is large, some would likely be missed by an analyst. Large amounts of data increase complexity of analysis and require additional manpower to analyze the data.

A case table is one of the main constructs in data mining. Case encapsulates everything about an entity that is being categorized, classified, or analyzed for trends. A simple case is, for example, a customer, who has the following attributes: age, martial status, and wealth.

Creating a Data-Mining Model

Before creating a new model, you should do the following:

- Define the problem. What columns or attributes should the model predict?
- Determine the location of the data to be analyzed. The source of data could be a SQL Server database or a cube.

- Decide the data-mining algorithm the model should use.

The data-mining model (DMM) designed to analyze the probability of a bike purchase for a customer of a certain age could be created with the following code:

```
CREATE MINING MODEL [BikePurchasePrediction]
(
    CustomerKey LONG KEY,
    BikeBuyer DOUBLE DISCRETE PREDICT,
    Age DOUBLE CONTINUOUS
)
```

Training DMM

To train DMM, "feed" it with data for which attributes to be predicted are known. For example

```
INSERT INTO [BikePurchasePrediction] (    CustomerKey,    BikeBuyer,    Age) OPENQUERY
(   [Adventure Works DW], 'SELECT CustomerKey, BikeBuyer, Age FROM vTargetMail')
```

NOTE

The first parameter for `OPENQUERY` is a named data source that exists on the Microsoft SQL Server 2005 Analysis Services (SSAS) database, such as `[Adventure Works DW]` used in this example.

17

DMM does not, usually, store inserted data; instead, it builds a statistical model (statistical patterns that the mining algorithm detected in the data). This statistical model is stored in a truth table, which contains each possible combination of examined parameters and the probability of each combination. In a "nutshell," a truth table looks similar to Table 17.2.

TABLE 17.2 Truth Table

Age	Probability of Buying a Bike
40	70%

As needed, DMM can be retrained or incrementally refined by using `TRUNCATE TABLE` and `DROP TABLE` statements.

Querying DMM

To query a DMM, you need to have input data that you want to analyze and a trained DMM. A query maps information between input data and a DMM and needs to specify what has to be predicted.

For example

```
SELECT
    age, PredictProbability([Bike Buyer])
FROM BikePurchasePrediction PREDICTION JOIN ProspectiveBuyer
    ON BikePurchasePrediction.age = ProspectiveBuyer.age
```

MDX and DMX

MDX is an acronym for Multidimensional Expressions. It is a statement-based scripting language used to define, manipulate, and retrieve data from multidimensional objects in SSAS. MDX is similar in many ways to the familiar Structured Query Language (SQL) syntax typically used with relational databases, but it is not an extension of SQL.

Data Mining Extensions (DMX) is a language that you can use to create and work with DMMs in SSAS. You can use DMX to create new DMMs, to train these models, and to browse, manage, and predict using those models. The DMX language is an extension of SQL, to create and work with models.

Advanced OLAP Concepts

First, you should understand a couple of definitions to become familiar with Analysis Services lingo. *Measure* or *fact* is a numeric value used to monitor (measure) business. Sales amount is an example of a measure. *Dimension* is an independent group of attributes of a measure. Each attribute within a group is called a *member*. Dimension has to be meaningful for business aggregations. For the member to be included in dimension, it should have a meaningful relationship to the dimension. Geography, date/time, and customer are examples of dimensions.

Measure can be analyzed by one or multiple dimensions. Table 17.1 earlier in this chapter is a simple example of aggregations or an OLAP report. In Table 17.1, Internet Sales-Sales Amount is a measure and Country-Region is a dimension. Therefore, the data in Table 17.1 is analyzed and aggregated by a single dimension. Data can also be analyzed by two dimensions, such as date and geography, as shown in Table 17.3.

TABLE 17.3 Two-Dimensional Data

Internet Sales Amount	**Calendar Year**				
Country-Region	**2001**	**2002**	**2003**	**2004**	**Grand Total**
Australia	1,309,047	2,174,285	3,033,784	2,563,884	9,061,000
Canada	146,830	621,602	535,784	673,628	1,977,844
France	180,572	514,942	1,026,325	922,179	2,644,018
Germany	237,785	521,231	1,058,406	1,076,891	2,894,312

TABLE 17.3 Continued

Internet Sales Amount	Calendar Year				
Country-Region	**2001**	**2002**	**2003**	**2004**	**Grand Total**
United Kingdom	280,335	583,826	1,278,097	1,195,895	3,338,173
United States	1,111,805	2,134,457	2,858,664	3,338,422	9,443,348
Grand Total	3,266,374	6,530,344	9,791,060	9,770,900	29,358,678

It is possible to add a third dimension (and so on) and, as in geometry, the structure will be a cube. A cube is basically a structure in which all the aggregations of measures by dimensions are stored.

Some dimensions can have one or many hierarchies for its members. For example

- A geography dimension might have a hierarchy: country, region (such as east, central, mountain, west), state (such as Texas, Florida, California), county, city, and postal code.
- Time might have a hierarchy: year, half-year (or semester), quarter, and month.

Figure 17.1 shows an example of a hierarchy.

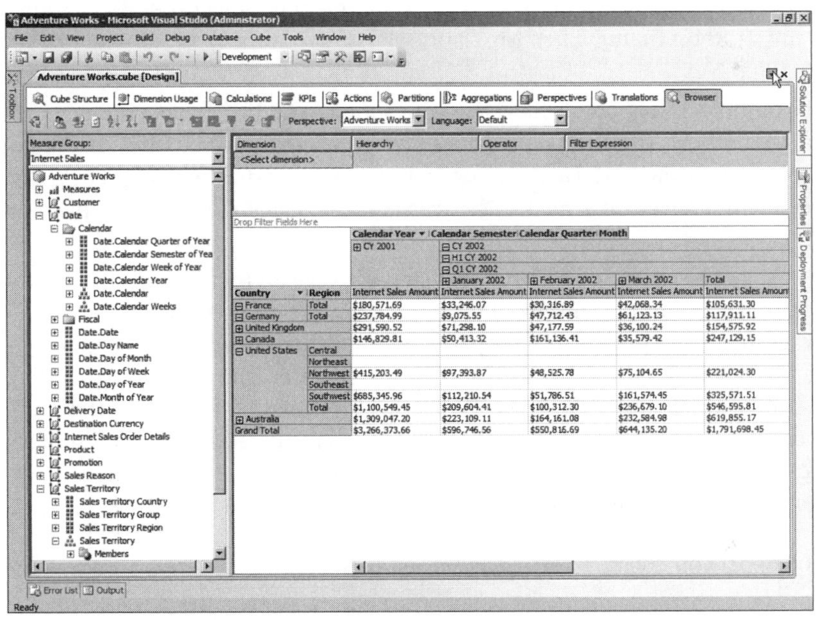

FIGURE 17.1 Multidimensional data with hierarchies.

The following walkthrough should help you achieve a better understanding of OLAP and its subsequent use by Reporting Services by developing a basic Analysis services cube. Later we will extend this with a data mining model.

1. Start Business Intelligence Development Studio (BIDS) and create a new Analysis Services project. Name it **`Analysis Services Project`**.
2. In Solution Explorer, right-click Data Sources, and select New Data Source from the shortcut menu. The Data Source Wizard begins. You can think of the data source as a connection to the database. Click Next on the Welcome screen.
3. On the Select How to Define the Connection screen, click the New button. Enter the requested information. To connect to SQL Server database, select Native OLE DB\SQL Native Client as the provider.
4. Enter the server name (for the local server, you can use either ***`server name`***, ***`localhost`*** or **`.`** [dot]). Select the authentication. (Windows authentication is preferred.) Select or enter AdventureWorksDW as the database.
5. Click Next. On the Impersonation Information screen, enter impersonation information. Selecting Use the Service Account should work in most cases. Leave the default name for the data source: Data Source.

Now that you have created a data source, you now want to create a Data Source view. To do so, follow these steps:

1. In Solution Explorer, right-click Data Source Views, and then select New Data Source View from the shortcut menu. Click Next and select Adventure Works DW as the data source. Click Next.
2. The wizard examines Data Source view, the data source, and brings up a dialog box in which tables or views from the data source can be selected. Select DimCustomer, DimGeography, DimTime, and FactInternetSales. Click Next. In the Completing the Wizard screen, enter **`Adventure Works DW Source View`**. Click Finish to complete the wizard.
3. BIDS brings up the design diagram. The next step is to create friendly names. Right-click FactInternetSales, and then select Properties from the shortcut menu. Remove the prefix Fact in the Friendly Name property. For all other tables in the diagram, remove the prefix Dim in the Friendly Name property. After completion of this step, BIDS looks similar to Figure 17.2. Figure 17.2 basically shows an essence of the UDM. You can connect to various data sources, create calculated fields, and establish relationships (all without any changes to the original data). Unlike in earlier versions, flattening and denormalizing of analysis data are no longer required.

Via the next set of steps, you create a new Analysis Services cube:

1. In Solution Explorer, right-click Cubes, and then select New Cube from the shortcut menu. After reading the information, click Next on the Welcome screen.

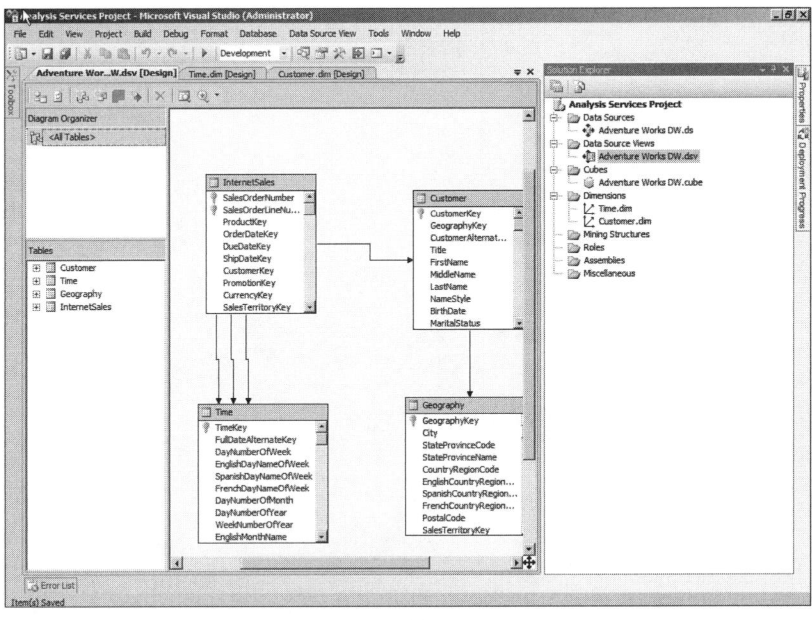

FIGURE 17.2 Unified Data Model.

2. On the next screen, select Use Existing Tables, and then click Next (see Figure 17.3).

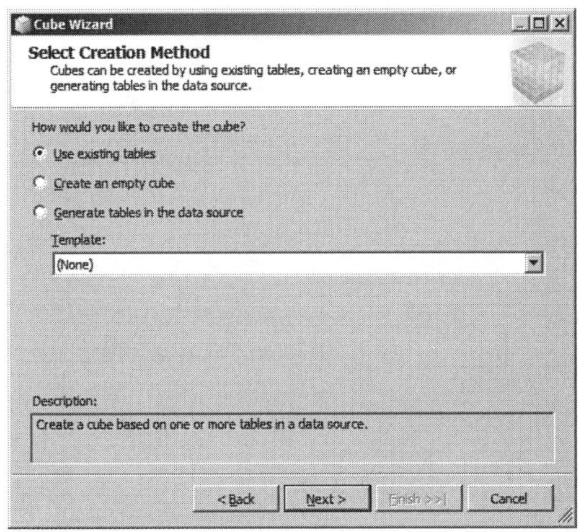

FIGURE 17.3 First step of the Cube Wizard.

3. This next screen asks us to pick our measure group tables. These are our fact tables. Select Internet Sales (see Figure 17.4) and click Next.

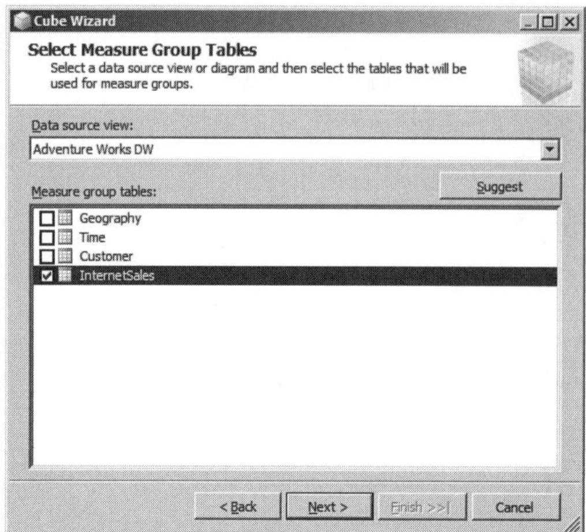

FIGURE 17.4 Selecting measure group tables.

4. The next screen asks us to pick the measures from our fact tables. Uncheck all existing check boxes besides Sales Amount, Order Quantity, Freight, Tax, and Internet Sales Count. Click Next (see Figure 17.5).

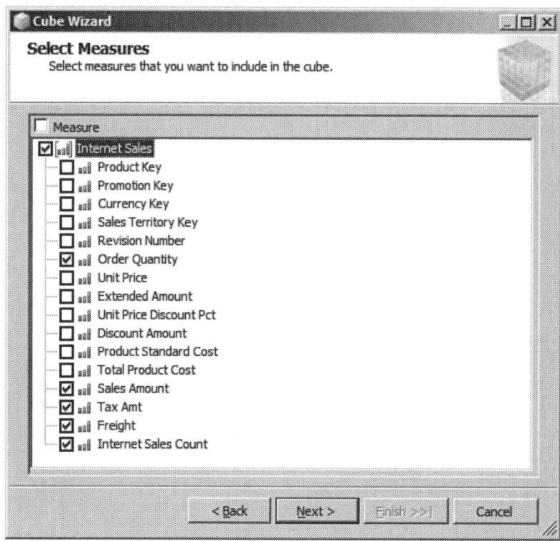

FIGURE 17.5 Selecting measures.

5. On this screen, we must select our dimension tables. These are going to be Time, Customer, and Geography. Make Sure Internet Sales is not checked. Click Next (see Figure 17.6).
6. Click Finish to create the initial cube.

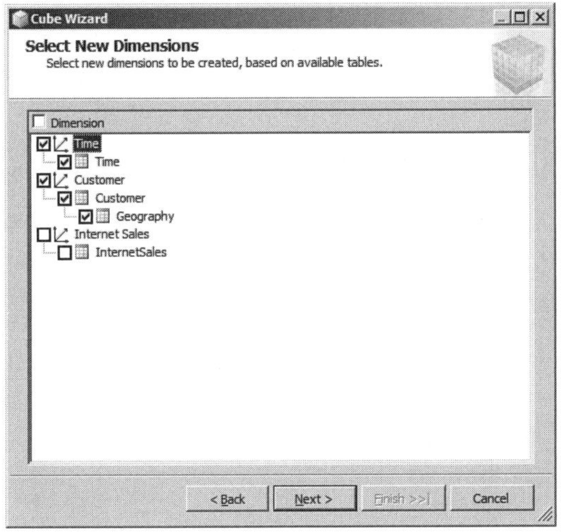

FIGURE 17.6 Selecting dimensions

Figure 17.7 shows the design surface after running the Cube Wizard. Our next steps will be to build the Time hierarchy to make it a little more user friendly.

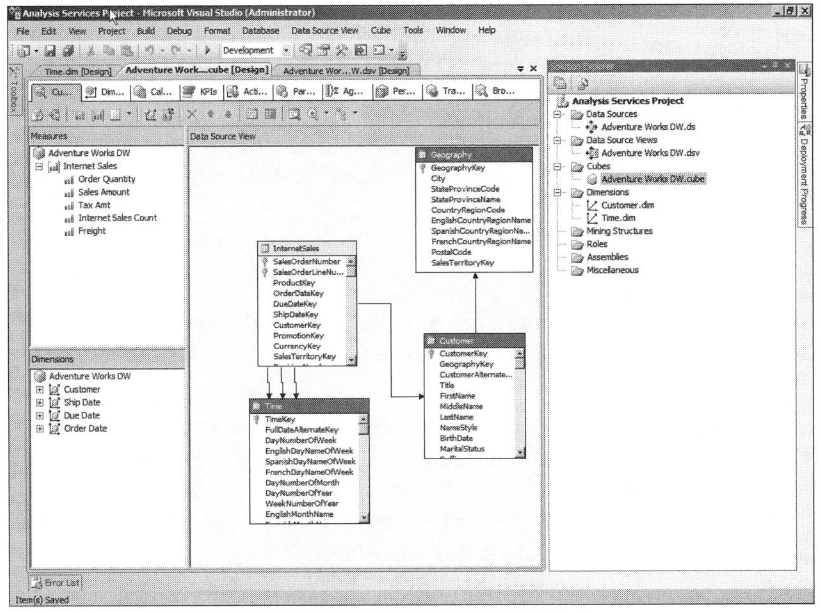

FIGURE 17.7 Design surface after running the Cube Wizard.

The change to the Time dimension includes making attributes such as Year, Month, Quarter, and so on so that we can sort and group on Time effectively. The other thing we will do is to create a hierarchy for calendar time. This allows us to easily aggregate up the Time dimension from Date to Month, Quarter, Half Year, and Year.

Here are the steps to modify the Time dimension:

1. Double-click the Time dimension to bring up the dimension designer. It should look like Figure 17.8.

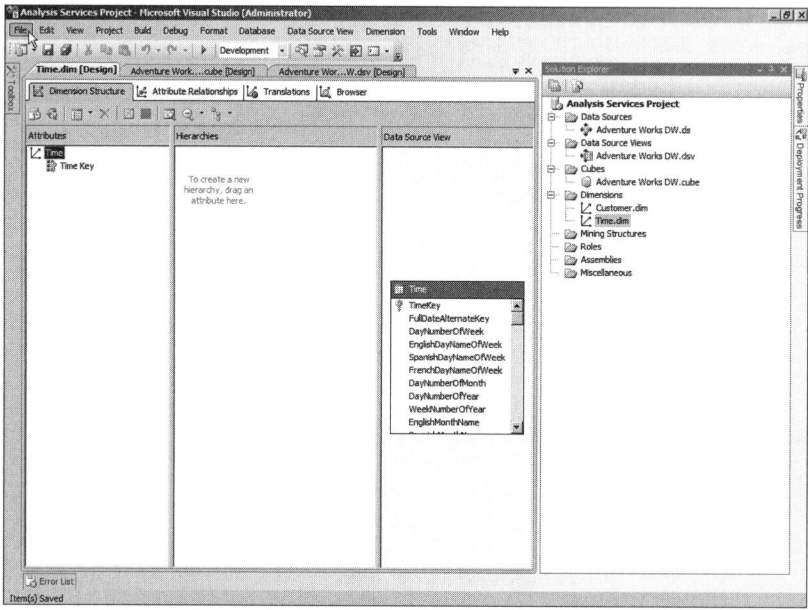

FIGURE 17.8 Time dimension design.

2. Drag Calendar Quarter, Calendar Semester, Calendar Year, English Month Name, and Full Date Alternate Key over to the Attributes pane. Figure 17.9 shows the results of doing so.
3. We'll create a new hierarchy by dragging attributes over to the Hierarchy pane. Attributes will be dragged over in order of granularity. Start with Year. This will automatically create a new hierarchy. Now drag Calendar Semester under Year, then Calendar Quarter, English Month Name, and then Full Date Alternate Key (see Figure 17.10). Finally, rename the new hierarchy **`CalendarTime`**.
4. Rename the attributes. You can do this by right-clicking each attribute and selecting Rename. You will need to do the same thing for the hierarchy. Name as follows:

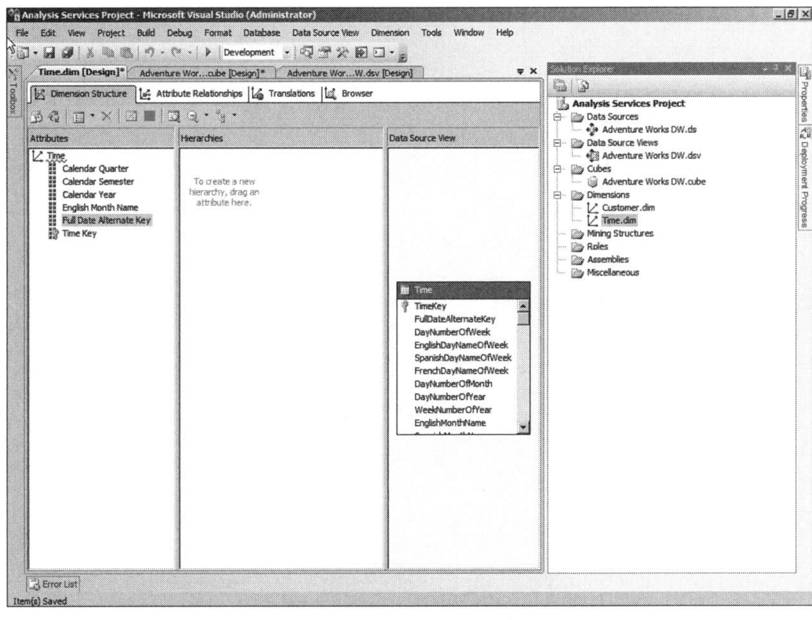

FIGURE 17.9 Time dimension attributes.

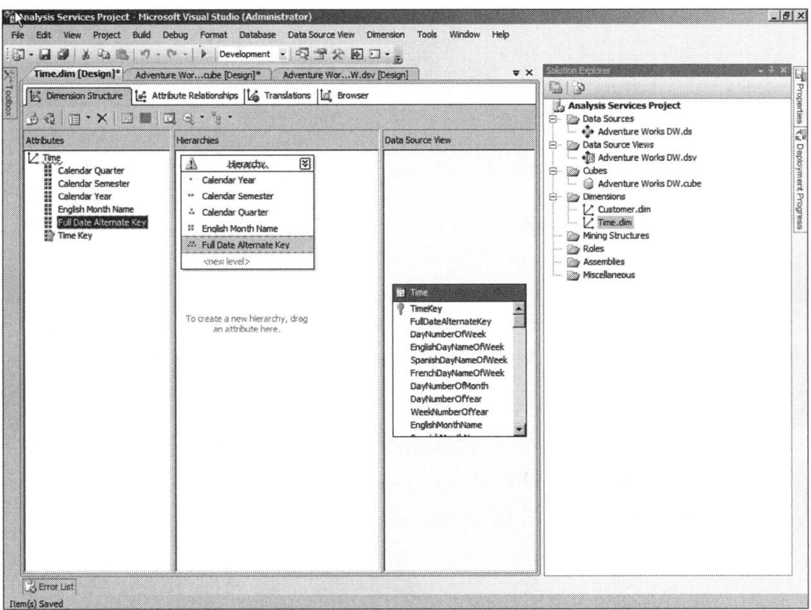

FIGURE 17.10 Time dimension attributes.

- Year: **CalendarYear**
- Half Year: **CalendarSemester**
- Quarter: **CalendarQuarter**
- Month: **EnglishMonthName**
- Date: **FullDateAlternateKey**

That completes the Time dimension (see Figure 17.11).

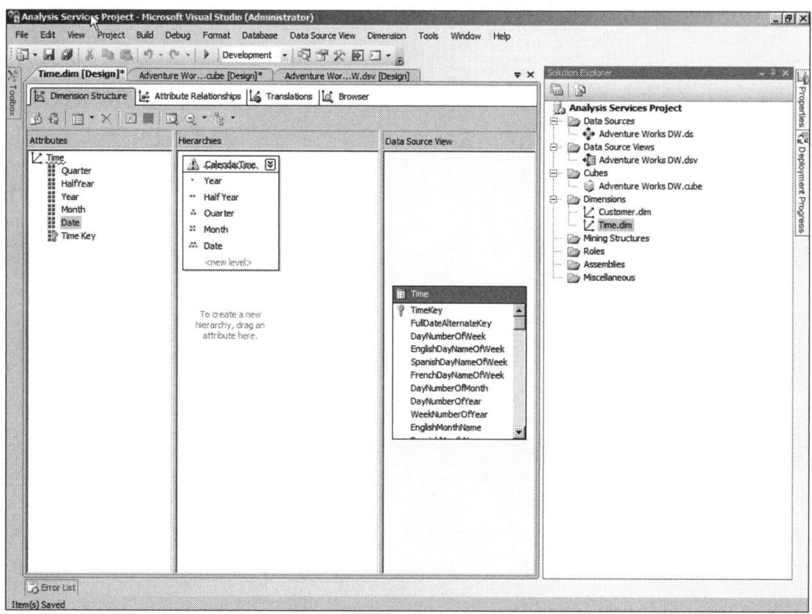

FIGURE 17.11 Completed Time dimension.

Now let's modify the Customer dimension to create a more logical geography hierarchy than the wizard detected for us. The following steps show how to modify the dimension:

1. Delete the Customer dimension. We will re-create this with the Dimension Wizard.
2. Right-click the Dimension folder in the Solution Explorer and select New Dimension. This will start the new Dimension Wizard.
3. Click Next on the Dimension Wizard Welcome screen.
4. On the Select Creation Method step, select Use an Existing Table.
5. On the Specify Source Information step, select Customer under Main Table. We will create a Customer dimension that we can get through by browsing the geography. Click Next.

6. The next screen shows a related table. Make sure Geography is selected. Click Next.
7. On the next screen, we select attributes. Go ahead and select all of them. Click Next.
8. Now we have to name the dimension. Name it **`Customer`** and click Finish.
9. Under the Dimension folder in Solution Explorer, double-click the Customer dimension. From the Attributes panel, drag the English Country Region Name attribute to the Hierarchy panel. Drag State Province Name under English Country Name, City attribute to the position right below the State Province Name level. When thinking about a hierarchy and at what level to place a particular attribute, consider what "contains" or "has" what. For example, country has many states and, therefore, should be on the higher level compared to state. Correspondingly, on the diagram, Country should receive less schematic "dots" than State.
10. Finally, drag Customer Alternate Key under City, and then rename it to **`Customer`**. Rename the hierarchy to **`Customer by Geography`** (see Figure 17.12).

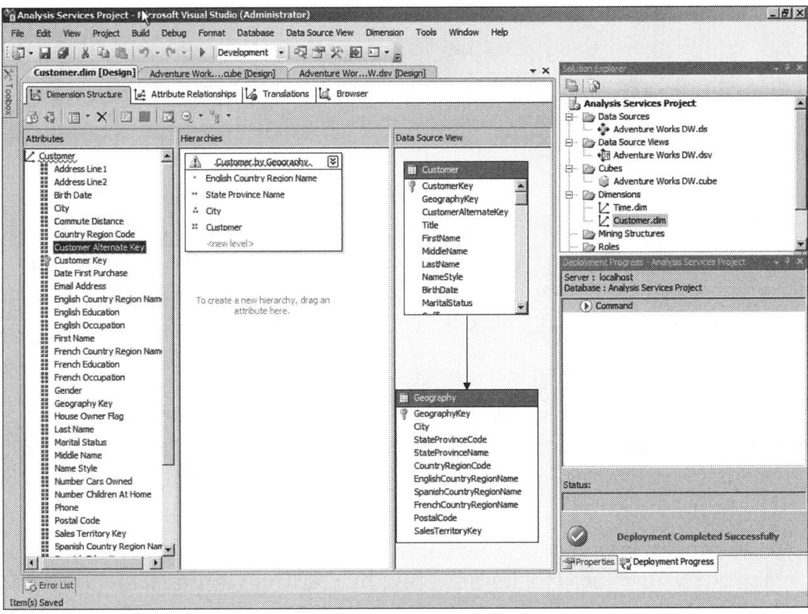

FIGURE 17.12 Dimension design screen.

11. Now we need to associate the new dimension to our measure group. Double-click the cube and select the Dimension Usage tab.
12. Click the Add New Dimension button on the toolbar. An Add Cube Dimension dialog box will then display. Select Customer and click OK. Figure 17.13 shows the final result.

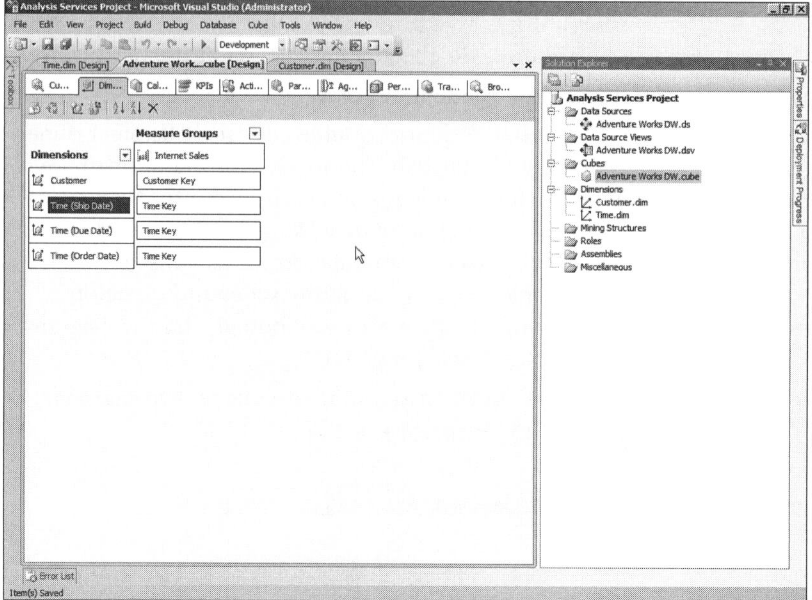

FIGURE 17.13 Added Customer dimension.

The following steps modify the Time dimension to properly order months of the year. Alphabetically, months are ordered as April, August, and so on. After ordering by key in place, you obtain correct ordering: January, February, and so on. You need this ordering when working with key performance indicators (KPIs) later in this chapter:

1. Double-click the Time dimension to open it.
2. In the Attributes pane, click the Month attribute of a Time dimension. In the Properties window (normally docked in the lower-right corner), click the KeyColumns property and click the ellipses (...). This brings up the Key Columns dialog box.
3. Click < to remove the EnglishMonthName column from the Keys list box. Next move MonthNumberOfYear into the Keys list box by clicking >. Click OK.
4. Next go to the NameColumn property and click the ellipses (...).
5. On the Name Column, make sure the binding type is Column Binding and that Time is selected in the Source Table drop-down. Select EnglishMonthName and click OK.
6. Now, right-click the Order By property and select Key from the resulting drop-down.

Now you are ready to deploy your solution. The following steps deploy to a local server:

1. From the main menu, select Build, Deploy Analysis Services Project. After deployment completes, double-click Adventure Works DW.cube in Solution Explorer, and then click the Browser tab, which is the last tab in the Adventure Works Cube [Design] window.

2. Click the Reconnect button to refresh the Browser tab. Keep in mind that after the cube structure is modified and changes are deployed, you should use the Reconnect button to browse the most recent updates. BIDS should show something similar to Figure 17.14.

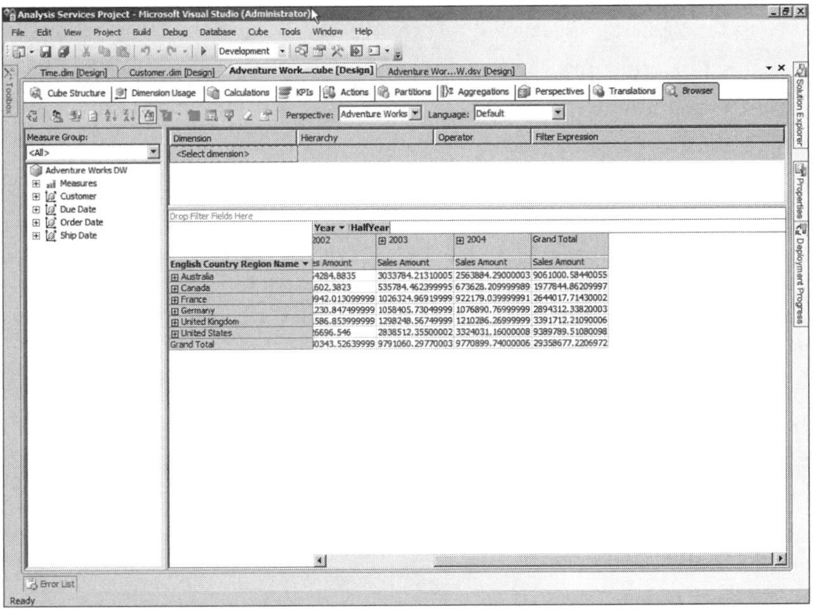

FIGURE 17.14 Cube browser.

To see the results of your work, drag and drop the Sales Amount from the Internet Sales measure to the center of the pivot table control, where it says Drop Totals or Details Fields Here. Drag and drop English Country Region Name from the Customer dimension on the row part of the pivot table control, where it says Drop Row Fields Here. The pivot table should display information similar to Table 17.1. You have now completed and verified the cube. This is a basic cube that will help you to understand how to use Reporting Services with Analysis Services. You can find more information about cubes and advanced features of Analysis Services in the SQL Server Books Online.

KPIs are designed to evaluate performance criteria that a business, usually, considers strategic in nature. Performance is evaluated against a specified goal and has to be quantifiable. Some of the KPI examples are stock performance, cost of operations, customer satisfaction, and so on.

Let's add a KPI to the just-completed cube:

1. In Solution Explorer, double-click the Adventure Works DW.cube. Click the KPIs tab. Right-click the surface of the KPI Organizer listview, and select New KPI from the shortcut menu. Name this KPI **`Average Item Price`**. This KPI is useful, for example,

if Adventure Works's management has determined that Internet sales have the minimum order-processing cost when an average price per item sold is $100 or more. In turn, maximum order-processing cost is when the average price per item sold is less than $10.

2. For the value expression, enter the following MDX query:

```
[Measures].[Sales Amount]/[Measures].[Internet Sales Count]
```

3. For the goal expression, enter **100**.
4. For the status, enter the following query:

```
Case
    When [Measures].[Sales Amount]/[Measures].[Internet Sales Count] < 10
        Then -1
    When [Measures].[Sales Amount]/[Measures].[Internet Sales Count] <= 50
Then 0
    When [Measures].[Sales Amount]/[Measures].[Internet Sales Count] >= 100
        Then 1
End
```

5. For the trend expression, enter the following MDX query. This query compares current values of the average order size to the previous time period. (Depending on the level of detail, this could be a year, month, and so on.) If the current period exceeds the previous one, the trend is good; otherwise, it needs improvement:

```
Case
When
    ([Order Date].[Date],
    [Measures].[Sales Amount])
    /
    ([Order Date].[Date],
    [Measures].[Internet Sales Count])
    >=
    ([Order Date].[Date].PrevMember,
    [Measures].[Sales Amount])
    /
     ([Order Date].[Date].PrevMember,
     [Measures].[Internet Sales Count])
Then 1
Else -1
End
```

6. Click the Browser View button on the KPI toolbar. Click the Process button on the KPI toolbar, and then click Run in the dialog box. Analysis Services processes the KPI. After the process has completed, close the Process Progress and Process Cube dialog box. In the Browser view, you should see KPI indicators similar to Figure 17.15.

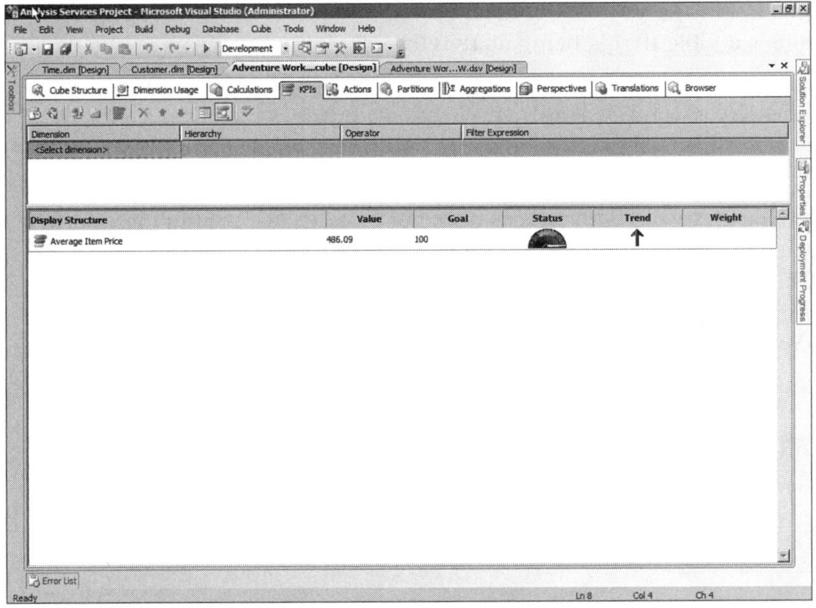

FIGURE 17.15 KPI browser.

Now let's create a mining structure. Adventure Works's management wants to create a targeting advertisement on the website to promote bicycle sales. Adventure Works has collected data from existing customers and can target those already, based on the existing data, but what about new customers making purchases? To be the most effective and unobtrusive in the advertising campaign, when should Adventure Works display links to bicycles? Similarly, what kind of customer should be targeted for a direct mail campaign?

1. In Solution Explorer, double-click Adventure Works DW Source.dsv. Right-click in the diagram area, and select Add/Remove Tables from the shortcut menu. Add the vTargetMail view. This is the view based on the data in Adventure Works DW tables, which adds a BikeBuyer field from the DimCustomer table. This field is derived from the Internet Sales table, where the product purchased was a bicycle.
2. In Solution Explorer, right-click Mining Structures, and then select New Mining Structure from the shortcut menu.
3. Click Next on the Welcome screen. Accept the default (From Existing Relational Database or Data Warehouse) by clicking Next.
4. Accept the default mining algorithm (Microsoft Decision Trees) on the Select the Data Mining Technique screen. Click Next.
5. Accept the default Adventure Works DW Source View for the Data Source view. Click Next.

6. Select vTargetMail as the Case table. Remember from earlier in this chapter that the Case table is a table that is being analyzed to determine patterns in the data. Click Next.
7. Leave CustomerKey as the key, and then select Bike Buyer as Predictable. Note that the Suggest button has become available. Click the Suggest button and note that based on the data sample, Age is the best input for the model.
8. Because the table that you have for tests does not have an Age column, and to simplify further efforts, let's use Birth Date rather than Age. It is possible to use the `DATEDIFF()` function to calculate the age of a customer, but because Birth Date provides essentially the same (time frame) information as Age, you can leverage Birth Date. You should see a screen similar to Figure 17.16. Click Next.

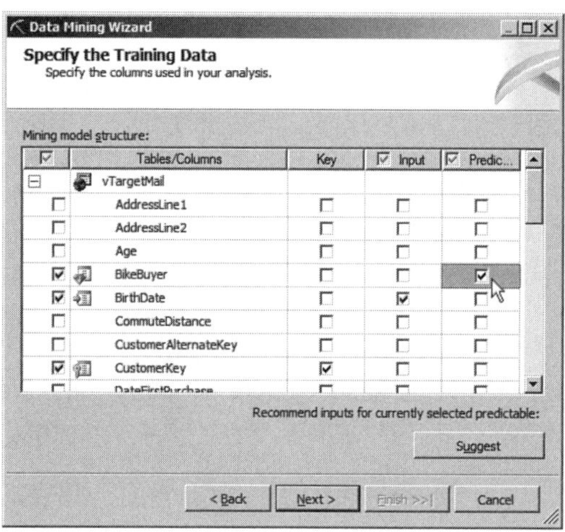

FIGURE 17.16 Data Mining Wizard.

9. On the Specify Columns' Content and Data Type screen, click Detect Columns' Content and Data Type. The wizard samples data. Note that the Bike Buyer's Content Type changed from Continuous to Discrete. The wizard queried the data and determined that the data is discrete, based on the fact that the Bike Buyer contains an integer value with just a few actual values: 1 and 0. Click Next.
10. On the Create Testing Set screen, leave the defaults.
11. For the mining structure name, enter **`Bike Buyer Structure`**, and for the mining model name, enter **`Bike Buyer Model`**. Select Allow Drill Through. Click Finish. Note that Customer Sales Structure appears under Mining Structures in Solution Explorer.

Now you are ready to deploy your DMM. Click Build, Deploy Solution. After deployment completes, click the Mining Model Viewer tab. Note the decision tree that was built. Based on the data, it should look similar to Figure 17.17.

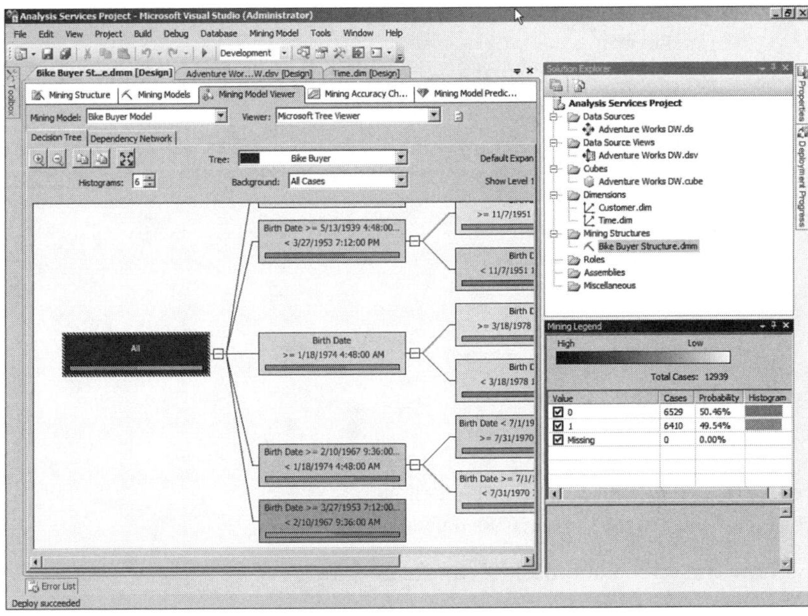

FIGURE 17.17 Decision tree.

The decision tree indicates that customers born in 1969 are almost three times as likely to purchase a bike as other customers and that customers born before 9/22/1931 are least likely to purchase a bike.

As an exercise to better understand data mining, click through other tabs, such as Mining Accuracy Chart. Click the Lift Chart tab under the Mining Accuracy Chart tab and note that the model provides at least 1.4 times better prediction than random guesses.

The following shows how to make a basic mining structure:

1. Click the Mining Model Prediction tab.
2. Click Select Case Table on the diagram and choose vTargetMail.
3. Drag and drop the BikeBuyer field from the Input Table (vTargetMail) onto the grid located below the diagram on the screen.
4. Drag and drop the Bike Buyer field from the Mining Model pane onto the grid.
5. On the third row of the grid, under the Source column, click and select Prediction Function from the drop-down menu that appears.
6. On the same row, click on the Field column and select Predict Probability from the drop-down menu.
7. Drag and drop Bike Buyer from the Bike Buyer Model onto the Criteria/Argument column of the third row. At this point the screen should look like Figure 17.18.

Click the drop-down next to the Switch to Query Result View (looks like a grid) button on the toolbar and select Query. The following query is displayed. This is a DMX query comparing the *actual* in the vTargetMail table and *value predicted* by a model.

```
SELECT
  [Bike Buyer Model].[Bike Buyer],
  PredictProbability([Bike Buyer Model].[Bike Buyer]),
  t.[BikeBuyer]
From
  [Bike Buyer Model]
PREDICTION JOIN
  OPENQUERY([Adventure Works DW],
    'SELECT
      [BikeBuyer],
      [BirthDate]
    FROM
      [dbo].[vTargetMail]
    ') AS t
ON
  [Bike Buyer Model].[Birth Date] = t.[BirthDate] AND
  [Bike Buyer Model].[ Bike Buyer] = t.[Bike Buyer]
```

Figure 17.18 shows how the screen should look in design mode.

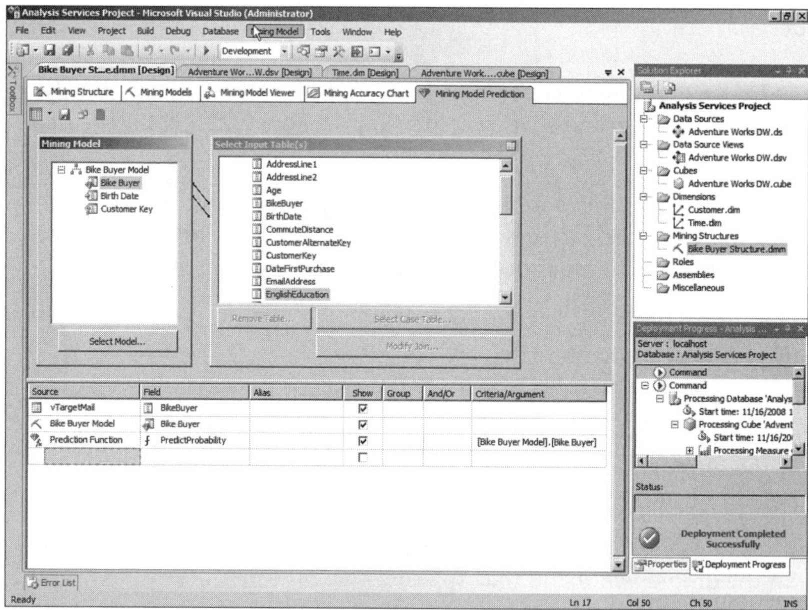

FIGURE 17.18 Mining model prediction.

Now you are ready to query OLAP data and data-mining structures from Reporting Services. Here's how:

1. From the File menu, select Add, New Project. Select Report Server Project from the list of installed Business Intelligence Projects templates. Name the new project

AnalysisServicesSamples. Click OK. Note that this is the same procedure as for creating any report project.

2. Right-click the Reports folder under the AnalysisServicesSamples project, and select Add New Report from the shortcut menu. The Report Wizard starts. Click the Next button to advance from the Welcome screen. On the Select the Data Source screen, select New Data Source, use the name AnalysisServicesData, and select Microsoft SQL Server Analysis Services as the type of data source. Use an appropriate connection string, as follows:

```
Data Source=localhost;Initial Catalog="Analysis Services Project"
```

3. Select Make This a Shared Data Source. The Report Wizard should look similar to Figure 17.19.

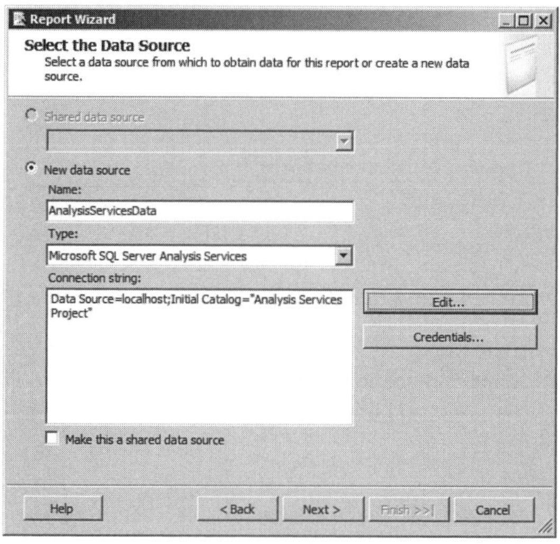

FIGURE 17.19 Analysis Services data source.

4. Click Next. Note that the Design the Query screen does not allow you to paste in a query. This is by design to avoid potential issues with complex MDX or DMX queries. Click the Query Builder button.

5. In the Metadata pane, expand Measures/Internet Sales and Customer hierarchies. Drag the Sales Amount from Measures and drop it on the area marked Drag Levels or Measures Here to Add to the Query. (We call this the Design area from now on.) Drag and drop English Country Region Name onto the Design area. So far, the process is not very different from working with pivot tables. However, in this case, Query Builder only allows you to design queries that produce table-like output. The Query Builder should look similar to Figure 17.20.

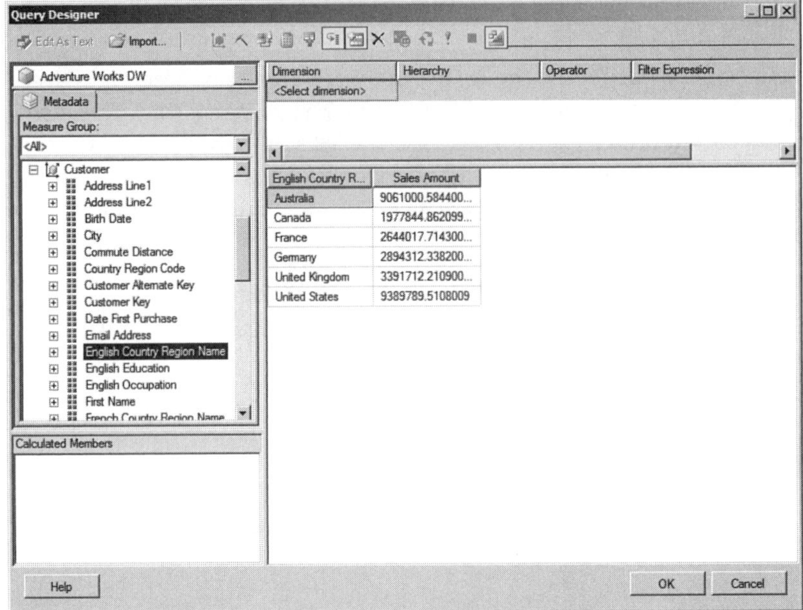

FIGURE 17.20 Multidimensional Query Designer.

6. Click OK and note the MDX query created by the Query Builder:

```
SELECT NON EMPTY { [Measures].[Sales Amount] } ON COLUMNS,
    NON EMPTY {([Customer].[English Country Region Name].
               [English Country Region Name].ALLMEMBERS)}
    DIMENSION PROPERTIES MEMBER_CAPTION,
    MEMBER_UNIQUE_NAME ON ROWS
FROM [Adventure Works DW Cube] CELL PROPERTIES VALUE, BACK_COLOR, FORE_COLOR,
      FORMATTED_VALUE, FORMAT_STRING, FONT_NAME, FONT_SIZE, FONT_FLAGS
```

7. Click Next.
8. On the Select the Report Type screen, accept the default: Tabular. Click Next. On the Design the Table screen, click the Details button to add the available fields to Displayed Fields. Click Next.
9. Select Bold on the Choose the Table Style screen. Click Next. Name this report **`Sales Report`**. Click the Finish button. Click the Preview tab. You should see a screen similar to the one shown in Figure 17.21.

You have just pulled data from the OLAP cube.

Let's make this report a bit more complicated and add a second dimension: Time. You will use the SalesReport that you have developed as a base for the following steps:

1. In Solution Explorer, right-click Sales Report and select Copy from the shortcut menu. Right-click the report project and select Paste from the shortcut menu. Rename Copy of SalesReport to **`TimedSalesReport`**.

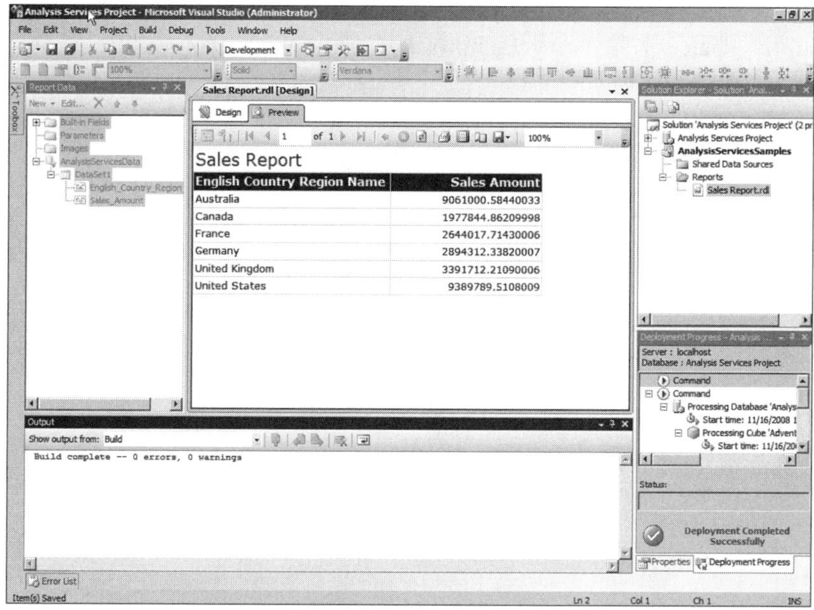

FIGURE 17.21 Result of a multidimensional report.

2. Double-click TimedSalesReport and click the Report Data pane in Report Designer.
3. Double-click DataSet1.
4. Click the Query Designer button.
5. Expand the Order Date dimension. From under OrderDate.CalendarTime, drag and drop Year onto the Design area. Once again, Query Builder flattens the OLAP output. Toggle the design mode and note that the MDX query now has a second dimension:

```
SELECT
NON EMPTY
    {[Measures].[Sales Amount] } ON COLUMNS,
NON EMPTY
    {([Customer].[English Country Region Name].[English Country Region
Name].ALLMEMBERS *
    [Order Date].[CalendarTime].[CalendarYear].ALLMEMBERS ) }
    DIMENSION PROPERTIES MEMBER_CAPTION, MEMBER_UNIQUE_NAME ON ROWS
FROM [Adventure Works DW]
CELL PROPERTIES VALUE, BACK_COLOR, FORE_COLOR, FORMATTED_VALUE,
  FORMAT_STRING, FONT_NAME, FONT_SIZE, FONT_FLAGS
```

6. Click the Layout tab and delete the table control from SalesReport. Place a Matrix control in place of the Table control. From the Datasets window, drag and drop Sales_Amount onto the data region of the Matrix control, drag and drop

CalendarYear onto the column area, and drag and drop English_Country_Region_Name into the Rows area of the Matrix control. Now you should see a screen similar to Figure 17.22.

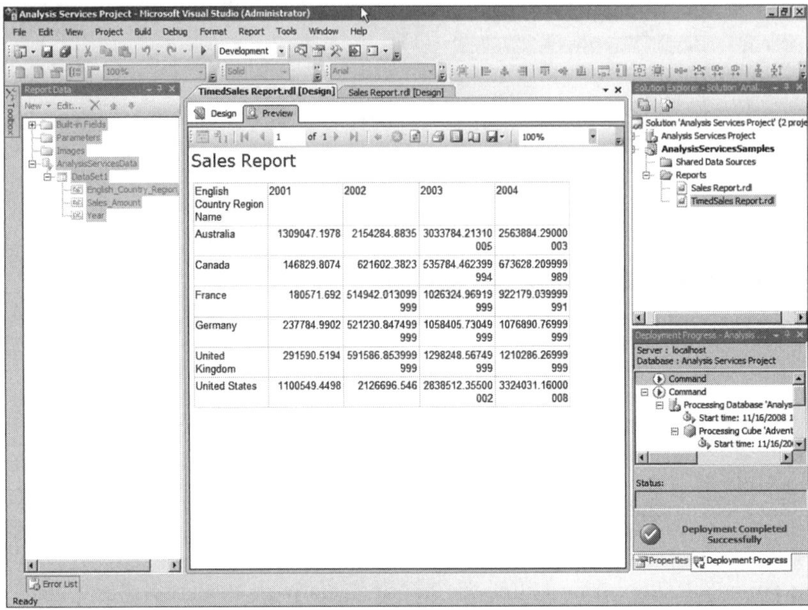

FIGURE 17.22 Result of a multidimensional report with Time dimensions.

Now let's create a report that leverages KPIs. Once again, you will use the SalesReport that you have developed as a base for the following steps:

1. In Solution Explorer, right-click SalesReport and select Copy from the shortcut menu. Right-click the report project, and select Paste from the shortcut menu. Rename Copy of SalesReport to **ItemPriceKPI**.
2. Double-click ItemPriceKPI and double-click on its data set in Report Designer. Execute the query and delete all columns from the results grid. This clears the query. In the metadata, expand KPIs. Drag and drop the Average Item Price KPI onto the Design area. The Design area now shows a grid with a single row with four columns corresponding to the details of the KPI: Average Item Price Value, Average Item Price Goal, Average Item Price Status, and Average Item Price Trend.
3. From the Customer dimension, drag and drop English_Country_Region_Name and State_Province_Name onto the query pane. Click Layout view, and if it has a Table or Matrix control, delete it. Add a new Table control. Add two more columns to the

table. Drag and drop English_Country_Region_Name, State_Province_Name, Average_Item Price_Value, Average_Item_Price_Goal, and Average_Item_Price_Status fields from the AnalysisServiceData data set to the Detail region of the table. Click the Preview tab. You should see a screen similar to Figure 17.23.

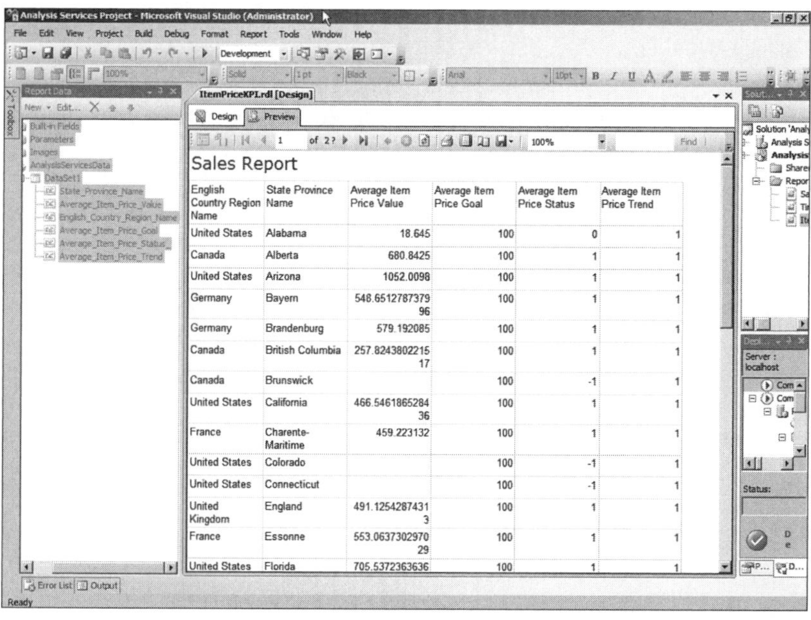

FIGURE 17.23 Result of a multidimensional report with KPIs.

You can validate the status works well and displays 1 when average order size > 100, 0, and when it is <= 50, and that it displays –1 when the average order size is < 10.

Note that all the KPI data is numeric. This version of Reporting Services does not include KPI controls, but KPI controls are easy to emulate. The following several steps show how to do it. You can create your own KPI graphics or leverage KPI controls from Visual Studio (by default located at `C:\Program Files\Microsoft Visual Studio 9\Common7\IDE\PrivateAssemblies\DataWarehouseDesigner\KPIsBrowserPage\Images`).

Let's embed three images (`Gauge_Asc0.gif`, `Gauge_Asc2.gif`, and `Gauge_Asc4.gif`) corresponding to three distinct states of the gauge's status: empty, half, and full. The steps to emulate KPI controls are as follows:

1. From the Toolbox, drag and drop an image control on the Detail area of the grid inside of the column Status. In the Properties dialog box that appears, select Embedded from the Select Image Source drop-down. Click the Import button, and

use the File Open dialog box to import one of the GIF images mentioned earlier. You will need to repeat this step two more times to import the other two images.

2. Click the image, and in the Properties window change the Value property from gauge_asc4 to the following:

```
=IIF (Fields!Average_Item_Price_Status_.Value=-1, "gauge_asc0",
        IIF(Fields!Average_Item_Price_Status_.Value=0,"gauge_asc2",
          "gauge_asc4"))
```

As you can tell by now, this expression directs Reporting Services to display an appropriate image. Note that image names are displayed as constants in the Expression Editor. Do not forget to include image names in double quotes, such as "gauge_asc0". You should see a screen similar to Figure 17.24.

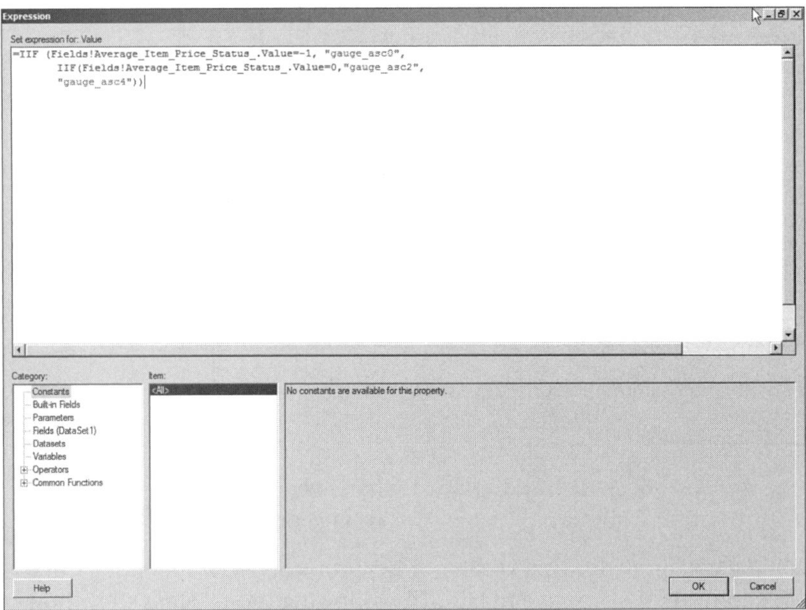

FIGURE 17.24 Adding graphical KPIs.

3. Click OK to close the Expression Editor.
4. If desired, you can modify formatting, such as the column headers, to improve the report's look. Click the Preview tab. You should see a screen similar to Figure 17.25. This approach to adding images works just as easily with reports from relational data.

You might have noticed that in the KPI example Brunswick in Canada, for example, does not have sales data; that is, nothing was sold there. In the real-life report, you should have

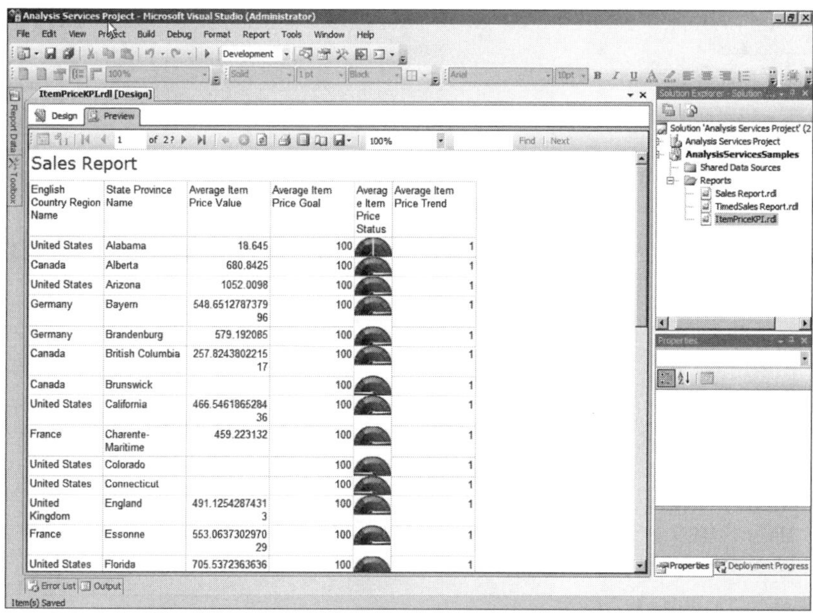

FIGURE 17.25 Resulting report after adding graphical KPIs.

excluded output of empty (or irrelevant data). Such filtering should be done, ideally, in a query. Report Server could be leveraged as well (for example, using the `Visibility` property of a report item).

Creating Data-Mining Reports

As a last exercise in this chapter, let's create a report that will leverage SQL Server data-mining capabilities:

1. In Solution Explorer, right-click the Reports folder and select Create New Report from the shortcut menu. Use the AnalysisServicesData shared data source that was created earlier in this chapter. Click Next.
2. On the Design the Query screen, click the Query Builder button. By default, Query Builder starts in MDX Query Design mode. To switch to DMX Query Design mode, click the third button on the Query Builder's toolbar, which is called Command Type DMX. (This button depicts a mining pickax.) This button switches between MDX and DMX Designer to correspondingly query OLAP cubes and DMMs. Click OK on the Warning dialog box.
3. In the Mining Model window, click the Select Model button. Expand the tree and select Bike Buyer Model. In the Select Input Table(s) window, click Select Case Table (see Figure 17.26).

FIGURE 17.26 Select Mining Model window.

4. Change the data source to Adventure Works DW, select ProspectiveBuyer (see Figure 17.27), and then click OK.

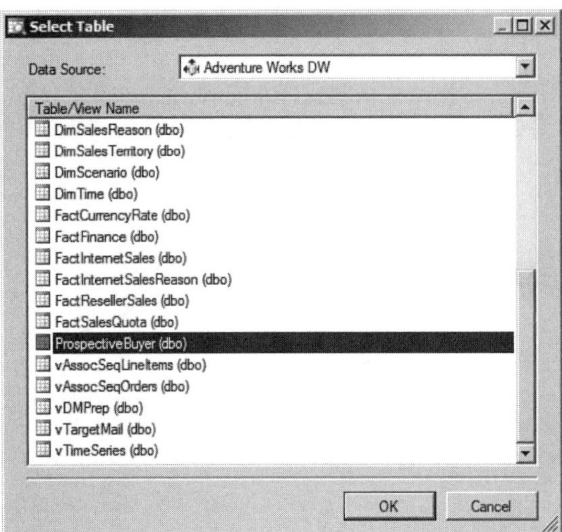

FIGURE 17.27 Selecting a table for analysis.

5. From under Bike Buyer Model, drag and drop Bike Buyer onto the grid below. In the Source column of the second row of the grid, select Prediction Function in the drop-down menu within a cell. In the Field column, select the PredictProbability function; and drag and drop the Bike Buyer field from the model to the Criteria/Argument column. Enter **`Probability`** as an alias for this expression.
6. From the ProspectiveBuyer table (located in the Select Input Table(s) window), drag the following fields: FirstName, LastName, and EmailAddress onto the grid pane.

This allows you to have a report that can be used for a personalized email campaign promoting Adventure Works's bikes. You should see a screen similar to Figure 17.28.

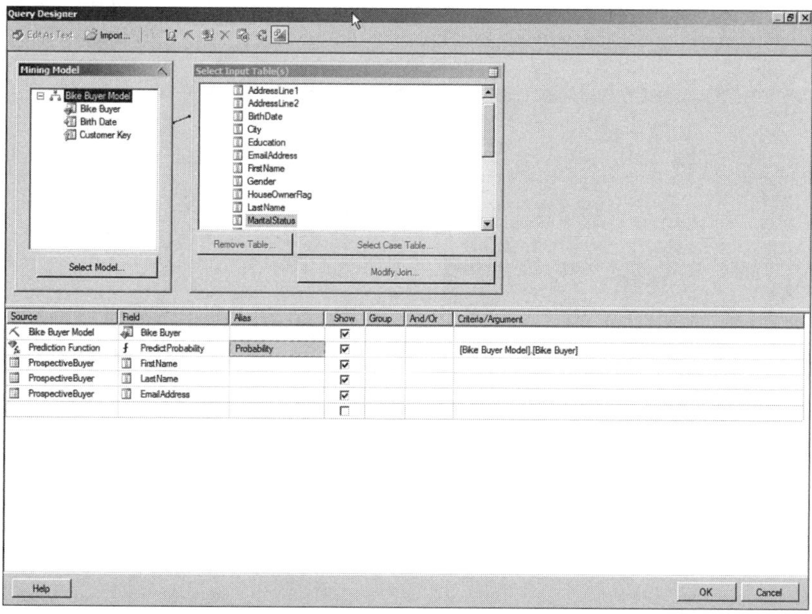

FIGURE 17.28 DMX Query Builder.

7. Click OK to complete the Query Builder. The following is the query:

```
SELECT
  [Bike Buyer Model].[Bike Buyer],
  (PredictProbability([Bike Buyer Model].[Bike Buyer])) as [Probability],
  t.[FirstName],
  t.[LastName],
  t.[EmailAddress]
From
  [Bike Buyer Model]
PREDICTION JOIN
  OPENQUERY([Adventure Works DW],
    'SELECT
      [FirstName],
      [LastName],
      [EmailAddress],
      [BirthDate]
    FROM
      [dbo].[ProspectiveBuyer]
    ') AS t
ON
    [Bike Buyer Model].[Birth Date] = t.[BirthDate]
```

8. On the Select Report Type screen, accept the default (Tabular) by clicking Next, and add all the fields displayed in the Fields section to the Details group. Click Next, and then accept the default style by clicking Next again. Name the report **`CampaignCustomerEvaluation`**. Format the fields to improve layout, and then click Preview. The screen should look similar to Figure 17.29.

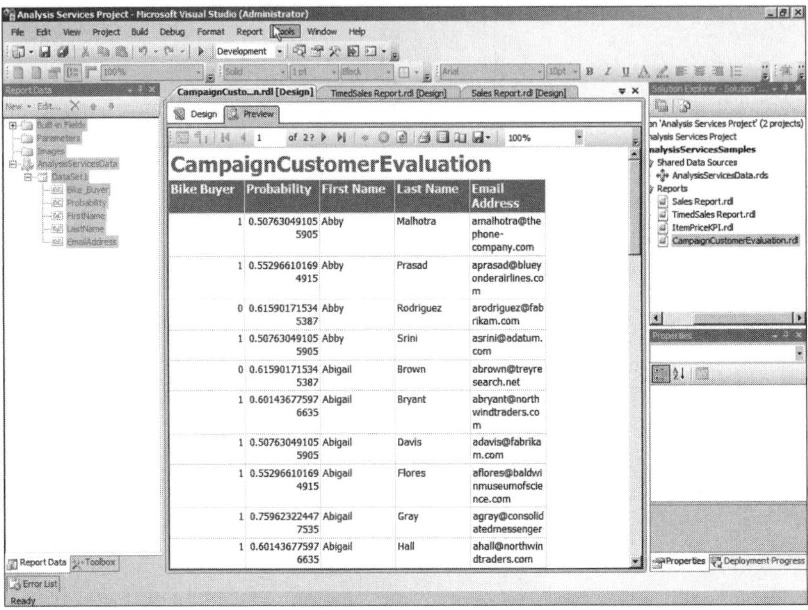

FIGURE 17.29 Data-mining report.

Summary

Analysis Services consists of two components: online analytical processing (OLAP) and data mining (DM). OLAP is designed to summarize data, and DM is designed to look for patterns and trends in data.

Key capabilities that SSRS can leverage include the following:

- UDM, which is designed to simplify access to data and combines the best of relational and analytical models.
- KPIs, which are designed to evaluate performance criteria that a business, usually, considers strategic in nature. Performance is evaluated against a specified goal and has to be quantifiable. KPI examples include stock performance, cost of operations, customer satisfaction, and so on.
- Graphical Query Builders for OLAP and DM are designed to simplify development of multidimensional and DM queries by providing a very intuitive graphical user interface.

CHAPTER 18

Ad Hoc Reporting

IN THIS CHAPTER

- Issues Facing Ad Hoc Reporting
- Client-Side Reporting with SSRS
- Report Models and the Model Designer

This chapter begins with a few words about needs and challenges for ad hoc reports and some definitions.

A lot of things have changed for business in the post dot-com era, but one thing that remains is the need for accurate and timely data. Most businesses want to analyze and report on up-to-the-minute data. Moreover, a lot of analysts want to analyze the data kept in their organization's data warehouses to test their theories or to spot trends. This kind of analytical reporting does not preclude the nicely printed and formatted reports for C-level executives, but rather serves as the foundation for new reports.

Issues Facing Ad Hoc Reporting

The challenge in doing this kind of analysis has often been with the technology. Technologists such as report developers are usually keen on SQL and their reporting tools. They know the ins and outs of relational databases, the different kinds of joins, and the concepts behind online analytical processing (OLAP). They might or might not be so keen on the business repercussions of certain trends.

The opposite is most likely true for business analysts. The typical analyst knows what he wants to see or at least has a theory that he wants to collect data for to prove or disprove. Analysts might not know or care that to get a typical sales order, he must join six or seven tables together. Analysts are not technologists.

What the analyst needs is a flexible, yet powerful tool to build his own reports and do his own analysis without overbearing technical terms.

Client-Side Reporting with SSRS

SSRS attempts to address these issues with two main tools: Report Builder and Model Designer.

Before a user can create a client-side report, an analyst or technologist must create a report model. The report model is built with the aid of Visual Studio, and contains metadata about the underlying database.

The purpose of the metadata is to describe the relationships between the various tables in the relational database management system (RDBMS) in terms of entities, attributes, and relationships (roles), which can then be used by Report Builder users to help them build ad hoc reports.

This helps to abstract the database management system (DBMS) into business objects that the nontechnologists should recognize.

The second part of the equation is the actual Report Builder. The Report Builder is the tool used to create ad hoc reports.

It is a Windows Forms-based .NET application that can be accessed through a URL (using the http://<localhost>/reportserver/reportbuilder/reportbuilder.application URL, where <localhost> is the name of the computer that is running Report Server) or from Report Manager (using the http://<webservername>/reports URL and then clicking Report Builder).

Report Builder uses the report model to present the end user with the abstracted view of business objects. Although Report Builder is a powerful report development application, Visual Studio provides many more features for report developers and is required to build models for Report Builder's consumption.

Report Models and the Model Designer

As previously mentioned, the first step in creating end-user reports is the creation of the report model. The model is written in a declarative language called Semantic Definition Model Language (SDML). SDML is based on the Unified Modeling Language (UML), and it contains many of the same paradigms. It is similar to the RDL in that it is an Extensible Markup Language (XML)-based communications language. The report model abstracts the RDBMS into business objects the end user would recognize.

To be effective for the end user, the model author must include some key pieces of information about the database. This type of information includes the following:

- A map of table names and column names into business objects
- Information about the relationships between tables that would otherwise be stored in primary keys or foreign keys

- Hierarchical information or logical groupings about your objects
- Permissions for users to see objects

From Report Builder, the model aids the user in selecting what information she wants to see, and, consequently, building the query for the data source of the resulting report.

To build these models, model developers must use a tool called Model Designer. Like Report Designer, it is built in to Visual Studio/Business Intelligence Development Studio (BIDS). The template project type is called Report Model Project. Models can be generated against SQL Server or Analysis Services.

NOTE

Model Designer and, subsequently, Report Builder can only build reports against SQL Server or Analysis Services. To build reports for other data sources, such as Oracle, you can use linked servers or the Unified Data Model (UDM). Both provide a thin abstraction layer.

Developers can generate models in two ways. The first way to generate models is based on a set of preexisting rules. This is the way the wizard and the autogenerate functionality work. The other way is to connect using a data source, and start designing the model by hand.

You will take a look at both methods later in this chapter.

Report Model Projects

As previously mentioned, report model projects are what the Model Designer uses to generate models. It uses three kinds of files to generate models. These files correlate to the major steps in models generation. The first kind of file is the data source (`.ds`) files.

The second type of file is the data source view (`.dsv`). The data source view provides the model information about the underlying data store. It is kind of like an entity relationship diagram, in that it provides information about the database schema, but is written in XML. The model uses the data source view to query the database, making the data source view the bridge between the model and the data source. The final type of file is the actual model file (`.sdml`). The model can only reference one data source and one data source view.

Model File Content

A report model contains three main sections:

- **Semantic model:** A semantic model is a collection of business objects in terms familiar to a business analyst.

The semantic model also contains the relationships of these business objects to one another.

- **Physical model:** The physical model outlines the database schema. This contains information about the tables and views in the data source.
- **Bindings:** The bindings map between the physical model and the semantic model.

The data source and data source view are used to make up the physical model. The semantic model is a combination of the physical model along with semantic objects and bindings.

Entities

The first of these objects is called an entity. The entity is really the crux of the semantic model because it maps tables and views.

An entity can map to multiple tables or views, and itself has a collection of objects called attributes, expressions, folders, and source fields. Entities should have names that are recognizable to a business analyst. For example, instead of the obscure table name `tbl_sls_ordr`, the entity would be named `Sales Order`.

As you add relational items to the data source view, you can map these items into entities. The binding property of the entity tells Report Builder the tables or views to which the entity refers.

Roles

In a way, roles take us back to Database Design 101. Roles store information about the relationship between entities. The relationship information is basically the cardinality between the objects. This can be one to one, one to many, or many to many. For example, a store entity can have only one address, whereas a customer can have many orders. Roles also contain information about which attributes in each entity are the defining ones in terms of the cardinality relationship. So, if the `AddressID` field on the store entity is what you need to obtain the proper address data from the address entity, the role that contains information about the relationship storing that `AddressID` is the field to use to correlate the two entities.

End users see the relationships play out when browsing entities in Report Builder. Roles are also what enable the infinite drill-down feature in Report Builder.

Source Fields and Expressions

If roles contain information about the primary and foreign fields, source fields contain information about the columns. A source field is an attribute that maps to a table column and gives the column a friendly name. Source fields can be added only after the parent entity's binding property has been set. For example, `LastName` on the `Person` table could be a source field on the person entity.

Expressions should have a familiar ring to them. Expressions in a report model take one or more source fields, and manipulate them with functions, operators, and constants to derive a calculated value. These expressions are just like expressions in Report Designer. They are based on VB.NET, and automatically provide access to `System.Math` and `System.Convert`. Functions from the `Microsoft.VisualBasic` namespace and references to other assemblies or custom code can be used, too.

A good example of what could be an expression is the combination of `FirstName` and `LastName` to create a new field called `Name`.

Folders

Folders allow you to group collections of entities. Folders can also contain other folders and perspectives. Folders allow you to add hierarchical information to the model. Folders can also be used to group items together regardless of hierarchical relationships. For example, because Report Builder users can navigate folders in a manner similar to Windows Explorer, you can move infrequently used items into a folder to hide them from the users.

Perspectives

Perspectives help to give us a narrower view or a view of a subset of the model. Perspectives can help limit users to see only information to which they have access. For example, a company might have a model that contains information about all the financial data items for that company. One of the things perspectives can help us do is to limit what budgetary information users can see to only information about their departments' budgets.

Perspectives are contained in the model, and the model designers and wizards don't create them for you. They have to be manually created, and model items must be placed in them. Perspectives can contain other model objects, such as entities folders, roles, source fields, and expressions. Just placing items into a perspective does not exclude them from the rest of the models. Items can still be placed in other folders and perspectives.

Creating a Model Project

To create a model, you need to complete a few steps. The first is to create a report model project. Then you give the project a data source and a data source view. Finally, you can create the models. In the following steps, you create a model based on the Adventure Works catalog:

1. Create a new project. Open Visual Studio or BIDS. Click File, New Project.
2. In the dialog box that opens, if not selected by default, select Business Intelligence Projects under Project Types.
3. Under Templates in the right pane in the active dialog box, select Report Model Project.

4. Call the project **First Model**. Make sure Create Directory for Solution is checked (see Figure 18.1).

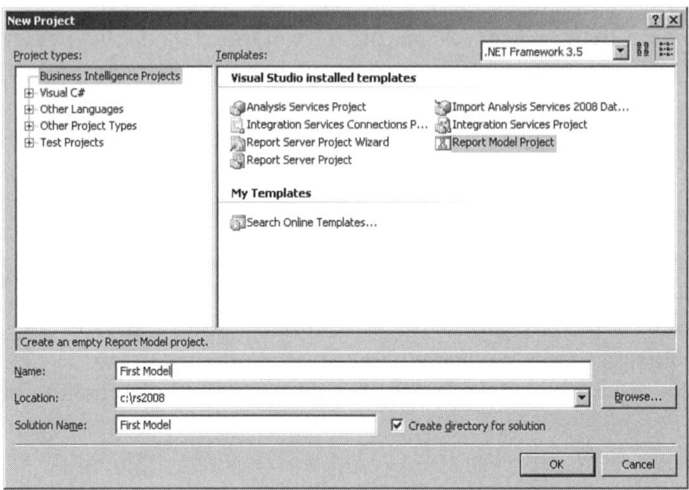

FIGURE 18.1 Creating new business intelligence projects.

Creating a Data Source

Now that you have an empty project, the next thing to do is connect it to a data source. Remember the data source has to be SQL Server (or abstracted through linked servers or UDM).

Unlike Report Designer, no other data sources are accepted directly:

1. Open Solution Explorer and right-click the Data Sources folder. Click Add New Data Source. This launches the New Data Source Wizard.
2. Skip the Welcome page by clicking Next.
3. On the next page, select Create a Data Source Based on an Existing or New Connection, and then click New.
4. Enter **localhost** as the name of the server to connect to.
5. Select Windows Authentication.
6. From the Select or Enter a Database Name list, select Adventure Works.
7. Click Test Connection; if you get an OK dialog box, click OK. If not, try to resolve the error using the debug information given, and then try again.
8. Click OK. At this point, you should have a screen that looks similar to Figure 18.2 (Data Source Wizard).
9. Click Next.
10. At this point, you could change the name of the data source. If it is not already, call the new data source **Adventure Works.**

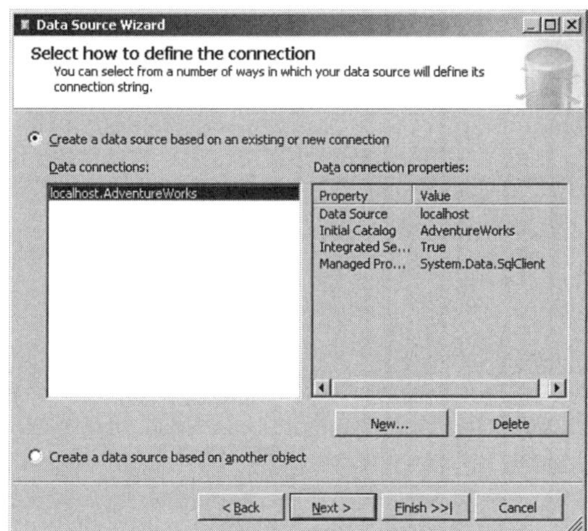

FIGURE 18.2 Defining the connection.

11. Click Finish.

A new data source called Adventure Works should appear in the Data Sources folder in Solution Explorer.

Creating a Data Source View

The next step in the creation of a model is the creation of the data source view. Recall, from earlier, that the data source view contains information about the physical layout of the database. To create a data source view, complete the following steps:

1. Open Solution Explorer and right-click the Data Source Views folder. Click Add New Data Source View. This launches the New Data Source View Wizard.
2. Select the Adventure Works data source and click Next.
3. The next screen asks you to select the tables and views that are going to be included in the semantic model. Click the >> button to move all the objects from the Available Objects list box to the Included Objects list box (see Figure 18.3).
4. Click Next.
5. Name the data source view **`Adventure Works DSV`**.
6. Click Finish.

A new data source view called Adventure Works DSV should appear in the Data Source Views folder in Solution Explorer.

The wizard is smart enough to detect whether the underlying data source has no foreign key constraints. In this case, the wizard gives you an extra screen before selecting which tables to include in the data source view. The screen gives you three types of matching logic so that it can infer relationships in the data store. If your DBMS does not follow any of these conventions, you will have to add the data source relationships yourself. Figure 18.4 shows the Name Matching screen.

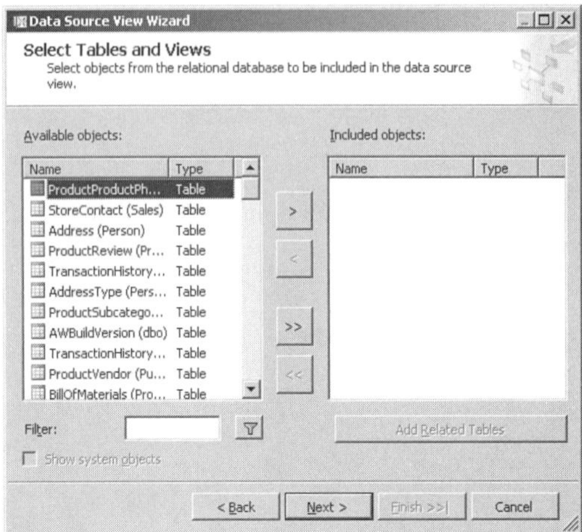

FIGURE 18.3 Selecting the tables and views.

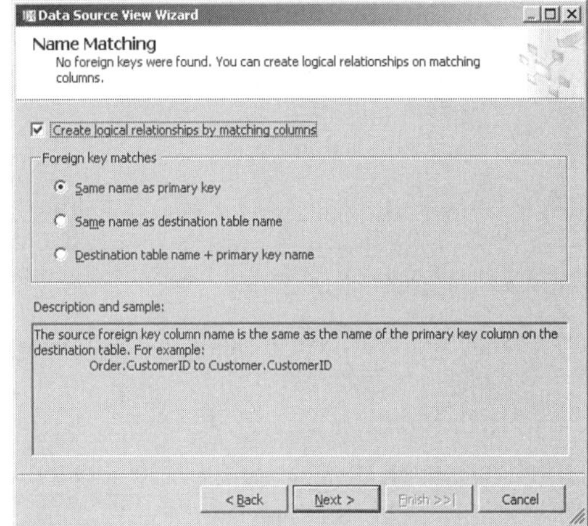

FIGURE 18.4 Name Matching screen of the Data Source View Wizard.

After the wizard is complete, double-click the `Adventure Works DSV.dsv` file in Solution Explorer. This opens a document showing you the relationships that the wizard has just inferred (see Figure 18.5).

To get the document to fit on one page, you might have to click the View menu, point to Zoom, and then click To Fit.

Creating a Report Model

Finally, you can create the actual model. To create the model, complete the following steps:

1. Open Solution Explorer and right-click the Report Models folder. Click Add New Report Model. This launches the New Report Model Wizard.

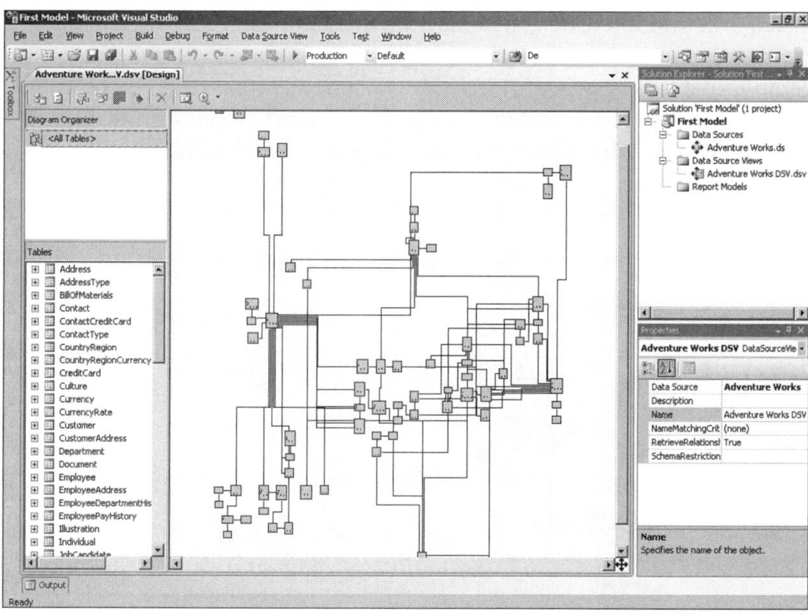

FIGURE 18.5 Data source view.

2. Click Next on the Welcome screen.
3. The next screen is the screen to select data source views. At this point, only the Adventure Works DSV should show up. Select this, and then click Next.
4. The next screen is the Model Generation Rules screen, which is shown in Figure 18.6. From this screen, you can select from a predefined set of rules to ease the model-generation process. For our purposes, the defaults are fine. Click Next.

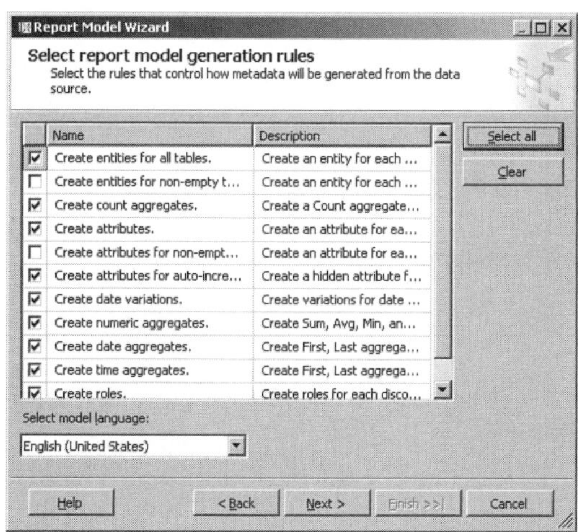

FIGURE 18.6 Selecting report model generation rules.

5. The next screen asks you to create statistics. Because Report Builder uses database statistics to aid it in the model-generation process, it is important to make sure your statistics are up-to-date. Otherwise, it might miscalculate some factors, such as drill down and aggregates. It is recommended to update statistics whenever the data source or data source views have changed. Click Update Model Statistics Before Generating, if necessary, on the Collect Model Statistics screen.

   Click Next (see Figure 18.7).

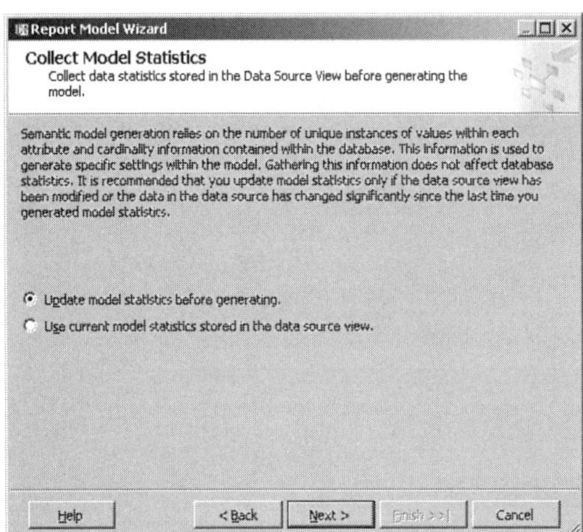

FIGURE 18.7 Collect Model Statistics screen of the Report Model Wizard.

6. Name the model **Adventure Works Model**, and then click Run. Figure 18.8 shows the resulting screen.

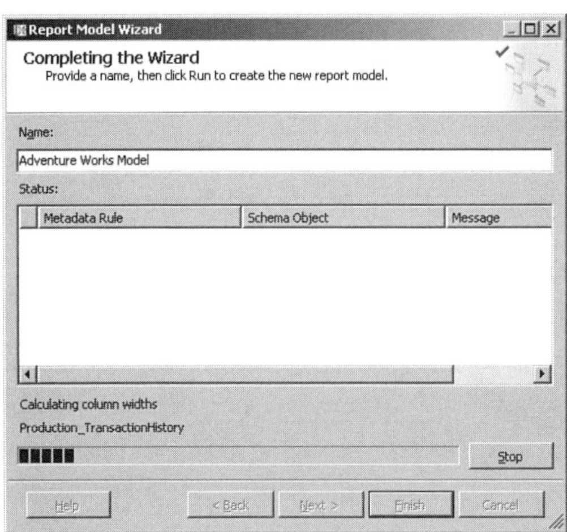

FIGURE 18.8 Completing the Wizard screen of the Report Model Wizard.

7. Click Finish. Figure 18.9 shows the completed model.

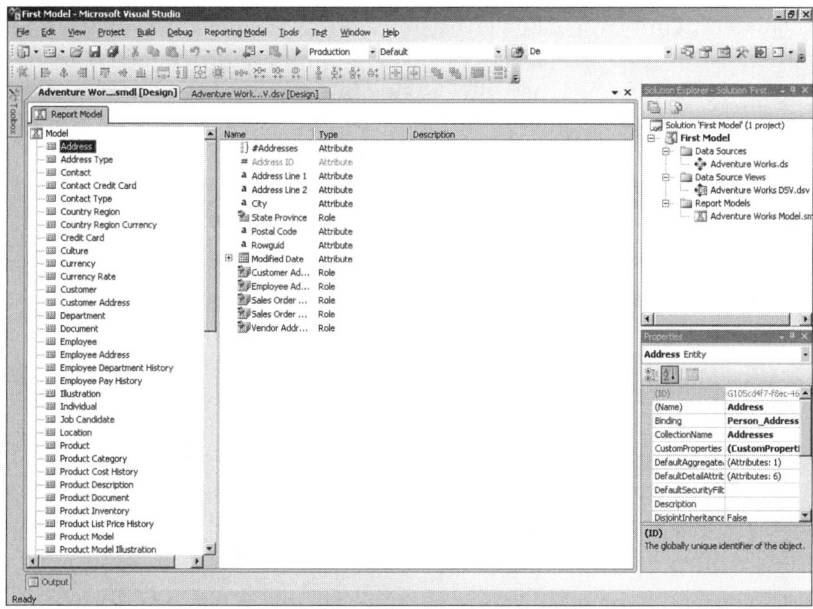

FIGURE 18.9 Completed database model.

Modifying Items in the Model

The way entities show up in the Model Designer reflects how they will show up in Report Builder. To make things more meaningful for the end user, many of the properties or entities can be customized. Working with the model involves some of the same basic concepts as working with Report Designer. The properties of any object can be modified from the Properties window.

Things you can customize include sorting, instance selection, and inheritance. What this means is that attributes can be set to come from other entities or that users can see a filtered list of instances of an entity. Entities can also predefine formatting of their attributes. For example, attributes that reflect currency can be formatted as currency depending on the user's localized settings. The order in which things appear in the entity browser can also be customized. By default, entities appear sorted in alphabetic order, but you can move certain entities to the top if users are going to report off them frequently.

To modify items in the model, it is just a matter of right-clicking in the tree view or list view. The Report Model menu in the Model Designer also gives the same menu options. To delete any item, just navigate to the item, right-click it, and choose Delete from the shortcut menu.

To add an entity, folder, or perspective, do the following:

1. Navigate to the top of the tree view.

2. From the Report Model menu, select New Entity, New Perspective, or New Folder.

From this point, each of these items has its own caveats.

If you choose to add a new entity, the name given to the entity is simply NewEntity. You must navigate to NewEntity, right-click it, select Rename from the shortcut menu, and rename it to what you want. To be effective, the binding information has to be set, too. When adding folders, a similar process has to be followed. You must navigate to the entity or to the top entity in the tree, right-click it, and select New Folder. A new folder called New Folder is created. The location of the new folder is dependent on where you were when you right-clicked to add the new folder. You must right-click it and select Rename from the shortcut menu to rename it.

To add a new role, attribute, or source field, click any detail item, and then select the option you need from the Report Model menu. When you add a new role, a pop-up appears with a list of entities. Select an entity, and then assign the bindings in the Properties window. Role bindings are nothing more than a list of relations defined in the data source view. When adding or modifying an expression, the Expression Editor is shown. From here, you can design the expression and name it. When adding a source field, select New Source Field from the Report Model menu. After adding the source field, you must rename it and set the bindings from the Properties window. Source field bindings refer to a list of columns from the data source view Model menu.

When you are adding or modifying perspectives, a specialized dialog box opens that enables you to add/remove items from the perspective.

When adding and removing perspectives, you might notice that adding one object seems to add others, and removing it removes other objects, too. This is because of the hierarchical nature of the items. When a parent item, such as a folder or attribute, with variations gets added or removed, all of its children get added and removed, too. The same thing applies for roles and identifying attributes. When a role is selected, the corresponding role is selected along with the entity it leads to. The reverse is also true. When an identifying attribute is deselected, any other entities that use that identifying attribute get deselected, too. To reselect those entities, the identifying attribute must get reselected.

Publishing the Model

When you are done creating or updating the model, you can publish the model just as you would a report. In a published model, the data source and the SMDL file are placed in the Report Server. Because the information in the data source view is incorporated into the semantic model, the data source view does not get published. If the information in the data source view, or for that matter, anything in the semantic model, needs to be updated, just publish an updated model.

After the model is published, it can be secured using Reporting Services role-based security. To use the model in Report Builder, a user must have access to it.

When you are ready to deploy the semantic model, the deployment steps closely resemble the deployment steps in Report Designer:

1. Right-click the project file in Solution Explorer, and select Properties.

2. Review the target folder's properties. There is one target folder for the data sources, and there is another target folder for the semantic models.
3. Verify that the Overwrite Data Sources option is on the intended setting. This option is similar in name and function to the one in Report Designer.
4. Click OK.

To deploy the model and data source, right-click the project file in Solution Explorer and select Deploy from the shortcut menu. To deploy just the model file, right-click the semantic model and click Deploy.

Creating Models from Report Designer

A second way to create a model is from Report Manager. Report Manager can take any SQL Server or Analysis Services data source and generate a model from it. You can complete the following steps to generate a model from Report Manager:

1. Go to the Report Manager web page. By default, it is located at http://localhost/Reports.
2. Click the New Data Source button.
3. Enter a name for this data source. Call this **`AdventureWorks DS`**. You can also enter a brief description.
4. Enter a connection type of **`Microsoft SQL Server`**.
5. Make sure that the Enable This Data Source check box is checked.
6. Enter **`Data Source=localhost;Initial Catalog=AdventureWorks`** in the Connection String text box.
7. Select Windows Integrated Security.
8. Click OK. You should return to the Folder View screen. Click the data source you just created (AdventureWorks DS).
9. Click the Generate Model button.
10. Enter a name for this model. Call it Adventure Works DS Model. If you want to, you can change where the model is located and give it a description. For now, just leave these fields blank.
11. Click OK.

Features of Report Builder

Report Builder is the second part of the two-part solution for end-user reporting. As previously mentioned, Report Builder is a click-once, client-side .NET application that can be launched from the Report Manager website. Report Builder uses Microsoft Office paradigms, so it should be easy for end users who use Microsoft Office to start using it, yet it still creates reports using standard Report Definition Language (RDL). Figure 18.10 shows how to access Report Builder.

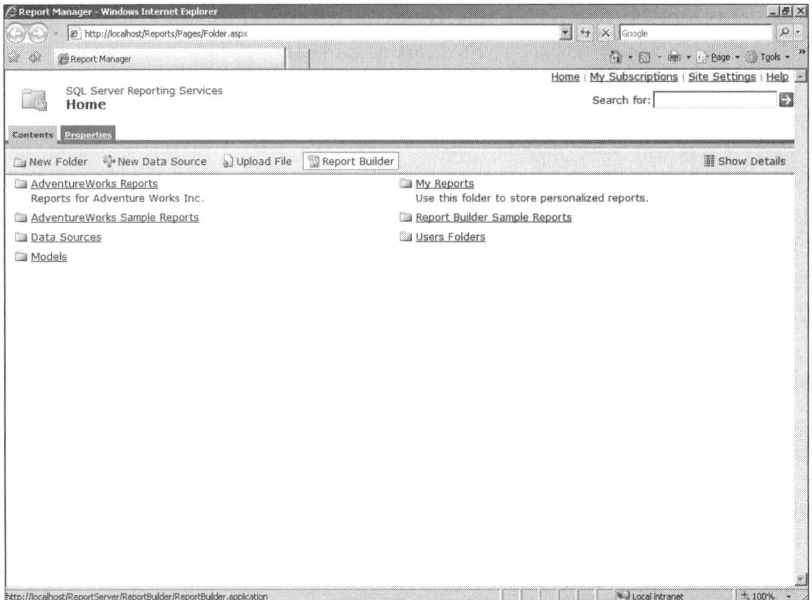

FIGURE 18.10 Starting Report Builder from the Report Manager web interface.

Report Builder uses the models stored on the Report Server. Report Builder calls these models. Through Report Builder, the end user knows nothing of the actual data source used by the model. End users will most likely be referring to the model as the data source, as shown in Figure 18.11. Keep in mind that because the models are secured by the Report Server, users will not be able to access models to use as data sources for their report if the appropriate permissions have not been set.

Report Builder has predefined templates available for matrix, table, and chart report layouts. Note that lists and rectangles are not supported. To use a template, the user just has to click a template in the left pane. Figure 18.12 shows the Report Builder interface.

After selecting a template, the end user simply has to drag and drop fields from the Report Data Explorer onto the data region provided. Report Data Explorer is nothing more than the entity explorer. Attributes and expressions make up the fields that are usable from within the entity explorer.

Some basic features are also available through Report Builder. Formatting can be done to any text box on the report layout. Data can be filtered, sorted, and grouped. A full range of export formats, such as PDF, TIFF, Excel, HTML, XML, CSV, and TIFF are also available to end users.

Report Builder saves reports to the Report Server. After being published, the reports can be managed like any other reports.

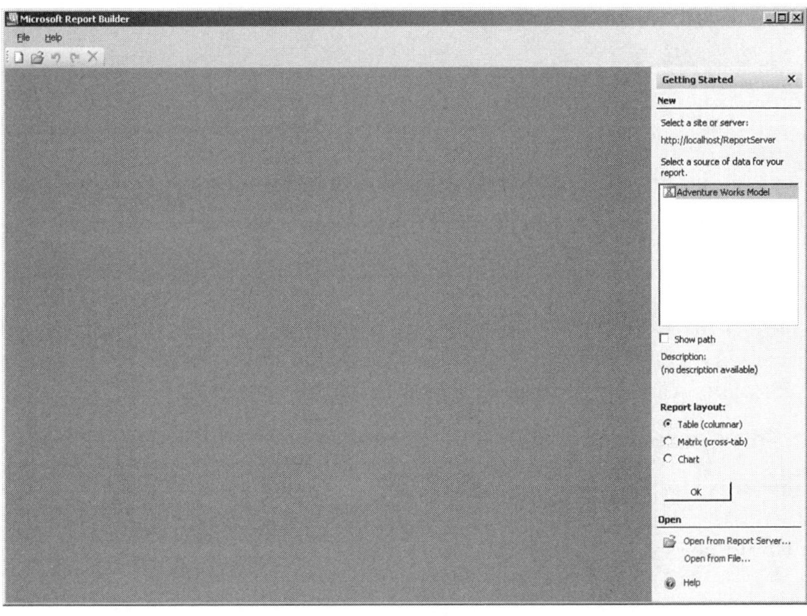

FIGURE 18.11 Selecting a model to use with Report Builder.

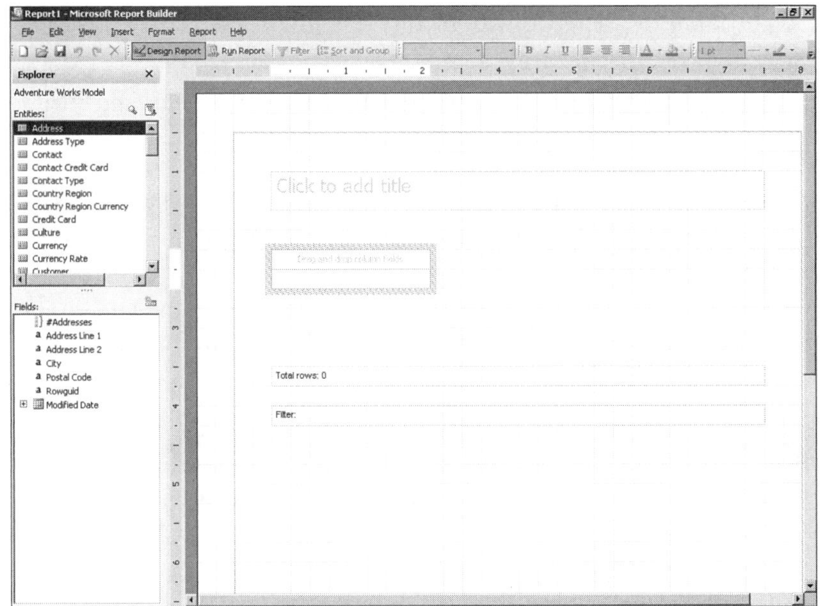

FIGURE 18.12 Report Builder after the model selection.

Building Reports with Report Builder

Building reports with Report Builder is fairly simple compared to Report Designer. The complexities of connecting to the data source and SQL Server are taken care of by the model. All that needs to be selected are attributes and expressions from the entity explorer.

First, launch Report Builder. After you launch Report Builder, a list of models appears that are available for you to use as your data source (see Figures 18.11 and 18.12). After you select the data source, Report Builder opens up to the report layout section. Figure 18.12 shows what the screen should look like in the default table view.

On the left side is the entity explorer. Below the entity explorer is the list of attributes and fields. On the right side is the list of style templates: Table, Matrix, and Chart. By clicking one of these templates, you can create a new report with that layout.

Now, let's try to build a simple report with Report Builder.

The requirements for this sample report are as follows: The marketing department wants to see the breakdown of subtotals for sales orders by quarter and by year. They are not sure what mechanism would be best to display the data, so they request it in tabular format and in a pivot table.

Tabular Report

Complete following steps to produce the report:

1. Select Table Report from the Report Layout menu on the right side.
2. Select Sales Territory from the entity explorer.
3. Under the Explorer pane, though still on the left side, is the list of fields and attributes. Select Name and drag it over to the layout view where it says Drag and Drop Column Fields.
4. After you drag Name over to the layout view, the entity explorer should have switched to entities that have a role relating to sales territory. From this list, select Sales Order Headers.
5. From the Attribute Fields menu, drag Order Year, which is located under Order Date, over next to the Sales Territory name. The mouse cursor should turn blue to signify that the table is ready to add a column.

NOTE

The Model Builder automatically creates expressions based on dates. These expressions are usually date parts.

Certain entities and attributes also might have a `#of <Entity>` expression. The rules chosen during the wizard are the driving factor behind these. The Model Builder also chooses whether to include a distinct count of values based on database statistics.

6. Drag Order Quarter (also located under Order Date) over next to Order Year.

7. Drag Total Sub Total over next to Order Quarter. After doing this, notice three total lines that appeared. One of the nice features of Report Builder is that it automatically groups and sums data for you.
8. Enter **`Total Product Sales by Quarter by Territory`** in the text box above the table where it says Click to Add Title.

Figure 18.13 shows what your report should look like.

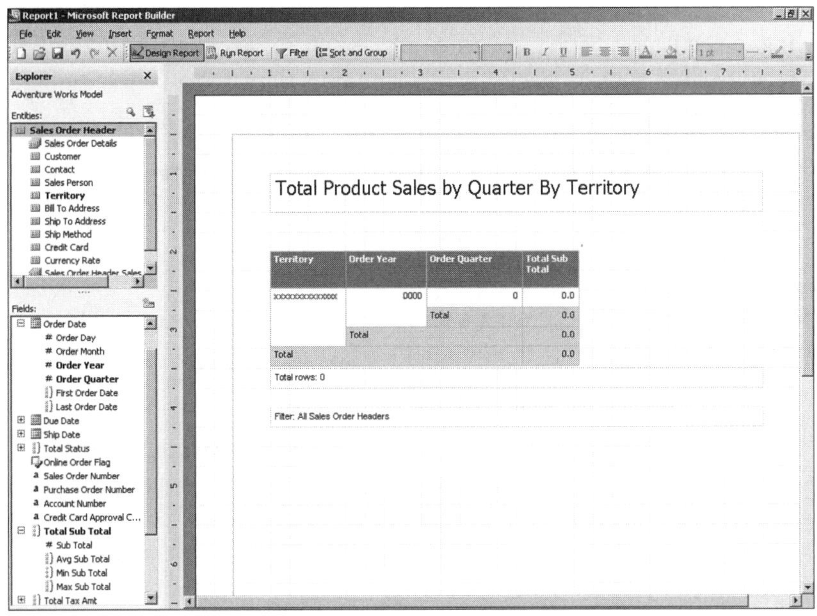

FIGURE 18.13 View of a report in Report Builder.

The report can be previewed by clicking the Run Report button on the toolbar.

Clickthrough Reports

When the report is in Preview mode, the end user can hover over the Sum of Sales Totals number and notice that it is actually a link to another report. This type of report is called a clickthrough report and is automatically generated by Report Builder.

Clickthrough reports are based on roles. After a user has selected to display a certain type of aggregate attribute, if the attribute has roles linking over to another entity, Report Builder automatically generates a report listing the contents of that aggregate. You could potentially drill down to the lowest level, and at each stage Report Builder will generate a report based on that entity. This feature is called infinite drill down. It is one of the benefits of putting work into generating models that contain information about all the relationships in the DBMS.

Saving/Publishing Reports

Now that you have completed this basic report, let's try to save it. Unlike in Visual Studio, the RDL file that has been generated by Report Builder cannot be saved on the user's hard drive. To save client-side reports, users must have access to publish reports in at least one folder on the Report Server. An easy way to enable this access is to enable the My Reports option on the Report Server.

This gives users permissions to their own My Report folder.

After enabling My Reports, saving a report is a simple matter. The menu options inside Report Builder are similar to the same commands in Microsoft Office. The only difference is that you are saving to the Report Server and not a file server. To save the existing report to the Report Server and call it Sales by Territory—Table, follow these steps:

1. Choose Save As from the File menu.
2. In the root folder of the Report Server, enter the filename **`Sales by Territory–Table`**, and then click OK.

Matrix/Pivot Table Report

Now, let's go on to make the same report using a pivot table or matrix. The concepts are the same; just the data region is different.

1. If you have already closed Report Builder, reopen it.
2. Select the Matrix Report style from the Report Layout section on the right pane.
3. From the entity explorer, select Sales Territory, and drag the Name attribute over to the matrix where it says Drag and Drop Row Groups.
4. From the entity explorer, select Sales Order Headers, and drag the Order Year under Order Date to the matrix layout where it says Drag and Drop Column Groups.
5. Similarly, select Order Quarter and drag it over to the matrix columns groups. Place it under Order Year. The mouse cursor should turn blue when it is ready to add a column group.
6. Select Total Sub Total and drag it to the Detail section of the matrix where it says Drag and Drop Totals.
7. Add a title to the report; call it **`Sales by Territory`**.
8. To make things easier to see, let's use some basic formatting to separate the quarters from the years. Right-click the inner 0, and select Format from the shortcut menu.
9. Go to the Fill tab and select Gold as the color. Then go to the Alignment tab and choose Center for the horizontal alignment. Do the same for the Adjoining Total text box. This should make all quarters-related information headers gold.
10. Do the same thing to the upper 0 and the adjoining total, except select Green as the color. Select Center for the horizontal alignment. On the Border tab, click the Outline button to put an outline border around the year.
11. When the report is previewed, it looks similar to Figure 18.14.

    Save this report on the Report Server as **`Sales by Territory Matrix`**.

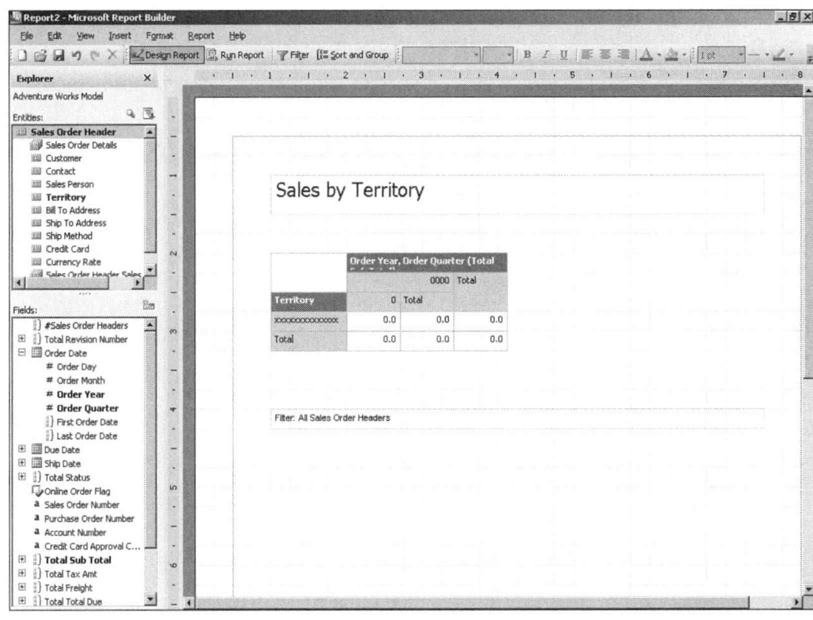

FIGURE 18.14 Preview of the report in Report Designer.

12. Right-click the Sum Sub Total text box, select Format from the shortcut menu, go to the Number tab, and select the currency format.

When everything is complete, your report design should look similar to Figure 18.15.

Report Builder 2.0

Report Builder 2.0 is a new client-side tool that can be installed on the end-user desktop. The design of Report Builder 2.0 takes a different take on ad hoc reporting. Report Builder 2.0 does not rely exclusively on report models for use as data sources. You can use data from SQL Server, Analysis Services, other OLE DB data sources, ODBC, SAP, SAP BI, NetWeaver, Hyperion Essbase, and Oracle. Connecting to a data source is a lot like when using BIDS. You can use either a shared data source or a report-specific data source.

Report Builder 2.0 can be used to create tabular, matrix, free-form and chart reports. The nice thing about it is that you can use Report Builder 2.0's Ribbon interface to place the data regions onto the layout surface. Report Builder 2.0 is a lot closer to being a full-featured report designer. Data can be manipulated by filtering, sorting, and grouping with queries or expressions. Rendering is also fairly open. Reports can be rendered and exported to HTML, Excel, Word, PDF, and TIFF.

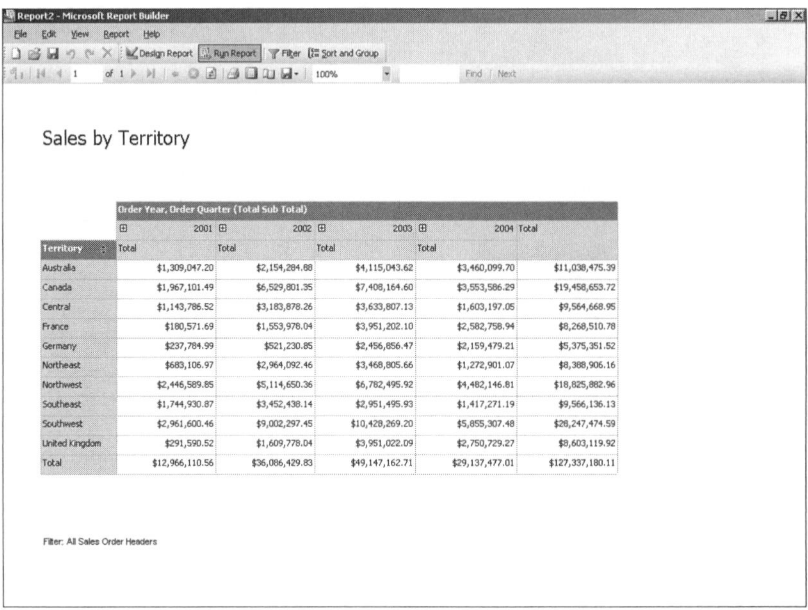

	Order Year, Order Quarter (Total Sub Total)				
	2001	2002	2003	2004	Total
Territory	Total	Total	Total	Total	
Australia	$1,309,047.20	$2,154,284.88	$4,115,043.62	$3,460,099.70	$11,038,475.39
Canada	$1,967,101.49	$6,529,801.35	$7,408,164.60	$3,553,586.29	$19,458,653.72
Central	$1,143,786.52	$3,183,878.26	$3,633,807.13	$1,603,197.05	$9,564,668.95
France	$180,571.69	$1,553,978.04	$3,951,202.10	$2,582,758.94	$8,268,510.78
Germany	$237,784.99	$521,230.85	$2,456,856.47	$2,159,479.21	$5,375,351.52
Northeast	$683,106.97	$2,964,092.46	$3,468,805.66	$1,272,901.07	$8,388,906.16
Northwest	$2,446,589.85	$5,114,650.36	$6,782,495.92	$4,482,146.81	$18,825,882.96
Southeast	$1,744,930.87	$3,452,438.14	$2,951,495.93	$1,417,271.19	$9,566,136.13
Southwest	$2,961,600.46	$9,002,297.45	$10,428,269.20	$5,855,307.48	$28,247,474.59
United Kingdom	$291,590.52	$1,609,778.04	$3,951,022.09	$2,750,729.27	$8,603,119.92
Total	$12,966,110.56	$36,086,429.83	$49,147,162.71	$29,137,477.01	$127,337,180.11

Filter: All Sales Order Headers

FIGURE 18.15 Finalized report design.

Report Builder 2.0 Features

Let's take a look at some of the features of Report Builder 2.0. A number of the features listed here are not part of Report Builder 1.0. Report Builder 2.0 is intended to be a full-featured report designer more akin to BIDS. (A lot of the differences between Report Builder 1.0 and Report Builder 2.0 can be attributed to that.)

- **Multiple data sources:** Report Builder 2.0 can use native SSRS data sources. Therefore, just as with reports you build in BIDS, you can use any OLE DB or ODBC data source. You can also use multidimensional data sources like Analysis Services or Essbase. You can also use XML data sources.
- **Report data regions:** You can use Report Builder 2.0 to create tabular, matrix, and free-form reports. You can also use charts, gauges, and all the features of the new SSRS Tablix feature.
- **Ad hoc reporting:** You can create and save reports and choose to save them directly to the Report Server or to your local desktop
- **Link to subreports:** With Report Builder, you can link to subreports and use report parameters just as you can with BIDS. This allows a certain level of interactivity. If you use a report model, you can use infinite clickthrough.
- **Rendering formats:** Report Builder 2.0 allows all rendering extensions used by SSRS. These include HTML, PDF, CSV, XML, TIFF, Word, and Excel.
- **Custom report items:** Custom report items can be used in Report Builder 2.0. Of course, this requires a certain amount of configuration.

- **Report navigation:** You can use document maps and add bookmarks to reports.
- **Graphics:** You can embed custom images and other resources into reports.
- **Aggregations:** You can group and summarize data in groups using either fields or expressions.

Installing Report Builder 2.0

Because Report Builder 2.0 comes with the feature pack, it must be installed outside of the normal installation. Remember that Report Builder 2.0 targets the end user or advanced analyst, so it does not get installed on the server, but on the end user's desktop.

The installation is fairly straightforward. The installation file is called `ReportBuilder.msi`.

Here are the steps to install Report Builder 2.0:

1. Double-click `ReportBuilder.msi` to start the install process.
2. Click Next on the first dialog box to start the install.
3. Accept the license agreement.
4. Enter the registration information.
5. For feature selection, make sure the Report Builder 2.0 feature is going to be installed completely, and then click Next (see Figure 18.16).

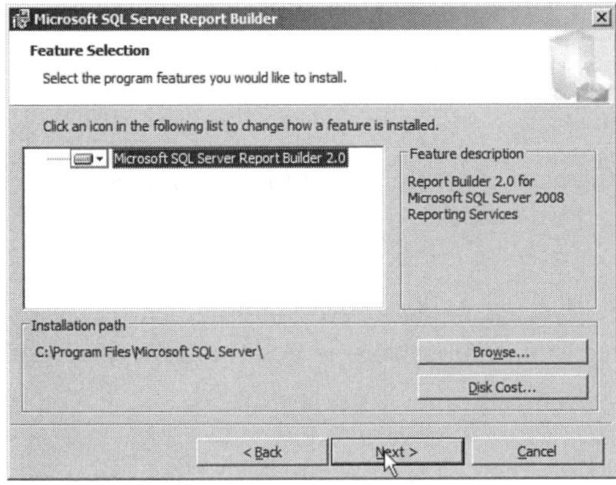

FIGURE 18.16 Report Builder 2.0 feature dialog box.

6. Now we have to pick the default target server. This is the server where Report Builder will automatically try to save to, and Report Builder will also look to this server for

shared data sources. Enter **`http://localhost/ReportServer`** (see Figure 18.17). Click Next.

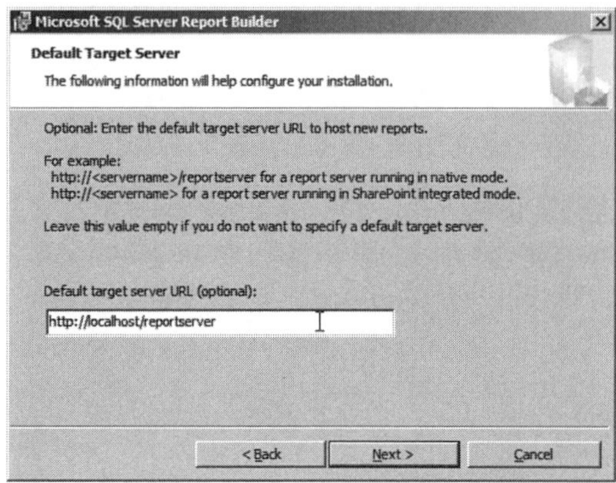

FIGURE 18.17 Report Builder 2.0 Default Target Server screen.

7. Click Install.
8. Click Finish when install completes.

When the install is complete, you can launch Report Builder 2.0 by clicking the Report Builder 2.0 shortcut in the Start menu. The program group is called Microsoft SQL Server 2008 Report Builder 2.0.

Design Surface

The design surface of Report Builder 2.0 is where most of the work of report authoring takes place. Similar to other report designers, this is where you add data regions, modify groupings, edit expressions, change visibility, and format reports.

Items from the data pane or from the Ribbon can be dragged onto the design surface. You can right-click anywhere on the design surface to edit report properties, and you can right-click any item to pull up its properties.

Page Size

One of the biggest issues faced by new users is reconciling page size with the printable page size. The page size on the design surface is based on the total available page size. However, the printing page size subtracts the margins from the total page size. You can use the Ruler from the Ribbons to get an idea about how large your reports are. Click the View tab on the Ribbon, and then check the Ruler check box. To set up the page size, click the Page Setup button in Preview mode.

To sum it up, if you have a printable page size of 8.5 x 11, and you use standard margins of 1 inch on all sides, your report body's size has to be 6.5 x 9. Therefore, you have to take 1 inch off of the page size from the right and left sides of the page, and 1 inch from the top and bottom.

Ribbons

One of the nice new features in Report Builder 2.0 is the intuitive Ribbons interface of Office 2007. There are four main tabs in the Report Builder 2.0 interface: Home, Insert, View, and Run.

The Home tab, as shown in Figure 18.18, contains useful commands to help design reports on the design surface. From this tab, you can run the report and change fonts, paragraph alignment, borders, and number formatting. Just like in BIDS, executing the report with the `run` command displays for you the report in HTML values. When you execute the report, you end up in the Run tab.

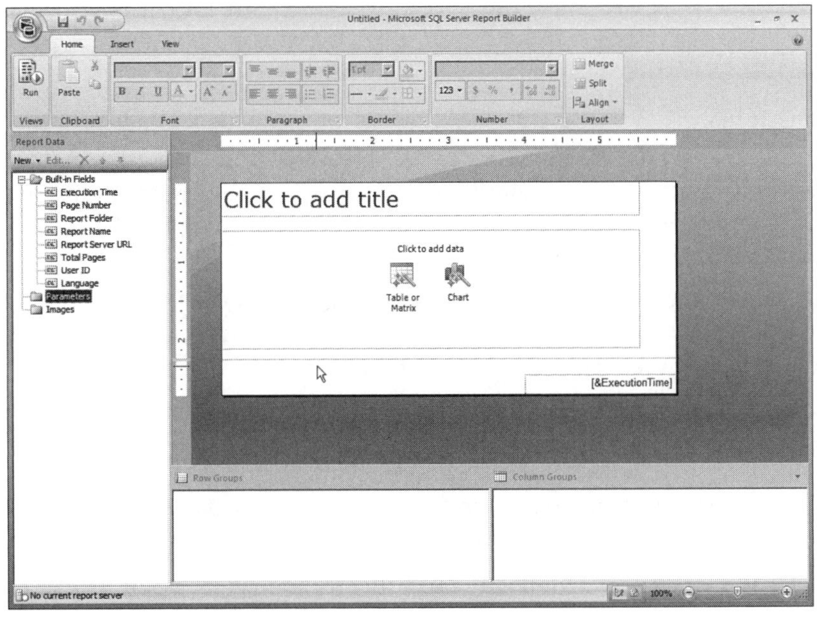

FIGURE 18.18 Home tab.

The Insert tab, shown in Figure 18.19, contains commands for adding report items. This Ribbon contains common data regions like Table, Matrix, Chart, Gauge, and List. It also contains common items such as Textbox, Image, Line, and Rectangle. In addition, you can add subreports and add a header and footer.

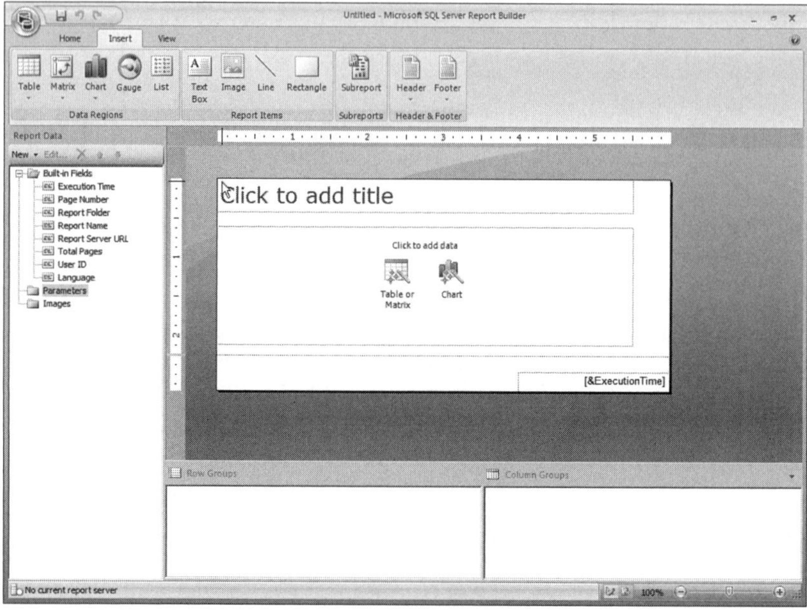

FIGURE 18.19 Insert tab.

The View tab, shown in Figure 18.20, contains items to help design reports. From this tab, you can turn off and on dialog boxes (for example, the Report Data, Grouping, Ruler, and the Properties dialog boxes).

From the Run tab, shown in Figure 18.21, you can get to crucial tools, such as the Print Layout, Page Setup, and Print functions. You can also use the Run tab and click the Export button to export into different rendering formats, such as XML, CSV, TIFF, PDF, MHTML, Excel, and Word. Clicking the Design button will send you back into design view.

Other Dialog Boxes

The data pane is there to manage data sources and data sets. From the data pane, you can also drag fields from common fields, or from the data sets.

The Properties dialog box enables you to modify properties for individual report items. You have to enable the dialog box from the View tab in the Ribbon. After you enable it, when you click any report item, modifiable properties will display. You can sometimes modify the properties just by editing text, or selecting a valid value from a drop-down. Other times, a custom dialog box may pop up.

The grouping pane in Report Builder 2.0 is similar to the grouping pane in BIDS. It contains two main groups: Row Groups and Column Groups. Groups can be created by

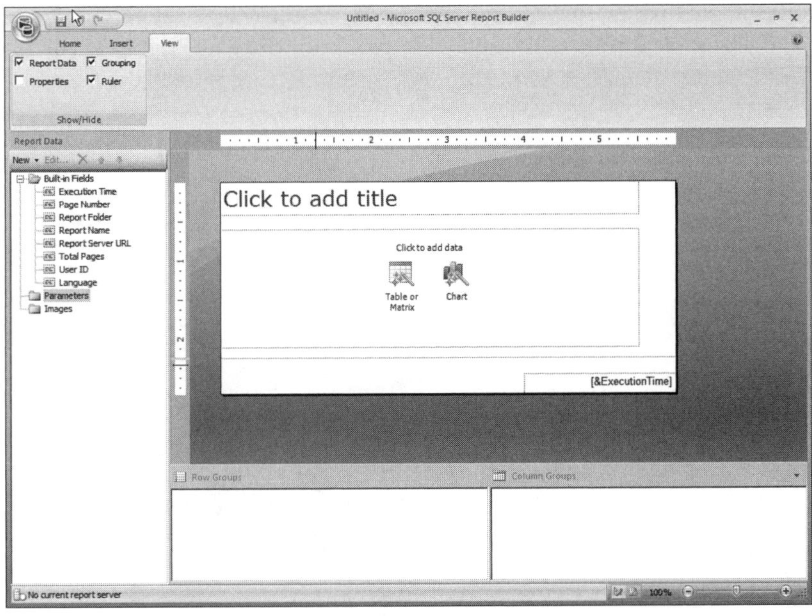

FIGURE 18.20 View tab.

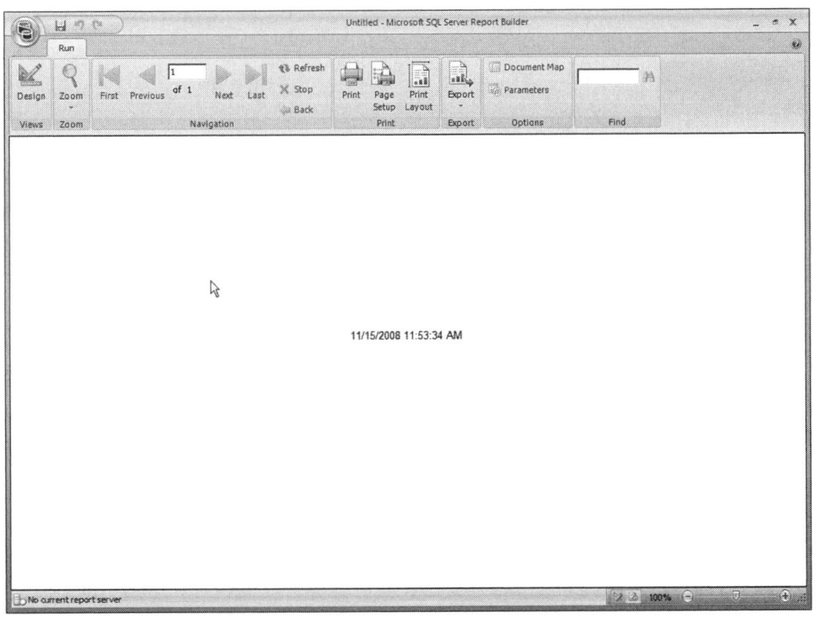

FIGURE 18.21 Run tab.

dragging fields from the data pane or by using expressions. As you select different data regions in a report, the grouping pane will display the group for the data region. If you do not want to see the grouping pane, you can turn if off by unselecting it from the View tab.

Figure 18.22 shows all the panes and dialog boxes.

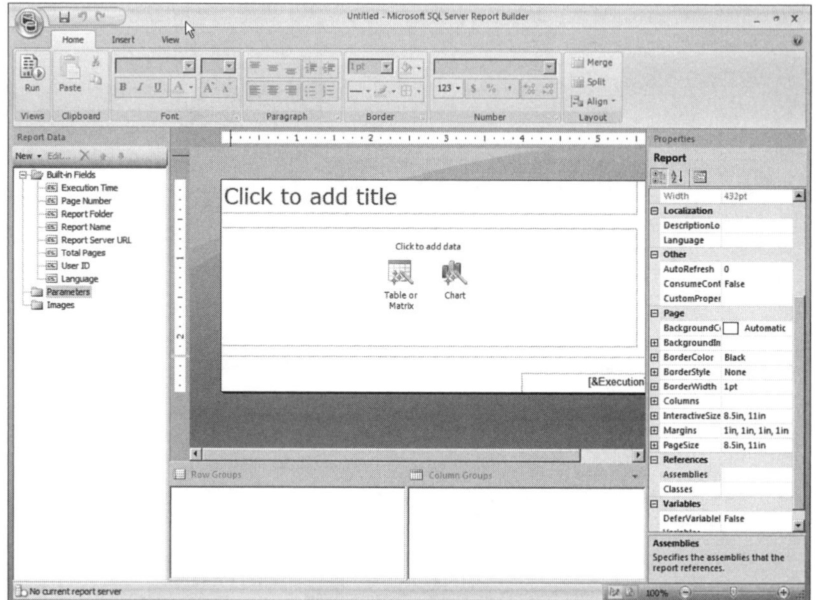

FIGURE 18.22 Report Builder 2.0 design surface.

Managing Data Sources and Data Sets

Reports created with Report Builder 2.0 use data sources and connections similar to those built with BIDS. Report Builder 2.0 actually has the capability to select shared data sources from the Report Server. If you do not choose one of those report data sources, you can still create and embed data sources with their own connection strings. Examples are similar to those mentioned in Chapter 11, "Accessing Data."

Data sources and data sets can be managed in the report data pane inside Report Builder 2.0. After you have created a data source or referenced a shared data source, you can design queries for that data source by using the Graphical Query Designer or the text-based Query Designer. Queries can also be imported from other report files (RDL files). Queries can use one or many parameters and have calculated fields. Queries can even have filters applied on the Report Server. Bear in mind, however, that these filters may use more system resources than filters applied at the database level. After you successfully define a data set, the data set will show up under a tree view in the data pane.

Here are the steps to create a basic data source and a data set:

1. Open Report Builder 2.0.
2. On the Report Data dialog box, click the New button and select Data Source.
3. In the Data Source Properties dialog box, enter a name for your data source. For this example, call it **`AdventureWorks`**.
4. Select Use a Shared Connection or Report Model.
5. Click the Browse button to browse data sources on the your Report Server. Select the AdventureWorks data source in the Data Sources folder. Click OK (see Figure 18.23).

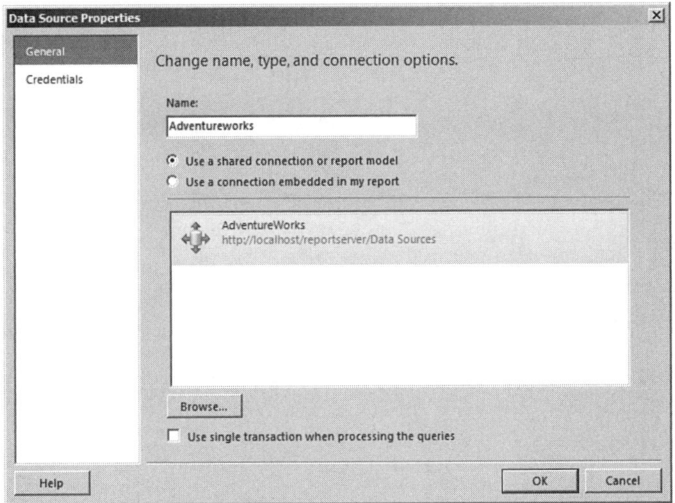

FIGURE 18.23 Data Source Properties dialog box.

Now that you have a data source defined, you need to add the actual data set. The Report Data pane contains a tree view, in which data sets are defined under the data sources they use. You should see an AdventureWorks icon in the tree view now. This signifies the data source. Here are the steps to create a data set:

1. Under the AdventureWorks icon, right-click and select Add DataSet.
2. Change the name of the data set to **`EmployeeInformation`**.
3. In the Dataset Properties dialog box, click the Query Designer button.
4. In the Query Designer dialog box, open the HumanResources folder and under Views, vEmployee, select Title, FirstName, LastName, Phone, and EmailAddress (see Figure 18.24). Click OK.

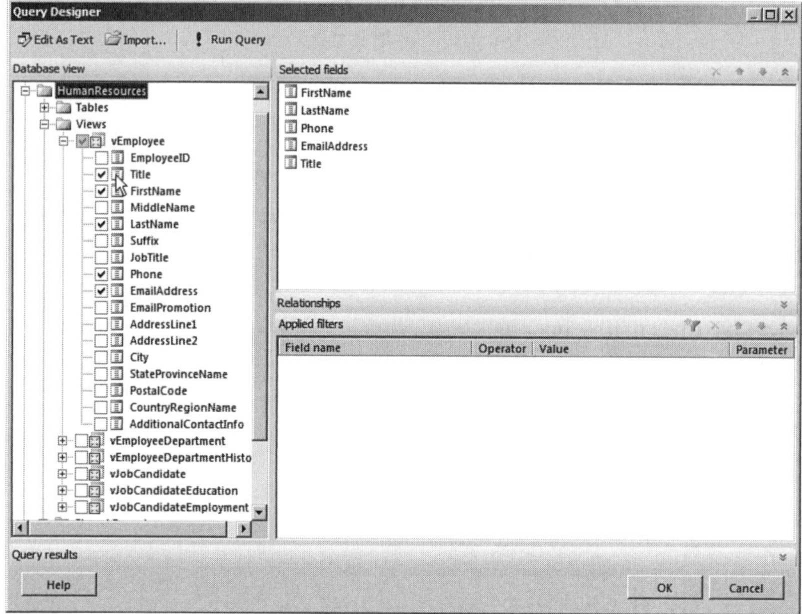

FIGURE 18.24 Query Designer.

5. Figure 18.25 shows the completed Dataset Properties dialog box. Click OK to exit the dialog box.

Report Layout

Report Builder 2.0 gives us a lot of flexibility when it comes to writing reports. One helpful new feature in Report Builder 2.0 is the Data Region Wizard. This wizard enables you to create data regions inside a report without having to regenerate the whole report, as in Report Builder 1.0. Another nice feature is that the default new report template automatically has a place to enter your report titles. It also places the report execution time expression in the lower-right corner of your page. All of this makes adding data regions and creating basic reports much easier.

Because Report Builder 2.0 is a new and more advanced ad hoc report builder, it can fully support common data regions such as Table, Matrix, and List. It also supports using Chart and Gauge controls with the reports.

Here are the steps to produce a simple tabular report from the data set you created earlier:

1. Select Table or Matrix from the center of the report to launch the Data Region Wizard.
2. Select Choose an Existing Dataset in This Report, and make sure the EmployeeInformation data set is selected (see Figure 18.26).

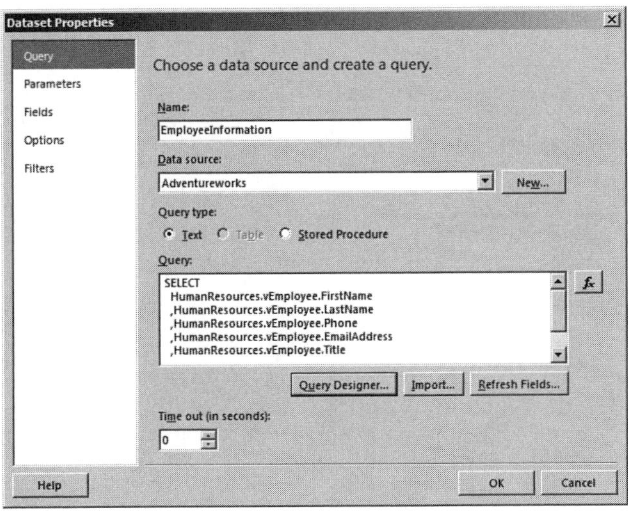

FIGURE 18.25 Dataset Properties designer.

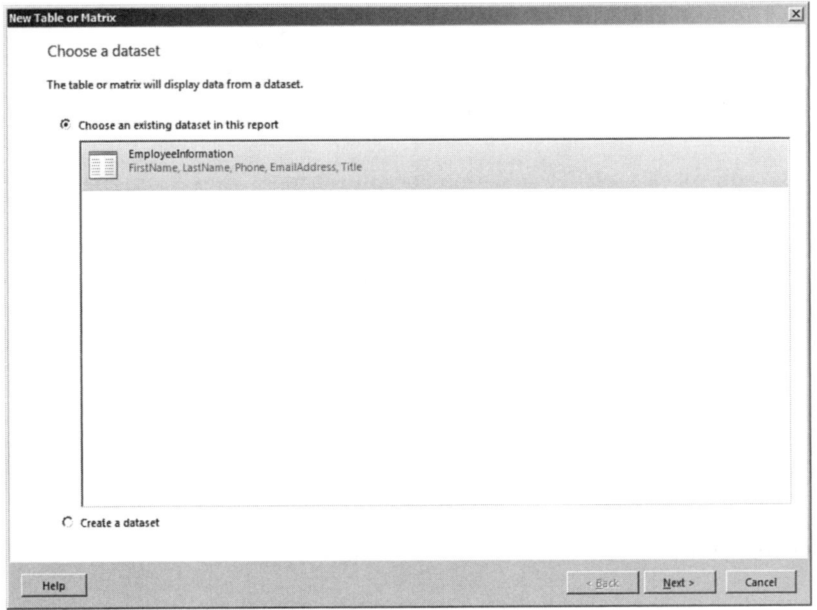

FIGURE 18.26 Table or Matrix Wizard.

3. On the next screen, we can create our groups. Drag FirstName, LastName, EmailAddress, and PhoneNumber over to the Values list box. Move Title over to Row Groups (see Figure 18.27).

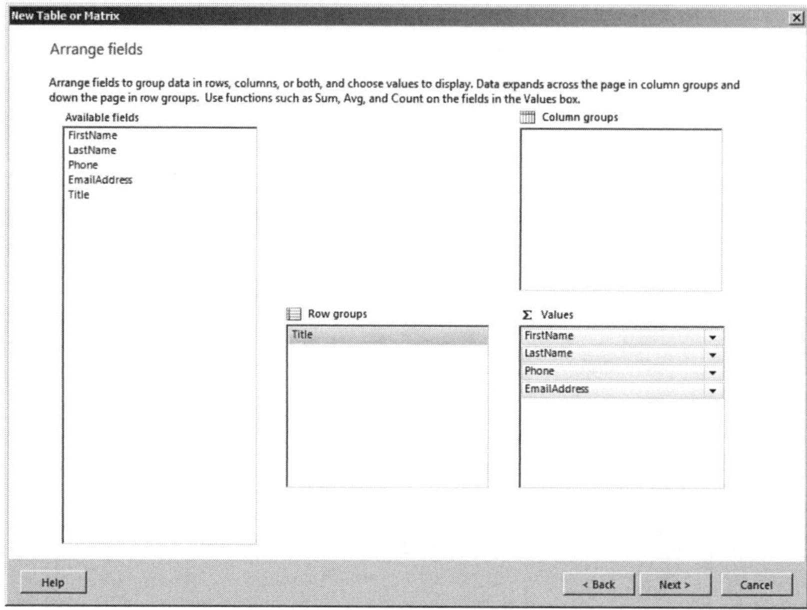

FIGURE 18.27 Grouping in Table or Matrix Wizard.

4. On the next screen, we can select the layout. For our purposes, make sure that Show Subtotals and Grand Totals and Expand/Collapse Groups are checked. Also make sure Blocked, Subtotal Below has been selected (see Figure 18.28).
5. On the next screen, we can select a style or color scheme. For this report, select Ocean (see Figure 18.29). Click Finish.

Now at this point, we can add a title. We can just modify the Click to Add Title text box. Change this to **`Employee Information`**. Figure 18.30 shows the completed report in the design windows. Figure 18.31 shows the completed report in Preview mode with the Title group expanded.

Now let's save this report:

1. Click the Report Builder button (round emblem at the upper-left corner of the screen).
2. Select Save As from the menu options.
3. The Save As Report dialog box will open. You'll notice this takes you directly to the Report Server if you have the Report Server configured. You can now save it in the My Reports folder if you have My Reports enabled. Otherwise, let's save it in the root. Change the name of the report to **`Employee Information`** and save it at the root (see Figure 18.32).

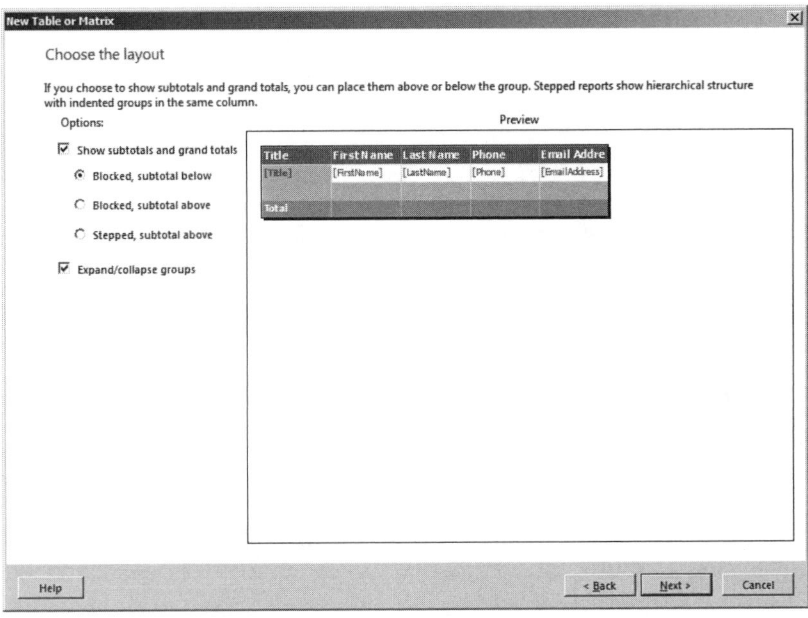

FIGURE 18.28 Grouping in Table or Matrix Wizard.

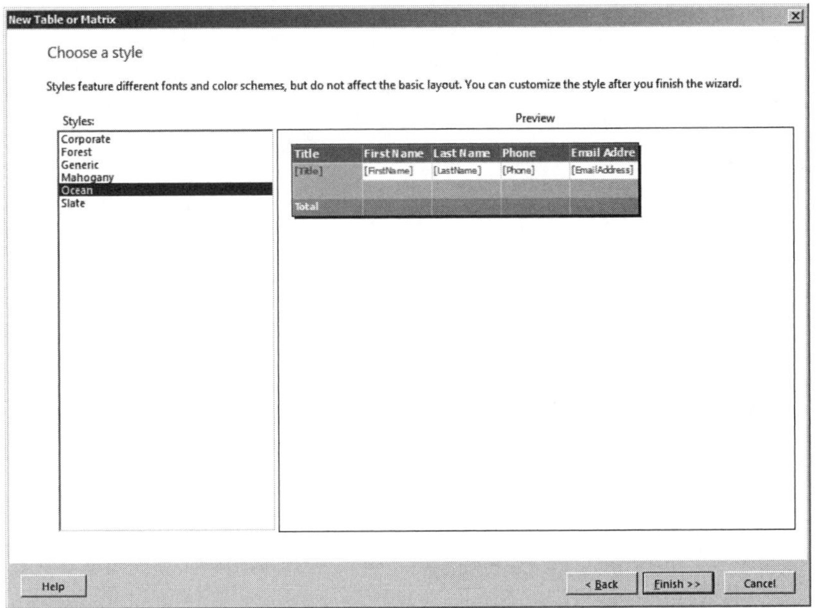

FIGURE 18.29 Grouping in Table or Matrix Wizard.

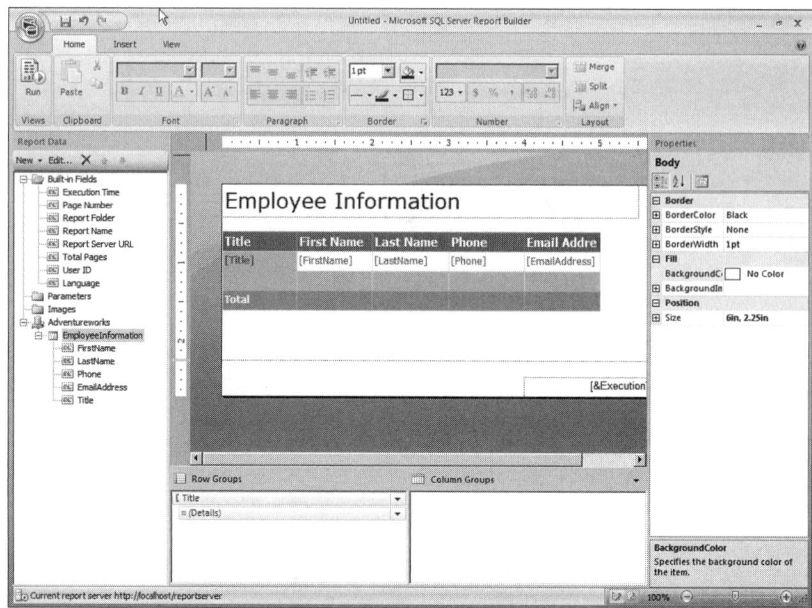

FIGURE 18.30 Completed Employee Information report.

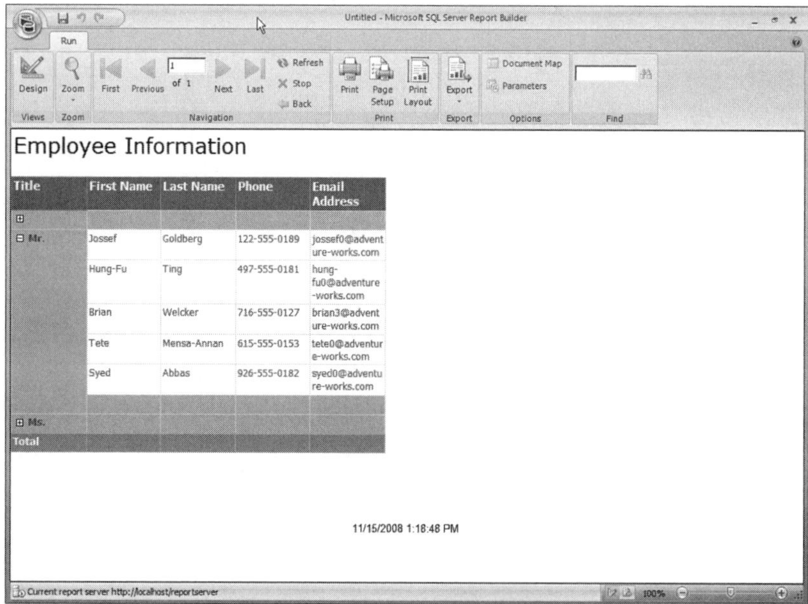

FIGURE 18.31 Employee Information report preview.

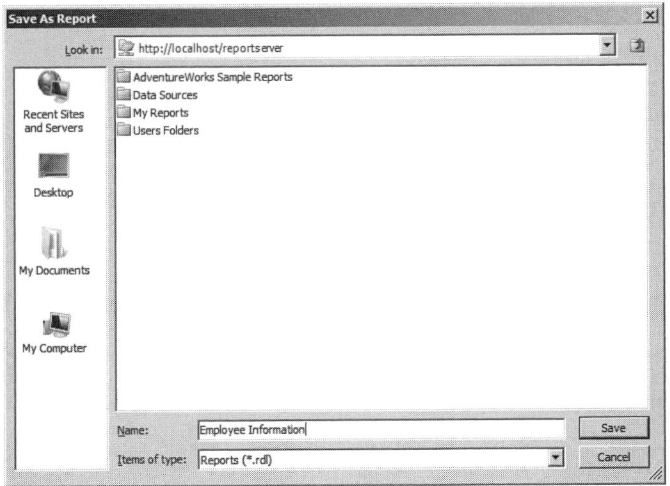

FIGURE 18.32 Save As Report dialog box.

As you have seen, Report Builder 2.0 works similarly to BIDS in a number of ways. The user interface includes an intuitive Ribbon-like interface. Apart from the Ribbons, Report Builder 2.0 has a very RDL-document-centered approach. It also includes new features such as enhanced charting and gauges that are not available in Report Builder 1.0. In addition, it does not depend on data source models. It can instead use embedded data sources and can use shared data sources from a central Report Server. Two other useful features are the Data Region Wizard and the Chart Wizard.

Summary

End-user reporting provides some fairly significant challenges. SQL Reporting Services answers this challenge with a combination of tools: the Model Designer and Report Builder.

The Model Designer is used by someone familiar with the data source to create a model that represents the database objects in terms of business objects.

The idea is to present end users with collections of objects that they can recognize.

Report Builder is a Windows Forms-based application that can be launched from the Report Manager website. It uses the report models as a data source, and, in combination with user input, it generates standard RDL documents as reports. Report Builder uses Microsoft Office paradigms, so end users who use Microsoft Office should find the product familiar. The reports can then be saved to the Report Server for later use.

CHAPTER 19

Managing Reports, Data Sources, and Models

IN THIS CHAPTER

- Deployment Options in Visual Studio
- Deployment Through Report Manager
- Changing Report Properties
- Setting Report History and Snapshots
- My Reports

Managing Report Server content on SSRS is fairly straightforward. After developing reports, the first thing you need to do is to learn how to deploy them. After reports are deployed, a number of options and properties can be set on the Report Server. These options range from the fairly mundane, such as moving reports from one folder to another, to more complex options, such as managing report histories and snapshots.

Deployment Options in Visual Studio

Because Visual Studio is the primary development tool, it should come as no surprise that it has the capability to deploy reports. You can actually set it up to deploy reports every time you build your projects. In addition, you can use Visual Studio to overwrite existing data sources on the server, hence setting the proper location for use in production.

Server Name

First, you need to set the server name for deployment of your project. You can do this by setting the project properties through the IDE. This is actually much simpler than it sounds.

1. Open the AdventureWorks Sample Reports reports project.
2. Open Solution Explorer (View, Solution Explorer).
3. Right-click the project and select Properties.

4. You should now have a screen that looks similar to Figure 19.1.

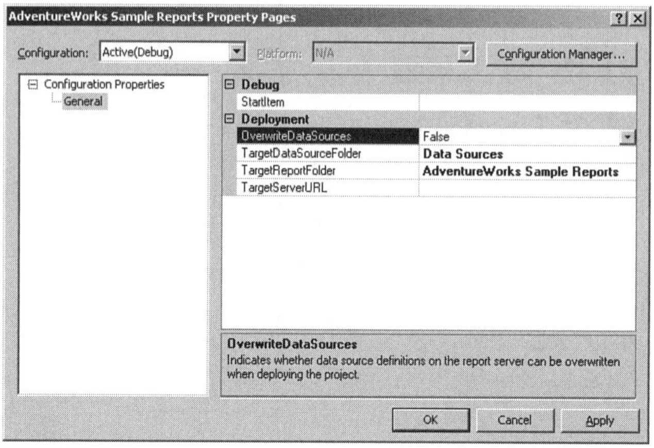

FIGURE 19.1 Deployment properties for the AdventureWorks project.

Now all you have to do is set the server name. The server name and virtual directory have to be placed in the `TargetServerURL` property. The format is `http://{ServerName}/{VirtualDirectory}`. By default, if you have installed the server locally, its property is filled in as `http://localhost/ReportServer`.

Report Folder Location

TargetReportFolder is another major property.

By default, it sets itself to the project name. The folder name is the name of the folder created on the Report Server to house your reports. You can leave it blank and reports will deploy on the root folder.

Overwriting Data Sources

One of the most important properties is OverwriteDataSources; it changes the location of the data source on the Report Server.

By default, when deploying via Visual Studio, it creates the data source for your reports. The key here is it creates the data source, but never updates it, even if you have updated the data source in your project. The exception to this is when the report has an embedded data source in its data sets.

The purpose of this switch is to force the upgrade of shared data sources. If you need to overwrite the data sources, set this to true and you will be on your way.

Target Folder for the Data Source

This property (TargetDataSourceFolder) is similar to the folder for reports. Remember this applies only to shared data sources.

Building and Deploying Reports

When you set all the properties, you should have a screen that looks similar to Figure 19.2.

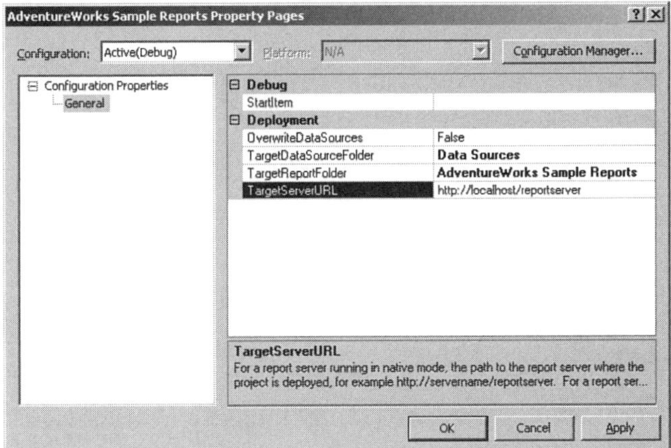

FIGURE 19.2 Completed deployment properties for the AdventureWorks project.

When you are ready to deploy the reports and data sources, complete the following steps:

1. From Solution Explorer, right-click the project.
2. Select Deploy.

After a quick permissions check with the chosen Report Server, Visual Studio should allow you to deploy the project. At this point, you should see the folders created in Report Manager (see Figure 19.3).

Deployment Through Report Manager

As covered in Chapter 1, "Introduction to SQL Server Reporting Services (SSRS)," the Report Manager web application is the main user interface. All administrative functions can be called from here. It also serves as the main user interface into the Report Server. Essentially, it checks user permissions, and if you have permission to do a task, it presents you with the interface to do it. By default, administrators on the machine on which the Report Server is installed have full permissions to all functions.

Creating a New Folder

First, you need to set up a folder into which you will deploy the reports. If you want, you can deploy it onto the root of the Report Server; however, it can get difficult to manage with a large number of reports.

In the Report Manager user interface, a row of buttons displays across the top (see Figure 19.3).

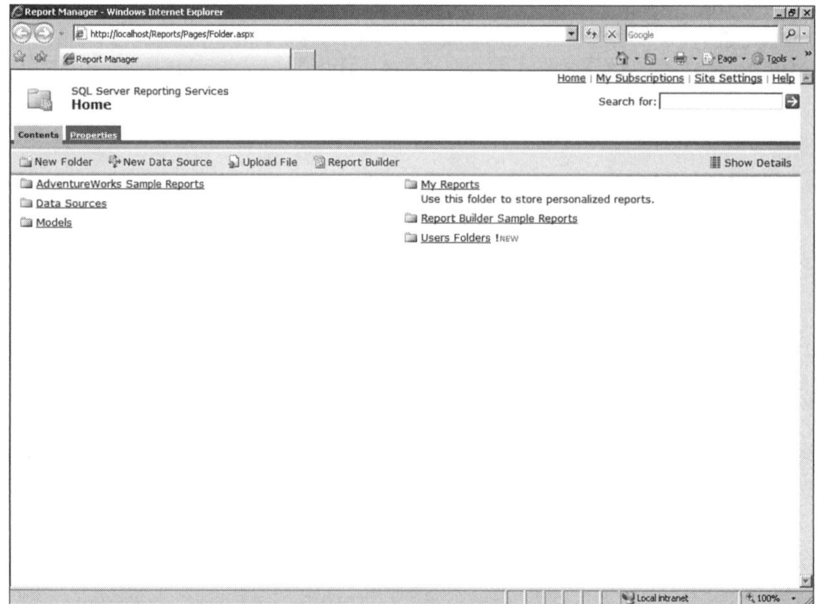

FIGURE 19.3 Deployed AdventureWorks project.

To get acquainted with Report Manager, let's use it to publish some reports manually. The first thing to do is to create a new folder by clicking the New Folder button. You should then see a screen similar to Figure 19.4.

Complete the following steps to finish adding the new folder:

1. Change the Name field to **`AdventureWorks Reports`**.
2. Change the Description field to **`Reports for Adventure Works Inc`**.
3. Click OK.

This should return you to the main screen, and you should see your folder present. If you click the folder, the user interface shows you its contents; however, it will be empty because it was just created and you haven't published anything yet.

Setting Up a Data Source

Now let's create a shared data source for the reports that you will be publishing. The shared data source is beneficial when you have many reports that use the same database catalog for information. To set up a shared data source, follow these steps:

1. If you haven't done so already, click the AdventureWorks Reports folder.
2. Click the New Data Source button on the toolbar. The contents of the browser window should look similar to Figure 19.5.

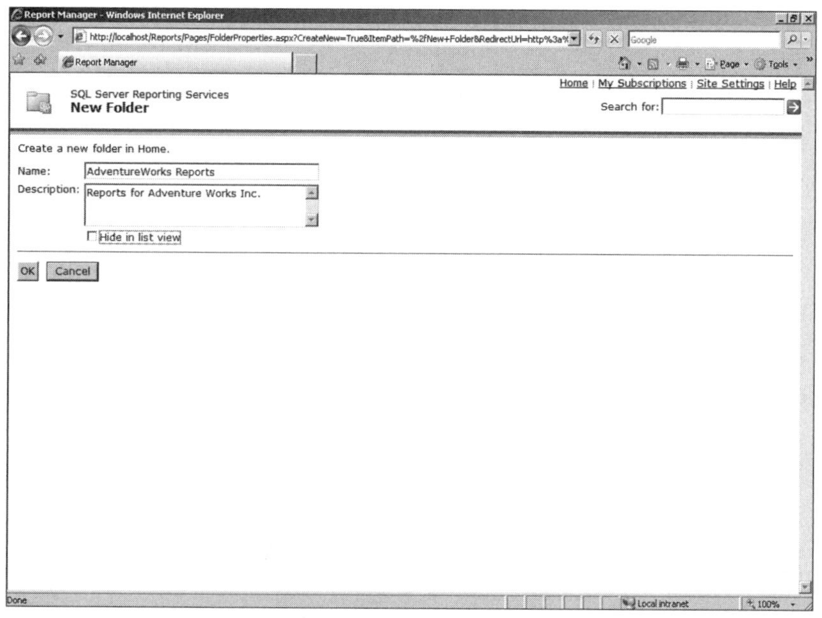

FIGURE 19.4 Creating a new folder.

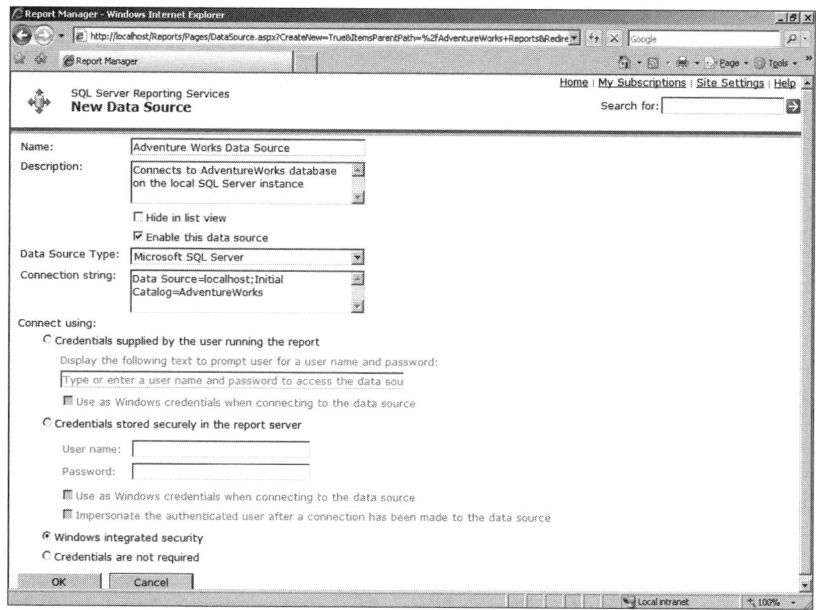

FIGURE 19.5 Creating a new data source.

3. In the Name text box, enter **`Adventure Works Data Source`**.

4. In the Description field, enter **`Connects to the AdventureWorks database on the local SQL Server instance.`**
5. Select Microsoft SQL Server for the connection type.
6. Enter the following connection string:

```
Data Source=localhost;Initial Catalog=AdventureWorks.
```

7. Select Windows Integrated Security.
8. Click OK.

Clicking the OK button should return you to the folder contents, and your data source should be displayed.

Uploading a Report

Now it is finally time to upload your reports. This is a pretty straightforward process, but you need to know the location of the Report Definition Language (RDL) files on your hard drive. If you do not remember, go back to the Visual Studio solution, click the report inside Solution Explorer and look at the properties for the report list. Take note of the `Full Path` property. This is the location of the RDL file on your PC.

Let's continue on and use the Report Manager to upload our reports. To upload reports, perform the following steps:

1. Click the Upload File button on the toolbar.
2. Click Browse and browse to the location of the RDL file.
3. Change the name (see Figure 19.6).

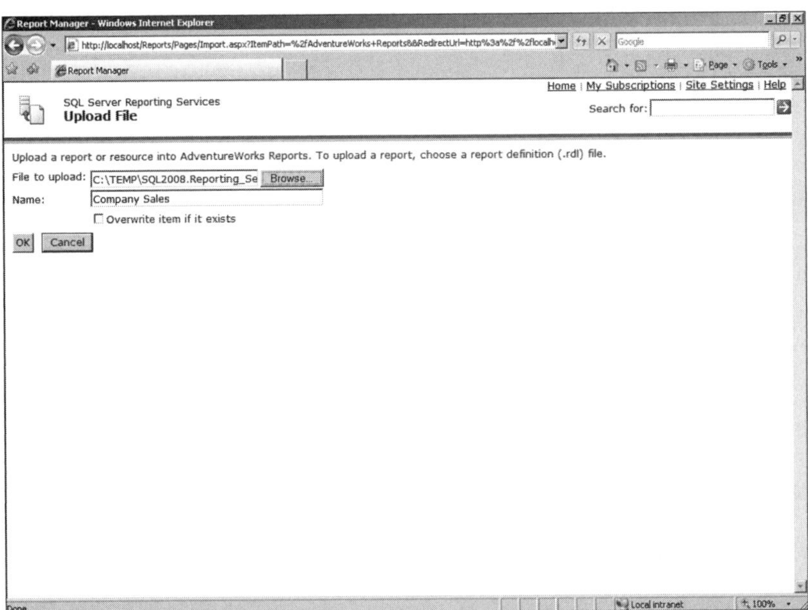

FIGURE 19.6 Uploading a file from the AdventureWorks project.

4. If you want to update an existing copy of the report, check the Overwrite Item If It Exists check box.
5. Click OK.

Report Manager should now display the folder contents with the report and data source in it.

Changing the Data Source

Because you are using a shared data source, it makes sense to change the report to use the shared data source. Changing the report to use the shared data source entails the following steps:

1. Click the report.
2. Click the Properties tab.
3. Go to Data Sources on the left menu.
4. Select the A Shared Data Source option.
5. Click Browse.
6. Drill down into the folder list until you see AdventureWorks Data Source and select it. You should now see a screen similar to Figure 19.7.
7. Click OK.
8. You should now be on the data source property window. Click Apply.

If you do not want to use the shared data source, you can choose to use a custom one.

In the data source Properties window, just select Custom Data Source as your Data Source option and fill in the values for the data source properties just as you would have if it had been a shared data source. Figure 19.8 shows an example of this. In place of using Windows security, it shows how to connect with a SQL Server logon and password. For simplicity's sake, the logon is sa; however, in a production environment, you should use more granular permissions sources.

Now if you click the report, it should render inside the window.

Changing Report Properties

Now that you have published the Adventure Works sample reports, let's change some properties. Most report properties can be changed.

Basic Properties

To start modifying properties, open any report by clicking it. Then select the Properties tab and click the General tab on the left (see Figure 19.9).

You can modify the name or description of any report. Just enter the new name/description and click Apply.

Some other options include the ability to retrieve and update the RDL definition of a report. Ideally, you should store RDL files in some form of source control, such as

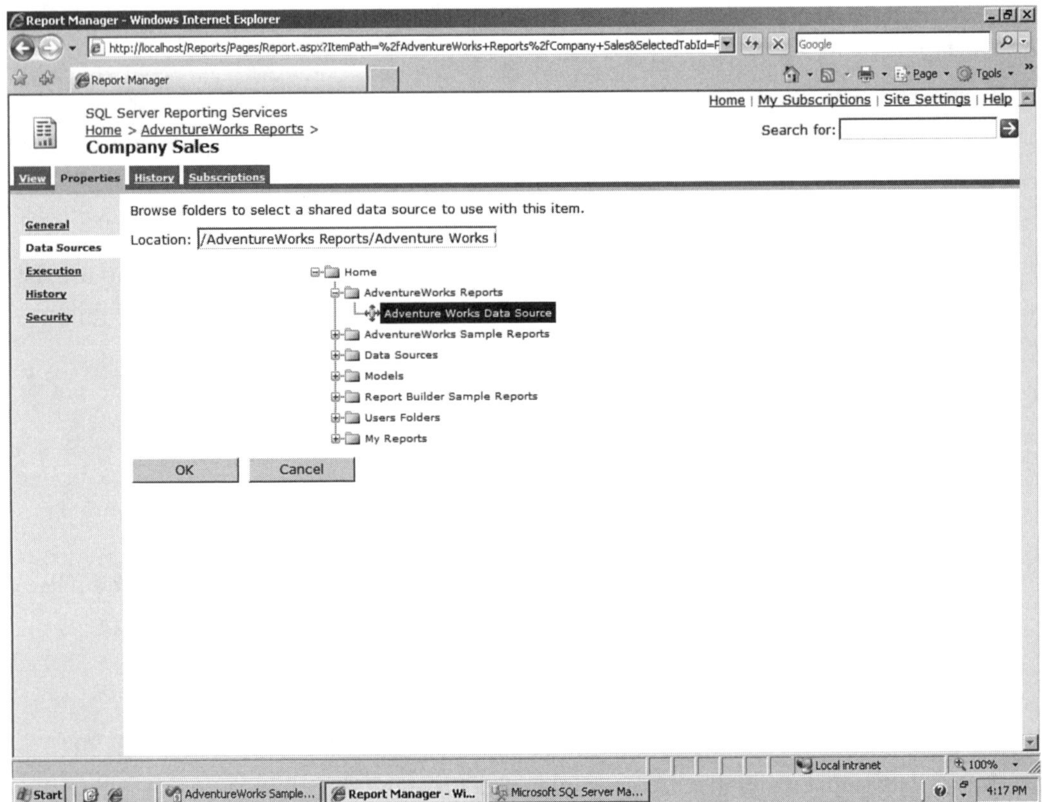

FIGURE 19.7 Setting the data source for a report through Report Manager.

Subversion or CVS. This helps not only with storage, but also with version control and history. However, because the RDL is stored in the Report Server database, you can also choose to download its files. To download the RDL file, click the Edit button and a File Download dialog box opens. If you want to update the RDL for any report, click the Update button.

Another obvious function is Delete, which deletes a report.

Moving Reports

The Move button enables you to move a report from one folder into another. To move a report, complete the following steps:

1. Click the report to be moved and select the Properties tab.
2. Under General on the menu on the left, click the Move button.

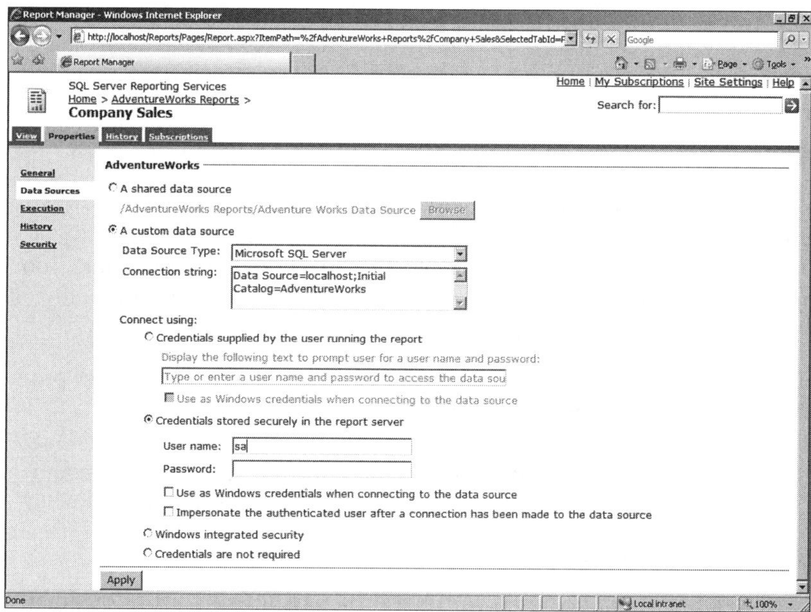

FIGURE 19.8 Defining a custom data source for a report through Report Manager.

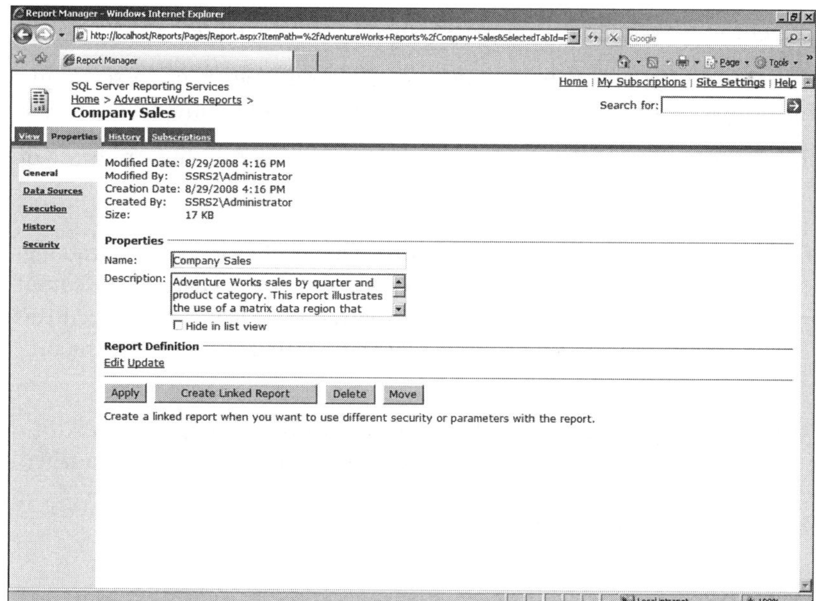

FIGURE 19.9 Report properties.

3. Choose the new location from the tree list.
4. Click OK.

Linked Reports

A linked report is a "copy" of a report with a different set of parameter values or other properties. Linked reports share the same RDL definition with the source report, and, therefore, when the parent report's RDL gets updated, the linked reports get updated, too. A single, nonlinked report can be the parent of any number of linked reports, but a linked report cannot be the parent of another linked report.

Linked reports may share the same RDL and data sources, but just about every other property can be modified. These include the following:

- **Name and Description:** Linked reports can have a completely different name and description. To the end user, it can look like a completely separate report.
- **Location:** Linked reports can exist anywhere in the catalog.
- **Parameters:** Linked reports can be used with a completely different set of parameter values from the originating report. This helps in presenting the linked report as a completely separate entity. This can also be the primary motivation for creating the linked report.
- **Security:** Different role assignments can be assigned to the linked report.
- **Report Execution and Report History:** The execution properties, report execution, and report history properties can vary from a linked report to the original.
- **Subscriptions:** Subscriptions to linked reports are completely separate from those of the parent.

After the linked report has been created, it can be treated like another item in the catalog. Linked reports can be deleted at will with no further repercussions. However, if the parent report of the linked report is deleted, all subsequent linked reports become invalid. At this point, either the linked report must be deleted or it must be pointed to a different report definition.

Creating a linked report is fairly straightforward, and it can be done through Report Manager. Complete the following steps to create a linked report through Report Manager:

1. Open the report and click the Properties tab.
2. Click the Create Linked Report button.
3. Enter a name and description. Just like any other report, the description is optional.
4. If you want to place the linked report in another folder, click the Change Location button and choose the new location.

5. When all the steps are complete, your screen should look similar to Figure 19.10. Click OK.

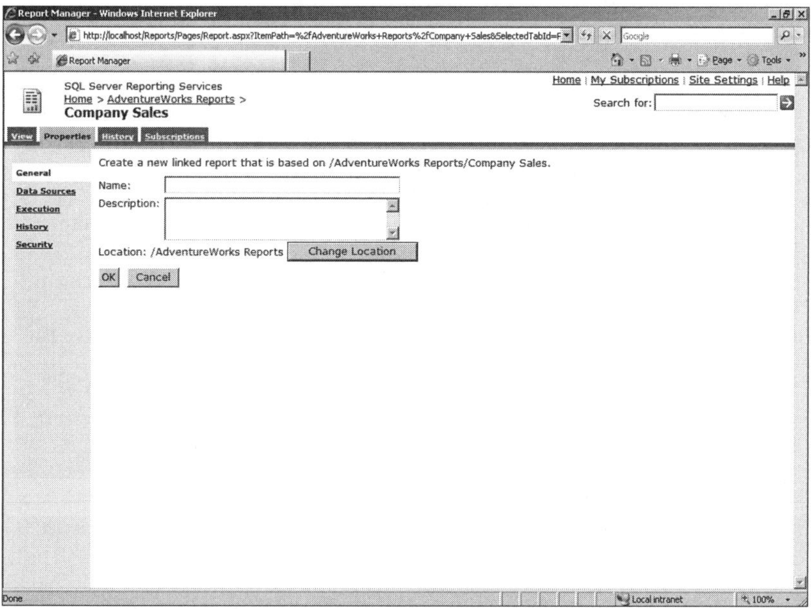

FIGURE 19.10 Creating a new linked report.

Setting Report History and Snapshots

Most of the reports, including many of the samples, don't really tax modern hardware. However, in some cases, there might be a report in production that could be hundreds of pages, or could tax the database server with expensive queries. In these cases, it would be helpful to be able to cache reports, so that the report-rendering engine and the database server don't waste resources.

SSRS attains the preceding goals by retaining something called a report history. The history is a collection of previously run reports called snapshots. A snapshot is a copy of the report at a point in time. If the report layout or data changes, the snapshot remains the same and does not reflect the update.

Report Server Settings to Affect Report History

There are two levels of settings when setting report history. The first level is Report Server–wide, and is accessible through the Site Settings link or by clicking the server itself. The other settings are at the report level, and can override the sitewide settings.

The only global parameter for the Report Server as a whole is how many snapshots to keep in history. By default, the sitewide settings are set to keep an unlimited number of snapshots in history. However, most reports are set to run on-the-fly, and not set to render from a snapshot. If an administrator decides to change this value, the old snapshots will be deleted as the maximum number of snapshots is reached.

The rest of the settings for snapshots are set at the report level, and can be set either through the Report Server or through SQL Server Management Studio. To access the setting through the Report Manager, click the report, select the Properties tab, and select History. The first option is Allow Report History to Be Created Manually.

This allows the New Snapshot button to appear on the History page in Report Manager. Using this button, users can then select to create a snapshot themselves.

The second option is Store All Report Execution Snapshots in History. This stores a copy of each snapshot in the report history. Users can then look back over time and see how the report has changed.

Another option allows users/administrators to generate report snapshots on a custom or shared schedule. The snapshots generated over time will help to form the history.

The last option defines how many snapshots are to be kept in history. This allows us to use the Report Server's default setting or override it by allowing a limited number or infinite number of copies.

From a security perspective, users must have the Manage Report History task inside their roles to generate snapshots. The end users must also have the View Reports role to view the report history. Report snapshots are not meant for, and not recommended to be used on, a report that contains secure or confidential data. If a report uses a data source that prompts the user for a password, or one that requires integrated security, the snapshot cannot be created.

Creating Snapshots

Snapshots contain the following data:

- A copy of the resultsets brought back by the data sources of the report.
- The report definition at the time when the snapshot was created. Keep in mind that this will not take into account any recent changes.
- Parameter values that were used while processing the reports/query.
- Any embedded resources for a report. If the report relies on an outside resource, that resource is not saved on the RS database.

To add a snapshot using Report Manager, follow these steps:

1. Open the report for which you want to create a snapshot, and click the History tab.
2. Click the New Snapshot button, as shown in Figure 19.11.
3. A new snapshot should appear, with the date it was created and the size.

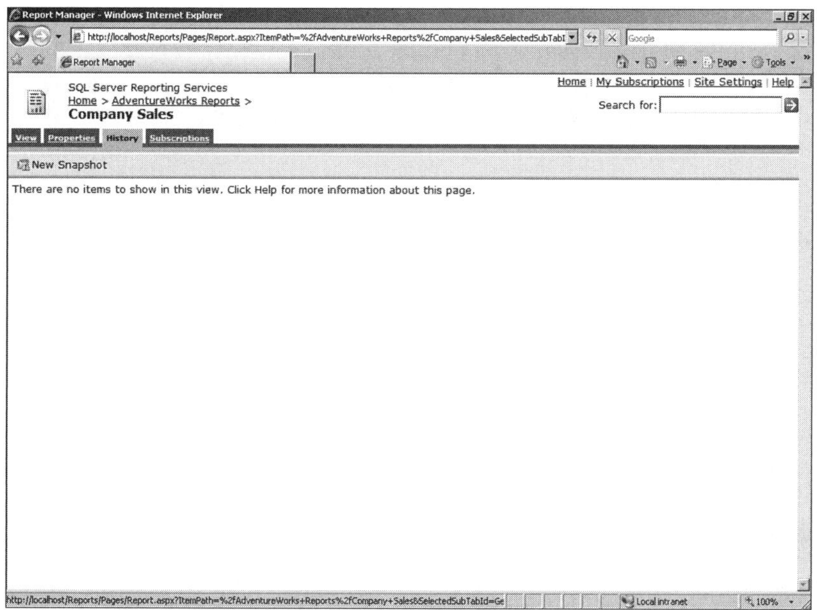

FIGURE 19.11 Creating a snapshot.

Deleting Snapshots

After snapshots have been created, they can only be deleted, not modified. There are two ways to delete a snapshot.

The first way involves using Report Manager to delete individual snapshots in the report history. From Report Manager, navigate to the report and click the History tab. Then select the check boxes next to the individual snapshots and click the Delete button. Right-clicking the History folder gives the user an option to Delete All Snapshots. Otherwise, right-click an individual snapshot and select Delete.

The second way to delete snapshots is to simply lower the number of snapshots the Report Server should keep. This forces the older snapshots to be deleted as needed.

My Reports

The My Reports folder creates an individual workspace for each user in the Report Server. Users can use it for any number of things as they see fit. These might include storage space for reports in progress, or as a holding area for reports not yet ready to be published. There is no way for an administrator to control the size or amount of content end users choose to place in their My Reports folder.

The structure of the My Reports folder is somewhat analogous to the My Documents folder in Windows. Just like My Documents is a pointer to `C:\Documents and Settings\...`, My Reports actually points to a folder called `/User Folders/<username>/My Reports`. This folder doesn't actually get created in the Report Server catalog until a user actually uses the My Reports feature.

Enabling My Reports

The My Reports feature is disabled by default in a new installation of SSRS. After being enabled, it is effective for the entire user base, meaning it cannot be enabled for some users but not others. A number of factors must be considered before enabling it.

First, you need to consider server resources. My Reports is a powerful feature. It is effectively like giving end users access to a file share with unlimited space. In SSRS 2000, end users only had Visual Studio to create reports (a not-so-appealing option for many end users). Now with Report Builder, end users can easily create new reports to suit their needs and store them on the Report Server.

Second, you need to consider security. With the My Reports feature turned on, end users can create new security policies and publish reports for other users from the My Reports folder. This might at first seem helpful for administrators, but the propagation of security policies could prove difficult to manage later.

If an administrator chooses to enable the My Reports feature, it is a fairly straightforward process. Here are the steps to enable My Reports:

1. Using SQL Server Management Studio, connect to your Reporting Services Server. You should see your folder in the Object Explorer. Your screen should look something like Figure 19.12.
2. Right-click the server name and select Properties.
3. Check the check box labeled Enable My Reports for Each User (see Figure 19.13).
4. Click Apply.

From this point forward, a user will see the My Reports folder pop up under the root folder in the catalog. In addition, administrators will see the User Folders folder, along with their My Reports folder. Of course, a user cannot create a folder called My Reports at the root folder level. The name My Reports has been reserved.

Disabling My Reports

Should My Reports have to be disabled, just deselect the check box from inside SQL Server Management Studio. From this point forward, users can create a folder called My Reports; however, no special redirection occurs. Any actual folder that has been created under the User Folders folder will remain.

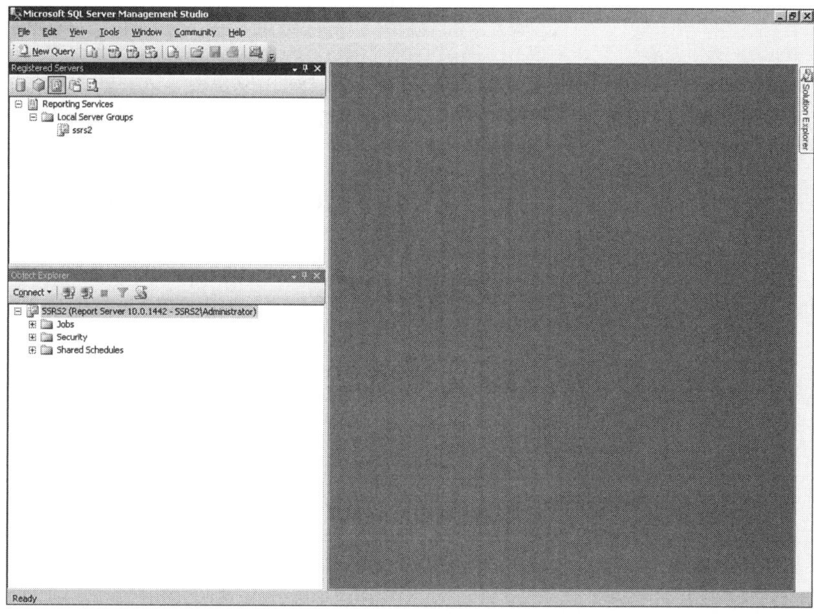

FIGURE 19.12 Server in the Object Explorer window.

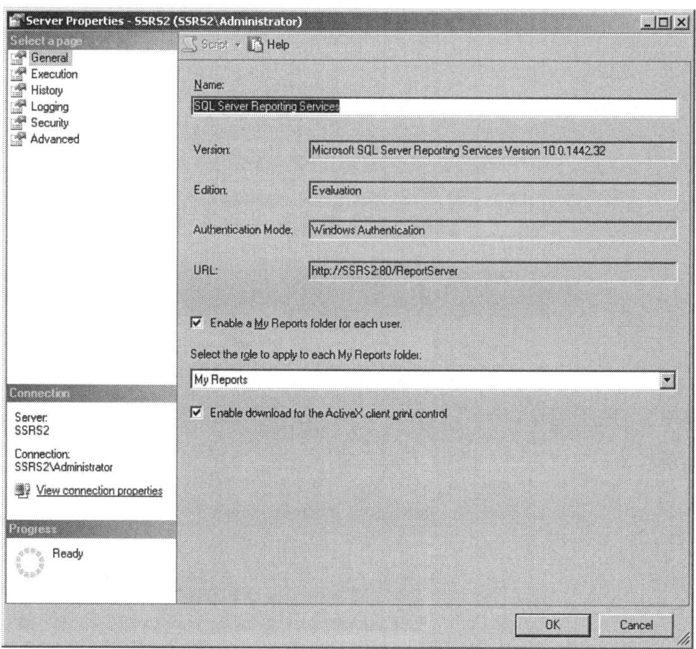

FIGURE 19.13 Enabling My Reports.

Summary

In this chapter, you have seen how to deploy reports through both Report Manager and Visual Studio. Report Manager allows end users to set basic report properties and modify a report's data source.

Report Manager also allows end users to link reports, move reports, and create report snapshots.

If administrators allow it, end users also can have their personal report repositories in their My Reports folders.

CHAPTER 20

Securing Report Server Items

IN THIS CHAPTER

Because SSRS is a .NET application, many of the existing .NET security paradigms come into play when securing access to the Report Server. From the end user's viewpoint, SSRS uses role-based authorization built on top of Windows authentication. If using a custom authentication mechanism, the underlying principals are the same. It is simply up to the authorization mechanism to define valid users and roles (called principals).

Reporting Services Security Model

Role-based authorization is not a new concept. It is a proven mechanism that is implemented in a variety of ways. One of the most common, everyday items that uses role-based authorization is the file system. If your PC's file system is based on NTFS, you have the ability to place access control lists (ACLs) on certain folders. ACLs specify users or groups of users (generically called principals), permissions to read, write, or execute items within a folder, or the folder itself. If a folder does not have ACLs placed on it, the folder then just inherits its permissions from the parent folder. The administrator of the computer can, of course, change access to certain folders, but is not allowed to place himself in the access pool.

Drawing from the file system's paradigm, SSRS security models it very similarly. Within SSRS, there are a fixed number of predefined roles, which can be assigned to users. These roles are used to give permissions to execute certain tasks on folders or other report items. Examples of some of the built-in roles include Browser, Content Manager, and System Administrator.

When SSRS installs, it sets up the local administrator pool with the System Administrator and Content Manager roles.

This is the absolute minimum security that can be applied. SSRS requires that at least one principal, a valid user or group, be assigned to the System Administrator role, and likewise to the Content Manager role. This ensures that the Report Server cannot be locked out from the outside.

There are no users added. Users cannot interact with the Report Server until someone in the local Administrators group assigns them to either one of the predefined roles, or a custom role.

When the time comes to start adding users, administrators have the choice to add users to a certain role, or to many roles. Users can even have different permissions on different report items. For example, a user might be a Content Manager, which allows the user to publish reports, in one folder, yet only be a Browser (read only) in another folder.

As mentioned in the chapter introduction, SSRS uses Windows authentication by default. The list of valid users and groups rests in the hand of the authentication services. When a user or group (referred to as a principal from this point forward) is added to a role, the principal is validated against the authenticating authority.

On a Report Server, authentication through the Windows security extension (default method) is performed by Internet Information Services (IIS). The user and group accounts that you specify in role assignments are created and managed through Active Directory.

If a custom security extension is used, it is up to the extension to validate the principal.

What Can Be Secured?

Although it might not be the most efficient approach, the reality is that just about every report item can be secured individually. Some things that don't follow this rule are subscriptions and schedules because they are used in conjunction with a report and not as an independent part of it. Table 20.1 describes how report items and their security work.

TABLE 20.1 Report Items and Effects of Security

Report Item	How Security Applies
Folder	Securing a folder usually ends up securing all the items within that folder. When SSRS is installed, only local administrators are Content Managers on the root folder. This ensures that no user can browse the catalog, unless given explicit rights to do so. The exception to this is the My Reports folder. My Reports, if it's enabled, creates a pseudofolder within the catalog in which users are given permissions to publish their own reports.

TABLE 20.1 Continued

Report Item	How Security Applies
Report	Reports and linked reports can be secured to control levels of access. For example, the View Reports task allows users to view a report as well as report history, whereas Manage Reports allows them to change report properties. Manage Report History allows users to generate snapshots.
Model	Primarily used to secure access to the model, it can also be used to secure reports for which the model acts as a data source. Models can also be secured internally by securing model items with perspectives, specifying role assignments on all or part of a model, and securing items such as the root node, folders, entities, and relationships within the model.
Resources	Resources are items in the Report Server that provide content to user. An example of a resource can be an HTML file or Word document. Securing a resource limits access to the resource and its properties. The View Resources permissions are needed to access the resources.
Shared data sources	Securing shared data sources limits access to the data source and its corresponding properties. To view the data source properties, users need the View Data Sources permission; likewise, Manage Data Sources gives permissions to modify them.

How Role Assignments Work

To continue with the file system analogy, one has to ask what are we actually putting limits on? The answer is who can read, write, and execute on objects within the file system. A cursory glance at Table 20.1 gives a similar perspective. By securing a report item, you are actually putting limits on what actions can be taken using that item. The actions are called tasks in SSRS.

SSRS comes with 25 different tasks. Tasks cannot be added to or taken away from. Table 20.1 has already mentioned the names of a few tasks, such as View Reports and Manage Reports.

Tasks themselves actually encompass a set of underlying permissions. For example, the Manage Folders task actually enables end users to create, delete, update, and modify a folder and its properties. If a user visits the Report Manager without the permissions to Manage Folders, none of the buttons or UI elements will be enabled.

The underlying permissions are nice to know about, but not very practical, as task is the lowest level of assignment. To get assigned permissions to complete an operation, the permissions have to be implemented into a task. The task or tasks have to then be placed in a role to be performed. Hence, if the View Models task is not included in a role, or the role is not included in a role assignment, users cannot view report models.

Tasks themselves come in two different categories, as follows:

- **Item-level tasks:** Tasks level that acts on an item in the Report Server catalog, such as folders, models, reports, and resources
- **System-level tasks:** Tasks level that can be performed on objects that are not in the catalog but are global in scope, such as site settings and shared schedules

As you might have already guessed, the role is the central tenet of role-based security. Roles are collections of tasks. SSRS comes with a few predefined roles, but administrators can also create roles to suit their needs. A single role can contain only one of the two task types; that is, either item-level tasks or system-level tasks. Because of this, there are item-level roles and system-level roles. A role is only active when it is assigned to a user.

When a user tries to perform an action, the Report Server checks what permissions are required to perform that action. The required permissions are expressed in the roles required for access. It then checks to make sure that the user requesting the action has sufficient privileges to perform that action. Again, the easiest way is to check whether the user is either a member of the specified role, or if the roles contain the required tasks and, hence, permissions.

Relationships Between Roles, Tasks, and Users

The relationship between items that need to be secured, roles, and users is called a policy. The policy is what is responsible for mapping out the minimum set of permissions required for securing a report item. An individual policy is a mapping of users or groups (principals) with a required role needed for access. Each item in the catalog can have multiple policies defined; however, no single item can have two policies that apply to the same principal.

For example, suppose you have a user named George and you need to grant George access to view reports in the Adventure Works folder. To do so, you specified that George can have the Browser role. After doing this, you created a policy. The policy can be modified by granting more roles to George, hence increasing George's permissions to, for example, Content Manager; however, you cannot create a second policy with George. What you can do is create a group, for example "Adventure Works Content Managers," and place George in that group. You can then give the group the role of Content Manager.

So, in the end, what are George's permissions? Well, because roles are really nothing more than a collection of tasks, George can perform all the tasks that Content Managers and Browsers can perform. This is why the policies are called additive.

By this point, you are probably thinking that security is a lot of trouble. If every item can have a policy, and polices are additive, granting permissions can quickly get out of hand. The thing to remember here is that just because you can do something doesn't mean that you should.

When you apply a policy to a folder, or some other items, you are, by default, applying the same policy to children of that folder/item. This makes it easy to change and apply policies. The recommended best practice is to secure folders within the Report Server catalog. By securing the folder, administrators are securing everything within that folder.

This is the same model used in NTFS. Every child item of a folder automatically inherits the parent folder's permissions. Whenever an item's permissions need to change, just break the inheritance and SSRS starts a new policy with that item.

Overview of Built-In Roles

For most organizations, the built-in roles should suffice. If they do not, keep in mind that the Report Server administrators can create custom role definitions. If you need to create a custom role definition, it might be helpful to stage that role definition in a development environment.

Tables 20.2 and 20.3 describe the predefined roles and their corresponding tasks. Keep in mind that when a task is called "Manage ...," that it implies the ability to create, modify, and delete.

TABLE 20.2 Item-Level Roles

Role Name	Description
Browser	Allows users to browse through the folder hierarchy, view report properties, view resources and their properties, view models and use them as a data source, and finally, execute reports, but not manage reports. It is important to note that this role gives Report Viewer the ability to subscribe to reports using their own subscriptions.
Content Manager	Allows users to manage folders, models, data sources, report history, and resources regardless of who owns them. This role also allows users to execute reports, create folder items, view and set properties of items, and set security for report items.
Report Builder	Allows users to build and edit reports using Report Builder and manage individual subscriptions.
My Reports	Allows users to build reports and store the reports in their own personal folder. They can also change the permissions of their own My Reports folder.
Publisher	Allows users to publish content to the Report Server, but not to view it. This role is helpful for people who are allowed to develop reports against a development or test data source, but are not allowed to view reports against the production data source.

TABLE 20.3 Tasks Assigned to Item-Level Roles

	Browser	Content Manager	My Reports	Publisher	Report Builder
Consume reports		X			X
Create linked reports		X	X	X	

TABLE 20.3 Continued

	Browser	Content Manager	My Reports	Publisher	Report Builder
Manage all subscriptions		X			
Manage data sources		X	X	X	
Manager folders		X	X	X	
Manage individual subscriptions	X	X	X		X
Manage models		X		X	
Manage resources		X	X	X	
Set security for individual items		X			
View data sources		X	X		
View folders	X	X	X		X
View models	X	X			X
View reports	X	X	X		X
View resources	X	X	X		X

There are two built-in, system-level roles. These roles follow the same pattern as the item-level roles in that one role allows view access to systems settings, and the other allows them to be modified. Keep in mind that you can also create new system-level roles. Tables 20.4 and 20.5 break down the system-level roles and tasks.

TABLE 20.4 System-Level Roles

Role Name	Role Description
System Administrator	Allows members to create and assign roles, set systemwide settings (Report Server properties and Report Server security), share schedules, and manage jobs
System User	Allows members to view system properties and shared schedules

TABLE 20.5 Tasks Assigned to System-Level Roles

	System Administrator	System User
Execute report definitions	X	X
Generate events		
Manage jobs	X	

TABLE 20.5 Continued

	System Administrator	System User
Manage Report Server properties	X	
Manage Report Server security	X	
Manage roles	X	
Manage shared schedules	X	
View Report Server properties	X	X
View shared schedules	X	X

After the Report Server is installed, the local Administrators group is assigned two roles. The first role is the Content Manager, and the second is the System Administrator role. Individually, the roles limit access to certain areas. The Content Manager role can manage everything within the Report Server catalog.

System Administrators can manage the Report Server. With the combination of these two roles, local administrators are able to do anything to the Report Server.

Assigning Built-In Roles

First, to use any method of authorization, you need to create some principals. As an example, you will use some Windows groups: AdventureWorksSalesManagers and AdventureWorksSalesPeople. Go ahead and create these Windows groups on your Report Server and place some users in them. The examples assume that the Adventure Works sample reports have been published to the Report Server and that there are two folders. There might be three folders if you have published the sample report model.

You can assign roles to an object either through the Report Manager website or through SQL Server Management Studio. The following sections cover steps to assign roles through the Report Manager.

Assigning Roles Through Report Manager

Role assignments can be done through either Report Manager or SQL Server Management Studio. Complete the following steps to assign roles through management studio:

1. Navigate to the Adventure Works Sample Reports folder.
2. Click the Properties tab. Then select Security from the left menu. The screen should resemble Figure 20.1.
3. Click the Edit Item Security button. A dialog box opens that looks similar to Figure 20.2. Click OK in this dialog box.
4. Click the New Role Assignment button, as shown in Figure 20.3.
5. Enter **`AdventureWorksSalesManagers`** in the Group or User Name text box, and select the Content Manager role, as shown in Figure 20.4.
6. Click OK.

To revert back to the parent security, click the Revert to Parent Security button, as shown in Figure 20.5.

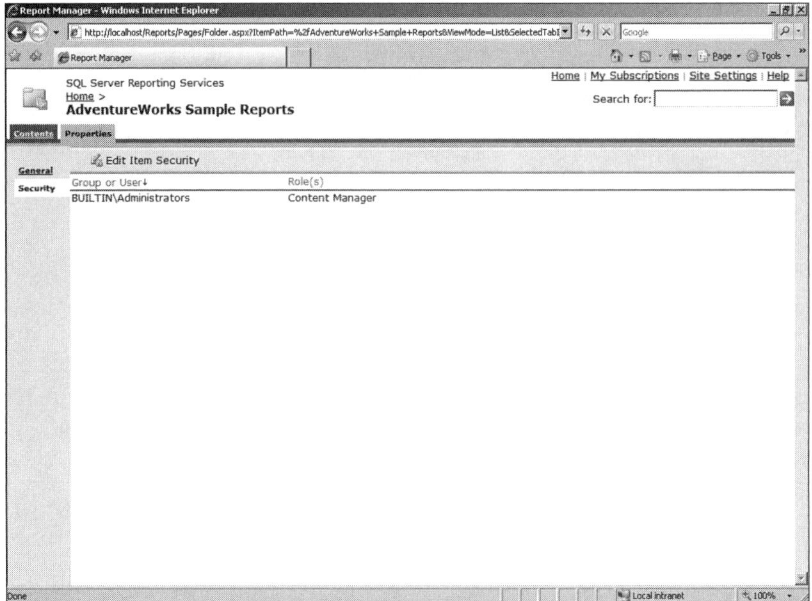

FIGURE 20.1 Item security on the Properties tab.

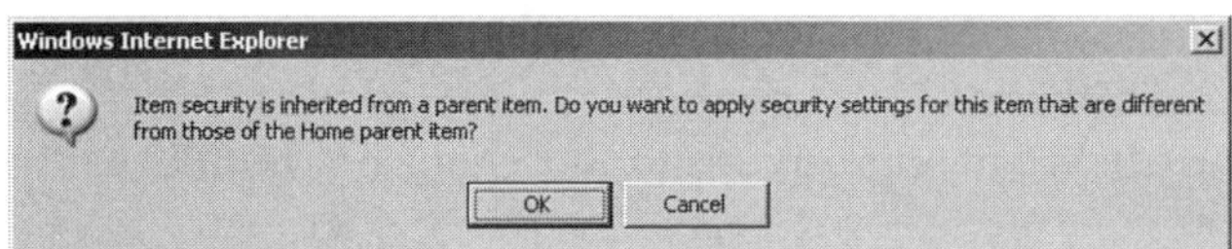

FIGURE 20.2 Confirmation dialog box to break security inheritance.

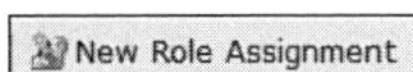

FIGURE 20.3 New Role Assignment button.

To modify an item's security, select a user or group by clicking the Edit check box next to the assigned principal under Security (on the left). This returns you to the role assignment screen, where roles can be added or removed.

To delete a role assignment, select the check boxes next to the principals to delete, and click the Delete button. Figure 20.6 illustrates how this can be done. A confirmation box appears asking users to confirm deletion of the items. Click OK.

To give Adventure Works's sales managers some visibility into the inner workings of the Report Server, let's outline the steps required to give the group the System Users role:

1. Click Site Settings.
2. Select Security from menu on the left. Figure 20.7 shows the resulting screen.

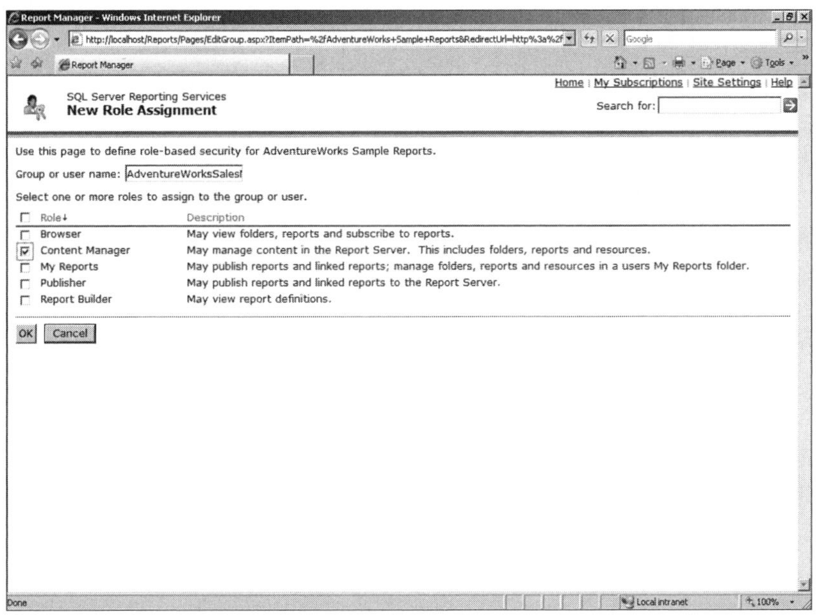

FIGURE 20.4 Granting AdventureWorksSalesManagers Content Manager roles.

Revert to Parent Security

FIGURE 20.5 Revert to Parent Security button.

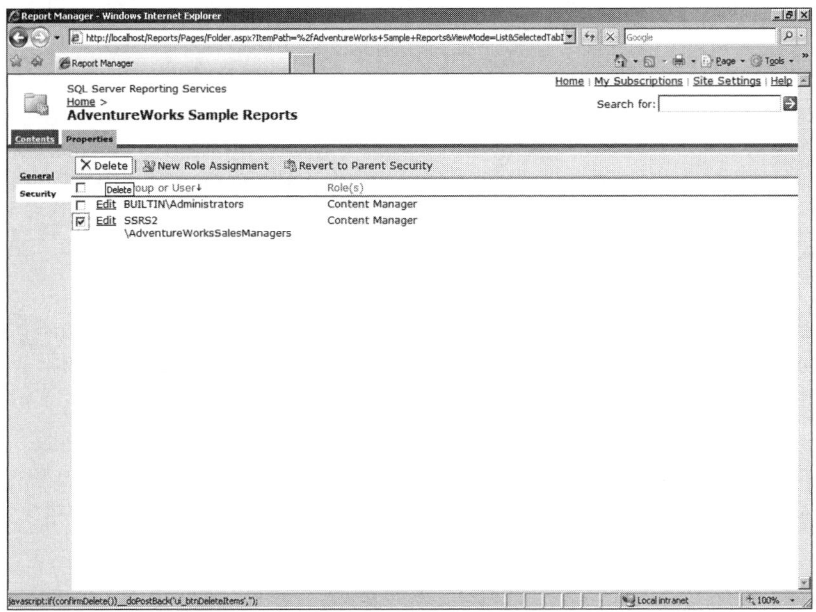

FIGURE 20.6 How to delete a role assignment.

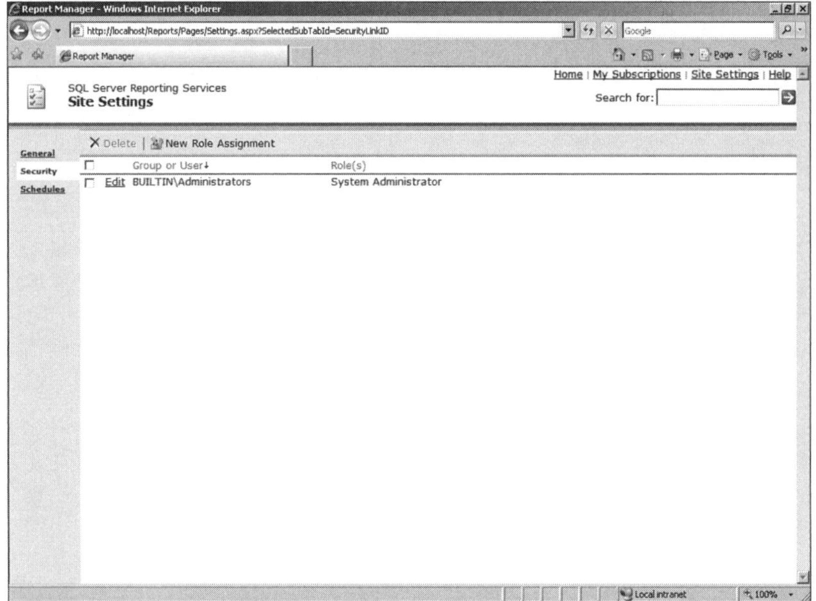

FIGURE 20.7 System Role Assignments screen.

3. From here, it is very similar to setting item-level security. Click the New Role Assignment button.
4. Enter **AdventureWorksSalesManagers** in the Group or User Name text box, and select the System User role, as shown in Figure 20.8.
5. Click OK.

To modify a role assignment, follow the steps to get to the appropriate property window. From the property window, select Permissions and update the lists of tasks. To delete a role assignment, select the role from the property window and click the Remove button.

Defining Custom Roles

SSRS allows administrators to create custom-defined roles to suit individual needs. This can be a helpful feature for organizations that desire a finer degree of granularity, or if the built-in roles simply do not suffice. Administrators can also modify any existing role.

Before jumping into creating new roles, a quick word of caution: It is very easy to get carried away with creating custom roles. There might only be 25 tasks altogether (16 item level and 9 system level), but there are many different combinations you could

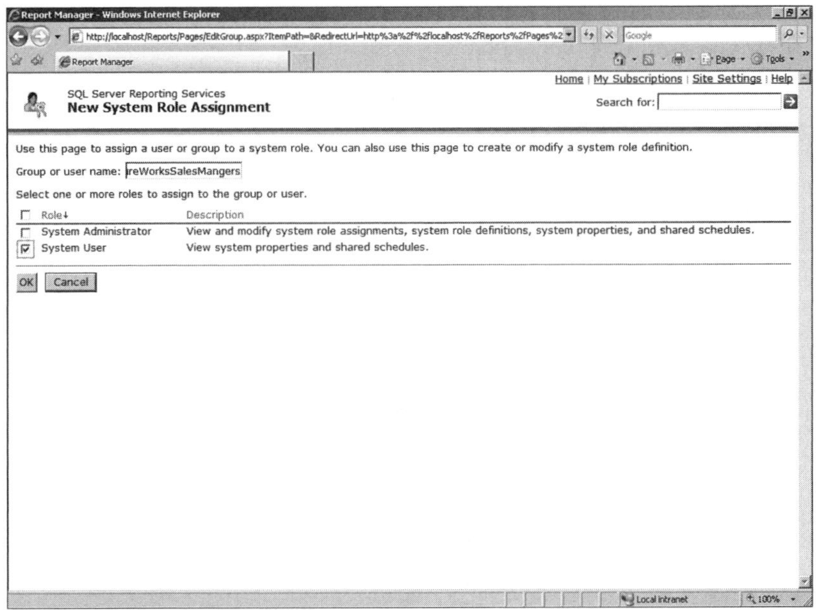

FIGURE 20.8 Adventure Works Sales Managers as System Users.

create. At this point, the management of roles might be just as cumbersome as managing individual tasks.

Creating/Modifying a Custom Role

One of the roles SSRS lacks is a true "view-only" type of role. The following steps outline how you could use Report Manager to create such a role. Later, you will use SQL Server Management Studio to do the same thing.

The following steps create a new View Only Role using SQL Server Management Studio:

1. Open SQL Server Management Studio.
2. Click File and then Connect Object Explorer.
3. Change the server type to Reporting Services.
4. Click the Connect button.
5. In Object Explorer, open the Security folder. At this point, if you want to create a system-level role, open the System Roles folder; otherwise, open the Roles folder.
6. Right-click the Roles folder and select New Role from the context menu.
7. Enter **`View Only Role`** in the Name text box and **`May view reports but not subscribe to them`** in the Description field.

8. Select View Folders, View Reports, View Models, and View Resources from the tasks. Figure 20.9 shows the resulting dialog box.

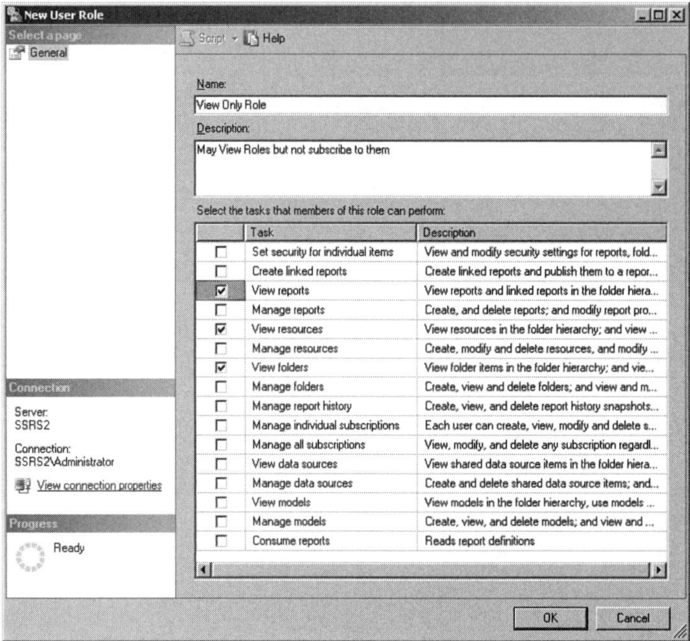

FIGURE 20.9 Creating a custom role with SQL Server Management Studio.

9. Click OK.

To modify a role, right-click any role and select Properties. The same screen appears as for adding a new role. Update the task list or description and click OK. To delete a role, select the role from Object Explorer, right-click the role, and select Delete from the context menu.

Summary

SSRS uses role-based security in a similar fashion as Windows itself. Roles are groups of tasks. SSRS contains two different types of tasks: system-level tasks and item-level tasks. Item-level tasks are actions that affect the catalog, such as View or Browse. System-level tasks are actions that can be taken on items outside the catalog, but are global in Report Server scope such as shared schedules.

The combination of principal, item, and role is called a policy. Every item in the catalog can either have a policy defined for it explicitly or will inherit the parent item's policy.

If the built-in roles do not suffice, administrators are free to make their own.

CHAPTER 21

Report Execution and Processing

IN THIS CHAPTER

- Managing Schedules
- Report Execution and Processing
- Report-Execution History

In this chapter, you explore some of the information that can be captured at runtime, and learn how to set up shared schedules that can be used to coordinate actions within the Report Server.

Managing Schedules

Schedules are used within SSRS to trigger executions of subscriptions and snapshots, generally classified as events. Schedules can trigger a one-time event, or cause events to run continuously at specified intervals (monthly, daily, or hourly).

Schedules create events on the Report Server. Actions within the Report Server, such as expiring a snapshot or processing a subscription, are triggered by the event. What SSRS actually does is create a scheduled job on the database server that hosts the SSRS database. The SQL Agent then runs the jobs, which usually contain nothing more than the command to execute a stored procedure to trigger an event. The other half of the scheduling and delivery processor within SSRS is the Report Server Windows Service referred to as SQL Server Reporting Services under Services in the Control Panel.

This service is responsible for querying the database server for events and running the processes that those events trigger. Both sides of the scheduling and delivery processor must be enabled for it to work. If the SQL Agent on the database server is turned off, the jobs do not run, and therefore the events do not fire and the corresponding actions are not taken. If the Report Server Service is down, the jobs show that they ran successfully, but no processing actually occurs.

Types of Schedules

There are two types of schedules used in SSRS: a shared schedule and a report-specific schedule. The relationship is analogous to the relationship between a shared data source and a custom data source. The shared schedule can be used to trigger a number of events throughout the Report Server. A report-specific schedule is used for one and only one specific event. A second event might occur at exactly the same time, but as far as SSRS is concerned, it is a different schedule. Because they are so similar, the question often brought up is "When should you use a report-specific schedule over a shared schedule?" In general, create a report-specific schedule if a shared schedule does not provide the frequency or recurrence pattern that you need.

Table 21.1 details the difference between shared schedules and report-specific schedules.

TABLE 21.1 Shared Versus Report-Specific Schedules

	Shared Schedule	Report-Specific Schedule
Permissions needed to create/modify	Needs system-level permissions	Can be created by individual users
Can be temporarily disabled?	Can temporarily pause and then resume shared schedules	Have to be modified to change the time
Manageability	Are managed centrally from the Site Settings tab in the Report Manager or Object Browser	Have to be managed by the individual items
Customizable	Cannot be customized for a specific item	Can be easily modified without any other down-stream implications

Creating/Modifying Schedules

The process of creating/modifying schedules is generally the same whether it is a shared or report-specific schedule. The only difference is the scope. For the shared schedule, it is created once and can be referenced in a subscription or property page when you need to specify schedule information.

From Report Manager or Object Explorer, administrators can specify which items use the shared schedule. Report-specific schedules are created and referenced by only that one report, subscription, or report-execution operation to determine cache expiration or snapshot updates.

To create a shared schedule using SQL Server Management Studio, follow these steps:

1. From Object Explorer, navigate to the Shared Schedules folder, right-click Shared Schedules, and select New Schedule.
2. Enter a name for the schedule.
3. Select how often you want the schedule to recur or select Once for a one-time event.
4. Click OK.

Alternatively, you can create a shared schedule from Report Manager by completing the following steps (see Figure 21.1):

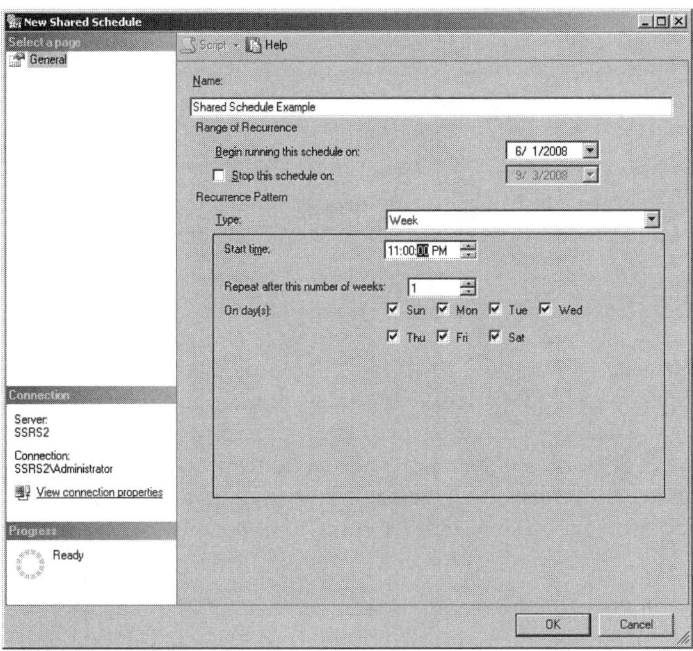

FIGURE 21.1 Creating a new shared schedule in SSRS.

1. Navigate to Site Settings.
2. Click Manage Shared Schedules under the Other section toward the bottom of the screen.
3. Click New Schedule.
4. Enter a name and how often the schedule should recur, and then click OK.

After being created, a schedule can be modified at any time. Modifying the schedule of a running process (subscription, snapshot, and so on) does not cause that process to stop. If the process that a schedule triggered is already running, modifying the schedule serves only to start the process again at the new time.

Deleting a schedule does not guarantee that the events that it triggers will stop firing. Deleting a shared schedule serves only to create report-specific schedules for any items that reference it. A better way to stop a schedule is to expire it, by putting an end date on it. Expired schedules are indicated as such by the Status field. Schedules that have been expired can be restarted by extending the end date.

Another alternative is to pause a shared schedule. A paused schedule can be resumed at a later date and time. Report-specific schedules cannot be paused. Pausing a schedule is similar to modifying it. Pausing the schedule of a process that is already running or of one that is in queue only stops the subsequent runs. It has no effect on the currently executing process.

NOTE

Administrators can pause schedules from Report Manager.

To pause a shared schedule, select it from the list of the Report Manager schedules and click the Pause button. The same process is used to delete a shared schedule.

Report Execution and Processing

Report processing is the process by which the instructions contained in the Report Definition Language (RDL) file are used to gather data, produce the report layout, and create the resulting report in the desired output format. Report processing is triggered by either on-demand report processing or from push access. Depending on the settings, the Report Server will perform either full processing where is goes through all the stages, or will perform the last stage of report processing (rendering the final document from the intermediate form).

The SSRS report processor generally executes reports in a three-stage process. Report processing retrieves the RDL and gathers the data. With the layout information and the base data, the report processor then does the following:

- **Retrieves the report definition:** This retrieval includes getting the report definition from the Report Server database, initializing parameters and variables that are in expressions, and other preliminary processing that prepares the report for processing its datasets. The data-processing extension then connects to the data source and retrieves the data.
- **Data processing:** Retrieves data from the data sources.
- **Layout processing:** Combines the report data with the report layout from the report definition. Data is aggregated for each section of the report, including header, footer, group headers and footers, and detail. The data is also used to process aggregate functions and expressions.

The output of this stage is the report intermediate format. For reports running as a snapshot or one that is to be cached, the output (intermediate format) is stored and used later.

- **Rendering:** Takes the intermediate format and the rendering extension, paginates the report, and processes expressions that cannot be processed during the execution stage. The report is then rendered in the appropriate device-specific format (MHTML, Excel, PDF, and so on).

Depending on the method of access, the server determines whether it needs to execute all stages or if it can skip one or two. The trick is in the report history. If the administrator specifies that the report should be rendered from a snapshot or cache, the report is rendered from the intermediate format stored in the database. Otherwise, the Report Server starts its processing from the data-gathering stage. Report processing for drillthrough reports is similar, except that reports can be autogenerated from models rather than report definitions. Data processing is initiated through the model to retrieve data of interest.

Report-Execution Timeouts

The time it takes to process a report can vary tremendously. While reports process, they take up time on the Report Server and possibly the report data source. As a matter of practice, most long-running reports take a long time to process because of a long-running query.

SSRS uses timeouts to set an upper limit on how much time individual reports can take to process. Two kinds of timeouts are used by SSRS: query timeouts and report-execution timeouts.

Query timeouts specify how long an individual query can take to come back from the data source. This value is specified inside the reports, by specifying the timeout property while creating a data set. Query timeouts can also apply to data-driven subscriptions.

The report-execution timeout is the amount of time a report can take to process. This value is specified at a system level, and can be overridden for individual reports. To set this setting, click the Site Settings tab and modify the Report Execution Timeout property. The default value is 1800 seconds.

SSRS evaluates the execution timeout for running jobs every 60 seconds. What this means is that every minute, SSRS enumerates through every running job and compares how long it has been running against how long it is supposed to run. The downside of this is that reports actually have a bit more time than the specified timeout value in which to run. If the timeout for a report is set to 30 seconds, SSRS does not check to see whether it exceeded the timeout until 60 seconds, so the report actually gets an additional 30 seconds of runtime.

Running Processes

A process in the Report Server is also called a job. The two kinds of jobs are user jobs and system jobs. User jobs are those jobs that are started by individual users or by a user's subscription.

Examples of user jobs include the following:

- Running an on-demand report
- Rendering a report from a snapshot
- Generating a new snapshot
- Processing a subscription

System jobs are those jobs that are started by the Report Server, including the following:

- Processing a data-driven subscription
- Scheduling a generation of a snapshot
- Scheduling report execution

As mentioned earlier, SSRS comes by every 60 seconds and checks on the status of any in-progress jobs. These jobs could be querying their data source, rendering into intermediate format, or rendering into final format. It drops the status of these jobs into the Report Server database. This generally means that a job has to be running for at least 60 seconds for it to be canceled or viewed. To cancel or view running jobs, click the Manage Jobs link under Site Settings. From here, administrators can view user and system jobs and cancel any running job.

NOTE

Canceling a running job does not guarantee that a query has stopped processing on the remote data server. To avoid long-running queries, specify a timeout for the query during the report development phase.

NOTE

The property `RunningRequestsDbCycle` in the `RSReportServer.config` file sets how often the Report Server evaluates running jobs.

Large Reports

Most of the reports shown so far in the examples are fairly small and easy to run. However, in the real world, you might run into a report that, when rendered, equals hundreds of pages. For these reports, you need to take into account some special considerations.

First, the amount of time a report takes to process is almost directly proportional to the number of rows returned from the database query, and how long it takes to get those rows back. It is a good idea to check with the DBA before running long-running queries against a database. Also, check the execution plan of the query before running it. Perhaps further indexing can be done. And finally, don't bring back any more rows than needed. Modern relational database management systems (RDBMS) are very good at sorting and grouping data. Let the RDBMS group and sort the data where it can; this saves CPU cycles on the Report Server and the network traffic.

Second, take into account the rendering. You should note that different rendering extensions have different effects on the Report Server. The fastest extensions and those that use the least amount of RAM are those whose output is essentially text (MHTML, CSV, and XML). Excel and PDF are very resource intensive, whereas TIFF and JPEG fall in between the two extremes.

Third, take into account the delivery method of the report. If a report uses pagination, it can be rendered like any other report. The default rendering format is HTML, which includes a soft page break. The page break is included intentionally and, in effect, produces a sort of poor man's paging. If a report is extremely large, this helps to deliver it via browser. If the report is delivered via subscriptions, it makes sense to deploy it to a file share and let the user's desktop be responsible for opening it. This takes the load off the Report Server and is the recommended course of action if using PDF or Excel.

The following list includes some general tips to help handle large reports:

- Make sure the report supports pagination.
- Run the report as a scheduled snapshot, and do not let it be run on demand. This lets the report perform data gathering and pagination without user involvement. Afterward, the report is rendered into its final form from the intermediate format.
- Set the report to use a shared data source. Shared data sources can be disabled, ensuring the report cannot be run on demand.
- Limit access to the report to ensure that only those who need to run it can run it.

Report-Execution History

In these days of endless audits, SOX (Sarbanes-Oxley), and now PCI (Payment Card Industry), it is becoming essential to know when someone within an organization accesses data. It is also helpful to know this information from an organizational and planning perspective. As more and more reports get published, how often reports get looked at and by whom could be essential information.

What Is the Execution Log?

To address these issues, SSRS keeps an execution log of reports that it has run. Because the database is what stores the data, the log is still good, even in a scale-out environment. The log has myriad useful information, such as what reports are run, who has run them, and how long they took to process. Other information it has includes the following:

- Name of the physical machine that ran the report (Report Server, not database server)

- Unique ID of the report
- Unique ID of the user running the report
- Whether the request came from a user or system process
- What rendering format was used
- Values of the report parameters
- When the report process started and when it finished
- Amount of time the server took to process the report in milliseconds
- Type of data used for execution (live, cached, snapshot, history)
- Final status code of the report processing (success or first error code)
- Final size of the rendered report in bytes
- Number of rows returned in the data sets of the rendered reports

How to Report Off the Execution Log

The downside of the execution log is that it is not in a human-readable format. To remedy this, Microsoft has distributed a SQL Server Integration Services package that can be used to port the data from the Report Server's internal execution log table to another database to be used for querying and reporting against the log. There are even some sample reports against the resulting execution log table. If you are still using SQL Server 2000, an equivalent DTS package does the same thing.

Three files are central to the extraction and reporting of the execution log. All three files should be located in the <Program Files\Microsoft Sql Server\100\Samples\Reporting Services\Report Samples\Server Management Sample Reports\Execution Log Sample Reports> directory. The first file is `Createtables.sql`, which is the script used to create the tables for the RSExecutionLog database. The second two files, `RSExecutionLog_Update.dtsConfig` and `RSExecutionLog_Update.dtsx`, form the integration package that pushes the data from the Report Server catalog into the RSExecutionLog database.

Creating the RSExecutionLog Database

You can create the RSExecutionLog database by completing the following steps (see Figure 21.2):

1. Open SQL Server Management Studio, connect to the database engine, and select Master as the default database.
2. Run the following query database:

```
create database RSExecutionLog
go
use RSExecutionLog
go
```

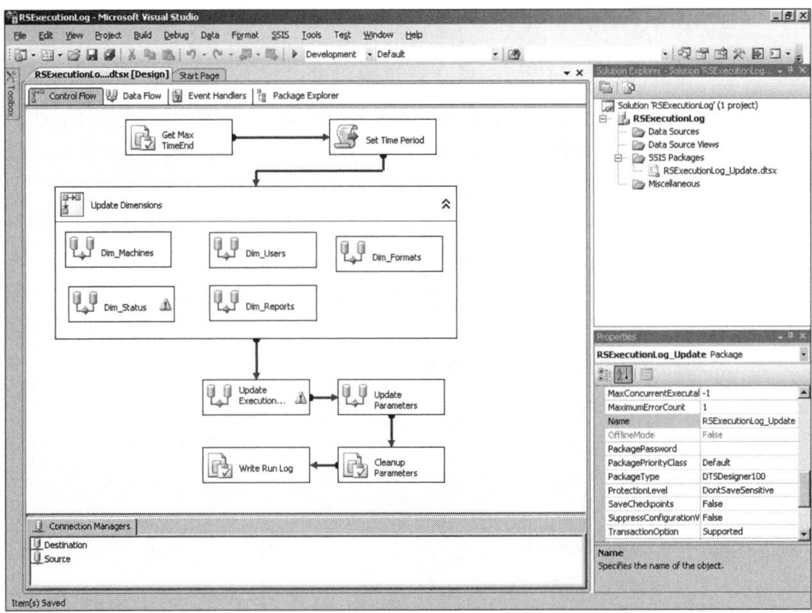

FIGURE 21.2 RSExecutionLog SSIS package.

3. Open the `Createtables.sql` file and execute it in the RSExecutionLog database. The results of the script should be as follows:

```
Dropping tables...
Creating ReportTypes...
Creating Reports...
Creating Users...
Creating Machines...
Creating RequestTypes...
Creating SourceTypes...
Creating FormatTypes...
Creating StatusCodes...
Creating ExecutionLogs...
Creating ExecutionParameters...
Creating RunLogs...
Script completed.
```

4. Double-click the DTSX file and click Execute to execute the package.

To keep data in the RSExecutionLog database current, periodically run the integration package. The package is designed to import new data, without overwriting or removing existing data. To remove old data in the RSExecutionLog database, run the `Cleanup.sql` script.

Overview of the Sample Reports

Three reports come included with the sample reports packages.

The first report (`Execution Status Codes.rdl`) includes a summary of reports run by the status they received. This shows the failure rate of reports on the server and why the processes failed.

The second report (`Execution Summary.rdl`) gives an overview of report executions. It includes some key metrics, such as the number of reports processed per day, the top ten most requested reports, and the longest-running reports. This report is shown in Figure 21.3.

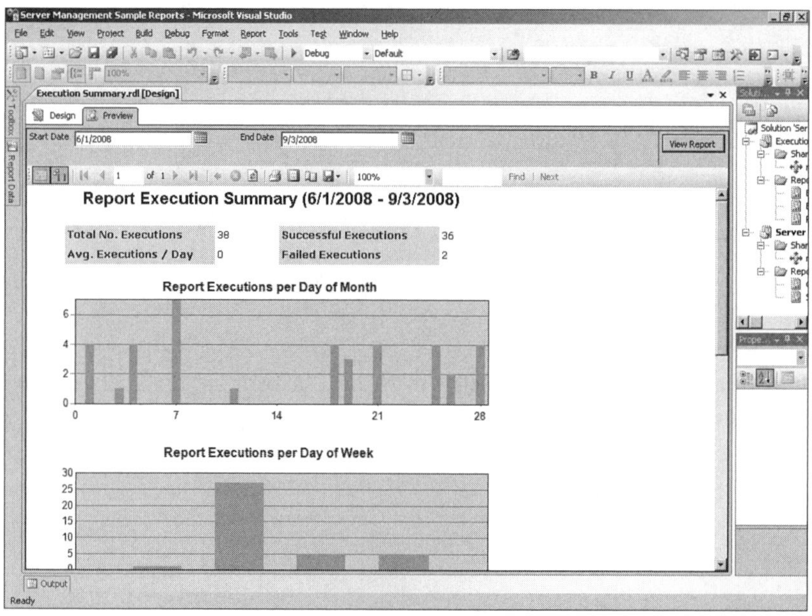

FIGURE 21.3 Report Execution Summary report.

The last report (`Report Summary.rdl`) is similar to the execution summary, but gives the execution overview of a specific report.

The sample reports can actually be published to the Report Server and accessed like any other report. (They get logged like any other report, too.) The only caveat with these reports is having to set the end date to one day ahead of the current date to include the current day's execution. The reason for this is that the date parameters have no way to accept time, and, hence, time defaults to 12:00 a.m. (start of the day). This might come up as an issue when you develop your own reports, too.

Summary

Report schedules allow the coordination of activities within the Report Server. There are two types of schedules: report-specific schedules and shared schedules. The relationship between the two is analogous to the relationship between a custom-defined data source and a shared data source.

A job is any process running on the Report Server. SSRS comes by every 60 seconds to poll which processes are running on the Report Server. Report-execution history enables end users to retrieve from SSRS who accessed what report, when, and using what parameters. Using an SSIS package, you can collect this information into a database for auditing purposes. SSRS comes with three sample reports to query this information from the catalog.

CHAPTER 22

Subscribing to Reports

IN THIS CHAPTER

One of the most convenient things about SSRS is its capability to deliver reports right to the end user without ever having to navigate to the Report Server through subscriptions.

If you have the Enterprise Edition of SSRS, the reports can even be customized based on data from queries. Another nice thing is that end users, if they have the appropriate permissions, can set subscriptions up for themselves. This chapter explores the ins and outs of subscribing to reports and managing subscriptions to reports.

Overview of Subscriptions

A subscription is akin to setting up a job on the Report Server to deliver a report to a user at a specified point in time. This provides a nice alternative to actively going to the Report Server and running the report.

Parts of Subscriptions

Subscriptions all have some common components/requirements. In addition to the following, you must have access to view the report and have a role assignment that includes the task Manage Individual Subscriptions before you can subscribe to the report. Common components/requirements of subscriptions include the following:

- The report has to be able to run independently; that is, the data sources must use either stored credentials or no credentials.

- The report must have a configured delivery method. The built-in ones include email and file sharing.
- You must specify a rendering extension for the subscribed report.
- Some trigger or event is required to run the subscription. Usually, this is a scheduled event, based on either a custom or shared schedule.
- The parameter values for any parameter in a report must be specified or defaulted.

Uses of Subscriptions

Subscriptions have a number of possible uses to meet a number of requirements:

- Deliver reports to end users (the most common use of subscriptions).
- Save reports for offline viewing. This is usually done using PDF or web archive formats.
- Send long-running reports or large reports directly to disk.
- Preload the Report Server's cache.

Standard Versus Data-Driven Subscriptions

SSRS has two different kinds of subscription options. The first kind is called the standard subscriptions. Users can create and manage standard subscriptions for themselves. All the information for the subscription is static, which means that the information has to be specified when the subscription is created (and that the information cannot be modified at runtime).

Data-driven subscriptions (DDS) are similar to standard subscriptions with one important difference. The data used for the subscription must come from a query. This makes DDS incredibly powerful. The list of recipients is derived via a query, which makes it ideal for recipient lists that may change frequently. Users can use DDS to create customized reports for recipients based on preferences of that recipient or that recipient's role within the organization. Even the delivery style and location can be customized. DDS are usually kept in the domain of report administrators and are typically not administered by end users.

NOTE

DDS are available only in SQL Server 2008 Enterprise and Developer editions.

Delivery Options

Reports are delivered using delivery extensions. Two delivery extensions come preloaded into SSRS and can be used by end users, although they cannot be configured. These are an email delivery extension and a file share delivery extension. Like many other parts of SSRS, end users can create their own delivery extensions if the existing ones are not sufficient. One kind of delivery extension an administrator can use that an end user cannot use is called the null delivery extension. As the name implies, it doesn't actually deliver a report anywhere. Instead, it is typically used to preload the Report Server cache or generate snapshots.

Subscription Processing

If you are familiar with SQL Server Notification Services, you might find the model that SSRS uses to process subscriptions familiar. SSRS responds to events. As events occur, SSRS matches these events to subscriptions that should be triggered by one or more of these events. When a subscription is triggered, the Report Server uses the information stored along with the subscription to process the report. When the report is done processing, the Report Server passes it along with the delivery information stored with the subscription to the appropriate delivery extension.

When processing a standard subscription, the Report Server's job is relatively simple. Because standard subscriptions contain only one report that does not vary by user, it just processes the report and sends it along.

The processing of DDS is considerably more complex. For DDS, the number of reports, deliveries, and even parameters to pass to those reports depends on the data passed in. The Report Server must generate a report and deliver it based on every record returned from the data set generated by the query.

Overview of Delivery Extensions

SSRS comes bundled with two main delivery extensions: email and file share. Although skilled developers can implement their own delivery extensions, the prepackaged ones should suffice for most people.

Email

Email can be used to deliver reports, or it can be used to deliver a hyperlink to the generated report; the contents of the message are based on the data included with the subscription.

The Subject line contains, by default, the Report Name (`@ReportName`) and the time it was run (`@ExecutionTime`). Of course, users can modify this to suit their needs.

The body text can contain an embedded report, or the report can come as an attachment. This depends on the rendering extension used. The HTML and MHTML extensions embed the report in the email body. All other extensions generate an attachment to the message.

The email extension is not available if the Report Server has not been set up for email. To set up email, use the Reporting Services Configuration tool.

From the RS Configuration Manager, select Email Settings, and then enter the sender address and name of the SMTP server.

The size limitations of email apply to subscribed reports, too. If the report is delivered as an attachment and the size of the attachment is too large, the report might not get delivered. Second, the Report Server does not validate the email addresses entered when creating the subscription or during runtime in the case of DDS.

Delivering to a File Share

The file share delivery extension drops rendered reports to a specified file share. The extension does not create a folder; however, it does drop files into any standard UNC share. As with any file share, the account that the Report Server service is running under must have access to the share to write to it successfully. The naming format for a UNC share is as follows:

```
\\<servername>\<sharename>
```

Remember not to include a trailing backslash.

After the report is rendered, a file is created using the specified delivery extension. For example, if the delivery extension specified is PDF, a PDF file is created on the file share.

Because a file is fairly static, an interactive feature in the rendered reports is made static. Hence, things such as matrixes and charts will retain the default views.

Creating a Simple Subscription

Report Manager is used to create a standard subscription, which uses both email and file share delivery. Complete the following steps to make an email-based subscription using Report Manager:

1. From Report Manager, open the report to be subscribed to, and select the Subscriptions tab.
2. On the Subscriptions tab, click New Subscription.
3. If necessary, select Report Server Email in the Delivered By drop-down list.
4. Enter the recipient list in the To text box. If you have multiple recipients in the list, the entries need to be separated by semicolons (;).
5. If the user has permissions to manage all subscriptions, the Cc and the Bcc text boxes and the Reply To text box appear. The same rules apply to these as to the To text box with regard to the formatting of email addresses.
6. Modify the Subject line as required.
7. To embed a copy or to attach a copy of the report, check the Include Report check box. Depending on the rendering format, the server will decide whether it can embed the report or include it as an attachment.
8. To send a link to the online version of the report, check the Include Link check box.
9. Pick the rendering format from the Render Format drop-down list. Remember that WebArchive embeds results in the report; everything else is an attachment.
10. Modify the priority and add a comment if desired.
11. If dealing with a parameterized report, set the parameters for the report.
12. Select a time to process the subscription. To set a new schedule, select the When the Scheduled Report Run Is Complete option and click the Select Schedule check box. If the report is executed from a scheduled snapshot, the subscription fires after

the snapshot has been executed by clicking the When the Report Content Is Refreshed option.

After you have completed entering the necessary information, the window should look similar to Figure 22.1.

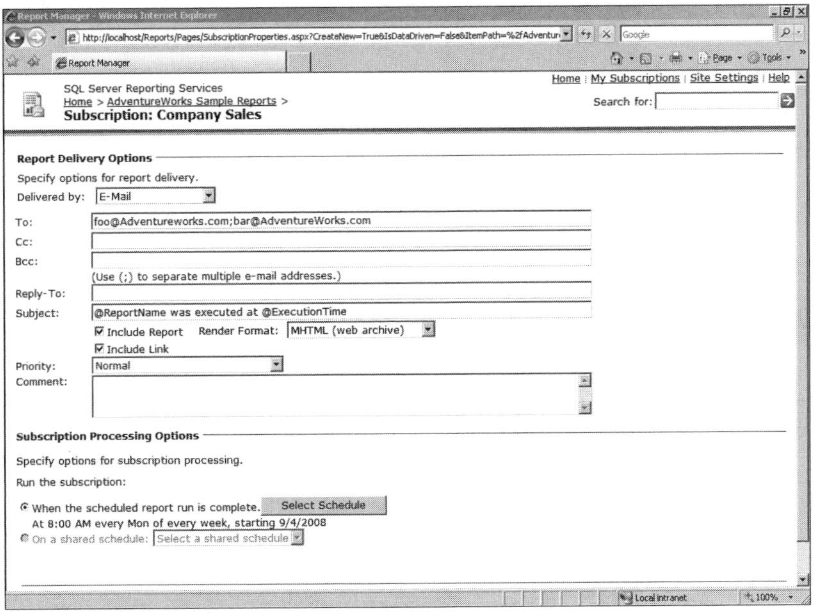

FIGURE 22.1 Email delivery subscription.

File Share Delivery

As previously mentioned, another way to deliver reports is directly to a file share. This can also be done through Report Manager. Complete the following steps to complete the task through Report Manager:

1. From Report Manager, open the report to be subscribed to, and select the Subscriptions tab.
2. On the Subscriptions tab, click the New Subscription button.
3. Select Report Server File Share in the Delivered By drop-down list.
4. Enter the desired filename in the File Name text box. The Add a File Extension When the File Is Created check box tells the server to add the extension when the file gets created. As long as it is checked, the end user should not add the extension to the file.
5. Enter the path to drop the report in the Path text box.

6. Select a render format from the Render Format drop-down list. Because the files are static, it is not recommended to pick a format that can be used interactively or might include multiple files. In other words, stay away from HTML.
7. Enter the credentials for a user with permission to access the share in the Username and Password text box. Use the <domain>\<username> format.
8. Specify file-overwriting options. Choosing the Do Not Overwrite the File If a Previous Version Exists option keeps delivery from occurring if a similarly named file exists. It is recommended to use one of the other two to keep such issues from becoming problematic.
9. If dealing with a parameterized report, set the parameters for the report.
10. Set the schedule as you did earlier when setting up email delivery.

When complete, the screen should look similar to Figure 22.2.

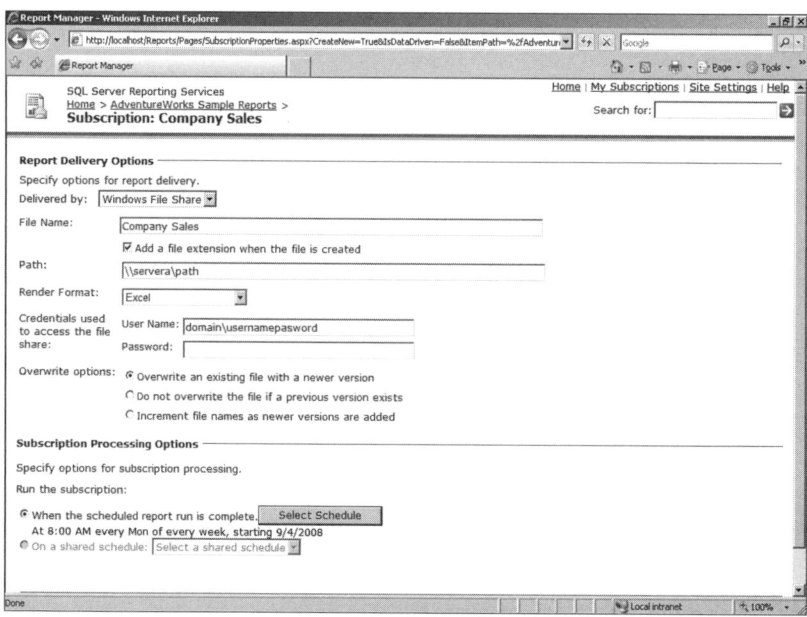

FIGURE 22.2 File share delivery subscription.

Creating a Data-Driven Subscription

The steps to create a new data-driven subscription are not too terribly different from the steps needed to create a standard subscription. The large difference in the DDS model is that the parameters for the recipient list and the rendering extension are all derived from a query. To aid end users in creating a data-driven subscription, both SQL Server Management Studio and Report Manager have wizards to set up all the information.

Remember that to use a subscription, the report's data sources must have stored credentials or no credentials.

Creating a Subscriptions Database

Before creating a data-driven subscription, the end user must create a data set that can be used to hold the information for the subscription. To create a Subscriptions database, open the SQL Management Studio and run the following script:

```
use master
go
if exists(select name from master.dbo.sysdatabases where name = 'Subscriptions')
begin
    drop database [Subscriptions]
end
    create database [Subscriptions]
go
use [Subscriptions]
go
create table [SubscriptionInfo]
    ([To] nvarchar(50),
     [Format] nvarchar(50),
     [EmailAddress] nvarchar(50),
     [EmployeeId] nvarchar(50),
     [Linked] nvarchar(50),
     [IncludeReport] nvarchar(50))
go
insert into [SubscriptionInfo] (
[To],[Format],[EmailAddress],[EmployeeId],[Linked],[IncludeReport])
select FirstName + ' ' + LastName [To],
    Format = case (EmployeeId%2) when 0 then 'MHTML' else 'PDF' end,
    EmailAddress,
    b.EmployeeId,
    Linked =  case (EmployeeId%2) when 0 then 'True' else 'False' end,
    IncludeReport =  case (EmployeeId%2) when 0 then 'True' else 'False' end
from AdventureWorks.Sales.SalesPerson a, AdventureWorks.HumanResources.Employee b,
    AdventureWorks.Person.Contact c
where a.SalesPersonId = b.EmployeeId
    and c.ContactId = b.ContactID
```

The preceding script creates a new database called Subscriptions. When setting up the data-driven subscription, a custom data source is created to connect to the table and pull the subscription information. It also pulls in the salespeople information from the AdventureWorks catalog, and sets some preferences.

Report Manager

You can use Report Manager to create data-driven subscriptions. The following steps show how to create a data-driven subscription using Report Manager:

1. Navigate to the Employee Sales Summary report from the Sample Reports included with SSRS, click the Subscriptions tab, and click the New Data Driven Subscription button.
2. Enter a description and choose Report Server Email for the delivery method. Select Specify for This Subscription Only under the prompt for the data source for the recipient information.
3. Enter the information needed to log in to the Subscriptions database.
4. Enter the following query to select information for the recipient list:

```
select *, datepart(m,getdate()) [month],
    datepart(yyyy,dateadd(yyyy,-1,getdate())) [year]
  from [SubscriptionInfo]
```

5. You can click the Validate button to execute the query on the Report Server and check to see whether it is valid.
6. Change the following values on the delivery settings from the defaults:
    - To gets its value from EmailAddress.
    - IncludeReport gets its value from the Include Report field.
    - Renderformat gets its value from Format.
    - IncludeLink gets its value from Linked.
7. Enter the parameters from the database query:
    - Month comes from the Month field.
    - Year comes from the Year field.
    - Employee comes from the EmployeeId field.
8. Finally, create a custom schedule for the subscription or choose whether it should be run on a shared schedule or after a new snapshot has been created. You can find more information about creating shared schedules in Chapter 21, "Report Execution and Processing."

Managing Subscriptions

Subscriptions can be managed with Report Manager. Report subscriptions are managed just like any other property of a report.

To view, modify, or delete subscriptions from Report Manager, navigate to the report, open it, and select the Subscriptions tab. From here, the Report Manager shows all the subscriptions for a particular report, including the description, how it is triggered, what the current status is, and when it was last run. Users can sort on any one of these fields to help find the subscription they are looking for. If a subscription does not exist, you have the option to create one. To modify any particular subscription, click the Edit button on the data grid. To delete a subscription, check the check box on that row of the data grid and click the Delete button. Click OK on the confirmation prompt.

My Subscriptions

Another feature in Report Manager is the My Subscriptions link next to Site Settings. This link consolidates all the subscriptions a user has created across the entire catalog.

This provides end users and administrators a single place to manage all of their subscriptions. The My Subscription page enables users to sort by report, description, folder, trigger, last run, and status. Just like the subscriptions page for any other report, the Edit button allows users to modify the subscription. To delete the subscription, check the check boxes on the rows corresponding to the subscription to be deleted and click the Delete button. Click OK on the confirmation prompt. Unlike the subscriptions page for any report, you cannot create a subscription. Figure 22.3 shows the My Subscriptions page.

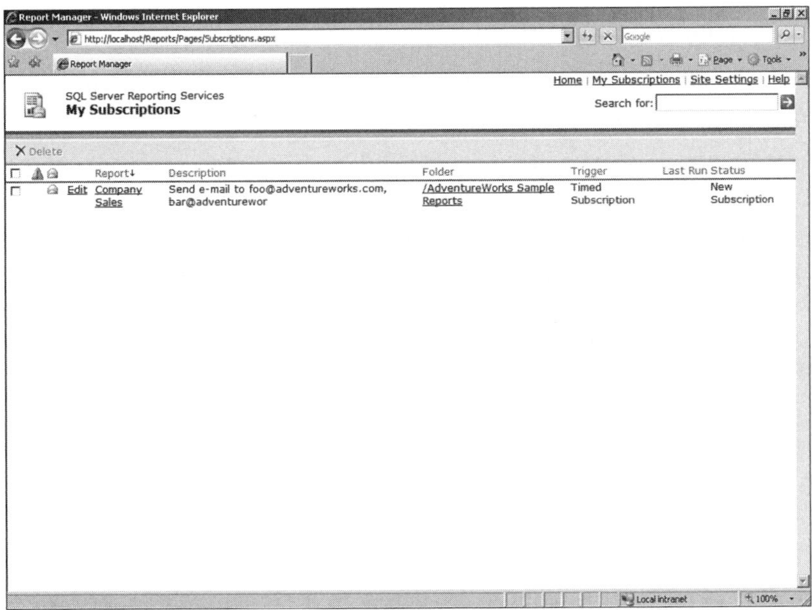

FIGURE 22.3 My Subscriptions page.

Monitoring Subscriptions

As mentioned previously, the individual subscription pages for a report, and the My Subscriptions page, have a Status column on them.

The Status column is crucial for monitoring the execution of a subscription in case the subscription runs into a processing error. If the Report Server detects a delivery error, the error is reported in the server's trace log. One case in which an exception might not be logged is if the trigger fails to occur, such as when a snapshot fails or a scheduled event does not run.

The Report Server service logs (located in `C:\Program Files\Microsoft SQL Server\MSRS10.MSSQLSERVER\Reporting Services\LogFiles`) include any information about delivery statuses. For example, if the delivery extension is email, these logs should include records from processing and delivery. The log does not tell you whether the email was opened.

Deleting/Inactivating Subscriptions

When a subscription fails to process, it is referred to as "inactive." These subscriptions should be taken care of or fixed immediately. The following are some common causes of inactive subscriptions:

- Changing the data source a report uses from having stored credentials or having no credentials to using integrated security or prompting the user for a username or password
- The removal or disabling of a delivery extension
- Changing the name or type of a report parameter after the subscription has already been created
- Changing how a report runs from being on demand, to executing a cached copy

When an event occurs that causes a subscription to later be inactive, the effect might not be immediately known. For example, if a scheduled subscription were to run on Sunday night, and the data source was changed to the next Friday, it would not be until the following Sunday that the subscription would become inactive. When the subscription does become inactive, a message is attached to the subscription to explain why and possibly what steps can be taken to resolve the issue.

Summary

Subscriptions are a powerful way to deliver reports directly to end users. There are two types of subscriptions: standard and data driven. The standard subscription uses static, hard-coded information to process the reports. The data-driven subscription retrieves all the information for processing the subscription (recipient list, report parameters, and so on) from a database query.

End users can manage their subscriptions from the My Subscriptions page. Administrators can monitor the status of the subscription processing through the Report Server log.

CHAPTER 23

SSRS Administration

IN THIS CHAPTER

- Monitoring SSRS
- Managing Active Jobs
- Key Management
- Configuring SSRS

A number of tools are used to monitor and configure SSRS, including basic tools such as Report Manager and SQL Server Management Studio. Other examples of tools are some of the more complex command-line utilities. In this chapter, we provide an overview of the tools available to monitor the Report Server and some of the switches we can tweak to optimize SSRS.

Monitoring

You can use a number of log files to monitor SSRS, including a trace log, execution log, and now even an HTTP log. You can also use performance counters to get an idea about how well the Report Server is performing and take action accordingly. In addition, through SQL Server Management Studio, you can view and monitor running processes.

Reporting Services Log Files

Reporting Services uses three main log files to provide information about the inner workings of the Report Server.

Report Server Execution Log

The first thing to know about this log is that it is stored in the database. This log file contains information about which reports were run, who ran them, when they were run, where reports were delivered, and which rendering format was used. The information for this log has to be obtained by running a SQL Server Integration Services (SSIS) package to gather data from the various table and internal mechanisms in SSRS. The package will drop all this information into a single table.

There are also reports that are included in the SQL Server samples that report on information included in the execution log.

The Report Server itself contains only about 60 days' worth of data. This limit is not configurable. If you want to keep a rolling history, schedule the SSIS package to running daily.

The execution log SSIS package and reports are located here:

```
<Program Files>\Microsoft SQL Server\100\Samples\Reporting Services\Report
Samples\Server Management Sample Reports\Execution Log Sample Reports
```

Trace Log

The Reporting Services trace log is primarily used for debugging applications. These files are written to as SSRS runs processes. The trace log contains very detailed information. Most of this information is redundant and can be found elsewhere. Nevertheless, the trace logs still serve as the single most useful source of debugging information.

The trace log files are ASCII files and can be found here (assuming default instance):

```
<Program Files>\Microsoft SQL Server\MSRS10.MSSQLSERVER\Reporting Services\LogFiles
```

The directory contains a number of files. Each file has its own timestamp in the filename. The trace files in their default setting will reach only 32MB, and the server itself will keep only 14 days' worth of files.

The level of tracing information itself is configurable from `ReportingServicesService.exe.config`. The location of the file, assuming the default instance, is `<Program Files>\Microsoft SQL Server\MSRS10.MSSQLSERVER\Reporting Services\Report Server\bin`. The two sections in the configuration file to pay particular attention to as far as tracing is concerned are `DefaultTraceSwitch` and `RSTrace`. They are shown here:

```
<system.diagnostics>
  <switches>
    <add name="DefaultTraceSwitch" value="3" />
  </switches>
</system.diagnostics>
<RStrace>
  <add name="FileName" value="ReportServerService_" />
  <add name="FileSizeLimitMb" value="32" />
  <add name="KeepFilesForDays" value="14" />
  <add name="Prefix" value="appdomain, tid, time" />
  <add name="TraceListeners" value="file" />
  <add name="TraceFileMode" value="unique" />
 <add name="Components" value="all:3" />
```

```
</RStrace>
```

If you want to turn off the trace, set `DefaultTracesSwitch` to `0`. Trace settings can vary from `0` to `4`. The levels are as follows:

- **`0`**: Turns off tracing
- **`1`**: Records only exceptions and restarts
- **`2`**: Records only exceptions, restarts, and warnings
- **`3`**: Records only exceptions, restarts, warnings, and status messages
- **`4`**: Verbose mode (most possible information)

Most of the other settings are self-explanatory. The most interesting setting is the Components setting. This enables us to specify which components to trace and the level to trace them at. The different components are as follows:

- **`All`**: Used to generate trace information for all components not included in the ones grouped into special categories. *All* is a bit of a misnomer; it really means everything except the other categories.
- **`Running jobs`**: Traces currently running reports.
- **`SemanticQueryEngine`**: Traces the processing of the semantic queries from model-based reports.
- **`SemanticModelGenerator`**: Traces semantic model generation.
- **`http`**: Traces Report Server HTTP requests. It is important to note that this is not enabled by default.

The settings can be modified to include one or more of these categories in a comma-separated list. The format is `<CategoryName>:<TraceLevel>`.

For example, to enable the web server logs and leave the rest of the trace file as is, use the following:

```
<add name="Components" value="all:3,http:4" />
```

More on web server logs later.

HTTP Log

Because SSRS 2008 no longer uses Internet Information Services (IIS) as a web server, it had to provide its own equivalent of the web server logs. The HTTP log contains information about the HTTP requests and responses handled by Report Manager and the Report Server Web Service. Remember from earlier that HTTP logging is disabled by default.

Like the other trace files, the HTTP log is an ASCII file. The HTTP log behaves like other trace files in that by default the size is limited to 32MB and it deletes itself after 14 days.

Once the HTTP log is enabled, you can find the files with the other trace files. It also contains familiar W3C fields, so you can use familiar parsers for IIS log files.

Remember that to benefit from HTTP logging you must enable it. As mentioned previously, one of the key steps is to add the `HTTP` category to the `Components` setting under `RSTrace`. There are other settings, too. These determine the filename prefix and the HTTP trace switches that determine which fields appear in the log file. A complete example of an `RSTrace` section with HTTP is shown here:

```
<RStrace>
  <add name="FileName" value="ReportServerService_" />
  <add name="FileSizeLimitMb" value="32" />
  <add name="KeepFilesForDays" value="14" />
  <add name="Prefix" value="appdomain, tid, time" />
  <add name="TraceListeners" value="file" />
  <add name="TraceFileMode" value="unique" />
  <add name="HttpTraceFileName" value="ReportServerService_HTTP_" />
  <add name="HttpTraceSwitches" value="date,time,
clientip,username,serverip,serverport,host,method,uristem,uriquery,protocolstatus,
bytesreceived,timetaken,protocolversion,useragent,cookiereceived,cookiesent,
referrer" />
  <add name="Components" value="all:3,http:4" />
</RStrace>
```

Viewing and Managing Jobs

Every so often, SSRS checks the status of all running jobs on the Report Server. When it gets the status of all these running processes, it continues to write that status into the Report Server database. The jobs it considers to be in progress are any jobs that are running a database query, processing the results of that query, or rendering reports.

Using the management tools available in SSRS, you can monitor these jobs and even cancel them. Being able to do so proves helpful when extremely large reports are weighing down a machine that has other processes running, too. It is also helpful to cancel processing to perform Report Server system maintenance.

User Jobs Versus System Jobs

Jobs are divided into user jobs and system jobs. User jobs are those that are started by an end user, such as an on-demand report. System jobs are jobs that are started by the Report Server itself, such as data-driven subscriptions.

View Running Jobs

SQL Server Management Studio (SSMS) enables you to view and cancel any job that is running on the Report Server. The Jobs folder in SSMS holds the key to this. After connecting SSMS to a Report Server, right-click the Jobs folder and refresh the list of running jobs. Right-click a running job and select Properties to pull up the job's Properties page to get more detailed status information for each job (see Figure 23.1). To view the status of every running job, right-click the Jobs folder and select Cancel All Jobs (see Figure 23.2).

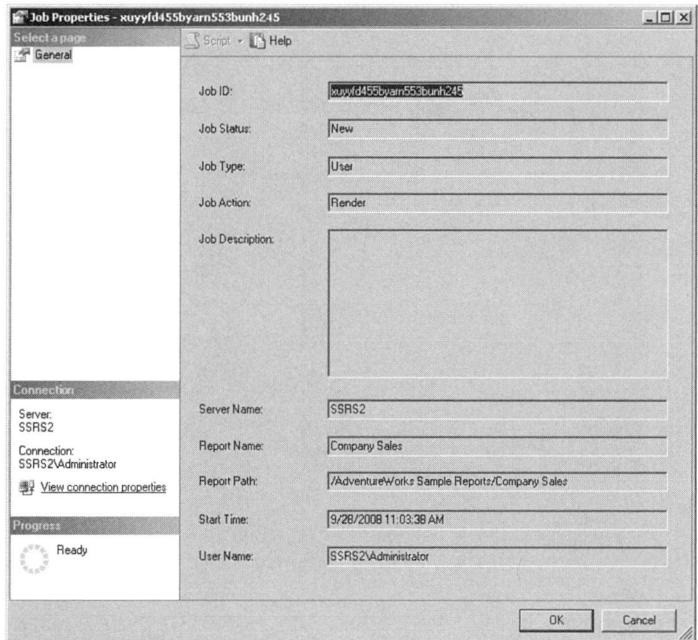

FIGURE 23.1 Job Properties dialog box.

Cancel Running Jobs

Only the following types of jobs can be canceled:

- On-demand reports
- Scheduled reports processed
- Standard subscriptions owned by individuals

An important thing to remember is that canceling a job cancels only the processes running on the Report Server. Therefore, if the report is running a query on a different database server, there is no guarantee that the query will stop processing on the remote server. If this becomes a concern, specify a timeout value for the query so that the query will automatically stop if it takes too long to execute.

Job Status Frequency

As mentioned previously, SSRS periodically scans all running processes and enters the information into tables in the Report Server database. One configuration setting controls how often the Report Server scans running jobs, and another one specifies the interval where a job is transitioned from New status to Running status. Both settings are in the `rsreportserver.config` file, which is located in the following directory (assuming the default instance):

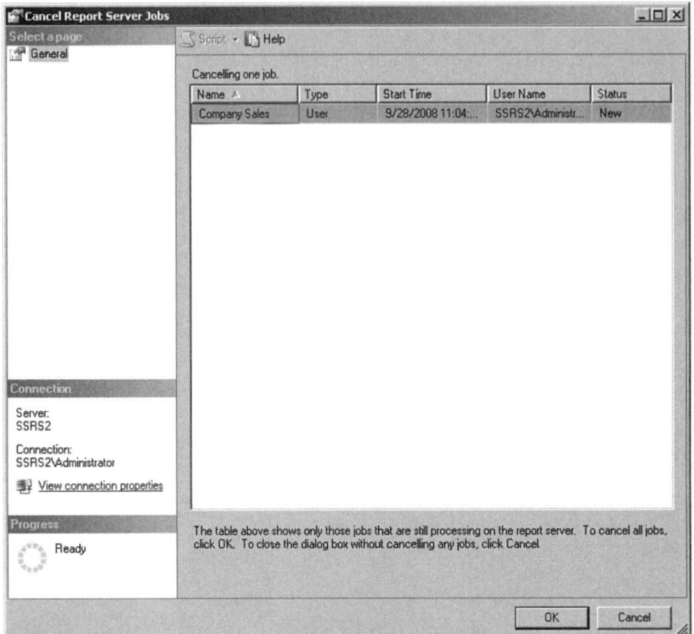

FIGURE 23.2 Cancel All Jobs dialog box.

```
<Program Files>\Microsoft SQL Server\MSRS10.MSSQLSERVER\Reporting Services\
ReportServer
```

An example of the settings is shown here. Both settings are shown with their default values:

```
<Add Key="RunningRequestsDbCycle" Value="60"/>
<Add Key="RunningRequestsAge" Value="30"/>
```

Performance

Many things can affect the performance of SSRS. The most common things include hardware, the number of concurrent users, the amount of data a report consumes and has to process, and even the rendering format.

There are also a number of ways to get performance data. Two of the most popular ways are the Windows Task Manager and Performance Console.

Task Manager can be used to provide information about your system's CPU and memory usage. It can also be used to compare processes against each other. The other popular way to obtain performance information is via Performance Console. Performance Console can be used in conjunction with Event Viewer to set up logs and alerts about report processing and resource consumption.

Performance Counters

SSRS has three performance objects:

- **MSRS 2008 Web Service:** This is used to track Report Server performance initiated through the Report Server's UI.
- **MSRS 2008 Windows Service:** This is used to track objects initiated from the scheduling and delivery processor. These are typically noninteractive processes.
- **Report Server Service:** This is used to monitor HTTP events that in earlier releases would have been relegated to IIS.

Most of the actual performance counters included in the MSRS Web Service and the MSRS Windows Service are actually the same. Most of these revolve around report processing and cache management. The biggest difference is that some of the counters for the MSRS Web Service reset when ASP.NET stops in the Report Server Web Service. A full description of each of the counters is available via Books Online.

Execution Mode

Report execution refers to how a report is processed: on demand, caches, or run from snapshots.

On Demand On-demand report processing requires the data source to be queried each time the report is run. Although this means that the report always gives you up-to-the-second data, it also means you can be putting an extremely heavy load on the data source.

Cached A cached report simply means that you can cache the report (and the data it needs) for a specified period of time. The cached copy of the report is then used for each of the users who access the report after the initial run. Cached report processing can be set to expire after an interval or after a specific date and time.

Snapshots Snapshots are reports that contain layout information and data that is retrieved at a specific point in time and later updated regularly. The information is stored in the Report Server database, and is used only when a user requests the report. As snapshots are updated, the snapshot is refreshed, and the old one is thrown away unless otherwise specified.

You need to be aware of a couple of caveats related to report snapshots. First, you cannot create a snapshot of a report that prompts the user for a data source that integrates Windows security. Second, the values for any parameters that require user input must be set first. If the user requests a snapshot report with a different set of parameter values than was specified, the report will re-query the database and render as if it were an on-demand report.

Large Reports

Very large reports have their own special concerns. They usually require substantial resources. To deal with them, here are a few tips:

- Make sure the report supports paginations. SSRS 2008 has a number of performance enhancements designed to help deliver paginated reports.
- Use a data-driven subscription to render the report as a snapshot to prevent it from being run during peak hours.
- Use CSV, XML, or HTML as a rendering format, if possible. These formats use the least amount of resources. PDF is fairly CPU intensive, relatively speaking, and Excel is RAM intensive and the slowest.

Timeout Values

Two kinds of timeout values can be set to limit system resources: query timeouts and report-execution timeouts:

- **Query timeouts:** These timeouts place a limit on the number of seconds a query to a data source can take. This timeout has to be defined inside a report. The default query timeout is 30 seconds.
- **Report-execution timeouts:** These timeouts are the maximum number of seconds a report can process before it is stopped. This is a system-level value, but it can be overwritten for each report. The default value is 1,800 seconds (or about 30 minutes). You can override the default on the report-execution Properties page for a report.

Configuration Items

You can configure a number of items through the log files. For example, some options, such as email delivery, can be configured with the Reporting Services Configuration tool; other things, such as memory and application domains, can only be configured by editing the configuration files.

Email Delivery

The easiest way to configure email delivery is via the Reporting Services Configuration Manager. Here are the steps to do so:

1. Open the Reporting Services Configuration Manager.
2. Connect to the Reporting Services instance, and click Email Settings.
3. Enter the name or IP address or name of the SMTP.
4. Enter the sender's email address.
5. Click Apply. The screen should look like Figure 23.3.

Unattended Execution Account

The unattended execution account, which is needed for batch processing, is just as easy to set up as email delivery. Just complete the following steps:

1. Open the Reporting Services Configuration Manager.
2. Connect to the Reporting Services instance and click Execution Account.
3. Enter the account username.
4. Enter the password and confirm the password.

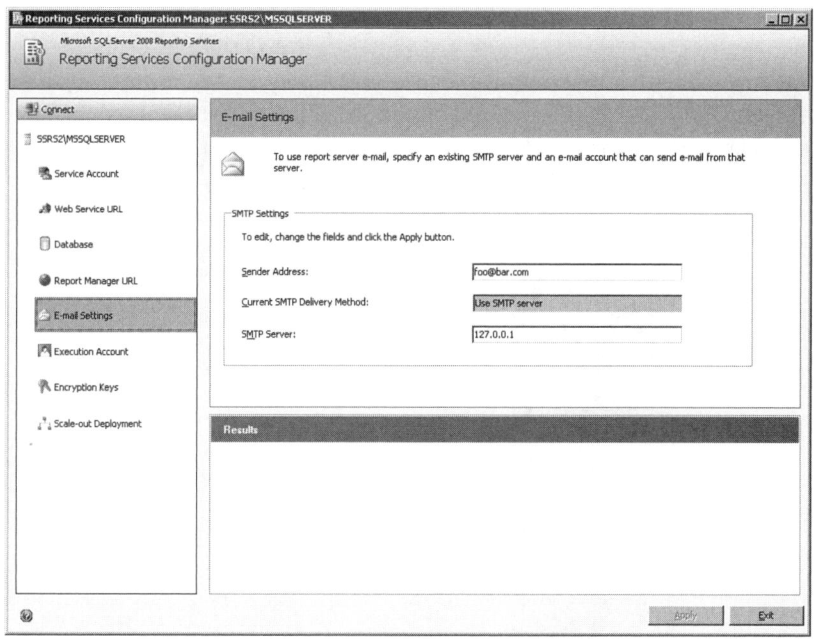

FIGURE 23.3 Email delivery settings.

5. Click Apply. The screen should look like Figure 23.4.

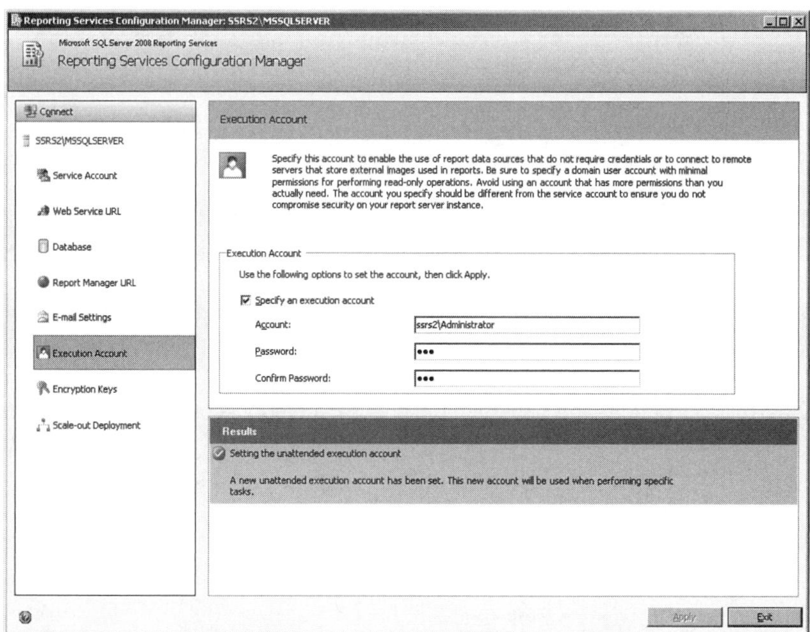

FIGURE 23.4 Unattended execution account settings.

Memory

You can configure memory settings (see Figure 23.5) only by editing the `RSReportServer.config` file with a text editor. Recall from Chapter 2, "Reporting Services 2008 Architecture," that four critical memory settings dictate the critical memory thresholds: `WorkingSetMaximum`, `WorkingSetMinimum`, `MemorySafetyMargin`, and `MemoryThreshhold`. Table 23.1 describes these settings.

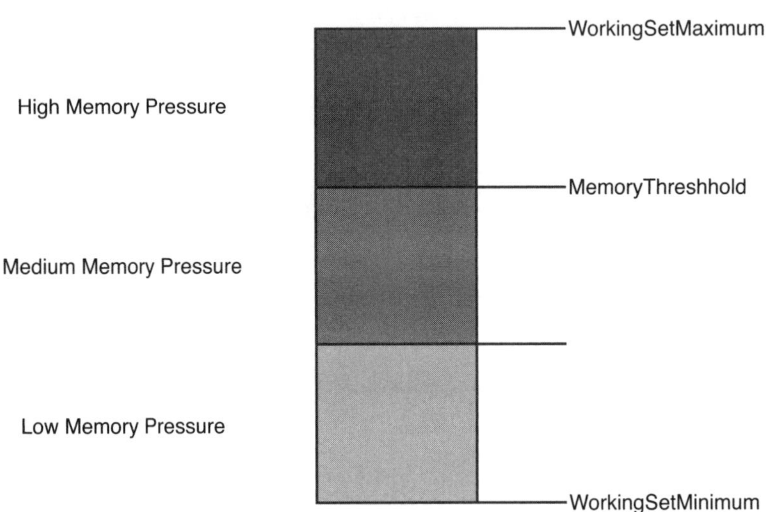

FIGURE 23.5 Memory threshold settings.

TABLE 23.1 Memory Threshold Settings

Configuration Option	Usage
`WorkingSetMinimum`	Defines the minimum amount of memory the Reporting Server Service can use
`WorkingSetMaximum`	Defines the maximum amount of memory the Reporting Server Service can use
`MemorySafetyMargin`	Defines the upper limit of the low-memory section
`MemoryThreshhold`	Defines the upper limit of the medium-memory pressure section

These are what filled settings in the file look like:

```
<MemorySafetyMargin>80</MemorySafetyMargin>
```

```
<MemoryThreshold>90</MemoryThreshold>
<WorkingSetMaximum>5000000</WorkingSetMaximum>
<WorkingSetMinimum>2500000</WorkingSetMinimum>
```

Key Management

As mentioned in Chapter 5, "Reporting Services Deployment Scenarios," the symmetric key is never exposed in an unencrypted fashion, and the public keys are tied to the account running the Report Server Windows Service and Web Service. The database knows nothing. Should a hardware failure happen, it is relatively easy to restore the database and hook a new Report Server to it. However, the new machine will not be able to decrypt the data stored in the catalog. What's one to do?

Thankfully, the developers who wrote SSRS gave you a tool called `rskeymgmt.exe`. The Reporting Services Configuration Manager also contains similar functionality. Both tools enable you to back up and restore the symmetric key. Effectively, these two tools allow end users to perform the following tasks:

- Perform a backup of the symmetric key. This provides safeguards against disaster recovery, and provides a helpful tool to perform a server migration.
- Restore a symmetric key from another Report Server instance over to the current installation.
- Change the symmetric key and re-encrypt all data in a Report Server database. This is helpful should the key ever get compromised, an important individual leave the organization, or as a proactive practice to safeguard the Data tab (see Figure 23.6).

Backing Up the Symmetric Key

Making a backup of the symmetric key should be performed immediately after installing SSRS. Because there is only one symmetric key for every Report Server database, the backup needs to be performed only once unless the key is changed or the backup is lost. Always have a backup of the symmetric key handy. The following list describes some situations in which the backup will become useful:

- Changing the service account under which the Report Server Windows Service runs, or changing its password
- Renaming the machine or changing the instance name of the SQL Server relational engine that hosts the Report Server database
- Migrating or changing the Report Server database of an existing installation
- Restoring the Report Server installation after a hardware failure

To back up the symmetric key, you must have a password to give to the utility. The password is used as an encryption key to encrypt the symmetric key before saving it. This ensures that the symmetric key is never seen unencrypted. Don't forget the password or let it be compromised.

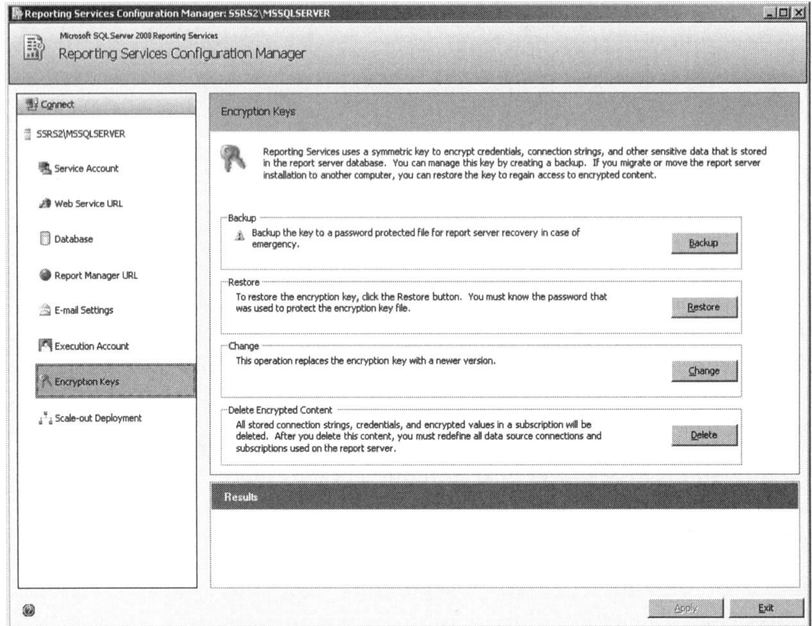

FIGURE 23.6 Encryption tab in the Reporting Services Configuration Manager.

You can complete the following steps to back up the symmetric key with the Reporting Service Configuration Manager:

1. Open the Reporting Services Configuration Manager and click the Encryption Keys tab.
2. Click Backup.
3. Enter a strong password, and enter the location in which to store the resulting file.
4. Click OK.

In a similar fashion, this can be done from the command line with the `rskeymgmt.exe` utility, as follows:

```
rskeymgmt -e -f rsdbkey.snk -p<password>
```

Restoring the Symmetric Key

Should disaster ever strike (such as accidentally deleting the keys, or corrupting the database) and you need to restore the key, you must have both the files with the key and the password for that file. Should the restored backup not contain a valid symmetric key for the Report Server database, the Report Server will not be able to unencrypt the data. In the absolute worst case, an administrator might have to delete all the encrypted data and then reenter it.

To restore the symmetric key with the Reporting Service Configuration Manager, follow these steps:

1. Open the Reporting Services Configuration Manager and click the Encryption Keys tab.
2. Click Restore.
3. Select the location of the file (in most cases this is the `*.snk` file), which contains the symmetric key. Type the password that unlocks the file.
4. Click OK.

To do the same thing from the command line, run the following command:

```
rskeymgmt -a -f rsdbkey.snk -p<password>
```


Changing the Symmetric Key

Changing the symmetric key involves generating a new key and reencrypting all encrypted data that was stored using the old key. It is certainly not something that needs to happen every day, although it is a good idea to do it from time to time as a best practice. Think of it as changing the administrator or sa password. The processes should also be done when the key has been compromised.

Changing the symmetric encryption keys is fairly straightforward. To change the symmetric key with the Reporting Service Configuration Manager, complete the following steps:

1. Open the Reporting Services Configuration Manager and click the Encryption Keys tab.
2. Click Change.
3. Click OK to acknowledge the computers, instance number, and installation ID.

The command to do this via the command line is also fairly simple:

```
rskeymgmt -s
```

Before changing the encryption key for a Report Server installation via the command line, you need to stop the Web Service and HTTP access. After the change is complete, you need to restart the Windows Service and reenable the Web Service. For a scale-out deployment, this needs to be done on all the Report Servers. After the key has been updated, the administrator can reenable web access.

Deleting the Symmetric Key

By deleting the symmetric key, you give up any hope of ever retrieving the encrypted data. All of it will have to be reentered from the ground up. In a scale-out situation, all the Report Servers deployed will have to be reinitialized. Proceed with extreme caution. After the keys have been deleted, the following items will definitely be affected:

- Data source connection strings
- Credentials stored in the catalog
- Reports that are based on Report Builder models (The models use shared data sources.)
- Subscriptions

To delete the symmetric key with the Reporting Service Configuration Manager, complete the following steps:

1. Open the Reporting Services Configuration Manager and click the Encryption Keys tab.
2. Click Delete.
3. Click OK.

The command to do this via the command line is also deceptively simple:

```
rskeymgmt -d
```

After deleting the encryption keys, you need to restart the Report Server Windows Service. For a scale-out deployment, you need to restart the Report Server Windows Service on all Report Server instances.

Scale-Out Deployment

As mentioned in previous chapters, SSRS allows multiple Report Servers to connect to a single shared database. Setting up a scale-out deployment is relatively easy. Just install SSRS on each computer that will be part of the same deployment, use the Reporting Services Configuration Manager to connect to each Report Server, and configure the server to use the same database. And then, use the Reporting Services Configuration Manager to complete the scale-out deployment by joining any new Report Server to that database that is already connected.

Here are the steps to join a server to an existing installation:

1. Open the Reporting Services Configuration Manager.
2. Connect to the existing server.
3. Click the Scale-Out Deployment link.
4. On the screen, you should see the machine waiting to be added to the instance. It will have a Waiting to Join status. Select that machine. The screen should look something like Figure 23.7.
5. Click the Add Server button.
6. Click Apply.

When Apply is clicked, a copy of the symmetric key is encrypted using the public key from the new server. It is then placed on the Symmetric Key column on the Keys table for the new server to use.

Removing a server from a scale-out deployment is pretty much the same process. Do most of the steps previously described, except select a server that has already been joined and click Remove Server.

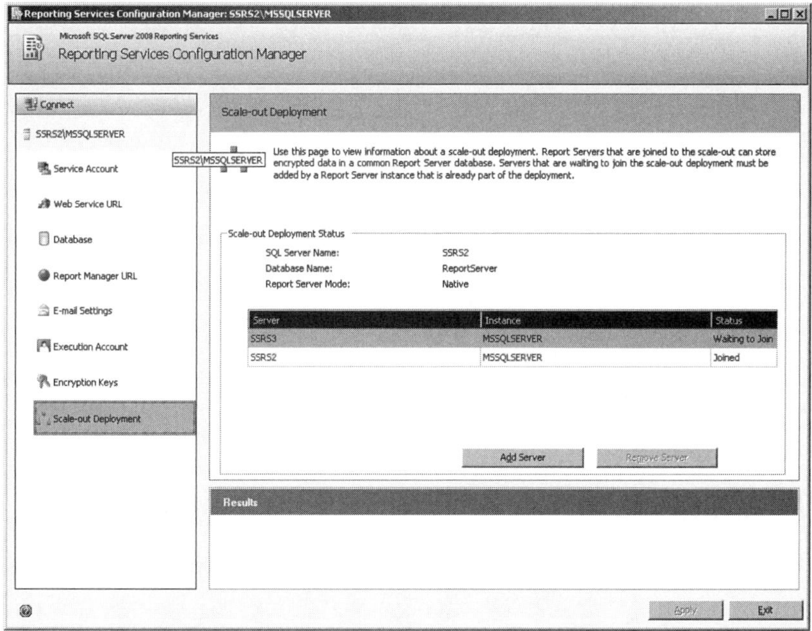

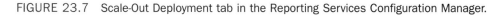

FIGURE 23.7 Scale-Out Deployment tab in the Reporting Services Configuration Manager.

Summary

A number of things can be configured and administered inside SSRS. Some administration can be done with SQL Server Management Studio, other things can be configured with Reporting Services Configuration Manager, and still more advanced functionality can be enabled or disabled simply by modifying configuration files. The trick to managing SSRS is to collect the information you need and then optimize accordingly. You can collect this information using performance counters and the RSExecutionLog.

CHAPTER 24

RS Utility

IN THIS CHAPTER

- Inside the Reporting Services Script Files
- Command-Line Arguments
- Sample Command Lines
- Code Examples

The RS utility is a handy little scripting utility that you can use to programmatically administer the Report Server. The utility basically executes a VB.NET script against the web service endpoints. It can be used to do things such as deploy reports, list running jobs, cancel running jobs, and configure system properties.

Inside the Reporting Services Script Files

The RS utility basically runs scripts that have an extension of `.rss` (RSS files). The script is essentially a Visual Basic.NET executable, in a single code file, which is written against the web service endpoint. The endpoint class can be reference as RS.

NOTE

The RS utility is not supported in SharePoint integrated mode.

The script can contain your own classes and functions if you find that useful. Like most command-line applications, it starts off executing the `Main()` function. You can access your own code from here.

The web service endpoint is basically already referenced for you in a module-level variable called RS. The web service endpoint that is used by default is http://<reportserver>/reportserver/ReportService2005.asmx. Via command-line options, you can make it use the ReportExecution2005.asmx endpoint.

Another handy feature is that you do not need to specify basic namespaces to import. The following namespaces are included when compiling the RSS script file:

- `System.Web.Service`
- `System.Web.Services.Protocols`
- `System.Xml`
- `System.IO`

The authenticating credentials for SSRS can be passed in via command-line options. If the credentials are passed in via command line, you do not need to set them. Because of security reasons, however, this is not the preferred method. The preferred method is to pass in the credentials within the script or use Windows integrated security.

Here is a sample script from SQL Server Books Online:

```
Public Sub Main()
    Dim items() As CatalogItem
    items = rs.ListChildren("/", True)
    Dim item As CatalogItem
    For Each item In items
        Console.WriteLine(item.Name)
    Next item
End Sub
```

This command line runs the script against a local server using integrated Windows security:

```
rs -i Sample.rss -s http://localhost/ReportServer
```

Variables can also be used in scripts. The variables can be passed in from the command lines. All the variables are typed as strings, and are passed like a name-value pair. More on that later.

Command-Line Arguments

You can use a number of command-line arguments with the RS utility, although only two are required. The two required are for the Report Server to execute the script and the filename of the script to execute.

Table 24.1 lists all the command-line arguments.

TABLE 24.1 RS Utility Command-Line Arguments

Argument	Required/Optional	Description
-?	Optional	Prints out a display listing all the command-line arguments and their proper usage.
-i	Required	This specifies the filename of the RSS file to execute. This can be a relative path if desired.
-s	Required	Specifies the URL of the Report Server web server to run the script against. The URL is the directory of the Report Server, not the Report Manager. For example, IE http://localhost/ReportServer for a local server using the default instance.
-u	Optional	Enter the username to use to authenticate against the Report Server. The username must be in the format `[domainname]\username`. If `-u` and `-p` are not used, the script handler defaults to Windows integrated security.
-p	Optional (unless `-u` is entered)	The password to use along with the `-u` argument for the username. Note that the password is case sensitive.
-l	Optional	This specifies a timeout value for the running script. By default, a script is allowed to run 60 seconds. If you enter value of `0`, the script never times out.
-b	Optional	Forces commands to be run in a batch. The whole batch is committed or it is rolled back. A quick note on exceptions: If an exception is thrown but not handled, it will cause the batch to roll back. If you handle the exception, and the script exits from `Main` normally, the batch is committed.
-e	Optional	Decides which endpoint to use while compiling the script. The only two options are `Mgmt2005` and `Exec2005`. By default, the `Mgmt2005` endpoint is used. Because the RS utility is not supported in SharePoint integrated mode, `ReportService 2006` cannot be used.
-v	Optional	Allows you to enter global string variables that can be used inside the RSS script. The `-v` option is used like a name-value pair. `IE -v Foo="Bar"` would result in a global string variable named `Foo` with a value of `Bar`.
-t	Optional	Output error message from executing the script into the Report Server's trace log. There are no options with -t.

A quick note: The RS utility is located in `<Program Files>\Microsoft SQL Server\100\Tools\Binn`. This path should be in your `PATH` environment variable.

Sample Command Lines

All of these samples use a local Report Server with the default instance. You may have to adjust the Report Server URL if you have a named instance.

Here is a basic example using a Windows username and password to authenticate to SSRS:

```
rs -i Sample.rss -s http://localhost/ReportServer -u SSRS2\Administrator -p Password1
```

Here is an example that shows batching all commands:

```
rs -i Sample.rss -s http://localhost/ReportServer -b
```

The following example passes in two variables, `Foo` and `Bar`:

```
rs -i Sample.rss -s http://localhost/ReportServer -v Foo="Foo Variable" -v
Bar="BarVariable"
```

Here is a sample command line with a script timeout of 5 minutes (300 seconds):

```
rs -i Sample.rss -s http://localhost/ReportServer -l 300
```

Code Examples

The following sample script uses the passed-in variable called `Foo`:

```
Public Sub Main()
       Console.WriteLine("The value of Foo is : {0}.",Foo)
End Sub
```

This can be called from the command line with double quotes in the string, as follows:

```
rs -i Sample.rss -s http://localhost/ReportServer -v Foo="Foo's Value with \"Double
Quotes\" inside"
```

The output from this is as follows:

```
The value of Foo is : Foo's Value with "Double Quotes" inside.
```

Here is an example that uses functions and displays running jobs:

```
Public Sub Main()
   Dim jobs As Job() = rs.ListJobs()
   ListRunningJobs(jobs)
End Sub

Public Function ListRunningJobs(jobs() As Job) As Boolean
   Dim runningJobCount As Integer = 0
```

```
    Dim message As String
    Console.WriteLine("Current Jobs")
    Console.WriteLine(("================================" + Environment.NewLine))
    Dim job As Job
    For Each job In  jobs
       If job.Status = JobStatusEnum.Running Or job.Status = JobStatusEnum.[New] Then
       ' New goes away soon
          Console.WriteLine("------------------")
          Console.WriteLine("JobID: {0}", job.JobID)
          Console.WriteLine("------------------")
          Console.WriteLine("Action: {0}", job.Action)
          Console.WriteLine("Description: {0}", job.Description)
          Console.WriteLine("Machine: {0}", job.Machine)
          Console.WriteLine("Name: {0}", job.Name)
          Console.WriteLine("Path: {0}", job.Path)
          Console.WriteLine("StartDateTime: {0}", job.StartDateTime)
          Console.WriteLine("Status: {0}", job.Status)
          Console.WriteLine("Type: {0}", job.Type)
          Console.WriteLine("User: {0}" + Environment.NewLine, job.User)
          runningJobCount += 1
       End If
    Next job
    If runningJobCount = 1 Then
       message = "There is 1 running job. "
    Else
       message = String.Format("There are {0} running jobs. ", runningJobCount)
    End If
    Console.Write(message)
    If runningJobCount > 0 Then
       Return True
    Else
       Return False
    End If
End Function
```

The example's output is shown here:

```
Current Jobs
================================

------------------
JobID: jgbfw045virghsnsgvbv4n55
------------------
Action: Render
Description:
Machine: SSRS2
```

24

```
Name: Company Sales
Path: /AdventureWorks Sample Reports/Company Sales
StartDateTime: 9/29/2008 8:39:17 PM
Status: New
Type: User
User: SSRS2\Administrator

There is 1 running job. The command completed successfully
```

Some other useful scripts that you can execute with the RS utility include the following:

- Deploy new reports (RDL files) and data sources
- Configure data sources
- Download contents of the Report Server
- Deploy to multiple servers simultaneously
- Set up subscriptions
- Refresh caches

As you can see, the RS utility can be used to accomplish almost anything you could use the Reporting Services web service to do. The work would be in developing script files to do it.

Summary

This chapter serves as an introduction to the RS utility. The RS utility can be used in conjunction with the web service endpoints to automate routine tasks or to script difficult deployments. Scripts written for the RS utility are basically VB.NET single code files. They start off by executing the `Main()` function. The web service endpoints are available in the script, and are referenced as the global web service proxy called RS. End users can use passed-in string variables that are available as global variables in the script. Script commands can be batched, and timeouts can be specified. The RS utility is a handy administrative and development tool.

CHAPTER 25

Implementing Custom Embedded Functions

IN THIS CHAPTER

- Adding Embedded Code
- Debugging Embedded Code

The simplest form of custom code available in SSRS is expressions, which were discussed in Chapter 10, "Expressions." The next level of coding complexity is custom embedded code in a report.

Adding Embedded Code

To get a better understanding of how embedded custom code is used in a report, report developers can assume all the code placed in the code window gets compiled into a make-believe class called `Code`. You can add properties and methods to the make-believe `Code` class, and call class members from expressions in the report, which has the class defined.

Embedded code is compiled into a report's intermediate format and gets executed as needed when the report is rendered. Report Designer provides a simple text area to allow editing of the embedded code. To access the code editor, complete the following steps:

1. From the Report menu, choose Report Properties. Alternatively, right-click the area surrounding the report's body and select the Properties menu.
2. Click the Code tab in the Report Properties dialog box.

You should see a window similar to that shown in Figure 25.1 and can type the code in the Custom Code area.

The code editor is basically a multiline text box, and it does not provide any productivity assistance, such as IntelliSense or debugging. You have to be extremely careful while using this code editor. For example, only one level of "undo" action is allowed, as compared to Visual Studio's infinite undo.

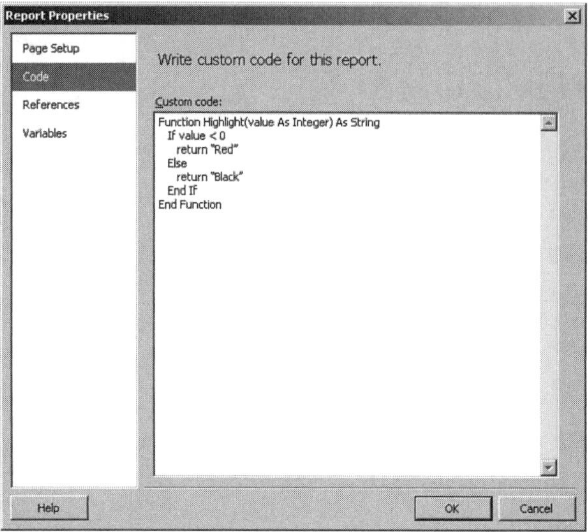

FIGURE 25.1 Code editor.

For all its difficulties, embedded code provides several key benefits for a developer, including the following:

- A more elegant approach (as compared to expressions) to medium-complexity coding scenarios
- A single repository for functions and methods that can be reused by multiple items within a single report, as opposed to complex copy-and-paste expressions
- Direct access to the exception-handling functionality of VB.NET

Every developer knows function reuse is beneficial over copy-and-paste programming. Consider the following fictitious example. Suppose two developers are assigned the parallel development of a single report. One developer uses embedded code, whereas the other one uses simple expressions. One of the initial goals was to highlight negative values in red. Later, this goal changed to a more complex requirement, such as color-coding numeric ranges. The developer who used embedded code could adapt to such change in requirements quickly.

Embedded functions must be written in VB.NET. If you prefer C#, you would have to develop a custom assembly. This topic is covered in Chapter 26, "Creating and Calling a Custom Assembly from a Report."

To add the function used in the preceding narrative, just follow these steps:

1. Open the report properties by either choosing Report Properties from the Report menu or right-clicking the area surrounding the report's body and selecting Report Properties.
2. In the Report Properties dialog box, display the Code tab and enter the following function in the Custom Code area:

```
Function Highlight(value As Integer) As String
   If value < 0
      return "Red"
   Else
      return "Black"
   End If
End Function
```

3. Drag a `Textbox` control from the Toolbox to the report and place the following code in the `Background Color` property:

```
=Code.Highlight(me.value)
```

4. Place `-1` (minus one) in the `Value` property of the text box.
5. Open the report in Preview mode to see the text box with a red background.

Embedded code can address more complex scenarios. For example, if you need to calculate a median, you can use the following approach:

1. Add the following embedded code, using the method described in the previous example:

```
Dim Data As System.Collections.ArrayList


Function AddData(newData As Decimal) As Decimal
   If (Data is Nothing)
      Data = new System.Collections.ArrayList()
   End If
   Data.Add(newData)
End Function

Function GetMedianInfo() As String
   Dim count As Integer = Data.Count
   If (count > 0)
      Data.Sort()
      GetMedianInfo ="Median: " & Data(count/2) & "; Total orders: " & count
    End If
End Function
```

NOTE

In our sample we use the `SalesOrderHeader` table from the Adventure Works database. We will calculate the median on the `TotalDue` field (or median order total). Adjust the code accordingly for different fields. The query to retrieve data is very simple:

```
SELECT TotalDue FROM Sales.SalesOrderHeader
```

2. Call the data set **`OrderTotals`**.
3. Add a table. (Note that in this example we use the table for calculations only, and we do not need to fill anything on the table's surface.)
4. Select the entire table by clicking the corner handler. Set the table's `Hidden` property to `True`.

NOTE

It is important to hide the table. Because of on-demand report processing enhancements in SSRS 2008, there is no guarantee that the `Code` class will maintain state across pages. You can experiment with this by making the table visible and seeing the changes in the results by applying `TOP N` clause to the query.

5. From the grouping pane, open Group Properties for the `Details` group, display the Variables tab, and enter the **`AddDat`** in the Name field and the following code in the Value field to populate `Data` array:

```
=Code.AddData(Fields!TotalDue.Value)
```

NOTE

You can enter any value you want in the Name field. In the case of this example, the value that you enter for the name does not matter because we are not going to use the variable in the sample's code. However the name is required, and SSRS will call the variable (and therefore the `AddData` function) every time the group variable changes. In this example, it happens for every row in the `OrderTotals` data set.

6. On the bottom of the report, add a text box with the following expression:

```
=Code.GetMedianInfo()
```

7. Run the report and see that the median order value in the `SalesOrderHeader` table is $865.20 and the total number of orders is 31,465.

You can take this example further and develop Excel-like functionality in terms of having calculations based on data in nonsequential Table cells, similar to `=$A$1/$B$5` in Excel.

To enable the previously described calculations, we can store the values from a data set in a two-dimensional array and use the array's members to perform calculations. Although for performance reasons we do not advocate this method on large data sets, the method can provide an elegant solution in some cases.

Debugging Embedded Code

SSRS does not provide any facilities to step through the embedded code, and therefore you have two options: You can either debug code in Visual Studio .NET or use some pre-Visual Basic tricks for debugging. The first trick is to label code lines. This is beneficial to locate both compile-time and runtime errors. The following code fragment shows how to label code lines. It also has errors that have been intentionally placed for demonstration purposes:

```
Function Add(n As Integer)
1: i = i + n
2: return i
End Function
```


When you build a report with the code snippet or try to preview the report that calls this code, SSRS reports two issues (one warning and one error):

- **Warning:** `There is an error on line 0 of the custom code: [BC42021] Function without an 'As' clause; return type of Object assumed.` Warnings display only if at least one error is found.
- **Error:** `There is an error on line 1 of the custom code: [BC30451] Name 'i' is not declared. Only the first error is displayed.`

With a small code fragment such as the preceding example, finding errors might not be an issue. For a code fragment that has a significant number of lines, locating the one with an error can prove burdensome.

NOTE

Keep in mind that labels can be present only inside of functions or subroutines and can repeat inside of different functions.

TIP

To properly determine line numbers, deliberately add an error and preview the report. The SSRS error indicates the line number.

TIP

To avoid laborious efforts of numbering and renumbering lines, you should only label key expressions or the first line of functions. Alternatively, you can use labeling to narrow down a line with an error.

The second trick is to locate a line that causes runtime errors by using a `Try-Catch` block:

```
Function DivByZero()
     Dim x As Integer
     Try   ' Set up structured error handling.
3:      x = x/ 0
      Catch ex As Exception
          Return ex.ToString() & vbCrLf & "Exception at Line: " & CStr(Erl)
      End Try
End Function
```

The result of the call to the function `DivByZero()` is as follows:

```
System.OverflowException: Arithmetic operation resulted in an overflow.
at ReportExprHostImpl.CustomCodeProxy.DivByZero()
Exception at Line: 3
```

Note that function `DivByZero()` uses the undocumented function `Erl` to return a line number for the line of code that produced the error. `Erl` really returns a label number. (In the preceding code, it is `3`.)

When you do not implement error handling, and then make a call to a function within the `Value` property of a report item, the report item shows `#Error` as a result.

Depending on the precision of a return value provided from a function, other potential results are `Infinity` or `NaN` (Not a Number).

TIP

Always check the Error List window after a build operation has completed, and make sure that there are no warnings. Best practice suggests eliminating all warnings in production code.

Exceptions within other properties can be caught during the build operation.

Summary

Custom embedded code can provide a more elegant approach to medium-complexity custom code than expressions through function reuse, centralized code repository, and additional error-handling options.

Custom embedded code is VB.NET code embedded in a report. Code is embedded as a part of a Report Definition Language (RDL) file and compiled together with the container report. Many errors are caught by the compiler when a reporting solution is built.

Although embedded code allows a developer to use the full object-oriented functionality of VB.NET, embedded code is mostly used for simple logic. It is possible to develop complex embedded code, but this is not usually done because of limited debugging facilities and limited functionality of the embedded code editor. The embedded code editor is a simple text box that does not have the advanced features, such as code completion, available in Visual Studio.

When functions are too complicated for embedded code to handle efficiently or you prefer to use C# instead of Visual Basic, you can develop and call a custom assembly from a report. The next chapter explains how to leverage a custom assembly within a report.

CHAPTER 26

Creating and Calling a Custom Assembly from a Report

IN THIS CHAPTER

- Initializing Assembly Classes
- Strong-Named Custom Assemblies
- .NET Security Primer for an SSRS Administrator
- Assemblies That Require Other Than `Execute` Permissions
- Debugging Custom Assemblies

SSRS comes with a comprehensive set of functions that can be used within reports. However, you might need to add custom functionality that is not covered by the set of common functions or is too complicated for embedded code to handle efficiently. In addition, if you, as a developer, are hard set on C# as a language of choice, a custom assembly is the way to go. A couple of examples of functionality that are better handled by a custom assembly are encryption and trend analysis.

NOTE

Trend plotting functionality is available in the full version of the Dundas chart. However, the chart does not provide trend calculation information to a report. In some cases, trend information might be needed to trigger some action, such as formatting on a report, and this is where trend analysis assembly might be useful.

Let's start with a simple example and develop a function `GetLibraryInfo()`, which returns a single string with a library version information.

Start Visual Studio 2008 and create a new Class Library Project (you can add this project to the report development solution you worked with previously). To create a Class Library Project, follow these steps:

1. Let's use C#, by selecting Visual C# from Project Types on a New Project dialog box.
2. Let's name the project **`RSCustomLibrary`**.

3. Make sure to select a version of .NET Framework you prefer the library to use.
4. Select the Add to Solution option.
5. See Figure 26.1 for the outcome of the previous actions.
6. Click OK to complete.

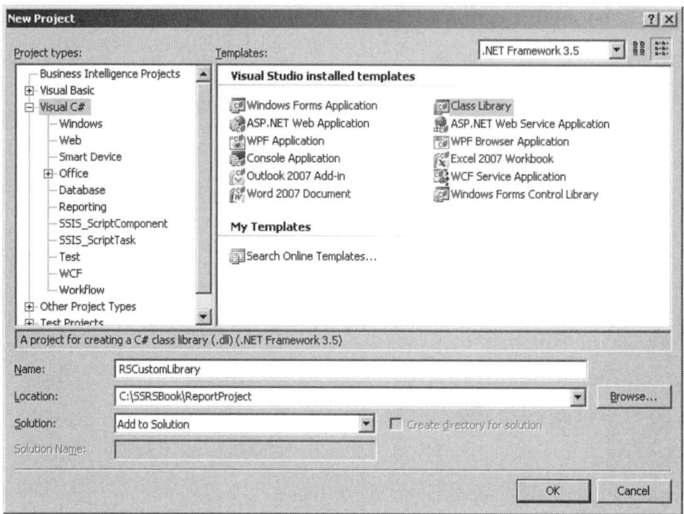

FIGURE 26.1 New library project.

Visual Studio creates a project with a single class `Class1`. Let's rename the file `Class1.cs` in Solution Explorer to **`MainClass.cs`**. Note how Visual Studio changed the name of the class in the code.

Substitute code in the class module with the following code:

```
using System;
//System.Reflection helps to get the assembly information
//using System.Reflection;
namespace RSCustomLibrary
{
    public class MainClass
    {
        //Method GetLibraryInfo() returns this custom assembly information
        //RSCustomLibrary, Version=1.0.0.0, Culture=neutral, PublicKeyToken=null
        public static string GetLibraryInfo()
        {
            //return Assembly.GetExecutingAssembly().GetName().ToString();
```

```
            return "RSCustomLibrary, Version=1.0.0.0, Culture=neutral, PublicKey
Token=null";
        }
    }
}
```

Now you may ask, "Why did they comment operations with the Reflection library? Wouldn't it be the best way to retrieve version information?" You are absolutely correct. The problem at this point is that our library only has `Execute` permission. This permission means that we have "access to the CPU" and we can do math and string operations, but we will get an error when accessing the Reflection library. (In this case, we added a call to the library as an expression in the `Textbox1`: `[rsRuntimeErrorInExpression] The Value expression for the textrun 'Textbox1.Paragraphs[0].TextRuns[0]' contains an error: Request for the permission of type 'System.Security.Permissions.FileIOPermission, mscorlib, Version=2.0.0.0, Culture=neutral, PublicKeyToken=b77a5c561934e089' failed.`)

NOTE

When a developer calls a .NET namespace, it might not be immediately clear whether the `Execute` permission is sufficient. For example, the `GetExecutingAssembly()` method requires `FileIOPermission`. However, it might be logically concluded that the `Execute` permission is sufficient because the method retrieves information about the assembly it is called from and the assembly should be loaded in the memory. Contrary to the conclusion, the call to this method does `PathDiscovery` to check the assembly's path and therefore requires `FileIOPermission`.

Later in this chapter, we discuss the actions that we need to take to allow an assembly to elevate its security from `Execute`-only permissions; see the "Assemblies That Require Other Than `Execute` Permissions" section.

NOTE

SSRS2K5 Report Designer allowed any permission for an assembly in the Preview mode. This would make developers wonder: "It worked in Preview mode, why doesn't it work anymore after I have deployed it to the server?" SSRS 2008 Report Designer fixed this discrepancy and will force you to deal with permissions in Preview mode, too.

TIP

To simplify a custom assembly test, developers can use a simple Windows application to call the assembly's methods. This allows testing the assembly's functionality prior to tests with SSRS.

The compiled assembly must be located in directories in which it is accessible by

- **Report Designer:** (The default directory is `C:\Program Files\Microsoft Visual Studio 9.0\Common7\IDE\PrivateAssemblies`.) This allows calling an assembly from reports in Preview mode.
- **Report Server:** (The default directory is `C:\Program Files\Microsoft SQL Server\MSRS10.MSSQLSERVER\Reporting Services\ReportServer\bin`.) This allows calling assembly from reports deployed on Report Server.

NOTE

Report Designer/Server reports an error if it can't find the library:

```
[rsErrorLoadingCodeModule] Error while loading code module:
'RSCustomLibrary, Version=1.0.0.0, Culture=neutral,
PublicKeyToken=null'. Details: Could not load file or assembly
'RSCustomLibrary, Version=1.0.0.0, Culture=neutral,
PublicKeyToken=null' or one of its dependencies. The system cannot find
the file specified.
```

Please compile the `RSCustomLibrary` project and let's now use our custom assembly in a report via the following steps:

1. First let's create an empty report. We can call it **`Ch26.CallingCustomAssembly.rdl`**. Then let's reference the assembly. Open the report properties by choosing Report Properties from the Report menu.
2. In the Properties dialog box, click the References tab.
3. Click Add under Add or Remove Assemblies.
4. Click the ellipsis (...) button and navigate to the RSCustomLibrary (see Figure 26.2).

   Developers can navigate to any location where the library is present, such as the bin directory of the library project. This operation records only the reference to the assembly and not a specific location of this assembly. Report Designer adds the following Report Definition Language (RDL) to reference an assembly:

   ```
   <CodeModules>
       <CodeModule>RSCustomLibrary, Version=1.0.0.0,
           Culture=neutral, PublicKeyToken=null
       </CodeModule>
   </CodeModules>
   ```

5. Enter a class name, such as **`RsCustomLibrary.MainClass`**. Filling in a class name and an instance name (such as **`myMainClass`**) is optional for static methods. When you specify a class name and an instance name, Report Designer creates an instance of the specified class and, subsequently, you can access the class inside of a report using the instance name of the class. Report Designer adds the following RDL:

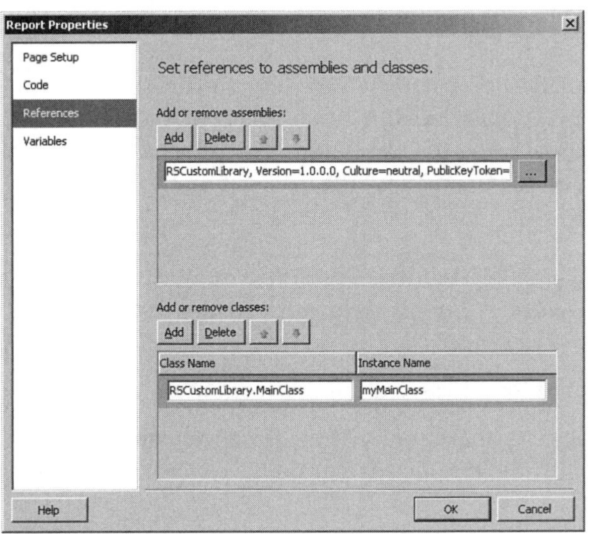

FIGURE 26.2 Reference custom assembly.

```
<Classes>
  <Class>
    <ClassName>RsCustomLibrary.MainClass</ClassName>
    <InstanceName>myMainClass</InstanceName>
  </Class>
</Classes>
```


When specifying a class name, you need to prefix the name of the class with its assembly, such as RSCustomLibrary.MainClass. Otherwise, the SSRS compiler returns an error: [rsCompilerErrorInClassInstanceDeclaration] Error in class instance declaration for class MainClass: [BC30002] Type 'MainClass' is not defined.

6. Call the assembly from one of the report's expressions. A static method can be called as =<AssemblyName>.<ClassName>.<StaticMethodName>; in this case, =RSCustomLibrary.MainClass.GetLibraryInfo(). An instance method can be called as =<Code>.<InstanceName>.<PublicMethodName>; in this case, =Code.myMainClass.GetLibraryInfo(). A static method does not require an instance, but can still be accessed through the instance if so desired.

Now that you have referenced a custom assembly in a report and copied binaries to the Report Designer's directory, the assembly can be called from the report in Preview mode of the Report Designer. To make the assembly work with a Report Server, also copy an assembly to its bin directory.

Initializing Assembly Classes

You might sometimes need to pass initialization parameters to a class in a custom assembly. This is done by overriding the `OnInit()` method of the `Code` object of a report. This can be done by editing the RDL directly or using the code editor. To open the code editor, choose Report Properties from the Report menu and click the Code tab in the Report Properties dialog box (see Figure 26.3).

To initialize a class, you can either

- Create a new instance of the class inside of `OnInit` and pass parameters to a class constructor.
- Write a public initialization method for a class and call this method from `OnInit`.

When you create a new instance of the class, make sure that the instance name used in the `OnInit` method does not conflict with the instance name you have created when you referenced an assembly:

```
<Code>
    Dim Public myMainClass1 As RSCustomLibrary.MainClass
    Protected Overrides Sub OnInit()
       myMainClass1 = new RSCustomLibrary.MainClass(Report.Parameters!Period.Value)
    End Sub
</Code>
```

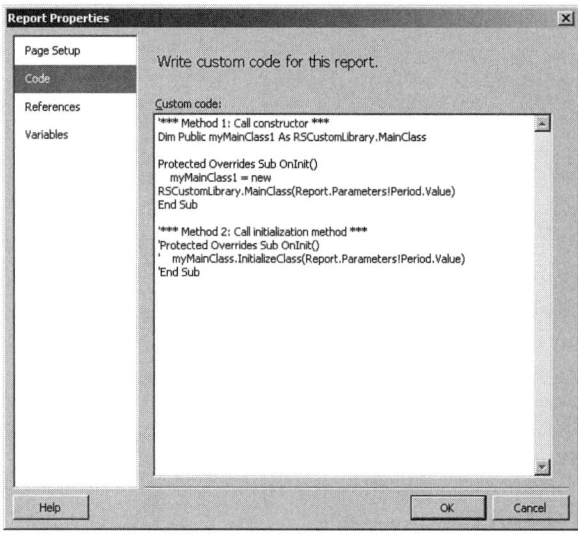

FIGURE 26.3 Using the code editor to override the **`OnInit()`** method.

To invoke this initialization method, from a report you can use the following expression: `=Code.myMainClass1.GetLibraryInfo()`.

NOTE

If a conflict exists between the instance created in a report's reference and any of the instances generated in the code, SSRS generates an error: `[rsCompilerErrorInClassInstanceDeclaration] Error in class instance declaration for class RsCustomLibrary.MainClass: [BC30260] 'myMainClass' is already declared as 'Private Dim myMainClass As <unrecognized type>' in this class.`

When you call a public initialization function, create an instance of the class by choosing Report Properties from the Report menu and then clicking the References tab.

You then call the initialization function from `OnInit`. Make sure that the instance name used in `OnInit` corresponds to the instance name used when you referenced an assembly:

```
<Code>
    Protected Overrides Sub OnInit()
        myMainClass.InitializeClass(Report.Parameters!Period.Value)
    End Sub
</Code>
```

To invoke this initialization method, you can use the following expression: `=Code.myMainClass.GetLibraryInfo()`.

NOTE

Because we are using parameters for initialization in this example, be sure to add a parameter Period to the report.

Within the `OnInit` method, you can use items from the `Globals`, `Parameters`, and `User` collections. The `Fields` and `ReportItems` collections are not available when the `OnInit` method is invoked.

NOTE

Do not forget to prefix the collection name with `Report` (such as `Report.Parameters`); otherwise, you will receive an error: `[rsCompilerErrorInExpression] The Value expression for the textbox 'textbox2' contains an error: [BC42024] Access of shared member, constant member, enum member or nested type through an instance; qualifying expression will not be evaluated.`

To take advantage of initialization, you need to add a constructor to the assembly. The updated assembly may have the following code:

```
using System;
//Need to have this so we can get the assembly information
//using System.Reflection;
namespace RSCustomLibrary
{
    public class MainClass
    {
        static int mPeriod = -1;
        public MainClass()
        {}
        public MainClass(int Period)
        {
            mPeriod = Period;
        }
        public void InitializeClass(int Period)
        {
            mPeriod = Period;
        }
        //Method GetLibraryInfo() returns this custom assembly information
        //RSCustomLibrary, Version=1.0.0.0, Culture=neutral, PublicKeyToken=null
        //AND initialization status:
        //
        public static string GetLibraryInfo()
        {
            //return Assembly.GetExecutingAssembly().GetName().ToString()
            return "RSCustomLibrary, Version=1.0.0.0, Culture=neutral,
➥PublicKeyToken=null"
                + (
                    (mPeriod != -1) ?
                        " Initialized with value=" + mPeriod.ToString()
                        : " Not initialized"
                   );
        }
    }
}
```

Note the operator ? (question mark) usage in the code. If you are not familiar with this operator, it is similar to the IIF function or the IF-THEN-ELSE statement.

NOTE

If you choose to use a constructor to initialize the class, an explicit default constructor (constructor with no parameters) is required. If no default constructor is defined, SSRS returns an error: `[rsCompilerErrorInClassInstanceDeclaration] Error in class instance declaration for class RsCustomLibrary.MainClass: [BC30455] Argument not specified for parameter 'Period' of 'Public Sub New(Period As Integer)'`.

It is very likely that the first deployed version of an assembly will not be perfect and one day you will need to update an assembly. You can update an assembly using one of four ways:

- Maintain the same assembly attributes (such as `Version` and `Culture`) and replace an assembly in Report Designer and SSRS directories. Maintaining assembly attributes is a key for this method because the report's RDL contains this information in the `<CodeModule>` descriptor. If an assembly's attributes change, the reports can no longer call it. This method is the best for frequent assembly updates, while maintaining classes and method signatures. This method of updates is especially relevant during debugging and testing.
- Update the assembly attributes and update all the references (using Report Designer or directly editing the `<CodeModule>` tags) to reference the new version of the assembly.
- Create a strong-named assembly (see the next section "Strong-Named Custom Assemblies" for more information) and store it in the Global Assembly Cache (GAC). The GAC allows multiple versions of an assembly. Reports can call any of the versions stored in the GAC. Thus, you can keep both versions of the assembly and refer to either one of the versions.
- As in the previous method, create a strong-named assembly, store a version of an assembly in the GAC, and force SSRS to redirect all the calls to the new assembly. In this case, an administrator would need to modify the `Web.config` and `ReportService.exe` configuration files to add the following entry:

```
<configuration>
   <runtime>
      <assemblyBinding xmlns="urn:schemas-microsoft-com:asm.v1">
         <dependentAssembly>
            <assemblyIdentity name="RSCustomLibrary"
                              publicKeyToken="..."
                              culture="..." />
            <bindingRedirect oldVersion="1.0.0.0"
                             newVersion="2.0.0.0"/>
```

```
            </dependentAssembly>
        </assemblyBinding>
    </runtime>
</configuration>
```

Strong-Named Custom Assemblies

The .NET Framework allows sharing of assemblies through the GAC. The GAC is a `%systemroot%\assembly` directory on a computer on which .NET Framework is installed. GAC can be managed through `%systemroot% \Microsoft.NET\Framework\version GACUTIL.exe` or the Assembly Cache Viewer extension of Windows Explorer (see Figure 26.4). You can find additional information about using this tool at http://msdn2.microsoft.com/library/34149zk3.aspx.

Assemblies must have a strong name to be stored in GAC; the .NET runtime can uniquely identify each assembly, even assemblies with the same name. A strong name is the combination of the assembly's name, the four-part version number, the culture (if provided), a public key, and a digital signature stored in the assembly's manifest.

Visual Studio 2008 made it very simple to sign an assembly through the Signing tab of the Project Designer. To access the Signing tab, select a project node in Solution Explorer, and then choose Properties from the Project menu. When the Project Designer appears, click the Signing tab.

By default, Reporting Services does not allow calls to strong-named custom assemblies directly from reports. This is probably a good thing because enabling SSRS to call strong-named assemblies poses security risks.

To enable calls to a strong-named custom assembly in Reporting Services, you can use one of the methods described in Table 26.1. Both methods described in Table 26.1 have security risks associated with them.

Security risks are especially relevant to the strong-named custom assemblies that require more than `Execute` permissions (as discussed in the "Assemblies That Require Other Than `Execute` Permissions" section").

.NET Security Primer for an SSRS Administrator

Although the details of .NET security are beyond the scope of this book, a brief security overview will help you to better understand the security of SSRS assemblies. You can find more security-related topics in the Microsoft .NET Framework documentation (http://msdn.microsoft.com/library/default.asp?url=/library/en-us/dnnetsec/html/netframesecover.asp).

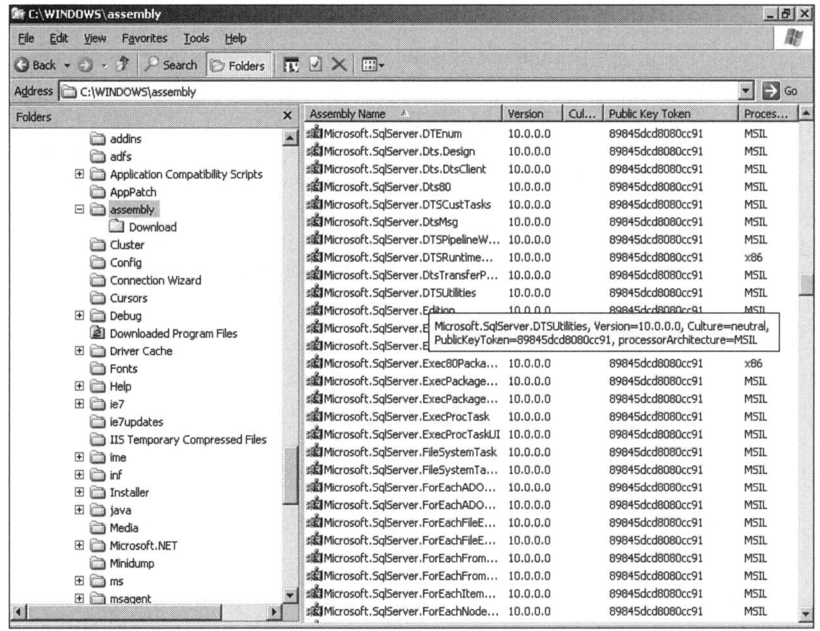

FIGURE 26.4 Assembly cache viewer.

By default, custom assemblies are granted `Execute` permission in Reporting Services. The `Execute` permission set enables code to run, but not to use protected resources. For example, the `Execute` permission allows string manipulations, but not access to the file system.

TABLE 26.1 Methods of Enabling a Strong-Named Assembly

Method	Accomplished By	Security Risk
Allow a strong-named assembly to be called by partially trusted code using the assembly attribute `AllowPartiallyTrustedCallers Attribute`.	In the assembly attribute file, add the following assembly-level attribute: `[assembly:AllowPartially TrustedCallers]` (`<assembly:AllowPartially TrustedCallers>` for VB projects).	Makes the assembly callable from any other assembly (partially or fully trusted)

TABLE 26.1 Continued

Method	Accomplished By	Security Risk
Grant `FullTrust` security permission to report expressions in Reporting Services. Caution! High security risk. *Never* use this method in the production environment.	Find the Report_Expressions_ Default_Permissions code group in RSPreviewPolicy.config and/or rssrvpolicy.config and modify PermissionSetName to state PermissionSetName="Full Access".	Grants `FullTrust` to all custom assemblies that are called in report expressions

The worst outcome of a malicious call to the assembly with `Execute` permission is a potential denial-of-service attack in which a malicious assembly causes excessive CPU and memory use, thereby impacting performance of other software components running on the computer on which such an assembly is installed.

After an assembly is enabled for additional permissions, the impact of a malicious call could be more dramatic, such as data loss.

.NET Common Language Runtime (CLR) employs code access security, which allows an administrator to assign permissions to an assembly. When an assembly makes a call to a protected resource (for example, file I/O), the runtime checks whether an assembly has appropriate permissions to do so. During the call, CLR evaluates all the assemblies in the call stack for permissions. This prevents an `AssemblyA` with restricted permissions (such as `Execute`) to call an `AssemblyB` with less restrictions to perform an operation on a protected resource.

An administrator sets the security policy by editing Extensible Markup Language (XML) configuration files. SSRS has three security configuration files: `rssrvpolicy.config`, `rsmgrpolicy.config`, and `RSPreviewPolicy.config` (outlined in Table 26.2). Depending on the end goal, one or more files should be edited.

TIP

An administrator should always create a backup of SSRS configuration files before making any modifications.

TIP

Refer to Microsoft Knowledge Base article KB842419 (http://support.microsoft.com/?kbid=842419) for the step-by-step process of working with security permission settings in SSRS.

TABLE 26.2 SSRS Configuration Files

Filename	Location (Default Installation)	Description
`rssrvpolicy.config`	`C:\Program Files\Microsoft SQL Server\MSRS10.MSSQLSERVER\Reporting Services\ReportServer`	The Report Server policy configuration file. This file contains security policies for the Report Server and affects execution of the following: ▶ Custom expressions and assemblies deployed to a Report Server ▶ Custom data, delivery, rendering, and security extensions deployed to the Report Server
`rsmgrpolicy.config`	`C:\Program Files\Microsoft SQL Server\MSRS10.MSSQLSERVER\Reporting Services\ReportManager`	The Report Manager policy configuration file. These security policies affect all assemblies that extend Report Manager (for example, subscription user-interface extensions for custom delivery).
`RSPreviewPolicy.config`	`C:\Program Files\Microsoft Visual Studio 9.0\Common7\IDE\PrivateAssemblies`	The Report Designer standalone preview policy configuration file. This file contains security policies for Report Designer and affects the following: ▶ Execution of custom expressions and assemblies in reports during preview in Report Designer ▶ Execution of custom extensions, such as data-processing extensions, that are deployed to Report Designer

Administrators can edit configuration files manually, using any text editor (possible, but not recommended method) or employ the help of the .NET Framework Configuration utility (`mscorcfg.mcs`). You can find more information about `mscorcfg.mcs` at http://msdn.microsoft.com/en-us/library/2bc0cxhc.aspx and at www.emmet-gray.com/Articles/CodeAccessSecurity.htm.

TIP

Use the .NET Framework Configuration utility (`mscorcfg.mcs`) to simplify permission creation and minimize the chances of malformed XML.

If you did not work with .NET Framework 2.0 before and just installed SQL Server and Visual Studio on a "clean" machine, then to leverage `mscorcfg.mcs`, you must install .NET Framework 2.0 Software Development Kit (SDK) from www.microsoft.com/downloads/details.aspx?FamilyID=FE6F2099-B7B4-4F47-A244-C96D69C35DEC&displaylang=en. Then you can enter **`mscorcfg.mcs`** at the SDK's command prompt. (To access the prompt, choose Start, Programs, Microsoft .NET Framework SDK v2.0, SDK Command Prompt.) Alternatively, you can double-click this file in the `C:\Program Files\Microsoft.NET\SDK\v2.0\Bin` directory. Figure 26.5 shows this tool.

NOTE

The latest version of `mscorcfg.mcs` is 2.0 and available from .NET Framework 2.0 SDK. You can use `mscorcfg.mcs` from version 2.0 to edit configuration for .NET Framework 3.0 and 3.5. This is possible because the later versions are incrementally built on a top of version 2.0.

The .NET Framework Configuration utility edits the computer's security policy file located at (make sure to adjust path for the proper version of .NET if you have used version 1.1 of the configuration utility) `C:\WINDOWS\Microsoft.NET\Framework\v2.0.50727\config\security.config`.

Instead of editing SSRS configuration files manually, an administrator can use the .NET Framework Configuration utility (`mscorcfg.mcs`) and then simply copy the `<PermissionSet>` and `<CodeGroup>` from the `security.config` file to an appropriate SSRS configuration file.

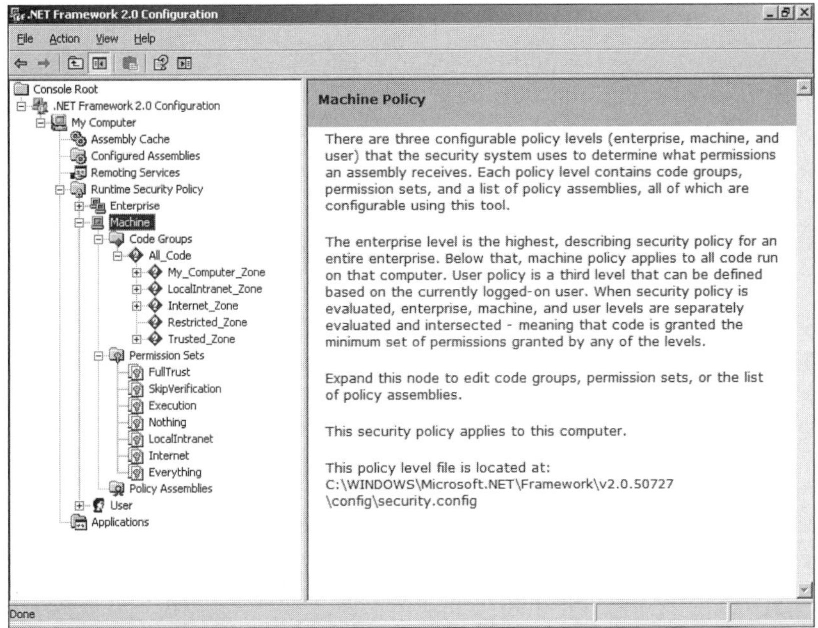

FIGURE 26.5 .NET Framework Configuration utility.

TIP

To simplify finding `<PermissionSet>` and `<CodeGroup>` elements that need to be copied to the SSRS configuration file, an administrator can choose to create a permission set and a code group with easily distinguishable names, which could be as simple as `PermissionSet` and `MyCodeGroup`. Then, an administrator can use a text editor to search and copy the appropriate permissions.

There are three levels of security policies:

- Enterprise level is the highest and applies to the entire enterprise.
- Machine policy applies to all code run on that computer.
- User policy applies to the currently logged-in user.

A lower level can place further restrictions on the policy settings from the highest level, but cannot expand the permissions. As a result, code is granted the minimum set of permissions granted by any of the levels.

To set permissions for an assembly, follow these steps:

1. Create a permission set or use one of the predefined sets, such as `Execution`. (Each assembly in SSRS gets this set by default.) Additional permission sets are `FullTrust`, `Internet`, `None`, and more.
2. Create a code group that maps a permission set to an assembly or, more specifically, uses `Membership Condition` to perform this mapping.

Figure 26.6 shows security permission configuration objects (configured as XML in `.config` files) for an assembly.

Each permission set contains zero or more permissions. A permission is a logical subdivision of system functionality (or access control to a protected resource). Examples of permissions are `Registry` (controls access to the computer's Registry, as a whole or by an individual key), `File IO` (controls access to a single file or a whole file system), `Printing` (controls access to printing resources), `SQL Client` (controls access to SQL servers), and more. (Peek under `Everything` permission set to see a complete list of permissions.)

Each permission supports one or more properties that provide more details for a permission. For example, the `File IO` permission allows specifying an individual file that can be accessed for either one or all of the following: `Read`, `Write`, `Append`, and `Path Discovery`.

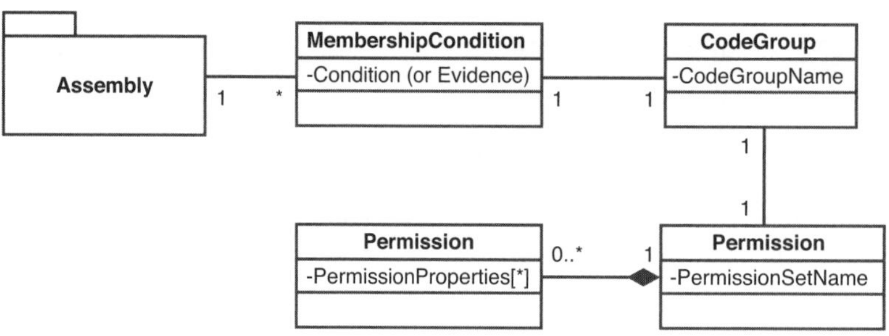

FIGURE 26.6 Assembly security permission objects.

`Security` is somewhat an obscure permission because its attributes are presented as security permissions.

Some of the permissions that `Security` allows to specify are `Enable Assembly Execution` (`Execute` permission) and `Assert Any Permission That Has Been Granted`. `Assert Any Permission That Has Been Granted` in turn enables an assembly to do exactly what the permission implies, that is, to assert security permissions, such as `File IO`.

A code group uses membership conditions to associate an assembly with a permission set. The most commonly used membership conditions are of `URL` and `Strong Name` type. `URL` membership uses a path to an assembly, and `Strong Name` uses exactly what it implies, the strong name of an assembly.

NOTE

Some literature uses the term *evidence* to refer to the membership condition type.

When SSRS calls an assembly, and the assembly, in turn, tries to access a protected resource, the .NET CLR checks whether administrators have set up the appropriate permissions. The CLR then checks the call stack to evaluate permissions for each assembly and makes sure that the minimum combined permission is applied. This prevents a malicious assembly with `Execute` permission from doing anything bad (for example, by calling another assembly with `FullTrust` permission).

Assemblies That Require Other Than Execute Permissions

A developer who wants to grant custom assemblies privileges beyond the `Execute` permission needs to edit one or both configuration files: `ReportServer\rssrvpolicy.config` and/or `RSPreviewPolicy.config`.

NOTE

Reporting Services 2000 used different configuration files (`RSReportServer.config` and `RSReportDesigner.config`). SSRS2K5 and SSRS 2008 both use `rssrvpolicy.config`, `rsmgrpolicy.config` and `RSPreviewPolicy.config` for permission-related configuration.

To have access to system resources, such as `File IO`, from the assemblies, you need to add the following to one or both `rssrvpolicy.config` and `RSPreviewPolicy.config` configuration files (refer to Table 26.2).

Correspondingly, this configuration setting ensures successful execution of the assembly deployed to the Reporting Services and assembly used by Report Designer:

```
<PermissionSet
   class="NamedPermissionSet"
   version="1"
   Name="MyPermissionSet"
   Description="A custom permission set to grant read access to a configuration
➥file.">
   <IPermission;custom assemblies, granting permissions>
      class="FileIOPermission"
      version="1"
      Read="C:\configuration.xml"
      Write="C:\configuration.xml"
```

```
   />
   <IPermission class="SecurityPermission"
      version="1"
      Flags="Execution, Assertion"
   />
</PermissionSet>
```

The preceding configuration section is a definition of a `NamedPermissionSet` with the name `MyPermissionSet`, which is located under the `<NamedPermissionSets>` tag in the configuration file (`rssrvpolicy.config` and/or `RSPreviewPolicy.config`). `MyPermissionSet` grants the assembly two security permissions:

- **Execute**: Allows executing code in the assembly. This permission was discussed earlier in this section.
- **Assert**: Allows asserting other defined permissions in the code. In this case, it allows asserting a `FileIOPermission`.

`MyPermissionSet` also grants the assembly a `FileIOPermission` permission to read and write configuration files. The named permission set is optional and used to create a fine granularity of permissions that are not already defined by built-in permissions.

In addition, the following `<CodeGroup>` configuration needs to be added to the configuration file (`rssrvpolicy.config` in this particular case):

```
<CodeGroup class="UnionCodeGroup"
   version="1"
   PermissionSetName="MyPermissionSet"
   Name="MyCodeGroup"
   Description="A special code group for my custom assembly.">
   <IMembershipCondition class="UrlMembershipCondition"
      version="1"
      Url="C:\Program Files\Microsoft SQL Server\MSSQL.3\Reporting
➥Services\ReportServer\bin\RSCustomLibrary.dll"/>
</CodeGroup>
```

Note that `CodeGroup` refers back to `MyPermissionSet`. Alternatively, `CodeGroup` could have used a predefined set, such as `FullTrust`: `PermissionSetName="FullTrust"`.

Note how the `Url` property of the `UrlMembershipCondition` condition points to the library that was deployed for use by SSRS. You might have spotted this because the `rssrvpolicy.config` configuration was edited and the library was deployed to the SSRS binary directory (`C:\Program Files\Microsoft SQL Server\MSSQL.3\Reporting Services\ReportServer\bin\`).

For Report Designer, the configuration file would have changed to `RSPreviewPolicy.config`, and the deployment directory (and thus the value of the `Url` property) would be `C:\Program Files\Microsoft Visual Studio 9.0\Common7\IDE\PrivateAssemblies\RSCustomLibrary.dll`.

The position of CodeGroup is extremely important. It has to be positioned like the following code fragment:

```
...
            </CodeGroup>

          <CodeGroup class="UnionCodeGroup"
           version="1"
           PermissionSetName="FullTrust"
           Name="MyNewCodeGroup">
            <IMembershipCondition class="UrlMembershipCondition"
               version="1"
               Url="C:\Program Files\Microsoft Visual Studio
➥9.0\Common7\IDE\PrivateAssemblies\RSCustomLibrary.dll"/>
          </CodeGroup>
        </CodeGroup>
    </CodeGroup>
</PolicyLevel>
...
```

This code fragment gives the RSCustomLibrary.dll FullTrust or unrestricted permission. As mentioned previously, because FullTrust is a predefined PermissionSet, it does not require you to specify anything in the <NamedPermissionSets> section of the configuration file.

26

For code to acquire the appropriate permission, it *must* first assert the permission:

```
FileIOPermission permission = new FileIOPermission(FileIOPermissionAccess.Read ¦
FileIOPermissionAccess.Write, @"C:\configuration.xml");
try
{
   permission.Assert();
   XmlDocument doc = new XmlDocument();
   doc.Load(@"C:\configuration.xml");
   ...
}
```

Alternatively, a method's attribute can carry an assertion:

```
[FileIOPermissionAttribute(SecurityAction.Assert, ViewAndModify=
                                                  @"C:\ configuration.xml")]
```

The details of what happens during Assert are beyond the scope of this book. You can find a very good explanation of Assert at http://blogs.msdn.com/shawnfa/archive/2004/08/23/219155.aspx.

What happens if you properly set all configurations, but did not do an `Assert`? In this case, .NET throws a `SecurityException`, such as the following:

```
Request for the permission of type 'System.Security.Permissions.FileIOPermission,
mscorlib, Version=2.0.0.0, Culture=neutral, PublicKeyToken=b77a5c561934e089' failed
```

Debugging Custom Assemblies

The best debugging tool for debugging custom assemblies, no surprise, is Visual Studio. There are two debugging options:

- **Debug with a single instance of Visual Studio:** This is done by creating a single solution that contains both a Reporting Services project and a custom assembly project. You would set breakpoints in a custom assembly and run the report in DebugLocal mode. The easiest way to start DebugLocal is to right-click the report that needs to be tested and select Run from the shortcut menu.
- **Debug with two instances of Visual Studio:** One has a report project and another custom assembly. Set breakpoints in the custom assembly, click Debug, and from the list of processes select the `devenv.exe` that corresponds to the report project. After you run a report that calls the assembly in Preview mode, the debugging session will break at defined breakpoints.

Debugging with a single instance of Visual Studio (DebugLocal method) requires several setup steps:

1. Include both the report project and a custom assembly project in a single solution.
2. Set breakpoints in a custom assembly.
3. Set up the report project as a startup project by right-clicking the project in Solution Explorer and selecting Set as StartUp Project from the shortcut menu.
4. Set up a report as a start item. Right-click the project in Solution Explorer and select Properties from the shortcut menu, select from the Start Item drop-down, and then select a report that you want to debug, as shown in Figure 26.7.
5. Start debugging by choosing Start Debugging from the Debug menu or by pressing F5. Use F11 to step through the report.

Running the `GetLibraryInfo()` example that was developed earlier in the chapter did not create any issues when you ran it in Preview mode (Report Preview tab). This is because Preview mode does not enforce security permissions. Let's try to run `GetLibraryInfo()` in DebugLocal mode. Visual Studio breaks on the `GetExecutingAssembly()` call and shows an exception:

```
System.Security.SecurityException was unhandled by user code Message="Request for the
permission of type 'System.Security.Permissions.FileIOPermission, mscorlib,
Version=2.0.0.0, Culture=neutral, PublicKeyToken=b77a5c561934e089' failed."
```

So, what happened with your code and why didn't it work?

First, you have to check whether the configuration was properly set. Reading of the configuration file was discussed earlier, but `GetLibraryInfo()` does not really read a configuration file. All it does is call the `GetExecutingAssembly()` function:

```
public static string GetLibraryInfo()
{
    return Assembly.GetExecutingAssembly().GetName().ToString()
        + (
            (mPeriod != -1) ?
                " Initialized with value=" + mPeriod.ToString()
                : " Not initialized"
          );
}
```

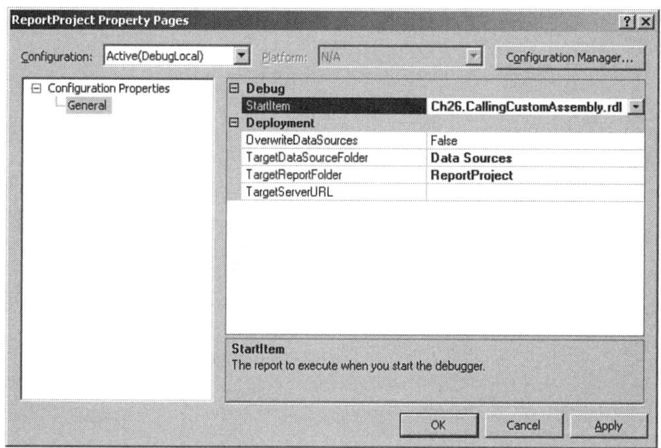

FIGURE 26.7 Project configuration dialog box.

The clue here is the fact that the assembly is trying to retrieve information about itself. So, it must mean that you need some kind of permission to that assembly file.

Earlier in this chapter, you learned that the `GetExecutingAssembly()` requires the `PathDiscovery` permission. To configure Report Designer for debugging of this library, copy the library to `C:\Program Files\Microsoft Visual Studio 9.0\Common7\IDE\PrivateAssemblies\` or, better yet, set an output path for the library in Visual Studio. In Solution Explorer, right-click the library project, select Properties, display the Build tab, and enter **`C:\Program Files\Microsoft Visual Studio 9.0\Common7\IDE\PrivateAssemblies\`** for the output path, as shown in Figure 26.8.

The benefit of setting an output path is that Visual Studio realizes that it was using this library (through Report Designer) and, thus, is able to replace it. If Visual Studio compiles the library to an alternative location and a developer is trying to copy to the `C:\Program`

Files\Microsoft Visual Studio 9.0\Common7\IDE\PrivateAssemblies\ directory, afterward he might not be able to do that. This is because Visual Studio will be "holding" this library during and after debugging. Visual Studio will require restart so that it can release the "hold" and so that the library can be replaced.

The next step is to create a <PermissionSet> with PathDiscovery permission in C:\Program Files\Microsoft Visual Studio 9.0\Common7\IDE\PrivateAssemblies\RSPreviewPolicy.config:

```
<PermissionSet
   class="NamedPermissionSet"
   version="1"
   Name="GetLibraryInfoPermissions"
   Description="A custom permission set to grant read access to a configuration
➥file.">
   <IPermission;custom assemblies, debugging>
      class="FileIOPermission"
      version="1"
```

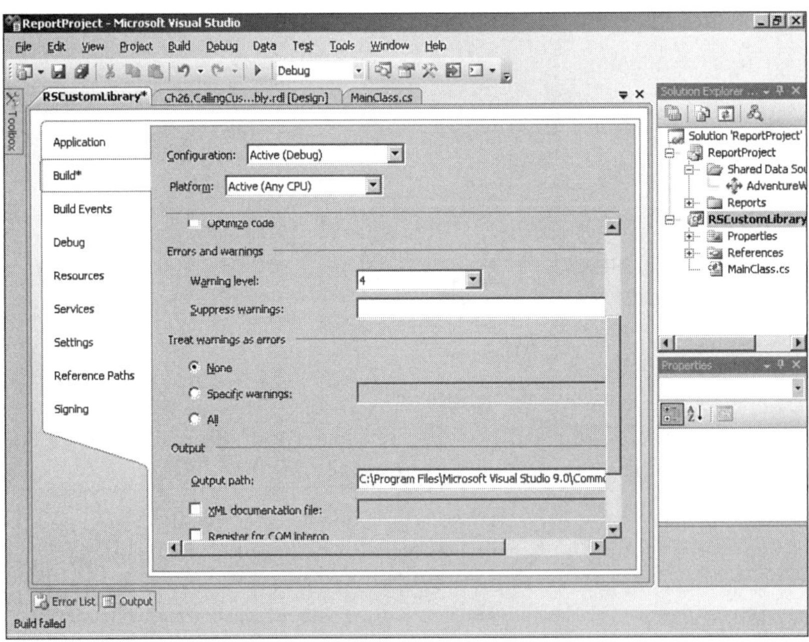

FIGURE 26.8 Library Properties interface.

```
      PathDiscovery=" C:\Program Files\Microsoft Visual Studio
                 ➥9.0\Common7\IDE\PrivateAssemblies"
   />
```

```
    <IPermission class="SecurityPermission"
       version="1"
       Flags="Execution, Assertion"
    />
</PermissionSet>
```

And in the same file, add the following:

```
<CodeGroup class="UnionCodeGroup"
 version="1"
 PermissionSetName="GetLibraryInfoPermissions"
 Name="MyNewCodeGroup">
  <IMembershipCondition class="UrlMembershipCondition"
     version="1"
     Url="C:\Program Files\Microsoft Visual Studio
➥9.0\Common7\IDE\PrivateAssemblies\RSCustomLibrary.dll"
</CodeGroup>
```

to this location:

```
...
   ADD HERE (before the second CodeGroup above the PolicyLevel)
        </CodeGroup>
    </CodeGroup>
</PolicyLevel>
...
```

The final step is to Assert the permission in the code, as follows:

```
public static string GetLibraryInfo()
{
    try
    {
        FileIOPermission permission = new Permission
                      (FileIOPermissionAccess.PathDiscovery,
                      @"C:\Program Files\Microsoft Visual Studio
                      9.0\Common7\IDE\PrivateAssemblies
                      \RSCustomLibrary.dll");
        permission.Assert();
    }
    catch (SecurityException ex)
    {
        return ex.Message;
    }
    return Assembly.GetExecutingAssembly().GetName().ToString()
              + ((mPeriod != -1)?
               " Initialized with value=" + mPeriod.ToString()
```

26

```
            : " Not initialized");
}
```

Now that we handled configuration and security, we can use reflection directly in our code without having a workaround with a string constant (as in the beginning of this chapter).

Summary

Custom assemblies greatly expand functionality (as compared to expressions and embedded code) that can be accessed from a report. A custom assembly can be written in any .NET language. Custom assemblies can leverage a full set of productivity enhancements available in Visual Studio .NET, such as IntelliSense, source code management, full debugging capabilities, and much more.

Custom assemblies can be used for complex code, where usage of expressions and embedded code is no longer elegant. If a custom assembly requires more than the default `Execute` permission, you need to have a good understanding of .NET security and SSRS configuration, modify configuration files to set the assembly's permissions, and assert the permissions in the assembly's code.

CHAPTER 27

Using URL Access

IN THIS CHAPTER

- How to Control Rendering Through URL Access
- How to Integrate URL Access in an Application

URL access is one of the easiest methods available to developers who want to incorporate SSRS functionality into custom applications. URL access is designed to provide the highest level of performance when used to view and navigate reports. URL access achieves this performance by bypassing the web service interface and communicating directly with the Report Server. On the other hand, because URL access does not access the web service, URL access functionality is limited to viewing and navigating reports.

NOTE

SSRS programmers who have implemented custom security extensions (Chapter 29, "Extending Reporting Services," discusses custom extensions) should know that SSRS still checks for permissions and a valid authorization cookie before allowing URL access to a report. In a practical sense, this means that before a report can be accessed through the URL, a call must be made to the `LogonUser` method in the SSRS web service, and the resulting cookie must be relayed to the client's browser.

How to Control Rendering Through URL Access

URL access accepts various parameters that affect a report's rendering. For example, some parameters affect the framing of a report and specify whether the toolbar and a document map are displayed. Other parameters specify a report's output format (HTML, Image, Excel, Word, CSV, PDF, XML). Commonly used parameters are discussed later in this chapter.

You can use URL access to render a report in a browser by typing the URL access command in the address bar or embedding URL access into applications that you develop.

Let's start from a simple example of URL access. One of the methods to discover what is possible through URL access is to actually navigate through the Report Viewer (Report Server web UI) and see how it works. Let's start at `http://localhost/ReportServer` (generic syntax would be `http://<server>/ReportServer`, where `<server>` is a NetBIOS name, a fully qualified domain name (FQDN), or an IP address of a server on which Report Server is installed). When a developer uses Report Designer to deploy a report, the name of the project becomes the name of the folder on a Report Server.

NOTE

If you deploy a solution that contains a report, the report's path is `/<Solution Name>/ <Project Name>/<Report Name>`. If you deploy a project (right-click the project and select Deploy from the shortcut menu), the report's path is `/<Project Name>/<Report Name>`.

For example, if you create a project with the name `Generic`, Report Designer creates a folder named `Generic`. When you navigate to the `Generic` folder, the address changes to `http://localhost/ReportServer?/Generic&rs:Command=ListChildren`. As can be inferred from `Command=ListChildren`, this command renders a list of children, such as reports, data sources, or any other items located in the `Generic` folder.

You do not have to URL encode a URL access string that you pass to a browser. Browsers should automatically encode it. The most common encoding is the space is replaced with a + (plus sign) or an escape sequence `%20`, `/` (slash) is replaced with an escape sequence `%2f`, and ; (semicolon) in any portion of the string is replaced with an escape sequence `%3A`.

URL access commands have corresponding calls in the Reporting Services web service. This case is no exception. The URL access command `Command=ListChildren` corresponds to the `ListChildren()` method call of the SSRS web service. When a user clicks one of the reports (let's use `SimpleReport` as a name of the report) in the SSRS web interface, you see the following URL address in a browser: `http://localhost/ReportServer/Pages/ReportViewer.aspx?%2fGeneric%2fSimpleReport&rs:Command=Render`.

`Render` perhaps is one of the most frequently used commands and has a corresponding web method call in the SSRS web service called `Render()`. `Render` is called to generate a stream of data (this stream is a rendered report) in the format specified by a parameter. By default, a browser receives an HTML stream.

When appropriate for a particular rendering, URL access uses implicit defaults. For example, by default a report is rendered with a toolbar. However, you do not see anything mentioning the toolbar in the URL address of the browser.

URL access uses the following syntax http[s]://<RSserver>/<RSpath>?/<Parameters>.

<RSserver> is a NetBIOS name, an FQDN, or an IP address of a server on which Report Server is installed.

<RSpath> is a virtual directory path on which Report Server is installed. (By default, it is installed to the Report Server virtual directory.)

<Parameters> consists of a relative path of an item (report or other resource) in relation to the SSRS virtual directory followed by one or more parameters with the syntax &prefix:parameter=value. Table 27.1 lists valid prefix values, and Table 27.2 shows valid parameters.

TABLE 27.1 Valid Parameter Prefixes

Prefix	Purpose	Example
No prefix	Treats this parameter as a report parameter. To pass a null value for a parameter, use ParameterName:isnull=true. Note: Report parameters are case sensitive.	&EmployeeID=123 &EmployeeID:isnull=true
rc	Denotes a report control parameter. Passes device information settings to rendering extensions. In the case of HTML (HTML Viewer), it is report framing information. Note: rc parameters are not case sensitive.	&rc:DocMap=True &rc:doCmaP=true &rc:Toolbar=True
rs	Denotes a Report Server parameter. Passes a parameter to SSRS. Note: rs parameters are not case sensitive and all have counterpart functions in the SSRS web service.	&rs:Command=Render
rv	Passes report parameters in a URL to a report in a SharePoint document library, for the Report Viewer web part. This is a new parameter prefix in SSRS 2008.	
dsu	Specifies a username with which to access a data source.	&dsu:MyDataSource=MyUser
dsp	Specifies a password with which to access a data source. Subject to limitations and risks of security exposures. Basically, avoid using it whenever possible.	&dsp:MyDataSource=Password

Syntax requires each prefix to be followed by a parameter. Report parameters do not have prefixes, and this is how URL access determines that a particular parameter should be treated as a report parameter. If a URL access command includes a report parameter that does not match any of the parameters defined in the report, SSRS reports an `rsUnknownReportParameter` error.

On the other hand, SSRS is lenient with prefixed parameters and uses a default value when the value specified in URL access is invalid. For example, `rs:Command= Reindeer` (note intentional misspelling of `Render`) defaults to `rs:Command=Render`. This is a mixed blessing because it might not be immediately clear why a certain URL access command does not work as you might have expected. However this handling minimizes errors.

`Command` is the most frequently used parameter and is used in almost all URL access commands. `Command`'s details and other available `rs:` parameters are shown in Table 27.2.

TABLE 27.2 **rs:** Report Server Parameters

`rs:` **Parameter**	**Purpose**

`Command`	Specifies the command to be executed. Valid commands include the following:
	`GetDataSourceContents`: Displays properties of a given shared data source as XML. Example:
	`http://localhost/ReportServer?/Samples/Adventure+Works&rs:Command=GetDataSourceContents`
	`GetResourceContents`: Renders a file in a browser. This is used to show images and other nonreport or data source files. Example:
	`http://localhost/ReportServer?/Samples/flogo.jpg&rs:Command=GetResourceContents`
	`ListChildren`: Lists items in a folder. Example:
	`http://localhost/ReportServer?/Samples&rs:Command=ListChildren`
	`Render`: Renders the specified report. Example:
	`http://localhost/ReportServer/Pages/ReportViewer.aspx/Samples/SimpleReport&rs:Command=Render`

`Format`	Specifies the format in which to render a report. Common values include `HTML3.2`, `HTML4.0`, `MHTML`, `IMAGE`, `EXCEL`, `WORD`, `CSV`, `PDF`, `XML`, and `NULL`.
`Parameter Language`	Provides a language for parameters passed in a URL. The default value is the browser language. The value can be a culture value, such as `en-us` or `de-de`. This is especially helpful for international deployments. For example, in Europe most of the countries reverse month and day position as compared with the United States.
`Snapshot`	Renders a report based on a report history snapshot.

Table 27.3 shows a partial set of report control parameters. Report control parameters target HTML Viewer to provide framing and the look and feel for a rendered report. More information about this topic is available in SQL Server Books Online.

TABLE 27.3 **rc:** Report Control Parameters

rc: **Parameter**	**Target Rendering**	**Value**
BookmarkID	HTML	Directs SSRS to position the report's viewing focus to the bookmark ID.
DocMap	HTML	Directs SSRS to show or hide the report document map. Valid values are true (default) or false.
DocMapID	HTML	Directs SSRS to position the report's viewing focus to the document map ID.
DpiX, DpiY	IMAGE	Specifies the resolution of the output device in x/y-direction; 96 is the default.
EndFind	HTML	Specifies the ending page for a search. Used in conjunction with the StartFind and FindString.
EndPage, StartPage	IMAGE, PDF	Directs SSRS to render the last/first page of the report. StartPage=0 renders all pages. Defaults: StartPage=1, EndPage=StartPage.
FallbackPage	HTML	Directs SSRS to render a page with a specified number when a search or a document map selection fails. The current page is the default.
FieldDelimiter	CSV	Specifies a URL-encoded delimiter string. The default value is a comma (,).
FindString	HTML	Specifies the text to search for in the report. The default is an empty string. When using this function, use rc:Toolbar=false. When rc:Toolbar=true (default), you view a report using the ReportViewer control, which, in turn, expects to handle the search.
JavaScript	HTML, MHTM	Indicates that JavaScript is supported in the rendered report.
HTMLFragment	HTML	Directs SSRS to return an HTML fragment rather than a full HTML document. An HTML fragment includes the report content in a Table element and omits the HTML and Body elements. The default value is false. Images for a report must be retrieved separately.

TABLE 27.3 Continued

rc: **Parameter**	**Target Rendering**	**Value**
LinkTarget	HTML	Specifies a target for hyperlinks in the report. LinkTarget=_blank opens a new target window. Other valid target names include a frame name, _self, _parent, and _top.
MarginTop, MarginBottom, MarginLeft, MarginRight	IMAGE, PDF	Specifies the margin value, in inches, for the report. It is an integer or decimal value followed by in (for example, 1in). Overrides the report's original settings.
NoHeader	CSV	Indicates whether the header row is excluded from the output. The default value is false.
OmitDocumentMap	EXCEL	Indicates whether to omit the document map for reports that support it. The default value is false.
OmitFormulas	EXCEL	Indicates whether to omit formulas from the rendered report. The default value is false.
OmitSchema	XML	Indicates whether to omit the schema name from the XML and to omit an XML schema. The default value is false.
OutputFormat	IMAGE	Specifies a report's rendering graphical format: BMP, EMF, GIF, JPEG, PNG, or TIFF.
PageHeight, PageWidth	IMAGE, PDF	Specifies a report's page height/width in inches. You must include an integer or decimal value followed by in. This value overrides the report's original settings.
Parameters	HTML	Shows or hides the parameters area of the toolbar. Parameters=true (default) shows, and Parameters=false hides the parameters area. Parameters=Collapsed hides the parameters area, but allows the end user to toggle.
Qualifier	CSV	Specifies a string to put around results that contain strings equal to FieldDelimiter or RecordDelimiter. If the results contain the qualifier, the qualifier is repeated. The Qualifier setting must be different from the FieldDelimiter and RecordDelimiter settings. The default value is a quotation mark (").
RecordDelimiter	CSV	Specifies the record delimiter for the end of each record. The default value is <cr><lf>.

TABLE 27.3 Continued

rc: **Parameter**	**Target Rendering**	**Value**
RemoveSpace	EXCEL	Directs an extension to eliminate small, empty cells from the result. A valid value is an integer or decimal value followed by in. The default value is 0.125in.
Schema	XML	Indicates to SSRS to render the XML schema definition (XSD) versus actual XML data. A value of true indicates that an XML schema is rendered. The default value is false.
Section	HTML	Sets the report's viewing focus page. A value greater than the number of pages in the report displays the last page; negative values display page one. The default value is 1.
SimplePageHeaders	EXCEL	Indicates whether the page header of the report is rendered to the Excel page header. A value of false indicates that the page header is rendered to the first row of the worksheet. The default value is false.
StartFind	HTML	Specifies the starting page for a search. Used in conjunction with the EndFind and FindString.
SuppressLineBreaks	CSV	Directs SSRS to suppress line breaks from the output. The default value is false. If the value is true, the FieldDelimiter, RecordDelimiter, and Qualifier settings cannot be a space character.
Toolbar	HTML	Shows or hides the toolbar. True is the default value. If the value of this parameter is false, all remaining framing options (except the document map) are ignored. The toolbar is not rendered through the SOAP API, but the Toolbar Device Information setting affects results of the SOAP Render method.
XSLT	XML	Specifies the path of an XSLT to apply to the XML output (for example, /Transforms/myxslt). The XSL file must be a published resource on the Report Server, and you must access it through a Report Server item path. This transformation is applied after any XSLT that is specified in the report. When used, the OmitSchema setting is ignored.

TABLE 27.3 Continued

rc: **Parameter**	**Target Rendering**	**Value**
Zoom	HTML	Sets the report Zoom value as an integer percentage (rc:Zoom=100 is the default) or in relation to the displayed page (Page Width [rc:Zoom=Page%20Width] or Whole Page). Supported by Internet Explorer 5.0 and later.

Table 27.4 presents the new SQL Server 2008 parameters for the Report Viewer web part in cases when Reporting Services is integrated with Windows SharePoint Services (WSS) 3.0 or Microsoft Office SharePoint Server (MOSS) 2007.

TABLE 27.4 **rv:** Report Viewer Web Part Control Parameters

rv: **Parameter**	**Value**
Toolbar	Sets the toolbar display for the Report Viewer web part: Full: Default; displays the complete toolbar Navigation: Displays only pagination in the toolbar None: Hides the toolbar
HeaderArea	Sets the header display for the Report Viewer web part: Full: Default; displays the complete header BreadCrumbsOnly: Presents a rudimentary navigation None: Hides the header
DocMapAreaWidth	Sets the display width, in pixels, of the parameter area in the Report Viewer web part.
AsyncRender	Controls whether a report is asynchronously rendered. A Boolean value with true (default) forces asynchronous rendering.

How to Integrate URL Access in an Application

You can use URL access to incorporate reports into Windows and web applications.

Several methods are available for web applications. The most common method is to use a URL access command string as a source or IFrame. In a simple case scenario, this could be an HTML file with the following code:

```
<IFRAME
    NAME="Frame1" SRC="http://localhost/ReportServer?/Samples/SimpleReport&
     rc:Toolbar=false&rc:LinkTarget= Frame1", width = 50%, height = 50%>
</IFRAME>
```

The preceding code creates a frame on the page that is located in the upper-left corner and takes 50% of the page's "real estate." The frame changes size as the browser window changes size. The purpose of `&rc:LinkTarget= Frame1` is to make sure that all the report's navigation happens inside of the frame called `Frame1`.

You can also add a link to a report in a web application or leverage the `rc:HTMLFragment` parameter.

You can also call the SSRS web service to obtain needed information and then incorporate the returned stream into the application's HTML stream. You can find more information about working with the SSRS web service in Chapter 28, "Using Reporting Services Web Services."

URL access methods for web applications described earlier, such as using a URL access command as a source for IFrame, have a common downside. They all use the `HTTP GET` method, which is equivalent to a form submission where `METHOD="GET"`.

There are a couple of potential issues with the `GET` method.

First, it might be easy to hack the URL string and make changes that would allow a malicious user to potentially get some proprietary information. A report's security restricts a user's access to a whole report, but does not prevent someone from experimenting with the parameters of a report.

By contrast, when you use URL access with `METHOD="POST"`, you can use hidden fields to prevent users from changing parameters used in URL access.

Second, the URL `GET` request's length is limited to the maximum allowed by the browser. Some browsers have this limit as low as 256 characters.

Internet Explorer's maximum URL request length is 2,083 characters, with 2,048 the maximum path length. This limit applies to both `GET` and `POST` methods. `POST`, however, is not affected by this limitation for submitting name-value pairs because they are transferred in the header and not the URL.

For more information, see the following Microsoft Knowledge Base article: http://support.microsoft.com/default.aspx?scid=kb;en-us;208427.

NOTE

Limits on the length of `POST` requests can also be controlled by Registry settings. For example, in IIS 6.0 and 7.0, `HKEY_LOCAL_MACHINE\System\CurrentControlSet\Services\HTTP\Parameters` subkeys `MaxFieldLength` and `MaxRequestBytes` control the size of the header, and subkeys `UrlSegmentMaxCount` and `UrlSegmentMaxCount` control segmentation. A segment is a part of a URL string separated by / (slashes). See http://support.microsoft.com/default.aspx?scid=kb;en-us;820129 for more information.

Changing the `GET` method to the `POST` method is fairly easy; for example, the following URL access `GET` method

```
http://localhost/ReportServer?/Samples/SimpleReport&rs:Command=Render
➥&rc:LinkTarget=main&rs:Format=HTML4.0& EmployeeID=0947834
```

can be translated to the following POST method:

```
<FORM id="frmRender" action=" http://localhost/ReportServer?/Samples/SimpleReport"
   METHOD="POST" target="_self">
   <INPUT type="hidden" name="rs:Command" value="Render">
   <INPUT type="hidden" name="rc:LinkTarget" value="main">
   <INPUT type="hidden" name="rs:Format" value="HTML4.0">
   <INPUT type="hidden" name="EmployeeID" value="0947834">
   <INPUT type="submit" value="Button">
</FORM>
```

To integrate URL access in a Windows application, you can embed a web browser control in a Windows form. An old-style COM component from the Internet Controls Library (shdocview.dll) can be used with Visual Studio versions earlier than Visual Studio 2005.

Starting from Visual Studio 2005, Visual Studio is sporting a .NET web browser control. Just drag and drop this control from the Visual Studio 2005 or 2008 Toolbox onto your Windows form, and then set the URL property of a control to a URL access string. It's that simple.

Summary

URL access provides simple and efficient access to a report's rendering functionality. URL access can be used through a simple HTML link, as a source of an IFrame, through web browser control in Windows and web applications, and in SharePoint web parts.

URL access is designed to provide the highest level of performance when used to view and navigate reports. URL access achieves this performance by bypassing the web service interface and communicating directly with Report Server. On the other hand, because URL access does not access the web service, URL access functionality is limited to viewing and navigating reports.

CHAPTER 28

Using Reporting Services Web Services

IN THIS CHAPTER

- Report Management Web Service (`ReportService2005.asmx`)
- How to Script Reporting Services (Using the RS Utility)
- Working with Report Parameters
- Security When Calling a Web Service (.NET 2.0 Style)
- Security When Calling a Web Service (.NET 3.x, WCF Style)
- Using SSL to Increase Security
- Some of the Commonly Used Methods with Short Code Snippets

In the preceding chapter, you learned about URL access functionality. URL access provides high-performance access to SSRS for report viewing and navigation. However, URL access does not provide sufficient access to SSRS management functionality. SSRS web services come to the rescue and complement URL access by providing full access to SSRS management and rendering functionality.

An application that needs to incorporate both report viewing and report management functionality will typically use both URL access and the SSRS web service. The two are often combined for a couple of reasons: URL access provides the best performance for the report-viewing experience and handles framing of a report. In contrast, SSRS web service provides comprehensive access to SSRS functionality, including management functionality, which is not available in URL access.

Because the web service uses Simple Object Access Protocol (SOAP) over Hypertext Transfer Protocol (HTTP), any SOAP-aware application or development tool can communicate with the SSRS web service. Technically, you can manually generate SOAP requests (which are basically Extensible Markup Language [XML] text written to SOAP specifications) and pass those requests to the SSRS web service. But why do all the work? Visual Studio generates a proxy and makes using a web service as easy as using any .NET namespace.

There are two common ways to access SSRS web services using Visual Studio 2008:

- The old style of accessing web services using a web services proxy. We refer to old style as Visual Studio 2005 style or .NET 2.0 style. As of time of writing SQL

Server Books Online use only the .NET 2.0 style and you may notice a statement: `This sample is not compatible with Visual Studio 2008`. This statement is a bit of a misnomer because you can still use .NET 2.0 style from Visual Studio 2008 provided that you have properly added a web service reference (as we show in the second example).

- The new style of accessing web services using Windows Communications Foundation (WCF). Later in this chapter we refer to this style as Visual Studio 2008, .NET 3.x (WCF became available in the .NET 3.0, albeit you may want to use .NET 3.5), or WCF style. Although conceptually much is the same as an old .NET 2.0 style (after all, SSRS web service is still a web service), WCF leverages a new programming model called the service model. Hence, as you see from the first example, you add `Service Reference` as opposed to `Web Service Reference`. The service model is designed to provide a developer with a unified experience across web services, .NET remoting, and other forms of remote communications.

What does the WCF style mean for a developer who wants to use the SSRS web service?

- Visual Studio 2008 will generate a service proxy.
- Although the method names will remain the same, the method signatures will change. For example, the .NET 2.0 web services call to the `Render()` method has 7 parameters, whereas the .NET 3.5 WCF style call has 10 parameters.
- A developer must deal with new configuration file entries and a couple of extra methods and properties, particularly around security.

Based on these notes and if you've already used SSRS web services in your applications using the .NET 2.0 style, you will see from the samples that there is a fair amount of differences between the .NET 2.0 and .NET 3.5 styles. The natural question is this: Does it make sense to upgrade? The answer depends on whether you see specific benefits for your application. If you do not, the answer is no. You can read a bit more about WCF at http://msdn.microsoft.com/en-us/library/ms731082.aspx. As an extra consideration, you may want to keep in mind that, as of today, there are few WCF samples for SSRS.

Let's start with a simple example and create a function that retrieves a report from SSRS as an XML string. In the following example, we use Visual Studio 2008 and .NET 3.5 WCF style of web service access.

This example accesses the SSRS web service, and then incorporates the resulting stream into a custom application. Much like parameter commands with the same name in URL access, `Render()` and `ListChildren()` are the most frequently used functions in the SSRS web service.

Here are the steps:

1. Open Visual Studio 2008.
2. Create a Visual C#, Windows Forms application project and call it **`EmbeddedReport`**.
3. Rename Form1 that Visual Studio created to **`MainForm`** in the Solution Explorer and change the form's **`Text`** property to `MainForm`, too.

4. Add a reference to the Reporting Services web service by expanding the project in Solution Explorer, right-clicking the project folder, and selecting Add Service Reference from the shortcut menu (see Figure 28.1). Alternatively you can also select Add Service Reference from the Project menu.

NOTE

You might have noticed that in Visual Studio 2008 the main method to communicate with servers is WCF (WCF is a part of .NET 3.5), and therefore Add Service Reference.

An option to add Web Reference is still available if you click the Advanced button of Add Service Reference dialog box. Add Web Reference generates code, based on .NET 2.0 web services technology. At the time of this writing, most, if not all, samples in the SQL Server Books Online are Visual Studio 2005 .NET 2.0 web services based.

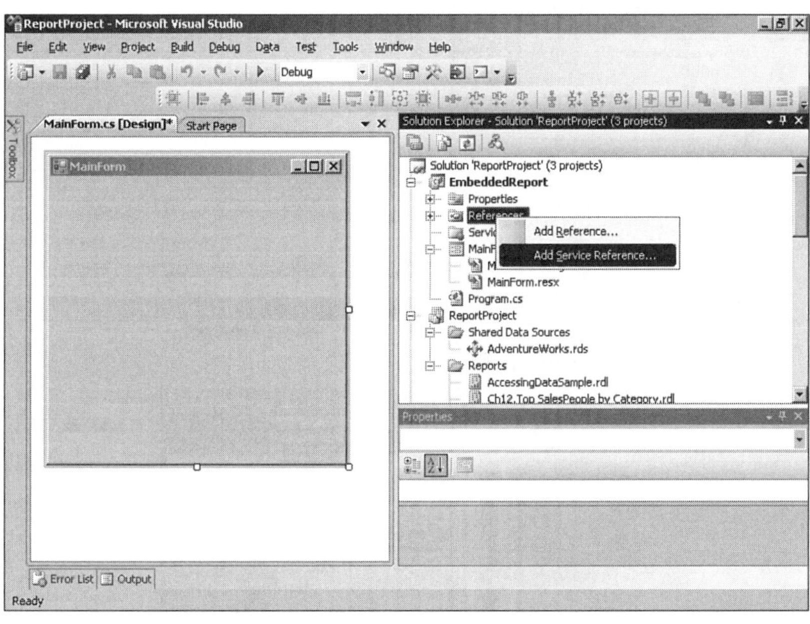

FIGURE 28.1 Adding service references in Visual Studio.

5. Select the most appropriate hyperlink or enter **`http://<server>/ReportServer/ReportExecution2005.asmx`** in the Address field of the Add Service Reference dialog box and click the Go button. Note **`<server>`** is the name of a server on which Report Server is installed. After Visual Studio completes this operation, it presents a selection such as the one shown in Figure 28.2.

   There are four SSRS services and corresponding endpoints (see Table 28.1). Note Services and Operations lists on the dialog box and, specifically, the function `Render`, which we use later in this chapter.

NOTE

If the browser does not show Web Service Description Language (WSDL) in a browser by default, try to add `?wsdl` after any of the SSRS endpoints' URLs (for example, `http://localhost/ReportServer/ReportService2005.asmx?wsdl`).

NOTE

SSRS 2000–compatible web service (`ReportService.asmx`) has been discontinued.

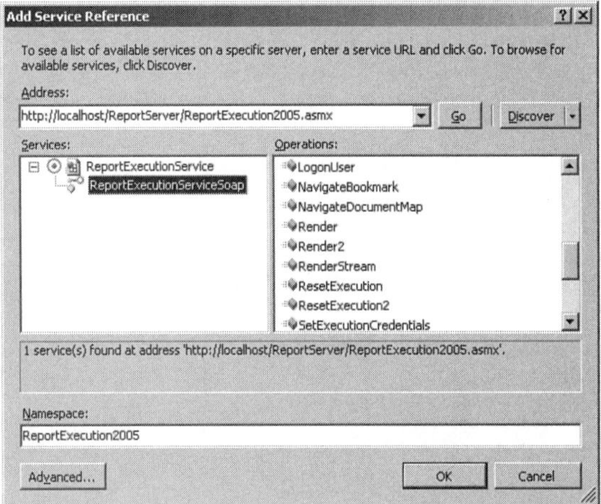

FIGURE 28.2 Add Service Reference dialog box.

TABLE 28.1 SSRS 2008 Web Services

Services	Typical Endpoint URL (SSRS Installed on `<ServerName>`)	Functionality

`ReportExecution2005`	Native mode:
	`http://<ServerName>/ReportServer/ReportExecution2005.asmx`
	SharePoint integrated mode:
	`http://<ServerName>/<SiteName>/_vti_bin/ReportServer/ReportExecution2005.asmx`
		Report-execution endpoint contains functionality to control report processing and rendering.

`ReportService2005`	Native mode:
	`http://<ServerName>/ReportServer/ReportService2005.asmx`
	SharePoint integrated mode:
	`rsOperationNotSupportedSharePointMode`
		Report and server management endpoint.

`ReportService2006` (New in 2008)	Native mode:
	`rsOperationNotSupportedNativeMode`
	SharePoint integrated mode:
	`http://<ServerName>/<SiteName>/_vti_bin/ReportServer/ReportService2006.asmx`
		Report and server management endpoint for a Report Server configured for SharePoint integrated mode.

`ReportServiceAuthentication`	Native mode:
	`rsOperationNotSupportedNativeMode`
	SharePoint integrated mode:
	`http://<ServerName>/<SiteName>/_vti_bin/ReportServer/ReportServiceAuthentication.asmx`
		Authentication endpoint for user authentication with a Report Server when the SharePoint web application is configured for forms authentication.

NOTE

A `ReportService2005` API call will return an `rsOperationNotSupportedSharePointMode` error when the Report Server is configured for SharePoint integrated mode.

A `ReportService2006` API call will return an `rsOperationNotSupportedNativeMode` error when the report server is configured for native mode.

6. Select one of the web services (SSRS endpoints) after Visual Studio completes this operation (web reference is found).
7. In the Namespace field replace ServiceReference1 with **`ReportExecution2005`**.
8. Click OK.

Solution Explorer now displays `ReportExecutionService` as one of the references in the Service References folder under the project folder. To permit the use of types in Reporting Services, you need to add a service reference to each module that uses a service. In a general case, the syntax of the reference looks like the following:

```
using <NamespaseUsingWebProxy>.<Namespace Name Given During Proxy Creation>;
```

In this specific example, you add the following before the code of `MainForm`:

```
using EmbeddedReport.ReportExecution2005;
using System.Web.Services.Protocols; //to handle SOAP xceptions
```

The second line is added to handle SOAP exceptions and requires us to add a reference to `System.Web` library:

1. Right-click the project folder.
2. Select Add Reference from the context menu.
3. In the Add Reference dialog box, display the.NET tab and scroll down and select the System.Web.Services component name.
4. Click OK to add the reference.

NOTE

Code fragments are presented for illustration purposes only and do not necessarily illustrate best practices.

The following code generates (renders) XML output (stream) for a report. You can use other formats supported by rendering extensions, such as Hypertext Markup Language (HTML):

```
static string GetReportXML_VS2008(string ReportPath)
{
    //creates a new web service (proxy) and sets its credentials
    ReportExecutionServiceSoapClient rs = new ReportExecutionServiceSoapClient();
    //Windows authentication
    rs.ClientCredentials.Windows.AllowedImpersonationLevel =
       System.Security.Principal.TokenImpersonationLevel.Impersonation;

    // Setup Render() call
    byte[] result = null;
    string encoding, mimeType, extension, DeviceInfo=null;
    Warning[] warnings = null;
    string[] streamIDs = null;

    try
    {
        string historyID = null;
        ExecutionInfo ExecInfo;
        ExecutionHeader ExecHeader;
        ServerInfoHeader SvrInfoHeader;

        //Note: set TrustedUserHeader = null, this is undocumented structure
        ExecHeader = rs.LoadReport(null, ReportPath, historyID,
                               out SvrInfoHeader, out ExecInfo);

        rs.Render(ExecHeader, null, "XML", DeviceInfo, out result,
                  out extension, out mimeType, out encoding,
                  out warnings, out streamIDs);

        //Gets a byte stream with Comma Separated Value (XML) layout
        return System.Text.Encoding.ASCII.GetString(result);
    }
    catch (SoapException e)
    {
        //Return exception message, if exception occurred
        return e.Message;
    }
}
```

Before we can use the preceding code, we must sort out security. Notice the following lines in the code:

```
    rs.ClientCredentials.Windows.AllowedImpersonationLevel =
       System.Security.Principal.TokenImpersonationLevel.Impersonation;
```

It is a request to WCF to impersonate the user. In addition to the code, we need to properly configure security in the `app.config` file. You can find the `app.config` file in your project's folder. Double-click it to edit, and ensure that it has the following in the security section. (Note that most of the security section is already set and you just need to fill missing items, such as `clientCredentialType`.)

```
<security mode="TransportCredentialOnly">
    <transport clientCredentialType="Windows" proxyCredentialType="None"
                            realm="" />
    <message clientCredentialType="UserName" algorithmSuite="Default" />
</security>
```

Note that `Windows` in the preceding code sample is case sensitive.

You may see the following exception if security is improperly configured:

```
Message="The HTTP request is unauthorized with client authentication scheme
'Anonymous'. The authentication header received from the server was 'Negotiate,NTLM'."
```

You may see this exception if you do not have sufficient privileges to access:

```
An unhandled exception of type 'System.Net.WebException'
occurred in system.web.services.dll. Additional information:
The request failed with HTTP status 401: Unauthorized.
```

The following is an exception if you do not request to impersonate a user:

```
Message="The HTTP request is unauthorized with client authentication scheme 'Ntlm'.
The authentication header received from the server was 'NTLM'."
```

Also notice:

```
<client>
    <endpoint address=http://127.0.0.1:80/ReportServer/ReportExecution2005.asmx
...
```

This is an address of the `ReportExecution2005` services end. In the preceding example, it is pointing to the `localhost` (127.0.0.1) port `80`. If you need to configure your application to use another SSRS, you can just modify the endpoint address.

A call to `GetReportXML_VS2008` as shown here demonstrates an assignment of the `/Samples/DemoList` report in the XML form to a text box `textBoxResult`:

```
textBoxResult.Text = GetReportXML_VS2008("/Samples/DemoList");
```

NOTE

If you want to incorporate the results of `Render()` in the web application, you can pass device information settings to retrieve an HTML fragment that does not contain a Body element (for example, `DeviceInfo="<DeviceInfo><HTMLFragment>True </HTMLFragment></DeviceInfo>"`).

Do not forget to change the format string to HTML if you need to get HTML output for the application.

Most parameters in the `Render()` function are optional and accept `null` values.

`Warning[] warnings;` contains an array of objects with information about errors and warnings for which SSRS did not generate exceptions. In production code, you need to make sure to incorporate handling for warnings.

The example uses part of the information available in `SoapException`. `SoapException` has four properties:

- **`Actor`**: The code that caused the exception.
- **`Detail`**: The XML describing application-specific error information. `Detail` is an `XMLNode` object, and inner text from `Detail` can be accessed for the flow control (for example, `if(ex.Detail["ErrorCode"].InnerXml == "rsItemNotFound") {/*handle the error*/}`).
- **`HelpLink`**: A link to a Help file associated with the error.
- **`Messsage`**: A message describing the error.

The Report Execution web service is very sensitive to the report's path, requires the path to start from / (slash), and does not accept URL-encoded strings. If the path is incorrect, the web service returns an `ItemNotFoundException` or `InvalidItemPathException` exception. For example, for a report with the name My DemoList (note the space after the word *My*) located in the Samples directory, the URL-encoded path `/Samples/My%20DemoList` is not acceptable. It would cause an error with an exception similar to the following:

```
System.Web.Services.Protocols.SoapException: The item
'/ReportProject/Top%20SalesPeople'
cannot be found. --->
Microsoft.ReportingServices.Diagnostics.Utilities.ItemNotFoundException:
The item '/ReportProject/Top%20SalesPeople' cannot be found.
```

If SSRS is configured in native mode and the path does not start with a slash, SSRS generates `InvalidItemPathException`:

```
System.Web.Services.Protocols.SoapException: The path of the item
```

28

```
'ReportProject/TopSalesPeople' is not valid. The full path must be less
than 260 characters long; other restrictions apply. If the report server is
in native mode, the path must start with slash. --->
Microsoft.ReportingServices.Diagnostics.Utilities.InvalidItemPathException
: The path of the item 'ReportProject/TopSalesPeople' is not valid. The
full path must be less than 260 characters long; other restrictions apply.
If the report server is in native mode, the path must start with slash.
```

The proper way to enter this path is `/Samples/My Demolist` (prefixed with slash when SSRS is in the native mode and without URL encoding).

Actions in `GetReportXML_VS2008 ()` should produce the same result as `http://localhost/ReportServer/ReportExecution2005.asmx?/Samples/DemoList&rs:Command=Render&rs:Format=XML`. The difference is that the web service call is not interactive, but the web service call allows an application to receive and process a report's XML internally.

`System.Text.Encoding.ASCII.GetString` is used to convert a `byte[]` array that `Render()` returns to a string. Note that ASCII is an option suitable for text-based formats, such as XML and CSV. Other converters (such as Unicode) are available in the `System.Text.Encoding` namespace.

As a comparison, to use .NET 2.0 web services style code, you follow steps 1 through 4 above to access the Add Service Reference dialog box and then complete the following steps:

1. Access the Add Web Reference dialog box by clicking the Advanced button on the Add Service Reference dialog box.
2. Enter **`http://<server>/ReportServer/ReportExecution2005.asmx`** in the URL field.
3. Click Go.
4. Set Web Reference Name to **`ReportExecution2005_VS2005`** (see Figure 28.3).
5. Click Add Reference. Under the project folder, note the Web References folder.
6. Add web references:

   ```
   using EmbeddedReport.ReportExecution2005_VS2005;
   using System.Web.Services.Protocols;
   ```

7. And add the following code:

```
static string GetReportXML2005(string ReportPath)
{
    //creates a new web service (proxy) and set its credentials
    ReportExecutionService rs = new ReportExecutionService();
    //windows authentication
    rs.Credentials = System.Net.CredentialCache.DefaultCredentials;

    //Assign web service URL. This is optional operation. Default URL
```

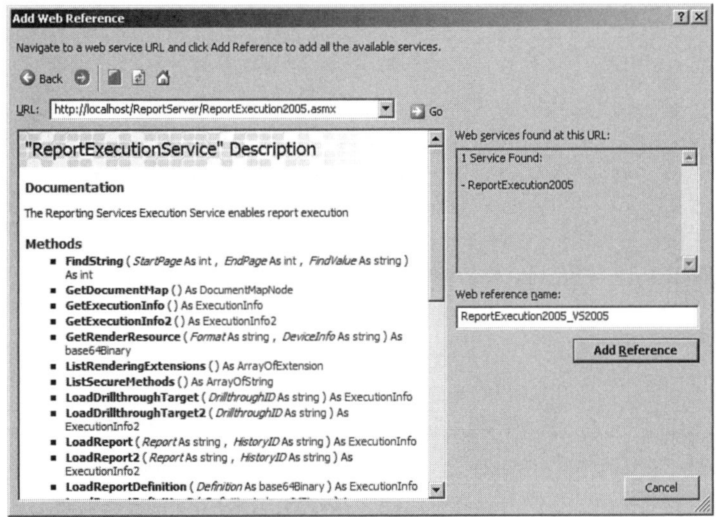

FIGURE 28.3 Add Web Reference dialog box.

```
    //is assigned during the creation of a proxy.
    //Typically http://<<server name>>/ReportServer/ReportExecution2005.asmx
    //rs.Url = ReportingServicesURL;

    // Setup Render() call
    byte[] result = null;
    string encoding, mimeType, extension;
    Warning[] warnings = null;
    string[] streamIDs = null;

    try
    {
        //Should be called prior to Render() to set report's path
```

```
            rs.LoadReport(ReportPath, null);

            //Gets a byte stream with Comma Separated Value (XML) layout
            result = rs.Render("XML", null, out extension, out encoding,
                               out mimeType, out warnings, out streamIDs);
            return System.Text.Encoding.ASCII.GetString(result);
        }
        catch (SoapException e)
        {
            //Return exception message, if exception occurred
            return e.Message;
        }
    }
```

The line `rs.Credentials = System.Net.CredentialCache.DefaultCredentials;` is very important. An application must supply credentials to the SSRS web service before the application can access a report. `DefaultCredentials` is the Windows authentication for the user.

Report Management Web Service (ReportService 2005.asmx)

Previously in this chapter, you saw an example of the Report Execution web service (`ReportExecution2005.asmx`). Most of the report-execution functionality is available using URL access.

In contrast, only a few URL access methods (such as `ListChildren()`) are available from the Report Management web service (`ReportService2005.asmx`). Thus, the Report Management web service is often used in combination with the Report Execution web service, and sometimes in combination with URL access. The combination of various access methods provides the most comprehensive access to SSRS.

NOTE

The following examples use Visual Studio 2005 .NET 2.0 style. We explained the difference between Visual Studio 2008 .NET 3.5 WCF-style samples and Visual Studio 2005 .NET-2.0 style samples previously in this chapter.

To access the Report Management web service, you can follow the same steps used earlier to access the Report Execution web service:

1. Add a web reference to the Report Management web service (`ReportService2005.asmx`).
2. Name the proxy **`ReportService2005`**.

3. Add a reference to the proxy in the code (using `EmbeddedReport.Report Execution2005;`).
4. Call Report Management web service methods.

The following is an example of a console application returning items stored on SSRS starting from the root/folder:

```
using System;
using System.Collections.Generic;
using System.Linq;
using System.Text;
using ConsoleApplication1.ReportService2005;
using System.Web.Services.Protocols;

namespace ConsoleApplication1
{
    class Program
    {
        static void Main(string[] args)
        {
            //creates new Web service (proxy) and set its credentials
            ReportingService2005 rs = new ReportingService2005();
            rs.Credentials = System.Net.CredentialCache.DefaultCredentials;

            try
            {
                CatalogItem[] items = rs.ListChildren("/", true);

                Console.Write("Item Path, Item Name, Item Type, MimeType");
                foreach (CatalogItem ci in items)
                {
                    Console.Write(ci.Path + "," + ci.Name + "," +
                                  ci.Type + "," + ci.MimeType + "\n");
                }
                return;
            }
            catch (SoapException e)
            {
                Console.Write(e.Message);
            }
        }
    }
}
```

Valid items include DataSources, Folders, LinkedReports, Reports, Resources, and Unknown items.

How to Script Reporting Services (Using the RS Utility)

The RS utility is a scripting utility that enables access to Reporting Services functionality using Visual Basic .NET scripts. In scripts, you can define classes and use other object-oriented functionality of Visual Basic .NET.

By default, the RS utility is installed in the C:\Program Files\Microsoft SQL Server\100\Tools\Binn directory. SSRS no longer comes with sample scripts, but you can download samples from the online community www.codeplex.com/MSFTRSProdSamples/Release/ProjectReleases.aspx?ReleaseId=16045. You can dissect and modify sample scripts to fit scenarios at hand. Scripting is a convenient way to automate repetitive administrative tasks or tasks that apply to a group of items.

Executing the rs /? command yields the following usage direction:

```
Microsoft (R) Reporting Services RS
Version 10.0.1600.22 ((SQL_PreRelease).080709-1414 ) x86
Executes script file contents against the specified Report Server.
RS -i inputfile -s serverURL [-u username] [-p password]
   [-l timeout] [-b] [-e endpoint] [-v var=value] [-t]

        -i  inputfile    Script file to execute
        -s  serverURL    URL (including server and vroot) to execute
                         script against.
        -u  username     User name used to log in to the server.
        -p  password     Password used to log in to the server.
        -e  endpoint     Web service endpoint to use with the script.
                         Options are:
                         Exec2005 - The ReportExecution2005 endpoint
                         Mgmt2005 - The ReportService2005 endpoint
        -l  timeout      Number of seconds before the connection to the
                         server times out. Default is 60 seconds and 0 is
                         infinite time out.
        -b               Run as a batch and rollback if commands fail
        -v  var=value    Variables and values to pass to the script
        -t  trace        Include trace information in error message
```

The following sample script gets a list of extensions registered with Reporting Services and, as a bonus, outputs the Report Server version and edition. For the purpose of an example, you can add the following code to the RsUtilTest.rss file:

```
Public Sub Main()
    Dim Extensions As Extension() = rs.ListExtensions(ExtensionTypeEnum.All)
    Console.WriteLine("Report Server Version Number:" &
                      rs.ServerInfoHeaderValue.ReportServerVersionNumber)
    Console.WriteLine("Report Server Edition:" &
                      rs.ServerInfoHeaderValue.ReportServerEdition)

    Dim Ext As Extension
    Dim Type As String
    Console.WriteLine("Type      Name")
    For Each Ext In  Extensions
        Select Ext.ExtensionType
                       Case ExtensionTypeEnum.Delivery
                       Type = "Delivery"
                Case ExtensionTypeEnum.Render
                       Type = "Render  "
        Case ExtensionTypeEnum.Data
                      Type = "Data    "
                Case Else
                      Type = "Other   "
        End Select
        Console.WriteLine(Type + "   " + Ext.Name)
    Next
End Sub
```

ReportServerVersionNumber and ReportServerEdition are properties of Reporting Services. You need to call Reporting Services before the properties are set. If you place this call after you access Reporting Services properties, those properties will be empty. This is what we are doing in the following line:

```
Extension()=rs.ListExtensions(ExtensionTypeEnum.All)
```

28

The scripting utility provides an internal reference to Reporting Services through the rs object, which is ready to be used in scripts without an explicit instance creation. The command to execute the script might look like the following:

```
rs -iRsUtilTest.rss -shttp://localhost/ReportServer
```

Working with Report Parameters

Report parameters are encapsulated by two classes: The ParameterValue class enables developers to set and retrieve report parameter values, and the ReportParameter class is used to get and set properties of a parameter. Both ParameterValue and ReportParameter are necessary to get complete information about a parameter. However, the ParameterValue class is sufficient to set and retrieve values of a parameter. The following code snippet shows how to pass parameters to render a function. You can incorporate this code into the GetReportXML2005() function written earlier in this chapter by adding the following code inside of the try block after LoadReport and through the call to the function Render, replacing the original Render call (Visual Studio 2005, .NET 2.0 style):

```
ParameterValue[] parameters = new ParameterValue[1];
parameters[0] = new ParameterValue();
parameters[0].Name = "SalesOrderNumber";
parameters[0].Value = "SO43659";

rs.SetExecutionParameters(parameters, "en-us");

result = rs.Render(format, devInfo, out extension,
                   out encoding, out mimeType,
                   out warnings, out streamIDs);
```

Or the following code for Visual Studio 2008, .NET 3.5, WCF style. Note that the main differences between WCF and .NET 2.0 style, in this case, are in the SetExecutionParameters and Render function signatures:

```
ExecutionInfo ExecInfo;
ExecutionHeader ExecHeader;

ParameterValue[] parameters = new ParameterValue[1];
parameters[0] = new ParameterValue();
parameters[0].Name = "SalesOrderNumber";
parameters[0].Value = "SO43659";

rs.SetExecutionParameters(ExecHeader, null, parameters, "en-us", out ExecInfo);

rs.Render(ExecHeader, null, "XML", DeviceInfo, out result, out extension,
                    out mimeType, out encoding, out warnings, out streamIDs);
```

In the previous examples, you can see two out of three string properties of the ParameterValue class: Name and Value. The third property is a Label and is used as an alternate name for a parameter.

Note the usage of the SetExecutionParameters() function that assigns the parameter and parameter's language (because this is optional, you can pass null) to the current execution of a report.

ReportParameter is used in conjunction with GetReportParameters() and SetReportParameters(). GetReportParameters() retrieves a report's parameters' properties (ReportParameter class) and can validate whether an array of ParameterValue values passed to this function are acceptable for a report. SetReportParameters() sets properties of parameters. Table 28.2 outlines commonly used public properties of the ReportParameter class.

TABLE 28.2 Commonly Used Public Properties of the `ReportParameter` Class

Name	Description
`AllowBlank`	Indicates whether an empty string is a valid value for the parameter
`DefaultValues`	Gets or sets the default value of the parameter
`DefaultValuesQueryBased`	Indicates whether the default values of the parameter are based on a query
`ErrorMessage`	Indicates the error message returned when a parameter value has failed validation
`MultiValue`	Indicates whether the parameter is a multivalued parameter
`Name`	Gets or sets the name of a parameter
`Nullable`	Indicates whether the value of the parameter can be `null`
`Prompt`	Gets or sets the text that prompts the user for parameter values
`PromptUser`	Indicates whether the user is prompted for the value of the parameter
`QueryParameter`	Indicates whether the parameter is used in a query
`ValidValues`	Indicates the available `ValidValues` objects for the parameter
`ValidValuesQueryBased`	Indicates whether the parameter's valid values are based on a query

As you can probably tell, the `ReportParameter` class properties directly correspond to the report parameter properties that were set during the design phase. See Chapter 12, "Report Parameters."

Security When Calling a Web Service (.NET 2.0 Style)

Out of the box, SSRS supports Windows authentication and authorization. If you need to have custom authentication, SSRS provides this through custom authentication (or security) extensions. You have to develop a new security extension to handle custom authentication.

.NET Framework greatly simplifies Windows and basic authentication handling through classes in the `System.Net` namespace.

Before deciding which authentication method to use, consider security implications of each type of authentication: anonymous, basic, and integrated/Windows.

As you might recall, we leveraged the .NET Framework to set Windows credentials in the `GetReportXML2005()` method earlier in this chapter:

```
rs.Credentials = System.Net.CredentialCache.DefaultCredentials;
```

To pass basic authentication credentials, you can substitute the preceding code with the following code:

```
rs.Credentials = new System.Net.NetworkCredentials("user name",
                                                   "password", "domain");
```

The credentials must be set before the use of any methods in the SSRS web service. Calls to a web service method before setting credentials receive an error: `HTTP 401 Error: Access Denied`.

Security When Calling a Web Service (.NET 3.x, WCF Style)

A detailed WCF security discussion is beyond scope of this chapter, but we do want to present you with some basic concepts to help you understand what we have done in our WCF example. You can find a detailed WCF security review at http://msdn.microsoft.com/en-us/library/ms732362.aspx and a pretty good short explanation at www.code-magazine.com/articleprint.aspx?quickid=0611051.

When we added the `ReportExecution2005` service reference, Visual Studio 2008 added a service reference and `<system.serviceModel>` configuration entries in the `app.config` file. There are several entries under the `<system.serviceModel>` tag:

- **`bindings`**: Describes communication configuration options, including protocol, configuration, and security.
- **`basicHttpBinding`**: Requests HTTP communications, and compatible with old-style (.NET 2.0, SOAP 1.1) web services. By default, the SOAP message is not secured and the client is not authenticated. You can use the `security` element to configure additional security options. There are other types of bindings: `NetTcpBinding` used for binary cross-machine TCP communications, and `WSHttpBinding` or `WSFederationHttpBinding` for web services that can support richer communication functionality.
- **`security`**: Describes security configuration. The security template that VS2008 adds is as follows:

  ```
  <security mode="None">
      <transport clientCredentialType="None" proxyCredentialType="None"
  realm="" />
  ```

```
        <message clientCredentialType="UserName" algorithmSuite="Default" />
    </security>
```

A complete set of options for basicHttpBinding can be expressed by the following configuration (curved brackets indicate that one of the options can be selected):

```
<security mode=
{"None" ¦ "Transport" ¦ "Message"
¦ "TransportWithMessageCredential" ¦ "TransportCredentialOnly"}>
    <transport clientCredentialType= {"None" ¦ "Basic"
                                     ¦ "Digest" ¦ "Ntlm" ¦ "Windows"}
     proxyCredentialType={"None" ¦ "Basic"
                                     ¦ "Digest" ¦ "Ntlm" ¦ "Windows"}
     realm="" />
    <message
        algorithmSuite=
        {
        "Basic128" ¦ "Basic192" ¦ "Basic256" ¦ "Basic128Rsa15" ¦
        "Basic256Rsa15" ¦ "TripleDes" ¦ "TripleDesRsa15" ¦
        "Basic128Sha256" ¦ "Basic192Sha256" ¦ "TripleDesSha256" ¦
        "Basic128Sha256Rsa15" ¦ "Basic192Sha256Rsa15" ¦
        "Basic256Sha256Rsa15" ¦ "TripleDesSha256Rsa15"
        }
        clientCredentialType=
        {"Certificate" ¦ "IssuedToken" ¦ "None" ¦
        "UserName" ¦ "Windows"
        }
/>
</security>
```

Let's look at additional configuration details:

- **mode**: Requests a specific mode of transfer security. basicHttpBinding allows the following options:
    - **None**: Default. The SOAP message is not secured during transfer.
    - **Transport**: HTTPS provides integrity, confidentiality, and server authentication. That is, the service is authenticated by the client using the service's Secure Sockets Layer (SSL) certificate. The service must be configured with SSL certificate. You control client authentication using the ClientCredentialType.
    - **Message**: SOAP message security provides security. For the BasicHttpBinding, the system requires that the server certificate be provided to the client separately. For BasicHttpBinding, the valid client credential types are UserName and Certificate.

- **TransportWithMessageCredential**: HTTPS provides integrity, confidentiality, and server authentication. That is, the service is authenticated by the client using the service's SSL certificate. The service must be configured with the SSL certificate. Client authentication is provided by means of SOAP message security. This mode is applicable when the user is authenticating with a `UserName` or `Certificate` credential, and there is existing HTTPS for securing message transfer.
- **TransportCredentialOnly**: We use this method in our example. It is, perhaps, the easiest one to use, but *use this mode with caution*. This mode does not provide message integrity or confidentiality; it provides only HTTP-based client authentication. You can use it in environments where other methods (such as IPSec) provide the transfer security and client authentication is provided only by the WCF infrastructure.

- **transport**: Configuration for `Transport` mode of security, including `TransportWithMessageCredential` and `TransportCredentialOnly`.
- **clientCredentialType**: Specifies the type of credential to be used when performing HTTP client authentication. Possible options for this configuration are as follows:
  - **None**: Anonymous authentication
  - **Basic**: Basic authentication
  - **Digest**: Digest authentication
  - **Ntlm**: Client authentication using NTLM
  - **Windows**: Client authentication using Windows
  - **Certificate**: Client authentication using a certificate
  - **proxyCredentialType**: Specifies the type of credential for client authentication in a domain using a proxy over HTTP. This attribute is applicable only when the `mode` attribute is set to `Transport` or `TransportCredentialsOnly`. The available options for this configuration are the same as for `clientCredentialType` (discussed earlier). In our example, we left this authentication as `None`, but it also works if you set it to the same value as `clientCredentialType`, or `Windows` in the case of our example.
- **realm**: A string that specifies a realm (or an independent resource partition) that is used by digest or basic HTTP authentication.

In our WCF example, we leveraged the .NET Framework `System.Security` class to set Windows credentials in the `GetReportXML2005()` method earlier in this chapter:

```
rs.ClientCredentials.Windows.AllowedImpersonationLevel =
   System.Security.Principal.TokenImpersonationLevel.Impersonation;
```

And Windows credentials were also reflected in the configuration as follows:

```
<security mode="TransportCredentialOnly">
    <transport clientCredentialType="Windows" proxyCredentialType="None"
```

Using SSL to Increase Security

To increase security, an administrator can use SecureConnectionLevel to configure SSRS and enforce web service client applications to leverage various levels of SSL communications for Report Server web service method calls. (This configuration also affects Report Manager.)

SSRS uses SecureConnectionLevel (located in RSReportServer.config) to determine which web service methods require an SSL connection. The default is 0 (noted in the configuration as <Add Key="SecureConnectionLevel" Value="0" />). SecureConnectionLevel has four levels that affect URL and SOAP interfaces that SSRS exposes:

- **0**: SSRS does not check for secure connections (SSL). Method calls can still be made over SSL (HTTPS) connections, if needed.
- **1**: SSRS checks for secure connections. If SSL is not available, the web service rejects the method (such as CreateReport() and GetReportDefinition()) calls that can pass sensitive information (such as user credentials). Because this setting is checked at the server, it is still possible to make a call that passes credentials before the web service handles the request. Method calls can still be made over SSL (HTTPS) connections, if needed. Because Render() is not restricted by this setting, it might be possible for a hacker to intercept sensitive data from a report.
- **2**: Most method calls, including Render(), are required to use SSL.
- **3**: All method calls are required to use SSL. In this case, SSRS requires SSL/HTTPS for all web service method calls.

You can find more information about using secure web service methods at http://msdn.microsoft.com/en-us/library/ms154709.aspx.

In addition, you can find information about how to configure SSRS with SSL at http://technet.microsoft.com/en-us/library/ms345223.aspx.

Some of the Commonly Used Methods with Short Code Snippets

All snippets require a proper SSRS endpoint reference as described earlier in the chapter, web and SOAP proxy references, and the following calls prior to calling any of the methods:

```
ReportingService2005 rs = new ReportingService2005();
rs.Credentials = System.Net.CredentialCache.DefaultCredentials;
```

Although the examples use VS2005 .NET 2.0 style, you can still use the style in Visual Studio 2008 as we have discussed earlier in this chapter, or you can modify the samples to use VS2008 .NET 3.5 WCF style.

- Find and cancel all jobs:

```
Job[] jobs = null;
jobs = rs.ListJobs(); //Get a list of current jobs.
foreach (Job job in jobs)
{
   if (job.Status == JobStatusEnum.Running || job.Status ==
JobStatusEnum.New)
   {
      rs.CancelJob(job.JobID);
   }
}
```

- Create a folder item:

```
rs.CreateFolder(strFolderName, strParentFolderName, null);
```

- Create a report item:

```
FileStream stream = File.OpenRead("sample.rdl");
Byte[] rdl = new Byte[stream.Length];
stream.Read(rdl, 0, (int) stream.Length);
stream.Close();
rs.CreateReport(strReportName, strFolderName, false, rdl, null);
```

- Delete an item:

```
rs.DeleteItem(strItemPath)
```

- Get an RDL of a report from SSRS:

```
System.Xml.XmlDocument doc = new System.Xml.XmlDocument();
byte[] reportDefinition = rs.GetReportDefinition(strReportName);
MemoryStream stream = new MemoryStream(reportDefinition);
```

```
    doc.Load(stream);
    doc.Save(@C:"\sample.rdl");
```

Method calls can also be grouped together and executed as a single transaction (for example, commit and roll back as a whole). The following code snippet shows how this could be accomplished:

```
BatchHeader bh = new BatchHeader();
bh.BatchID = rs.CreateBatch();
rs.BatchHeaderValue = bh;
rs.<<MethodCall, like DeleteItem>>;
rs.<<MethodCall>>;
...
rs.ExecuteBatch();
```

Summary

SSRS web service complements URL access with full access to SSRS management and configuration functionality. An application that incorporates both report viewing and report management functionality would typically use both URL access and the SSRS web service. SSRS web service's function `Render()` enables you to retrieve a byte stream of a rendered report and use it for SSRS integration. SSRS comes with the `rs.exe` utility for scripting of the SSRS web service access using Visual Basic .NET scripts. The `rs.exe` utility is frequently used to automate high-volume management tasks: report deployment, security management, and so on.

CHAPTER 29

Extending Reporting Services

IN THIS CHAPTER

SSRS is designed for extensibility. In the previous chapters, you learned how to extend SSRS reporting capabilities by writing custom code that can be called from a report. Extensions, on the other hand, are called by SSRS. Extensions are composed of four key categories: security, delivery, data processing, and rendering (see Chapter 2, "Reporting Services 2008 Architecture"). SSRS 2008 adds a new type of extension called Report Definition Customization Extension (RDCE), which allows customization of Report Definition Language (RDL) at runtime. RDCE is explained later in this chapter.

Typical extensions installed with SSRS are as follows:

- **Data processing:** Microsoft SQL Server, Microsoft SQL Server Analysis Services, Oracle, SAP NetWeaver BI, Hyperion Essbase, Teradata, OLE DB, ODBC, XML, SAP BW, Essbase, and Teradata.
- **Delivery:** File share, email, document library, null. Note that not all delivery extensions are compatible with all rendering extensions; for example, most of the delivery extensions exclude null rendering from the processing.
- **Render:** Excel, MHTML, HTML 4.0 (Microsoft Internet Explorer 5.0 or later), PDF, Image (graphical image output, such as TIF, GIF, JPG), CSV, XML, null (used to place reports in cache and in conjunction with scheduled execution and delivery), RGDI (format used for Windows Forms `ReportViewer` control), and RPL. (Report Page Layout format is an intermediate format that the processing engine creates and that is used by each renderer to show the report. It gives

consistency across rendering format. The object model for RPL is not publicly exposed in the 2008 release.)

- **Other:** `SemanticQuery` and `ModelGeneration` to extend Report Builder's functionality. `EventProcessing` to act on the events generated by Report Server.
- **Security:** By default, SSRS uses Windows integrated authentication.

A complete list of extensions installed on a particular instance of SSRS can be retrieved by calling `ReportingService2005.ListExtensions (ExtensionTypeEnum.All)` or by examining the `rsreportserver.config` file.

Rendering is, perhaps, the most developed category of extensions. With a wide range of rendering extensions and a multitude of applications (including Microsoft Office) that "understand" HTML, it is hard to think of a new rendering extension that would be immediately useful.

Some of the SSRS capabilities that customers are frequently looking for and that are currently not available "out of the box" are as follows:

- **Printer (fax) delivery:** An ability to print (fax) batches of reports without human interactions
- **Custom authentication:** An ability to authenticate non-Windows clients

It is possible to work around the need to have certain functionality. For example, instead of delivery to a printer directly from SSRS, an administrator can configure delivery of a report to a file share and have a separate process monitoring and printing from such a file share by using the Windows `PRINT` command (for example, `PRINT /D:\\<server URL>\<printer name> <files to print>`).

It is also possible to work around the scenario in which users cannot use Windows authentication. An administrator can create a Windows account for a user, configure Internet Information Services (IIS) to accept basic authentication (must enable Secure Sockets Layer [SSL] for better security), and ask the user to enter Windows credentials to access a report.

Although it is possible to work around some of the limitations, custom extensions can offer elegant solutions to supplement missing functionality.

A custom extension is a private or shared .NET assembly with a *unique* namespace (the specific assembly name is not important, but it must be unique), and a class that implements the `IExtension` interface and one or more interfaces shown in Table 29.1. To improve chances for an assembly to have a unique name, you can prefix it with the name (or abbreviation) of your company.

As with any .NET implementation, Visual Studio is the most frequently used development tool for development of assemblies and, therefore, extensions. Unless we specified otherwise, an interface mentioned in the Table 29.1 is a part of the following .NET library: `Microsoft.ReportingServices.Interfaces`.

TABLE 29.1 Frequently Used Subset of Interfaces for Custom Extensions

Interface(s)	Applies to an Extension Category	Description
`IAuthenticationExtension`	Security	Implementation of this interface extends the authentication feature of SSRS. This interface extends `IExtension`.
`IAuthorizationExtension`	Security	Implementation of this interface extends the authorization feature of SSRS. This interface is not Common Language Specification (CLS)-compliant. This means that not all .NET languages can call or implement this interface; also C# and VB.NET can deal with this interface just fine. This interface extends `IExtension`.
`IDbConnection`, `[IDbConnectionExtension]`, `IDbTransaction`, `[IDbTransactionExtension]`, `IDbCommand`, `[IDbCommandAnalysis]`, `[IDbCommandRewriter]`, `IDataParameter`, `[IDataMultiValueParameter]`, `IDataParameterCollection`, `IDataReader`, `[IDataReaderExtension]`	Data processing	(Optional) and required interfaces of a class that implements a data-processing extension. Those interfaces are modeled after .NET data provider interfaces and defined in the `Microsoft.ReportingServices.DataProcessing` namespace.
`IDeliveryExtension`	Delivery	Implementation of this interface interacts with SSRS to share and validate an extension's settings and to execute delivery. This interface extends `IExtension`.
`IDeliveryReportServerInformation`	Delivery	Implementation of this interface is used in conjunction with `IDeliveryExtension`. SSRS supplies information about itself through this interface.
`IExtension`		You can use `IExtension` to build custom data, delivery, and rendering extensions. Implementation of `IExtension` provides localized extension name and extension-specific configuration information from the Reporting Services configuration file.

TABLE 29.1 Continued

Interface(s)	Applies to an Extension Category	Description
IParameter		Implementation of this interface contains information about a parameter: Name, IsMultivalue, and Values.
IRenderStream	Rendering	Implementation of this interface provides support for multiple streams rendering from a rendering extension.
IRenderingExtension	Rendering	Implementation of this interface is required for a rendering extension so that the extension is recognized by SSRS. This interface is defined in the Microsoft. ReportingServices.ReportingRenderi ng namespace.
IReportDefinition CustomizationExtension, IReportContext, IUserContext, IParameter	Report-definition customization extension	Implementation of the IReport DefintionCustomizationExtension interface gets an RDL as input, and returns modified RDL and True if the report was modified. This interface extends the IExtension interface. IReportContext, IUserContext, and IParameter provide the report and user context and parameters for the RDL being processed.
[ISubscriptionBaseUIUser Control]	Delivery	Implementation of this interface provides a subscription UI for the Report Manager. This interface is what shows data-entry fields. For example, in the case of an email, it displays an interface to enter a To: email address and so on. This interface extends IExtension. This interface is optional because a subscription can be created using SOAP API methods CreateSubscription and CreateData DrivenSubscription. The class that inherits from this interface must also inherit from System.Web. UI.WebControls.WebControl.

Common Considerations for Custom Reporting Services Extensions: Implementation, Deployment, and Security

The reporting library provides three namespaces that supply interface definitions, classes, and value types that allow extensions to interact with SSRS:

- **`Microsoft.ReportingServices.DataProcessing`**: Used to extend the data-processing capability of SSRS.
- **`Microsoft.ReportingServices.Interfaces`**: Used to build delivery and security extensions.

  This namespace also enables you to maintain a cross-connection state. A class that implements the `IExtension` interface from this namespace is kept in memory for as long as SSRS is running.
- **`Microsoft.ReportingServices.ReportRendering`**: Used to extend the rendering capabilities of SSRS. This namespace is used in conjunction with the `Microsoft.ReportingServices.Interfaces` namespace.

Before you can successfully compile an extension, you must supply the reference to one or more `Microsoft.ReportingServices` namespaces as follows:

```
using Microsoft.ReportingServices.Interfaces;
```

A namespace can have optional interfaces, such as `IDbConnectionExtension` in `Microsoft.ReportingServices.DataProcessing`, and required interfaces, such as `IDbConnection` in the same extension's namespace. When an interface is required and a developer chooses not to implement a particular property or method of the interface, it is a best practice to throw a `NotSupportedException`. `NotSupportedException` is most appropriate for this purpose as it indicates methods (and properties) that did not provide implementation for methods described in the base classes (interfaces). The next best alternative is `NotImplementedException`. Note that optional interfaces do not require implementation at all.

NOTE

If you have chosen not to implement a particular property or method of the *required* interface, choose `NotSupportedException` for clear identification.

Optional interfaces do not require implementation at all.

Any CLR application interacts with the CLR security system. This book briefly covered the basics of .NET security in Chapter 26, "Creating and Calling a Custom Assembly from a Report," specifically in the section ".NET Code Access Security Primer for an SSRS

Administrator." The same principles apply to extensions. Local security settings and SSRS configuration files define the code permissions that an extension's assembly receives. SSRS extensions must be a part of a code group that has the `FullTrust` permission set.

To deploy an assembly, an SSRS administrator must have appropriate permissions to write to the Report Server directory, Report Designer directory, and configuration files.

When a Report Server first loads an extension in memory, the Report Server accesses an assembly using service account credentials. Service account credentials are needed so that an extension can read configuration files, access system resources, and load dependent assemblies (if needed). After an initial load, the Report Server runs an assembly using credentials of the user who is currently logged in.

An extension can be deployed for use by the Report Server, Report Manager, Report Designer, or all of these. This is provided that the extension can be used by a tool. For example, Report Manager uses only delivery extensions.

The deployment procedure for an extension used by the Report Server, Report Manager, or Report Designer is basically the same. The only difference is the deployment directory and configuration files that need to be modified. To simplify further discussion, this book uses the following abbreviations:

- **`{AssmDir}`**: To abbreviate assembly deployment directories. The default Report Server binary directory is `C:\Program Files\Microsoft SQL Server\MSRS10.MSSQLSERVER\Reporting Services\ReportServer\bin`. The default Report Designer binary directory is `C:\Program Files\Microsoft Visual Studio 9.0\Common7\IDE\PrivateAssemblies`. The default Report Manager binary directory is `C:\Program Files\Microsoft SQL Server\MSRS10.MSSQLSERVER\Reporting Services\ReportManager\bin`.
- **`{ConfigFile}`**: To abbreviate configuration files (note the default file path). The default location for the Report Server configuration file is `C:\Program Files\Microsoft SQL Server\MSRS10.MSSQLSERVER\Reporting Services\ReportServer\RSReportServer.config`. The default location for the Report Designer configuration file is `C:\Program Files\Microsoft Visual Studio 9.0\Common7\IDE\PrivateAssemblies\RSReportDesigner.config`. A separate Report Manager configuration file (`RSWebApplication.config`) has been deprecated in this release, and the Report Manager uses `RSReportServer.config` configuration instead.
- **`{SecConfig}`**: To abbreviate security configuration files. The default location for the Report Server security configuration file is `C:\Program Files\Microsoft SQL Server\MSRS10.MSSQLSERVER\Reporting Services\ReportServer\RsSrvPolicy.config`. The default location for the Report Designer security configuration file is `C:\Program Files\Microsoft Visual Studio 9.0\Common7\IDE\PrivateAssemblies\RSPreviewPolicy.config`. The default location for the Report Manager security configuration is `C:\Program Files\Microsoft SQL Server\MSRS10.MSSQLSERVER\Reporting Services\ReportServer\RsMgrPolicy.config`.

To deploy an extension, a report administrator can use the following steps:

1. Copy an extension assembly to the {AssmDir} directories. Remember that {AssmDir} is an abbreviation that denotes three different directories. If an assembly with the same name that you are trying to deploy exists in one of the {AssmDir} directories, stop the Report Server Service, copy an assembly, and then restart the Report Server Service.
2. Locate an entry in the {ConfigFile} under the <Extensions> tag that corresponds to a category ({ExtCategory}) of an extension: <Delivery>, <Data>, <Render>, <Security> (authorization), <Authentication>, or <DeliveryUI>.
3. Add an entry for a newly created extension to a {ConfigFile}:

```
<Extensions>
   ...
   <(ExtCategory}>
      <Extension
          Name="{Unique extension name up to 255 characters}"
          Type="{Fully qualified name of the class implementing IExtension},
                {AssemblyName without .dll}"
          Visible="{false¦true; false indicates that extension is not visible
in UI}"
      >
      {optional configuration data}
      </Extension>
   </(ExtCategory}>
   ...
   </Extensions>
```

An example of PrinterDeliveryProvider for rsreportserver.config is as follows:

```
<Extensions>
      <Extensions>
          <Delivery>
               <Extension Name="Printer Delivery Sample"
Type="Microsoft.Samples.ReportingServices.PrinterDelivery.Printer
DeliveryProvider,Microsoft.Samples.ReportingServices.PrinterDeliverySample">
                    <Configuration>
                         <Printers>
                              <Printer>HPOfficeJet</Printer>
                         </Printers>
                    </Configuration>
               </Extension>       ...
   ...
```

SSRS “knows” what library and class to use based on the preceding configuration. Microsoft.Samples.ReportingServices.PrinterDeliverySample is the name of the library, PrinterDeliveryProvider is a class that implements IExtension and

IDeliveryExtension, and Microsoft.Samples.ReportingServices.PrinterDelivery is the namespace where PrinterDeliveryProvider resides.

When interacting with PrinterDeliveryProvider, SSRS calls two methods of the IExtension interface: SetConfiguration and LocalizedName. SSRS passes an XML fragment between <Configuration> and </Configuration> tags in the configuration file as a parameter to SetConfiguration, so the extension can take advantage of the flexibility that configuration offers.

The LocalizedName property targets user interface implementations (such as Report Manager) and should return values for various languages. This way, an extension can be used around the world and does not have to be recompiled every time the extension is deployed in a new locale.

4. Finally, an administrator can grant FullTrust permission for an assembly by modifying the {SecConfig} file:

```
<CodeGroup
          class="FirstMatchCodeGroup"
          version="1"
          PermissionSetName="Execution"
          Description="This code group grants MyComputer code Execution per-
mission. ">
     <IMembershipCondition
               class="ZoneMembershipCondition"
               version="1"
               Zone="MyComputer" />
<!— Above existing configuration —>
<!— add below to ensure successful access to delivery extension—>
     <CodeGroup class="UnionCodeGroup"
             version="1"
             PermissionSetName="FullTrust"
             Name="PrinterDeliveryCodeGroup"
             Description="Code group for my delivery extension">
          <IMembershipCondition class="UrlMembershipCondition"
             version="1"
             Url="C:\Program Files\Microsoft SQL Server\MSRS10.MSSQLSERVER\
Reporting Services\ReportServer\bin\Microsoft.Samples.ReportingServices.
➥PrinterDeliverySample.dll"
                                        />

       </CodeGroup>
```

NOTE

Although a separate configuration file for a Report Manager has been eliminated, security configuration files continue to be separate. To achieve a successful deployment for delivery extensions, ensure that both `RsSrvPolicy.config` and `RsMgrPolicy.config` contain `FullTrust` security configuration for a custom extension. Also ensure that the `Url` element points to a proper path: `C:\Program Files\Microsoft SQL Server\MSRS10.MSSQLSERVER\Reporting Services\ReportServer\bin\` and `C:\Program Files\Microsoft SQL Server\MSRS10.MSSQLSERVER\Reporting Services\ReportManager\Bin` correspondingly.

5. An administrator can verify deployment of an extension by using the `ListExtensions` method.
6. Most of the delivery extensions will have additional options that will be entered during subscription configuration. For example, the email address is a part of the configuration a subscription administrator would enter. To integrate into Report Manager's graphical interface, you add a functionality to render an HTML control, much like the printer delivery example does:

```
<DeliveryUI>
    <Extension Name="Printer Delivery Sample" Type="Microsoft.Samples.
➥ReportingServices.PrinterDelivery.PrinterDeliveryUIProvider,Microsoft.
➥Samples.ReportingServices.PrinterDeliverySample"/>
...
  </DeliveryUI>
```

NOTE

Additional details about security are covered in Chapter 26, specifically in the section ".NET Code Access Security Primer for an SSRS Administrator."

To debug a deployed extension, complete the following steps:

1. Determine the processes that access the extension. For example, for a delivery extension that is accessed by Report Manager (because Report Manager runs in the content of IIS), the process is `ReportingServicesService.exe`, or `aspnet_wp.exe` or `w3wp.exe` when SSRS installed on IIS.
2. Set breakpoints in the extension's code.
3. Attach Visual Studio to the calling process using, for example, Debug, Attach to Process. The Attach to Process dialog box opens. You need to make sure that the Show Processes from All Users check box is selected, after which you can select a process to attach to, and then click Attach.

4. As the extension is invoked, Visual Studio breaks at set breakpoints, and you can step through the code.

Report Definition Customization Extension

Report Definition Customization Extension (RDCE) is a new feature of SSRS 2008. It lets the developer customize the RDL at runtime.

The motivation behind this feature is to help ISVs support scenarios where RDL needs to be customized based on context. You may want to show different columns or layouts for the report based on the user's role, company, country, or language. Here are some examples:

- If a user prefers French, show labels and descriptions of a report in French. Otherwise, show them in English.
- If the user is from Canada, add a GST tax to the sales orders to show the total bill report. If a user is from a U.S. state, however, add the relevant state sales tax to get the total bill report.
- If a user is a manager, show the salary and bonus columns in an employee report. Otherwise, hide those columns.

Here are the mechanics of how the feature works:

- A developer publishes the original RDL to the Report Server and sets a property (RDCE) on the report to identify that report execution for this report will result in a call to the RDCE extension.
- The developer deploys an RDCE extension by implementing the method `processReportDefinition` for the `IReportDefinitionCustomizationExtension` interface. The extension implementation gets as input the RDL from the server along with the user context (username, authentication mode, security token) and report context (report name/path, parent report name/path, query parameters, whether report is a subreport or a linked report, linked target name/path). The implementation logic uses these inputs to customize the RDL and returns the custom RDL as output.
- The custom RDL is rendered by the report engine for the user session that requested the report execution.

NOTE

Inputs such as user and report context provide some useful context to customize report layouts, but there is a lot of additional context that would be useful such as language, company, country, and so on. The way to get such information across to the extension is to use parameters. Query parameters (including hidden parameters) are provided to the extension as part of the ReportContext. As long as you make sure that the UsedInQuery property is set on a parameter, it will get sent to the extension. Therefore, you can preserve any information that drives your customization logic, such as language or company, via hidden parameters and use the information to generate the desired custom RDL in the RDCE extension implementation.

As you can probably imagine, the RDCE extension has a lot of potential. However, there are limits to the level of customization and the Report Server features supported with this extension. Some key features such as snapshots, caching, and history are not supported for reports that are processed via the RDCE extension. Therefore, you really have to weigh the pros and cons of using RDCE for your customization scenario.

Limits on Customization

- Data sources and parameters cannot be changed by the extension. Other sections of the RDL such as `Body`, `Page`, `PageHeader`, `PageFooter`, and `DataSets` may be customized.
- The customization implementation needs to output the same RDL version as the input. For example, if a 2008 RDL was sent to the server, the RDCE extension implementation needs to output 2008 RDL. It cannot return a 2005 or 2000 version of RDL.

Limits on SSRS Features Supported with RDCE

- SSRS won't support snapshots, caching, or history on reports on which the RDCE property is set. This is actually an existing limitation of SSRS for any reports where query results depend on the user value.
- The RDCE extension is supported only with Report Server. You cannot use just the report design environment for debugging and testing. You have to set up a Report Server in your development and test environment to ensure the extension implementation works as expected.

Steps to Deploy and Use Your RDCE Implementation

You can create an implementation of the RDCE extension by implementing the `IReportDefinitionCustomizationExtension` .NET interface. For most developers, this will be done via Visual Studio to generate an RDCE implementation DLL:

1. Copy your implementation (for example, `RdceImpl.dll`) to the following:

   ```
   %ProgramFiles%\Microsoft SQL Server\MSSQL.<n>\ReportingServices\Report
   Server\bin
   ```

2. Register your extension in the Report Server `reportserver.config` file:

   ```
   <Service>
      <IsRdceEnabled>True</IsRdceEnabled>
   </Service>
   <Extensions>
      <ReportDefinitionCustomization>
         <Extension Name="RdceImpl" Type="RdceImpl.RdceImpl, RdceImpl"/>
      </ReportDefinitionCustomization>

      </Extensions>
   ```

3. Configure code access security.
4. Elevate CAS security for the extension assembly in `rssrvpolicy.config`:

   ```
   <CodeGroup
             class="UnionCodeGroup"
              version="1"
              PermissionSetName="FullTrust"
              Name="Rdce Impl"
              Description="This code group grants Rdce Impl code full trust. ">
               <IMembershipCondition
                         class="UrlMembershipCondition"
                         Url="file://C:\Program Files\Microsoft SQL Server\
   ➥MSSQL.2\Reporting Services\ReportServer\bin\RdceImpl.dll"
                 />

      </CodeGroup>
   ```

5. Enable the `RDCE` property on desired reports.
6. Even though after the first three steps the Report Server is configured to use the RDCE extension, the extension is not used by default. Developers/IT have to explicitly identify whether they want a report to be sent to the RDCE implementation for customization. This can be done by setting an `RDCE` property on the report.

   Here is a simple Visual Basic script that can be used to carry out this step using the `rs.exe` command-line utility:

   ```
   Public Sub Main()


             Dim props(0) As [Property]
   ```

```
        Dim SetProps As New [Property]
        SetProps.Name ="RDCE"
        SetProps.Value = "RdceImpl"
        props(0) = SetProps
        rs.SetProperties("/<REPORT PATH>/<REPORT NAME>", props)

    End Sub
```

7. Run the script to enable RDCE on the report:

```
%ProgramFiles%\Microsoft SQL Server\MSSQL.<n>\Tools\Binn\RS.exe
        -s <server url> -i <script name>.rss
```

This needs to be done for each report that you want to be run via the RDCE extension.

Keep in mind that there are feature limitations on reports that are run via RDCE. Therefore, one idea is to keep the original report around to enjoy features such as snapshots, caching, and history on the report for most users and then deploy a copy of the report with RDCE enabled to benefit from runtime customization for select users.

Delivery Extension

A delivery extension spends part of its "life" responding to subscription-related requests from SSRS and part responding to SQL Server Agent–triggered scheduled delivery-related requests from SSRS.

For an enterprise deployment, we recommend that Report Server Windows service runs under domain account credentials. A domain account allows an appropriate access control for delivery extensions. For example, a domain account would allow permission for the file system delivery extension to write to a network share, whereas `Local System` account would not.

In addition to the `IExtension` interface (See Table 29.2), a delivery extension should also implement the `IDeliveryExtension` interface (See Table 29.3).

The delivery extension example is one of the five samples supplied by Microsoft. As mentioned previously, SQL setup does not incorporate the install of SSRS samples. To install samples, visit www.codeplex.com/MSFTRSProdSamples/Release/ProjectReleases.aspx?ReleaseId=18649, download an appropriate platform sample, and install it. SSRS sample setup will install samples into the directory `C:\Program Files\Microsoft SQL Server\100\Samples\Reporting Services\Extension Samples\PrinterDelivery Sample` by default.

TABLE 29.2 Members of the `IExtension` Interface

Property or Method	Name	Description

P	`LocalizedName`	Allows an application, such as Report Manager to get a localized name (string) of an extension. You can examine a locale and return an appropriate name understandable in the locale.
		`System.Globalization.CultureInfo.CurrentCulture.Name` provides a name of a culture, such as `en-US`.
		We recommend that you add `LocalizedNameAttribute` attribute to every extension:
		`namespace My.Samples.ReportingServices.PrinterDelivery`
		`{`
		`[LocalizedName("PrinterDelivery")]`
		`...`
		If you do not, SSRS will construct the extension and examine `LocalizedName`, resulting in some negative performance impact, and it is a bit annoying during extension debugging.

M	`SetConfiguration(string XMLConfiguration)`	SSRS will call this function to pass a custom configuration (<Configuration> element of `rsreportserver.config`) XML string to an extension: ... <Extensions> <Delivery> <Extension Name="Printer Delivery Sample" Type="Microsoft.Samples.ReportingServices.PrinterDelivery.PrinterDeliveryProvider,Microsoft.Samples.ReportingServices.PrinterDeliverySample"> <Configuration> <Printers> <Printer>HPOfficeJet</Printer> </Printers> </Configuration> </Extension> ... The <Configuration> element itself is not included as a part of an XML string, and in essence you would need to parse an XML inside of <Configuration>. If the <Configuration> element is not provided for an extension, SSRS will pass an empty string to this method.

TABLE 29.3 Members of the `IDeliveryExtension` Interface

Property or Method	Name	Description
P	`ExtensionSettings`	Provides a list of settings to SSRS. The settings are used by both subscription and delivery mechanisms. Report Manager uses these settings and an implementation of `ISubscriptionBaseUIUserControl` to present a UI to enter settings. For example, in the case of email delivery, this is To:, Subject:, Priority, and so on. In the case of file share delivery, it is Path:, Render Format:, and credentials to access the file share, and so on. So that the settings are available during delivery, SSRS stores settings in a `Notification` object and passes `Notification` as a parameter to the `Deliver` method.
P	`IsPrivilegedUser`	Indicates whether the user is allowed access to all the functionality of the extension. This property is required so that SSRS can manage the extension. SSRS sets this property to `false` (default) if the user accessing the extension does not have the `Manage All Subscriptions` permission as a part of her role.
P	`ReportServerInformation`	Contains the names of rendering extensions supported by an SSRS instance.
M	`Deliver`	Delivers the report to a user based on the contents of the notification. The notification contains information retrieved through the `ExtensionSettings` property, such as an email address for the email delivery.
M	`ValidateUserData`	Determines whether specific delivery extension settings are valid. For example, this method can validate whether an email address provided as a setting is properly formatted.

At the time of this writing, the samples were written for Visual Studio 2005; however, Visual Studio 2008 will successfully upgrade samples when you open a solution. To ensure that an extension compiles, you need to create a key file by executing

```
sn -k SampleKey.snk
```

from the command prompt in the `C:\Program Files\Microsoft SQL Server\100\Samples\` directory.

Interactions Between User, SSRS, and a Delivery Extension

When a user interacts with SSRS to create a subscription, the interaction could be done from a

- Custom application using a SOAP API call to the SSRS web service method `CreateSubscription()`.
- Or more typically, from the Report Manager, which performs the following:
  - Interacts with `ISubscriptionBaseUIUserControl` implementation inside of a delivery extension to present a UI for data entry
  - Collects data and passes data as `CreateSubscription()` parameters
  - Interacts with SSRS to create a subscription

Along with other parameters, `CreateSubscription()` accepts the full pathname of the report and the `ExtensionSettings` object, which, in turn, contain `ParameterValue` objects. `ParameterValue` objects contain name-value pairs with information that a delivery extension expects. For example, for email delivery, one of the parameter values is `"TO:"` information:

```
extensionParams(0) = New ParameterValue()
extensionParams(0).Name = "TO:"
extensionParams(0).Value = "administrator@adventure-works.com"
```

SSRS then fills settings with information from `ParameterValue` and passes settings to a delivery extension for the validation `ValidateUserData()` call. After being validated, SSRS stores settings with the subscription in the Report Server database and returns a `SubscriptionID` string to a user.

For each subscription, there is either a shared or dedicated schedule in a form of the SQL Server Agent job that inserts an event in the Report Server database Event table.

NOTE

When working with delivery extensions, always ensure that SQL Server Agent is running. Some error messages related to a stopped SQL Server Agent could be cryptic: `An error occurred within the report server database. This may be due to a connection failure, timeout or low disk condition within the database. (rsReportServerDatabaseError) Get Online Help SQL Server blocked access to procedure 'sys.xp_sqlagent_enum_jobs' of component 'Agent XPs'....`

SSRS monitors the Event table and routes subscription events to the scheduling and delivery processor.

The scheduling and delivery processor receives a notification event, matches it to the subscription, creates a `Notification` object (see Table 29.4), and calls the `Deliver` method in a delivery extension associated with a subscription, passing `Notification` as a parameter of the call.

TABLE 29.4 Members of the `Notification` Class

Property or Method	Name	Description
P	`Attempt`	Counter of notification attempts.
P	`MaxNumberOfRetries`	Maximum attempts that Report Server will make to deliver notification.
P	`Owner`	Notification owner in a form domain\user.
P	`Report`	`Report` object, report information associated with a subscription.
P	`Retry`	Boolean indicating whether notification delivery should retry.
P	`Status`	Status for the subscription user interface. You set it in an extension to help identify various stages of processing.
P	`UserData`	An array of `Setting` objects, extension settings for the notification set in `IDeliveryExtension.ExtensionSettings()`.
M	`Save`	Save changes to the `UserData` and `Status` properties back to the subscription. Does not require re-creating a subscription.
M	Various names	Inherited from `Object`: `Equals`, `GetHashCode`, `GetType`, `ReferenceEquals`, `ToString`.

NOTE

To examine how the delivery mechanism works, set a breakpoint on `Deliver` method.

The delivery extension leverages SSRS rendering extensions, using the `Notification.Report.Render` method. (See Table 29.5 for more information about `Report` class members.) The `Notification.Report.Render` method returns the `RenderOutputFile` object. The `RenderOutputFile.Data` property contains a `Data` member with `Microsoft.ReportingServices.Library.RSStream` with a rendered report. When you get a stream, you can decide in your delivery extension what to do with the stream. In the case of the printer delivery extension sample, the stream is converted to a metafile using the `System.Drawing.Graphics` class (because most of the reports are more complex than simple text) and printed using functionality from the `System.Drawing.Printing` namespace (see the `PrintReport` function of the sample).

TABLE 29.5 Members of the `Report` Class

Property or Method	Name	Description
P	`Date`	Server date and time of the report execution (usually a few seconds after the subscription event).
P	`Name`	The name of the report.
P	`URL`	Full URL of a report, including `http://IP Adress/ReportPath/`.
M	`Render (String render Format, String deviceInfo )`	Takes `renderFormat` (for example, `"HTML"`) and `deviceInfo` (for example, `<DeviceInfo><OutputFormat>emf</OutputFormat> </DeviceInfo>"`). Returns an array of `Microsoft.Reporting Services.Interfaces.RenderedOutputFile` objects. `RenderedOutputFile[0]` is the rendered report; `RenderedOutputFile[1+]` outputs resources that must be delivered with the report data (such as associated images).
M	Various names	Inherited from `Object`: `Equals`, `GetHashCode`, `GetType`, `ReferenceEquals`, `ToString`.

Custom Report Items

A custom report item extends rendering capabilities of RDL. Although many custom report items can be purchased today from various software vendors, you may be faced with a situation where you need to write your own. Some of the custom report items that you can purchase are map, calendar, barcode, and other controls.

A custom report item consists of the following:

- **A runtime component**
    - Implemented as .NET assembly (and therefore can be written in any .NET-compliant language).

- Called by the report processor at runtime.
- Implements `Microsoft.ReportingServices.OnDemandReportRendering.ICustomReportItem` interface, which is defined in `C:\Program Files\Microsoft SQL Server\MSRS10.MSSQLSERVER\Reporting Services\ReportServer\bin Microsoft.ReportingServices.ProcessingCore.dll`.
- Configured in `Rsreportdesigner.config`, `Rsreportserver.config`, and `Rsssrvpolicy.config` (to grant code access permissions).

- **A design-time component**
  - Implemented as .NET assembly.
  - Provides a graphical representation in SSRS Report Designer and design-time activities: accepts drag and drop, provides a custom property editor.
  - Inherits from the `Microsoft.ReportDesigner.CustomReportItemDesigner` class.
  - Defines the `CustomReportItem` attribute in addition to the standard attributes used for a .NET Framework control. The `CustomReportItem` attribute must correspond to the name of the custom item defined in the `reportserver.config` file.
  - Configured in `Rsreportdesigner.config` and `Rsssrvpolicy.config` (same configuration entry as for the runtime component).
- **Optionally, a design-time item converter component when you extend an existing report item**

Microsoft developed a custom report item sample, called `PolygonsCustomReportItem`. When you download and install samples (as described in the "Delivery Extension" section of this chapter), the default directory for this sample is `C:\Program Files\Microsoft SQL Server\100\Samples\Reporting Services\Extension Samples\PolygonsCustomReportItem`.

Summary

SSRS supplies an infrastructure (interfaces, classes, value types, and customizable configurations) to enable developers to extend SSRS capabilities. Developers can write extensions to extend security, delivery, data-processing, and rendering functionality of SSRS.

Although extensions require more in-depth understanding of SSRS inner workings and its supporting infrastructure, the need to provide custom functionality sometimes takes a developer to the realm of extensions. Although developing extensions is quite a bit more complex than developing reports, the experience to see an extension coming to "life" is certainly very rewarding.

CHAPTER 30

Reporting Services Integration with SharePoint

IN THIS CHAPTER

- SharePoint Technology
- Reporting Service Integration with SharePoint
- Planning for SharePoint Integration
- Unsupported Features
- Sample Reports Integrated with SharePoint

SharePoint Services is Microsoft's foundation platform for building web-based applications. In recent years, SharePoint has rapidly become the standard front-end browser-based tool for teams and companies to manage documents and to collaborate online. Even if some users don't know it, there is a high probability that their intranet or extranet web pages are SharePoint websites. SharePoint sites simplify collaboration activities such as uploading and sharing documents, making lists, and creating surveys.

Microsoft's business intelligence strategy is centered on two key suites of products: SQL Server and Office. SQL Server is used as the data and reporting platform, and Office provides popular easy-to-use front-end tools for end users to view and manage the data and analysis. This includes products such as Excel, Word, and SharePoint. You'll find more information about SharePoint products and capabilities later in this chapter. The key point is that SharePoint provides a central way to collaborate online.

Reports are designed with the purpose of sharing information and trends about a business or process. If SharePoint is the central collaboration tool for your organization, it makes sense for users to be able to view and manage reports within SharePoint. That is the key motivation behind Reporting Services integration with SharePoint. The initial mechanism to integrate reports into SharePoint sites that was made available in the SSRS product was via SharePoint 2.0 web parts called Report Explorer and Report Viewer.

NOTE

Microsoft documentation refers to the SharePoint Report Explorer and Report Viewer web parts as the SharePoint 2.0 web parts because they were first developed for use with SharePoint 2.0. However, note that you can use them against SharePoint 3.0 if you choose to do so.

However, the level of integration with web parts is useful only for browsing and running reports. Report management, security, and administration are still very SSRS oriented. You still end up using Report Manager and managing security settings for reports and users.

Microsoft enabled deep integration between Reporting Services and SharePoint in SSRS2K5 SP2 and enhanced it incrementally in SSRS 2008. This was done via an RS add-in for SharePoint and the capability to configure Report Server in SharePoint integrated mode. This integration enables an end user to view and manage reports completely from within SharePoint document libraries. This part of the book is dedicated to this deeper integration approach between SSRS and SharePoint. Chapters 31 through 37 cover the architecture and tools and the reporting life cycle in SharePoint integrated mode.

NOTE

If your team or corporation has adopted Microsoft SharePoint technology as its portal solution, we recommend installing SSRS in SharePoint integrated mode. Doing so will enable your reporting end user and administration experience to occur entirely from within your SharePoint portal environment.

SharePoint Technology

SSRS integrates with Windows SharePoint Services 3.0 and Office SharePoint Server 2007. This section provides a brief introduction (including the acronyms used) to these SharePoint technologies.

Microsoft Windows SharePoint Services 3.0 (WSS) provides a foundation for building web-based business applications and is available as a free download for basic team-based SharePoint sites. Notable collaboration features provided via WSS include the following:

- A workspace to upload and organize documents and coordinate schedules
- Document management features such as versioning and security and an option to require check-in and check-out for shared editing
- Alerts when changes to existing information or documents are made
- Collaboration features such as announcements, surveys, and discussion boards
- Templates for implementing weblogs (for blogging) and wikis (websites that can be quickly edited by teammates)

- Synchronization through Microsoft Office Outlook 2007 to manage document libraries, lists, calendars, contacts, tasks, and discussion boards

See http://office.microsoft.com/sharepointtechnology for more information about WSS.

Microsoft Office SharePoint Server 2007 (MOSS) includes collaboration and workflow functionality and builds on top of WSS. It enables forms and business processing, personal sites, enterprise search, and more. Notable features provided via MOSS include the following:

- Site templates for corporate intranet, Internet, and application portals
- Enhanced tools for managing navigation and security of sites
- Search capability for more than 200 file types and all enterprise data
- Business document workflow, including document review, approval, and issues tracking
- Policy-based management, including retention and auditing policies
- Creation and management of business forms via InfoPath forms

See http://office.microsoft.com/sharepointserver for more information about MOSS.

Reporting Services Integration with SharePoint

By default, reports are hosted in the SSRS reports catalog database and managed via Report Manager. This type of setup is called *native mode* for SSRS.

Starting with SSRS2K5 SP2, Microsoft added deeper integration with SharePoint Server by providing a SharePoint integrated mode for SSRS. In this mode, reports are stored as SharePoint documents and are viewed and managed via the SharePoint user interface.

Key benefits of SharePoint integrated mode include the following:

- Report-authoring tools such as Report Designer, Model Designer, and Report Builder can publish reports and models directly to a SharePoint library.
- Report subscriptions can be delivered directly to SharePoint libraries.
- Users and IT can use a single SharePoint user experience for viewing and managing reports (and that includes managing reports, models, data sources, schedules, subscriptions, and report history).
- Dynamic reporting and visualization via a customizable Report Viewer web part
    - Supports page navigation, print, search, and export features.
    - Can be used in full-page view or dashboards.
    - Can be linked with the SharePoint Filter web part or Library web part.

- Standard SharePoint features, such as workflow, versioning, and collaboration, can be used on reports because they are just another type of document in the SharePoint document library.
- The SharePoint security model applies to reports just like other documents in the SharePoint document library.
- Reports still get executed from SSRS Report Server and take advantage of all its capabilities.
- SharePoint deployment topologies can be used to distribute reports over the Internet or intranet.

Planning for SharePoint Integration

After a Report Server is deployed in a particular mode (native or SharePoint integrated), there is no easy way to switch modes and still keep the original report metadata. Therefore, it is good to understand the deployment modes available to you. See Table 30.1 for a comparison.

TABLE 30.1 Deployment Mode Options

SSRS Release	Deployment Mode	Description
SSRS 2000+ (all releases)	Native (default installation mode)	Report Server is deployed as a stand-alone application and manages report execution, processing, and delivery. The default UI is Report Manager.
SSRS 2000 SP2+ (all releases thereafter, including SSRS 2005 and SSRS 2008)	Native mode with SharePoint web parts	Report Server is deployed in stand-alone native mode. However, customers can add a Report Explorer and a Report Viewer web part in SharePoint to navigate reports from the Report Server and view them in SharePoint. These web parts work with Windows SharePoint Services 2.0, Windows SharePoint Services 3.0, SharePoint Portal Server 2003, or Office SharePoint Server 2007.
SSRS 2005 SP2+ (all releases thereafter, including SSRS 2008)	SharePoint integrated mode	Report Server runs within a SharePoint server farm. A SharePoint site provides the user experience, while the Report Server handles report execution, processing, and delivery. SharePoint integrated mode works with Windows SharePoint Services 3.0 or Office SharePoint Server 2007.

If you decide that you want your users to view reports from SharePoint, you have the choice to use the SharePoint Report Explorer and Viewer web parts with native mode or go for a SharePoint integrated mode deployment. If you have to use an SSRS release version older than SSRS2K5 SP2 or if you are using SharePoint Services 2.0, your only choice is to use the SharePoint web parts. However, with later versions, you can pick between the two options. The web parts are good enough for simple report-viewing needs. However, they don't provide the deep security and database-level integration with SharePoint or the report-management experience via SharePoint that gets enabled with SharePoint integrated mode. If you need more information about these two choices, refer to "Comparing Integration Support for 2.0 and 3.0 Releases" via Microsoft SQL Server Books Online (http://msdn.microsoft.com/en-us/library/bb326405.aspx).

We recommend using SSRS 2008 with WSS 3.0 or MOSS 2007 to integrate your reports with SharePoint sites. Doing so will enable you to take advantage of all the benefits of SharePoint integrated mode. Make sure you install an edition of SSRS that supports SharePoint integrated mode (such as Developer, Evaluation, Standard, or Enterprise).

NOTE

SSRS2K5 SP2 was the first release to support SharePoint integrated mode and can be used for integration with WSS 3.0 or MOSS 2007. SSRS 2008 added support for data-driven subscriptions (DDS) and support for passing parameters over URL.

The architecture and different deployment topologies (for example, single machine versus a server farm deployment) are covered in the next chapter. The installation steps and information about how to use SSRS tools and management features in SharePoint integrated mode are covered in the remaining chapters.

Unsupported Features

When SSRS is set up in SharePoint integrated mode, these features are not supported:

- Report Manager cannot be used for a server in SharePoint mode. This is to ensure that only the SharePoint UI is used for report management.
- The My Reports feature is available only in Report Manager, which is not available in SharePoint mode.
- Linked reports.
- Custom security extensions are not supported because the Report Server uses SharePoint authentication.
- The SSRS role-based authorization model is not supported because SharePoint permissions and groups are always used to control access to Report Server content.

- RS.EXE command-line utility.
- Batching methods.
- Migration of Report Server content between Report Server databases that are configured for different modes is not supported.

Some of the SharePoint site features cannot be used with reports either:

- Cannot use SharePoint web application with anonymous access with Report Server
- Cannot use the Alternate Access Mapping feature for SharePoint zones with Reporting Services (although support expected in the next version of SSRS after 2008)
- Cannot use SharePoint Outlook calendar integration, SharePoint scheduling, or personalization for Report Server document files

Sample Reports Integrated with SharePoint

The following figures show some examples of reports being viewed directly from SharePoint. Figure 30.1 shows a SharePoint site with reports in the document library. Figure 30.2 shows an SSRS 2008 Report Viewer web part in SharePoint full-page view. And, Figure 30.3 shows an SSRS 2008 Report Viewer web part in the SharePoint dashboard.

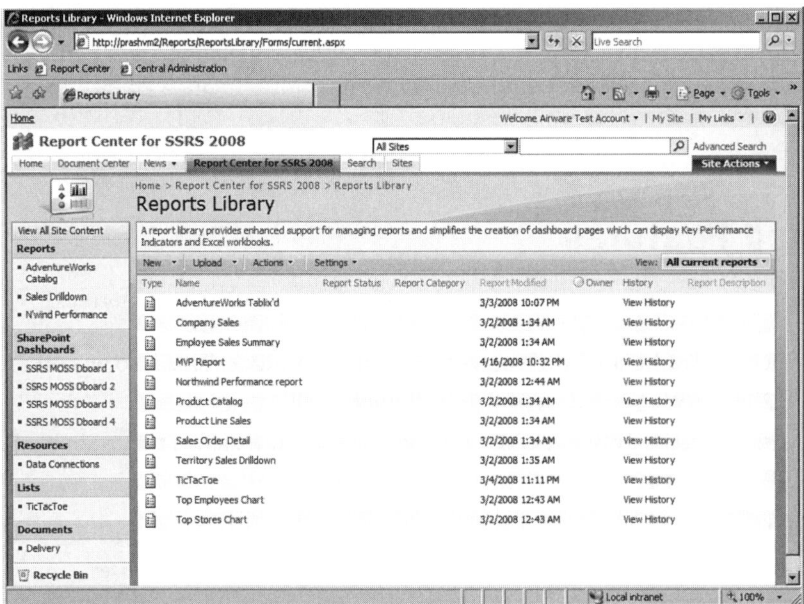

FIGURE 30.1 SharePoint site with reports in the document library.

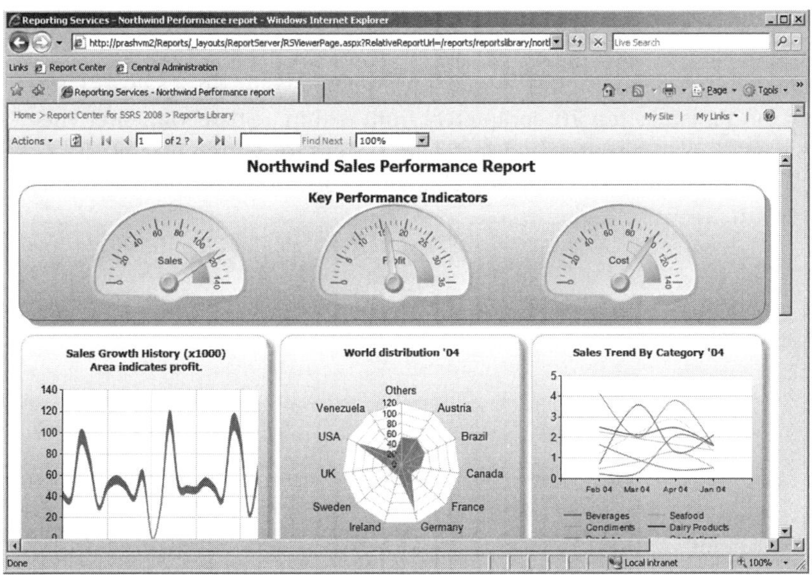

FIGURE 30.2 SSRS 2008 Report Viewer web part in SharePoint full-page view.

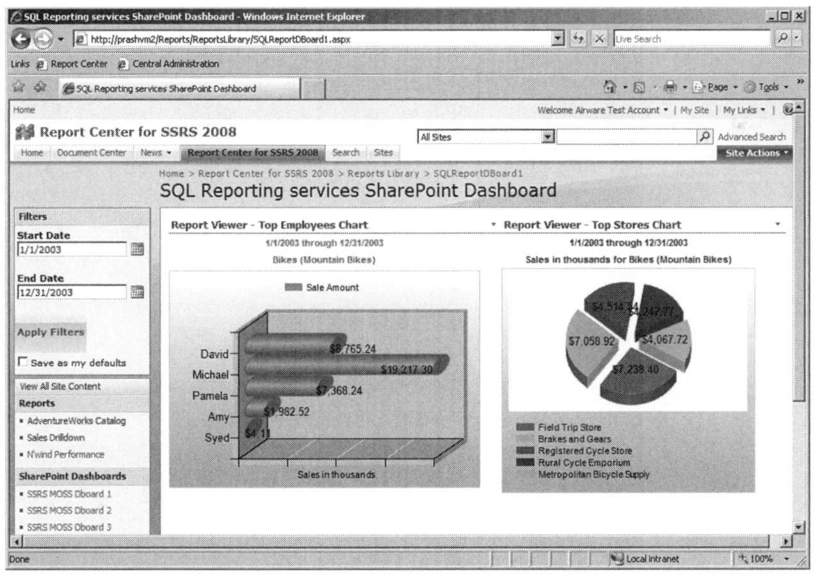

FIGURE 30.3 SSRS 2008 Report Viewer web part in the SharePoint dashboard.

The remaining chapters guide you through the architecture, installation, administration, tools, and report-management experience for integrating Reporting Services with SharePoint.

Summary

Microsoft has enabled deep integration between SSRS and SharePoint since SSRS2K5 SP2. Users can now view and manage reports completely from within a SharePoint site. The next two chapters cover the architecture and installation steps for setting up SSRS in SharePoint integrated mode, and the remaining chapters explain how to run and manage reports from SharePoint.

CHAPTER 31

SSRS 2008 SharePoint Integration Architecture

IN THIS CHAPTER

Understanding the basic architecture of how SSRS 2008 integrates with SharePoint will help you to plan your deployment topology, carry out a successful installation, and troubleshoot problems when you choose to deploy Reporting Services in SharePoint integrated mode.

The key point to remember is that the integration with SharePoint has been done at the document library level. Essentially, reports become just another document on your SharePoint site. Therefore, SharePoint document features such as workflow, versioning, permissions, and collaboration apply to reports just like any other document.

Some of the benefits of SharePoint integration mentioned in Chapter 30, "Reporting Services Integration with SharePoint," provide clues about the basic needs of the architecture, including the following:

- The ability to treat reports like traditional SharePoint documents implies that reports need to be saved in the SharePoint Content database.
- Running reports through Report Server to benefit from all server features implies communication between SharePoint Content database and Report Server.
- The user interface to view and manage reports in SharePoint implies adding a `ReportViewer` control and report administration UI pages to the SharePoint site.

Figure 31.1 shows the architecture of Reporting Services integration with SharePoint. The box on the left represents a SharePoint Server installation (WSS 3.0 or MOSS 2007), and the one on the right represents a SQL Server Reporting Services installation (2005 SP2 or 2008).

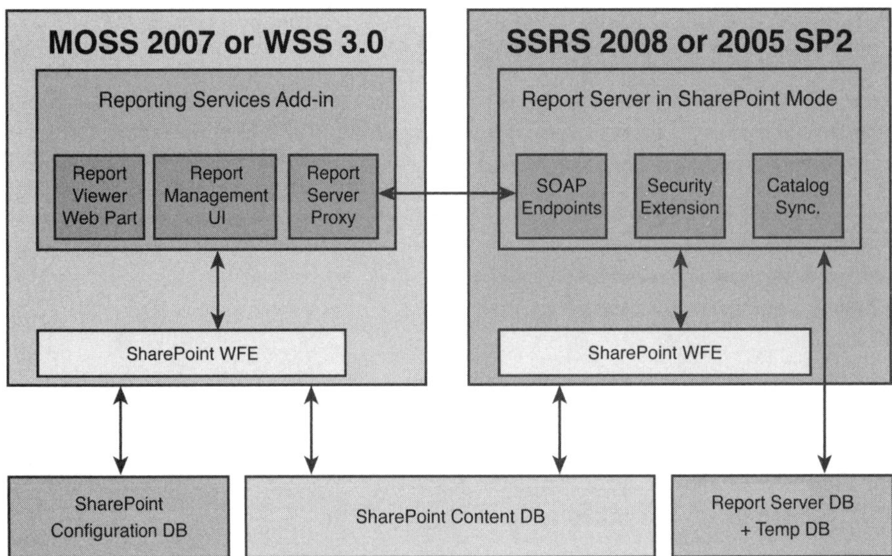

FIGURE 31.1 SSRS 2008 SharePoint integration architecture.

The primary components that enable the integration are as follows:

- On the SSRS box

  Report Server: To run reports and support standard reporting features such as caching and subscriptions (needs to be installed and configured in SharePoint integrated mode)

  SharePoint Object Model: For Report Server to communicate with SharePoint Server (needs to install MOSS Web Front End [WFE] for integrating with MOSS 2007 or WSS WFE for integrating with WSS 3.0)

- On the SharePoint box

  RS SharePoint add-in: To enable SharePoint with SSRS reporting (needs to be installed on each SharePoint WFE that will be used to view and manage reports)

Report Server in SharePoint integrated mode and the RS SharePoint add-in work together to ensure that SharePoint sites can be used as the front end for viewing and managing reports. The Report Server functions as the back end for rendering reports and managing features such as caching and subscriptions.

Reporting Services Add-In for SharePoint

Starting with the SSRS2K5 SP2 release and updated for SSRS 2008, a Reporting Services add-in for SharePoint is available as a public download. It is usually referred to by the shorter name of *RS add-in*.

To find the RS add-in, go to www.microsoft.com/downloads and search for "Microsoft SQL Server 2008 Reporting Services add-in." Besides the MSI file download, you will find an overview and instructions on how to install and configure the RS add-in.

From the perspective of the SharePoint administrator, the RS add-in is the piece of software that allows customers to extend their SharePoint sites with SSRS reports. The RS add-in needs to be installed on each MOSS or WSS WFE that needs to be integrated with SSRS in the SharePoint farm.

Figure 31.1 shows some of the key components that are available via the RS add-in on the SharePoint Server. These are the key features that the RS add-in provides to the SharePoint sites:

- **Report Server content types:** Additional SharePoint content types are installed for ad hoc reports, data sources, and models. After these have been added as standard SharePoint content types, they become just another type of document, and SharePoint features such as document management, collaboration, security, and deployment apply to them, too.
- **Context-sensitive menus:** Menu options are added for Report Server items that show up in SharePoint sites. For example, when you click a report, you may see menu options like Manage Parameters and Manage Subscriptions.
- **Report Viewer Web Part:** This is the traditional Report Viewer control that provides report-viewing capability, an option to save the report in different rendering formats, pagination, search, print, and zoom. This Web Part communicates with the Report Server (in SharePoint integrated mode) to execute reports and display them in SharePoint full-page view or dashboards.
- **Report management pages:** These are traditional SharePoint web application pages that are added to the SharePoint site to manage reports, models, and data sources and to create subscriptions and schedules.
- **Report Server proxy endpoint:** The proxy is responsible for connecting to the Report Server, creating a session for report execution, and displaying it in the Report Viewer Web Part.

Report Server Integrated Mode

Starting with the SSRS2K5 SP2 and applicable to SSRS 2008, Report Server can be installed in SharePoint integrated mode (besides the default native mode). Report Server provides the core functionality of SSRS, such as report rendering and execution, in either mode.

To support SharePoint integrated mode, the following features were added to the Report Server:

- **Catalog synchronization:** Ability to sync reports from SharePoint Content databases to Report Server databases.
- **Security synchronization:** Ability to map SharePoint site and document permissions to authorize Report Server operations.

- **ReportExecution2005 SOAP endpoint:** The traditional web service application programming interfaces (APIs) for report execution in native mode were updated to also work in SharePoint integrated mode.
- **ReportService2006 SOAP endpoint:** A new web service for managing content in Report Server in SharePoint integrated mode.
- **ReportServiceAuthentication SOAP endpoint:** A new web service to authenticate users against a Report Server when the SharePoint web application is configured for forms authentication.
- **SharePoint delivery extension:** The ability to deliver reports to SharePoint libraries via subscriptions and the ability to publish reports and models from Report Designer and Model Designer to SharePoint libraries.
- **Report Builder support from SharePoint:** The ability to open reports and models in Report Builder from a SharePoint library and save them back to SharePoint libraries.

In addition to the changes in Report Server, the Reporting Services Configuration tool was updated in SSRS 2008 to allow configuration of Report Server for SharePoint integrated mode. Also with SSRS 2008, SQL Server Management Studio (SSMS) can be used to manage a Report Server in SharePoint integrated mode. These changes are covered in Chapter 34, "Tools Support for SSRS Integrated with SharePoint."

Database management and security management are the key differences between native mode and SharePoint integrated mode.

Database Management

Figure 31.1 identifies three underlying databases:

- **SharePoint Configuration DB:** SharePoint web applications have a configuration database to store application settings. Chapter 33, "SharePoint Mode Administration," covers settings that need to be configured to get SharePoint to work with Report Server. These settings are stored in the SharePoint Configuration database.
- **SharePoint Content DB:** SharePoint web applications have content databases to store documents that are managed through the SharePoint Server. For a Report Server configured for SharePoint integrated mode, the SharePoint Content database provides the primary storage for reports, report models, and shared data sources. Figure 31.1 shows that SharePoint Content DB is the master copy for reports and is accessible by both the SharePoint Server and the Report Server. Any time a user requests a report operation, the latest copy of the report in the SharePoint Content DB is used.
- **Report Server DB:** SSRS typically has a Report Server DB to store persistent reports metadata and a Report Server Temp DB to store transient session and report-processing data. In SharePoint integrated mode, the master copies for reports, models, and data sources live in the SharePoint Content DB, and internal copies are created in

Report Server DB. Report Server ensures that the copy of the reports in Report Server DB is kept in sync with the master copy in the SharePoint Content DB via a catalog-synchronization feature. Any metadata associated with the reports such as schedules, subscriptions, and snapshots for report history or report execution is stored only in the Report Server DB.

Figure 31.1 shows catalog synchronization as a feature in Report Server in SharePoint integrated mode. This is a background process that is triggered automatically whenever a report item is created, updated, or retrieved. It ensures that the copies kept in Report Server DB are in sync with the SharePoint Content DB.

When report items are deleted from the SharePoint site, the Report Server performs periodic verification and removes any copies from the Report Server database along with any associated report snapshots, subscriptions, and other metadata for the report. At daily intervals, the Report Server runs a cleanup process to verify that items stored in the Report Server database are associated with a report in the SharePoint Content database. The frequency of the cleanup process is controlled by the `DailyCleanupMinuteofDay` property in the `RSReportServer.config` file.

Security Management

For authentication, both the Windows integrated and trusted account modes are supported between SharePoint Server and Report Server. Figure 31.2 shows how the authentication information flows between the SharePoint and Report Server.

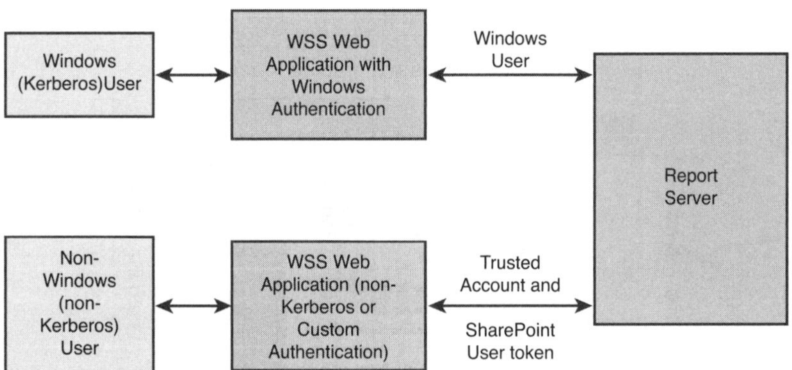

FIGURE 31.2 Security authentication modes.

In SharePoint integrated mode, SSRS uses a security extension to maintain report security in MOSS or WSS. SharePoint security features can be used to access report items from SharePoint sites and libraries. Once you integrate Report Server and SharePoint, the existing site and list permissions for your users automatically give them permissions for Report Server operations. For example, the SharePoint View Item permission means the user can also view reports, whereas the Add Item permission translates to rights for creating new reports, data sources, and report models on the SharePoint site. A list of SharePoint permissions and how they map to Report Server operations is provided in Chapter 33.

Deployment Architecture

Prerequisites for SSRS to integrate with SharePoint include the following:

- Install SSRS 2008 in SharePoint integrated mode, which is available in the following editions: Developer, Evaluation, Standard, and Enterprise.
- Install the same type and version of SharePoint WFE on the Report Server machine as is on the SharePoint Server that will be used for integration. Integration is supported for WSS 3.0 and MOSS 2007 Standard or Enterprise editions. If you integrate with WSS, install the WSS WFE on the Report Server machine; for MOSS, install the MOSS WFE.
- Install the RS add-in on each SharePoint WFE that will be used to view and manage reports.

To plan your system architecture, here are the variations of deployment topologies to consider:

- **Single machine:** Figure 31.3 shows all SSRS and SharePoint components working together on the same machine. Putting everything on a single computer may not be practical for an enterprise production deployment, but it is attractive in a development or testing environment to save costs (for example, hardware and software licensing costs).

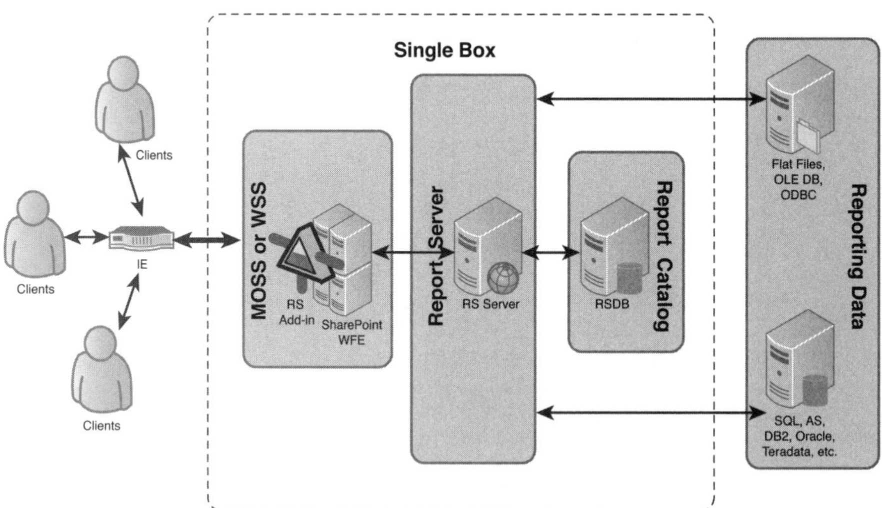

FIGURE 31.3 Single-machine deployment of SSRS and SharePoint.

- **Distributed servers:** It is common to separate the application server and database server on separate machines even for a single instance of SSRS or SharePoint Server.

For example, you may have all the databases for SharePoint and Report Server on one machine, Report Server on another machine, and the SharePoint web application on a third machine. As long as you install a SharePoint WFE on the Report Server machine and the RS add-in on the SharePoint web application, the deployment topology is sound and provides better resource isolation between the servers.

- **Scalable deployments:** To support a large number of users or workloads, multiple instances of the same server component can be deployed, such as multiple Report Servers or multiple SharePoint sites (also called a SharePoint farm). Figure 31.4 shows a series of computers being used for SSRS scale out and a series of computers being used for a SharePoint farm. NLB in Figure 31.4 stands for network load balancer. The entire SharePoint farm must be configured to use a virtual Report Server URL as a single point of entry. Individual SharePoint sites in a farm cannot be configured against different Report Servers. SSRS does not provide load-balancing features or the ability to configure a virtual server URL out of the box. Therefore, a hardware or software load-balancing solution must be used.

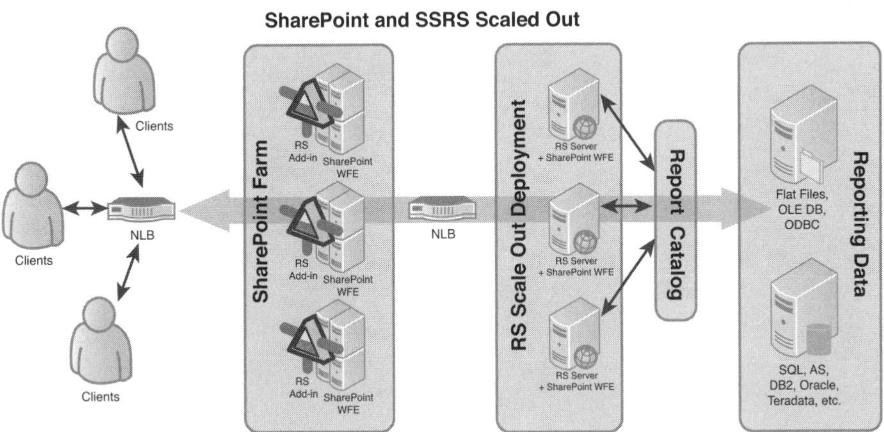

FIGURE 31.4 Multiple-machine deployment in a scale-out farm.

Summary

SSRS SharePoint integration is enabled via deep database and security integration between Report Server and SharePoint via the Report Server SharePoint integrated mode. An RS add-in is required to be installed on the SharePoint web application to view and manage reports and to interact with SSRS. All user actions are initiated via the SharePoint UI, which uses a proxy to communicate with Report Server and complete any actions on report items. A variety of deployment topologies can be picked for integration between SharePoint and SSRS, such as single machine, distributed servers, and scalable deployments.

CHAPTER 32

Installation of Reporting Services Integrated with SharePoint

IN THIS CHAPTER

- Installing Reporting Services
- Installing SharePoint
- Configuring Report Server in SharePoint Integrated Mode
- Installing Reporting Services Add-In for SharePoint
- Configuring Report Server Integration Via SharePoint Central Administration
- Upgrading from SSRS2K5 SP2
- Scaling-Out Deployments
- Troubleshooting

The preceding chapter covered deployment architectures, which can help you to decide whether to integrate SharePoint with Reporting Services on a single machine, distributed servers, or scalable farms.

Traditionally, you can launch Microsoft software installation by clicking `setup.exe` without much planning and troubleshoot if something goes wrong. Customers have found that installation and configuration of the integration between SharePoint and Reporting Services can be hard to troubleshoot. There might also be additional steps needed to configure your specific deployment environment. Therefore, we highly recommend that you spend some time planning the list of tasks for your integrated deployment before you actually start installation.

The recommended order for setup and configuration is as follows:

1. Install Reporting Services.
2. Install SharePoint.
3. Configure Report Server for SharePoint mode.
4. Install the RS add-in for SharePoint.
5. Configure SharePoint to work with Report Server.

NOTE

Basic (default) installation of SharePoint Server will install an Embedded Edition of SQL Server that is used for storing the SharePoint Content and Configuration databases. If you are installing SharePoint Server and Reporting Services on the same machine, note that Reporting Services cannot use the Embedded Edition of SQL Server for storage. You will have to install a database engine from the SQL Server CD along with Reporting Services.

Installing Reporting Services

Follow the steps from Chapter 6, "Installing Reporting Services." Step 10 and Figure 6.9 show how to specify the installation mode on the Reporting Services Configuration page.

To pick the default configuration for SharePoint integrated mode installation, select the Install the SharePoint Integrated Mode Default Configuration option. This option will configure the Report Server web service, Report Server database, the service account, and connections needed for access.

An alternative is to pick the Install, but Do Not Configure the Report Server option. This is called a Files Only mode of installation. This will require post-installation configuration steps that provide more opportunities to pick URLs, port numbers, and names for web services and databases.

Installing SharePoint

You can do a fresh install of Windows SharePoint Services 3.0 (WSS) or Microsoft Office SharePoint Server 2007 (MOSS) or use existing SharePoint deployments to integrate with Reporting Services. Refer to tutorials or books on WSS and MOSS for information about topics such as administration of SharePoint farms. For many readers, you are likely to have existing installations of WSS or MOSS, and your SharePoint administrator can help you with the integration tasks.

If you are installing a new SharePoint Server, you can reduce the number of database engines to manage by reusing the SQL Server 2008 database you just installed with SSRS 2008 as your storage location for SharePoint.

NOTE

If your deployment topology includes installing the Report Server and SharePoint Server on separate machines, remember to install a SharePoint Web Front End (WFE) on the Report Server computer, too. The WFE type and version should be the same as on the SharePoint Server (WSS or MOSS) that you are integrating with SSRS. Follow steps 1 through 3 described in the instructions to set up WSS 3.0.

Here are the basic steps to set up WSS 3.0 to use for reporting integration:

1. WSS 3.0 is available as a free download as a setup file called `SharePoint.exe`. Download it and launch `SharePoint.exe`.
2. Click the Advanced installation type and select Web Front End.
3. To configure the WFE, use the SharePoint Configuration Wizard. If you are installing just a WFE on the machine, choose the Connect to an Existing Server Farm option and you should be done.
4. To continue to set up a new SharePoint Server, choose the Create a New Server Farm option.
5. Pick the database server where the SharePoint Configuration database should live. Note that if you have installed SSRS 2008 already, you can try to use the same database as Reporting Services. You will need to specify Windows account credentials for WSS to connect to the database. We recommend using a domain account.
6. Create a web application and site collection via the SharePoint Central Administration application.
7. From the Application Management tab, click the Create or Extend Web Application link and choose Create a New Web Application.
8. Choose the Use an Existing IIS Web Site option to use the default website.
9. Choose to Create New Application Pool and select the Network service account as the security account for the application.
10. Click the Create Site Collection link on the Application Created page and pick a name for the portal site.
11. Enter a Windows domain account as your primary site collection administrator. A new site collection is created with a top-level site (for example, `http://servername`).
12. If you want, you can create a new subsite (for example, reports) from the top-level site using the Site Actions drop-down menu on the top right. Now `http://servername/reports` is ready to host any documents (in this case, reports).

Configuring Report Server in SharePoint Integrated Mode

You can use the Report Server Configuration tool to create a Report Server database in SharePoint integrated mode and configure the Report Server Service.

Chapter 34, "Tools Support for SSRS Integrated with SharePoint," is about using tools with SharePoint mode, and Figure 34.3 shows the Report Server Database Configuration Wizard, which you can use to create the Report Server database in SharePoint mode.

Note that you have to configure the Report Server Service to run under a domain account if Report Server and application databases are on one computer and the SharePoint web application is on another computer. Chapter 33, "SharePoint Mode Administration," provides more information about security.

32

Installing the RS Add-In for SharePoint

Go to www.microsoft.com/downloads and search for "Reporting Services add-in for SharePoint."

> **NOTE**
>
> There are multiple versions of the SSRS add-in. You need to download the 2008 Reporting Services add-in for SharePoint for the language of your choice. Version 10.00.2531.00 released on April 7, 2009 is the most current update and includes the Report Builder 2.0 Click Once update (www.microsoft.com/downloads/details.aspx?displaylang=en&FamilyID=58edd0e4-255b-4361-bd1e-e530d5aab78f).

Run the `rsSharePoint.msi` on each SharePoint Web Front End (WFE) that is part of your SharePoint farm and will be used to run and manage reports. Doing so requires SharePoint farm administrator privileges.

Configuring Report Server Integration Via SharePoint Central Administration

Launch your SharePoint 3.0 Central Administration and click the Application Management tab (see Figure 32.1).

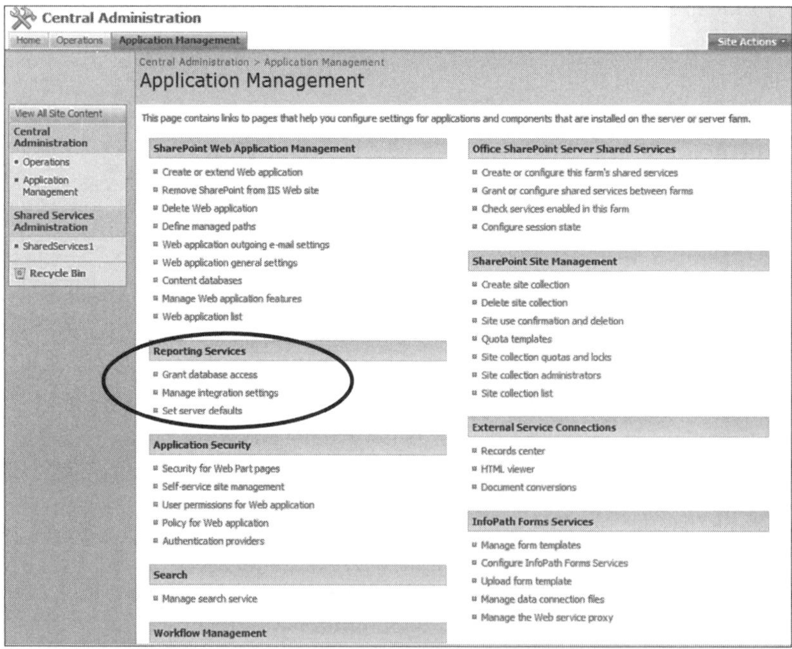

FIGURE 32.1 SharePoint Central Administration: Reporting Services management.

If the RS add-in for SharePoint was properly installed and activated, you should see a section for Reporting Services with the following links: Grant Database Access, Manage Integration Settings, and Set Server Defaults. If you don't see these links, navigate to Site Actions, Site Settings, Site Collection Features, and find Report Server Integration Feature in the list and click Activate (see Figure 32.2 and Figure 32.3).

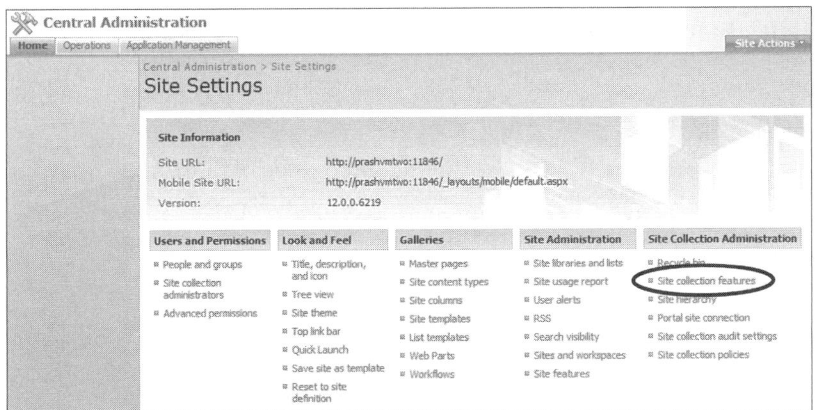

FIGURE 32.2 SharePoint Central Administration: Site Collection Features.

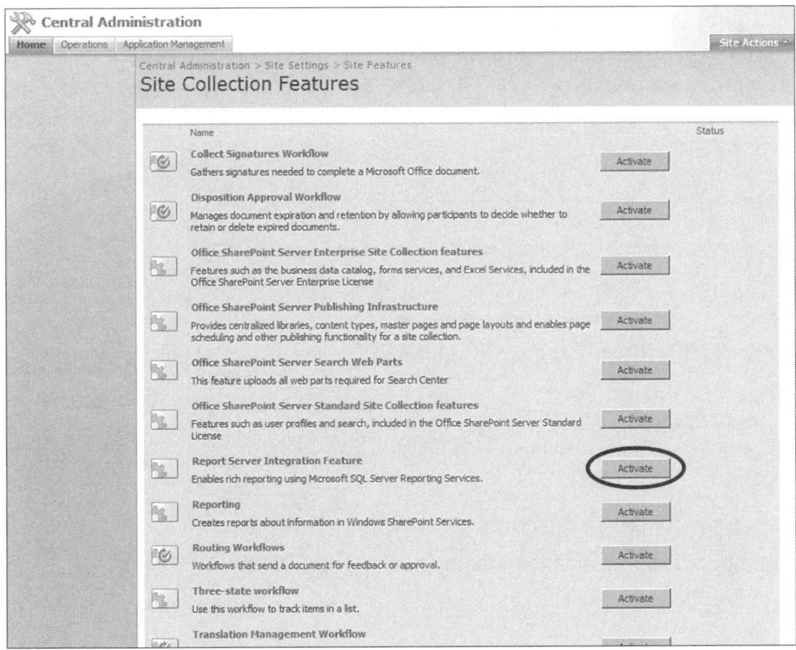

FIGURE 32.3 SharePoint Central Administration: Activate Report Server Integration Feature.

Once the Reporting Services section shows up under Application Management, you can use the various links under it to configure SharePoint to talk to Report Server.

First, click Manage Integration Settings (see Figure 32.4). In the first field, you can specify the Report Server web service URL, which represents the target Report Server in SharePoint mode. This is the same value as the web service URL from the Reporting Services Configuration tool. The second field is a drop-down choice for authentication mode (between Windows authentication or trusted authentication), which can be selected based on what type of authentication mode is used for the SharePoint web application.

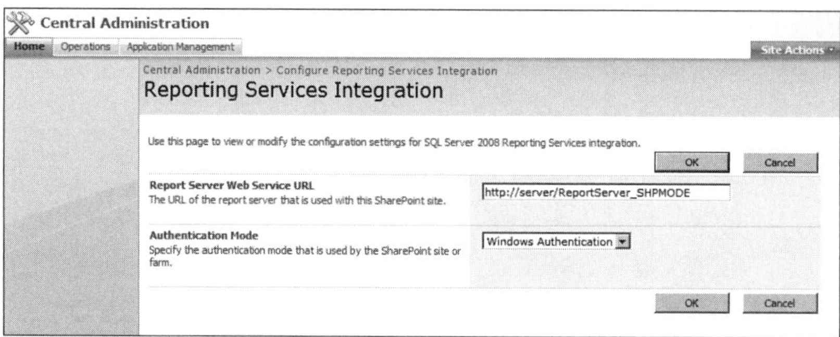

FIGURE 32.4 Reporting Services Application Management: Manage Integration Settings.

Now, click Grant Database Access (see Figure 32.5) to allow the Report Server Service to access the SharePoint Configuration and Content databases. Specify the Report Server name and database instance name. When you click OK, a pop-up dialog will request credentials for connecting to the Report Server.

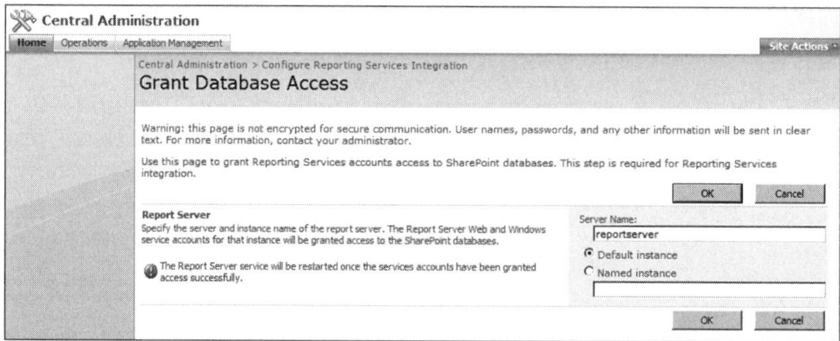

FIGURE 32.5 Reporting Services Application Management: Grant Database Access.

The last link under Reporting Services Application Management is Set Server Defaults (see Figure 32.6).

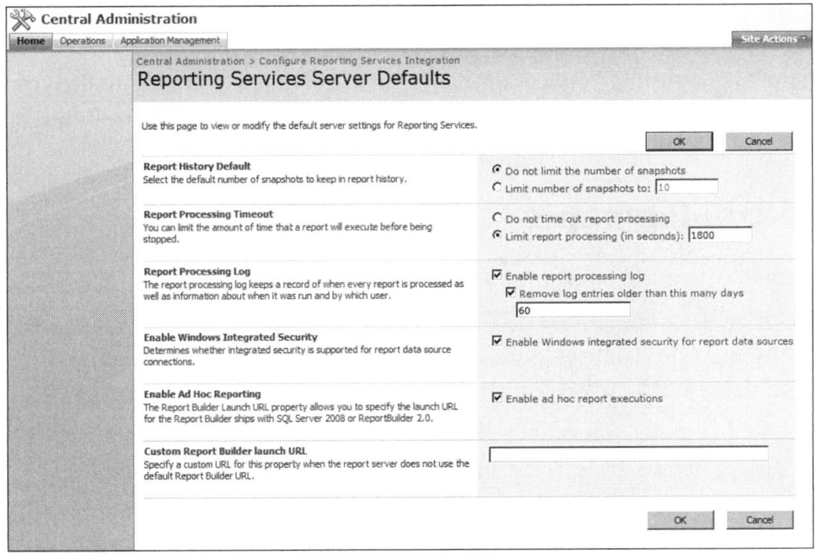

FIGURE 32.6 Reporting Services Application Management: Set Server Defaults.

The Set Server Defaults option enables you to specify the default for the following Reporting Services features:

- **Report History Default:** The ability to limit the default number of snapshots that can be stored for each report.
- **Report Processing Timeout:** The ability to time out report processing after certain number of seconds.
- **Report Processing Log:** The ability to generate trace logs for report processing.
- **Enable Windows Integrated Security:** The ability to connect to report data sources with the user's Windows security credentials.
- **Enable Ad Hoc Reporting:** The ability to control whether users can perform ad hoc queries from a Report Builder report. If this is not set, the Report Server will not generate clickthrough reports for reports that use a report model as a data source.
- **Custom Report Builder Launch URL:** The ability to specify the launch URL for the Report Builder that ships with SQL Server 2008 or Report Builder 2.0.

If you are using a SharePoint farm or a scale-out reporting deployment topology and don't want to repeat these configuration steps manually on each server, you can use SSRS programmability to create configuration scripts. Chapter 33 shows a code sample of how to do that.

Upgrading from SSRS2K5 SP2

If you were already using Reporting Services 2005 SP2 in SharePoint integrated mode, you can upgrade the 2005 SP2 Report Server to 2008, and you can also do an in-place upgrade of the 2005 SP2 Reporting Services add-in for SharePoint with the 2008 version.

Scaling-Out Deployments

Here are some security account prerequisites for multiple-server deployments:

- Create or use an existing domain user account to connect the SharePoint WFE to the SharePoint Configuration database. Server farms require that you use domain accounts for services and database connections. Otherwise, you will get `Access Denied` errors.
- Create a SQL Server database login for the domain account with DBCreator permissions.
- Configure the SharePoint application pool process account to run as a domain user.
- Configure the Report Server Service to run as a domain user account.

Traditional steps for setting up SharePoint farms (refer to SharePoint documentation or books) and scale-out Reporting Services can be applied. Here are some additional principles that have to be followed for SSRS scale-out deployments with SharePoint:

- All Report Servers in a scale-out deployment must run in SharePoint integrated mode. It is not possible to mix and match modes.
- The instance of the SharePoint product (WSS 3.0 or MOSS 2007) that you install on the Report Server must be the same version as the other nodes in the farm.
- There must be a single URL for the scale-out deployment that is used for configurations in SharePoint farms because there is no support for configuring an individual SharePoint WFE with individual Report Servers. You can create a single point of entry to the scale-out deployment via a URL that resolves to a virtual IP for the NLB cluster for Report Server instances.

Make sure you install the minimum SharePoint installation such as WFE on the SSRS machines. Otherwise, you will see the error `The Report Server cannot access settings in the SharePoint Configuration database.`

NOTE

SQL Server Books Online has a helpful article available titled "How to Configure SharePoint Integration on Multiple Servers" (http://technet.microsoft.com/en-us/library/bb677365.aspx).

There is also a helpful blog post on distributed server deployment for SharePoint integrated mode at http://mosshowto.blogspot.com/2009/03/reporting-services-sharepoint-multiple.html.

Troubleshooting

As mentioned at the beginning of this chapter, customers find various challenges (installation and configuration) when integrating SharePoint with Reporting Services. Some useful tips are listed here. If you run into further problems, see Appendix A, "References and Additional Reading," for a list of resources (white papers, blogs, and newsgroups) that may help you to resolve various issues.

- **Problems on domain controllers:** If the "Grant database access" step fails with A new member could not be added to a local group because the member has the wrong account type error, make sure your Report Server services accounts are domain accounts on a domain controller. Otherwise, you will get an error when you try to add the account to the local WSS_WPG group.
- **Problems installing the RS add-in for SharePoint:** If you see User does not have permission to add feature to site collection, locate the installation log created by the RS add-in MSI in the Temp folder (<Drive>:\Documents and Settings\<user_name>\Local Settings\Temp\RS_SP_<number>.log). You should be able to locate log entries such as the following:

```
Activating feature to root site collection: <sharepoint_site_collection>
******* User does not have permission to add feature to site collection:
➥<sharepoint_site_collection>
```

  This means that the RS integration feature was installed, but the feature might not be activated for the <sharepoint_site_collection>, because the user who ran the MSI was not a site collection administrator. To view the RS integration feature in the site, you need the site collection administrator to activate the Report Server feature.

NOTE

There is a white paper titled "Troubleshooting Integration with SQL Server 2005 and Microsoft SharePoint Technologies" at http://msdn.microsoft.com/en-us/library/bb969101.aspx. Even though it was created for 2005 SP2, it is relevant for 2008 integration, too.

Summary

Plan your deployment architecture for integrating Reporting Services with SharePoint carefully and follow these setup steps in this order:

1. Install Reporting Services.
2. Install SharePoint technology.
3. Configure Report Server for SharePoint mode.
4. Install the RS add-in for SharePoint.
5. Configure SharePoint to work with Report Server.

CHAPTER 33

SharePoint Mode Administration

IN THIS CHAPTER

Installation and configuration of Reporting Services integrated with SharePoint is more than half the challenge for administration.

Here is a basic checklist that you should have completed during installation:

- Install a SharePoint Web Front End (WFE) on the Report Server machine.
- Install the Reporting Services add-in on the SharePoint Server.
- Activate the Report Server feature in SharePoint Central Administration.
- Create or point to a Report Server database in SharePoint integrated mode via the Reporting Services Configuration tool.
- Configure Report Server integration via SharePoint Central Administration.

If you did not complete any of those steps, refer for instructions to Chapter 32, "Installation of Reporting Services Integrated with SharePoint."

The other challenges for administration are security, authorization, and programmability. The rest of the chapter covers these areas.

Security Overview

For SharePoint integrated mode, the Report Server uses the authentication and authorizations defined in the

SharePoint web application to control access to report operations. This makes administration much simpler and primarily driven by the SharePoint administrator.

Reporting Services will process requests based on the SharePoint web application authentication settings, such as the following:

- Windows with integrated security (Kerberos enabled)
- Windows without impersonation
- Forms authentication

Kerberos is better compared to NTLM when multiple hops are required. So, it is good for single-server or multiserver deployment scenarios and when external data sources are involved that use Windows integrated credentials.

Custom security extensions for Reporting Services are not supported with SharePoint integrated mode. All access to a Report Server in SharePoint Integrated mode originates from the SharePoint web application. Report Server just sticks to the SharePoint authentication scheme.

Authorization to access Report Server items from SharePoint sites and libraries is mapped to the built-in permission model for SharePoint. This means that after SharePoint is integrated with Reporting Services, the existing permission levels of SharePoint users (for example, Read, Contribute, or Full Control) for the site will apply to report operations, too. This allows users to publish reports, view reports, create subscriptions, or manage report items such as data sources.

Reports (`.rdl`), report models (`.smdl`), and report data sources (`.rds`) are SharePoint document library items. One of the various menu actions available on these report items is Manage Permissions. This enables users to set individualized permissions on report items and is described further in Chapter 36, "Managing Reports in SharePoint."

User Authentication with SharePoint

Reporting Services process requests are based on the SharePoint web application authentication settings. Two basic authentication workflows are used between SharePoint and the Report Server:

- Windows integrated security
- Trusted account

So how do you choose between Windows integrated or trusted account authentication? Use the Windows Integrated option for Kerberos-enabled environments and in single-box deployment scenarios. Use Trusted Account mode for forms-based authentication, Windows authentication when impersonation is not enabled, and other scenarios. If you are having trouble setting up Kerberos, consider using Trusted Account mode to at least set up and verify that RS integration with SharePoint works. After you have fixed your Kerberos issues, you can choose to switch to using Windows integrated. For help with Kerberos, see the section on setting up Kerberos authentication.

An understanding of the various security connections that are involved in completing a reporting request from a SharePoint site comes in handy when planning or troubleshooting security for your deployment.

Windows Integrated Security

Figure 33.1 shows the authentication workflow for a SharePoint application that is configured to use Windows integrated security and is integrated with Reporting Services. The components in the diagram should be familiar from the chapter on the architecture of SharePoint integration with Reporting Services.

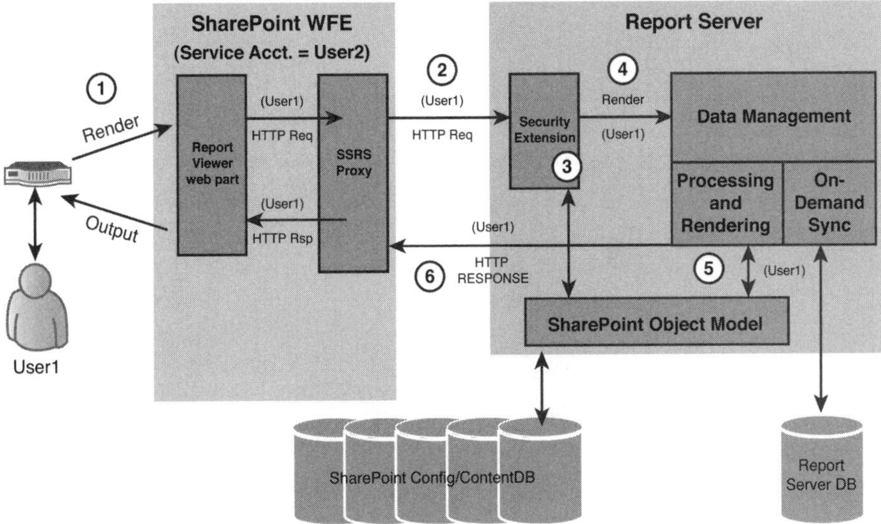

FIGURE 33.1 Authentication workflow using Windows integrated security.

To understand the various connections involved in the workflow, follow the numbered arrows in Figure 33.1:

1. Windows User1 makes a request to render a report from the Report Viewer web part via SharePoint.
2. The Reporting Services proxy connects to Report Server using the Windows User1 credentials and token.
3. If the connection is successful, Report Server needs to verify whether User1 has permissions to access and render the report. This is done by connecting to the SharePoint object model to verify the SharePoint permissions for User1 for the report.
4. If access is allowed, the Report Server proceeds to render the report.
5. Report Server will use the User1 credentials to retrieve and sync the latest copy of the report from the SharePoint Content DB and then execute the report.
6. The report results are sent back to be displayed in the Report Viewer.

Trusted Account with Windows or Forms Authentication

Figure 33.2 shows the authentication workflow for a SharePoint application that is configured to use forms authorization or Windows without Kerberos. It relies on a predefined trusted account that has permission to impersonate a SharePoint user on the Report Server.

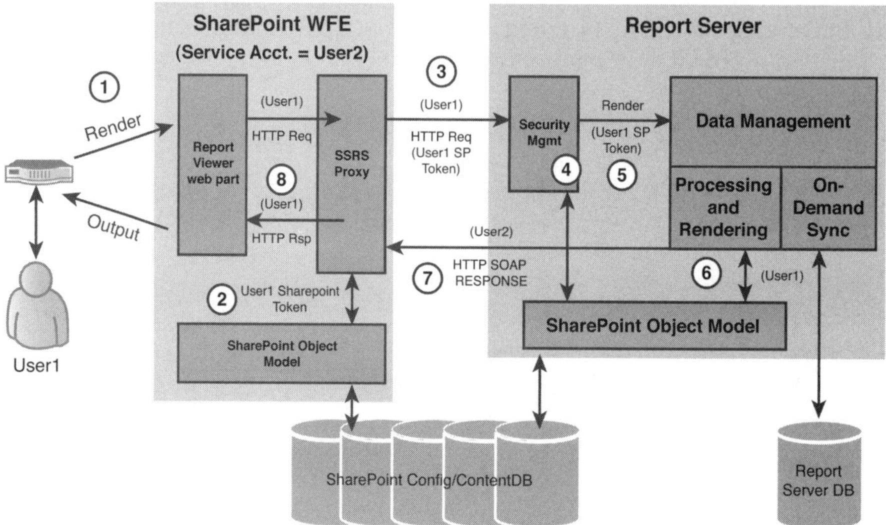

FIGURE 33.2 Authentication workflow using trusted account authorization.

To understand the various connections involved in the workflow, follow the numbered arrows in Figure 33.2:

1. Windows User1 makes a request to render a report from the Report Viewer web part via SharePoint.
2. The SharePoint web application authenticates User1 against the SharePoint object model and creates a SharePoint user token that contains the user identity and group membership for User1.
3. The Reporting Services proxy connects to Report Server using User2, the trusted Windows service account under which the SharePoint web farm is running, and sends along the User1 SharePoint user token.
4. The Report Server validates whether the connection request is from a trusted account by comparing User2 to account information that the Report Server retrieved from the SharePoint Configuration databases when the Report Server started.
5. If the authentication is valid, the rendering request can proceed along with the User1 SharePoint user token.
6. Report Server needs to verify whether the User1 SharePoint token contains the user identity and permissions needed to access and render the report.

7. If access is allowed, the Report Server retrieves and syncs the latest copy of the report from the SharePoint Content DB, and then executes the report.
8. Report Server returns the report results back to the SharePoint WFE using the Windows trusted account, User2.
9. Reporting Services proxy returns the report results back to the Report Viewer web part via the original User1 connection.

User Authorization with SharePoint

Authorization to access Report Server items from SharePoint sites and libraries is mapped to the built-in permission model for SharePoint. So, you need to start with a basic understanding of the SharePoint permissions model, which allows securing SharePoint sites and documents. Inheritance is supported to apply permissions from the site level to all subsites and from folders to all its documents. Permissions are grouped into sets of permission levels that can be granted to SharePoint users or groups. Five default permission levels are available in SharePoint: Full Control, Design, Contribute, Read, and Limited Access. Think of these as default roles that can be applied to users. SharePoint also provides default groups that map to some of the predefined permission levels. Adding users who need to use reports to these default groups is the easiest way to give them the appropriate level of access to reports. Most of the SharePoint users may already belong to one of more of these groups:

- **Visitors:** This group has the Read permission level. Visitors can view reports and create subscriptions.
- **Members:** This group has the Contribute permission level. Members can create new reports, models, report data sources, and other report items in SharePoint or publish them from design tools to SharePoint.
- **Owners:** This group has Full Control. Owners can create, manage, and secure all report items and operations.

Another way to look at it is to map traditional Reporting Services roles from native mode to SharePoint groups:

- **Content Manager:** This role has full permissions to all items and operations. This can be mapped to the Owners group in SharePoint.
- **Publisher:** This role allows adding and editing of reports, models, and data sources. This can be mapped to the Members group.
- **Browser:** This role allows viewing reports and managing individual subscriptions. This can be mapped to the Visitors group.
- **Report Builder:** This role allows viewing reports, managing individual subscriptions, and opening and editing reports in Report Builder. The Members and Owners groups provide these rights, but they provide other privileges, too. If you don't want your Report Builder users to have those privileges, you can create a custom group in SharePoint and assign limited permissions.

- **System User, System Administrator, My Reports:** These roles don't have an equivalent mapping because they are not relevant in SharePoint mode.

Table 33.1 is a reference list of SharePoint permissions, regardless of whether they are included in default SharePoint groups, and the Report Server operations that get enabled with the permission.

TABLE 33.1 SharePoint Permissions

SharePoint Permission	Owners	Members	Visitors	Report Server Operation
Manage Lists	X			Create a folder in a SharePoint library Manage report history
Add Items	X	X		Add reports, report models, shared data sources, and external image files to SharePoint libraries Create shared data sources Generate report models from shared data sources Start Report Builder and create a new report or load a model into Report Builder
Edit Items	X	X		Edit or replace report, model, data source, and dependent report items Create report history snapshots or view past versions of report history snapshots Set report processing options and parameters Open model or model-based report in Report Builder and save changes Assign clickthrough reports to entities in a model Customize Report Viewer web part for specific report

TABLE 33.1 Continued

SharePoint Permission	Owners	Members	Visitors	Report Server Operation
Delete Items	X	X		Delete reports, report models, shared data sources from library
View Items	X	X	X	Render report or report model
Open Items	X	X	X	View a list of shared data sources View clickthrough reports that use a report model Download a copy of the source file for report definition or report model
View Versions	X	X	X	View past versions of a document or report snapshots
Delete Versions	X	X		Delete past versions of a document and report snapshots
Manage Alerts	X	X	X	Create, change, and delete subscriptions

Programmability

Simple Object Access Protocol (SOAP) endpoints are available to enable developers to directly program against Report Server:

- **`ReportService2006.asmx`**: Enables developers to programmatically manage objects on a Report Server that is configured for SharePoint integrated mode.
- **`ReportExecution2005.asmx`**: Enables developers to programmatically execute report objects on a Report Server in either native or SharePoint mode.
- **`ReportServiceAuthentication.asmx`**: Provides classes for authenticating users against a Report Server when the SharePoint web application is configured for forms authentication.

These web services are used by the official Reporting Services tools, too.

The Reporting Services 2008 Windows Management Instrumentation (WMI) provider has been updated to work in SharePoint integrated mode, and you can use it to configure and manage Report Server programmatically.

Configuration Code Sample

Chapter 32 described the steps that can be carried out via the SharePoint Central Administration to configure Report Server integration. Here is a sample of the three steps for configuration done via code.

```
using System;
using System.Collections.Generic;
using System.Text;
// For #1 - manage integration settings
using Microsoft.SharePoint.Administration;
using Microsoft.ReportingServices.SharePoint.Common;
// For #2 - grant database access
using System.Runtime.InteropServices;
// For #3 - set server defaults
using System.Web.Services.Protocols;
using RSShpConfig.ReportServer;

namespace RSShpConfig
{
 class Program
 {
  [DllImport("netapi32.dll", CharSet = CharSet.Unicode,
              CallingConvention = CallingConvention.Winapi,
              SetLastError = false)]
  public static extern NET_API_STATUS NetLocalGroupAddMembers(
            string serverName,
            string groupName,
            int level,
            LOCALGROUP_MEMBERS_INFO_3[] buf,
            int totalEntries);
        [StructLayout(LayoutKind.Sequential)]
  public struct LOCALGROUP_MEMBERS_INFO_3
        {
            [MarshalAs(UnmanagedType.LPWStr)]
            public string strRSServiceAccount;
        }
  public enum NET_API_STATUS
        {
            NERR_Success = 0,
            ERROR_MEMBER_IN_ALIAS = 1378,
        }

  static void Main(string[] args)
```

```
{
  try
  {
   // 1. Manage Integration settings
   // Setting the URL and Authentication Type
   SPRSServiceConfiguration rsConfig =
SPFarm.Local.Services.GetValue<SPRSServiceConfiguration>
➥(SPRSServiceConfiguration.RSServiceName);
   rsConfig.RSServerUrl = "http://<your server name>/Reportserver";
   rsConfig.AuthenticationType = RSAuthenticationType.Trusted;
   rsConfig.Update();

   // 2. Grant Database Access
   String strRSServiceAccount = "<domain\user>";
     // a) Provisioning the RS service account to access sites in the SharePoint
Farm
     SPWebServiceCollection svcColl = new SPWebServiceCollection(SPFarm.Local);
       foreach (SPWebService svc in svcColl)
       {
          foreach (SPWebApplication app in svc.WebApplications)
          {
               app.GrantAccessToProcessIdentity(strRSServiceAccount);
          }
       }
     // b) Add RS Service Account to "WSS_WPG" Windows group
     LOCALGROUP_MEMBERS_INFO_3[] LgMIArr = new LOCALGROUP_MEMBERS_INFO_3[1];
     LgMIArr[0].strRSServiceAccount = strRSServiceAccount;
     NetLocalGroupAddMembers("", "WSS_WPG", 3, LgMIArr, LgMIArr.Length);

   // 3. Set Report Server defaults
   ReportingService2006 RSService = new ReportingService2006();
   RSService.Credentials = System.Net.CredentialCache.DefaultCredentials;
     // Example of increasing Report Processing Timeout from default to 2000 seconds
     Property[] props = new Property[1];
     Property setProp = new Property();
     setProp.Name = "SystemReportTimeout";
     setProp.Value = "2000";
     props[0] = setProp;
     RSService.SetSystemProperties(props);
  }
  catch (Exception exp)
  {
    Console.WriteLine(exp.ToString());
  }
```

33

```
    }
  }
}
```

Setting Up Kerberos Authentication

Kerberos is an authentication protocol that provides mutual authentication between clients and servers and between servers and other servers. It is considered more secure, flexible, and efficient than NTLM.

You must have already enabled Kerberos on your SharePoint farm or single-server installation.

Here are the steps to enable SSRS for Kerberos authentication:

1. Create a service principal name (SPN):

   ```
   setspn.exe -A HTTP/SSRS_Server domain\RS_Service_Login
   ```

   For more information about registering SPNs for RS, see http://msdn.microsoft.com/en-us/library/cc281382.aspx.
2. Enable Trust for Delegation.
3. Open Active Directory (AD) as a user with domain administration rights. For SPNs, find the account and computers, click Properties, and choose Trust This User/Computer for Delegation to Any Service (Kerberos) from the Delegation tab.
4. In the RSreportServer.config file, set up authentication to be Negotiate:

   ```
   <Authentication>
        <AuthenticationTypes>
             <RSWindowsNegotiate/>
             <!—RSWindowsNTLM/—>
        </AuthenticationTypes>
        <EnableAuthPersistence>true</EnableAuthPersistence>
   </Authentication>
   ```
5. Try to connect to Report Server from the client machine. If you have problems connecting, enable Kerberos logging to see what is going on with the client machine. To enable Kerberos logging, refer to http://support.microsoft.com/kb/262177.

Summary

Administration focuses primarily on installation and configuration of the integration between Reporting Services and SharePoint. After the system has been set up, authentication and authorization are the key ongoing administration tasks. Reporting Services in SharePoint integrated mode maps to SharePoint authentication providers and permissions models. authentication between SharePoint and Report Server is carried out via Windows integrated security or via a trusted Windows account (depending on how SharePoint is set up). Standard SharePoint groups such as Owners, Members, and Visitors provide support for some of the default roles for Reporting Services. Individual SharePoint permissions can be mapped to users or custom SharePoint groups for finer-grain control on report operations.

For developers, Reporting Services provides a couple of SharePoint-specific web services for SharePoint forms-based authentication and for managing Report Server objects in SharePoint mode. The web service for executing reports is the same for Report Server in native mode and SharePoint integrated mode.

CHAPTER 34

Tools Support for SSRS Integrated with SharePoint

IN THIS CHAPTER

- Reporting Services Configuration Tool
- SQL Server Management Studio
- Administration and Management Pages
- Report-Authoring Tools

Each server involved in the integration has its own set of tools that continue to carry out their intended functions. For example, SharePoint Server administration and management tools are used to administer SharePoint sites with or without reporting integration. The primary difference between SSRS in native mode and in SharePoint integrated mode is that the portal used to view and manage reports in native mode is Reports Manager, whereas in SharePoint mode it is the SharePoint site.

For more information about SSRS tools, refer back to Chapter 3, "Getting Started with Reporting Services Tools." Most SSRS tools function the same way with Report Server in SharePoint integrated mode as with Report Server in native mode:

- The Report Server Configuration tool can be used to set up and configure the Report Server. It has the option to create the Report Server database in native or SharePoint mode.
- SQL Server Management Studio (SSMS) can be used by administrators to monitor and manage security and roles for the Report Server and for job management.
- Business Intelligence Development Studio (BIDS), Report Builder, and Model Builder continue to be the development tools for creating reports and models. The only difference is that reports and models can be published to a SharePoint site as opposed to Report Manager.

Some SSRS tools not supported in SharePoint integrated mode:

- SSRS Report Manager is disabled in SharePoint integrated mode because users need to use SharePoint sites to view and manage reports.
- The `RS.EXE` command-line utility is not supported against SharePoint mode. This utility is useful to automate Report Server deployment and administrative tasks. Microsoft has not yet gotten around to supporting it in SharePoint integrated mode.

Report Services Configuration Tool

This tool is used to configure an initial installation of SSRS or to fix existing Report Server configuration settings such as report service accounts, web service URLs, and the Report Server database.

The Report Server mode is prominently displayed on the Report Server Status page and Database page (see Figure 34.1 and Figure 34.2).

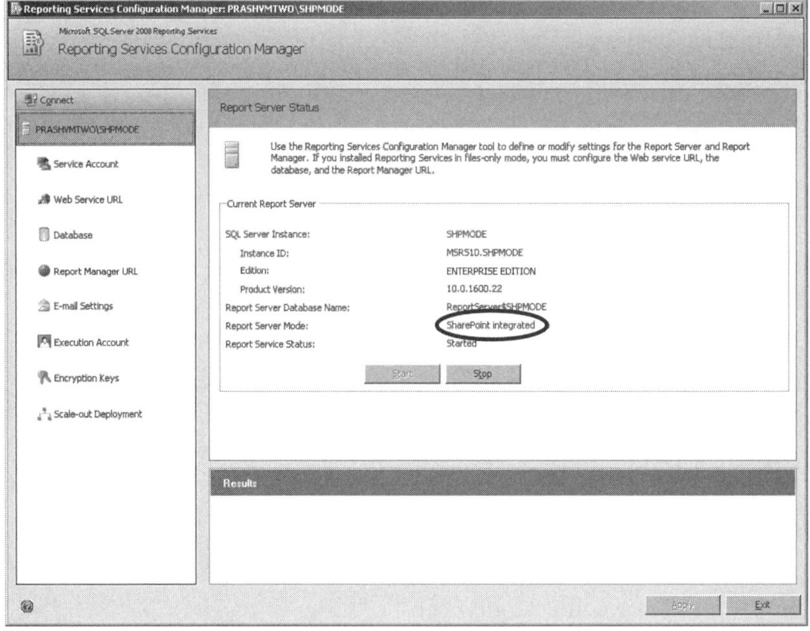

FIGURE 34.1 Report Server Configuration Tool Status page.

If you want to create a new Report Server database in SharePoint mode, go to the Database tab and click the Change Database button. The Report Server Database Configuration

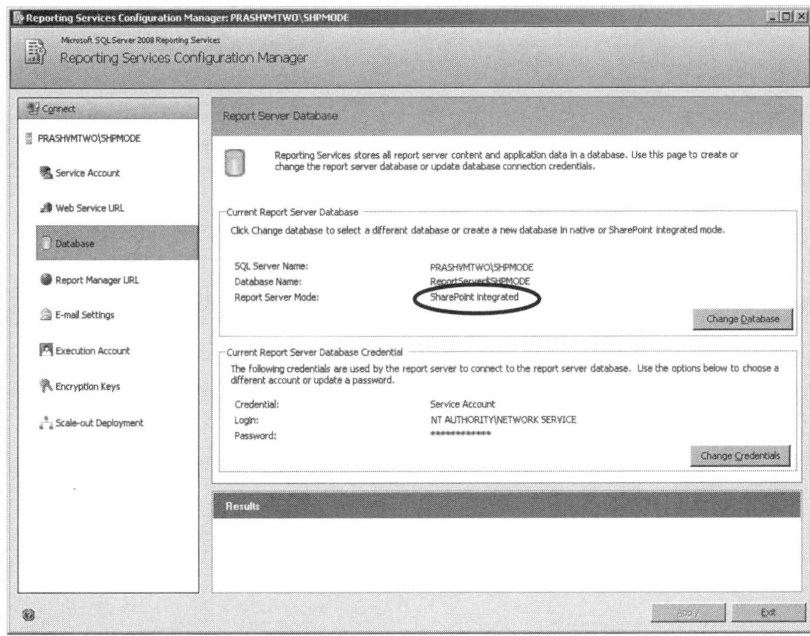

FIGURE 34.2 Report Server Configuration Tool Database page.

Wizard is launched. While you are creating a new database, you can select from two mode options: Native Mode or SharePoint integrated Mode (see Figure 34.3).

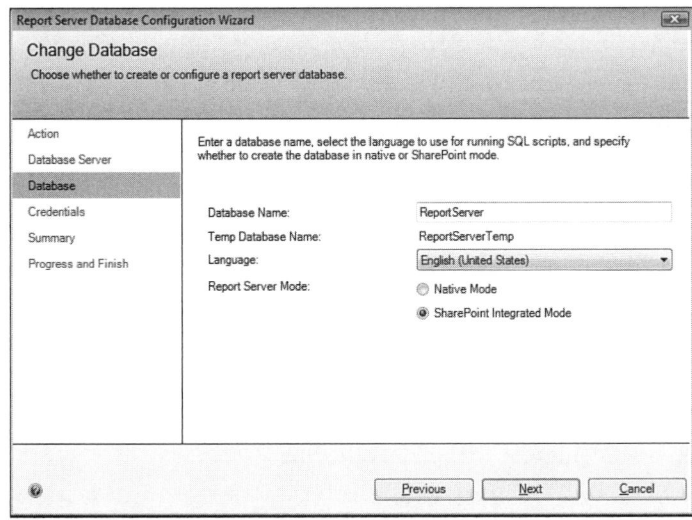

FIGURE 34.3 Report Server Database Configuration Wizard.

SQL Server Management Studio

Starting with the SQL 2008 release, SQL Server Management Studio (SSMS) supports management of Report Server in SharePoint integrated mode (see Figure 34.4). You can connect to a Report Server in SharePoint mode by entering the URL to the SharePoint site in the Connect to Server dialog box (example syntax: `http://<server>/<site>`) and entering the appropriate credentials.

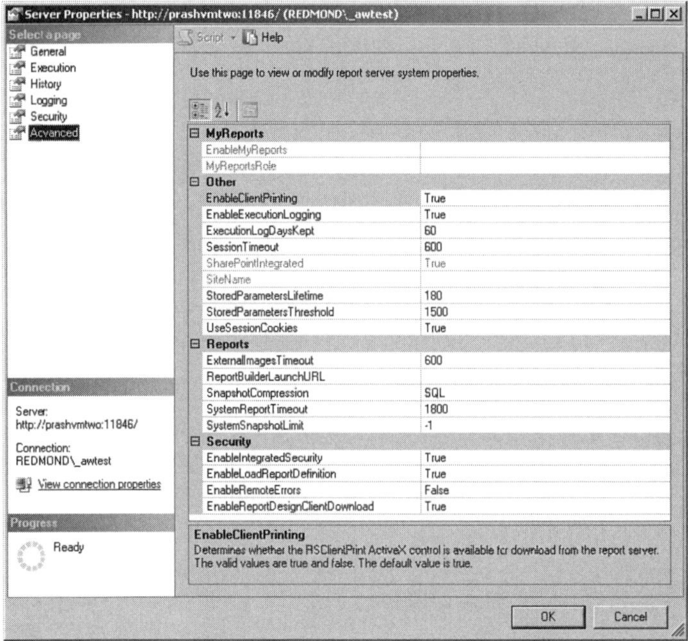

FIGURE 34.4 SSMS connected to Report Server in SharePoint integrated mode.

The following administration tasks can be performed via SSMS:

- View and set Report Server properties. Figure 34.4 shows SSMS connected to a Report Server in SharePoint integrated mode. The menu option for Properties on the connected Report Server brings up the dialog box for the Report Server properties, as shown in Figure 34.4.
- View and cancel jobs. You can show a list of reports currently running in the Report Server and may cancel them.
- Create and manage shared schedules for the SharePoint site.

- View permission levels defined for the SharePoint site. Note that standard SharePoint roles are used, and the read-only dialogs show the automated mappings to permissions for reporting tasks (see Figure 34.5).

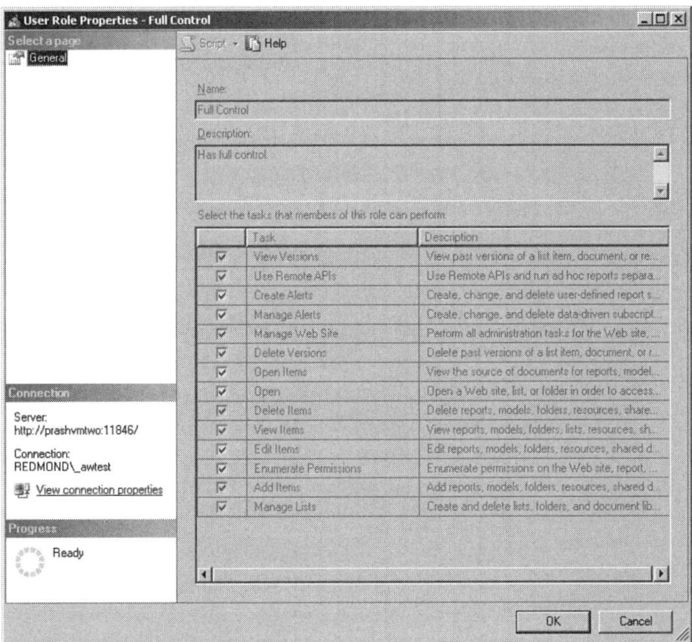

FIGURE 34.5 SSMS security permissions for Report Server in SharePoint integrated mode.

Administration and Management Pages

SharePoint site pages for Report Server administration and report management tasks are added as part of the SSRS add-in for SharePoint.

Figure 34.6 shows the location of the administration pages for Report Server integration. Information about each page is discussed in Chapter 33, "SharePoint Mode Administration."

Figure 34.7 shows some of the menu options for reports that launch relevant management pages. Information about each page is discussed in Chapter 36, "Managing Reports in SharePoint."

Report-Authoring Tools

Reporting Services authoring tools include the following:

- **Report Designer:** Available in BIDS
- **Report Model Designer:** Also in BIDS

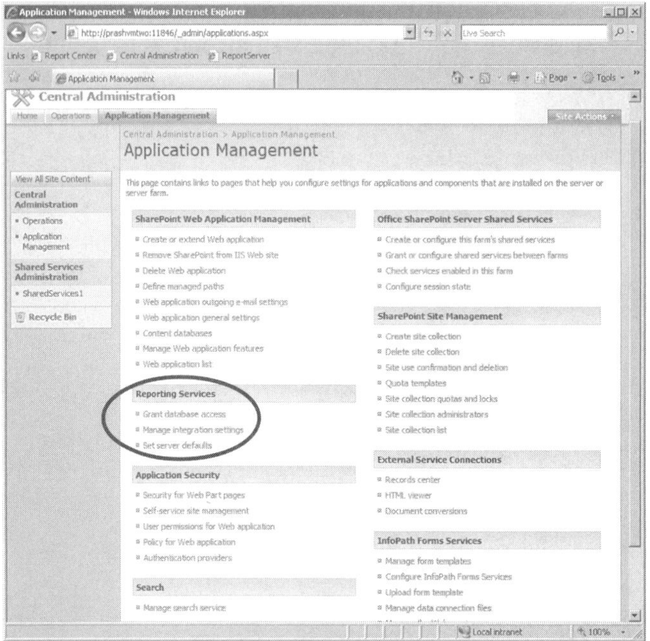

FIGURE 34.6 SharePoint administration pages for Report Server integration.

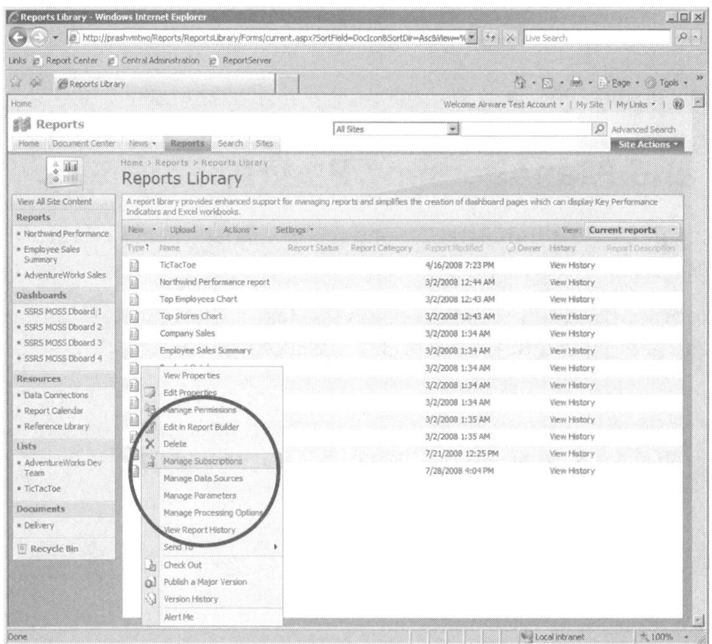

FIGURE 34.7 Report management menu options in a SharePoint document library.

- **Report Builder:** Launched from the SharePoint site and covered in Chapter 37, "Ad Hoc Reporting in SharePoint"

These tools continue to be the primary tools for development of reports, models, and data sources. In native mode, when report development is completed, the developer publishes the report to the Report Server. The difference for SharePoint mode is that the report or model is published to a desired SharePoint library.

A SharePoint library contains documents or folders. Reports, report models, shared data sources, and external images are treated like documents and get stored in SharePoint libraries. SSRS automatically takes care of syncing up SSRS report items from the SharePoint content database to the SSRS Report Server database.

Develop or edit your report or model in BIDS just like you are used to. The only difference is the deployment step. Right-click the project in the Solutions Explorer in BIDS, choose Properties, and specify the target SharePoint reports library site location (see Figure 34.8).

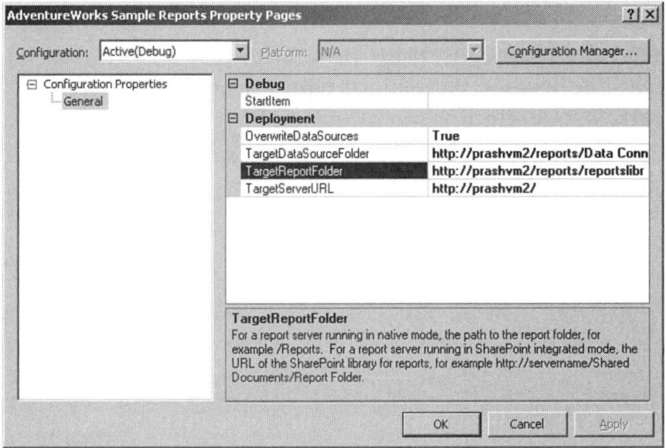

FIGURE 34.8 Publishing reports from BIDS to a SharePoint document library.

As shown in Figure 34.8, the SharePoint library location needs to be specified via a full URL. By default, on WSS 3.0, the library appears after the server name (for example, http://*servername*/Documents), whereas on MOSS 2007, the library appears after the site and subsite (for example, http://*servername*/*site*/Documents). Of course, this can vary based on how you set up your MOSS URLs.

NOTE

Relative paths cannot be used for deployment to SharePoint sites. In fact, deployment will update references to report data sources and images in the Report Definition Language (RDL) file to use absolute paths.

Remember that reports, data sources, and report models are just like another SharePoint document. Therefore, you may also choose to directly upload your RDL file to the document library by using SharePoint site actions (just like you would add an Excel or Word document). The difference between this approach and publishing directly from report-authoring tools is that the tools validate report items before publishing to SharePoint, whereas direct upload does no validation and you will find out whether there are any problems with the report only when you try to run or manage it.

Summary

Most SSRS tools function the same way with Report Server in SharePoint integrated mode as with Report Server in native mode. The primary difference is that Report Manager is replaced by the SharePoint site as the tool for viewing and managing reports in SharePoint integrated mode.

The Reporting Services Configuration tool allows creation of a Report Server database in SharePoint integrated mode. SQL Server Management Studio allows jobs, schedules, and Report Server properties management for Report Server in SharePoint integrated mode. Standard SSRS report-authoring tools continue to be used for report development and enable you to publish report items to SharePoint document libraries.

CHAPTER 35

Viewing Reports in SharePoint

IN THIS CHAPTER

- Report Viewer Web Part
- Connect the Report Viewer Web Part with Other SharePoint Web Parts
- URL Access Parameters
- Viewing Reports with SharePoint 2.0 Web Parts

Reporting Services integration with SharePoint enables reports to be uploaded to SharePoint document libraries. See Figure 30.1 in Chapter 30, "Reporting Services Integration with SharePoint," for a view of a reports document library in a SharePoint site. This chapter focuses on all the ways reports can be viewed from SharePoint.

Reports can be viewed in a full page of the browser or as part of SharePoint dashboards.

Reporting Services add-in for SharePoint installs a Report Viewer web part to SharePoint that is used to view and run reports. This web part is configured to have a file association with Report Definition Language (RDL) files so that reports are automatically opened in the Report Viewer web part in SharePoint.

If you click a report from a SharePoint document library, it will automatically open in full-page view. This means the browser page shows up with the Report Viewer web part as the only control on the page. One of the examples in Chapter 30 shows a report in full-page view (see Figure 30.2).

Reports can also be viewed as part of SharePoint dashboards. Developers can add multiple reports or a mix of reports and other objects in dashboards by placing a Report Viewer web part in each location of the dashboard where they want to run a report. Figures 35.4 and 35.5 show examples of reports running in dashboards.

One way to customize the default report-viewing experience in a SharePoint site is to use URL access parameters to change default report parameter values or to change the default report-viewer rendering experience in the full-page view of the report. This is a newly supported feature in SSRS 2008 and is discussed in this chapter.

Finally, it is possible to view reports in SharePoint without using the SharePoint integrated mode deployment option. Table 30.1 in Chapter 30 lists the alternative option of deploying Report Server in native mode but using the SharePoint 2.0 web parts. The mechanics of how to do that are addressed in this chapter.

Report Viewer Web Part

The Report Viewer web part gets installed through the Reporting Services add-in for SharePoint setup package and is named `ReportViewer.dwp`. It is a custom SharePoint web part wrapper around the traditional `ReportViewer` control that supports viewing and printing reports, navigating to different pages, and exporting the report to other formats. Figure 35.1 highlights the drop-down menu options for actions on the web part, such as Print and Export.

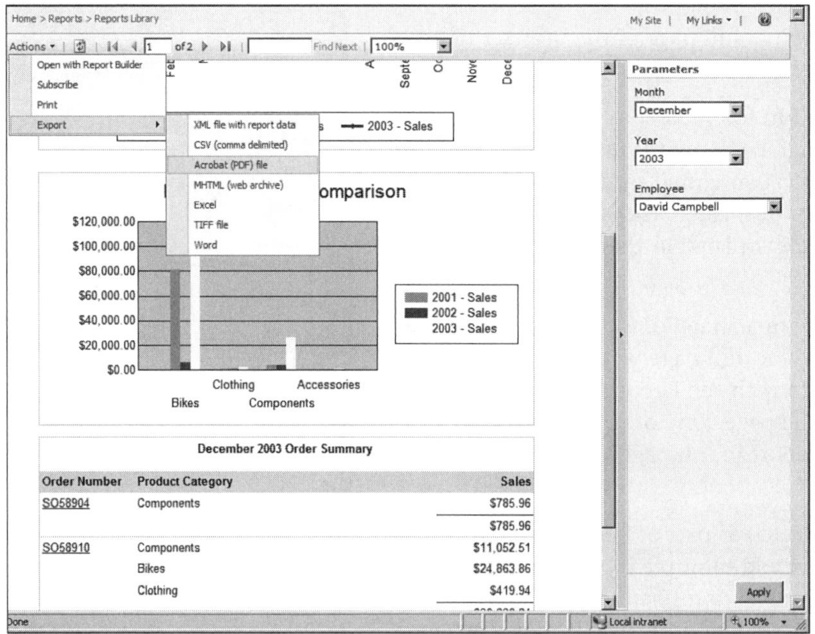

FIGURE 35.1 Report Viewer web part for SharePoint.

To add the Report Viewer web part to a dashboard page, launch the Add Web Parts Wizard and expand the All Web Parts Miscellaneous section to find the SQL Server Reporting Services Report Viewer web part (see Figure 35.2).

Report Viewer web part properties can be customized to control the appearance and features available on the toolbar and the view areas. Some of the properties are general

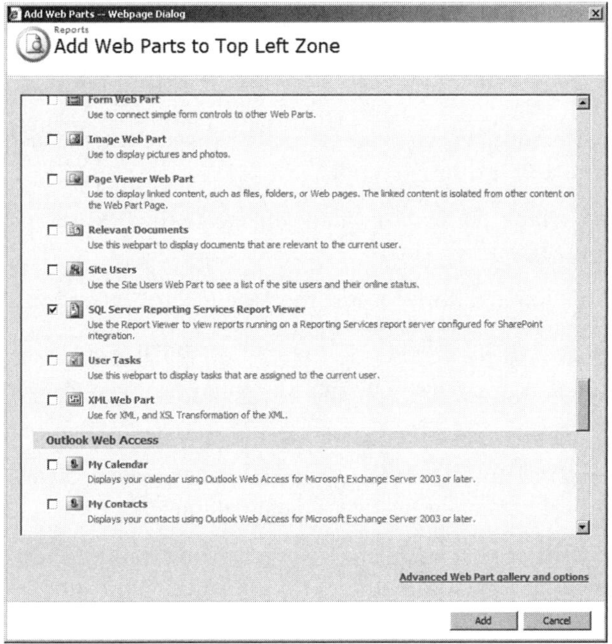

FIGURE 35.2 Adding the Report Viewer web part to a SharePoint dashboard.

SharePoint web part properties such as title, height, width, chrome type, and zone; others are specific to the Report Viewer web part. Figure 35.3 shows the Report Viewer properties.

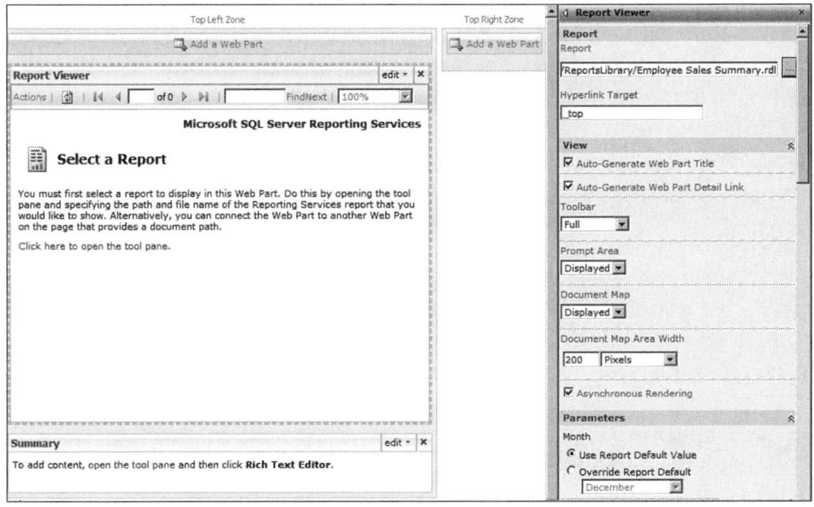

FIGURE 35.3 Report Viewer web part properties.

Here are some of the notable properties:

- **Report:** Specifies the URL for the report on the SharePoint site that is to be run in the web part.
- **Hyperlink Target:** Specifies standard HTML for how to display linked content, such as another report referenced from a drill-through report.
- **Auto-Generate Title and Link check boxes:** Automatically create the title for Report Viewer and a link for launching the report.
- **Toolbar:** Options to show the full toolbar, none, or just the page navigation options.
- **Prompt Area:** Choose whether to display, collapse, or hide the parameters area.
- **Document Map Area:** Choose whether to display, collapse, or hide the Document Map area.
- **Parameters:** If there are parameters defined for the reports, a Load Parameters button retrieves them, and you can set the default value for each parameter.

It is that simple to add a report to a dashboard. If you want to, you can add multiple reports to the dashboard or mix and match by adding different types of web parts in different parts of the page.

Connect the Report Viewer Web Part with Other SharePoint Web Parts

If you are integrating SSRS with MOSS 2007 Enterprise Edition, you can connect the Report Viewer web part to the SharePoint Filter web part or the SharePoint Documents web part.

By connecting with the Filter web part, users can pick filter values in a Filter web part, which are then sent as parameter values to reports in the Report Viewer web part. The report must have parameters defined for it that are compatible with the values, data type, and format sent by the Filter web part. To set this up, pick Connections from the drop-down menu of edit on the Filter web part, and pick Send Filter Values To and select the appropriate report in the dashboard. Figure 35.4 shows an example of a Date Filter web part connected to two reports that require date parameters. Figure 35.5 shows an example of a Date Filter web part connected to a Report web part and an Excel web part.

By connecting with the Documents web part, users can click reports in the documents library and view the report in an adjacent Report Viewer web part. This can be done by selecting Connections from the Edit menu on the Report Viewer web part and selecting Get Report Definitions From and connecting to a Documents web part on the dashboard. Figure 35.6 shows such a dashboard.

NOTE

If you need more help with connecting Report Viewer web part to the Filter or Documents web parts, see http://technet.microsoft.com/en-us/library/bb283248.aspx.

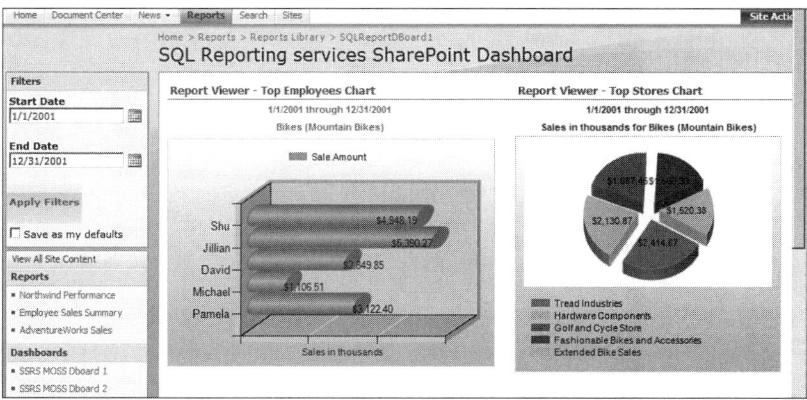

FIGURE 35.4 Filter web part connected to Report Viewer web parts in a SharePoint dashboard.

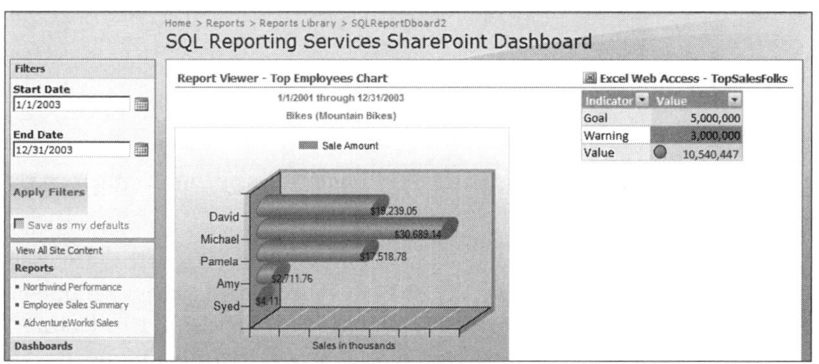

FIGURE 35.5 Filter web part connected to a Report Viewer web part and an Excel web part in a SharePoint dashboard.

URL Access Parameters

URL access to the Report Server is a way to access individual reports in a customized fashion. URL requests contain parameters that are processed by the Report Server and impact how the URL request will be handled.

There are several types of parameters that can be sent via the URL:

- Parameters for Report Server commands are prefixed with `rs:` and can be used to specify properties such as the rendering export format or the history snapshot to use for running the report.
- Parameters for the HTML Viewer are prefixed with `rc:` and can be used to specify properties such as style sheet and visibility of toolbar and parameters.
- Parameters specific to the SharePoint Report Viewer web part are prefixed with `rv:` and can be used to specify properties such as Document Map area width and visibility of the toolbar and Header area.

35

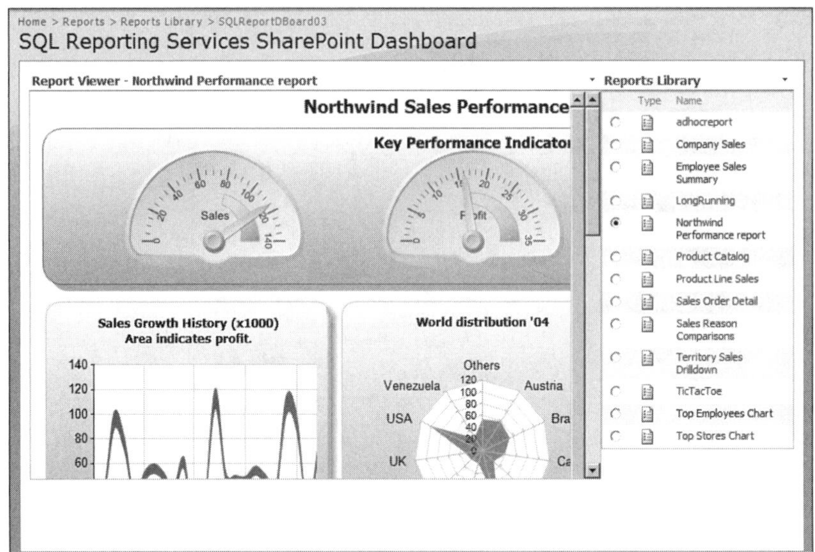

FIGURE 35.6 Documents web part connected to a Report Viewer web part.

For more information about using URL access parameters, refer to http://msdn.microsoft.com/en-us/library/ms152835.aspx.

We just looked at using URL access parameters against Report Server URL paths. There is an additional feature that has been added in SSRS 2008 to support URL access parameters against SharePoint document library URL paths. The key intent behind this feature is to allow specifying nondefault report parameter values when rendering a report in full-page view.

When a report is rendered in full-page view in SharePoint, the URL is displayed in the following format:

```
http://<SharePoint_site>/_layouts/ReportServer/RSViewerPage.aspx?rv:
➥RelativeReportUrl=/<SharePoint_Document_Library>/<Report_Name>.rdl
```

In SSRS 2008, you can specify a report parameter name and value pair by explicitly specifying the prefix `rp:`. Here is an example to add on a parameter with the name Month that accepts a string value:

```
http://<SharePoint_site>/_layouts/ReportServer/RSViewerPage.aspx?rv:
➥RelativeReportUrl=/<SharePoint_Document_Library>/<Report_Name>.rdl&rp:Month=January
```

You can also specify a fixed set of Report Viewer parameters to alter the full-page rendering experience. These Report Viewer parameters need to be explicitly prefixed by rv:. Here is an example of rendering the report with the Parameters area collapsed:

```
http://<SharePoint_site>/_layouts/ReportServer/RSViewerPage.aspx?rv:
➥RelativeReportUrl=/<SharePoint_Document_Library>/<Report_Name>.
➥rdl&rv:ParamMode=Collapsed&rp:Month=January
```

Here are examples using the AdventureWorks sample reports as if they were stored in a SharePoint document library, http://<SharePoint_site>/Reports/ReportsLibrary.

- Render the AdventureWorks Employee Sales Summary report for Syed Abbas for January / 2004 with theReport Viewer toolbar showing pagination only:

  ```
  http://<SharePoint_site>/Reports/_layouts/ReportServer/RSViewerPage.aspx?rv:
  RelativeReportUrl=/Reports/ReportsLibrary/Employee%20Sales%20Summary.
  ➥rdl&rv:ToolBar=Navigation&rp:EmpID=288&rp:ReportMonth=1&rp:ReportYear=2004
  ```

- Render the AdventureWorks Product Catalog report with the Document Map area collapsed and no Header area:

  ```
  http://<SharePoint_site>/Reports/_layouts/ReportServer/RSViewerPage.aspx?rv:
  RelativeReportUrl=/Reports/ReportsLibrary/Product%20Catalog.
  ➥rdl&rv:HeaderArea=None&rv:DocMapMode=Collapsed
  ```

Table 35.1 lists Report Viewer parameters and their values for controlling full-page report rendering.

TABLE 35.1 Report Viewer Parameters

Report Viewer Parameter	Description	Values
rv:HeaderArea	Control how the Report Viewer web part's header is displayed in full-page view	Full, None Default: Full
rv:ToolBar	Control how the Report Viewer web part's toolbar is displayed in full-page view	Full, Navigation, None Default: Full
rv:ParamMode	Control how the Report Viewer web part's header is displayed in full-page view	Full, Collapsed, Hidden Default: Full
rv:AsyncRender	Control whether the report is rendered asynchronously or synchronously	true, false. Default: true
rv:DocMapAreaWidth	Control the display width in pixels of the Report Viewer web part's Document Map area	Non-negative integer
rv:DocMapMode	Control the display of the Document Map area of a report	Displayed, Collapsed, Hidden Default: Displayed

Viewing Reports with SharePoint 2.0 Web Parts

Table 30.1 in Chapter 30 lists the alternative option of deploying Report Server in native mode but using the SharePoint 2.0 web parts to view reports in SharePoint. These are the Report Explorer and Report Viewer web parts that have been included with SSRS since SSRS 2000 SP2 release. These web parts were originally created to work against SharePoint 2.0 and got their name accordingly. After installation of SSRS, these web parts are available from `\Program Files\Microsoft SQL Server\100\Tools\Reporting Services\SharePoint\RSWebParts.cab`.

NOTE

There is potential for some name-related confusion with the SharePoint 2.0 Report web parts. Even though they are called 2.0 web parts, they can work against WSS 3.0 and MOSS 2007, too. Another potential for confusion is with the name of Report Viewer web part, which is one of the two SharePoint 2.0 Report web parts. This is a different web part from the Report Viewer web part that is included in the SharePoint RS add-in and used in the SharePoint integrated mode.

The Report Explorer web part is used to explore the Report Server folder hierarchy. It connects to Report Manager on the Report Server computer and allows browsing available reports. Access to individual items and folders throughout the Report Server folder hierarchy are controlled through role assignments on the Report Server. When you select a report, it opens in a new browser window and uses the HTML viewer on the Report Server to display the report.

The Report Viewer web part can be added to a SharePoint web part page to show a specific report or you can connect it to Report Explorer to display reports that are opened through that web part.

Instructions for installing and using these web parts are available at http://msdn.microsoft.com/en-us/library/ms159772.aspx.

Summary

Reports can be run and viewed in SharePoint via the Report Viewer web part, which gets installed as part of the SSRS add-in for SharePoint. Reports can be launched in full-page view or be run as part of SharePoint dashboards. For MOSS 2007 environments, the Report Viewer web part can be connected to other SharePoint web parts, such as the Filter web part and the Documents web part.

Starting with SSRS 2008, URL access parameters are supported by Report Server in SharePoint integrated mode, which helps when integrating with custom web applications.

CHAPTER 36

Managing Reports in SharePoint

IN THIS CHAPTER

- Managing Properties
- Managing Permissions
- Managing Data Sources
- Managing Parameters
- Managing Report Processing Options
- Managing Report History
- Managing Shared Schedules
- Managing Subscriptions
- SharePoint Document Management

Reports get published to the SharePoint document library via report-authoring tools or simply get uploaded as a Report Definition Language (RDL) file. Once reports are available in the SharePoint document library, various menu options allow interaction with the integrated Report Server to manage report capabilities such as subscriptions, report history, parameters, and report-processing options (see Figure 36.1).

In a similar fashion, report data sources and report models, which are treated as documents, have associated menu options (see Figure 36.2 and Figure 36.3).

All the management actions are being done via the SharePoint UI. However, the underlying functionality of report management remains the same as native mode.

As you read in Chapter 31, "SSRS SharePoint Integration Architecture," reports, report models, and report data sources are treated as SharePoint documents. These get stored in the SharePoint Content database and synchronized with Report Server database. What about all of the additional Report Server capabilities, such as subscriptions, report history, parameters, and report-processing options? Such report metadata is stored only in the SSRS Report Server catalog.

The RS add-in for SharePoint added a proxy to communicate with Report Server using a Simple Object Access Protocol (SOAP) web service. Therefore, all the report management can happen from the SharePoint UI. The proxy just asks Report Server to update its report metadata via SOAP calls.

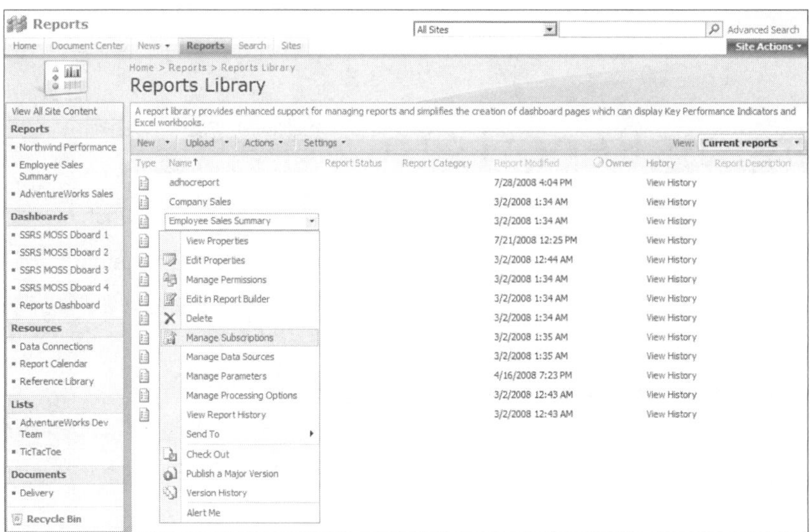

FIGURE 36.1 Report management menu options in SharePoint.

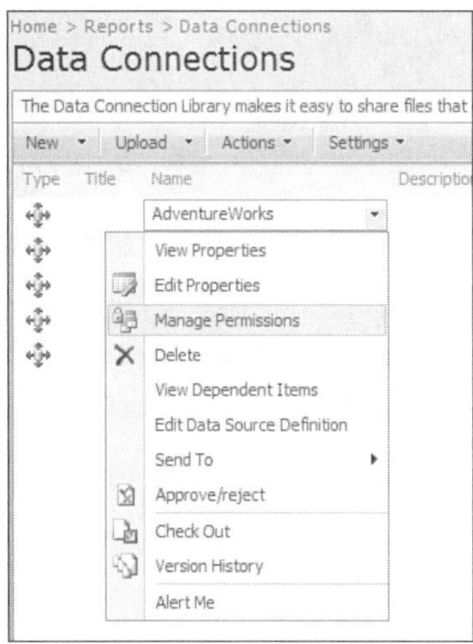

FIGURE 36.2 Report data source menu options in SharePoint.

Managing Properties

View Properties and Edit Properties options are available to manage basic document-level properties for selected reports, report data sources, or report models. Figure 36.4 shows an example of document properties for a report.

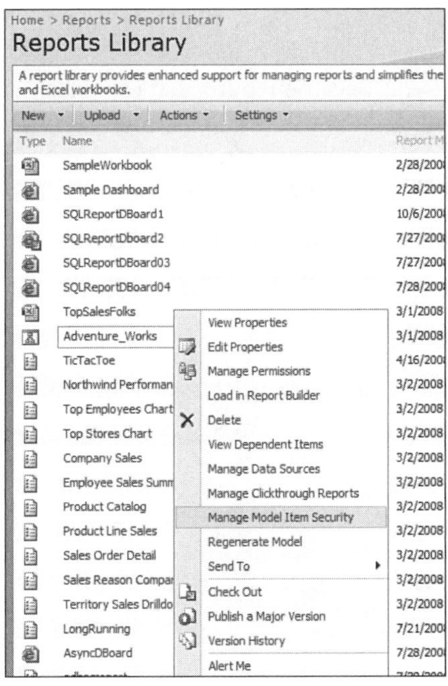

FIGURE 36.3 Report model menu options in SharePoint.

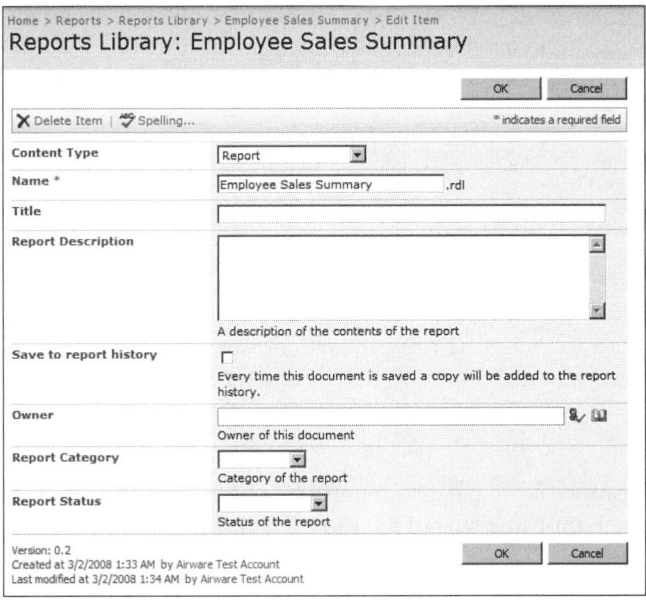

FIGURE 36.4 SharePoint document properties for a report.

Managing Permissions

Existing SharePoint site permissions apply to report items because reports, data sources, and models are fundamentally the same as SharePoint documents. See the sections on security and permissions in Chapter 33, "SharePoint Mode Administration," for information about how each SharePoint permission maps to Report Server permissions.

Permissions are inherited from the parent site but can be customized for each report, model, or data source. To manage permissions, click the report item and select Manage Permissions from the list of menu options.

You can select an action to Edit Permissions (see Figure 36.5) to create customized permissions for the report. This breaks inheritance, and future changes to permissions for the parent site are not applied to the report item.

FIGURE 36.5 Customize permissions for report items.

If you choose to customize permissions for a report item, you can add new users, edit existing user permissions, or go back to inheriting from the parent (see Figure 36.6).

Managing Data Sources

Report data sources specify the location of the data for reports via connection strings and security credentials. Reports can be built using shared data sources or a custom data source that is only used for the selected report.

To add a shared data source, you can navigate to the document library that will contain data sources (for example, the Data Connections library) and pick the document library menu option to create new report data source.

FIGURE 36.6 User permissions for report items.

To manage a data source for a single report, click Manage Data Sources on the menu option for the report. You can select a shared data source (see Figure 36.7) or create a new custom data source (see Figure 36.8).

Home > Reports > Reports Library > Employee Sales Summary > Manage Data Sources > Data Source

AdventureWorks: Employee Sales Summary

Warning: this page is not encrypted for secure communication. User names, passwords, and any other information will be sent in clear text. For more information, contact your administrator.

Use this page to edit the data source connection information used by this report or model.

OK Cancel

Connection Type
Specify whether connection information is specific to this report or shared with other reports.

A shared data source can be shared by this report and other reports or models.

Shared data source
Custom data source

Data Source Link *
Select the shared data source file to use with this report.

ports/Data Connections/AdventureWorks.rsds

OK Cancel

FIGURE 36.7 Manage data sources for a selected report: shared data source.

Managing Parameters

Parameters are defined when a report is created to filter data based on input values. To change parameter values or properties, select the report and choose Manage Parameters from the menu. You can change existing parameters, but you cannot add or remove parameters. To add or remove parameters for a report, you must change the report definition.

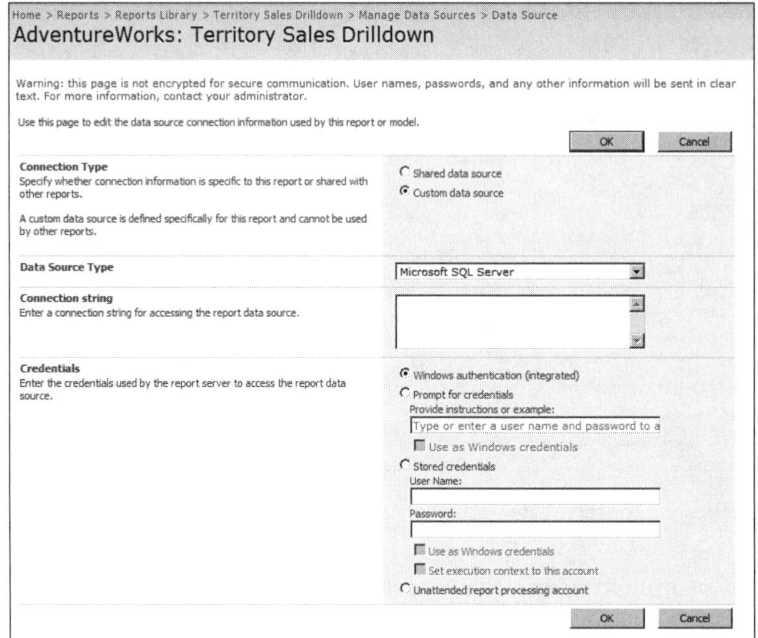

FIGURE 36.8 Manage data sources for a selected report: custom data source.

To manage an existing parameter, click the parameter name to view these parameter properties (see Figure 36.9):

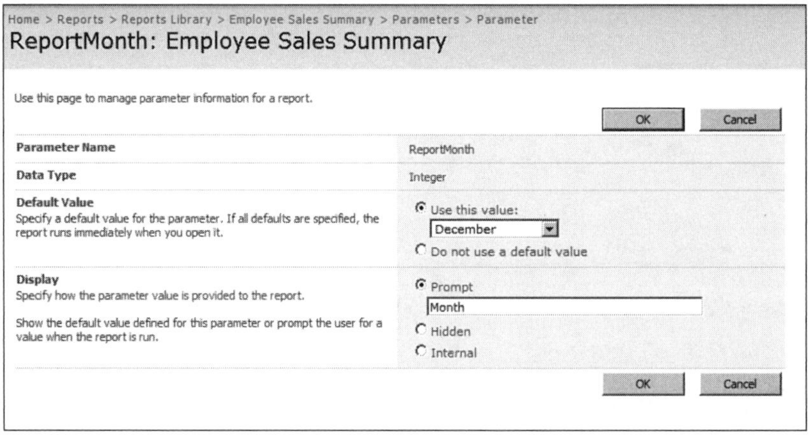

Home > Reports > Reports Library > Employee Sales Summary > Parameters > Parameter
ReportMonth: Employee Sales Summary
Use this page to manage parameter information for a report.
OK Cancel
Parameter Name — ReportMonth
Data Type — Integer
Default Value — Specify a default value for the parameter. If all defaults are specified, the report runs immediately when you open it. — Use this value: December; Do not use a default value
Display — Specify how the parameter value is provided to the report. Show the default value defined for this parameter or prompt the user for a value when the report is run. — Prompt: Month; Hidden; Internal
OK Cancel

FIGURE 36.9 Manage report parameters.

- **Parameter Name:** The name of the parameter as it is defined in the report. This property is set during report definition.

- **Data Type:** The type of data expected by the parameter. This property is set during report definition.
- **Default Value:** Set a default value to use or leave it blank. The domain of values is specified during report definition.
- **Display:** Pick how you would like the parameter to prompt the user for a value, or let it be hidden or internal.

Managing Report Processing Options

Report Server provides processing options to cache reports and to save snapshots of report executions. These report results can be used to view the report execution from a particular time as opposed to processing the report every time someone wants to view the report. The snapshots can be refreshed periodically, and timeouts can be set to ensure that report processing doesn't use up computing resources for long periods of time.

To set processing options, you can select the report, and then select Manage Processing Options from the menu.

Figure 36.10 shows the various options that are available:

- **Data Refresh Options:** Pick how the selected report get its data:
  - **Use Live Data:** Query the data source for the latest data.
  - **Use Cached Data:** If cache exists, use cached data to run the report. Otherwise, use live data. Cache is maintained based on parameter values selected by the user.

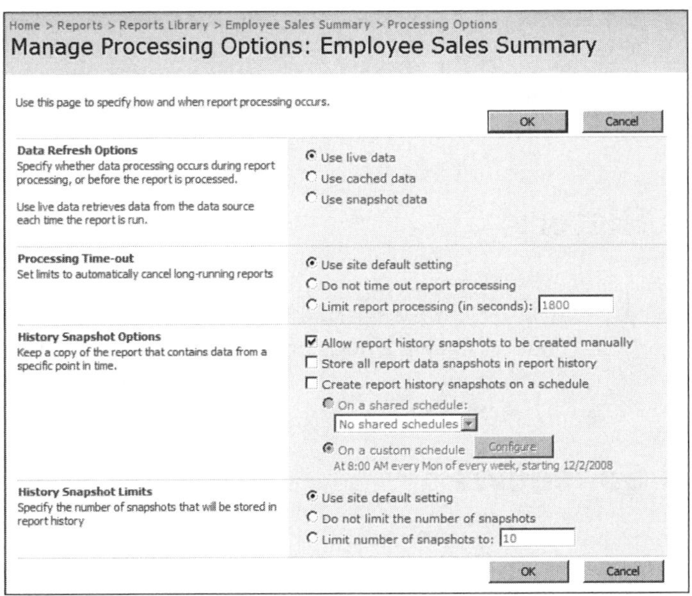

FIGURE 36.10 Manage report-processing options.

    - **Use Snapshot Data:** Use data from the time a snapshot was taken.
- **Processing Time-out:** A timeout to prevent a single report from using too much server resources:
    - **Use Site Default Setting:** Use the timeout setting that is configured in the Set Server Defaults option in the Reporting Services application under the SharePoint Central Administration site.
    - **Do Not Time Out Report Processing:** Run without any time limits.
    - **Limit Report Processing (in seconds):** Run report for the number of seconds specified and then time out.
- **History Snapshot Options:** Select options for how you would like historical report snapshots to be taken and stored:
    - **Allow Report History Snapshots to Be Created Manually:** Allows users to create snapshots on an ad hoc basis for the selected report.
    - **Store All Report Data Snapshots in Report History:** Stores snapshot data in history.
    - **Create Report History Snapshots on a Schedule:** Creates history snapshots at a predefined interval.
- **History Snapshot Limits:** Limit the number of snapshots for the selected report to control storage in server:
    - **Use Site Default Setting:** Use the snapshot limit setting configured under the Set Server Defaults option in the SharePoint Reporting Services application.
    - **Do Not Limit the Number of Snapshots:** Stores snapshot data in history.
    - **Limit the Number of Snapshots To:** Limits the number of snapshots to a specified value.

Managing Report History

Report history shows a list of all snapshots that have been taken for a report. The View Report History menu shows all snapshots taken for the selected report, including the date and time (see Figure 36.11). There is an option to create new snapshots and delete existing ones.

Managing Shared Schedules

A shared schedule allows creation of a schedule that can be used by multiple reports or subscriptions as a trigger to perform actions at a specified time and frequency. Shared schedules can be centrally managed, paused, and resumed.

Home > Reports > Reports Library > Employee Sales Summary > Report History

Report History: Employee Sales Summary

Use this page to manage report history.

Close

New Snapshot | Delete

Date Processed

12/2/2008 7:33 PM

12/2/2008 7:34 PM

Close

FIGURE 36.11 Manage Report History menu.

You must be a site administrator to manage shared schedules on a SharePoint site.

To create shared schedules, click Site Actions at the upper right on the site, pick Site Settings, Modify All Site Settings, and then click Manage Shared Schedules under the Reporting Services section (see Figure 36.12).

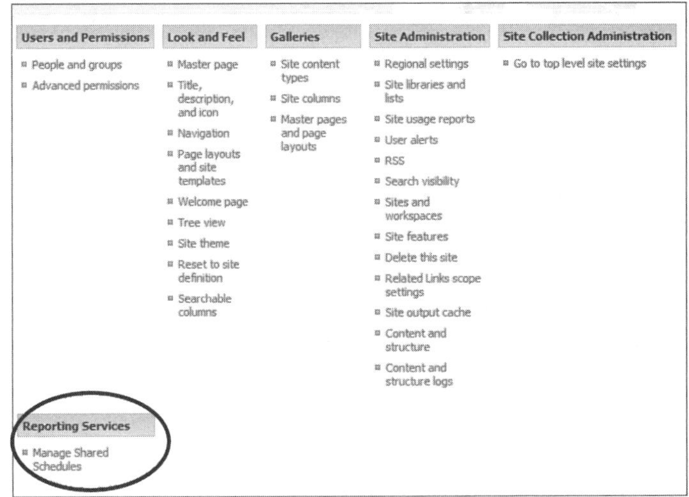

FIGURE 36.12 Manage shared schedules.

Click Add Schedule to create a shared schedule. You can specify a descriptive name, frequency, and a start and end date (see Figure 36.13).

Shared schedules rely on the SQL Server Agent service. Once the schedule is created, reports and subscriptions associated with the schedule are triggered to run in a timely fashion. The

Home > Reports > Manage Shared Schedules > Schedule Properties

Schedule Properties

Use this page to edit schedule properties that are available for report operations on this site.

OK Cancel

Schedule Name — Test_Schedule

Frequency
Define a schedule that runs on an hourly, daily, weekly, monthly, or one-time basis.
Hour / Day / Week / Month (selected) / Once

Schedule
Times are expressed in (GMT-08:00) Pacific Time (US and Canada).
Select Months: Jan, Apr, Jul, Oct, Feb, May, Aug, Nov, Mar, Jun, Sep, Dec (all checked)
On calendar day(s): 1, 3-5
Start time: 8:00 A.M. (selected) P.M.

Start and End Dates
Specify the date to start and optionally end this schedule.
Begin running this schedule on: 12/2/2008
Stop running this schedule on (checked): 12/3/2008

OK Cancel

FIGURE 36.13 Create shared schedules.

shared schedule can be paused or resumed (see Figure 36.14). If it is paused, reports executions associated with the schedule will not get triggered until the schedule is resumed.

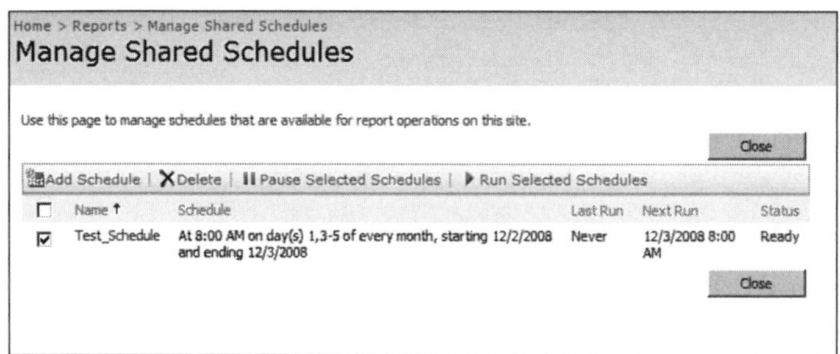

FIGURE 36.14 Pause and resume shared schedules.

Managing Subscriptions

There is a Manage Subscriptions menu option when you select a report from the SharePoint document library. Subscriptions enable you to receive reports through a variety of delivery methods beyond the simple interactive report execution via a browser.

Two types of subscriptions are supported: Standard Subscriptions and Data Driven Subscriptions (New in 2008 for SharePoint integrated mode; see Figure 36.15). Standard subscriptions produce one instance of a report and deliver it to a preconfigured destination. Data-driven subscriptions can produce many report instances and deliver them to multiple destinations dynamically.

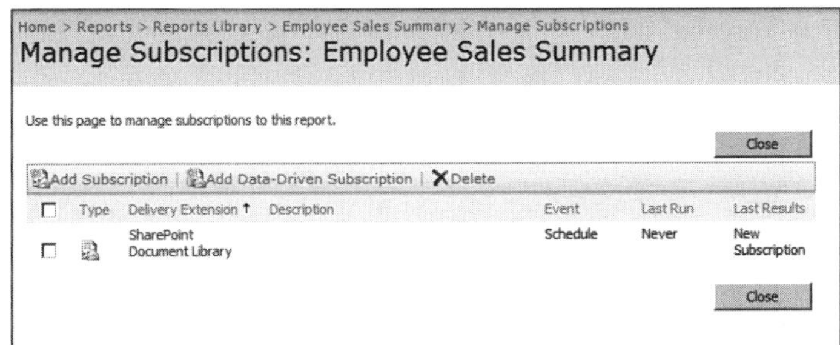

FIGURE 36.15 Manage subscriptions.

Subscription delivery methods include the following:

- **Email:** Send a report via email. You can also configure fields such as To, CC, BCC, and Subject.
- **Windows File Share:** Send a report to a Windows file share with the filename and security credentials.
- **Null Delivery Provider:** Generate subscriptions that preload the report cache. This can help increase report performance.
- **SharePoint Document Library:** Send reports to a specified SharePoint document library.

NOTE

You must configure your report data source to use stored credentials or the unattended report-processing account as a prerequisite to creating subscriptions on the report. The credentials can be a Windows user account or a database user account.

Figure 36.16 shows the UI for creating a standard subscription.

Data-driven subscriptions (DDS) are more powerful and have been enabled for *SharePoint integrated mode* in Reporting Services 2008. DDS provide a way to dynamically filter results, decide on an output format, and generate a list of subscribers at runtime.

The DDS feature is available only in the SQL Server Developer and Enterprise editions and not available in Standard, Web, or Express editions.

Besides report and delivery extension information, a DDS includes information such as the subscriber data source and query to use for generating the dynamic subscription information at runtime.

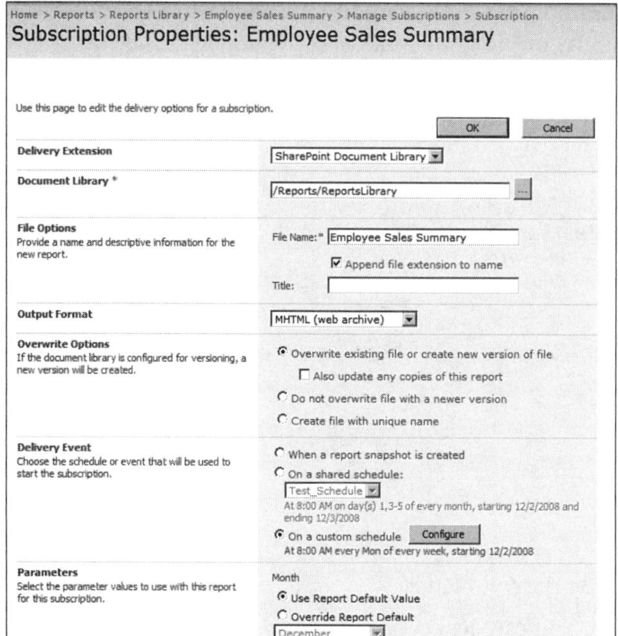

FIGURE 36.16 Standard subscription in SharePoint integrated mode.

Figures 36.17 through 36.20 show the various steps in the SharePoint UI for setting up a DDS from the Create a Data-Driven Subscription option.

Step 1 is to define the data source and query that will provide the dynamic list of recipients, delivery settings, and report parameter values for each recipient.

Step 2 is to specify the parameter values to use with the report subscription. It can be the report default, a static value, or a dynamic value returned from the query specified in step 1.

Step 3 is to specify the delivery options to use with the report subscription, including location and rendering format.

Step 4 is to specify the schedule for delivering the subscription. Delivery time can be based on a shared schedule, customized schedule, or whenever a report snapshot is created.

Once a data driven subscription is created, when you click it to view details in SharePoint, there is a nice summary page that can be used to view and edit the various parts of the subscription, such as data definition, parameters, delivery options, and scheduling info (see Figure 36.21).

SharePoint Document Management

One of the key advantages of SSRS integration with SharePoint is that you can leverage popular SharePoint document management features such as versioning, content approval, alerts, permissions, and workflows.

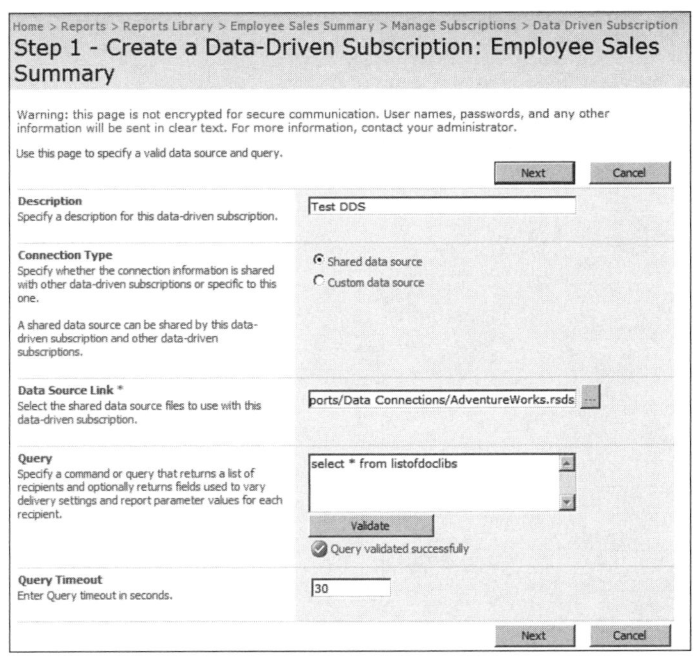

FIGURE 36.17 Create a data-driven subscription in SharePoint integrated mode: Step 1.

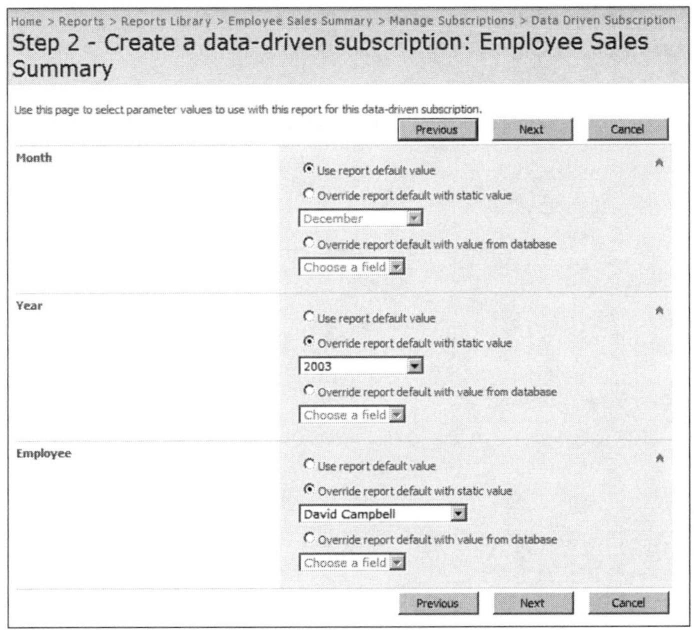

FIGURE 36.18 Create a data-driven subscription in SharePoint integrated mode: Step 2.

Home > Reports > Reports Library > Employee Sales Summary > Manage Subscriptions > Data Driven Subscription
Step 3 - Create a data-driven subscription: Employee Sales Summary
Warning: this page is not encrypted for secure communication. User names, passwords, and any other information will be sent in clear text. For more information, contact your administrator.
Use this page to select delivery options to use with this report for this data-driven subscription.
Previous Next Cancel
Delivery Type
Select a delivery type and configure its delivery options for the data-driven subscription.
SharePoint Document Library
File name *
Specify a static value
EmpSalesSubs.pdf
Select a value from the database
Choose a field
Path *
Specify a static value
Select a value from the database
DocLib
Render Format *
Specify a static value
Acrobat (PDF) file
Select a value from the database
Choose a field
Write mode *
Specify a static value
Overwrite
Select a value from the database
Choose a field
File Extension
Use no value
Specify a static value

FIGURE 36.19 Create a data-driven subscription in SharePoint integrated mode: Step 3.

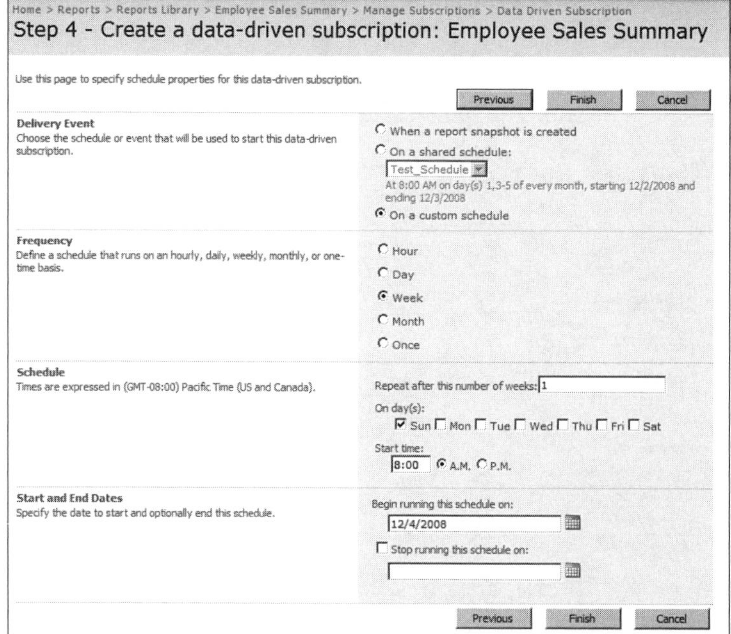

FIGURE 36.20 Create a data-driven subscription in SharePoint integrated mode: Step 4.

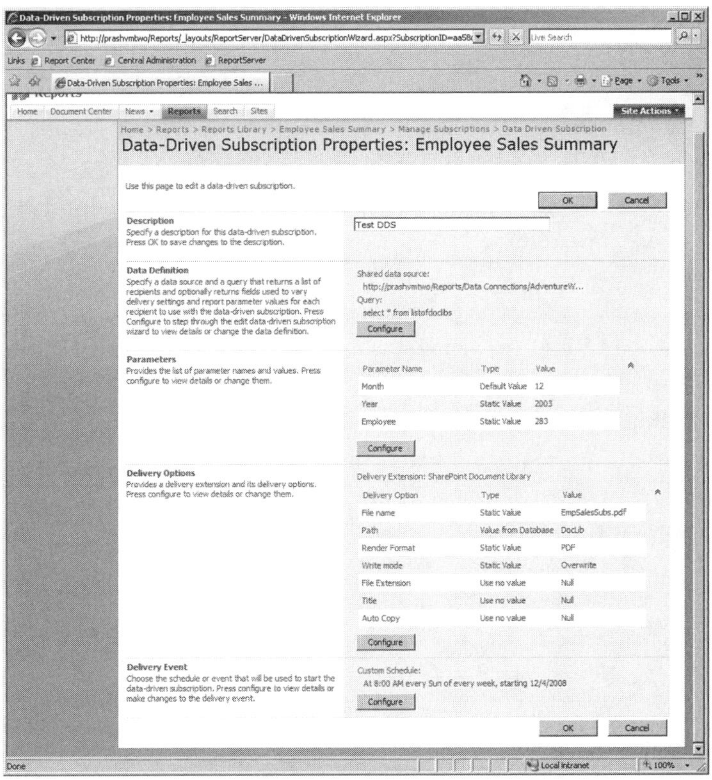

FIGURE 36.21 Create a data-driven subscription in SharePoint integrated mode: Summary.

For example, you can send an alert every time a report definition is updated on the SharePoint site in the same way SharePoint enables you to send alerts when a Word or Excel file is updated.

No wonder that IT departments want to deploy SSRS in SharePoint integrated mode. Users are already trained in uploading, sharing, and securing documents via SharePoint, and they can now treat reports just like any other document and take advantage of SharePoint document management features.

If you are new to SharePoint and want to learn more, you can find a helpful white paper on SharePoint document management at http://go.microsoft.com/fwlink/?LinkID=92638.

Summary

Report management is done in the SharePoint UI via the menu options on reports in the SharePoint document library. These include the management of report properties, permissions, data sources, parameters, processing options, history, schedules, and subscriptions. DDS support has been enabled in SharePoint integrated mode with the Reporting Services 2008 release.

CHAPTER 37

Ad Hoc Reporting in SharePoint

IN THIS CHAPTER

- Report Builder Reports in SharePoint
- Data Sources in SharePoint
- Report Models in SharePoint
- Report Builder 2.0
- Tips for Report Builder Usage

Report Builder is supported in SharePoint integrated mode and can be launched from SharePoint sites to create new reports or to edit existing reports and report models.

By default, SSRS 2008 RTM release shipped with Report Builder 1.0, which relies on building reports on top of models. If you want to use Report Builder 2.0, you can install SQL Server 2008 Service Pack 1 and get 2.0 with Click Once capability. More information is available later in this chapter.

As part of the SSRS add-in for SharePoint installation, new content types for Report Builder Report, Report Model, and Report Data Source are made available to SharePoint. These content types can be added to any document library to enable creating new documents of these types in that library. If you have a new document library that you want to enable with SSRS content types, go to the library settings, select Add from Existing Site Content Types, and select the reporting content types (see Figure 37.1).

When you go to the New menu on the document library, you will now see options to create a new Report Builder Report, Report Data Source, or Report Model (see Figure 37.2).

Thus, the end user is enabled to do ad hoc reporting by creating data sources, models, and Report Builder reports directly on the SharePoint site.

NOTE

With SSRS integration, the correct menu option in the SharePoint document library for creating new ad hoc reports is called New Report Builder Report.

Do not get confused by a default New Report menu item that shows up in SharePoint Reports Center. It is a SharePoint-specific concept, and it does not refer to SSRS reports. Instead, use the New Report Builder Report menu option for your ad hoc reporting needs.

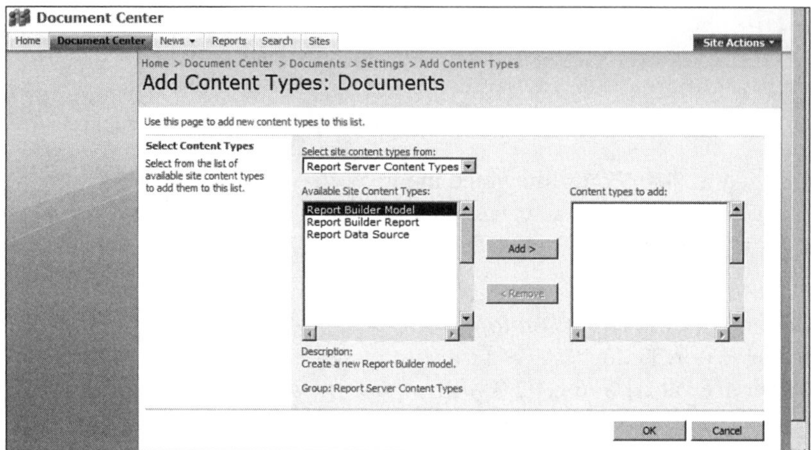

FIGURE 37.1 Add SSRS content types to a SharePoint document library.

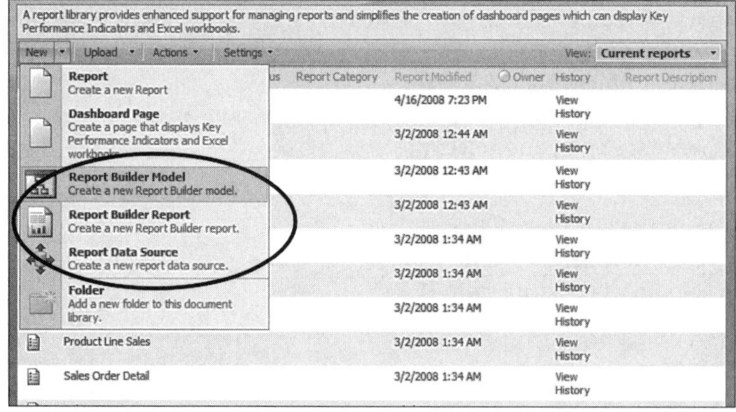

FIGURE 37.2 New menu options for report items in a SharePoint document library.

Report Builder Reports in SharePoint

When the New Report Builder Report menu option is selected, it will start the download of a click-once Report Builder application from the Report Server in SharePoint Integrated mode (see Figure 37.3).

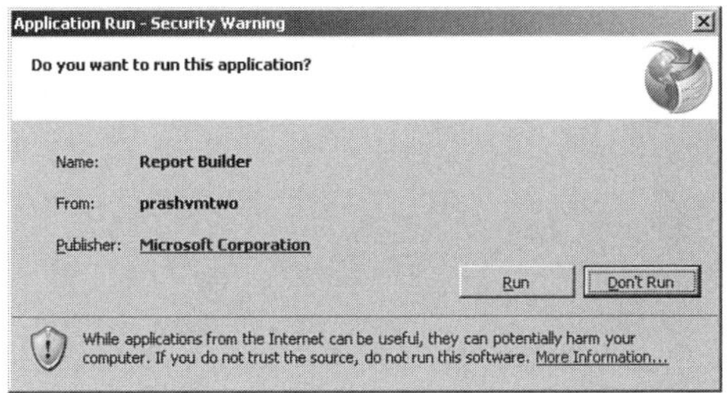

FIGURE 37.3 Click-once installation of Report Builder from Report Server.

With SSRS 2008, Report Server has a property setting called `ReportBuilderLaunchURL`. Based on the value of this property set by the administrator, the Report Builder 1.0 or Report Builder 2.0 application may get downloaded for the end user. Report Builder 1.0 reports need to be created against report models, whereas Report Builder 2.0 reports can be created from scratch. Figure 37.4 shows a new Report Builder 1.0 report being created against an existing report model.

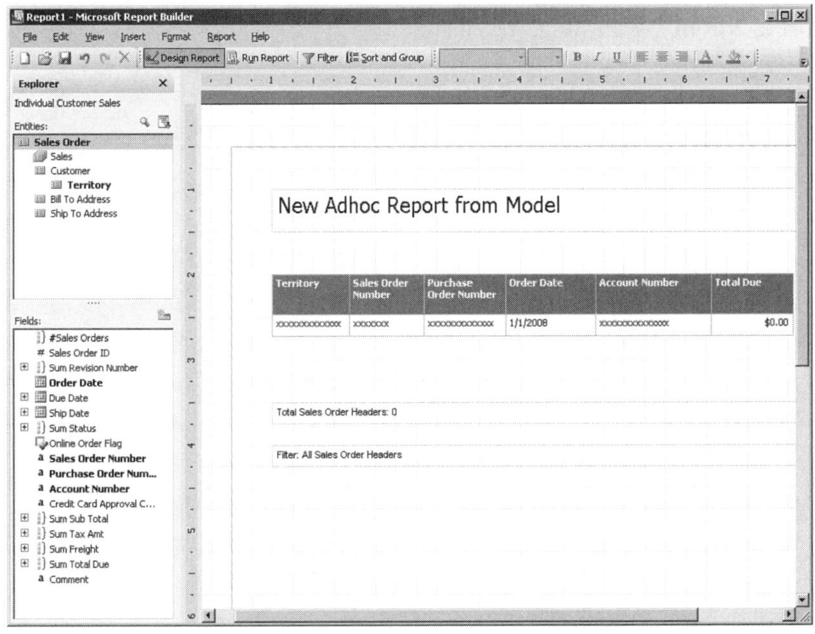

FIGURE 37.4 Report Builder 1.0 launched from SharePoint to create an ad hoc report.

After the report has been developed, the Save option allows publishing the report directly to the SharePoint document library as an RDL file (see Figure 37.5).

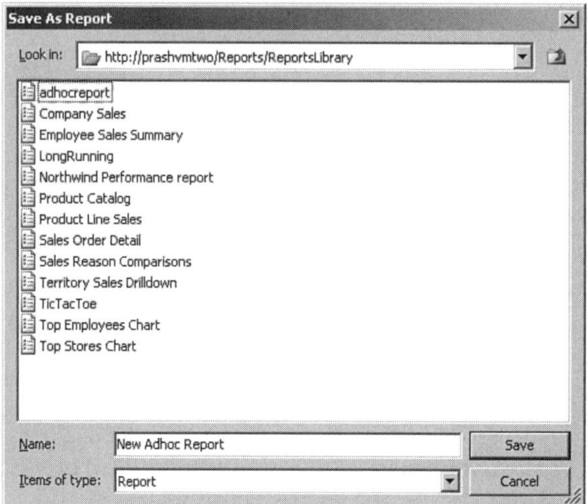

FIGURE 37.5 Save the Report Builder report by publishing to a SharePoint document library.

In the same spirit, reports that are already published on the SharePoint document library can be opened in Report Builder for editing and then be resaved. This is done by selecting a report and choosing Edit in Report Builder (see Figure 37.6).

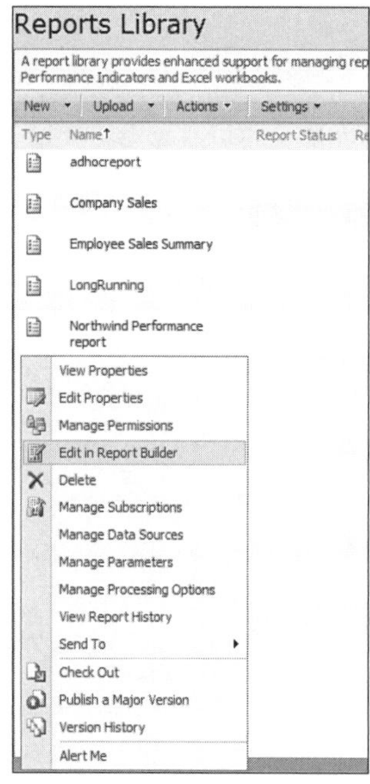

FIGURE 37.6 Edit a report from a SharePoint document library in Report Builder.

Data Sources in SharePoint

An RSDS file represents a report data source, and it is generally created via Report Designer or Model Designer, from where it can be published to a SharePoint library. A new shared data source can also be created directly from the SharePoint document library. Figure 37.2 showed the Report Data Source option available on a SharePoint document library. This brings up a SharePoint page for creating a shared report data source (see Figure 37.7).

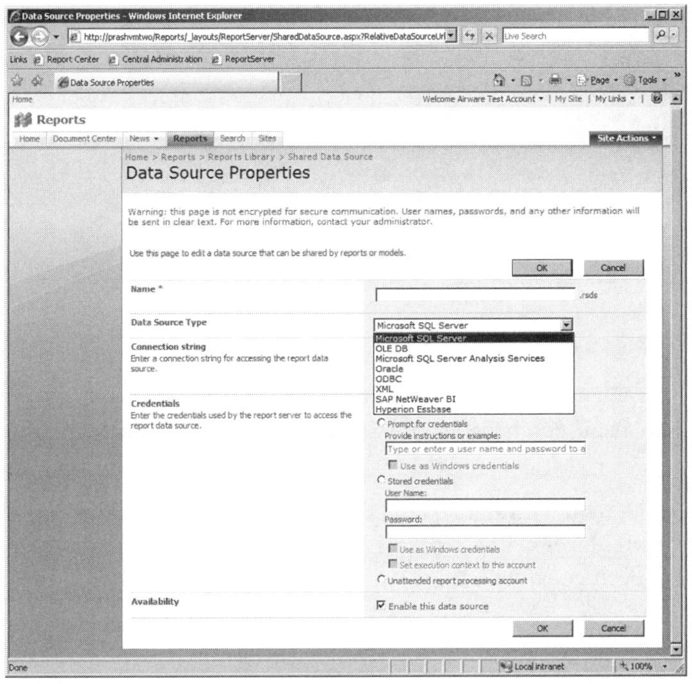

FIGURE 37.7 Create a new report data source from a SharePoint document library.

Note that the SharePoint Data Connections document library is a logical place to save the shared report data sources. However, you can save them in any document library where reporting content types are enabled.

NOTE

It is also possible for reports in SharePoint integrated mode to use Office Data Connection (ODC) files rather than report data sources in limited scenarios (such as connecting to OLE DB or ODBC data sources). If you have existing ODC files that you want to use with reports, be sure to first review the limitations by reading the Microsoft SQL Server Books Online article titled "How to Use an Office Data Connection (.odd) with Reports" at https://technet.microsoft.com/en-us/library/bb326418.aspx.

Report Models in SharePoint

Report Builder 1.0 requires reports to be built on top of report models. An SMDL file represents a Report Builder model, and it is generally created via Model Designer, from where it can be published to a SharePoint library. New Report Builder models can also be created directly from the SharePoint document library. Figure 37.2 showed the Report Builder Model option available on a SharePoint document. This brings up a SharePoint page for creating a model (see Figure 37.8).

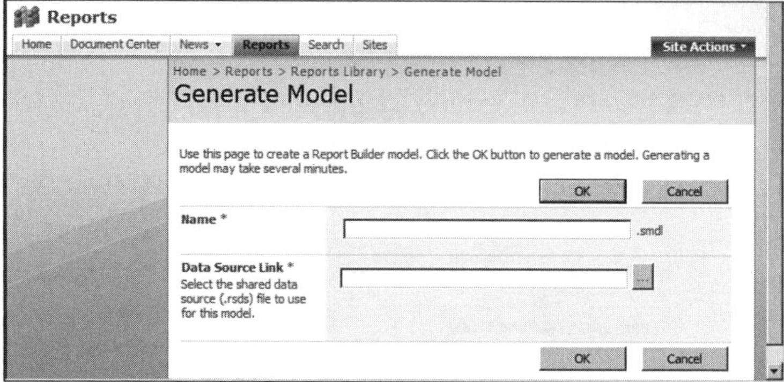

FIGURE 37.8 Create a new Report Builder model from a SharePoint document library.

Creation of a Report Builder model requires a shared data source to be available on the SharePoint site. The rules for the model generation are pretty much hidden from the user's perspective. After the model has been generated, there is an option to regenerate it if needed.

Report Builder 2.0

Report Builder 2.0 delivers an Office-like report-authoring environment and supports most of the report designer functionality found via Business Intelligence Development Studio (BIDS). Chapter 18, "Ad Hoc Reporting," has more information about Report Builder 2.0

If you are using the SSRS 2008 RTM release, you won't find Report Builder 2.0 in the box. It was made available as a web download after the RTM release. The download link is available from www.microsoft.com/sqlserver/2008/en/us/report-builder.aspx.

NOTE

We recommend installation of SQL Server 2008 Service Pack 1 on top of your SSRS 2008 RTM deployment because the service pack includes Reporting Builder 2.0 with Click Once capability. To download the service pack, go to: www.microsoft.com/downloads and search for "SQL Server 2008 Service Pack 1."

There is a new property in SSRS 2008 for Report Server called `ReportBuilderLaunchURL` that can be modified to point to Report Builder 2.0 rather than the default for Report Builder 1.0.

Tips for Report Builder Usage

To enable Report Builder to launch from a SharePoint document library when using forms authentication, follow these steps:

1. Add the following entries to the `Web.config` file for the SharePoint web applications where you want to allow Report Builder to be launched from your reports document libraries:

```
<location path="_vti_bin/ReportBuilder/ReportBuilder.application">
  <system.web>
    <authorization>
      <allow users="*" />
    </authorization>
  </system.web>
</location>
<location path="_vti_bin/ReportBuilder/ReportBuilder.exe.manifest">
  <system.web>
    <authorization>
      <allow users="*" />
    </authorization>
  </system.web>
</location>
<location path="_vti_bin/ReportBuilder/ReportBuilder.chm.deploy">
  <system.web>
    <authorization>
     <allow users="*" />
    </authorization>
  </system.web>
</location>
<location path="_vti_bin/ReportBuilder/ReportBuilder.exe.deploy">
  <system.web>
    <authorization>
      <allow users="*" />
    </authorization>
  </system.web>
</location>
```

2. For non-English sites, ensure that you also add the appropriate LCID and culture entries to the `Web.config` file. For example, to enable launching in Japanese in addition to English, add the following:

```
<location path="_vti_bin/ReportBuilder/1041/ReportBuilder.chm.deploy">
```

37

```
    <system.web>
      <authorization>
        <allow users="*" />
      </authorization>
    </system.web>
  </location>
  <location path="_vti_bin/ReportBuilder/ja/ReportBuilder.resources.dll">
    <system.web>
      <authorization>
        <allow users="*" />
      </authorization>
    </system.web>
  </location>
```

3. For information about LCIDs and cultures supported by the Reporting Services add-in for SharePoint, refer to the Install folder under `%programfiles%\Common Files\Microsoft Shared\web server extensions\12\ISAPI\ReportBuilder`.
4. Enable anonymous access on the ReportBuilder folder via IIS Manager. For more information, see "How to Enable Anonymous Access on the ReportBuilder Folder" at http://msdn.microsoft.com/en-us/library/ms365173(SQL.90).aspx.

If users encounter an `HTTP 401` or `400` error when launching Report Builder with basic authentication, you need to ensure that users select the Remember Password check box when they see the User Credentials dialog box at login time. The root cause is that the login via the User Credentials dialog box results in SharePoint creating a `WSS_KeepSessionAuthenticated` cookie to ensure this user remains authenticated for the duration of the session. Report Builder is launched using click-once, which is not aware of this `WSS_KeepSessionAuthenticated` cookie and results in this error from SharePoint during launch of Report Builder.

Summary

Ad hoc reporting is supported in SharePoint via Report Builder, which enables SharePoint users to create new reports or edit existing reports from the SharePoint document library. Report Builder reports are built on top of data sources and report models.

The SSRS add-in for SharePoint adds new content types on the SharePoint site for reports, report data sources, and Report Builder models. This enables creation and sharing of these report items in the SharePoint document library. These report items can then be used via Report Builder for ad hoc reporting.

APPENDIX A

References and Additional Reading

IN THIS APPENDIX

- MSDN Websites
- SQL Customer Advisory Team Technical Notes
- Microsoft SQL Server 2008 Samples
- SQL Server Reporting Services 2008 Forum
- Blogs
- White Papers
- SharePoint Integration Links
- Additional Books

MSDN Websites

- Microsoft SQL Server 2008 Books Online

  http://msdn.microsoft.com/en-us/sqlserver/cc514207.aspx

- MSDN aggregator page for SQL Server Reporting Services (has links to newsgroups, blogs, white papers, videos, and tutorials)

  http://msdn.microsoft.com/en-us/sqlserver/cc511478.aspx

SQL Customer Advisory Team Technical Notes

http://sqlcat.com/

Search for "Reporting Services" to find gems such as the following:

- Scaling Up Reporting Services 2008 vs. Reporting Services 2005: Lessons Learned
- Reporting Services Scale-Out Deployment Best Practices
- Reporting Services Performance Optimizations
- Reporting Services Scale-Out Architecture
- New Best Practices Articles Published - Scaling Up Reporting Services 2008 vs. Reporting Services 2005: Lessons Learned

- Report Server Catalog Best Practices
- Technet Webcast: Building SQL Server Reporting Services 2008 Large-Scale Solutions (Level 400)

Microsoft SQL Server 2008 Samples

www.codeplex.com/MSFTRSProdSamples/Release/ProjectReleases.aspx?ReleaseId=18649

SQL Server Reporting Services 2008 Forum

If you get stuck, you can get your questions answered at http://social.msdn.microsoft.com/Forums/en-US/sqlreportingservices/threads/.

Blogs

- SSRS Team blog

  http://blogs.msdn.com/sqlrsteamblog/
- Report Engine, report design blog

  http://blogs.msdn.com/robertbruckner
- SharePoint integration blog

  http://blogs.msdn.com/prash
- Report Server, report management, security blogs

  http://blogs.msdn.com/lukaszp

  http://blogs.msdn.com/jgalla

  http://blogs.msdn.com/jameswu/
- Data visualization blogs

  http://blogs.msdn.com/seanboon

  http://blogs.msdn.com/alexgor/
- Architect's blog

  http://blogs.msdn.com/chrishays
- Report Builder PM blog

  http://blogs.msdn.com/bobmeyers
- Rendering PM blog

  http://blogs.msdn.com/chrisbal

- Former group program manager's blog

  http://blogs.msdn.com/bwelcker

- BI consultant blog

  http://blogs.msdn.com/bimusings

White Papers

- *SQL Server 2008 Reporting Services Overview*

  http://download.microsoft.com/download/a/c/d/acd8e043-d69b-4f09-bc9e-4168b65aaa71/RSinSQL2008.doc

- *SQL Server 2005 Integration with Microsoft SharePoint Products and Technologies*

  http://technet.microsoft.com/en-us/library/bb969100.aspx

- *Using SQL Server 2008 Reporting Services with SAP NetWeaver Business Intelligence*

  http://msdn.microsoft.com/en-us/library/cc974473.aspx

- *Using SQL Server 2008 Reporting Services with.NET Framework Data Provider for Teradata*

  http://msdn.microsoft.com/en-us/library/dd182005.aspx

- *Reporting Services: Using XML and Web Service Data Sources*

  http://msdn.microsoft.com/en-us/library/aa964129(SQL.90).aspx

- *Extending SQL Server Reporting Services with SQL CLR Table-Valued Functions*

  http://msdn.microsoft.com/en-us/library/cc655659(SQL.90).aspx

- *Using SQL Server 2005 Reporting Services with Hyperion Essbase*

  http://download.microsoft.com/download/4/7/a/47a548b9-249e-484c-abd7-29f31282b04d/UsingSSRSandESSbase.doc

SharePoint Integration Links

- Learn about SharePoint integrated mode

  http://msdn.microsoft.com/en-us/library/cc281021.aspx

- Configure Reporting Services integration with SharePoint

  http://msdn.microsoft.com/en-us/library/bb326356.aspx

- White paper: *SQL Server 2005 Integration with Microsoft SharePoint Products and Technologies*

  http://technet.microsoft.com/en-us/library/bb969100.aspx

Additional Books

- *Microsoft SQL Server 2008 Analysis Services Unleashed*

  By Irina Gorbach, Alexander Berger, Edward Melomed (Sams Publishing, 2008)

  ISBN: 0672330016

  www.informit.com/store/product.aspx?isbn=0672330016

- *Pro SQL Server 2005 High Availability*

  By Allan Hirt (Apress, 2007)

  ISBN: 159059780X

- *Microsoft SQL Server 2008 Analysis Services Step by Step*

  By Scott Cameron (Microsoft Press, 2009)

  ISBN: 0735626200

APPENDIX B
Glossary

action
An end-user-initiated operation that, for example, can launch another report, open a URL, or transfer focus to a bookmark.

aggregate function
A function that performs a summary calculation on a series of data and returns a single value. Each aggregate function uses the `Scope` parameter, which defines the scope (such as grouping, data set, or data region) in which the aggregate function is performed.

assembly
A managed application module that contains class metadata and managed code.

authentication
The process of validating that the user attempting to connect to Reporting Server is authorized to do so.

authorization
The operation that verifies the permissions and access rights granted to a user to securable report items, such as folders, reports, (report) models, resources, and shared data sources.

BIDS
Abbreviation for SQL Server Business Intelligence Development Studio.

collation
A set of rules that determine how strings of character data are compared, ordered, and presented. Character data is sorted using collation information, including locale, sort order, and case sensitivity.

column

In a table, the area in each row that stores the data value for some attribute of the object presented in the table. For example, in an `Employee` table, a `FirstName` column would contain the first name of an employee.

Common Language Runtime (CLR)

The engine that supplies managed code with services such as cross-language integration, code access security, object lifetime management, and debugging and profiling support.

configuration

In SSRS, a name/value pair that controls certain behaviors of SSRS, such as directing SSRS to load specified extensions or to use a specified encryption key.

connection

An interprocess communication (IPC) linkage established between a SQL Server application and an instance of SQL Server.

connection string

A string supplied to a data provider that provides information sufficient to connect to the data. An example of a connection string is `Data Source=MyServer\MyInstance;initial catalog=AdventureWorksDW`.

constant

A group of symbols that represent a specific data value. For example, `'abc'` is a character string constant, `'123'` is an integer constant, `'April 19, 1999'` is a date-time constant, and `'0x02FA'` is a binary constant.

cube

A set of data that is organized and summarized into a multidimensional structure defined by a set of dimensions and measures.

custom report item

A custom report item extends rendering capabilities of the Report Definition Language (RDL). Some of the custom report items that you can purchase (not included as standard items in SSRS) are map, calendar, barcode, and other controls.

data mart

A subset of the contents of a data warehouse. A data mart tends to contain data focused at the department level, or on a specific business area.

data-processing extension

A component in Reporting Services that provides query processing and data retrieval for a data source type that can be used in a report.

data set

A set of data that is the result of executing Transact-SQL `SELECT`, Data Mining Expressions (DMX), or Multidimensional Expressions (MDX) statements.

data source
An object containing information about the location of data. The data source leverages a connection string. See *connection string*.

Data Source view
An abstraction layer for a data source. Data Source view acts similarly to SQL Server view and allows joining multiple tables from a data source, creating calculated fields, and "renaming" fields from a data source. Data Source view describes this abstraction in XML and does not cause any modification to a data source.

data type
An attribute that specifies what type of information can be stored in a column, parameter, or variable. There are two different data types: system supplied and user defined.

data warehouse
A database designed for reporting and data analysis. A data warehouse typically contains data representing the business history of an organization.

database
A collection of information, tables, and other objects organized and presented to serve a specific purpose, such as searching, sorting, and recombining data. Databases are stored in files.

decision support
The systems designed to support the complex analytic analysis required to discover business trends for managerial decision making.

default
A value (data value, option setting, collation, or name) assigned or an action taken automatically by the system if a user does not specify the value or the action.

default database
The database the user is connected to immediately after logging in to SQL Server.

default instance
The copy of SQL Server that uses the computer name on which it is installed as its name.

`DELETE` **query**
A query (SQL statement) that removes rows from one or more tables.

delivery extension
A component in Reporting Services that is used to distribute a report to specific devices or target locations (for example email delivery, shared folder delivery, or printer delivery).

dimension
A structural attribute of a cube upon which the user wants to base an analysis (for example, geography dimension). Dimension describes data in a fact table.

dimension hierarchy
One of the hierarchies of a dimension.

dimension table
A table that contains the data from which dimensions are created.

drill through
An action or a technique used to retrieve the detailed data by (for example, clicking a report item that contains summarized data).

enterprise
The word *enterprise* is used in several different connotations throughout this book. When enterprise describes a business, it implies (according to Encarta dictionary) "organized business activities aimed specifically at growth and profit." According to the definition, an enterprise could be a company with a few employees or thousands of employees. However, typically, people think of an enterprise as a company that has a hierarchical management structure; division of responsibilities, such as operations, financial, sales, marketing, and so on; and more than a handful of employees.

Enterprise Edition
An edition of a product that provides more powerful features than a product labeled as "standard." In addition to providing extended features, "enterprise" products are also designed to handle large user loads, scale up (use more memory and a large number of CPUs), scale out (have the capability of adding more servers to the installation), and have provisions for high availability.

expression
In SSRS, a combination of variables, constants, functions, and operators that evaluate to a single data value. Simple expressions can be a constant, variable, column, or scalar function. Complex expressions are one or more simple expressions connected by operators.

fact
A row in a fact table in a data warehouse. A fact contains values that define a data event such as a sales transaction.

fact table
A central table in a data warehouse schema that contains numeric measures and keys relating facts to dimension tables. Fact tables contain data that describes specific events within a business, such as bank transactions or product sales.

field
An area in a data set that stores a single data value.

foreign key (FK)
The column or combination of columns whose values match the primary key (PK) or unique key in the same or another table.

function

A piece of code that operates as a single logical unit. A function is called by name, accepts optional input parameters, and returns a status and optional output parameters. Many programming languages support functions, including C, Visual Basic, and Transact-SQL. Transact-SQL supplies built-in functions, which cannot be modified, and supports user-defined functions, which can be created and modified by users.

Hypertext Markup Language (HTML)

A system of marking up a document so that it can be published on the World Wide Web. HTML provides formatting tags and can be viewed using a web browser (such as Microsoft Internet Explorer).

index

In a relational database, a database object that provides fast access to data in the rows of a table, based on key values. The primary key of a table is automatically indexed.

inner join

An operation that retrieves rows from multiple source tables where values from columns shared between the sources tables match to each other.

`INSERT` **query**

A query that copies specific columns and rows from one table to another or to the same table.

instance

A copy of SQL Server or SSRS running on a computer. A computer can run multiple instances of SQL Server.

interface

A defined set of properties, methods, and collections that form a logical grouping of behaviors and data. Classes are defined by the interfaces that they implement. An interface can be implemented by many different classes.

job

A specified series of operations, called steps, performed sequentially by SQL Server Agent.

join

A process or a result of combining the contents of two or more tables and producing a resultset that incorporates rows and columns from each table.

key

A column or group of columns that uniquely identifies a row (primary key), defines the relationship between two tables (foreign key), or is used to build an index.

key column

A column referenced by a primary, foreign, or index key.

linked server
A definition of an OLE DB data source used by SQL Server distributed queries. The data exposed by a linked server is then referenced as tables, called linked tables.

local server
An instance of SQL Server running on the same computer as the application.

local variable
A user-defined variable that is used within the statement batch or procedure in which it was declared.

locale
A set of Windows operating system behaviors related to language, such as the code page, the order in which characters are sorted, the format used for dates and time, and the character used to separate decimals in numbers. SQL Server collations are similar to locales in that the collations define language-specific types of behaviors for instances of SQL Server.

measure
A set of usually numeric values from a fact table that is aggregated in a cube across all dimensions.

Messaging Application Programming Interface (MAPI)
An email API.

metadata
The information describing the properties, such as the type of data in a column (numeric, text, and so on), the length of a column, the structure of database objects, such as tables, measures, dimensions, and cubes, and so on.

Multidimensional Expressions (MDX)
A syntax used for defining multidimensional objects and querying and manipulating multidimensional data.

multiple instances
Multiple copies of SQL Server or SSRS running on the same computer.

.NET Framework
The .NET Framework is an integral Windows component for building and running applications. .NET Framework includes the Common Language Runtime (CLR) and the .NET Framework class library (ADO.NET, ASP.NET, Windows Forms, Windows Communication Foundation [WCF], and Windows Presentation Foundation [WPF]).

`null`
An entry that has no explicitly assigned value. `null` is not the same as zero or blank.

numeric expression
Any expression that evaluates to a number.

object

In databases, one of the components of a database: a table, index, trigger, view, key, constraint, default, rule, user-defined data type, or stored procedure. In object-oriented programming, an instance of a class.

object variable

A variable that contains a reference to an object.

OLE DB

A COM-based API for accessing data. OLE DB supports accessing data stored in any format (databases, spreadsheets, text files, and so on) for which an OLE DB provider is available.

OLE DB consumer

Any software that calls and uses the OLE DB API.

OLE DB for OLAP

Formerly, the separate specification that addressed online analytical processing (OLAP) extensions to OLE DB. Beginning with OLE DB 2.0, OLAP extensions are incorporated into the OLE DB specification.

OLE DB provider

A software component that exposes OLE DB interfaces. Each OLE DB provider exposes data from a particular type of data source, such as SQL Server databases, Microsoft Access databases, or Microsoft Excel spreadsheets.

online analytical processing (OLAP)

A technology that uses multidimensional structures that aggregate data to provide rapid access to data for analysis. The source data for OLAP is commonly stored in data warehouses.

online transaction processing (OLTP)

A data-processing system designed to record all the business transactions of an organization as they occur. An OLTP system is characterized by many concurrent users actively adding and modifying data. Typically, OLTP systems perform large numbers of relatively small transactions.

Open Database Connectivity (ODBC)

A data access API that supports access to any data source for which an ODBC driver is available.

outer join

A join that includes all the rows from the joined tables that have met the search conditions, even rows from one table for which there is no matching row in the other join table.

parameterization

The act of using parameters or parameter markers rather than constant values.

parameterized report
A published Reporting Services report that accepts input values through parameters.

path
A locator information to access a file, such as `c:\myfile.txt`.

pivot
The act of rotating rows to columns, and columns to rows.

pivot table
A visual control that displays rows and columns in a cross-tabular structure. Pivot tables are mostly used to display multidimensional data (cubes).

primary key (PK)
A column or set of columns that uniquely identifies all the rows in a table.

property
A named attribute of a control, field, or database object that defines one of the object's characteristics (such as size or color) or an aspect of its behavior (such as visible or hidden).

property pages
A tabbed dialog box that allows specifying values for properties.

realm
A partition of protected resources; each partition can have its own authentication scheme/authorization database. Realms are used only in basic and digest authentications.

relational database
A collection of information organized in tables.

relational database management system (RDBMS)
A system that organizes data into related rows and columns. SQL Server is an RDBMS.

relationship
A link between tables that references the primary key in one table to a foreign key in another table.

rendered report
A fully processed report that contains both data and layout information, in a format suitable for viewing.

rendering extension
A component in Reporting Services that is used to process the output format of a report. Rendering extensions included in Reporting Services are HTML, TIFF, XML, Excel, PDF, CSV, and Web archive.

report definition

A Report Definition Language file (`.rdl`) that contains information about the query and layout for a Reporting Services report.

report model

A metadata description of business data used for creating ad hoc reports in Report Builder.

report-processing extension

A component in Reporting Services that is used to extend the report-processing logic beyond SSRS "out-of-the-box" capabilities to process `List`, `Table`, `Matrix`, `Chart`, `Textbox`, `Line`, `Rectangle`, and `Image`. Developers can build or purchase a third-party report-processing extension to support custom data-bound controls embedded in reports.

Report Server administrator

A user who is assigned to the Content Manager role, the System Administrator role, or both for a Report Server.

report snapshot

A report that contains data captured at a specific point in time. A report snapshot is stored in an intermediate format containing retrieved data rather than a query and rendering definitions.

resultset

The set of rows returned from a `SELECT` statement. The format of the rows in the resultset is defined by the column list of the `SELECT` statement.

row

A horizontal line in the table that contains all attributes of a single object modeled in the table.

script

A collection of Transact-SQL statements used to perform an operation. Transact-SQL scripts are stored as files, usually with the `.sql` extension.

Secure Sockets Layer (SSL)

A protocol that supplies secure data communication through data encryption and decryption.

security extension

A component in Reporting Services that authenticates a user or group to a Report Server. The default security extension in Reporting Services is Windows authentication. Custom extensions can be created to support forms-based authentication or to integrate with third-party single sign-on technologies.

security identifier (SID)

A unique value that identifies a user who is logged in to the security system. SIDs can identify either one user or a group of users.

`SELECT` query
The Transact-SQL or DMX statement used to return tabular data or the MDX statement that returns multidimensional data.

server name
A name that uniquely identifies a server computer on a network. SQL Server applications can connect to a default instance of SQL Server by specifying only the server name. SQL Server applications must specify both the server name and instance name when connecting to a named instance on a server.

shared dimension
A dimension created within a database that can be used by any cube in the database.

sort order
The set of rules in a collation that define how characters are evaluated in comparison operations and the sequence in which they are sorted.

SQL collation
A set of SQL Server collations whose characteristics match those of commonly used code page and sort order combinations from earlier versions of SQL Server. SQL collations are compatibility features that let sites choose collations that match the behavior of their earlier systems.

SQL expression
Any combination of operators, constants, literal values, functions, and names of tables and fields that evaluates to a single value. For example, use expressions to define calculated fields in queries.

SQL query
A SQL statement, such as `SELECT`, `INSERT`, `UPDATE`, `DELETE`, or `CREATE TABLE`.

SQL Server authentication
One of two mechanisms for validating attempts to connect to instances of SQL Server. Users must specify a SQL Server logon ID and password when they connect. The SQL Server instance ensures the logon ID and password combination are valid before allowing the connection to succeed.

SQL Server Business Intelligence Development Studio (BIDS)
A Visual Studio shell with Business Intelligence project templates: Analysis Services, Integration Services, Report Server, and Report Model.

SQL statement
See *SQL query*.

SSRS
Abbreviation for SQL Server Reporting Services.

stored procedure
A precompiled collection of Transact-SQL statements stored under a name and processed as a unit.

string
Contiguous character-based (letters, numbers, special characters) or binary (string of bytes) data value.

string functions
The functions that perform operations on character or binary strings. Built-in string functions return values commonly needed for operations on character data.

Structured Query Language (SQL)
The language understood by RDBMSs and used to create and manage database objects and perform data manipulations (`INSERT`, `UPDATE`, `DELETE`, and `SELECT` queries). SQL Server uses a version of the SQL language called Transact-SQL.

subscription
A request for a copy of a report to be delivered to a subscriber. The subscription defines what reports will be received, where, and when.

table
A two-dimensional object, consisting of rows and columns, used to store data in a relational database. Each table stores information about one of the types of objects modeled by the database, such as information about sales orders.

time dimension
A dimension that breaks time down into levels such as year, quarter, month, and day. In Analysis Services, a special type of dimension created from a date/time column.

tool
An application, ideally with a graphical user interface, designed to perform common tasks.

Transact-SQL
The language understood by SQL Server and used to create and manage database objects and perform data manipulations (`INSERT`, `UPDATE`, `DELETE`, and `SELECT` queries).

transaction
A group of database operations combined into a logical unit of work that is either wholly committed or rolled back. A transaction is atomic, consistent, isolated, and durable.

transaction processing
The data processing used to efficiently record business transactions, which are of interest to an organization (for example, sales, orders for supplies, or money transfers).

trigger
A stored procedure that executes in response to a Data Manipulation Language (DML) or Data Definition Language (DDL) event.

underlying table
A table referenced by a view, cursor, or stored procedure.

update
The act of modifying one or more data values in an existing row or rows, typically by using the `UPDATE` statement. Sometimes the term *update* refers to any data modification, including `INSERT`, `UPDATE`, and `DELETE` query operations.

utility
An application that can be executed from a command prompt to perform common tasks.

variable
A read/write container for variable values.

VS200x
Visual Studio 2005 or Visual Studio 2008.

`WHERE` **clause**
The part of a SQL statement that specifies which records to retrieve.

wildcard characters
The characters, including underscore (_), percent (%), and brackets ([ ]), used with the `LIKE` keyword for pattern matching.

Windows Management Instrumentation (WMI)
An interface that provides information about objects in a managed environment, with extensions for SQL called WMI Query Language (WQL).

WMI Query Language (WQL)
A subset of ANSI SQL with semantic changes adapted to Windows Management Instrumentation (WMI).

APPENDIX C

Frequently Asked Questions and Additional Information

The intention of this appendix is to share answers to some common questions about SSRS. The appendix is presented in the Q&A (question-and-answer) fashion.

Q Can I connect Report Builder 1.0 to an Oracle database?

A direct connection between Report Builder 1.0 and Oracle is not supported; however, you can connect to an Oracle database by leveraging link servers or the Analysis Services Unified Data Model. Both provide a thin layer of abstraction and allow usage of any OLE DB- or ODBC-compliant data source, including Oracle.

Q Can I join two separate data sets in a report?

Although it is not possible to join two data sets directly, it is possible to simulate this feature. Depending on what you are trying to accomplish, there might be options. For example, you can align two data regions, such as tables, and make sure that rows properly match. You can also synchronize two data sets by using the same query parameter as was done in the sample included with this book.

Q Can I use SSRS to update my sales data?

Although it is possible to update a database using SSRS, developers should refrain from using SSRS in this fashion. For example, it is possible to create a report that passes parameters to a stored procedure (or a query), which, in turn, updates a database (and might return some data back to a report). Such a report produces an "unexpected behavior." Expected behavior of a report is to retrieve and display information.

Q I would like to embed Report Builder in my custom application. Is it possible?

The current release of SSRS does not provide this functionality. It is possible to develop an RDL generator that will provide functionality similar to Report Builder.

Q Does the Printer icon on the Report Manager's toolbar invoke the Printing extension?

No. This is the ActiveX `RSPrintClient` control. This control provides client-side printing for reports viewed in HTML Viewer. The control presents the Print dialog box for a user to initiate a print job, preview a report, specify pages to print, and change the margins. Developers can use this control in the code to enable report-printing functionality.

Q Is there a 64-bit version of SSRS?

Yes, SSRS 2008 Enterprise Edition supports both Itanium (IA64) and Extended Complex Instruction Set (x64; supported CPUs AMD64: Opteron and Athlon64; EM64T: Xeon). SSRS 2008 Standard Edition does not support IA64. Business Intelligence Development Studio (BIDS) is not supported on IA64.

Q How can I get the history of report executions?

You can find a sample of report execution history report in Microsoft SQL Server 2008 Samples, www.codeplex.com/MSFTRSProdSamples/Release/ProjectReleases.aspx?ReleaseId=18649. SSRS comes with a sample of packages and reports. By default, samples that provide administrators with a set of tools to view report execution history and performance characteristics are installed at `C:\Program Files\Microsoft SQL Server\100\Samples\Reporting Services\Report Samples\Server Management Sample Reports`.

You can also look through SSRS execution log files in a text editor. By default, SSRS execution log files are written to the `C:\Program Files\Microsoft SQL Server\MSRS10.MSSQLSERVER\Reporting Services\LogFiles` directory. An entry for a report execution may look like this: `webserver!ReportServer_0-4!eac! 11/16/2008-23:29:52:: i INFO: Processed report. Report='/ReportProject/Top SalesPeople...'`. Note that entry has a time associated with it.

Q What is WMI used for in SSRS?

Windows Management Instrumentation (WMI) is a set of management interfaces to retrieve and modify configuration information for SSRS. For an unnamed instance, the root namespace can be found in `\root\Microsoft\SqlServer\ReportServer\RS_MSSQLSERVER\v10\Admin`. For a named instance, replace `RS_MSSQLSERVER` with an instance name.

Q What are the classes under the root namespace?

There are two classes under the `\root\Microsoft\SqlServer\ReportServer\RS_MSSQLSERVER\v10\Admin` WMI namespace for SSRS. The first is the `MSReportServer_ConfigurationSetting` class, which contains configuration information for the Report Server. Note: Due to the merging of Report Server and Report Manager configuration files, the `MSReportServerReportManager_ConfigurationSetting` class is no longer available.

Q What is the purpose of the WMI provider for SSRS?

The Reporting Services WMI provider exposes an object model that enables you to configure all aspects of a local or remote Reporting Services installation, including specifying the service account, configuring Report Server web service and Report Manager URLs, creating and configuring the Report Server database, configuring scale-out deployment, backing up encryption keys, and configuring a Report Server for email delivery. You have to write custom code to use the WMI provider. SQL Server Books Online has several examples of using WMI provider as well as alternatives to writing custom configuration code.

Q When I try to set up a subscription, I get the error `SQL Agent service is not running. This operation requires the SQL Agent service. (rsSchedulerNotResponding)`. What should I do?

Make sure that the SQL Agent service is running. The agent must be running on the SQL Server that hosts the SSRS catalog.

Q When I click the Print icon on the Report Manager's toolbar, nothing happens. What should I do?

Because this button invokes an ActiveX control, make sure that the browser you are using supports ActiveX and that the browser's security allows downloading and running of signed ActiveX controls. After you allow your browser to run signed ActiveX, clear temporary Internet files, including offline content. If your browser asks your permission to download a print control, allow your browser to do so.

APPENDIX D

What's New in SQL Server SP1?

IN THIS APPENDIX

- What's New in SP1?

As we were ready to wrap up editing of this book, Microsoft released Service Pack 1 (SP1) for SQL Server 2008 and a couple of additional cumulative updates. The impact of SP1 on SQL Server Reporting Services (SSRS) is relatively small.

What's New in SP1?

For the Reporting Services developers and users, SQL Server 2008 SP1 delivers bug fixes and support for Report Builder 2.0 click-once deployment. Chapter 37, "Ad Hoc Reporting in SharePoint," briefly mentions SP1 updates for Report Builder 2.0, and this appendix expands on that information.

In terms of bug fixes, SP1 incorporates rollup of cumulative updates 1 through 3 (http://support.microsoft.com/kb/956717, http://support.microsoft.com/kb/958186, http://support.microsoft.com/kb/960484), Quick Fix Engineering (QFE) updates, and other fixes.

Overall, notable SP1 improvements include the following:

- **Slipstream deployment:** Allows you to combine basic SQL Server installation with service pack and fix deployments, and thus reduces the effort required to a single installation step.
- **SP uninstall:** Allows you to uninstall only the service pack or cumulative updates, preserving the originally installed SQL Server components. You can do this from Programs and Features in Control Panel. Click View Installed Updates under Tasks on the left side and select SP1 and Fixes to uninstall from there.

- **Report Builder 2.0 click-once deployment:** Allows you to easily change SSRS configuration to enable click-once deployment of Report Builder 2.0.

To install SP1 on a single machine, download SP1 setup from http://www.microsoft.com/downloads/details.aspx?displaylang=en&FamilyID=66ab3dbb-bf3e-4f46-9559-ccc6a4f9dc19 and run the appropriate install executable for your platform (x86, x64, or IA64). For multi-server deployments, you can leverage your favorite software distribution tool, such as Microsoft System Center, or slipstream deployment.

Much like most of the software that you install, you must have administrative rights on the computer to install SP1.

Manual installation requires just a few steps, as follows: Run the install executable, and accept the license terms and select features where you want SP1 to be applied. By default, SP1 is applied to shared features, such as connectivity, Books Online, management tools, and so on. You can additionally select to apply SP1 to the Database Engine, Analysis Services, and Reporting Services, which you likely want to do. To avoid a complete restart, you can close applications and stop services that may be using SQL-related files. You do not need to stop any SQL Services, such as Database Engine or SQL Server Analysis Services (SSAS); the SP1 setup will take care of those automatically.

Setup, in turn, performs some checks and displays a Ready to Update dialog (summarizing the features that SP1 installation will affect). At this point, you have a Final opportunity to proceed (Click Update) or cancel the update process.

Depending on the performance of the machine and installed SQL features, the SP1 setup may take a while. When SP1 setup completes, you can issue a query `SELECT @@VERSION` and should see the following as a result:

```
Microsoft SQL Server 2008 (SP1) - 10.0.2531.0 (Intel X86)   Mar 29 2009
10:27:29   Copyright (c) 1988-2008 Microsoft Corporation  Enterprise Edition
on Windows NT 6.0 <X86> (Build 6001: Service Pack 1) (VM)
```

To check a version of SSRS, you can connect to an instance of SSRS using SQL Server Management Studio. Right-click the instance, select Properties from a context menu, and under the General tab you will see a version of SSRS:

```
Microsoft SQL Server Reporting Services Version 10.0.2531.0
```

You can find versions of the installed SQL features in a few other places, too. For example, you can find the SQL Server Installation Center under Start, All Programs, Microsoft SQL Server 2008, Configuration Tools. If you display the Tools tab, you will see the Installed SQL Features discovery report, which shows all the installed SQL features and their versions.

Now that we have SP1 installation out of the way, let's look at the click-once deployment scenario for Report Builder 2.0.

When you open a Report Manager and have proper permissions, you will see a Report Builder button on the header. This button launches Report Builder (Report Builder 1.0

by default). If you right-click it, you will see that it points to the following URL: http://<ServerName>/ReportServer/ReportBuilder/ReportBuilder.application.

NOTE

If you do not see the button or a header, check your security permissions. For a thorough troubleshooting walkthrough, refer to http://social.msdn.microsoft.com/Forums/en-US/sqlreportingservices/thread/e8da121a-c0ac-4d0b-8774-abd5128d88fe/.

SP1 deploys Report Builder 2.0 on the server for click-once deployment scenarios with no additional effort required on your part. Much like an earlier version of Report Builder, the new version is deployed into the following directory:

C:\Program Files\Microsoft SQL Server\MSRS10.MSSQLSERVER\Reporting Services\ReportServer\ReportBuilder

There, after you complete the SP1 installation process, you should see two manifests: ReportBuilder.application and ReportBuilder_2_0_0_0.application.

If you are running SSRS in native mode, just change the Custom Action URL on the Site Settings page of the Report Manager (see Figure D.1) to /ReportBuilder/ReportBuilder_2_0_0_0.application.

Note that there are underscores between numbers in the path. An incorrect path results in an error message: The Report Builder launch URL is not valid. It can be an absolute or relative URL and must include the .application file extension.

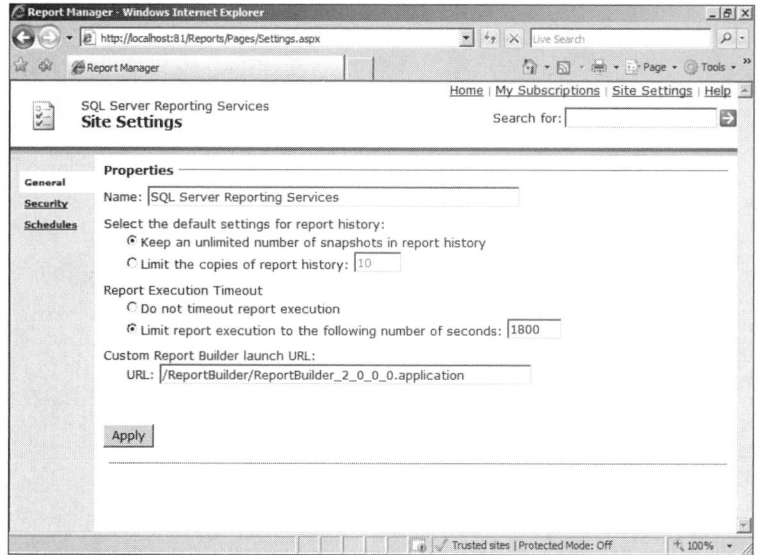

FIGURE D.1 Click in the Report Manager.

Click Apply to commit changes. Notice that the link associated with the Report Builder button changes to http://<ServerName>/ReportServer//ReportBuilder/ReportBuilder_2_0_0_0.application (see Figure D.2).

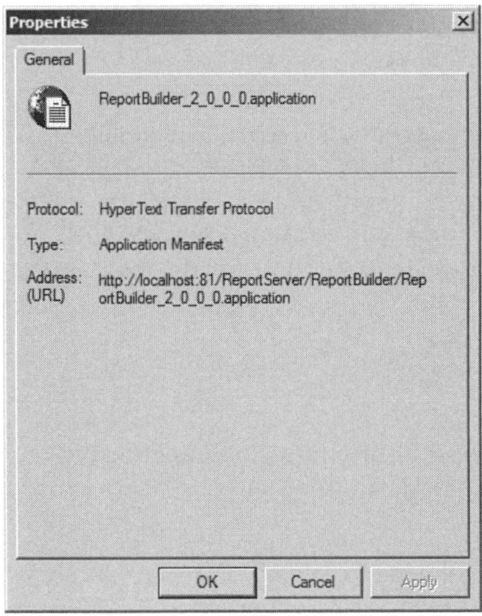

FIGURE D.2 The link behind the Report Builder button.

Alternatively, you can set up this property using the Advanced tab of the Server Properties dialog in SQL Server Management Studio (see Figure D.3). To display the dialog, right-click the server that want to set up and select Properties from the context menu.

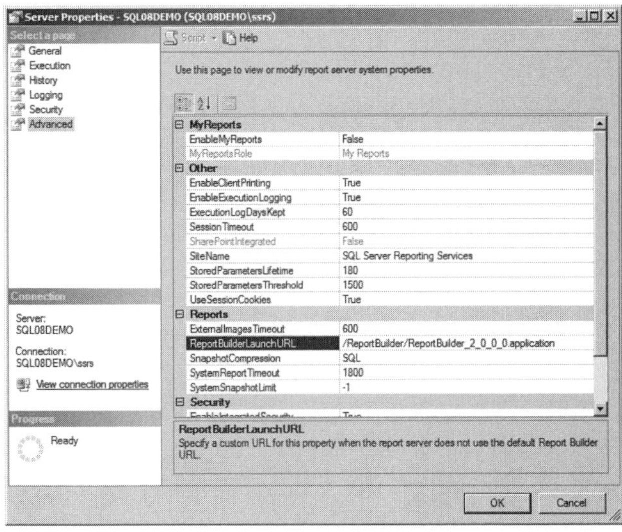

FIGURE D.3 Click in the SQL Server Management Studio.

If you are running SSRS in SharePoint integrated mode, you must first download the Microsoft SQL Server 2008 Reporting Services add-in for Microsoft SharePoint Technologies, April 2009, from http://www.microsoft.com/downloads/details.aspx?FamilyID=58edd0e4-255b-4361-bd1e-e530d5aab78f&displaylang=en. Then, you can change the Custom Action URL to /_vti_bin/ReportBuilder/ReportBuilder_2_0_0_0.application, similar to the instructions for native mode.

NOTE

For the Report Builder 2.0 click-once to function properly, it is important to install the add-in for Microsoft SharePoint, as described in the "Microsoft SQL Server 2008 Report Builder 2.0 ClickOnce for SharePoint" readme at http://download.microsoft.com/download/7/0/1/701890C9-2990-4AB2-A41B-21F7152A3082/Readme_rsclickonceaddin.htm.

After you set up Report Builder 2.0 click-once, users can install Report Builder 2.0 on their workstations without having administrative privileges on their machines. This proves especially beneficial in corporate environments, where elevated permissions for employees are typically restricted. To run click-once, the only requirement on client machines is .NET 3.5 SP1.

The click-once installation includes several available languages. The click-once installation process selects a language based on the client's workstation display language.

Those users who have administrative permissions on their machines can also install Report Builder 2.0 by downloading and installing the product from http://www.microsoft.com/downloads/details.aspx?FamilyID=dbddc9b6-6e19-4d4b-9309-13f62901b0d5&displaylang=en.

Note that Microsoft has also released an updated April 2009 Feature Pack (http://www.microsoft.com/downloads/details.aspx?FamilyID=b33d2c78-1059-4ce2-b80d-2343c099bcb4&displaylang=en) and two additional post-SP1 update packages: Package 4 (http://support.microsoft.com/kb/963036) and Package 5 (http://support.microsoft.com/kb/969531). Both have updates that address Reporting Services issues.

APPENDIX E

What's New in SQL Server 2008 R2?

IN THIS APPENDIX

- Map and Spatial Visualizations
- Grab and Go Reporting
- Report Builder 3.0 and Ad Hoc Reporting
- SharePoint Integration Enhancements
- Report Manager Facelift
- Report Viewer Control Updates
- ATOM Data Renderer
- Other Features in R2

As we publish this book, Microsoft is getting ready to release a Community Technology Preview 2 (CTP2) preview of the next version of SQL Server called SQL Server 2008 R2. The release is also known by its code name Kilimanjaro.

SQL Server 2008 R2 will add important new features for data visualization, report design, and end-user reporting. This appendix provides an overview of the expected features in the R2 release. We plan to keep our readers informed about R2 updates online at http://www.informit.com/store/product.aspx?isbn=0672330261 as new information becomes available and new features are implemented in the SQL Server 2008 R2 CTP releases.

New Reporting Services features in SQL Server 2008 R2 include the following:

- Map and spatial visualization
- Grab and go reporting
- Report Builder 3.0 and ad hoc reporting
- SharePoint integration enhancements
- Report Manager facelift
- Report Viewer update
- ATOM renderer
- Other improvements

Map and Spatial Visualizations

The ability to visualize data related to geographic locations is an intuitive reporting need. Think, for example, about all the reports and charts showing red states and blue states from the 2008 U.S. presidential election. Common business reporting needs come to mind, too (for instance, showing sales territories on a map, comparing sales and profits, showing inventory volumes of particular product by store locations around a city, and showing customer demographic projections in different regions).

In the 2008 R2 release, maps in a report enable you to view your data against a geographic or geometric background. Map data can be spatial data from a SQL Server query, an Environmental Systems Research Institute, Inc. (ESRI) shapefile, or image tiles from Microsoft Virtual Earth Tiles. Spatial data consists of sets of coordinates that define polygons that represent shapes or areas, lines that represent routes or paths, and points that represent markers. You can associate aggregate data with map elements to automatically vary their color and size. Figure E.1 shows sample types of map data visualizations enabled in SQL Server 2008 R2.

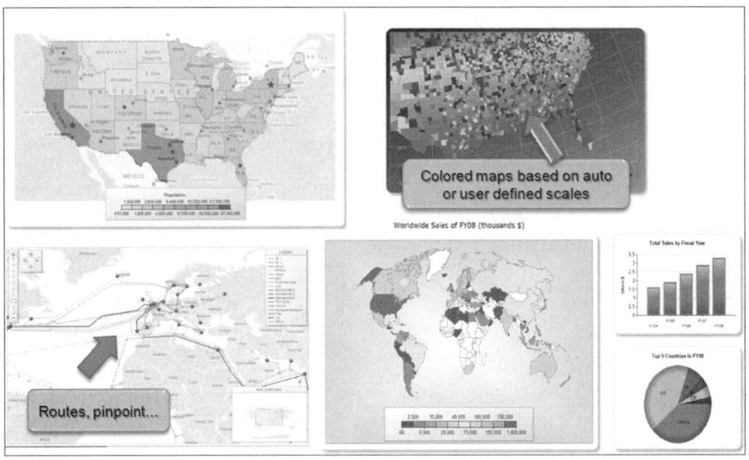

FIGURE E.1 Examples of map data visualization in SSRS 2008 R2.

Think for moment about the power of these new features. You can mash up business information with geographic information on a report to gain new insights. For example, if customer numbers are steeply rising on the west side of town and declining on the east side, you may want to redistribute your sales offices.

Grab and Go Reporting

Microsoft acquired the small company 90 Degree Software because of its strength in grab and go reporting. This feature may also be referred to as Report Component Library.

The idea behind grab and go reporting is to provide easy reusability of key report components such as data sets, charts, gauges, and so on. These components can be reused across multiple reports and are maintained in a central library. This saves time for report authors and enables end users to rapidly deploy custom reports by reusing common components.

NOTE

Every time a component is used in a report, a copy is made for the report, but the server maintains the component's metadata link to the component library.

Another way to think about this feature is that report designers can focus on creating reusable data sets and visual components and publish them to the Report Server. Other reporting users can then search for these components via Report Manager or the SharePoint portal and use them to create more interesting reports.

See Figure E.2 to get a feel for how the component library will show up for report authors and how they can drag and drop a component into a report they are authoring.

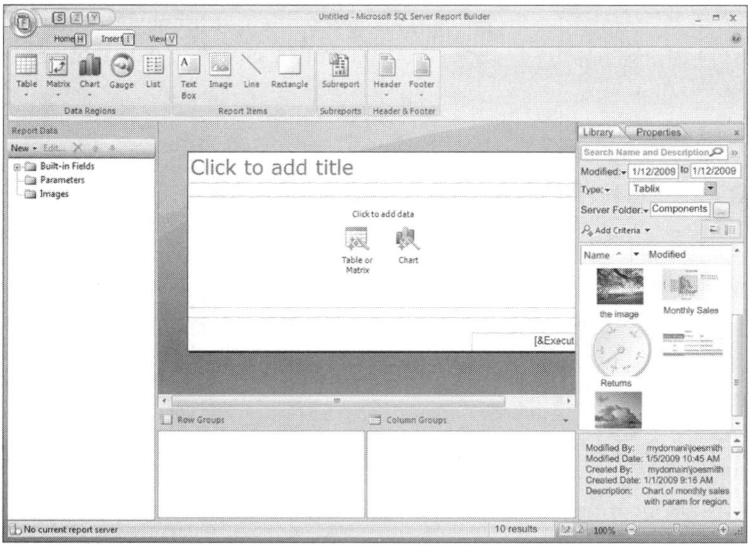

FIGURE E.2 Using components in report design.

The concept of sharing visual report components such as charts and gauges in different reports seems intuitive. However, it is good to understand that you can also reuse the underlying data sets. To get an idea about how the new feature of shared data sets fits into the reuse story, see Figure E.3. Caching will be supported on the shared data sets to provide better performance on reuse.

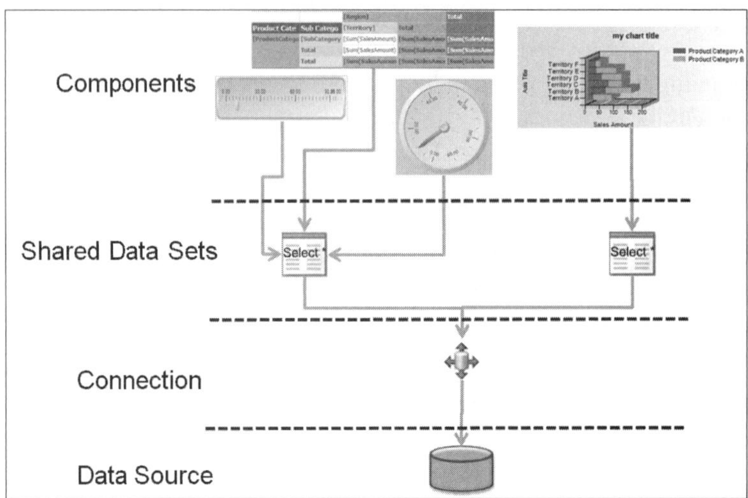

FIGURE E.3 Components and shared data sets.

Shared data sets and the visual components can be managed by Report Manager or the SharePoint user interface, just like reports or models. You can list, move, or delete them and secure them with permissions.

Report Builder 3.0 and Ad Hoc Reporting

At the time of publication, Report Builder 3.0 in the SQL Server 2008 R2 release is expected to be similar to Report Builder 2.0 in the 2008 release. It will also support report models and include support for the new features added in R2, such as Map.

Report Builder 3.0 includes enhancements for designing and editing reports when it is connected to the Report Server:

- All server-supported credentials options work for query design and preview.
- Users can test data source connections through the server.
- Users experience better performance because of the caching infrastructure. For example, switching between layout and preview mode will be faster.
- Relative references to server items such as subreports and external images will now work.

Report Builder 3.0 will also focus on the ad hoc reporting experience, such as user-friendly semantic query features and a model explorer.

SharePoint Integration Enhancements

Some of the long-standing feature requests for SharePoint integration will be enabled in the 2008 R2 release, including support for Alternate Access Mappings (also called multi-zone support) and reporting against SharePoint lists.

The Reporting Services SharePoint add-in will become a prerequisite for the Office 14 SharePoint release. Therefore, starting with SharePoint 14, the SharePoint servers will be ready for Reporting Services integration out of the box. This is good news for administrators.

Report Manager Facelift

Report Manager is finally getting a facelift in SQL Server 2008 R2, with new colors and a new look and feel. Folder and item properties and workflows will be updated to be more user friendly. The concept of context menus on reports (which should be familiar to SharePoint UI users) will be introduced so that users can view and manage report properties without having to render the report first. For example, if a user wants to create a subscription for a report, she can just select a Subscriptions option from the context menu on the report name.

Report Viewer Control Updates

The Report Viewer Control is being updated in 2008 R2 to operate on ASP.NET Ajax-enabled pages. More events will be exposed to developers and generally give developers more control and customization capability over both the functional and cosmetic aspects of the viewer.

ATOM Data Renderer

Reporting Services in 2008 R2 will be able to render reports as standards-compliant ATOM data feeds. Besides other ATOM clients, this will allow Gemini clients (available with SQL Server 2008 R2 Analysis Services) to use reports as a first-class source of data. This is a big win for the integration story between Reporting Services and Analysis Services.

Other Features in R2

Even more features are likely to make it into the R2 release. Features will be incrementally rolled out in Customer Preview releases, such as CTP2 in July 2009 and CTP3 around September 2009.

Some of the features include integration with Analysis Services key performance indicators (KPIs) and support for sparklines (a way to visualize a trend without the details).

For developers, there will be a new Simple Object Access Protocol (SOAP) namespace for report management called ReportService2010, which will work for both native and SharePoint mode. It will essentially combine the features of the ReportService2005 and ReportService2006 web services with additional support for R2 features.

Index

A

B

C

D

E

F

G

H

I

J - K

L

M

N

O

P

Q

R

S

T

U

V

W

X - Y - Z

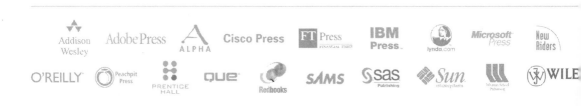